GUIDE
TO
THE
PILGRIM
HYMNAL

GUIDE TO THE PILGRIM HYMNAL

ALBERT C. RONANDER
ETHEL K. PORTER

UNITED CHURCH PRESS
Philadelphia • Boston

PREFACE

"For here the saying holds true, 'One sows and another reaps.' I sent you to reap that for which you did not labor; others have labored, and you have entered into their labor." These words of Jesus to his disciples express perfectly the feeling of the editors as they complete their work on this *Guide*. To engage in an enterprise of this kind is to be made aware of the many sowers and laborers who preceded this study and made it possible: saints and prophets, writers and musicians, reformers and theologians, poets and teachers, lawyers and doctors, ministers and evangelists, priests and statesmen, and hosts of others. These are the authors, translators, composers, and arrangers of the hymns, an exceeding great company. Some are renowned, others are remembered only because of one hymn or tune. Following after them are the scholars and publishers who discovered and preserved these treasures of the past. To their number should be added the hymnologists and students of history who sought out the original sources and put their findings into writing that later generations might know the origin and story of the hymns. Finally, there is the multitude of faithful believers who have joyously sung God's praises down through the centuries. To all these the editors owe a debt of incalculable magnitude.

Simply as a pleasurable exercise, nothing more is required in hymn singing than a sound voice and the ability to read. Information about the authors and composers and knowledge of how the hymns came to be is not essential for this simple enjoyment. In fact, when such knowledge leads to a pedantic concern with petty details it can actually get in the way of making "a joyful noise to the Lord." However, to enter fully into the deeper meaning and wider context of hymns demands some understanding of their background. Hymns are illumined by their associations and gain in power and import when something is known of their history and the situations out of which they have come.

Great care has been taken to include only such information as can by reasonable standards be held to be historically accurate. Undoubtedly some errors have crept in and some apocryphal incidents have been repeated, although every effort has been made to keep these to a minimum and, indeed, to expunge them altogether. But research was not always able to uncover the original sources, and obscurities still cling to some hymns. Much of the information in this *Guide* can be found in other commentaries, but it is scattered here and there among many different sources. The *Guide* endeavors to bring together this rich store of facts and insights into a readily available and convenient form and, at the same time, to break new ground in what can be discovered about the texts and the tunes.

The *Guide* is intended: (1) as an aid to ministers and choir directors who may wish to provide their congregations and choirs with information about the background of the hymns and tunes; (2) as a help in selecting hymns for worship or for hymn festivals and special services; (3) as a resource for study groups exploring church music and hymnody; (4) as a companion to the *Pilgrim Hymnal* for use in the church school and in the home; and (5) as a reference work for general library use.

These prefatory remarks would be incomplete without an expression of gratitude to the many persons who helped with the preparation of the *Guide*: Ruth E. Messenger, late editor of *The Hymn* and professor of classical languages at Hunter College, for her research on the original sources and versions of the hymns; Harriett T. Ronander for her invaluable assistance in preparing the text commentaries and introductory articles; John Ferris, organist and choirmaster at Harvard University, and Carl Wolff of Brock University, Canada, for their thorough study of the original manuscript and their many critical suggestions; Ross Cannon, minister of Second Church in Newton, West Newton, Massachusetts, for his generous counsel in planning and developing the general outline for the *Guide*; Robert Beach, librarian of Union Theological Seminary, and members of his staff for their help at all times; Louise Wilhelm for her typing of the tune comments; H. Earle Johnson, musicologist, for planning and preparing the Index; Mildred L. Curtis of the staff of the United Church Press for her experienced work of copy editing the manuscript; Grace W. Ingalls of the United Church Press staff for her highly efficient handling of copyright requirements, permission, and acknowledgments; Charles A. Butts, Director of Production for the United Church Press, for his unfailing patience, encouragement, and willingness to let what was to have been a slim book grow to its present proportions and without whose generous support this *Guide* would never have been completed.

Albert C. Ronander
Ethel K. Porter

CONTENTS

Preface   v

Hymns in Christian Worship   ix

Music of the Hymns   xiii

Isaac Watts and Congregational Hymnody   xix

Uses of the Hymnal   xxiii

The Hymns   1

Acknowledgments   423

Bibliography   425

Index   426

Hymns in Christian Worship

Of all the characteristic features of Christian worship, hymns are among the oldest and most enduring. Before there were sacred scriptures, formal creeds, fixed liturgies, or special buildings, Christians met regularly to sing their songs of faith. The earliest description of Christian worship, contained in a second-century letter from Pliny the Younger, governor of Bithynia and Pontus, to the Roman Emperor Trajan, recounts how Christians "were in the habit of meeting on a certain fixed day before dawn, when they sang in alternate verses a hymn to Christ, as to a god."

The first songs were undoubtedly psalms, taken from the Hebrew psalter, particularly those having a messianic import, but soon a distinctively Christian note was introduced by adding the *Gloria Patri* at the end of each psalm. This became an established practice by the close of the fourth century, thereby sealing the Old Testament with a Christian affirmation of praise while extolling the one God of both covenants. The three canticles found in the opening chapters of the Gospel according to Luke, the *Magnificat* (1:46–55), the *Benedictus* (1:68–79), and the *Nunc Dimittis* (2:29–32), are probably the earliest examples of Christian hymns, albeit derived from older Jewish models. Three other early and well-known canticles are the *Sanctus,* based on the seraph's words heard by Isaiah (6:3), the *Gloria in excelsis,* inspired by the angels' song at Bethlehem (Luke 2:14), and the *Te Deum laudamus,* the greatest of all the nonbiblical hymns of praise, which has seldom, if ever, been equalled and never surpassed (see No. 559). Throughout Paul's letters are portions of what undoubtedly were early Christian hymns, as in Ephesians 5:14, Philippians 2:6–11, and 1 Timothy 3:16, illustrating and adding force to his admonition that Christians are to "sing psalms and hymns and spiritual songs with thankfulness in your hearts to God" (Colossians 3:16). Before the creeds took final form, when they were still in the process of being shaped, "they were sung," according to Millar Patrick, "as often as not defiantly, in hymns that were like banners flung out challengingly on the breeze."

In the earliest days of the church, the hymns were sung in the common language by the entire congregation. These were not cast into metrical form and sung with instrumental accompaniment, such as is known today, but were more in the nature of free-flowing rhythmic and poetical prose, what might be called "sung speech." Worship at first was informal and even spontaneous and much was made of congregational singing in the vernacular. Gradually, however, worship assumed a more formal character and trained choirs increasingly did most of the singing. In both the East and the West, from about the sixth century until the Reformation, congregational participation in the music of the church was largely suppressed, except for brief responses. Hymns, defined in the broadest sense as religious songs of a rhythmical character designed for use in public worship, continued to be sung by clergy and choirs in the Divine Liturgy and in the mass and by monks in the monasteries. Some of the finest hymns of the church came from the monasteries in connection with the observance of the canonical hours, beginning with matins and ending with compline, or from those associated with the monastic orders. Among these hymns are "Come, Holy Ghost, our souls inspire" (*Veni Creator Spiritus*), "The day of resurrection!" "Come, ye faithful, raise the strain," and "O what their joy and their glory must be." Hymns were also sung by the people in connection with pilgrimages, festive celebrations, processions and on other extraliturgical occasions. However, within the church, the congregation of believers had little opportunity to join in the singing.

One of the major accomplishments of the Reformation was the restoration to Christian worship of congregational singing in the language of the people. To Luther primarily belongs the credit for effecting this change and thereby releasing a great new power into the life of the church. A century earlier the Bohemian Brethren had introduced hymns into their worship and issued the first Protestant hymnal but their example had not extended much beyond their own communion. It was Luther who made congregational singing a normative part of the corporate praise of the church. Out of his profound study of the Bible, especially the Psalms and the New Testament, he came to see that the exclusion of the laity from participation in the church's music in worship was a fundamental violation of early Christian teaching and practice. Writing to Spalatin, a friend, in 1523, he said, "Unquestionably, in the early church, the people sang much which only the priests and clerics now sing. I propose after the example of the prophets and early fathers to write for the people some hymns and spiritual songs that by the help of song, the Word of God may abide among them." Luther not only did that, writing thirty-seven hymns, but he also utilized the folk songs of the German people and brought them into the service of the church, adapting them to sacred texts, as the psalmists had done centuries earlier. From this came the magnificent German chorales which later were to blossom so gloriously in the music of Bach, Mendelssohn, and Brahms. Luther ranked music next in importance to the Word of God, and as a result of his labors, in the words of George Adam Smith, "there broke forth from all lands of the Reformation, as though it were birds in springtime, a great burst of hymns and prayers with the clear notes of the Gospel in the common tongue." This elicited the petulant remark of a Jesuit at the time that "Luther's songs have damned more souls than all his books and speeches."

Nevertheless, it must not be supposed that the transformation from a clergy-dominated to a congregation-inspired form of worship took place overnight. Actually, decades were to pass before the full effect of Luther's ideas were to prevail. Even at the time of Johann Sebastian Bach, most of the music in the church was vested in the organ and the choir. The people listened more than they sang. However, an impetus had been given to congregational singing that could not permanently be stayed or denied. New leaders in Germany and in other countries on the continent emerged to further Luther's reforms; in England, Isaac Watts and Charles Wesley elevated the hymn to a high and permanent place in the worship of English-speaking communions. Although Calvin and those who followed him confined the praises of the church to a strict psalmody, they actively promoted congregational singing and prepared the way for a rich flowering of hymnody in later decades within all Reformed bodies.

In every significant upsurge of renewal that has taken place within the church during the past two centuries, from the early revivals to the present ecumenical movement, hymn singing has played an important role. It is of more than passing interest that the Roman Catholic church in its current program of radical reexamination and reform, *aggiornamento,* is encouraging the singing of hymns in the vernacular by the people in the mass. A leading Catholic spokesman has declared, "Active participation of the faithful in song is the most noble form of worship and is an important emphasis that will radically alter the history of Catholic church music." One of the surest signs that the church of the mid-twentieth century may be in a period of reawakening and renewal is the quickened interest in a revitalized hymnody.

Hymns serve a many-faceted purpose in Christian worship. They are first and primarily, in Erik Routley's phrase, "the congregation's response to the great movements of the service." If worship is the reenactment and celebration of the mighty events recounted in the biblical drama, beginning with creation and ending with the final consummation of all things in Christ, then hymns are the people's fitting response to what is said and done. Words alone can convey meaning and music by itself can stir the emotions, but together they have the power to elevate both mind and heart to an exalted level of praise and adoration beyond anything either could attain separately. There is no higher form of worship, when all the faculties combine to extol God's power and goodness.

Hymns are inherently expressions of praise or affirmations of faith which the people themselves offer to God in response to his mighty acts in the past and renewing grace in the present. In this fundamental sense, hymns serve an essential liturgical function uniting the whole congregation of believers in one corporate act of praise and prayer. Anthems and choral selections are primarily *aids to worship,* recognizing that they are and should be offered in the spirit of prayer and praise and never as a performance or, what is worse, as entertainment. Hymns, on the other hand, are basically *acts of worship.* Corporate praise without the rich embroidery of organ and choir can be threadbare and thin, but worship which reduces the people to passive listeners and observers is theatrical and sterile. If the liturgy is the "work of the people," as defined in its original meaning, then hymns take their place among the highest and most authentic parts of Christian worship. They are not embellishments added to the service but indispensable ingredients of the service, what Pope Pius X, referring to church music, called *parte integrante,* a "functional part." The late Bernard Manning, writing as a Free Church layman, expressed what is now held rather widely as a consensus among many Christians when he described hymns as "the framework, the setting, the conventional, the traditional part of divine service as we use it."

He said further: "We mark times and seasons, celebrate festivals, express experiences, and expound doctrines by hymns. . . . Every clause in the Nicene and in the Athanasian Creed has its parallel in our hymn-

xi

books; and if we use no crucifix, no stations of the Cross, no processions, no banners, no incense, you must attribute it not to the fancy that we have neither need nor understanding of what these things represent. We do not use these things because our hymns revive the sacred scenes and stir the holy emotions with a power and a purity denied to all but the greatest craftsmen." (*The Hymns of Wesley and Watts.*)

As an essential part of Christian worship, hymns properly come at those points in the service where the whole congregation is called upon to respond to what is said and done. After the opening sentences, extolling God's power and majesty and summoning the people to worship, a hymn should be sung in celebration of God's sovereignty and in gratitude for the promise of his renewing grace. This should be affirmative, outgoing, and joyous, as with Henry Lytes' hymn, "Praise the Lord, his glories show," or William Kethe's paraphrase of Psalm 100, "All people that on earth do dwell." As all creation joined in singing God's praises upon coming into being, and continues still the *musica mundana*, "the music of the spheres," so man echoes the song of earth and heaven in the *musica humana*, "the music of humanity," as he comes to celebrate God's creative might and redeeming presence with hymns.

Another appropriate place for a hymn, although not exclusively so, is in connection with the reading and preaching of the Word. This should be in preparation for receiving God's truth. Good examples of such hymns are "O Word of God incarnate" and "Come, gracious Spirit, heavenly Dove." When a hymn precedes the sermon, it may fittingly and probably should be chosen to accord with the text and message of the day. The closing hymn, like a bugle call, should sound the note of thanksgiving, commitment, and victory. It should "repeat the sounding joy" of the songs of the redeemed in the heavenly Jerusalem which bring the whole biblical drama to a triumphant and soaring conclusion. The words and music should be like banners flying. Among such hymns one would surely include "Glorious things of thee are spoken," "Jesus shall reign," "Soldiers of Christ, arise," and "God of grace and God of glory."

In addition to their primary liturgical function, hymns also serve to instruct believers, preserve the faith, win converts, awaken the indifferent, promote fellowship, and unite Christians of all communions. The church possesses no greater asset in its store of spiritual gifts than its treasury of hymns. Indeed hymns constitute one of the distinctive and almost unique marks of the Christian faith in its corporate worship. All religions have made use of music and song, but this usually has taken the form of hymns sung or recited by individuals in private devotions or of instrumental or choral works performed by trained musicians and singers. Congregational singing, the lifting up of heart and voice by the people in common praise, is peculiarly Christian, without parallel in other world religions, exclusive of Judaism, save as these have been influenced by Christian example and practice. The church began in song and has been singing its hymns of praise and adoration through the centuries and, we dare believe, will continue to do so to the end of time and even into God's own eternity.

A. C. R.

Music of the Hymns

A hymnal is a fascinating book to explore whether it is approached by way of words or music. On virtually every page there are waymarks pointing to areas of interest which, when explored, broaden one's outlook in many directions. For instance: The headings of "Our God, our help in ages past," the first hymn in the *Pilgrim Hymnal,* refer to Psalm 90, Isaac Watts, and William Croft. One of the most striking facts to emerge from the study of hymns and tunes is that the psalms — that inexhaustible treasury of devotion — are at the heart of Jewish, Catholic, and Protestant worship. Their influence on hymnody is immeasurable. For generations, congregations in Protestant churches which followed the Calvinist traditions in public worship, sang only metrical versions of the psalms and a few scriptural paraphrases. A glance at pages 561 and 562 in the *Pilgrim Hymnal*'s Index of Authors, Translators, and Sources, will show what a large number of the hymns in the book are based on psalms. For well over two hundred years "psalm tune" rather than "hymn tune" was the accepted term for the music sung by Protestant congregations. Many of our finest tunes are from the Genevan, English, and Scottish psalters.

How firmly the tradition of psalm-singing took hold in churches is discovered as one reads of the long and determined opposition to Isaac Watts' "hymns of human composure" which were written to liberate congregations from the stranglehold of psalmody. This was a momentous chapter in the history of English hymnody and one that affected American congregations as well. The celebrated tune ST. ANNE appeared originally with a metrical version of Psalm 42. Not until 1861 was it set to "Our God, our help in ages past," Watts' paraphrase of Psalm 90. This one hymn introduces us to Isaac Watts, a key figure in English hymnody, to his distinguished contemporary, William Croft, and to the engrossing subject of psalmody.

Once a person's interest is kindled in hymnody he discovers that its ramifications are endless. Hymnody did not develop apart from the mainstream of life but in the midst of transforming movements in the history of mankind. Bound up with man's deepest emotions and experiences, it is intensely alive, full of human interest, drama, adventure. It puts one in touch with history, biography, poetry, music. It would be hard to prescribe a better way to sense the excitement and power of the Reformation than through a study of the music which played such a crucial part in its growth and carried it from country to country. Luther's enemies said that his followers were singing their way into the new doctrines. His hymns and tunes penetrated where his writings were excluded. Calvin's influence at Geneva owed much to the enthusiastic singing of French psalm versions set to Bourgeois' melodies.

Practically every great religious revival in the church has been sung as well as written and preached into the minds and hearts of people. Each movement has made its distinctive contribution to hymnody. Tunes as well as words reflect the times in which they were created. More than a singing

xiii

acquaintance with them is necessary if one is to appreciate them at their full value. To follow a melody from country to country, from denomination to denomination, from century to century, and to learn of its alterations and associations along the way, is absorbing and stimulating. Familiarity with the characteristic types of tunes associated with successive periods in the history of the church opens one's eyes to the richness and diversity of the music in a hymnal. Instead of thinking in terms of a comparatively small number of familiar tunes one becomes cognizant of the larger framework of history that is mirrored in the music of hymnody. When members of congregations, church musicians, directors of religious education, ministers, take time each week to learn something about the background of the hymns and tunes sung on Sunday, they find the hymnal coming to life in a new way. Their sympathies and interests are enlarged, their devotion is quickened, their outlook on religion and worship broadened, and a new perspective on hymns is gained. Such interest and effort does not fail to add vitality to individual and corporate worship.

Program notes for symphony concerts, operas, ballets, plays, are an accepted part of the American cultural scene and add considerably to an audience's understanding and appreciation of what is heard and seen. When ministers or church musicians provide informative notes on hymns and tunes in the weekly or monthly church bulletins, congregations begin to take a more lively interest in the hymns they sing. Those who prepare such notes discover new riches in their hymnals. Involvement in any aspect of hymnody discloses unsuspected treasure. This wealth comes to light with the continued study of texts and tunes in conjunction with handbooks, guides, and other reference books. There are enough fine tunes in a good hymnal to provide an almost limitless supply of ideas for special musical services and hymn festivals.

Hymn-sings, hymn festivals, rehearsals, with choirs and congregation participating, quicken interest in hymnody. A hymnal and a guide in the home is an incentive to make frequent use of them. Children and young people who study music should be encouraged to learn how to play hymn tunes, even if at first they can manage only the melody. To play hymns well requires practice and skill; the earlier one starts, the better.

HYMNS IN CHRISTIAN EDUCATION

The singing of first-class hymns and tunes should be given a major part in Christian education. Dr. Henry Sloane Coffin's recommendation is that "children should be familiarized with the best music that the Church knows, music that they will proudly carry with them as a standard of good taste all their days." The longer one knows and sings the great hymns of the church, the more he finds to admire in them. The best place to improve congregational singing is in the church school.

Children are responsive and receptive to the best in texts and tunes and have no inhibitions about undertaking something new. As they sing the hymns the fundamentals of faith are impressed vividly in their memories and affections. Words of hymns provide wonderful springboards for discussion through which new concepts are gained and familiar ones clarified.

Hymns awaken and strengthen the sense of wonder, love, and praise. From third grade on, along with hymn singing, there should be some instruction in hymnody — in small amounts. Children can be given an awareness of the central place that psalms have held in worship and hymnody, of people and movements that have shaped church and denominational history, of authors and composers. They need experience in finding their way through the hymnal from cover to cover, of browsing through its indexes, of considering headings, meters, tune names. The contribution that the singing of fine hymns and tunes can make to childrens' lives is unique and incalculable.

The hymn text rightly takes priority over the tune and is the justification for a hymnal's existence. Some who think of a hymnal primarily in terms of the tunes may forget that the mission of hymns is religious, not musical. However, the tune is as essential as the text in the actual practice of hymnody; for a hymn, as St. Augustine said, is "the praise of God in singing." Walford Davies believed that in hymnody melody "is the actual carrier of wonderment and devotion." Certainly the tune is of vital importance in public worship. A hymn read is entirely different from a hymn that is sung. To know how true this is, imagine a congregation reading "A mighty fortress is our God" instead of singing it. In hymnody, text and tune supplement each other and form an indivisible whole. The music intensifies the meaning of the text and in many instances goes beyond it, inspiring thoughts and feelings too profound for utterance in words. The greatest tunes have enduring qualities and power past telling and add something indefinable and distinctive to every text with which they are associated.

Tunes have individuality and personality. Some are found in a variety of forms with a variety of names. The source of many is unknown. They come from many different communions and transcend the barriers of race, nationality, and time. Only a few have been indissolubly associated with one text. EIN' FESTE BURG is one of these. Through the tunes one meets a varied company: court and church musicians, renowned composers and "one tune" men, amateurs and professionals, instrumentalists and singers, ministers and laymen.

A hymn tune is one of the shortest and simplest musical forms, often no more than eight measures long. But one has only to think of ST. ANNE or DUNDEE to realize how moving eight measures can be. In an essay on William Shrubsole, composer of the hymn tune MILES LANE, Vaughan Williams asks: "What does size matter? Who would not rather have drawn eight bars straight from the fountainhead than have compiled whole symphonies strained very thin through the medium of the best foreign models?" Probably because of their brevity hymn tunes receive less attention than they deserve. By some they are considered an insignificant musical form and little thought is given to their structure. However, analyzing the melody, tonality, rhythmic pattern, harmonies, and form of hymn tunes can be a profitable exercise. There is more musical substance and greater diversity in them than is commonly supposed. The finest have simplicity, strength, dignity.

By directing attention to the make-up of hymn tunes musicians can give children and adults in their choirs and classes an understanding of music fundamentals and musical form. More than thirty hymns in the *Pilgrim*

Hymnal have two musical settings. In some cases the two tunes are matched in quality though different in character. In others there is considerable disparity. A comparison of the two can aid in developing greater sensitivity to musical quality and to the effect that a tune has on the text. One of the striking examples of this is found in the settings for William W. How's hymn "For all the saints" at Nos. 306 and 307. Comments on the structure of a number of melodies in the *Pilgrim Hymnal* have been included in the *Guide* in order to encourage a closer look at hymn tunes in general.

If a church musician shares Luther's conviction that music is "one of the most beautiful and most precious gifts of God," he will do all he can to promote interest in it. Obviously, hymn tunes are not to be thought of principally from the point of view of teaching music fundamentals. But the more ways in which a musician can get children and adults to focus their attention on the hymn tunes they sing, the better for congregational singing and the better for church music. Approaching hymn tunes from several different angles helps enormously in teaching them and in deepening their impact. In *Praises with Understanding* the English hymnologist A. S. Gregory says: "As with hynms, so with tunes, the informed critical faculty is not the enemy, but the friend of true religion. . . . Music . . . may be itself a means of grace, and not merely, as is so often supposed, the handmaid of another means; further, the capacity to discern and to love the best . . . in music is one that can and ought to be cultivated by all who seek in hymns to glorify God."

There is abundant evidence to show that when a director of music places a high value on hymns and makes a consistent effort to acquaint his choirs and congregation with them, there is generally an eager response. Peter C. Lutkin, who did much to further the cause of church music in the United States, says in a pamphlet on hymn-singing and hymn-playing that "with a little enterprise congregations may be shown quite obviously the difference between the good and the poor" but "cannot rise above their own standards without help." Many people in churches have a genuine interest in hymns and welcome informative comments on the background of texts and tunes, the make-up of a hymnal, the history of hymnody. Invariably they express surprise that it is such a many-sided subject. A hymn-study group (no matter how small) formed each year in churches, with every member of the group taking an active part, could lead to a more intelligent use of the resources in a hymnal and eventually to more spirited congregational singing. Ideally, every church library should have a shelf of books on hymnody which would include hymnals of different denominations, handbooks, reference books. In *A Short Bibliography for the Study of Hymns,* published in 1964 by The Hymn Society of America, the editors have designated books which might form the nucleus of such a reference shelf. This bibliography is available from the society's offices at 475 Riverside Drive, New York City.

Musical examples have been included in the *Guide* for their historical interest and with the hope that some will be used by choirs and other groups. It is sometimes more instructive to see the early form of chorale melodies and Genevan tunes than to read about them. To hear and sing them is even better, for in this way their free rhythm and distinctive tonal flavor are more clearly discerned. Singing chorales and Genevan psalm tunes to the

German or French texts with which they have had long association is an enriching experience. Through it one senses the significance of these melodies in the Lutheran and Reformed traditions and in hymnody in general. To sing Luther's words to EIN' FESTE BURG in its original form seems to put one in closer touch with his thought, with the music of his time, and with the stirring events of the early days of the Reformation. Similarly, the glorious tune, OLD 124th, has new meaning for those who have sung it with de Bèze's French version of Psalm 124 and know something of what the text and tune meant in the lives of the Huguenots.

APPEAL OF CHORALES AND GENEVAN TUNES

It would be worthwhile, and in keeping with the current emphasis on language study in the schools, to have children's and young people's choirs learn the German and French texts to chorales and Genevan tunes for special occasions, such as Reformation Sunday. Children and young people learn songs in foreign languages readily and find it a challenging assignment. If they were to master only one chorale or one Genevan tune a year, they would gradually build up a repertoire of classic texts and tunes to prize for a lifetime. If choir directors have not studied German or French, they can usually find someone in the congregation or in the schools to help in such an undertaking.

At the present time more of Johann Sebastian Bach's compositions are being sung and played in churches than ever before. He made lavish use of chorale melodies in his choral and organ works. Twenty-one hymns in the *Pilgrim Hymnal* are set to chorales harmonized by him. In addition a considerable number are set to melodies which appear in his organ works, cantatas, passions, motets, and chorale collections. Throughout the *Guide* comments on these harmonizations and melodies mention the specific works in which they have been used by Bach. A program of his chorale preludes can be made much more intelligible to laymen if before each work the melody on which it is based is sung by the choir, preferably in German and in unison. It might also be sung in English by the congregation. If a chorale has roots in a Gregorian chant and a Genevan tune as well, these could precede the German version. There is no more telling way to show how the traditional melodies of the Roman Catholic Church were used by the Bohemian Brethren, Calvinists, and Lutherans for some of the new vernacular hymns of the Reformation. Such an introduction points up the fact that tunes, like words, have interesting derivations.

Many people are puzzled by the German titles of chorale preludes for organ which are played in services and at recitals. They don't know their meaning — often no translation is given — nor that the titles are from the first line of the chorale on which the prelude is based. Paul Henry Lang calls the chorale "the Ariadne's thread in Bach's works." Those who are familiar with the chorale used in the prelude have little difficulty following the thread of melody which is woven into the fabric of the work. But the members of many congregations in the United States have sung comparatively few chorales. Hence the need to acquaint them with the melody of the chorale before the prelude is played so that they can identify it by sound.

xvii

Seeing "Vater unser im Himmelreich" on a program might mean little to the majority of people in our churches; but knowing that the words mean "Our Father in heaven" and are the first line of Luther's version of the Lord's prayer, set by him in 1539 to an anonymous melody which was sung later with English versions of the same prayer in England, Scotland, and in parts of New England, adds fresh meaning to the melody and the work in which it appears.

METER DESIGNATIONS

One feature in the headings of hymns, the meter designations, may need clarification for some readers. Even Mendelssohn, when asked by an English friend to write a tune in L.M., replied that he couldn't comply with the request because he didn't know what the letters meant. The abbreviations C.M., L.M., S.M., found to the right of the tune name in the *Pilgrim Hymnal* stand for Common Meter, Long Meter, Short Meter, the three metrical patterns most commonly used in English and American hymnody. A four-line hymn in Common Meter has the pattern 8.6.8.6. — eight syllables in the first and third lines, six in the second and fourth, as in "Our God, our help in ages past." The pattern for Long Meter is 8.8.8.8. as in "Praise God from whom all blessings flow." That for Short Meter is 6.6.8.6. as in "Blest be the tie that binds." These three hymns are useful to remember as models in case one forgets the numerical patterns for the abbreviations. The letter D. after letters or numbers stands for "double" as in C.M.D. (Common Meter Double), the meter of the eight-line hymn "O beautiful for spacious skies." Metrical patterns other than these are given in numbers. In the Metrical Index, page 567 of the *Pilgrim Hymnal,* all the meters used in the book are listed with the tunes to which they have been set. In nineteenth-century American hymnals and tune-books one finds the abbreviations P.M. for Peculiar or Particular Meter and H.M. for Hallelujah Meter, both of which appear in a variety of combinations. These are no longer used. Children enjoy learning the metrical patterns, their abbreviations, noting the meters of the hymns they sing, singing familiar texts to unfamiliar tunes in the same meter, finding the meter of unfamiliar texts. In this way they learn some of the basics of hymnody.

Because of the necessary limitations of space, a hymnal guide or handbook can be little more than an introduction to the vast and varied subject of hymnody. It is hoped that the comments on tunes in the *Pilgrim Hymnal* will generate sufficient interest to whet the reader's appetite for additional detail and spur him to further study. It should be emphasized, however, that hymns, and tunes, and information about their background are not to be thought of as ends in themselves. The purpose of a hymn is to direct thought Godward and a hymnal exists for the worship of God through the singing of "psalms, and hymns, and spiritual songs." A hymnal guide fulfills its true function only in the degree to which it gives worshippers new eyes for the visibles and invisibles on the pages of their hymnals and new joy in singing their Creator's praise.

E. K. P.

Isaac Watts and Congregational Hymnody

Protestant hymnody at the time of the Reformation ran in two main streams: the Luthern and the Reformed. The first was characterized by the sturdy German chorales. These were biblical paraphrases and sacred texts set to adaptations of plainsong melodies, folk songs, or original compositions. Two of the most familiar are "A mighty fortress is our God" and "O sacred Head, now wounded." The chief architect of the chorales was Martin Luther. The second great stream emanated from Geneva under the influence of John Calvin and consisted of metrical versions of the psalms, usually cast in a quite literalistic form. Clément Marot and Théodore de Bèze (Beza) were the chief versifiers of the texts while Louis Bourgeois was primarily responsible for the music.

The Lutheran hymnals and Genevan psalters appeared in numerous versions and constituted the main sources of congregational hymns and songs during and following the Reformation. These two streams flowed in separate channels for more than two centuries, with some intermingling, and then gradually converged to form one cascading river of Protestant hymnody.

Of those writers who came out of the psalter tradition and pioneered in broadening the church's praises, Isaac Watts is preeminent. By the hymns he wrote, the role he played in emancipating Protestant worship from a rigid psalmody, and by the principles he enunciated, he stands out as a pivotal figure. If nothing else had come from his pen but his magnificent hymn, "Our God, our help in ages past" (see comments at No. 1), he would for that reason alone deserve to rank with the greatest of all hymn writers. Congregational hymnody owes its distinctive character to him. One can trace at least five distinguishing features in his work which have shaped Congregational hymnody, marking it off from those traditions which have been primarily oriented to a strict psalmody or to a purely liturgical or aesthetic use of hymns in worship.

1. ITS CHRISTOCENTRIC CHARACTER. The first hymn which Isaac Watts wrote, prompted by his dissatisfaction with the metrical psalms sung in the chapel he attended in Southampton, reveals both his motivating concern and guiding passion, namely, that Christ is to be enthroned and adored above all else in the worship of the church.

> Behold the glories of the Lamb
> Before His Father's throne;
> Prepare new honors for His name,
> And songs before unknown.

Watts initiated his movement of reform largely because the psalmody of his time allowed no place for the explicit showing forth of the glory of Christ in the praises of the church. He gave as his reason for altering and rephrasing the psalms: "When we are just entring into an Evangelic Frame, by some of the Glories of the Gospel presented in the brightest Figures of Judaism, yet the very next Line perhaps which the Clerk parcels out unto us, hath something in it so extremely Jewish and cloudy, that darkens our Sight of God the Saviour: Thus, by keeping too close to David in the House of God, the Veil of Moses is thrown over our Hearts." It was to remove this "veil" and allow "the light of the knowledge of the glory of God in the face of Christ" to be revealed in its fullness and majesty that Watts wrote his hymns.

This distinctively Christian emphasis which characterized all of Watts' work, firmly anchoring it in the mainstream of classical Christianity, has remained as a continuing mark of Congregational hymnody. Even during the height of the social gospel movement, with its more "liberal" type of Christology, and in the heyday of Unitarianism, with its broader theological interpretations, both of which contributed much to an ampler and improved hymnody, this basic orientation has never been lost. So, a later Congregationalist, Ray Palmer, expressed it:

> My faith looks up to thee,
> Thou Lamb of Calvary, Savior divine!
> Now hear me while I pray; Take all my guilt away;
> Oh, let me from this day Be wholly thine.

Congregational hymnody has been centered in a high valuation of Christ, consonant with historic Christianity.

2. ITS CHURCHLY INTENT. Watts wrote many hymns suitable for personal use and private devotions, for family gatherings and children's instruction, yet his hymns were written primarily to be sung in church and were inspired in the setting of worship. His efforts were prompted not by aesthetic considerations nor the requirements of large evangelistic meetings nor the more personal needs of individual Christians but solely by his desire to furnish the house of God in its corporate worship with acceptable and worthy songs of praise. Watts was a churchman, first and last. His most notable admirer in New England during the Revolutionary period, Timothy Dwight, in writing what some have called the first great hymn produced in America, expressed as completely as anyone could the dominant concern and kindling spirit of hymnody's great emancipator:

> I love thy kingdom, Lord,
> The house of thine abode,
> The Church our blest Redeemer saved
> With his own precious blood.
>
> . . . .
>
> Beyond my highest joy
> I prize her heavenly ways,
> Her sweet communion, solemn vows,
> Her hymns of love and praise.

Congregational hymnody, throughout its history, avoiding the extremes of a pietistic subjectivism and a revivalistic emotionalism, has made the service of Christ in the worship of his church its major and controlling goal.

3. ITS SCRIPTURAL BASE AND QUALITY. One of Watts' most significant and enduring contributions to hymnody was to emancipate the

church not only from an inordinate and exclusive preoccupation with psalmody but also from a strict and confining biblical literalism. In thinking of hymns as a human offering of praise to God, he maintained that each age should fashion its songs of faith in its own language: "By reading we learn what God speaks to us in his word; but when we sing, especially unto God, our chief design is, or should be, to speak our own hearts and our words to God." Watts was no scriptural literalist.

Nevertheless, recognizing this, it must also be said that everything he wrote, from his paraphrases to his lyric poems, was inspired, shaped, and informed by a profound grasp of biblical revelation and imagery. His magnificent communion hymn, "When I survey the wondrous cross," regarded by some as the greatest Christian hymn ever written, gains its power from and is steeped in the pungent language of the New Testament, so that there is hardly a line which cannot be traced back to one of Paul's impassioned epistles. Even where Watts is not explicitly paraphrasing one of the psalms or basing a hymn on a particular passage of scripture, his language and thought are saturated with biblical phrases and allusions. If he fought for a more liberal attitude toward the Bible in the use made of it in hymnody, he did so only that the Bible, abetted by the fires of human imagination and the wings of pure poetry, might thereby be enabled to speak its word of truth with an even greater thrust of meaning, power, and beauty. In this he not only established the prevailing mind-set of succeeding generations of Congregational hymn writers, men like Philip Doddridge, Timothy Dwight, Ray Palmer, Washington Gladden, and John Oxenham, but also anchored Christian hymnody in the common ground of biblical experience, from which it has ever derived its greatest strength and grandeur.

4. ITS SOCIAL VIGOR AND SENSITIVITY. If it would be incorrect to attribute to Watts a passionate concern about social problems, which reflected itself in his hymns, it would be equally misleading to think that he devoted his efforts purely to scriptural, doctrinal, and liturgical themes. Although the latter unquestionably received the major portion of his attention and talents, he never forgot that where Christ truly reigns, there:

> The prisoner leaps to lose his chains;
> The weary find eternal rest,
> And all the sons of want are blest.

For Watts, Christian worship and praise could never be divorced from the common life nor remain detached from the problems of the here and now. The emphasis he gave was to influence greatly the work of later authors and give to Congregational hymnody one of its essential qualities, a bold and forthright confrontation of the social implications of the Christian gospel which it has retained to the present day.

5. ITS COMPREHENSIVE REACH AND SCOPE. In all that Watts wrote, there was a broad sweep and spaciousness to his outlook. Nothing merely sectarian or trivial was allowed to intrude or to limit the range of his interests and creative efforts. He drew his inspiration from a wide variety of sources and in his hymns and songs lifted up those basic and common affirmations in which all Christians could join. The catholicity of his spirit was informed by a profound sense of the universal and cosmic significance

of the Christian gospel. It is for this reason that he eschewed everything petty and encompassed the whole universe in his offerings of praise. This note is frequently struck, as in the lines from his hymn "Come let us join our cheerful songs."

> Let all that dwell above the sky
> And air, and earth and seas,
> Conspire to lift Thy glories high,
> And speak Thine endless praise;
>
> The whole creation join in one
> To bless the sacred name
> Of Him that sits upon the throne,
> And to adore the Lamb.

No one could accuse Watts of being narrow or cramped or stunted. What he did for his own day and generation, in giving a broadened and elevated vision of the joy and comprehensiveness of the gospel, has remained and made its mark on the developing tradition of Congregational hymnody, as it has on all Protestant hymnody. Henry Hallam Tweedy, in his prize-winning missionary hymn written for The Hymn Society of America in 1929, caught the feel and spirit of the vision which motivated Watts and those who followed after him:

> Eternal God, whose pow'r upholds
> Both flower and flaming star,
> To whom there is no here nor there,
> No time, no near nor far,
> No alien race, no foreign shore,
> No child unsought, unknown,
> O send us forth, thy prophets true,
> To make all lands thine own!

Congregational hymnody, with its firm anchorage in the mainstream of classical Christianity, as exemplified in its continuing fidelity to Christ, the church, and the Bible, and with its awareness of the social dimensions and outreach of the Christian faith, has at the same time retained a broad, inclusive, and comprehensive point of view both with respect to the best in other traditions and the sweep and range of the gospel it proclaims.

A. C. R.

Uses of the Hymnal

The primary purpose of the hymnal is to provide the congregation with a readily available body of hymns suitable for singing in public worship throughout the Christian year. Although there have been individuals and church groups so familiar with the hymns that they could sing them from memory, most congregations would be lost without the hymnal. It is an indispensable aid in Protestant worship. The present *Pilgrim Hymnal* has been so conceived and put together that if a person in charge of a service of worship had no other resource available it would contain everything required to plan and conduct the service.

The minister bears the major responsibility of using the hymnal effectively in worship, since he usually selects the hymns and sets the example for the congregation. Nothing contributes more to spirited worship than vigorous congregational singing, and the minister can be the quickening, inspiring force. As much study and thought should be given to the choice of the hymns as to the scripture readings and prayers. A record should be kept of the hymns sung each week so as to avoid overworking a few old favorites and neglecting worthy but less familiar ones. With the wealth of good hymns to draw upon, no hymn should normally be sung more than two or three times in the course of a year and at least one new or less well known hymn should be introduced each month. For its part, the congregation should participate vigorously in the singing and give as much attention to the words as to the music, taking note of what is being sung. Sung with understanding, a hymn achieves its full potential and brings its intended reward.

In addition to its primary use in worship, the hymnal is also an excellent resource as a devotional aid in preparing for worship. Before the service members of the congregation can engage in no better exercise than to read and study the texts of the hymns to be sung. There is almost certain to be a thought or a phrase to enable the worshipper to enter into the service in the right spirit. By their very nature hymns deal with the greatest themes of Christian faith in the most direct and compelling manner and convey the highest truths with the utmost simplicity. Those hymns that have endured, those that represent an ecumenical consensus in their usage, are inexhaustible mines of poetic imagery and profound insight. To know their thought and to meditate on their meaning is to engage in prayer. Such a discipline, followed Sunday after Sunday, will not only enrich the individual worshipper but will also contribute to the vitality and value of the service itself.

If the main function of a hymnal is to serve as a repository of hymns for congregational singing, of almost equal importance is its potential in providing a wealth of homiletical insights. Carefully and appropriately chosen, lines of a hymn can bring home the truth of an idea with luminous intensity and make clear in a few words what before may have remained tenuous and indistinct. Paul's letters were filled with quotations from hymns, giving dramatic and pointed immediacy to his thought. Throughout Christian history preachers, both well-known and obscure, have followed Paul's example and drawn upon hymns for the vivid summation of a homiletical idea and for inspiration. Philip Doddridge regularly wrote the closing hymn for the services he conducted to "bring home" and make real the theme of the sermon. It is said that Phillips Brooks knew more than two hundred hymns by heart and often quoted them in his preaching. Often a few lines from a hymn can express the deepest truths in the fewest words. When Theodore Dwight Woolsey, president of Yale University from 1846 to 1871, sought in an address to dispel the prevailing skepticism of his time, he made his point and won his audience in a memorable and telling manner by pausing and suddenly quoting the first stanza of the familiar hymn, "O where are kings and empires now." Such effective use of hymns in preaching demands constant study of their content and requires great familiarity with their thought.

Since the preference of adults for certain hymns is largely determined by what they have learned in their formative years, the use made of the hymnal in the religious nurture of children and young people is of decisive importance. From their earliest years children should be taught to know and appreciate the great hymns of the church so that by the time they are ready to become full members they will be familiar with its finest hymns. One of the best ways to introduce such hymns is to tell the stories connected with them, the interesting accounts of the lives of the authors and composers and the occasions that prompted them to write. Every church school library should have one or more reference books on hymnody, such as the present *Guide* and Armin Haeussler's *The Story of Our Hymns*. Another valuable resource is Millar Patrick's *The Story of the Church's Song,* American edition, 1961, giving a swift, fascinating, and scholarly survey of hymnody through the centuries.

Like the Bible, the hymnal is designed for use in the home as well as in church and is intended for private devotions as well as for congregational worship. Many hymns are prayers and touch upon the great themes of faith with a simplicity and beauty that often match and sometimes surpass the classic prayers of the church. Every home should have a copy of the hymnal and the *Guide,* and families should be encouraged to use hymns for grace at meals, for devotions, and for singing together.

The uses to which the hymnal can be put creatively are almost endless, and the resources it contains for a strong, jubilant faith almost inexhaustible. To know, think about, and sing the lines of notable hymns is to engage in prayer with the church universal.

A. C. R.

THE HYMNS

1 Our God, Our Help in Ages Past

Isaac Watts (1674–1748) wrote this hymn, based on Psalm 90, while he was serving as pastor of Mark Lane Independent (Congregational) Church in London. At the time, approximately 1714, Queen Anne was near death and there was widespread anxiety about her successor, many fearing that England would be torn by civil strife. The hymn first appeared in his *Psalms of David, Imitated in the Language of the New Testament, and Apply'd to the Christian State and Worship,* 1719, with the heading, "Man frail and God eternal." Frequently the first stanza begins with "O" instead of "Our," a change introduced by John Wesley, but it is given here as Watts wrote it, in the more personal style of the Lord's Prayer. Frederick J. Gilman has said that it "has become the great ceremonial hymn of the English nation, and if nothing else had come from his pen, it justifies its author's memorial in Westminster Abbey." It was sung at Sir Winston Churchill's funeral on January 30, 1965, in St. Paul's Cathedral, London.

Because of ill-health, Watts lived for the last thirty-six years of his life as a semi-invalid in the home of Sir Thomas Abney, one of his wealthy parishioners, ministering to his people with the aid of an assistant and devoting most of his time to writing. He was the author of approximately sixty volumes, including a standard textbook on logic long used at Oxford, but his fame today rests on his hymns and paraphrases. Many of the finest of these were written while he was in his early twenties. Known as the father of modern English hymnody, he wrote more than six hundred hymns and paraphrases and enabled Protestantism in England and New England to emancipate itself from a rigid and exclusive use of literalistic, metrical versions of the psalms in its congregational singing, despite strenuous and long-continued opposition. His poetic gifts were such as to prompt Samuel Johnson to include him in his *Lives of the Poets,* 1781. Most of his hymns were published in four major collections: *Horae Lyricae,* 1706; *Hymns and Spiritual Songs,* 1707; *Divine Songs,* 1715; and *The Psalms of David,* 1719.

ST. ANNE   Referring to ST. ANNE, Calvin Laufer wrote: "As a musical setting for Watts' words it will never be superseded. The words and music fit as hand in glove." Yet this tune and these words did not appear together until

1

1861 in *Hymns Ancient and Modern.* Earlier associations of the text were with BANGOR (149), ST. MARY (497), DUNDEE (85). In early nineteenth-century American hymnals the tune is found with a wide variety of texts. Its first appearance in England was in the sixth edition of *A Supplement to the New Version of Psalms,* 1708 (Tate and Brady), named ST. ANNE'S TUNE and set to a paraphrase of Psalm 42.

The tune bore no composer's name but from 1720 on was attributed to William Croft (1678–1727) who is thought to have had a part in editing the *Supplement,* published while he was organist at St. Anne's Church in Soho, London. In Abraham Barber's *Book of Psalm Tunes,* 1715, the tune was called LEEDS and ascribed to a Mr. Denby, but this is now considered to be a four-part rearrangement of Croft's tune. The first phrase of ST. ANNE seems to have been common property in the seventeenth and eighteenth centuries. Two of Henry Lawes' psalm tunes start with it, and three of them contain its first four-note motif. The phrase appears in Handel's sixth Chandos anthem, "O praise the Lord with one consent," and is the first subject of Bach's great organ fugue in E flat major, known to English and American organists as the St. Anne Fugue.

Croft(s) was a boy chorister in the Chapel Royal and a student of Dr. John Blow. In 1700 he was sworn in as a gentleman of the Chapel Royal and in the same year became organist, probably the first, at St. Anne's Church, Soho, to which William III had presented an organ in 1699. For three years Croft and Jeremiah Clark (No. 78) served as joint organists of the Chapel Royal. After Clark's death in 1707 Croft remained as sole organist. In 1708 he succeeded Dr. Blow as organist of Westminster Abbey, master of the children, and composer to the Chapel Royal. In 1713 Croft received the Doctor of Music Degree at Oxford. He died at Bath in August, 1727, and was buried in Westminster Abbey.

Although in his earlier years Croft wrote music for the theater, for the harpsichord and other instruments, and for voice, it was as a composer of church music — psalm tunes, anthems, services — that he attained distinction. In 1724 he published *Musica Sacra . . . Select Anthems in Score . . . to which is added the Burial-Service* in order to show musicians the "Benefit and Advantage" of having the music "laid before them in a complete and correct score." In the Preface he wrote that this was "the first Essay of publishing *Church-Musick* in England, after the *Manner* of *Printing"* — that is, engraved on plates. In his day, choristers had to sing from separate vocal parts which were full of printers' and copyists' mistakes, with no score available for reference. Croft wrote that it was "difficult to find in the Cathedrals, any one Antient valuable Piece of *Musick,* that does not abound with Faults and Imperfections." His hope that *Musica Sacra* would induce some "able Hand . . . to procure and publish correct Copies in Score, of all that is valuable in the Church-Way" was not fulfilled until Boyce's *Cathedral Music* was published in 1760. (See No. 562.)

Croft's "Burial Service," which contains Purcell's setting of the graveside sentence, "Thou knowest, Lord, the secrets of our hearts," is considered one of the masterpieces of English church music. Its opening sentences were sung at the funeral service for Sir Winston Churchill at St. Paul's Cathedral on January 30, 1965.

2 All Glory Be to God on High

Based on the ancient canticle, *Gloria in excelsis,* this hymn is attributed to Nicolaus Decius (d. 1541), a Catholic monk who was greatly influenced by Luther and became an Evangelical preacher in Stettin, Germany. Both the text and tune are ascribed to him. Since many of the Reformation pastors were poets and musicians as well as preachers, following Luther's example, it was not uncommon for them to write both the words and the music for their hymns. The translation, derived from the High German version of 1539, was made by Catherine Winkworth (1827–1878), distinguished English scholar, translator, and educator who was largely responsible for introducing the treasures of German hymnody to the English-speaking world. Active all her life in educational and social work, especially in fostering greater educational opportunities for women, she possessed both a keen, inquiring mind and an intensely devout spirit. It was the latter quality that undoubtedly attracted her to the German chorales with their warm, personal character. Her first published volume of translations of German hymns, *Lyra Germanica,* which appeared in two series, 1855 and 1858, ran to twenty-five editions and has become a devotional classic. She later published two other notable volumes, *The Chorale Book for England,* 1863, and *Christian Singers of Germany,* 1869. Bishop Percival, then headmaster of Clifton College, said of her, "She was a person of remarkable intellectual and social gifts and very unusual attainments; but what specially distinguished her was her combination of rare ability and great knowledge with a certain tender and sympathetic refinement which constitutes the special charm of the womanly character." [1]

ALLEIN GOTT IN DER HÖH' (STETTIN; DECIUS; TO GOD ON HIGH)   The name most frequently found with this chorale is from the first line of Decius' German paraphrase of the *Gloria in excelsis:* "Allein Gott in der Höh' sei Ehr' " ("To God alone on high be praise"). The melody first appeared with Decius' text in Valten Schumann's *Geistliche Lieder,* 1539, a collection of early Reformation hymns and tunes. It is an adaptation, generally attributed to Decius, of a tenth-century plainsong setting of the Gloria in the Paschal or Easter mass. (*Lux et origo.*) This melody had appeared in Thomas Münzer's *Deutsche evangelische Messe,* 1524, with a German version of the text. Parts of Decius' adaptation are identical with parts of the plainsong and show clearly how writers and musicians of the Reformation drew freely and openly on the liturgical texts and melodies of the Roman Catholic Church. The first and second phrases of the chorale are almost identical with the plainsong melody for "Et in terra pax hominibus" which was traditionally sung by the choir in response to the priest's intonation of "Gloria in excelsis Deo." In time, Decius' German version, sung by the congregation, replaced the choir's traditional response.

Bach used the melody in Cantatas 84, 104, 112, 128, and in ten chorale preludes for organ: three in the *Clavierübung,* three in the *Eighteen Chorales,* four among the miscellaneous Preludes. There is one harmonization of the melody in the *Choralgesänge.* The first chorale in Mendelssohn's oratorio *St. Paul* is ALLEIN GOTT IN DER HOH'. The 4/2 or 4/4 rhythm of the melody, used by Bach and Mendelssohn, is found in various German hymnals of the former Reformed Church in the United States and the Evangelical

3

Synod of North America. The setting in the *Pilgrim Hymnal,* except for passing notes and two chords, is from *The Hymnal,* 1941 (Evangelical and Reformed).

Decius' adaptation of the melody had the following form (Zahn 4457), still found in most Lutheran hymnals.

Al - lein Gott in   der Höhe sei Ehr und Dank für sei - ne Gna - - - - - de
da - rum dass nun und nim-mer-mehr uns rüh-ren kann kein Scha - - - - de

ein Wohl-ge-fall'n Gott an   uns hat; nun   ist gross Fried ohn Un - ter - lass, all

Feh - de   hat   nun   ein   En   -   de.

3 God Himself Is With Us

Stressing the immediacy of God's presence, Gerhard (or Gerhardt) Tersteegen (1697–1769), a profound German mystic, devoted his life to prayer, writing, and good works. Concerned about the low spiritual estate of the church of his time, he gave up his career as a silk weaver and began to hold informal prayer meetings and discussions of the Bible in his home. People came to him from great distances and other lands to seek his company and advice, so that his modest home in Mühlheim became the center of a vital religious movement and was known as the Pilgrims' Cottage. Conducting spiritual retreats and traveling each year to Holland to hold preaching services, he was everywhere known as the physician of the poor and forsaken. The letters he wrote ran into the thousands and he published an important collection of hymns, *Geistliches Blumen-Gärtlein,* 1729, from which the present hymn was taken, entitled "Remembrance of the Glorious and Delightful Presence of God." He also produced many translations of medieval authors and French mystics. Congregational singing was given a large place in his ministry and he urged his listeners to "sing with the spirit of reverence, with sincerity, simplicity and hearty desire." The translation given here is largely the work of Bishop Frederick W. Foster (1760–1835), editor of the *Moravian Hymn Book,* 1826 (revised edition), and a member of the English Moravian Church.

ARNSBERG (WUNDERBARER KÖNIG; GOTT IST GEGENWÄRTIG; GRÖNINGEN) This tune, attributed to Joachim Neander (1650–1680), was originally the setting for his hymn, "Wunderbarer König," published in a collection of his texts and tune, *Glaub-und-Liebesübung,* 1680.

Tersteegen's hymn, "Gott ist gegenwärtig," given here in translation, was written to fit Neander's tune. Both hymns are still sung with this melody in Germany, and appear with it in hymnals published in the United States for churches of the Reformed and Lutheran traditions. Neander's melody (Zahn 7854) has undergone a number of changes in contour and rhythm. The present version, the one in most common use in the United States, is also found in hymnals published on the Continent. See No. 15 for comments on Neander.

4 All People That on Earth Do Dwell

Among the well-known English psalm paraphrases now in common use, this is the earliest. It is based on Psalm 100. Written by William Kethe (d. 1953?), reportedly a native of Scotland and a refugee in Frankfurt and Geneva during the persecutions of Queen Mary, 1553–1558, it was one of twenty-five paraphrases contributed by him to the Anglo-Genevan Psalter of 1561 and was included in the Scottish Psalter issued in 1564–1565. It is printed exactly as he wrote it save that the word "mirth" has been substituted for "fear" in the first stanza as more in keeping with the original Hebrew. This change was introduced by the Scottish Psalter of 1650 and is now commonly accepted. Kethe served as an envoy from Geneva to fellow exiles on the continent during the time that Mary reigned in England and later was chaplain to the English troops under the Earl of Warwick. The latter years of his life seem to have been spent in the parish church of Childe Okeford, Dorsetshire.

OLD HUNDREDTH, the best-known and most widely used of all psalm tunes, has survived "all the changes of thought or fashion that the progress of four centuries has witnessed." In the 1551 Genevan Psalter it was set to Théodore de Bèze's version of Psalm 134, the psalm with which it is still sung in France and on the Continent. The original form of the melody, with English text, is given at No. 514. The tune came into English use in 1561 with Kethe's paraphrase of Psalm 100 and has been associated with it ever since. Its name, OLD HUNDREDTH, and the rhythm of its last phrase in the version given here are peculiar to English hymnody. OLD in the name indicates that it was the tune for Psalm 100 in Sternhold and Hopkins' Psalter, known as the Old Version after publication of Tate and Brady's *New Version of the Psalms* in 1696. The present form, with the same rhythmic pattern in each of its four phrases, became the accepted English version after inclusion in Ravenscroft's *Whole Booke of Psalms,* 1621. In the original melody the fourth phrase starts with three long notes instead of one. The version in which all the notes are of equal length (No. 515) seems to have been introduced around the middle of the eighteenth century. In American collections the tune was often called OLD HUNDRED and attributed to Martin Luther, as it had been in some English books.

In Germany the tune, in its original form, was sung in Reformed churches with Lobwasser's version of Psalm 134, and in Lutheran churches, after 1567, with "Herr Gott dich loben alle wir," and also with other texts. Bach used the melody in the first and last movements of Cantata 130. How much of the tune originated with Louis Bourgeois is not known. Using a well-known phrase to start a melody and then developing it along independent lines, was an accepted practice of the time. The first phrase of OLD HUN-DREDTH is said to be from a fifteenth-century secular chanson. It seems to have been a popular melodic formula of sixteenth-century composers, for it has been found in a number of psalm tunes published on the Continent and in England.

Louis Bourgeois, to whom OLD HUNDREDTH is attributed, was born in Paris c. 1510. Little is known of his activities before his residence in Geneva. He was there from 1545 to 1557, serving as choirmaster at the churches of St. Pierre and St. Gervais, teaching, composing, writing, selecting and arranging the tunes for successive French psalters, working closely with Calvin. He lived in the *chantrerie,* a house near the church of St. Pierre, maintained by the city for the precentor and the choir school. In collaboration with the ministers, Bourgeois worked out a *Table pour trouver les pseaumes,* a kind of chart on which the psalms were arranged in three columns (for a 28-week period) so that one could tell which would be used at the morning and evening services on Sunday and the service on Wednesday. It was posted at the door of the church so that members of the congregation would have no excuse for not knowing which psalms were to be sung. For his part in this innovation Bourgeois was rewarded with a gift of money. In 1547 the Council of Geneva granted him rights of citizenship in recognition of his loyal services, and in order to give him more time for study exempted him from serving as a town guard and working on fortifications, duties normally required of a citizen. In 1550 Bourgeois was given permission to publish, at his own expense, a book on music and singing, *Droict chemin de musique.* After the publication of the 1551 Psalter he was put in prison for having altered some of the tunes without authorization, but through Calvin's intervention was released after twenty-four hours. In the same year his salary, and that of other city employees, was reduced because of a depleted treasury. His repeated requests for the restoration of his former wages and for a possible increase were unsuccessful even though Calvin interceded in his behalf. In 1547 and 1554 collections of psalm tunes harmonized by Bourgeois were published at Lyons, a center of Protestant activity. Calvin did not permit the printing or singing of harmonized tunes at Geneva. It is thought by some that Bourgeois may have left that city because of the strong opposition to part-singing. In 1560 he was living in Paris, and on May 27th of that year attended the baptism of a daughter, Suzanne, at the Catholic church of St. Côme. Nothing is known of him after 1560.

It is not known with certainty which melodies in the French psalters were adapted or composed by Bourgeois. All were anonymous. Some bear traces of secular and liturgical melodies. The final form of the melodies for Marot's psalm versions in the 1551 Psalter is generally attributed to Bourgeois. All were retained in the completed Psalter of 1562, which contained 125 melodies. The finest are those for which Bourgeois seems to have been responsible.

The French or Genevan Psalter, which evolved in 1539–1562, has had immense influence on psalmody and hymnody. With its psalm versions translated into Dutch and set to the Genevan tunes, it was adopted by the Reformed Church of the Netherlands; and with Lobwasser's German versions set to the same tunes, it was used by the Reformed Church in Germany for more than two centuries. A considerable number of its tunes passed into Lutheran use and into the early English and Scottish psalters. In recent years more of the Genevan tunes in their original form have been included in hymnals, and there is a new awareness and appreciation of their intrinsic quality and beauty.

5 All People That on Earth Do Dwell

See No. 4 for comments on the text.

OLD HUNDREDTH   This setting of OLD HUNDREDTH appeared in Este's Psalter, 1592, which contained tunes arranged for four voices by ten of the leading composers of the day. In sixteenth- and seventeenth-century English usage, the term *faux-bourdon* was applied to simple harmonizations of psalm tunes with the melody in the tenor. The congregation sang the simple tune, while trained voices sang other parts which harmonized with it.

John Dowland (1562–1626), the greatest lutenist of his age and the most famous of the Elizabethan lutenist song writers, was unrivaled as a virtuoso. His success on the Continent was even greater than in England, not only as a performer on the lute, but as a singer and composer as well. Little is known of his early years or education. Before he was twenty he was in the service of Sir Henry Cobham, the English ambassador in Paris, remaining with him from 1580 to 1583. During this time he was persuaded by friends to become a Roman Catholic. Back in England in 1584, he married, and in 1588 received the Bachelor of Music degree at Oxford. When his application for a place among Queen Elizabeth's musicians was unsuccessful (c. 1594) he concluded: "My religion was my hindrance, whereupon my mind being troubled I desired to get beyond the seas." He went to Germany at the invitation of the Duke of Brunswick who treated him royally. Later, after service with the Landgrave of Hesse, he set out for Italy in the hope of studying in Rome with Luca Marenzio. When he discovered during a stay in Florence that he was among English Roman Catholics who were plotting against Queen Elizabeth and her government, he promptly forsook them and their religion and returned to Germany in spite of being promised a pension from the Pope and the patronage of several cardinals. From 1598 to 1606, he was lutenist to the King of Denmark, who honored him in many ways and paid him a salary equal to that of high ministers of state; but his extravagance and irresponsibility in money matters brought about his dismissal. Returning to England, he met with considerable neglect, but in 1612 was appointed one of the king's musicians for the lutes at the court of Charles I.

When preparations were being made for the coronation of Queen Elizabeth II on June 2, 1953, Ralph Vaughan Williams suggested that a hymn be sung by the congregation. This proposal was welcomed by the Archbishop of Canterbury, and accordingly OLD HUNDREDTH was sung at the Offertorium, the first congregational hymn ever to be sung at an English coronation. Vaughan Williams' arrangement of the tune for this occasion included

Dowland's harmonization from Ravencroft's Psalter, 1621, with the melody in the tenor. It was intended that while this was sung by the choir, the congregation would be silent; but since no directions to that effect were given in the printed order of service for the coronation, "the congregation proceeded on its way unabashed" and "the whole Abbey was flooded with the unison of the great hymn, thus triumphantly justifying the innovation." (*Musical Times*, 1953)

6   O Worship the King, All Glorious Above

Inspired by William Kethe's paraphase of Psalm 104 (see No. 4), Sir Robert Grant (1779–1838) wrote this majestic hymn in 1833, one year before being knighted and appointed governor of Bombay. His hymn was first published in Edward Bickersteth's *Christian Psalmody*, 1833, and was later included in his own posthumous *Sacred Poems*, 1839. Grant, after graduation from Magdalen College, Oxford, was called to the bar in 1807 and became King's Sergeant in the court of the Duchy of Lancaster. Entering Parliament in 1818, he successfully put through a bill for the emancipation of the Jews and was made a Privy Councillor in 1831 and judge advocate general in 1832. Shortly after his death at Dalpoorie, India, in 1838, a medical college was built in Bombay as a memorial and named in his honor.

LYONS Although LYONS is generally attributed to Johann Michael Haydn, younger brother of Franz Joseph Haydn, its source has never been found in any of his works. Marked *Adagio e Maestoso,* with the heading "Subject Haydn," it appeared in Vol. 2 of William Gardiner's *Sacred Melodies from Haydn, Mozart and Beethoven Adapted to the best English Poets and appropriated to the use of the British Church,* 1812–1815. Gardiner hoped that these texts and melodies would be used in church and displace the psalm versions of Sternhold and Hopkins, Tate and Brady, and the tunes to which they were sung. His hopes were not fulfilled, but through *Sacred Melodies* he introduced much good music and provided subsequent editors with what has been called a veritable gold mine of tunes. Gardiner sent a copy of his collection to Beethoven with the introductory statement: "Allow me to present to you the first volume of my 'Sacred Melodies' which contain your divine Adagios appropriated to the British Church." He was puzzled by the fact that Beethoven never acknowledged the gift, but Alexander W. Thayer says in his *Life of Ludwig van Beethoven:* "Evidently he did not realize that Beethoven was not the man to feel complimented by having his 'divine Adagios' turned into hymn tunes."

William Gardiner (1770–1853), musical amateur, composer, author, editor, was the son of a Leicester hosiery manufacturer whose business he inherited. He described himself as one "entangled in the toils of a manufactory all his life." He managed, however, to combine a successful business career with a passionate devotion to music and was acquainted at home and abroad with professional and amateur musicians. On business trips to the Continent he made every effort to hear the works of leading composers, particularly of those in Germany, and learned to know their productions well, especially

8

those of Beethoven. In *Music and Friends* Gardiner tells of hearing a work of Beethoven for the first time (1794), an early trio for violin, viola, and cello brought to England by Abbé Dobler, a refugee. "This composition, so different from anything I had ever heard," he says, "awakened in me a new sense, a new delight in the science of sounds. . . . When I went to town, I enquired for works of this author, but could learn nothing more than that he was considered a madman and that his music was like himself." Such opinions did not affect Gardiner's enthusiasm. He predicted that Beethoven "would extend the art in a way never contemplated by Haydn or Mozart." Unexpected recognition came to Gardiner when the Beethoven statue was unveiled in Bonn on August 12, 1848. A university professor who caught sight of him in the vast crowd suggested that this Englishman, who was born in the same year as Beethoven and was the first to introduce his music into England, should sign the dedicatory parchment which was to be sealed in the base of the statue. It had been signed by the king and queen of Prussia, by Queen Victoria and Prince Albert, and by other dignitaries. The professor's suggestion was acclaimed, Gardiner was called to the platform and directed to write his name beneath those of Victoria and Albert.

LYONS came into American use through the *Boston Handel and Haydn Society's Collection of Church Music,* 1822, whose editor, Lowell Mason, drew heavily on Gardiner's *Sacred Melodies* and acknowledged the source. In the Boston collection LYONS was set to "O praise ye the Lord, prepare a new song," the text with which it had appeared in Gardiner's book, and with which it continued to appear in many early nineteenth-century collections of tunes. It is not found in English hymnals.

7 Immortal, Invisible, God Only Wise

A distinguished minister and scholar in the Free Church of Scotland, Walter Chalmers Smith (1824–1908) included this hymn in his *Hymns of Christ and the Christian Life,* 1867, based on Timothy 1:17, "Now unto the King eternal, immortal, invisible, the only wise God." Smith was the minister from 1876 to 1894 of the Free High Church in Edinburgh and served as the Moderator of the Assembly of the Free Church of Scotland in its Jubilee Year in 1893. A man of catholic and scholarly interests, his published works include *The Bishop's Walk,* 1860; *North Country Folk,* 1883; *A Heretic, and Other Poems,* 1891; and *Poetical Works,* 1902. Since its appearance in Horder's *Congregational Hymns,* 1884, where it was slightly revised, this hymn has become a great favorite. W. Garrett Horder (1841–1922), a Congregational minister in England, was a man of exceptional endowments and influence. Percy Dearmer says that many of our finest hymns "would never have become known but for the learning and discernment of Garrett Horder in his *Worship Song,* and other collections which struck a new note and began a new era." [2]

ST. DENIO, known in Wales as JOANNA, is based on a traditional Welsh secular melody which dates from the end of the eighteenth or the beginning of the nineteenth century. It was associated with a song about the cuckoo,

9

"Y Gog Lwydlas," and with "Can Mlynedd i 'Nawr' " ("A hundred years ago"). Its first use as a hymn tune was in *Caniadau y Cyssegr* (Songs for Worship), 1839, edited by John Roberts who simplified the melody considerably. Hearty and straightforward, the hymn tune has the form characteristic of many folk songs, with its first, second, and fourth phrases alike, the third providing the needed variety. In the last phrase the melody starts out a third higher than in the first two phrases, and this simple change is effective. It is interesting to notice how the melody in the third phrase goes up by skips in contrast to the descending figure in the other three phrases. Thus, even in this simple tune, we have the elements of unity and variety — repetition and contrast.

ST. DENIO appeared with Dr. Smith's text in the *English Hymnal*, 1906, the first English hymnbook to include it. Gustav Holst has been credited with introducing the tune to that book.

8 Joyful, Joyful, We Adore Thee

Following his graduation from Princeton Theological Seminary in 1877 and his ordination in 1879, Henry van Dyke (1852–1933) became the minister of the United Congregational Church in Newport, Rhode Island, serving in that position for four years. From 1883 to 1889 he was the pastor of Brick Presbyterian Church in New York City, where the vigor and originality of his preaching attracted large congregations. Because of his literary skills and interest, he was appointed Murray Professor of English literature at Princeton University in 1899, remaining there until his retirement in 1923. His home "Avalon," with its remarkably extensive library, became a gathering place of authors and intellectuals. In 1912 he was elected president of the National Institute of Arts and Letters, and from 1913 to 1916 served as Minister to the Netherlands and Luxembourg from the United States, the latter appointment coming to him because of his close friendship with President Woodrow Wilson. A prolific writer, he published approximately twenty-five books, including *The Reality of Religion*, 1884; *The Poetry of Tennyson*, 1889; *The Story of the Other Wise Man*, 1896; and *The Gospel for an Age of Doubt*, 1896. During a preaching visit to Williams College in 1907, he penned the words of this hymn and placed them before the college president at the breakfast table, saying as he did so: "Here is a hymn for you. Your mountains [the Berkshires] were my inspiration. It must be sung to the music of Beethoven's 'Hymn to Joy.' " The hymn was later published in *Poems of Henry van Dyke,* 1911.

HYMN TO JOY (BEETHOVEN; BONN; JOY) The source of this hymn tune is the principal theme of the choral finale of Beethoven's Ninth Symphony in which it is set to selected stanzas from Schiller's *Ode to Joy.* Vaughan Williams has called this "one of the greatest melodies of the world." Although it has the simplicity of a folk song, the theme reached its present form not through sudden inspiration, but step by step through some two hundred sketches. After the first performance of the symphony in Vienna on May 7, 1824, the totally deaf Beethoven, who had been standing near the conductor, was turned around by one of the soloists so that he could see the waving of hats and handkerchiefs and thus become aware of the enthusiastic applause which he could not hear. The Ninth Symphony has been described as an open and fervent declaration of belief in the brotherhood of man. The joy theme was used as a hymn tune long before its association with van Dyke's words. In *The Mozart Collection,* New York, 1846, edited by Elam Ives, Jr., there were three arrangements of it, all named BONN. "Rise, my soul, and stretch thy wings," one of the texts to which it was set, appeared with the tune in American hymnals as late as 1921, generally with Edward Hodges' arrangement, published in Tuckerman's *Trinity Collection of Church Music,* 1864. When the present hymn first appeared with Beethoven's theme in *The Hymnal* (Presbyterian), 1911, the adaptation used was basically Ives' although no source was given for it. Since 1911 various composite arrangements, such as the one given here, have appeared with the text.

Ludwig van Beethoven (1770–1827), "one of the most tragic and at the same time one of the most commanding figures of all history," was born in Bonn where his grandfather and father were musicians at the electoral court. He had early musical training from his father and other court musicians, played in public at seven, composed in a variety of forms, substituted for the court organist at eleven, and served as accompanist for the court orchestra at twelve, playing from score, and conducting rehearsals. At fourteen he was appointed assistant court organist with a salary, and from 1788 to 1792 played viola in the theater orchestra. His home life was wretched because of poverty and his father's addiction to alcohol, but devoted, influential friends helped him in numerous ways. During his first visit to Vienna in 1787 he had a few lessons from Mozart who remarked to friends, on hearing him improvise: "Keep your eyes on him; some day he will give the world something to talk about."

When Haydn stopped in Bonn on his way home from England in 1792, he praised a cantata composed by Beethoven and encouraged him to continue his studies. Later that year Beethoven went to Vienna to study with Haydn, and remained there for the rest of his life. His brilliant piano playing and improvisations won the friendship and affection of the music-loving Viennese aristocrats who gave him generous and loyal support in spite of his unpredictable ways and his uncompromising independence. He became the most renowned pianist and composer in Europe. Deafness, first noticeable in 1798, grew progressively worse and forced him to give up public performances in 1814. When he confided to a friend that he was losing his hearing, he wrote: "I will seize fate by the throat; it shall never drag me down." Emil Ludwig comments, "The miracle in Beethoven's destiny is that his works became more glorious with his increasing deafness."

During the last difficult years when Beethoven was completely deaf, harassed by ill health, fear of poverty, and the care of his nephew Karl, he composed some of his greatest works — the last five piano sonatas, the *Missa Solemnis,* the *Diabelli* variations, the Ninth Symphony, the last string quartets. Donald Tovey refers to these works as "the crowning mystery and wonder of musical art." Through Beethoven's genius instrumental forms were given new dimensions and new content. His influence on later com-

11

posers is immeasurable. Donald Jay Grout has said of him: "Beethoven was the most powerful disruptive force in the history of music. His works opened the gateway to a new world."

9 Before Jehovah's Aweful Throne

This paraphrase of Psalm 100 by Isaac Watts was first published in his *Psalms of David,* 1719, and was altered by John Wesley (1703–1791) in his *Collection of Psalms and Hymns,* Charles-Town, 1737. The latter was the first hymnbook, as distinguished from the psalters, to be published in America. Wesley intended the hymnal to be used in Christ Church, Savannah, while he was on a mission in Georgia for The Society for the Propagation of the Gospel. The paraphrase has since become almost as well known as Kethe's version of the same psalm, "All People That on Earth Do Dwell" (No. 4). "Aweful" has been spelled with an *e* to emphasize the original meaning. John Wesley was the outstanding preacher and evangelist of the eighteenth century who initiated the founding of the Methodist Church and who, by his ministry to the working classes, is credited by some with sparing England the horrors of the French Revolution. In hymnody he is best known for his translations of German hymns, particularly those of the Moravians, and also for the alterations, usually improvements, which he introduced in the hymns of his brother Charles and those of Isaac Watts. See No. 1 for comments on Watts.

WINCHESTER NEW (CRASSELIUS; FRANKFORT; BARRE) Judging from its name and character, one might assume that this is an English tune; but its source is an anonymous melody (Zahn 2781) from *Musicalisch Hand-Buch,* Hamburg, 1690, in which it was set to "Wer nur den lieben Gott lässt walten." (For English translation see text of No. 83.) In early American collections the tune was in 3/2, named WINCHESTER, and sometimes attributed to Dr. Croft, as it was in the *Boston Handel and Haydn Society Collection of Church Music,* 1822, in the following form, with Isaac Watts' paraphrase of stanza two of Psalm 141:

The tune seems to have been introduced into English hymnody through John Wesley's *A Collection of Tunes, Set to Music, as they are commonly Sung at the Foundery,* 1742. Named SWIFT GERMAN TUNE and set to a hymn of Charles Wesley's, it was one of fourteen German melodies included in the first tune book compiled for the Methodists. Its title recalls their first London meetinghouse, built on the site of a government foundry which had been abandoned in 1716 after an explosion occurred during the recasting of guns captured by the Duke of Marlborough. The building was wrecked and lay in ruins until John Wesley bought it in 1739. In the *Foundery* tune book the German melody was in 2/2; in George Whitefield's *Divine Musical Miscellany,* 1754, it was in 3/4 and called WINCHESTER NEW TUNE.

The present form of WINCHESTER NEW (except for the omission of half notes at the beginning and end of each line of the text) is from William H. Havergal's *Old Church Psalmody,* 1847.

10 Before Jehovah's Aweful Throne

See No. 9 for comments on the text.

PARK STREET (VENUA)   This is another tune (see No. 6) which came into American hymnody from Gardiner's *Sacred Melodies* by way of Lowell Mason's first collection of church music. It was named PARK STREET and set to "Hark! how the choral song of Heaven" with which it was associated in subsequent nineteenth-century American tune books. In *Sacred Melodies* it appeared with "Thee will I love, O Lord my strength" in an arrangement for strings, organ, harp, and voices. Writing of the tune in *Music and Friends,* Gardiner said that it was "an adagio dance by Venua who formerly led the ballet in the Opera." In the same book Gardiner told of standing next to Venua when Paganini gave his first concert at the London Opera House.

Frédéric Marc-Antoine Venua (1786–1872), born in Paris of Italian parents, was enrolled as a student at the Paris Conservatory in 1800, went to London in 1805 to study violin and composition, and stayed for nearly sixty years. Part of this time he was musical director of the ballet at the King's Theatre. R. G. McCutchan says in *Hymn Tune Names* that PARK STREET was named for the Park Street Church, Boston, "an old Puritan meetinghouse, citadel and stronghold of orthodoxy." Lowell Mason directed its music for a time after he came to Boston from Savannah.

11 From All That Dwell Below the Skies

Inspired by the shortest chapter in the Bible, Psalm 117, this free paraphrase was first published by Isaac Watts in his *Psalms of David,* 1719. Percy Dearmer has described this as "the classic of English doxologies." See No. 1 for comments on Watts.

OLD HUNDREDTH   See No. 4 for comments on this tune.

12 From All That Dwell Below the Skies

See No. 11 for comments on the text. The Alleluias were not in the original but were added to match the tune.

LASST UNS ERFREUEN (VIGILES ET SANCTI; EASTER ALLE–LUYA)   This tune, in the following form, was set to an Easter hymn "Lasst uns erfreuen herzlich sehr" in *Geistliche Kirchengesäng,* a Catholic hymnbook published at Cologne in 1623. (Bäumker, Vol. I, No. 280.) Like many other hymn tunes, it is thought to have been derived from a folk song. Its first phrase is identical with that of the tune for Psalms 36 and 68 in the Genevan Psalters. (See No. 577.)

Lasst uns er - frew - en hertz - lich sehr, Al - le - lu - ia.
Ma - ri - a seufftzt und weint nit mehr, Al - le - lu - ia.

Ver-schwun-den al - le Ne - bel seyn, Al - le - lu - ia.
Jetzt scheint der lie - be Son-nen - schein, Al - le - lu - ia.

Al - le - lu - ia, Al - le - lu - ia, Al - le - lu - ia.

This early form of the melody, set to an English paraphrase of a twelfth-century Easter hymn, is given in *Songs of Syon,* 1910, at No. 96 B, and with slight rhythmic changes is the setting for "All creatures of our God and King" in *Cantate Domino,* 1951, the hymnbook of the World's Student Christian Federation. The wide use of the hymn among Roman Catholics of southern Germany is indicated by its inclusion in a number of their hymnals published before 1700. It did not enter into German Protestant hymnody, and apparently for a long time was forgotten. Its present melodic form, with some differences in rhythm, is from David Gregor Corner's hymnals (Catholic) of 1631 and 1649. It was published with the original German text in Heinrich Reimann's *Das deutsche geistliche Lied,* 1895, a collection of sacred songs from the fourteenth through the nineteenth centuries. The tune came into English and American hymnody through *The English Hymnal,* 1906, where it appeared in its present form with "Ye watchers and ye holy ones" (No. 30). Since then it has been sung with Watts' version of Psalm 117 and also with "All creatures of our God and King" (No. 64).

13 Praise the Lord! Ye Heavens, Adore Him

This hymn by an unknown author, based on Psalm 148, was originally found in a four-page folder pasted as an insert into copies of *Psalms, Hymns, and Anthems of the Foundling Hospital,* music edition, 1796, a hymnal compiled for use in the chapel of the hospital. This was an orphan asylum in London where music and singing played a large role in rehabilitating the children and in providing support for the institution by means of special concerts. The latter were attended by crowds of fashionable society people. For nearly a century, from 1782 to 1877, choirs from the home sang at St.

Paul's Cathedral. Handel gave a benefit concert in the hospital in 1749 to raise funds for the completion of the chapel, and later presented the hospital with an organ. During the latter part of his life, when his health permitted, he conducted a yearly performance of the *Messiah* in the chapel.

HYFRYDOL was written by Rowland H. Prichard (1811–1887) when he was about twenty years old. A grandson of the bard Rowland Huw, Prichard was born at Graienyn, Bala, North Wales, where he spent most of his life and was well-known as a precentor and composer of tunes. At sixty-nine, because of reduced circumstances, he moved to Holywell and worked as a loom tender's assistant in a flannel mill. HYFRYDOL (the word means "pleasant") is a strong, simple melody within the compass of a fifth except for one note in the last phrase. It has had long association with Wesley's words, "Love divine, all loves excelling" in Welsh churches where English hymns are sung. Its first appearance in English hymnody seems to have been in *The English Hymnal,* 1906, set to "Alleluia, sing to Jesus" and "Once to every man and nation."

14 The God of Abraham Praise

Many individuals had a share in the making of this hymn in its present form. The first was Moses Maimonides (1130–1205), a great Hebrew scholar, who summed up the essential doctrines of Judaism in thirteen articles of faith. Two centuries later, Daniel ben Judah, a medieval writer of whom little is known, arranged these articles in a metrical version which became known as the *Yigdal* or Doxology. It was, and still is, sung antiphonally by precentor and congregation in Jewish worship, usually at the close of the service on the eve of the Sabbath and at festivals. Thomas Olivers (1725–1799), a Wesleyan preacher from Wales, wrote an English version of the *Yigdal* after hearing it sung in the Great Synagogue, Duke's Place, London. It was published in 1772 and was so popular that it appeared in thirty editions by 1799. Max Landsberg (1845–1928), a rabbi, and Newton Mann (1836–1926), a Unitarian minister, both of Rochester, New York, collaborated in preparing the present translation. The opening line is from Olivers' version; otherwise it is as Mann and Landsberg wrote it. The hymn is especially appropriate for use in interfaith services.

LEONI (YIGDAL; JUDEA; JERUSALEM) is an adaptation of the melody to which the Yigdal was sung when Thomas Olivers, hearing it, was so captivated by it that he determined to adapt it for use in Christian congregations. Through his version the hymn and tune passed into Christian hymnody. It is said to have been used in all Methodist hymnals since 1785. All twelve stanzas of Olivers' original paraphrase were included with LEONI in *The Christian Lyre,* New York, 1831. Before that, the tune had appeared in a number of American hymnbooks with other texts. It was Olivers who stipulated that the tune be called LEONI for Meyer Lyon (Meier Leon), cantor of the Duke's Place synagogue, who transcribed the tune for him and whose singing of it may have been as much responsible as the tune itself for the impression it made on him.

15

Lyon (1751–1797 or 1800?), whose voice attracted Gentiles as well as Jews to the synagogue, had a turn in opera; but because of his unwillingness to sing on Friday nights and during religious festivals, and his lack of acting ability, he did not succeed in that field. In 1787, when the Ashkenazic (German and English) congregation in Kingston, Jamaica, needed a reader (cantor, precentor) for their new synagogue, Lyon took the position and remained in Kingston until his death.

In *Jewish Music*, 1929, A. Z. Idelsohn tells of a collection of songs prepared in 1791 by Ahron Beer for use in Jewish services. LEONI is one of twelve songs listed as compositions of Leon Singer (Lyon). Idelsohn shows in a chart of folk melodies how Lyon's YIGDAL tune incorporates motives common to Jewish, Spanish-Basque, and Slavic song.

15 Praise to the Lord, the Almighty

After leading the carefree, boisterous life of a student, so common in Germany in the seventeenth century, Joachim Neander (1650–1680) came under the influence of Theodore Undereyk, pastor of St. Martin's Church in Bremen, and as a result identified himself with the Pietists. Because of his zealous religious practices and preaching, he was frequently in trouble with the church authorities, from which he sought release in communion with nature, in prayer, and in composing hymns. Although he died of tuberculosis at the age of thirty, he wrote some sixty hymns as well as the tunes. He is widely regarded as the first poet of the Reformed Church in Germany and the greatest of the Reformed hymn writers. This thanksgiving hymn is a free paraphrase of Psalms 103:1–6 and 150. The translation is by Catherine Winkworth from her *Chorale Book for England*, 1863. See No. 2 for comments on Miss Winkworth.

"Praise to the Lord, the Almighty" was the opening hymn sung by the choir and congregation of a hundred thousand worshippers at the evening mass celebrated by Pope Paul VI in Yankee Stadium, New York City, on October 4, 1965.

LOBE DEN HERREN (PRAISE TO THE LORD) has been associated with Neander's hymn of praise and thanksgiving since 1680, the last year of his life, when the text and tune appeared in the following form in his *Glaub- und Liebesübung*. (Zahn 1912)

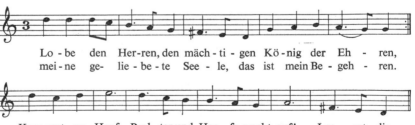

16

Mu - si - cam hö - ren!

Neander adapted the tune from an anonymous melody in a 1665 Stralsund hymnbook. Zahn suggests that it was based on an earlier secular song. The present form of the melody is a composite of the 1665 version and several later modifications. Bach used the melody of LOBE DEN HERREN in Cantatas 57 and 137, in the unfinished Cantata "Her Gott, Beherrscher aller Dinge," and in the choral prelude "Kommst du nun, Jesu," No. 6 of the Schübler Chorales. The harmonization given in the *Pilgrim Hymnal* is from *The Chorale Book for England,* 1863, in which chorale melodies were set to Catherine Winkworth's English translations of two hundred German hymns.

16   Praise, My Soul, the King of Heaven

Taken from his collection, *The Spirit of the Psalms,* 1834, containing over 280 paraphrases of the psalms, this hymn based on Psalm 103 by Henry Francis Lyte (1793–1847) was written for his congregation in the small fishing village at Lower Brixham, Devonshire, where he remained as curate for the last twenty-four years of his life. Having been "jostled from one curacy to another" in his early ministry and never in robust health, Lyte died at Nice, France, worn out by his labors among folk who were not fully able to appreciate his sensitive and dedicated spirit. His works include *Tales On the Lord's Prayer in Verse,* 1826; *Poems, chiefly Religious,* 1833; and *The Spirit of the Psalms,* 1834. In explaining why he wrote his hymns and poems, Lyte expressed himself in these words:

> Might verse of mine inspire
>   One virtuous aim, one high resolve impart —
> Light in one drooping soul a hallowed fire,
>   Or bind one broken heart,
>
> Death would be sweeter then,
>   More calm my slumber 'neath the silent sod,
> Might I thus live to bless my fellowmen,
>   Or glorify my God.

Erik Routley has said of him in *Hymns and Human Life,* "Lyte was an obscure country curate who has no claim to fame beyond his saintly character and a handful of hymns."

PRAISE MY SOUL (BENEDIC ANIMA MEA; LAUDA ANIMA) was written for Lyte's words by Sir John Goss (1800–1880), one of England's foremost nineteenth-century church musicians. The tune has been credited with making the hymn popular. Goss, the son of an organist, was one of the children of the Chapel Royal for five years and was later a pupil of Thomas Attwood (No. 517) whom he succeeded as organist of St. Paul's

17

Cathedral in 1838, remaining there until 1872. In 1827 Goss was appointed professor of harmony at the Royal Academy of Music, a post which he filled for forty-seven years with remarkable success. One of his students was Arthur Sullivan, who wrote of him: "I am eternally grateful to him; he had a wonderful gift of part-writing, and whatever facility I possess in this respect, I owe entirely to his teaching and influence." Goss' *Introduction to Harmony and Thorough-Bass,* 1833, went through thirteen editions. In 1856 he was appointed composer to the Chapel Royal and in 1872 was knighted by Queen Victoria. Cambridge University granted the honorary Mus.D. to both Goss and Sullivan in 1876.

Goss composed much church music but is best known for his anthems which reveal expert craftsmanship and a gift for melody. One of the most familiar, "O Saviour of the world," is described by Fellowes as "hardly more than a miniature . . . admirably fitted to the words, and perfectly phrased." It was said that Goss never began writing an anthem without asking a blessing upon his work, and that he meant every anthem to be a sermon in music. He was music editor of Mercer's *Church Psalter and Hymn Book,* 1854, the first important general hymnal in England to include tunes as well as words, and notable for the large number of German chorale melodies contained in it. Commenting on the wide use of this hymn and tune in England, Erik Routley says that it "combines the dignities of being, nowadays, *the* Royal wedding hymn with being our national hymn of thanksgiving." It was one of the hymns sung at the wedding of King George VI, and was chosen by Queen Elizabeth II for the processional at her wedding in 1947.

17 Praise Thou the Lord, O My Soul, Sing Praises

Johann Daniel Herrnschmidt (1675–1723) belonged to the older Pietistic school in Germany and was the author of many hymns. He was long associated with the University of Halle and held the position of professor of theology during the last eight years of his life. This is undoubtedly his most popular hymn, based on Psalm 146. Carl F. Pfatteicher (1882–1957), the translator, edited the excellent collection *Oxford American Hymnal for Schools and Colleges,* 1930, as well as several other volumes in church music, and served as professor of music at Phillips Academy, Andover, Massachusetts, from 1912 to 1947. He was an authority on Bach and for many years conducted outstanding choral concerts featuring works of Bach and other great composers.

LOBE DEN HERREN, O MEINE SEELE   In *The Handbook to the Lutheran Hymnal,* 1942, this anonymous tune is described as "one of the most brilliant gems in our chorale treasury." It has been inseparably united with the German hymn from which its name is derived ever since the publication of Freylinghausen's *Neues Geistreiches Gesangbuch,* Halle, 1714. There are numerous versions of the melody. (Zahn 4995)

Johann A. Freylinghausen (1670–1739), pastor, poet, and musician, has been called the Charles Wesley of the Pietistic movement which did for Germany what Methodism did for England. Although forty-four hymns and twenty-two tunes are attributed to him, his name is most often remembered for the collections of hymns and tunes which he edited, the most widely circulated of German hymnbooks in the eighteenth century. They were epoch-making for German hymnody and influenced English hymnody as well. Through his collections published in 1704 and 1714, many fine tunes, different in character from the older chorales and better suited to the sentiments expressed in the new Pietistic hymns, were introduced and were liberally drawn on by later editors. His hymnbooks were used by the Moravians whose fervent singing, deep faith, and piety impressed and greatly influenced John Wesley. Wesley's copy of Freylinghausen's *Gesangbuch* is still preserved in the library of the Wesleyan College in Richmond, England. See No. 75 for further comments on Freylinghausen.

18 O God, We Praise Thee, and Confess

This metrical and abbreviated version of the "Te Deum laudamus" is from the Supplement to the *New Version*, 1703, and is a paraphrase of the first part of the "Te Deum." The author is unknown. See No. 81 for comments on the *New Version* and No. 559 for comments on the "Te Deum laudamus." The latter source gives the complete text with a musical setting; see also "Unison Readings," No. 137 (page 549 in the hymnal).

TALLIS' ORDINAL is one of nine "broad, simple, and effective" tunes composed and harmonized in four parts by Thomas Tallis (c. 1505–1585) for *The Whole Psalter* (c. 1560) of Matthew Parker, chaplain to Queen Anne Boleyn and Henry VIII, and archbishop of Canterbury under Queen Elizabeth I. During enforced retirement (1553–1558) in the reign of Queen Mary, Parker translated the whole Psalter, the canticles, and the "Veni, Creator," into various meters. The tune's name comes from its association with his Common Meter version of "Veni Creator Spiritus" (No. 575), the hymn prescribed for ordinations in the *Book of Common Prayer*. For comments on Tallis see No. 56.

19 Praise the Lord, His Glories Show

Based on Psalm 150, this hymn by Henry Francis Lyte is from his *Spirit of the Psalms*, 1834 and consisted originally of two eight-line stanzas. The Alleluias were added to make the hymn suitable for use with LLANFAIR. See No. 16 for comments on Lyte.

LLANFAIR (BETHEL) This simple Welsh hymn melody, in AABA form, was introduced to English congregations through the *English Hymnal*, 1906, set to "Hail the day that sees him rise," with the present harmonization. The tune, dated July 14, 1817, and named BETHEL, is from a manuscript book of the Welsh singer Robert Williams (c. 1781–1821), composer of tunes and gifted musician, who was blind from his birth. Born at Mynydd Ithel on the island of Anglesey in North Wales, Williams spent his whole life there, earning his living as a skilled basketmaker. He is said to have had such a sharp ear that if he heard a tune once he could jot it down without a single mistake. It is not known whether he composed LLANFAIR or noted it in his book after hearing it sung. There are others who have claimed the tune as their own. LLANFAIR is the first part of the long name of a little village in Montgomery County, Wales. One of the longest words in any language, it is given in full, with the meaning, in *Hymn Tune Names*, 1957. The tune appeared with Lyte's words in *The Church Hymnary*, revised, 1927.

20 Sing Praise to God Who Reigns Above

A lawyer and a fervent Pietist, Johann Jacob Schütz (1640–1690) lived at Frankfort-am-Main and there published a collection of hymns, *Christliches Gedenckbüchlein*, 1675, in which this hymn, originally beginning "Sei Lob und Ehr dem höchsten Gut," first appeared. He was an intimate friend of Philipp J. Spener (1635–1705), and it was as a result of one of his suggestions that Spener founded his *Collegia Pietates*, or prayer meetings, which really started the Pietistic movement. Schütz eventually became a Separatist and refused to attend the Lutheran services. Frances Elizabeth Cox (1812–1897), English poet and author, translated this hymn in her *Hymns from the German*, 1864. She also published *Sacred Hymns from the German*, 1841, and according to Robert Guy McCutchan "shares with Catherine Winkworth the honor of being among the best translators of German hymns into English."

MIT FREUDEN ZART (BOHEMIAN BRETHREN)   This fine melody, set to the words of a hymn for Easter, had the following form in a hymnbook of the Bohemian Brethren (Unitas Fratrum) published in 1566. (Zahn 8186)

Mit Freu-den zart   zu   die-ser Fahrt   lasst   uns   zu-
beid Gross und Klein von Her-zen rein   mit   hel-lem

gleich   fröh-lich   sin-gen,   Das   e-wig   Heil   wird
Ton   frei   er-klin-gen.

uns   zu   teil;   denn   Je-sus   Christ   er-stan-den

ist,   welchs   er   lässt   reich-lich   ver-kün-den.

20

It has much in common with the tune for Psalm 138 in the 1562 Genevan Psalter, which begins with a phrase almost identical with that of a French secular song published in 1529–1530 by Attaignant. (The tune for Psalm 138 and the chanson are given in *Le Psautier Huguenot*, 1962, by Pierre Pidoux.) The present harmonization, by the Rev. Maurice F. Bell, is from *The English Hymnal*, 1906, in which the tune is set to "O dearest Lord, by all adored."

21 We Gather Together

Written by an unknown Dutch patriot at the end of the sixteenth century, this hymn celebrates the freedom of the Netherlands from Spanish domination after a century of oppression and strife. It was first published in 1626 in a collection of Dutch songs edited by Adrian Valerius, *Neder-landtsch Gedenckclanck*. The English translation by Theodore Baker (1851–1934) was originally printed in Coenraad V. Bos's *Dutch Folk-songs*, 1917. Baker was for many years literary editor and translator for G. Schirmer, Inc., in New York City, and he is credited with making the first thorough study of the music of the American Indian.

The tune KREMSER is also from Valerius' collection of Dutch songs, and has practically the same rhythmic and melodic form that it had in 1626. Before that, it had been associated with secular words, "Hey wilder dan wild." After long neglect, the tune seems to have been discovered and put into circulation again by Edward Kremser (1838–1914), Viennese choral director, composer of operettas and works for piano and voice. In 1877 he arranged and published *Sechs Altniederländische Volkslieder*, a selection of six Old-Netherlands melodies from Valerius' collection. This is the best known of the six. The Dutch words for this hymn are given in *Cantate Domino* (No. 80), hymnal of the World's Student Christian Federation. In *Music Education in America*, 1926, Archibald T. Davison, commenting on the use of folk songs in an army camp during World War I, wrote that "If frequency of request, and spirit in performance, are criteria, the most popular of all was . . . the Netherlands folk song, the 'Prayer of Thanksgiving.' "

22 We Praise Thee, O God

Mrs. Julia Bulkley Cady Cory (1882–   ), daughter of one of New York City's distinguished architects, J. Cleveland Cady, wrote this hymn in 1902 at the invitation of J. Archer Gibson, organist of Brick Presbyterian Church in New York City, who thought that the older words to KREMSER were too militaristic. Mrs. Cory's text is not a translation or paraphrase but was written to fit the music, so as to provide the tune with an appropriate set of Christian words. Several minor changes have been made by Mrs. Cory since the first version.

KREMSER   See comments at No. 21.

23   Ye Holy Angels Bright

Among a galaxy of outstanding Puritan divines in England in the seventeenth century, Richard Baxter (1615–1691) ranks as one of the greatest. Irenic in spirit and yet courageous in his convictions, he was a moderating influence in a time of religious stress and fanaticism. Judge Jeffreys who sentenced him to prison for two years for his refusal to comply with the Act of Uniformity complained that he wrote "books enough to fill a cart." Two of his books, *The Saints' Everlasting Rest,* 1650, and *The Reformed Pastor,* 1656, have become Protestant classics. This hymn was appended by Baxter to his *Poor Man's Family Book,* 1672, "with a request to Landlords and Rich Men to give to their Tenants and poor Neighbours, either this or some fitter Book." Originally containing sixteen stanzas, it was partly rewritten by John Hampden Gurney and others.

DARWALL'S 148th   Written originally for Psalm 148 in Aaron Williams' *New Universal Psalmist,* 1770, this tune has been associated with Baxter's words since 1889. Its composer, John Darwall (1731–1789), was clergyman, poet, and enthusiastic amateur musician whose compositions included music for the piano and tunes in two parts, treble and bass, for each of the 150 psalms in the *New Version,* 1696. Several of these were published but this is the only one that has continued in use. Darwall went to St. Matthew's Parish Church in Walsall, Staffordshire, as curate in 1761, became vicar in 1769, and remained there until his death.

24   Now Let Every Tongue Adore Thee

Renowned in his day as a brilliant Lutheran preacher, Philipp Nicolai (1556–1608) is today chiefly remembered as the author and composer, a remarkable achievement, of two of the finest chorales, "Wake, Awake, for Night Is Flying" and "O Morning Star, How Fair and Bright," known respectively as the king and the queen of chorales. They first appeared in his *Mirror of Joy,* a series of meditations published in 1598, the year of a devastating plague. Nicolai wrote in the Preface, "Then day by day I wrote out my meditations, found myself, thank God! wonderfully well, comforted in heart, joyful in spirit, and truly content." The present hymn was originally the third stanza of "Wake, Awake, for Night Is Flying" (see No. 108), and is here given as translated by Paul England (d. 1932), for many years a translator for the English publishers, Boosey and Hawkes. See Nos. 108 and 145 for further comments on Nicolai.

WACHET AUF (SLEEPERS, WAKE)   Nicolai's melody for this so-called king of chorales was in the free rhythm characteristic of his time and is still found in that form in some hymnals published on the Continent and in the United States. Nicolai's version of the melody follows (Zahn 8405 a)

Wa-chet auf, ruft uns die Stim - me   der Wäch-ter sehr hoch
Mit-ter - nacht heisst die- se Stun - de,   sie ru - fen uns mit

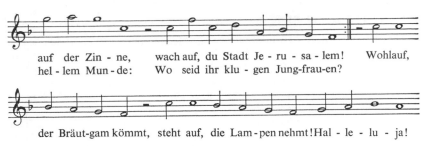

auf der Zin - ne,   wach auf, du Stadt Je - ru - sa - lem!   Wohlauf,
hel - lem Mun - de: Wo seid ihr klu - gen Jung-frau-en?

der Bräut-gam kömmt, steht auf, die Lam-pen nehmt! Hal - le - lu - ja!

Macht euch be - reit   zu der Hoch-zeit! Ihr müs - set ihm ent - ge - gen gehn.

Although attributed to Nicolai, WACHET AUF is generally thought to be his adaptation of older material. Bach used the melody in three movements of Cantata No. 140. The first of Schübler's *Sechs Choräle* for organ is an adaptation of the fourth movement of the cantata.

John Sebastian Bach (1685–1750), who has been called the most distinguished member of the most distinguished family in musical history, was little known outside of Germany in his day, and then mostly as an organist and teacher. Not until the nineteenth century was his greatness as a composer widely recognized. Since then, appreciation of his incomparable music has steadily increased. G. Wallace Woodworth has said of him: "Not only through his development of organ style and his varied use of the chorale, but also because of his commanding musical genius and the sincerity and virility of his sacred style, Bach stands as the greatest figure in the history of Protestant church music." [8]

The term "Bach chorale" is somewhat misleading. Bach composed only a few chorale melodies but his matchless harmonizations of existing tunes have led people to assume that he was responsible for all their beauty. By Bach's time the chorale melodies had lost their original rhythmic flexibility which gave them such distinctive individuality and vitality. They had gone through a process of gradual transformation at the hands of successive editors of chorale collections who wanted to bring them up-to-date and altered them accordingly. Rhythmic freedom was made captive to regular accent and bar lines and much of the modal flavor was lost in tonal harmonizations. Bach's settings compensate in large part for these alterations. In *Music, History and Ideas* Hugo Leichtentritt comments:

"Through four centuries these Protestant choral tunes have been the most precious material of German church music. One cannot imagine Bach's art without the *cantus firmus* of these glorious spiritual folk songs. No cantata, no Passion music, no Bach motet, no organ chorale prelude without these tunes. They are the center of all Bach's church music, its deepest and most solid foundation." [9]

For further comments on Bach see Nos. 281 and 233.

23

25 Stand Up and Bless the Lord

The son of a Moravian minister, James Montgomery (1771–1854) was a poet by nature and a champion of human rights by vocation. As editor of *The Sheffield Iris* in Sheffield, England, for thirty-one years, a newspaper which he took over at the age of twenty-five, he was twice imprisoned in York Castle, once for printing a poem in celebration of the fall of the Bastille and again for describing the details of a political riot in Sheffield. He wrote over four hundred hymns, of which more than a hundred are still in use. This hymn was written for the anniversary service of the Sheffield Red Hill Wesleyan Sunday School on March 15, 1824. He later changed "children" to "people" in the first stanza in his *Christian Psalmist,* 1825. Julian said of him: "The secrets of his power as a writer of hymns were manifold. His poetic genius was of a high order, higher than most who stand with him in the front rank of Christian poets. His ear for rhythm was exceedingly accurate and refined. His knowledge of Holy Scripture was most extensive. His religious views were broad and charitable. His devotional spirit was of the holiest type. With the faith of a strong man he united the beauty and simplicity of a child. Richly poetic without exuberance, dogmatic without uncharitableness, tender without sentimentality, elaborate without diffusiveness, richly musical without apparent effort, he has bequeathed to the Church of Christ wealth which could only have come from a true genius and a sanctified heart."

CARLISLE (INVOCATION) has been called one of the most exhilarating of short-meter tunes. Composed by Charles Lockhart (1745–1813), it was named INVOCATION and set to "Come, Holy Spirit, come" in Martin Madan's *Collection of Psalm and Hymn Tunes,* 1792, compiled for use at Lock Hospital, an institution "for the restoration of unhappy females." It appeared with the same name and text in several early nineteenth-century American collections. In some it was called CARLISLE.

Lockhart, blind from birth, served as organist in three churches and at Lock Hospital, and was well known as a trainer of childrens' choirs. The Lock Hospital *Collection,* to which Lockhart contributed a number of tunes, was one of the earliest and most celebrated of the hymn books compiled for use in various charitable institutions established in London during the eighteenth century under the impetus of the Evangelical movement. Music played an important part at these centers, and through them, hymn singing gained ground at a time when it was still opposed by the conservatives in the Church of England.

Madan (1726–1790), a brother of the bishop of Peterborough and a cousin of the poet Cowper, was educated at Oxford and admitted to the bar in 1748. One day, in a London coffeehouse, he was delegated by his companions to hear John Wesley preach in order to mimic his ways for their amusement. When Madan returned and was asked if he had "taken off the old Methodist" he replied, "No gentlemen, but he has taken me off." He gave up law, took holy orders, and despite his evangelical tendencies was ordained in the Church of England. He preached in a number of towns under the auspices of the Calvinist Methodists and served for many years as chaplain of Lock Hospital, which he and friends had founded. His popularity as a preacher was such that a chapel had to be built at the hospital

to accommodate the crowds that came to hear him. The musical performances there drew large and fashionable audiences.

Hymns and tunes from Madan's collections were widely circulated and appropriated by editors of hymn books in England and America. His influence
on English and American hymnody was considerable, and his is one of the
names that appears most frequently in American collections of the first
decades of the nineteenth century. His tune HOTHAM for "Jesus, lover
of my soul" was the accepted setting for over a century in both England
and America.

26   O Be Joyful in the Lord

Based on Psalm 100, this hymn was one of several submitted by Curtis
Beach (1914–   ) for consideration by the editorial committee of the new
Pilgrim Hymnal. The committee selected two of these original hymns, the
other being "O How Glorious, Full of Wonder" (No. 74). Mr. Beach is the
only author to have more than one of his original hymns accepted for in-
clusion. Formerly the minister of the Neighborhood Church in Pasadena,
California, he became the minister of the Smithfield Congregational Church
(United Church of Christ) in Pittsburgh, Pennsylvania, in 1959.

ROCK OF AGES is the traditional melody for the hymn "Mooz tsur"
which is sung during Hanukkah, the Jewish Feast of Dedication (Festival of
Lights) instituted by Judas Maccabaeus, his brothers, and the congregation
of Israel in 165 B.C., to commemorate the rededication of the temple at
Jerusalem after the victory over Antiochus Epiphanes. This feast, mentioned
in John 10:22, is celebrated for eight days. The melody with its Hebrew text
is given in A. Z. Idlesohn's *Jewish Music,* 1929. (No. 10, p. 168)

Idlesohn believed that the first two measures of phrases one and two originated in the anonymous fifteenth-century German melody used by Luther for
"Nun freut euch, lieben Christen g'mein" and that the third phrase was derived from a popular German battlesong called the *Benzenauer,* composed in
1504. He writes: "The two German songs penetrated into the Ghetto, and
were fused in the mind of some Jewish singer into one tune and used for the
joyous theme of the victory of the Maccabees. It was first sung at the home-
service of kindling the Hanukkah lights, and was later introduced into the
synagogue. The poem, however, was sung long before the invention of the
present tune." [4] See No. 271 for comment on the tune NUN FREUT EUCH.

27   O Be Joyful in the Lord

See No. 26 for comments on the text.

FINLAY was composed for these words in 1957 by Harold Friedell
(1905–1958) and named for the Rev. Terence J. Finlay who, in 1955, became rector of St. Bartholomew's Church in New York City where Mr.
Friedell was organist and choirmaster from 1946 until his death. He was born

in Jamaica, New York. After graduation from high school, he studied organ with David McK. Williams, theory with Clement Gale, and composition with Bernard Wagenaar. He was organist and choirmaster of Calvary Episcopal Church in New York City from 1928 to 1931, and of St. John's Episcopal Church in Jersey City from 1931 to 1939, and later taught theory and composition at the Guilmant Organ School, the Juilliard School of Music, and the school of sacred music at Union Theological Seminary. A Fellow of the American Guild of Organists, he served as its treasurer for ten years, was chairman of the examination committee (1947–1955), and was its delegate to the International Congress of Organists in London in 1957. He was a Fellow of Trinity College, London, and the recipient of an honorary doctorate in music from Missouri Valley College. His compositions include anthems, carols, hymns, and service music.

Thirteen original hymn tunes composed by Friedell were included in *Hymns for Children and Grownups,* 1953, which he edited with Dr. Lee Hastings Bristol, Jr.

In FINLAY characteristic elements of American folk-hymn melodies are combined with those of the modern unison hymn tune. The mode, the flow of the melody, the simple form (basically A A B A), the unhackneyed rhythmic pattern, the unison setting with diatonic harmonies (only one accidental), add up to a tune that is fresh, distinctive, and singable. Those who play FINLAY should observe that each of the four phrases ends with a whole note which receives two pulses, not four. To hold the final note of the third phrase for four pulses deprives the tune of the slight irregularity of phrase length which gives it a certain freshness.

28 We Worship Thee, Almighty God

Johan Olof Wallin (1779–1839) Sweden's greatest sacred poet, holds the same place in Swedish hymnody that Isaac Watts does in English hymnody. A gifted preacher who became primate of the church in Sweden, he was responsible for editing the official Swedish hymnal in 1819, called the *Psalmbook,* which remained in use for more than a century. Wallin contributed 128 of his own hymns and twenty-three translations in addition to revising a number of others. In the 1937 edition of the *Psalmbook,* more than one third of the hymns were either written, translated, or revised by him. His famous Christmas hymn, "All Hail to Thee, O Blessed Morn," is sung in almost every church in Sweden at dawn on Christmas Day. The present hymn is a metrical version of the "Te Deum laudamus" and has been called the Swedish "Te Deum."

See No. 559 for comments on this early Latin hymn. Charles Wharton Stork (1881–   ) is the translator.

VI LOFVE DIG, O STORE GUD   Known also as WALLIN, for the great Swedish poet Johan Wallin, this melody appeared in the 1819 *Psalmbook* of the Church of Sweden with 1529 as the date of its first use as a hymn tune. The book was edited by the poet-clergyman, whom Henry W. Longfellow called "the sublime Wallin of David's harp in the Northland."

29 Now Thank We All Our God

Written during the period of the Thirty Years' War (1618–1648), this hymn has become the German "Te Deum" and is sung on all national occasions of rejoicing and thanksgiving. It was also sung at the Diamond Jubilee of Queen Victoria in 1897. Martin Rinkart (1586–1649), who for thirty-two years served as the Lutheran pastor in Eilenburg, Saxony, the town of his birth and childhood, wrote the first two stanzas, based on Ecclesiasticus 50:22–24, to be sung as a grace at table by his own family, and added the third stanza as a doxology, based on the *Gloria Patri*. It was first published in his *Jesu-Hertz-Büchlein*, Leipzig, 1636. Since Eilenburg was a walled city, it became a refuge for thousands fleeing the horrors of war. During one year, following a terrible pestilence and famine, Pastor Rinkart buried over four thousand people. Yet in the midst of these calamities he maintained his courage and good cheer. The translation is by Catherine Winkworth from her *Lyra Germanica*, 1858. See No. 2 for comments on Catherine Winkworth.

This was the closing hymn sung at the evening mass celebrated by Pope Paul VI in Yankee Stadium, New York City, on October 4, 1965.

NUN DANKET has been associated with Rinkart's hymn "Nun danket alle Gott" since its appearance, anonymously, in *Praxis pietatis melica* ("The musical practice of piety") 1647, a famous collection of hymns and tunes which went through more than forty editions and "constituted the mainstream of Lutheran hymnody" in the seventeenth century. In use for over a century, by 1736 it included more than thirteen hundred hymns. Its original editor, Johann Crüger (1598–1662), called the finest melodist of the century, was well known in his day as composer, editor, cantor, and the author of a number of theoretical works. With the help of other first-rate collaborators, Crüger not only introduced through his collections fine new material but also included much good music previously published, thus preserving it and in some cases giving it new form and life. He is known to most people as the composer of some of the most beautiful chorale melodies and as one of the most notable figures in the history of the chorale. NUN DANKET, the best-known of his tunes, was used by Bach in No. 7 of the *Eighteen Chorals* for organ, in No. 3 of the *Wedding Chorales,* in the Reformation Cantata, No. 79, where it is the basis for the stirring extended chorale in the third movement, and in Cantata No. 192, "Nun Danket alle Gott." There is one harmonization of it in the *Choralgesänge*. There are a number of different versions of the melody. The melody and harmonization given in the *Pilgrim Hymnal* are based largely on Mendelssohn's version in his *Lobgesang* ("Hymn of Praise"), Op. 52.

The son of a prosperous innkeeper and grandson of the local pastor of the Prussian village Gross-Breesen where he was born, Crüger attended various schools before going to the Jesuit college at Olmütz and the Poet's School in Regensburg. There his major studies were in music with the cantor, Paul Homberger, who had been a pupil of Giovanni Gabrieli. After travels in Moravia, Bohemia, and Saxony, Crüger settled in Berlin (1615) and became tutor for the children of Christoph von Blumenthal, captain of the guard of Elector Frederick Wilhelm I. From 1620 to 1622 he studied theology in

Wittenberg, where his fine bass voice and ability as a composer brought him recognition and considerable reputation as a musician. In 1622 he became cantor of the Church of St. Nicolai in Berlin and teacher at the gymnasium of the Gray Friars. He remained at St. Nicolai until his death, and during those forty years became the leading musical figure in Berlin. One of his colleagues at St. Nicolai was Paul Gerhardt, who came there as deacon in 1657. NUN DANKET had the following form originally. (Zahn 5142)

Nun dan-ket al-le Gott mit Her-zen, Mund und Hän-den,
der gro-sse Din-ge thut an uns und al-len En-den,

der uns von Mut-ter-leib und Kin-des-bei-nen an un-zäh-lig

viel zu gut und noch jet-zund ge-than.

30 Ye Watchers and Ye Holy Ones

One of the leading figures in the preparation of *The English Hymnal,* 1906, was J. Athelstan Riley (1858–1945). He wrote three original hymns and translated seven Latin hymns for this epochal hymnal, edited by Percy Dearmer and Ralph Vaughan Williams. This collection, "offered as a humble companion to the Book of Common Prayer for use in the Church," was a pioneer among twentieth-century hymnals in recovering the great classic hymns of earlier centuries, in reawakening an interest in authentic folk music, and in introducing new hymns and tunes by modern authors and composers, and it set a standard of editorial excellence that greatly influenced later hymnals. One of Riley's original contributions was the present hymn, many phrases of which were derived from ancient Greek liturgies. He was educated at Eton and Pembroke College, Oxford, B.A., 1881, M.A., 1883, and traveled extensively in Persia, Turkey, and Kurdistan. The latter experiences provided him with material for several pamphlets and magazine articles on Greek Orthodox, Nestorian, and other Eastern Christian churches, as well as material for his book, *Athos, or the Mountain of Monks,* 1887. For most of his life he was a member of the House of Laymen of the Province of Canterbury.

LASST UNS ERFREUEN   See No. 12 for comments on the tune. In two hymnals of the Protestant Episcopal Church in the United States of

America, *The New Hymnal,* 1918, and *The Hymnal 1940,* this German tune has a Latin name, VIGILI(ES) ET SANCTI, obviously coined from the first line of the present English text.

31 Worship the Lord in the Beauty of Holiness

Educated at Trinity College, Dublin, and eventually rector of St. Nicholas, Guildford, John S. B. Monsell (1811–1875) wrote more than three hundred hymns and urged that hymns should be more fervent and joyous. "We are too distant and reserved in our praises," he said. "We sing not as we should sing to Him and of Him who is Chief among ten thousand, the Altogether Lovely." This hymn was taken from his *Parish Hymnal,* 1873. A devout and happy man, he had an ideal home that has been described as "full of the beauty of holiness, with genial brightness and gaiety playing like sunshine over all the troubles of life." There are two conflicting stories of his sudden and untimely death, one that he fell from the roof of his church while watching the repairs being made, the other that he was struck by a falling stone while inspecting the rebuilding operations. Shortly before, he had written a hymn which contained a startling premonition of his death:

> Dear body, thou and I must part;
> Thy busy head, thy throbbing heart
> Must cease to work and cease to play,
> For me at no far distant day.

MONSELL was composed by William Fiske Sherwin (1826–1888), who was selected by Dr. John J. Vincent, founder of the Chautauqua Assembly, Lake Chautauqua, New York, to organize and direct the choruses there. He continued as choral conductor at Chautauqua from its founding in 1874 until 1888. Sherwin, born in Buckland, Massachusetts, had little formal schooling. He received his early musical training in singing schools, and later studied in Boston with Lowell Mason and George Webb. At eighteen he started to teach and subsequently had positions in North Adams, Massachusetts, Hudson, New York, and Albany, where he directed the music at the Pearl Street Baptist Church for ten years and was professor of music at the Albany Female Seminary. Subsequently he was a voice teacher, choral director, and lecturer at the New England Conservatory of Music in Boston, and a highly successful director of amateur choral groups.

32 Awake, My Soul, and With the Sun

The most frequently sung words in Protestant worship are undoubtedly those of the familiar doxology, "Praise God From Whom All Blessings Flow." They were written by Bishop Thomas Ken (1637–1711) for the schoolboys at Winchester College and appeared as the concluding stanza to his "Three Hymns for Morning, Evening and Midnight," published as an Appendix to the 1695 edition of his *Manual of Prayers for the Use of the Scholars of Winchester College.* Ken referred to the hymns in the following note in the 1674 edition of his *Manual,* although they do not appear there: "Be sure to sing the Morning and Evening Hymn in your chamber devoutly, remembering that the Psalmist, upon happy experience, assures you that it is a good thing to tell of the loving kindness of the Lord early in the morning and of his truth in the night season." It is likely that they were sung by the scholars from printed or manuscript sheets for twenty years or more before their appearance in the 1695 edition of his *Manual.* In 1692 the morning and evening hymns were published in garbled form in an unauthorized pamphlet which so provoked Ken that he was led to publish all three hymns "in his own Defence" in a pamphlet dated 1694. The present hymn is a cento from the morning hymn, the original having fourteen stanzas and ending with the doxology. His biographer, Dr. Hawkins, commented that Ken used to "sing his Morning Hymn, to his lute, daily before he put on his clothes." Ken wrote with typical modesty of his hymns:

> And should the well-meant songs I leave behind
> With Jesus' lovers an acceptance find,
> 'Twill heighten e'en the joys of Heaven to know
> That in my verse the saints hymn God below.

Left an orphan in early childhood, Ken was brought up by Isaak Walton, who had married Ken's older sister, Ann. Ken was as brave as he was devout. When Charles II came to Winchester with his mistress, Nell Gwynne, Ken refused her the use of his house; and the dissolute king, out of respect or possibly as a whim, shortly thereafter appointed him to the see of Bath and Wells. He was later deprived of his bishopric for refusing to take the oath of loyalty to the new sovereign, William III. His last remaining years were spent in the home of a friend, Lord Weymouth of Longleat, Wiltshire.

MORNING HYMN (MAGDALENE; HIPPOLYTUS), published in *A Supplement to the Asylum Hymns &c* (undated) was written between 1785 and 1789 for Bishop Ken's hymn by François Hippolyte Barthélémon at the request of the chaplain of the Asylum for Female Orphans in London. Barthélémon (1741–1808), the son of a French colonial officer and "an Irish lady of wealth," held a commission in the Irish brigade of the Duke of Berwick's regiment. His varied accomplishments in fencing, music, and languages (including Hebrew and Greek) led the colonel of the regiment to introduce him to the Earl of Kelly, amateur composer, violinist, and music enthusiast, who persuaded the young man to become a professional musician and did much to further his career. After study in France, Barthélémon went to London, had considerable success as a composer, conducted at the King's Theatre, at Marylebone and Vauxhall Gardens (where much good music was performed in the eighteenth century), and became a noted violinist. Through his wife, Mary Young, a gifted and prominent singer, Barthélémon was related to Thomas Arne and Johann Lampe, the latter a famous bassoonist who composed tunes for a number of Charles Wesley's hymns.

In 1776 Barthélémon and his wife gave concerts in Germany, Italy, and France, performing several times for the Queen of Naples who gave them a letter of introduction to her sister, Marie Antoinette. They were invited to perform for a select party at Versailles and were urged to remain at the

French court. Haydn became their close friend during his second visit to London, gave lessons to their only daughter, and on one occasion accompanied Mrs. Barthélémon at a benefit concert. In the latter part of his life, Barthélémon withdrew more and more from society, did little with music, and died after several unhappy years. MORNING HYMN is the one tune by which he is known.

The Anglican clergyman who asked Barthélémon to write a new tune for Bishop Ken's hymn, was Jacob Duché (1737–1798), a native of Philadelphia and a member of the first class to graduate from the College of Philadelphia (now the University of Pennsylvania). He was a classmate and brother-in-law of Francis Hopkinson, one of the signers of the Declaration of Independence. After two trips to England for study at Cambridge, Duché served as rector of Christ Church and St. Peter's in Philadelphia. An enthusiastic supporter of the Revolution, he was invited to give the opening prayer at the First and Second Continental Congresses held in Philadelphia in 1774 and 1775; after proclamation of the Declaration of Independence, he was appointed chaplain, but resigned after three months. In 1777, when the British entered Philadelphia, Duché became a Loyalist and wrote to George Washington urging him and others to reaffirm their allegiance to the crown. The letter was shown to members of Congress, Duché was called a traitor and left for England in December, 1777. In London he preached for a time in Bow Church, Cheapside, before being appointed, in 1782, secretary and chaplain of the Asylum and House of Refuge for Female Orphans. The Barthélémons attended services in the chapel of that institution, and heard Duché preach the doctrines of Swedenborg, which he and they eventually embraced. The three played a leading role in the establishment of the first New Church in London. After Duché was finally permitted to return to Philadelphia in 1792, he had one visit with George Washington. MORNING HYMN has one more link with American history, in that Barthélémon's younger brother, a lieutenant colonel in the French army, was killed in the latter part of the American Revolution.

33 As the Sun Doth Daily Rise

Nephew of the renowned and celebrated Admiral Viscount Nelson, Horatio Nelson (1823–1913) recast and included this hymn in his *Hymn for Saint's Day, and other Hymns*, 1864. Based on a Latin hymn, beginning with the words "Matutinus altiora," it was first published in translated form, according to John Julian, by J. Masters (no date) who referred to it as King Alfred's hymn and credited the words to "O.B.C." and the music to "Dr. Smith." There is no evidence that King Alfred wrote it, and the author is unknown. Nelson was an intimate friend of John Keble (see comments at No. 36) and was active in the Home Reunion Society. He succeeded to the earldom in 1835 and published two devotional books, *A Form of Family Prayer, with Special Offices for the Seasons*, 1852, and *A Calendar of Lessons for Every Day of the Year*, 1857.

INNOCENTS (DURHAM; ALL SAINTS; AN ANCIENT LITURGY) appeared in its present form in *The Parish Choir*, 1850, a monthly journal of

The Society for Promoting Church Music (1846–1851), an organization of Anglican Church musicians associated with the Oxford Movement and interested especially in improving the portions of the service sung by the choir. The melody, called *An Ancient Litany,* was set to "Little flowers of martyrdom," a hymn for the Feast of Holy Innocents — December 28. (See Matthew 2:16.) There has been much speculation about the origin of this bright little tune. It has been attributed to Handel (compare it with the first half of No. 362), to Samuel Webbe the Younger, and to a Joseph Smith. After commenting on these varied claims, Erik Routley assigns the form of the tune, as we know it, to William Monk, editor of *The Parish Choir* in 1850 and music editor of *Hymns Ancient and Modern,* 1861, in which INNOCENTS appeared and quickly gained favor.

34 Awake, Awake, to Love and Work

Famed as a chaplain in the British Army during World War I and known affectionately to thousands of soldiers as "Woodbine Willie," Geoffrey A. Studdert-Kennedy (1883–1929) was later appointed chaplain to the king and attained immense popularity in England and the United States as a forceful and eloquent preacher. His sermons were marked by a refreshing originality and candor. Taken from his book *The Sorrows of God and Other Poems,* 1921, this hymn is made up of the last three stanzas of the poem, "At a Harvest Festival."

MORNING SONG (CONSOLATION) was set to Isaac Watts' "Morning Song" — "Once more my soul, the rising day" — in *Kentucky Harmony,* 1816, a shape-note hymnal edited and printed by Ananias Davisson, a Presbyterian singing master, hymn writer, and publisher of Harrisonburg, Virginia. The tune was named CONSOLATION and attributed to a Mr. Dean whose original setting, with the melody in the tenor and rather stark harmonies, may be seen at No. 156 in *The Hymnal 1940 Companion.* The present harmonization was made by C. Winfred Douglas for *The Hymnal 1940.* See No. 371 for comments on Douglas, and No. 576 for comments on Davisson.

35 When Morning Gilds the Skies

Appearing with varying texts in two nineteenth-century German Roman Catholic hymnals, a *Gesangbuch* of 1828, and F. W. Ditfurth's *Fränkische Volkslieder,* 1858, this hymn, originally beginning "Beim frühen Morgenlicht," is a cento from a translation by Edward Caswall (1814–1878) which was first published in Henry Formby's *Catholic Hymns,* 1854, and later published with added stanzas in Caswall's *Masque of Mary,* 1858. The original author is unknown. Caswall was a convert to Catholicism and joined the Oratory at Edgbaston, near Birmingham, founded and directed by John Henry Newman, where he devoted himself to ministering to the sick and the poor and to writing original hymns and translating early Latin hymns from the Roman breviaries.

LAUDES DOMINI was composed for these words by Joseph Barnby (1836–1896), organist, conductor, composer, whose name comes to mind immediately in any discussion of Victorian hymn tunes. He wrote quantities of church music: anthems, services, chants, vocal solos, and 246 hymn tunes, many of which were popular at the turn of the century. He was music editor of five hymnals, the most notable of which was *The Hymnary*, 1872, edited for the High Church party by Benjamin Webb (see No. 150), Vicar of St. Andrew's Church, where Barnby was organist and choirmaster from 1863 to 1871. Under his direction the choir attained a place second to none in London.

The son of an organist, Barnby was a chorister at York Minster when he was seven, an organist and choirmaster at twelve, and a student at the Royal Academy of Music at sixteen. In competition for the first Mendelssohn Scholarship in 1856, he lost by a slim margin to Arthur Sullivan. After serving in three London churches and for eight years at St. Andrew's Church, he became organist and choirmaster at St. Anne's, Soho, in 1871, remaining there fifteen years. An outstanding choral conductor, Barnby did much to stimulate interest in Bach's music. He presented the *St. John Passion*, with orchestra, annually, at St. Anne's, and in 1871 conducted the *St. Matthew Passion* with full orchestra in Westminster Abbey, the first performance of that work in an English church. He was musical adviser to Novello and Company; precentor, organist, and director of music at Eton for fifteen years, and principal of the Guildhall School of Music from 1892 until his death. He was knighted in 1892.

36 New Every Morning Is the Love

Beginning his career as a brilliant student at Oxford where he won double first class honors, a rare achievement, John Keble (1792–1866) was ordained a priest in the Church of England and served relatively obscure parishes all his life. Yet, through his writings, he effected a spiritual awakening in the church of his time. His volume of religious poems, *The Christian Year: Thoughts in Verse for the Sundays and Holydays throughout the Year*, 1827, which he modestly published anonymously, was recognized almost immediately as a literary masterpiece and went through ninety-six editions in his lifetime. The proceeds from its sale provided funds for Keble to restore his church at Hursley. It has been called the Prayer Book in poetry. He preached a famous sermon at Oxford in 1833 on "National Apostasy," which started the Oxford Movement. See No. 215 for comments on the Oxford Movement. This hymn, based on Lamentations 3:22–23, is taken from the morning hymn in Keble's *Christian Year*.

MELCOMBE (NAZARETH) This fine tune appeared anonymously in *An Essay on the Church Plain Chant*, 1782, a collection of music for use in the Roman Catholic chapels of London. It was printed in plainsong notation and set in two parts to "O salutaris Hostia" for use at Communion. In R. Harrison's *Sacred Harmony*, 1791, the first Protestant book to include it, the tune was named MELCOMBE and assigned to Samuel Webbe (1740–

1816). A year later in Webbe's *Collection of Motetts* it was one of the tunes printed "by Permission of Mr. Webbe" which leaves little doubt as to its source. It is thought that Webbe compiled the first two parts of the *Essay,* the earliest known book to contain ADESTE FIDELES in printed form. The association of MELCOMBE with Keble's words dates from *Hymns Ancient and Modern,* 1861, for which the present harmonization, based largely on Webbe's, was made by William H. Monk. (See No. 209.) In the year that Webbe was born in England, his father died in Minorca where he had gone by government appointment. This left the boy's mother with little income and at eleven he was apprenticed to a cabinet maker. At the end of his seven-year term of service, he gave up cabinet making and started to study Latin, French, and Italian, supporting himself by copying music for a London publisher. This employment led him into music as a profession. He was given lessons by the organist of the Bavarian chapel, but largely through his own initiative and industry became a first-rate musician and gained proficiency in several languages. A Roman Catholic, he served as organist for many years at the Sardinian chapel and composed much music for the Catholic Church. Before the Catholic Emancipation Bill of 1829, the chapels of foreign embassies were the only legal places for the celebration of the Roman rites, so their services took on a public importance they might not otherwise have had. Webbe is celebrated for his catches (English rounds of the seventeenth and eighteenth centuries) and glees, a distinctively English form of unaccompanied choral composition for mens' voices, popular in the eighteenth century.

MELCOMBE may have been introduced into American hymnody by Lowell Mason — at least, the name NAZARETH, given to it in his collections (as early as 1828), appears with it also in books of several other editors.

37 Still, Still with Thee

Famed as the author of *Uncle Tom's Cabin,* Harriet Beecher Stowe (1812–1896) was also a gifted hymn writer. When her distinguished brother, Henry Ward Beecher, published his notable *Plymouth Collection of Hymns and Tunes,* 1855, it contained three of her hymns, including this one, inspired by the line from Psalm 139:18, "When I awake, I am still with thee." Much of her writing was prompted by the need to supplement the meager salary of her husband, who was in poor health. Later, writing of this period, she said, "If I sit by the open fire in the parlor, my back freezes, if I sit in the bedroom and try to write, my head and my feet are cold." Her husband, Calvin Ellis Stowe, was a professor of natural and revealed religion at Bowdoin College and later taught at Andover Theological Seminary. Her father, Lyman Beecher, was one of the most eloquent and forceful preachers of his day.

CONSOLATION (BERLIN; EPIPHANY) In the celebrated *Plymouth Collection,* 1855, "Still, still with Thee" was assigned to REST, a tune composed by the Rev. Charles Beecher, who was largely responsible for editing the music in the book. Since then the words have appeared with a variety of tunes.

The present setting for the hymn is an adaptation of one of Mendelssohn's *Songs without Words* (Op. 30, No. 3), entitled CONSOLATION in some editions although no name was given to it by the composer. It was marked simply "Adagio non troppo." In the 1864 edition of *The Church Psalter and Hymn Book* there was an arrangement of the first half of this short piano piece, named BERLIN, harmonized by John Goss and set to Lyte's "Abide with me." In Hopkins' *Temple Church Hymn Book*, 1869, the same piece, arranged by Adolphus Levy, Esq., and named EPIPHANY, was the setting for "Brightest and best of the sons of the morning." In the *Bristol Tune Book*, 1876, an arrangement much like that of Goss and named BERLIN was the first of two tunes printed with the first stanza of Mrs. Stowe's hymn. The original rhythm of Mendelssohn's composition was modified in these adaptations, as it is in the present arrangement which is largely that of Goss. See No. 120 for further comments on Mendelssohn.

38 Morning Has Broken

These words were written by Eleanor Farjeon (1881–   ), English author and poet, at the request of Percy Dearmer, editor of *Songs of Praise*, 1931, for the tune to which it has been set here. She also wrote *Nursery Rhymes of London Town* and *Singing Games from Arcady*. See No. 112 for comments on Dearmer.

BUNESSAN, a Gaelic melody, taken down from a wandering Highland singer by Alexander Fraser and published in *Songs and Hymns of the Gael*, 1888, was used for "Child in the Manger," a Christmas hymn, in the Irish *Church Hymnal*, 1917. It appears with those words in the *Church Hymnary, Revised*, 1927, harmonized, as at No. 38, by Dr. David Evans (1874–1948), one of Wales' most distinguished musicians. He was born in Rhos, educated at Arnold College, Swansea, and University College, Cardiff. When he was twenty-one he was granted his D.Mus. degree at Oxford. For a time he was organist and choirmaster at Jewin Street Welsh Presbyterian Church in London. He was professor of music at University College, Cardiff (1903–1939), organist, choral conductor, composer, editor of music and of the music journal, *Y Cerddor* ("The Musician"), 1916–1921, and a leading adjudicator at the National Eisteddfodau. He conducted many of the psalmody and hymn-singing festivals which had been founded by John Roberts (1822–1877) to strengthen and raise the standard of congregational singing in Wales and which had a deep influence on its religious life as well. The night before his death Evans conducted four thousand choristers at the Rhos Choir Eisteddfod.

39 O Splendor of God's Glory Bright

Elected bishop of Milan in 374 by public acclamation, although at the time he was only a catechumen, Ambrose (340–397) was the greatest churchman of his day. Earlier in his life he had distinguished himself as a lawyer and as an administrator. He courageously and successfully defied the Roman rulers in their repeated attempts to dominate the church, and he was largely responsible for winning over St. Augustine to the Christian faith. His most notable contribution to the Western Church was the introduction of congregational and antiphonal singing into the services of worship. His own hymns and the Latin texts which he set to simple metrical tunes had a powerful appeal and spread throughout western Europe. Augustine included a moving tribute to the power and beauty of Ambrose's hymns in his *Confessions*, Book IX, 7. C. S. Phillips says in *Hymnody Past and Present*, "Not only do we owe to St. Ambrose the recognition of hymns as an integral part of the public worship of the Western Church, but also . . . it was he who laid down the lines on which Latin hymnody was mainly to develop in the centuries succeeding." This hymn was written for lauds, one of the early morning offices or services observed in the monastic orders. The translation is by Robert Bridges from his *Yattendon Hymnal*, 1899. See No. 430 for comments on Bridges.

PUER NOBIS NASCITUR ("Unto us a boy is born"), sometimes called SPLENDOUR because of its use with the present text, was set to "Geborn ist Gottes Söhnelein" in Vol. VI of *Musae Sioniae*, 1609, an important collection of choral music for Protestant services compiled by Michael Praetorius (1571–1621). The present form of the tune, in triple time, is undoubtedly Praetorius' adaptation of an older carol "Puer nobis nascitur." (See No. 142.) *Musae Sioniae*, published in nine volumes between 1605 and 1610, contains chorale arrangements of more than 1,200 compositions, from simple chorale harmonizations to polychoral settings. The son of a Lutheran pastor who had been a pupil of Johann Walther (see No. 498), Praetorius attended the Latin school of Torgau and the University of Frankfurt an der Oder, serving as organist of St. Mary's Church while he was a student at the university. In 1589 he left Frankfurt to be organist at the Castle Church in Gröningen for Bishop Heinrich Julius of Halberstadt, later duke of Brunswick and Lüneburg. His association with this music-loving nobleman was a long and fruitful one. In 1594 he went with the duke to Wolfenbüttel, where he served as court organist and *kapellmeister* and had his own home from 1612 until his death. In 1596, on the occasion of the dedication of a new organ built by David Beck of Halberstadt, the duke, at great personal expense, arranged to have more than fifty well-known organists come to Gröningen to hear and try the new instrument. Through this unusual gathering, Praetorius met the leading organists of Germany.

His education in music started late. He was largely self-taught but learned much from musicians whom he met at the courts of Prague, Halle, Magdeburg, and Dresden, where official duties took him. He expressed regret more than once that he had never been instructed by a great master nor had the opportunity to study the new music at its source in Venice. Nevertheless, as one of the pioneers who embraced the new trends in music stemming from Italy and combined them with the distinctive elements of the German tradition, Praetorius became an outstanding figure of the early Baroque. He wrote secular as well as sacred music and was one of the most versatile, industrious, and productive musicians of his time. His output was enormous, an extraor-

36

dinary achievement for an organist, choir director, theorist, composer, author, and editor who died on his fiftieth birthday. His *Syntagma Musicum* ("Musical Treatise"), 1615–1619, is a remarkable three-volume work of great historical value because of the light it casts on the musical knowledge and practices of his day. Volume II, which deals with instruments and instrumental music, is of particular interest to contemporary organists and organ builders because of the detailed descriptions of typical German organs of that time.

40 O Splendor of God's Glory Bright

See No. 39 for comments on the text.

SPLENDOR PATERNAE, the traditional melody for St. Ambrose's text (and used also with other hymns at lauds) is given here in the form found in the *Sarum Antiphoner*. "Sarum Use" or "Sarum Rite" refers to the liturgical practices or the order of divine service of Old Sarum, the diocese of Salisbury, which differed in some ways from the Roman rite and was the order in most general use in England in the later Middle Ages. Antiphonal, antiphonary, antiphoner, were names given to books which contained the plainsong melodies sung by the choir at services other than the mass. The tune name is from the first line of the Latin text of Ambrose's morning hymn. The harmonization is by Winfred Douglas, outstanding American Protestant authority on plainsong and liturgical music. See No. 371 for comments on Douglas.

41 Father, We Praise Thee, Now the Night Is Over

Pope Gregory I (540–604), known familiarly as Gregory the Great, holds the honor of sending the first missionary to England, Augustine of Canterbury, and of reorganizing and decisively shaping the liturgy and music of the Roman Catholic Church. The officially approved music of Catholic liturgy is named after him, "Gregorian chant" or plainsong (see comments at No. 111 on the tune SPLENDOR PATERNAE). This hymn for matins, originally beginning "Nocte surgentes vigilemus omnes," is generally attributed to him, although some scholars credit it to Alcuin, the leading intellectual in Charlemagne's court. The translation was made by Percy Dearmer for *The English Hymnal,* 1906. See No. 112 for comments on Dearmer.

CHRISTE SANCTORUM The tune name is from a Medieval Latin office hymn "Christe sanctorum, decus angelorum" ("Christ, the fair glory of the holy angels") which may be seen in an English translation with its traditional plainsong melody in *The Hymnal 1940* (No. 123). The tune, an anonymous French Church melody, has been traced to a Paris antiphoner of 1681 where it was associated with another Latin hymn, "Ceteri numquam." It was the setting for the present words in the *English Hymnal,* 1906, with its source given as La Feillée's *Méthode du plain-chant,* 1782. This manual of instruction for choirmasters, written by a priest and singer connected with the choir of Chartres Cathedral in the mid-eighteenth century, would seem to have little relevance for English or American Protestant hymnody. But it continued to be printed and augmented by other editors well into the nineteenth century and was the source of seven melodies in the *Hymnal Noted* (1852, 1854) and of a number in the *English Hymnal,* 1906.

Although printed as plainsong, these so-called church melodies were measured, predominantly major and minor in tonality, and had their source in seventeenth- and eighteenth-century French breviaries. La Feillée, aware of the changes taking place in the music of his time (modal to tonal harmonization, free to isometric rhythm), included in his *Méthode* instruction not only in singing the traditional plainsong but in singing the new music, *le chant figuré,* as well. In a 1777 edition of the *Méthode,* a copy of which is in the New York Public Library, its author tells the Bishop of Poitiers, to whom it is dedicated, that the book contains the praises of our Lord and the way to sing them. One wishes that this musician-priest knew how far and wide his little book would carry these praises! The harmonization at No. 41 is from the *Church Hymnary, Revised,* 1927. For further comments on French church melodies see No. 59.

42 High O'er the Lonely Hills

Best known for her popular, wartime novel, *Mrs. Miniver,* 1940, Jan Struther (1901–1953) published a collection of essays and sketches, *Try Anything Twice,* 1938, one volume of serious poems, *The Glass-Blower,* 1941, and several collections of light verse. Her professional name was a pseudonym formed from her maiden name, Joyce Anstruther. She was married to Anthony Maxtone Graham in 1923. During the war years she and her two children lived in New York City where she was in great demand as a lecturer. On one occasion she remarked about her experiences: "My children are delighted when they hear taxi drivers say 'foist' and 'thoid' just as in films. They say, 'Gosh, aren't the cops tough!' with the very greatest admiration. It is good, too, to hear European languages freely spoken without people making notes and whispering, 'Fifth Columnists.'" Her novel, previously printed in serial form in the London *Times,* was a series of sketches on the ordinary, day-by-day incidents in a typical English middle-class household just prior to World War II. She was invited to write this hymn for *Songs of Praise,* 1931, as an Advent hymn, and eleven other of her lyrics were included in this noteworthy hymnal.

DAWN, so named in *The Hymnal 1940,* is called WATCHMAN in the English hymnals which include it, because of its earlier association with an Advent hymn, "Hark! 'Tis the watchman's cry." The editors of *Songs of Praise,* 1931, eager to have this tune in their book, invited Jan Struther to write words for it. Percy Dearmer, one of the editors, comments, "The result was this beautiful lyric, which gives a fresh charm to the tune." No information about T. H. Ingham (1878–1948) is available at the present time.

43 Christ, Whose Glory Fills the Skies

Charles Wesley (1707–1788), the "sweet singer" of Methodism, was the youngest son of Samuel and Susannah Wesley, in a family of nineteen children, and together with his brother John effected one of the greatest religious revivals in English history. Traveling hundreds of miles on horseback, he preached to crowds of thousands, often in open fields and on city streets. Although critical of the established church, he remained a loyal Anglican all his life and disapproved of the separatists among the Methodists and of his brother's informal ordinations. His most memorable contribution to Christendom was made through his hymns — of which he is said to have written more than 6,500 — several of them being among the choicest treasures in the hymnody of the church. This hymn, based on Malachi 4:2, was first published in the Wesleys' *Hymns and Sacred Poems*, 1740, and was described by James Montgomery as "one of Charles Wesley's loveliest progeny."

RATISBON was adapted by William H. Havergal from a melody in Johann G. Werner's *Choralbuch*, Leipzig, 1815. (Zahn 6801) Werner (1777–1822), organist, choirmaster, teacher, composer, author, and editor, evidently reconstructed the melody from a tune in Freylinghausen's *Gesangbuch*, 1704, based on an earlier melody by Joachim Neander. (Zahn 3947) The first two phrases of these melodies seem to bear some relation to the first half of the Easter chorale "Jesus meine Zuversicht" published in 1653 and often attributed to Johann Crüger. In some hymnals RATISBON is given as an alternative name for this tune of which there are two harmonizations by Bach, one in the *Choralgesänge*, one in Cantata No. 145. The tune was printed with the first stanza of "Christ whose glory fills the sky" in *Old Church Psalmody*, 1847, from which the present harmonization, with minor changes, is taken.

44 Lord Jesus, in the Days of Old

James Ashcroft Noble (1844–1896), English journalist and literary critic, wrote this evening hymn for the girls at Wintersdorf, a school in Southport, Lancashire, where he lectured on English literature. It was published in his *Verses of a Prose Writer*, 1887, in the section entitled "Poems of the Inner Life."

VATER UNSER (OLD 112TH) This anonymous German melody appeared with Luther's version of the Lord's Prayer, "Vater unser im Himmelreich" in Valten Schumann's *Geistliche Lieder*, 1539. (Zahn 2561) Luther is said to have discarded a tune of his own composition in favor of this melody, first found in a manuscript part-book given him in 1530 by the musician Johann Walther. (See No. 498.) In the Appendix of *Psalmes of David in Englishe Meter*, 1560, it was set to Bishop Cox's English version of the Lord's Prayer. In later English and Scottish Psalters it was also associated with Kethe's version of Psalm 112, hence its alternative name. The Pilgrims must have known this tune, for in Ainsworth's Psalter, 1612, it was assigned to Psalms 34, 82, 133, and 149. Apparently congregations in the Massachusetts Bay Colony were also familiar with it, for in the "Admonition" printed at the end of the *Bay Psalm Book*, 1640 (which contained no music), Psalm 112 or the Pater Noster was given as the tune to which the versions of Psalms 85 and 138 could be sung.

Va-ter un-ser im Him-mel-reich, der du uns al-le hei-ssest

gleich Brü-der sein und dich ru-fen an und willst das

Be-ten von uns han, gieb, das nicht bet al-lein der Mund,

hilf, dass es geh von Her-zen Grund.

VATER UNSER, a great favorite of John Wesley, was one of the German tunes included in the *Foundery* tune book, 1742 (see No. 9), where it was called "Playford's Tune." Bach used the melody in Cantatas 90, 101 (it appears in six movements), 102, in the *St. John Passion* (Part I, No. 9), and in four chorale preludes for organ, one in the *Orgelbüchlein,* two in the *Clavierübung,* one in the miscellaneous Preludes. There is one harmonization in the *Choralgesänge.* All the movements of Mendelssohn's "Sixth Organ Sonata" are based on this chorale.

45 Day Is Dying in the West

Associated with the Chautauqua movement most of her adult life, Mary A. Lathbury (1841–1913) wrote these lines in the summer of 1877 for Bishop John H. Vincent, founder of the famous Chautauqua Assembly. The daughter of a Methodist minister, she contributed frequently to periodicals for children and young people and served as the assistant editor under Bishop Vincent of several Methodist publications, *Sunday School Advocate, Classmate,* and *Picture Lesson Paper.* A gifted artist as well as a poet, she often illustrated her own books. She founded the Look-Up Legion in Methodist Sunday schools which had a membership of four thousand boys and girls in 1885 and was inspired by Edward Everett Hale's four rules:

> Look up, and not down;
> Look forward, and not back;
> Look out, and not in,
> And lend a hand.

Later, Hale added the line, "In His Name." Later in life she was attracted to the thought of Emanuel Swedenborg, due in large measure to his emphasis on the close relationship between science and religion which had also played so prominent a part in the Chautauqua program. She joined The Church of the New Jerusalem in Orange, New Jersey, in 1895. Because of her literary talents, Miss Làthbury was known popularly as the poet laureate of Chautauqua. Following her death at East Orange, New Jersey, on October 20, 1913, the *New-Church Messenger* published a tribute to her with this comment: "For several years Miss Lathbury superintended a large Chinese Sunday school in New York City, and when her labors there came to an end she became the friend, advisor and guide of the colored people of the Oranges, who have in her removal to the higher realms of life lost one of their best and most sympathetic friends. It was through the disinterested efforts of Miss Lathbury that some of the brightest of our young colored people were enabled to pass through the higher schools of this country and enter upon the work which they are now doing."

CHAUTAUQUA was written for Miss Lathbury's hymn by William F. Sherwin in 1877 (see No. 31). "So completely has this tune become fixed in the musical memory of Americans that it and the words 'Day is dying in the west' have become synonymous" (R. G. McCutchan). A writer in *The Independent* once said that Sherwin "was a genial tyrant of the baton, who would scold his chorus till they cried, and then heal all hearts with his 'Day is dying in the west.' " In *The Chautauqua Movement,* 1886, Bishop John H. Vincent, telling of the meetings of the Chautauqua Literary and Scientific Circle each afternoon at five for discussion, wrote: "As this hour draws near its close 'The Song of Evening Praise,' "Day is dying in the west," is invariably given out or called for. . . . No one can hear it sung at the close of a Round Table or Vesper service at Chautauqua without feeling its power."

CHAUTAUQUA is still sung at the five o'clock vesper services held each Sunday during the eight-week season of Chautauqua Institution and at the sacred song service on Sunday evenings in the amphitheater.

46 Again, as Evening's Shadow Falls

Born in Portland, Maine, where he also died, Samuel Longfellow (1819– 1892), brother of the famous poet, was equally distinguished as a Unitarian minister and as a writer of hymns. While pastor of the Second Unitarian Church in Brooklyn, he instituted a series of vesper services, which became widely popular in many other communions. He wrote this hymn for those services. The present Unitarian and Universalist hymnal is named after one of his compilations, *Hymns of the Spirit,* 1864, which he published in collaboration with Samuel Johnson and which one writer facetiously referred to as "The 'Sam' Book."

CANONBURY   The source of this tune is No. 4 of Robert Schumann's set of piano pieces, *Nachtstücke* (Nocturnes), Op. 23, 1839. Its form at No. 46 (arranged for this hymnal) differs slightly in measures one, five, and seven from the more familiar arrangement at No. 397, but is closer to the original. Because a crippling injury to his hand made a career as a concert pianist impossible, Schumann's gifts were diverted to composition and he became one of the greatest composers of the Romantic school and one of its leading spokesmen. His works include a wealth of pieces for piano, the medium through which he expressed himself most naturally; songs (over one hundred of them were written in one year) which have taken their place alongside those of Schubert; chamber music, symphonies, choral works, and a piano concerto. Schumann (1810–1856) had literary as well as musical gifts. He was one of the founders and, for ten years, the editor of *Die Neue Zeitschrift für Musik,* a periodical created to combat the mediocrity and superficiality of much of the music of that time, drawing attention to the best in the past and encouraging new talent. The rare faculty of being able to recognize true greatness among contemporaries was his, and two of his most famous essays are those in which he acclaims the genius of Chopin and Brahms. Some of his essays and criticisms are available in English under the title *Music and Musicians.* His wife, Clara, daughter of Friedrich Wieck, his piano teacher, was one of the great pianists of her time and did much to make her husband's music known. All accounts of Schumann mention the magnanimity and generosity of his spirit and his high idealism.

47 The Day Thou Gavest, Lord, Is Ended

John Ellerton (1826–1893), Anglican clergyman and the author of many books, is today best remembered as a hymnologist, translator, and hymn writer. He wrote this evening hymn for *A Liturgy for Missionary Meetings,* 1870. It was sung in thousands of churches throughout the British Empire, at Queen Victoria's request, on the occasion of her Diamond Jubilee Service in 1897. He was a contributor to *Hymns, Ancient and Modern,* 1889 edition, and was frequently consulted for his wide knowledge in hymnody. Julian said of him, "His sympathy with nature, especially in her sadder moods, is great; he loves the fading light and the peace of eve, and lingers in the shadows." (*Dictionary of Hymnology.*)

LES COMMANDEMENS DE DIEU (COMMANDMENTS; OLD 125TH; BAVA)   This, one of the best-known tunes adapted or composed by Louis Bourgeois (see No. 4), was set to Marot's version of the Ten Commandments in the 1547 and subsequent editions of the Genevan Psalter. It had appeared with the same text in a Strasbourg psalter of 1545 and in Bourgeois' *Pseaulmes cinquante de David,* 1547, a collection of four-part harmonizations of psalm tunes published at Lyons.

Le - ve   le cueur, ou - vre l'au - reil - le   Peuple en - dur - cy, pour es - cou - ter

De ton Dieu la voix nom-par - eil - le   Et ses com-man-de-mens gou-ster

LES COMMANDEMENS was also used for Psalm 140 in later editions of the French Psalter. In *One and Fiftie Psalmes,* 1556, the first musical edition of the English Psalter, it was adapted to William Whittingham's Long Meter (L. M.) version of the Decalogue, "Attende my people and give eare." After 1556 the tune was included in English and Scottish psalters with versions of the Commandments and in Este's (1592), Ravenscroft's (1621), and Playford's (1671) psalters with Psalm 125 as well. In nineteenth-century English hymnals LES COMMANDEMENS was generally in 4/2 or 4/4 with notes of equal length throughout, set to Long Meter texts. Ralph Vaughan Williams, music editor of *The English Hymnal,* 1906, restored the original rhythm and form of the melody and set it to the present text. LES COM–MANDEMENS was known to the early settlers in New England. It was set to Psalm 5 in Ainsworth's Psalter, 1612, and was recommended by the editors of the *Bay Psalm Book,* 1640, for use with L. M. versions, as one of the tunes "most familiar to us." In *The National Psalmist,* 1848, and *Cantica Laudis,* edited by Lowell Mason and George Webb, LES COMMANDE–MENS, in Long Meter, with a long note at the beginning and end of each phrase, harmonized by Havergal, was named BAVA (Old "Ten Commandments" Tune).

In Germany, LES COMMANDEMENS, with no melodic or rhythmic alterations, was set to the Decalogue and Psalm 140 in Lobwasser's Psalter, 1573, for use in the Reformed Church. (Zahn 750) From 1567 on, the tune, with slight changes, was used by Lutherans for Paul Eber's "Wenn wir in höchsten Nöthen sein" ("When in the hour of utmost need"), and later with other hymns as well. In a contemporary German hymnal it is the setting for six texts. There are two harmonizations of the melody in Bach's *Choralgesänge* (in 4/4) and two chorale preludes for organ on it. One is in the *Orgelbüchlein,* the other is the last of the *Eighteen Chorales* on which Bach worked during his last illness when he was revising some of his earlier works. For further comments on Bach's use of the tune see *Bach's Chorals,* Part III, 1921 (pp. 316–324), and *Bach: A Biography,* 1928 (pp. 263–264), by Charles Sanford Terry.

48 The Day Thou Gavest, Lord, Is Ended

See No. 47 for comments on the text.

ST. CLEMENT was composed for the present text by the Rev. Clement C. Scholefield (1839–1904) and first published in *Church Hymns with Tunes,* 1874, edited by Arthur Sullivan. Scholefield, a self-taught musician was conduct (chaplain) at Eton College; vicar of Holy Trinity, Knightsbridge; and had been curate for eight years at St. Peter's Church, South Kensington, where Sullivan was organist for a time.

49 O Gladsome Light

One of the oldest Christian hymns, this was sung in the early Greek Church at the lighting of the lamps in the evening service and is therefore known as the "Candlelighting Hymn." It is still sung at this service in the Greek Church, which is in keeping with the early Christian practice of singing hymns at the rising and setting of the sun. St. Basil, who died in 379, quotes it as of unknown authorship and date. It was first published in Archbishop Ussher's *De Symbolis*, 1647. This translation was made by Robert Bridges for his *Yattendon Hymnal*, 1899. There are many other translations. See No. 430 for comments on Robert Bridges.

NUNC DIMITTIS was composed or adapted by Louis Bourgeois (see No. 4) for Marot's metrical version of the "Song of Simeon" (*Nunc dimittis* — Luke 2:29–32) in the Genevan Psalter, 1549. Sung regularly after Communion, it and the versified Ten Commandments (No. 47) were the two exceptions to the early ruling in the Reformed Church that all congregational singing be restricted to versions of the Psalms. The harmonization is an adaptation of a four-part setting by Claude Goudimel (c. 1505–1572) outstanding sixteenth-century French composer of secular and sacred songs, masses and motets, and of a large number of harmonizations of the Genevan psalm tunes. In these, originally, the melody was in the tenor. The 1565 edition of his settings for the whole psalter contained simple note-for-note harmonizations which appeared in nearly all of the seventeenth- and eighteenth-century psalmbooks printed on the Continent in a variety of languages for the churches of the Reformed tradition. They are coming back into use in contemporary hymnals. *The Hymnal for Colleges and Schools,* published in 1956 by Yale University Press, contains more than twenty of Goudimel's settings. In the eighteenth century, Jean Jacques Rousseau wrote of the singing of the peasants of Neuchâtel, "One of their common amusements is to sing the psalms in four parts, with their wives and children, and one is astonished to hear the vigorous and manly harmonies of Goudimel, so long forgotten by our learned musicians, issuing from these country cottages." Goudimel, a Protestant convert, was killed with fellow Huguenots at Lyons in August, 1572, when the St. Bartholomew massacre spread from Paris to the provinces.

50 Sun of My Soul, Thou Savior Dear

Inspired by the text, "Abide with us: for it is toward evening, and the day is far spent" (Luke 24:29), John Keble wrote this evening hymn for his *Christian Year,* 1827. The original hymn had fourteen stanzas. See No. 36 for comments on Keble.

HURSLEY (STILLORGAN; PASCAL; FRAMINGHAM), derived from "Grosser Gott, wir loben dich" (No. 247), was named by the editors of *Hymns Ancient and Modern,* 1861, for the village near Winchester, England, where Keble was vicar for thirty years. Its association with the present text dates from *The Metrical Psalter,* 1855, of Irons and Lahee. In the ninth edition of the *Boston Handel and Haydn Society Collection,* 1830, edited by Lowell Mason, HURSLEY, in a slightly different form, set to "Come hither, all ye weary souls," was called FRAMINGHAM, a name given by Mason in later collections to two other tunes.

51 Now the Day Is Over

Famous for his hymn, "Onward, Christian Soldiers," Sabine Baring-Gould (1834–1924) is described by James Moffatt (*Handbook to the Church Hymnary*) as "a man of an extraordinary range of interests, and of inexhaustible versatility and industry." [1] Ordained in the Church of England, he served successively as curate of Horbury and Dalton, both in Yorkshire, and as rector of East Mersea, Essex, and Lew Trenchard, Devon. Having inherited the family estate in Lew Trenchard upon the death of his father in 1872, he combined the life of a country squire and parson after going to his last charge in 1881. He published over eighty-five volumes in such diversified fields as travel, mythology, poetry, fiction, biography, history, folk songs, and popular theology, and is reported to have had more book titles listed after his name in the literary catalogue of the British Museum than any other author of his time.

This hymn was written for the children of Horbury Bridge, near Wakefield, Yorkshire, while Baring-Gould was the curate of Horbury parish. It was included in the Appendix to *Hymns Ancient and Modern*, 1868.

MERRIAL was set without a name to this text in Joseph Barnby's *Original Tunes for Popular Hymns*, 1869. Although widely used in America it does not appear in contemporary English hymnals. In them, EUDOXIA (No. 510), composed by the author of the hymn, is the accepted setting. The name MERRIAL was given to the tune by an American, Charles S. Robinson, who allegedly invented it from his daughter's name and initial: Mary L. (*Hymn Tune Names*, R. G. McCutchan.)

See No. 35 for comments on Barnby.

52 Now, on Land and Sea Descending

Samuel Longfellow wrote this hymn for a small book of verses which he published in 1859, *Vespers*, intended for use in the vesper services in his church in Brooklyn. See No. 46 for comments on Longfellow.

VESPER HYMN, familiar to many as the tune for "Hark, the vesper hymn is stealing, O'er the waters soft and clear," first appeared with Thomas Moore's words in Sir John Stevenson's *Selection of Popular National Airs,* London, 1818, where it was called RUSSIAN AIR. A footnote said that Stevenson had added the fourth line. Although the tune is attributed to Dimitri Bortniansky, nothing resembling this "Russian Air" has been found in his published works. As early as 1819 the tune appeared in sheet form in New York City and became a popular glee club number. It was included in the *Christian Lyre,* 1831, named "Vesper Hymn" and set to "Lord, with glowing heart I'd praise Thee." In two other early nineteenth-century American collections of church music, Abner Jones' *Harmonia sacra*, 1831, and Lowell Mason's *Modern Psalmist,* 1839, it appeared with Moore's words, not among the congregational hymns but in the choir section, arranged for solo voice, with the choir coming in on "jubilate." In these books it is named VESPER HYMN and listed as a Russian Air.

53 The Duteous Day Now Closeth

Combining elements of both the older, more objective type of hymnody, as represented by Luther, with the newer, more subjective type, as represented by the Pietists, Paul Gerhardt (1607–1676) was a bridge between two eras. A beloved and popular Lutheran preacher, he has been called the greatest hymn writer after Luther. His life was marked by much suffering which severely tested but did not vanquish his courageous spirit and serene faith. Beneath his portrait in the Lutheran church in Lübben, his last pastorate, is the inscription, "Theologus in cribro Satanae versatus" ("A divine sifted in Satan's sieve"). The present hymn, originally beginning "Nun ruhen alle Wälder," first published in Johann Crüger's *Praxis pietatis melica,* 1647, is widely sung by children in Germany as an evening prayer. Robert Bridges wrote this English paraphrase for his *Yattendon Hymnal,* 1899. See No. 430 for comments on Bridges.

INNSBRUCK (O WELT ICH MUSS DICH LASSEN; NUN RUHEN ALLE WÄLDER; IN ALLEN MEINEN THATEN), now generally considered to be an anonymous, traditional German melody of the fifteenth century, is often attributed to the Flemish musician, Heinrich Isaak (c. 1450–c. 1527), one of the most notable and versatile composers of his time. INNS–BRUCK was the top voice of a four-part polyphonic setting of the *Wanderlied* (traveler's song) "Innsbruck, ich muss dich lassen" ("Innsbruck, I must leave thee") which appeared in Georg Forster's *Teutschen Liedlein,* Nürnberg, 1539, an important collection of 130 German secular melodies, three of which were used later as hymn tunes. This setting, the first known printed form of INNSBRUCK, has been ascribed to Isaak. From 1598 on, the melody was associated with "O Welt, ich muss dich lassen" ("O world, I must leave thee"), Johann Hesse's hymn for the dying, based on the secular words, as shown below. (Zahn 2293a)

wo ich im E - - - - - - - - - - - - - - - - - lend bin.
set - zen gnä-dig in - - - - - - Got - - - - - - tes Hand.

In the seventeenth century the melody came to be associated also with the German original of the present text, and with Paul Flemming's hymn "In allen meinen Thaten." Bach used the melody in Cantatas 13, 44, 97, twice in the *St. Matthew Passion* (Nos. 16, 44), once in the *St. John Passion* (No. 8). There are four harmonizations of it in the *Choralgesänge*. Brahms wrote two chorale preludes on it in Opus 122. Like most chorale melodies this one has a number of variants. In *The National Psalmist*, 1848, edited by Lowell Mason and George Webb, it was named CLINTON, with the heading "Arranged from an old Tune by H. Isaac, 1490."

Isaak wrote sacred and secular, vocal and instrumental music in a variety of forms. He has been called the first international composer because much of his music reflects the character and the stylistic idioms of the different countries in which he lived. His most significant work, *Choralis Constantinus*, contains polyphonic settings of the proper of the mass for practically the entire liturgical year and is said to sum up the polyphonic craft of an era. Nothing is known of Isaak's activities before c. 1477 (1480, 1484?) when he was appointed organist and director of music at the court of Lorenzo the Magnificent in Florence. He served that great patron of art and music until Lorenzo's death in 1492. Included in his official duties was the giving of music instruction to Lorenzo's children, one of whom, Giovanni, became Pope Leo X in 1513. From 1497 until his death, Isaak was court composer (*Hofkomponist*) to Emperor Maximilian I. Since this position did not require continuous attendance at the imperial court, Isaak had considerable freedom and lived by turns in Augsburg, Innsbruck, Vienna, Torgau, Neustift, and Constance. In 1515 he was given permission by Maximilian to remain permanently in Florence where he died in 1517. Isaak's associates and pupils were among the greatest musicians of the day. The composer Ludwig Senfl (c. 1492–c. 1533), whose works were greatly admired by Martin Luther, was one of Isaak's students and his successor at the Vienna court.

INNSBRUCK, set to "O Esca viatorum" ("O Food of men wayfaring") is frequently sung in Roman Catholic churches as a Eucharistic motet during mass, as it was during the requiem mass for President John F. Kennedy in St. Matthew's Cathedral, Washington, D.C., on November 25, 1963. Bäumker gives the German version of the Latin hymn in Vol. IV, No. 407a.

54 Now Cheer Our Hearts This Eventide

Usually attributed to Nicolaus Selnecker (1528–1592), this hymn is composite in character. The first stanza, published as a broadsheet in 1579, is a translation of Melanchthon's "Vespera jam venit," based on Luke 24:29. Philipp Melanchthon (1497–1560), one of Luther's closest friends and advisers, was a reconciling influence in the bitter disputes between various Protestant groups and between Protestants and Catholics at the time of the Reformation.

The Augsburg Confession is from his pen, and he published the first major Protestant work in systematic theology, *Loci Communes (Common Topics)*, 1521. The second stanza resembles a rhymed prayer found in Selnecker's *Der Psalter*, 1572, but it is not certain that he wrote it. Originally this hymn contained nine stanzas in its final form, as given in Selnecker's *Geistliche Psalmen*, Nürnberg, 1611, the last seven stanzas of which are definitely his. Selnecker was a noted Lutheran preacher and theologian and the leading figure in developing the great Motet Choir in St. Thomas' Church, Leipzig, later made famous by J. S. Bach. This hymn first appeared in English in the *Yattendon Hymnal*, 1899, edited by Robert Bridges. See No. 430 for comments on Bridges.

ACH BLEIB BEI UNS (CALVISIUS) This melody, found in *Geistliche Lieder*, 1589, was the alto in a four-part setting of "Danket dem Herrn, heut' und allzeit" (Zahn 439) in a 1594 collection of Latin and German hymns edited by Seth Calvisius (1556–1615). It is attributed to him in some books. Bach used a variant of the melody in Cantata No. 6 for a soprano aria which he later arranged for No. 5 of Schübler' *Sechs Choräle* for organ. His harmonization at No. 54 appears in the *Choralgesänge* with two texts, "Ach bleib bei uns" and "Uns ist ein Kindlein heut geborn."

Calvisius (Seth Kallwitz), the son of a poor peasant, attained eminence as astronomer, chronologer, musician, theorist, mathematician, theologian, poet, author. Through singing and teaching he earned enough money to attend the gymnasiums in Frankenhausen and Magdeburg, the University of Helmstedt, and with the help of a wealthy patron was enabled to continue his studies at the University of Leipzig. For a year he directed the music at the Paulinerkirche in Leipzig. During twelve years as cantor of the Fürstenschule in Schulpforta, he established high standards of scholarship and brought new distinction to that famous humanistic classical school. From 1594–1615 he was cantor at the Thomasschule and director of music at the Nicolaikirche and Thomaskirche in Leipzig, one of Bach's distinguished predecessors. In 1611 he was offered the chair of mathematics at Wittenberg but chose to remain in Leipzig. He composed and arranged music, edited collections of motets and psalm tunes, and wrote a number of treatises on music.

55 At Even, Ere the Sun Was Set

While headmaster of a large grammar school, the Godolphin School, Hammersmith, England, Henry Twells (1823–1900) was invited by Sir Henry Baker to contribute an evening hymn for the Appendix to *Hymns Ancient and Modern*, 1868. He complied, as he later confided in a letter to a friend, by writing these words "one afternoon while the boys were under examination [paper work] and I was supposed to be seeing 'all fair.' I am afraid I could not have been very energetic or lynx-eyed in my duties that day." He later retired to Bournemouth, because of failing health, where he built and endowed with his own means a new church, St. Augustine, which he served as priest-in-charge until his death. This hymn is based on the healing incident described in Mark 1:32. See No. 79 for comments on *Hymns Ancient and Modern*.

ANGELUS (WHITSUN HYMN) from Part II, *Cantica Spiritualia,* Munich, 1847, is derived in part from a melody attributed to Georg Joseph, mid-seventeenth-century court musician in the employ of the prince-bishop of Breslau. The original tune was set to "Du meiner Seelen güldne Zier" in *Heilige Seelenlust,* 1657, a collection of Johann Scheffler's poems for which Joseph supplied the music. Scheffler, poet and mystic from Breslau, Silesia, took the name Angelus Silesius when he became a Roman Catholic in 1653. ANGELUS came into English hymnody in 1863 and was set to the present text in the Appendix to *Hymns Ancient and Modern,* 1868.

56 All Praise to Thee, My God

This is a cento of the first three stanzas and the concluding doxology of Bishop Ken's evening hymn taken from his *Manual of Prayers,* 1695 edition. The first stanza as Ken wrote it began, "Glory to thee, my God, this night" and often appears in this form. There were originally eleven stanzas in addition to the familiar doxology. Archibald Jacob has said that "Ken's hymn has been known in part and loved by many millions" and "has been divided, subdivided, and rearranged in a great variety of ways." See No. 32 for comments on Ken.

TALLIS' CANON (BERWICK; CANON; BRENTWOOD; SUFFOLK; and others) In a form twice as long, with each phrase repeated, TALLIS' CANON was set to Psalm 67 in Archbishop Parker's *Whole Psalter* (c. 1561) for which Tallis supplied nine tunes arranged in four parts. A facsimile of the original setting is given on page 122 of *The Hymnal 1940 Companion.* Its transcription in modern notation appears in *Historical Companion to Hymns Ancient and Modern,* 1962, at No. 23. The present short four-phrase form dates from Ravenscroft's *Whole Booke of Psalmes,* 1621, in which it was set to "A Psalme before Morning Prayer." Presumably it was first printed with Bishop Ken's words in the *Harmonious Companion,* 1732. Originally, the tenor took the lead in the canon, followed by the soprano. *The Harvard Dictionary of Music* defines a canon as "a polyphonic composition in which all parts have the same melody throughout, although starting at different points."

Thomas Tallis (c. 1505–1585), one of the most distinguished Tudor musicians, was a composer of extraordinary gifts, who, as a gentleman of the Chapel Royal for over forty years and one of its organists, served in the reigns of Henry VIII, Edward VI, Queen Mary, and Queen Elizabeth I. Reliable records of his early life are lacking, but it is known that before the dissolution of the monasteries in 1540, he served as organist and master of the choristers at Waltham Abbey where Henry VIII was a frequent visitor, and where the king's musical interests must have brought him into contact with Tallis. After leaving Waltham Abbey, Tallis was at Canterbury for a time, serving as a lay clerk. He was appointed a gentleman of the Chapel Royal about 1542. For a number of years he and William Byrd (thirty years his junior) served as joint organists of the Chapel Royal. In 1575 Queen Elizabeth granted these two musicians a special license which gave them the sole right for twenty-one years to print and publish music and ruled music paper.

Their first publication, *Cantiones Sacrae,* 1575, dedicated to the queen, contained thirty-four motets, sixteen by Tallis, eighteen by Byrd. All were set to Latin texts. The only other works by Tallis published during his life were five anthems set to English words in Day's *Certain Notes,* 1560.

Most historians agree that Tallis' finest music was written before the Reformation, for Latin texts: masses, magnificats, motets. His most famous motet, "Spem aliam non habui" is in forty parts, for eight five-part choirs. Although his sympathies seem to have remained with the Roman Catholic faith, he was one of the first to respond to the need for simple musical settings of the liturgy, anthems, and psalm paraphases in English and much of the music he wrote for the Anglican choral service is still in use. For many years he was known principally for his harmonizations of the preces, responses, and litany, his Short Service in D minor (the Dorian), simple anthems with English texts, and two psalm tunes from Archbishop Parker's Psalter. But there has been a much greater appreciation of Tallis in recent years since musical research and the publication of many of his great polyphonic works have revealed the true musical stature of this composer often referred to as the father of English cathedral music.

57 All Praise to Thee, My God

See No. 56 for comments on the text.

TALLIS' CANON is given here in the form in which it is normally printed. One can see that the tenor part is the same as the soprano but starts four notes later and is completed in the first measure. This can be sung effectively as a canon between men and women, between choir and congregation, or between the two sides of a church choir and congregation.

58 God That Madest Earth and Heaven

A friend of Sir Walter Scott, Robert Southey, and other distinguished authors and poets, Reginald Heber (1783–1826) is credited not only with popularizing the use of hymns in the Anglican communion but with giving a new literary quality to the hymnody of the church. His book *Hymns written and adapted to the Weekly Church Service of the Year,* published posthumously in 1827, a year after his death, introduced a type of hymnody characterized by great poetic beauty and contained fifty-seven of his own hymns, including this evening hymn. Having attained fame as a poet, preacher, and scholar, he was appointed bishop of Calcutta in 1822, a see which included all of British India, and there gained the distinction of ordaining the first Indian to the Christian ministry. After three years of arduous labors marked by much traveling and notable success, he died suddenly in Trichinopoly at the close of a day in which he had confirmed forty-two persons. The second stanza of this hymn was written by Frederick L. Hosmer for the *Hymn and Tune Book,* 1914. See No. 383 for comments on Hosmer.

AR HYD Y NOS A facsimile of this familiar Welsh melody, as first found in printed form in Edward Jones' *Musical Relicks of the Welsh Bards,* 1784, is given in *The Hymnal 1940 Companion.* In that arrangement of the tune, three variations for harp follow the ballad which was to be sung by the harpist to a simple accompaniment, with the listeners (chorus) coming in on the refrain, "Ar hyd y nos" ("The livelong night"). It is said that Heber wrote the first stanza of this hymn during a visit in Wales. One evening while listening to a harper play "Ar hyd y nos" in the hall of his host's home, he withdrew from his friends to write down the words inspired by the melody.

In England the melody of AR HYD Y NOS was sung to "Here beneath a willow, weepeth poor Mary Anne." In Wales it is still sung only to the words of the ballad for which it is named. In *Companion to Congregational Praise* Erik Routley says that hymn books did not dare print Heber's hymn with this tune, because of its secular associations, until "the *English Hymnal* in doing so made one of its boldest strokes." In that book it was set to Heber's words with a second stanza by Archbishop Whately. In the United States the tune was printed in Volume I of *The Christian Lyre,* 1831, with "There's a friend above all others, Oh how he loves" which was captioned "The love of Jesus." It was named WELSH MELODY and had the following footnote: "This is a favorite piece among the Welsh and much used in their revivals. It was sent in Ms. from Bristol to a gentleman in New York who kindly gave it for the Lyre." In Henry Ward Beecher's *Plymouth Collection,* 1855, AR HYD Y NOS was called WALES and assigned to "There's a friend above all others" and "When the spark of life is waning, Weep not for me" which appeared with it in *The Choir,* 1832, edited by Lowell Mason.

59 Now God Be With Us

One of the most significant pre-Reformation religious groups in Bohemia and Moravia was that known as the Unitas Fratrum, also called Unity of Brethren or Bohemian Brethren. Many of the essential doctrines and principals of Luther and Calvin were antedated in this movement. Petrus Herbert (d. 1571), whose exact birth date and birthplace are unknown, belonged to this group, which was the first religious body to place a hymnal in the common language in the hands of the people. The first version appeared in 1501. It was from this movement that the Moravian Church was later to come. In the preface to *The Liturgy* of the Unitas Fratrum is this comment:

> The hymns of the Brethren were a power in the Church and the land.
> They gave life to public worship; they were familiarly sung in the homes
> of the nobles and of peasants; they set forth the pure Gospel in strains
> that captivated thousands of hearts in the Roman Catholic Church and
> brought them to a knowledge of free grace in Christ Jesus.

Petrus helped to compile the enlarged hymnbook of the Brethren, *Kirchengeseng,* 1566, and contributed some ninety hymns, including the present one. An ordained Brethren minister and a member of the Select Council, he went on many important missions, involving consultations with Calvin, the Duke of Württemberg, and the Emperor Maximilian. The Moravian communities in

Winston-Salem, North Carolina, and Bethlehem, Pennsylvania, have contributed greatly to keeping alive the rich heritage of Moravian music and hymnody. The translation is by Catherine Winkworth from her *Chorale Book for England*, 1863. See No. 2 for comments on Miss Winkworth.

DIVA SERVATRIX, a French Church Melody, has been traced to a 1739 Bayeux antiphoner where it appeared with the Latin hymn for which it is named, "Diva Servatrix" ("Divine Helper"). This was a hymn to the Virgin Mary. The present form of the melody and the harmonization are from *Congregational Praise*, 1951.

The so-called French Church Melodies came into use in the seventeenth and eighteenth centuries in churches and cathedrals of a number of French Roman Catholic dioceses where they were sung to new Latin hymns based on classical models and included in the neo-Gallican breviaries and missals. These had been compiled by leaders in the French Church who were critical of the existing breviaries and missals of the Roman rite and were eager for liturgical reform. They reflect a church deeply conscious of its national character during that brilliant period of French history. From 1680 to 1789 these breviaries and missals continued to appear. By 1791 eighty dioceses had abandoned the Roman rite in their favor, and their use continued into the nineteenth century. After 1838 there was a gradual return to the older rites.

The tunes, which were sung in unison, may have had their roots in plainsong or in secular melodies — their composers or arrangers chose to remain anonymous. They reflect the musical trends of their times in being measured and predominantly major or minor, thus differing from traditional plainsong in rhythm and tonality. Although conventionally printed in the guise of plainsong, their notes had definite time values. Some carried a time signature and were barred and in triple time throughout. Accidentals (sharps and flats) were more in evidence. Some, printed in modern hymnals in straight 4/4 time, originally had a free alternation of duple and triple rhythm. The *English Hymnal*, 1906, introduced a number of these melodies which are direct, straightforward, and appealing. (See No. 41.)

In *The French Diocesan Hymns and Their Melodies*, Cyril E. Pocknee gives an excellent account of their background and has reprinted some of the melodies in the form in which they appeared in the French breviaries.

60   Savior, Again to Thy Dear Name

Written by John Ellerton as the concluding evening hymn for a choir festival at Nantwich, Cheshire, England, in 1866, this hymn was later shortened from six to four stanzas and revised by him for the Appendix to *Hymns Ancient and Modern*, 1868. The last stanza was sung at his funeral in 1893. See No. 47 for comments on Ellerton.

ELLERS was written for this text in 1869 by Edward J. Hopkins (1818–1901). The original setting was for voices in unison with an organ accompaniment that varied with each stanza. In 1872 Dr. Hopkins made a four-part harmonization of the tune which the present arrangement follows, except for one passing note in the bass of measure five and the substitution in several measures of half notes for repeated quarters in the three lower voices. Hopkins had a long and distinguished career in church music, starting out at eight as a chorister in the Chapel Royal. At sixteen he was appointed organist of the Mitcham Parish Church (he had played services in Westminster Abbey before that), and after appointments in two other churches, served for fifty-five years (1843–1898) as organist of the Temple Church in London. Evidently he had energy and endurance as well as musical gifts, for two of his church positions involved walking sixteen miles each Sunday. He was noted for his improvisations and service playing and was unrivaled as an accompanist, playing often for Jenny Lind's concerts.

Dr. Hopkins composed a great deal of church music, taught organ in the Royal Normal College for the Blind, gave organ recitals until his seventy-eighth birthday, contributed articles to *Grove's Dictionary,* and was one of the founders of the Royal College of Organists (1864) and Trinity College of Music (1872). With E. F. Rimbault he wrote *The Organ, its History and Construction,* 1855, a standard work for half a century. The success of his *Temple Church Choral Service,* 1867, was such that he was engaged to edit hymnals for several denominations.

61   God Be With You Till We Meet Again

After graduation from Andover Theological Seminary in 1854, Jeremiah E. Rankin (1828–1904) served Congregational churches in New York, Vermont, and Massachusetts before being called to the First Congregational Church in Washington, D.C., where he remained for fifteen years. It was during the last pastorate that he wrote this hymn, based on the familiar "Good-bye," which is a contraction of "God be with you." Rankin later said that it was written as a Christian good-bye for use at gospel meetings or Sunday nights. It was published in his compilation *Gospel Bells,* 1883, and became a great favorite with Christians of all denominations, and especially with the British soldiers during the South African War. The hymn in the present version has been shortened by the omission of the refrain. Rankin edited a number of gospel song books and later became president of Howard University in Washington, D.C.

RANDOLPH was composed for these words by Ralph Vaughan Williams and first published in the *English Hymnal,* 1906. Two directives given with the tune in that book were inadvertently omitted in the *Pilgrim Hymnal.* Measures one, two, seven, and eight are to be sung in unison, measures three, four, five, and six in harmony. See No. 239 for comments on the composer.

62   God Be With You Till We Meet Again

See No. 61 for comments on the text.

GOD BE WITH YOU   After writing the first stanza of this hymn, Jeremiah Rankin sent copies of it to two musical friends, and chose the present tune composed by one of them, William G. Tomer (1833–1896), who was then in charge of the music at Grace Methodist Episcopal Church in Washington, D.C. Tomer's musical background was slight, acquired in singing schools and in the village choir at Finesville, New Jersey, where he started teaching school at seventeen. During the Civil War he served in the Union Army on the staff of Gen. Oliver O. Howard, for whom Howard University was named. The general also traveled all over the country to raise funds for building First Congregational Church in Washington, where Rankin became pastor in 1869. After Tomer's release from the Army he taught school for a time in New Jersey, then returned to Washington, where he was employed in government and newspaper work for seventeen years. He spent the last years of his life in New Jersey. At the time of his death he was editor of the *Hunterdon Gazette*.

63 Lord, Dismiss Us With Thy Blessing

Deeply impressed, when he was sixteen years of age, by a sermon preached by George Whitfield, John Fawcett (1739/40–1817) was later ordained (1763) as a Baptist minister and devoted his entire ministry to two small Baptist churches at Wainsgate, Yorkshire, and Hebden Bridge, near Halifax. He had several opportunities to go to larger parishes and more important positions, but he declined all such invitations. It is said that he wrote a hymn for every sermon he preached. He also published several theological works, devotional books, and volumes of poetry. The present hymn appeared anonymously in *A Supplement to the Shrewsbury Hymn Book*, 1773, but is generally attributed to him. Brown University in Providence, Rhode Island, conferred a Doctor of Divinity degree upon him in 1811.

SICILIAN MARINERS (SICILY; DISMISSAL) In English, German, and American hymnals this tune is listed as a Sicilian melody, although no one has been able to find its source in Sicilian or Italian folk songs. Sung to "O du fröhliche, o du selige," it is a favorite Christmas hymn of Germans everywhere. The German version of the melody has a dotted rhythm in several measures and an extra note in measures nine and ten which give it a certain lilt and added charm. In nineteenth-century American collections, generally, the dotted rhythm was retained and the tune was named DISMISSAL or DISMISSION because of its association with the present words. The name O SANCTISSIMA comes from its use with the Latin text "O sanctissima, O piissima," a hymn to the Virgin Mary called the "Prayer of the Sicilian Mariners." It was with the Latin words that the German poet Johann G. von Herder first heard the tune during a trip to Italy in 1788–1789. He wrote in his *Stimmen der Volker in Liedern* ("Voices of Nations in Song"), 1807, that the words and music were "An die Jungfrau Maria. Ein sicilianisches Schifferlied" (Bäumker, Vol. IV, No. 199). Earlier, however, the tune had appeared in England with Merrick's version of Psalm 19 in Tattersall's *Improved Psalmody*, 1794, and in America with the Latin words in Ralph Shaw's *The Gentleman's Amusement*, 1794–1795, Philadelphia. From that time on the tune was included in numerous collections abroad and in this country, with English texts and "O Sanctissima."

64 All Creatures of Our God and King

Written by St. Francis of Assisi (1182–1226) while he lay sick and temporarily blind in a straw-thatched hut at San Damiano, Italy, where he had taken refuge from the fierce heat during the summer of 1225, this hymn has been referred to variously as the "Canticle of the Sun," "Hymn of the Creation," "Sun Song," and "Song of all the Creatures" ("Cantico di fratre sole, laude della creature"). The great-hearted saint drew his inspiration from the *Benedicite*. (See comments at No. 73.) It was translated from the early Italian and freely paraphrased by William H. Draper for a schoolchildren's Whitsuntide festival at Leeds. See No. 168 for comments on Draper. St. Francis founded the order of the Franciscans which sent out its emissaries, two by two, to preach the gospel and aid the needy. His hymns are among the earliest metrical songs written in the Italian vernacular, and he was largely responsible for preserving and adopting the troubadour style of music in the popular music of the church. His great love of nature in all its forms and his compassionate, unpretentious nature make him one of the most revered of all the saints.

LASST UNS ERFREUEN   See No. 12 for comments on this tune.

65 Glory Be to God on High

Theodore C. Williams (1855–1915), author of this hymn, was the minister of All Souls' Unitarian Church in New York City and later served as headmaster of Hackley School, Tarrytown, New York. The hymn is presumed to have first appeared in print in a collection compiled by Mrs. Williams, *Hymnal Amore Dei*, 1890.

GWALCHMAI (the name of a Welsh bard and also of a town) was set to a poem of George Herbert's in the *English Hymnal*, 1906. Since then it has been used with several other texts. It appeared in *Llyfr, Tonau ac Emynau*, 1868, a collection of hymns and tunes which Joseph D. Jones (1827–1870) helped to edit. Although Jones' parents were so poor that they could give him only one year of schooling, he learned all that he could about music through his own initiative, taught himself to play the cello, and before he was twenty published a collection of original tunes. Funds from the sale of these enabled him to go to a training college in London. Several hymn collections published by him became both popular and remunerative. One of his sons, the Rev. J. D. Jones, was a celebrated English Congregational minister, another, Sir H. Haydn Jones, a member of Parliament. Like many Welsh hymns this is simple structurally, with the first, second, and fourth phrases alike, and the third providing contrast.

66 For the Beauty of the Earth

Inspired to write this hymn on a lovely spring day near his native city of Bath, England, Folliott Sandford Pierpoint (1835–1917), English classicist and poet, intended it to be sung in the communion service as a hymn of joy

55

and thanksgiving. Originally containing eight stanzas and including references to the Lord's Supper, it was subsequently shortened and revised and is now used most frequently as a hymn of praise and as a children's hymn. It was first published in Orby Shipley's *Lyra Eucharistica,* 1864, under the heading, "The Sacrifice of Praise." The refrain, as Pierpoint wrote it, read:

> Christ, our God, to thee we raise
> This our sacrifice of praise.

DIX   Composed by Conrad Kocher (1786–1872) for the text "Treuer Heiland wir sind hier," this melody is known in English hymnody as DIX because of its arrangement by W. H. Monk in *Hymns Ancient and Modern,* 1861, for William C. Dix's hymn "As with gladness men of old." (See No. 119.) In order to fit the music to that text, Monk omitted one phrase of the original melody.

Kocher, a native of Ditzingen, in Württemberg, intended to make teaching his profession and at seventeen went to St. Petersburg as a tutor. There he studied piano and counterpoint and for the first time heard the music of Haydn and Mozart played well. With the encouragement of the great pianist Clementi, he decided to become a musician. After his return to Germany, he won recognition with some compositions and was sent to Italy by a publishing firm. Through study of the great Italian choral works, particularly those of Palestrina, he became deeply interested in sacred choral music. On his return to Stuttgart (where he was organist in the Stiftskirche from 1827 to 1865) he organized the *Gesangvereins Liederkranz* which had great influence in furthering the cause of sacred choral music, popularizing four-part singing, and improving church music throughout Württemberg. Kocher composed an oratorio, two operas, sonatas, a variety of vocal and instrumental works, and wrote a treatise on church music, but is remembered chiefly for the chorale collections which he edited and to which he contributed a number of original tunes. In 1852 he was given an honorary Ph.D. degree by Tübingen University.

67   God of the Earth, the Sky, the Sea

This was one of the hymns included by Samuel Longfellow in his notable collection, *Hymns of the Spirit,* 1864, which he published in collaboration with Samuel Johnson.

See No. 46 for comments on Longfellow.

HERR JESU CHRIST, MEIN'S LEBENS LICHT   This chorale, the final movement of Bach's Cantata No. 153, is based on an anonymous German melody from *As Hymnodus Sacer,* 1625, a collection of twelve German hymns and eight tunes. There are many variants of the melody. (Zahn 533a) Time signatures of 2/4, 3/4, 4/4 appear with it in Bach's works. He used the melody with "Ach Gott, wie manches Herzelied" in Cantatas 3, 44, 58, 153, and with "O (Herr) Jesu Christ, mein's Lebens Licht" in Cantata 118.

BRESLAU, No. 538, is a later form of this melody.

68 I Sing the Mighty Power of God

Taken from Isaac Watts' *Divine Songs attempted in Easy Language for the use of Children,* 1715, the first hymnal written exclusively for children, and later called *Divine and Moral Songs,* this hymn originally consisted of eight stanzas, under the heading, "Praise for Creation and Providence." See No. 1 for comments on Watts.

ELLACOMBE has been traced to an anonymous melody found in a number of hymnals in use among German Roman Catholics in the nineteenth century. Its earliest known roots are in an anonymous melody from a collection of hymns and tunes used in the chapel of the Duke of Württemberg. A facsimile of the title page of the book and of the tune was printed in *The Hymn,* January, 1961, in connection with Maurice Frost's article, *"Origins of the Tune Ellacombe."* No words appeared with the tune but Frost "suspected" that it was sung with the *Marienlied* "Ave Maria klarer" to which it was set in a number of later books. In *Das katholisches deutsche Kirchenlied* (Vol. IV, No. 145), Bäumker gives five versions of this melody with five texts that appeared with it in Catholic hymnals. The present harmonization by William H. Monk was set to "Come, sing with holy gladness" in the Appendix to *Hymns Ancient and Modern,* 1868. Ellacombe is a place name in Devonshire.

69 Let the Whole Creation Cry

An Anglican clergyman, with liberal views and a poetic inclination, Stopford A. Brooke (1832–1916) served several Church of England parishes with distinction and in 1867 was appointed chaplain to the queen. Although he later resigned his orders, he remained an Anglican all his life and was greatly in demand as a preacher and a lecturer. During his ministry at Bedford Chapel, he published a collection entitled *Christian Hymns,* 1881, for his congregation, containing several of his own compositions, including the present hymn. The original had ten stanzas and was an imitation of Psalm 148.

SALZBURG The melody of this chorale appeared anonymously in *Praxis pietatis melica,* 1678, with "Alle Menschen müssen sterben" ("All men are mortal"), a hymn written for the funeral of a Leipzig merchant in 1652. The melody was attributed to Jacob Hintze after his initials "J. H." appeared with it in 1690, in one of the editions of the *Praxis* which he edited after Crüger's death. (See No. 29.) Hintze (1622–1702), German composer and editor, highly regarded in his day as a contrapuntist, was court musician to the Elector of Brandenburg at Berlin from 1666 to 1695. The harmonization of the chorale is from Bach's *Choralgesänge* where it appears with "Alle Menschen müssen sterben" in 87.87.88.77. meter. When it was set to an English text in 77.77.D in *Hymns Ancient and Modern,* 1861, a few changes in the melody (substitution of half notes for quarters at the end of measures 2,6,8,10) were made. These have been retained at No. 69. A version of the melody, dating from 1690, with an ascending figure in the next to the last measure, was used for three texts in *The Chorale Book for England,* 1863, and appears in some contemporary hymnals. The name SALZBURG was given the tune by English editors. Bach used two other melodies with "Alle Menschen," one in the concluding chorale of Cantata No. 162, and one for a chorale prelude in the *Orgelbüchlein*.

70 Let Us With a Gladsome Mind

Of nineteen psalm versions from the pen of John Milton (1608–1674), this is the only one to have attained wide use and popularity. Written when he was fifteen years of age, while a student at St. Paul's School, London, it consisted originally of twenty-four stanzas, closely following the lines of Psalm 136, and was first published in *Poems of Mr. John Milton, both English and Latin,* 1645. He was a staunch supporter of Oliver Cromwell and wrote vigorously in defense of the Commonwealth and the freedom of the press, his most famous prose pamphlet being *Areopagitica,* 1644. His greatest and most enduring poetic works, *Paradise Lost,* 1667, *Paradise Regained,* 1671, and *Samson Agonistes,* 1671, were written, or rather dictated, when he was totally blind. He was much admired by Isaac Watts; and Dr. Henry Bett in *The Hymns of Methodism,* 1913, revised edition, 1945, wrote that "his influence upon the poetic style of the Wesleys is greater, perhaps, than that of any other writer."

INNOCENTS See No. 33 for comments on the tune.

71 Let Us With a Gladsome Mind

See No. 70 for comments on the text.

CHINESE MELODY (P'U T'O) Dr. Frank W. Price (see Nos. 486, 487), who was born in China and served there as a missionary for thirty years, tells of having heard this ancient Buddhist melody sung to several different Chinese Christian hymns. It appeared with Milton's words, and with the present harmonization, in *Cantate Domino,* 1951, hymnbook of the World's Student Christian Federation, which contains texts (all in English, French, and German versions) and tunes from all over the world. Although "originally created to meet a student need, . . . it has found its way into many ecumenical organizations and assemblies." The harmony is a western addition to the melody which was sung originally in unison and is most effective that way. Except for the note *d* in measure six, it is in the pentatonic or five-tone scale, found the world over in primitive and early musical cultures. Many Chinese, Japanese, Korean, African, Scottish, American Indian, and Negro spirituals are in this mode. One may play its most common form by striking only the black keys of the piano or by omitting the *f* and the *b* of the C major scale, or the fourth and seventh degrees of any major scale. The alternative tune name means "Buddha."

72 The Spacious Firmament on High

Described by Isaac Watts as "the most authentic judge of fine thought and language that our age has produced," Joseph Addison (1672–1719), English man of letters and poet, is today chiefly remembered for his essays in *The Spectator.* In the issue for August 23, 1712, he appended this hymn, based on Psalm 19:1–6, at the close of an article entitled "An Essay on the Proper Means of Strengthening and Confirming Faith in the Mind of Man." Although he wrote only five hymns, they were all of high literary quality and set a standard that influenced generations of later hymn writers. Samuel Johnson concluded his sketch of Addison in his *Lives of the Poets,* 1781, by writing, "Whoever wishes to attain an English style, familiar but not coarse, and elegant but not ostentatious, must give his days and nights to the volumes of Addison."

CREATION is adapted from parts of "The heavens are telling," the last chorus of Part I of Haydn's oratorio *The Creation.* Its use as a hymn tune is confined to American hymnody. But it was an Englishman, William Gardiner of Leicester (No. 6), who first arranged Haydn's music for Addison's hymn. The combination appeared in the following form in Vol. I of *Sacred Melodies,* 1812. Marked *Allegro,* it was scored for clarinets, trombones, tympani, strings, organ, and voices.

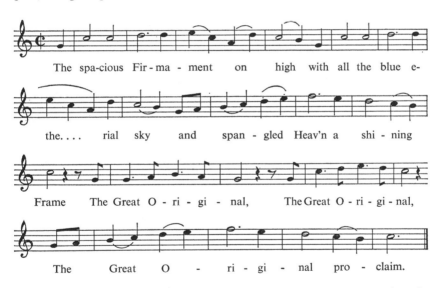

The tune appeared in numerous nineteenth-century American collections in a variety of forms and with a variety of hymns, most often with six-line texts which required no repetition of the first eight measures. In *The Choir,* 1833, edited by Lowell Mason, an anthem captioned THANKSGIVING was described as "an adaptation of the celebrated chorus from Haydn's *Creation* . . . to a versification of the 149th Psalm." Its first two phrases, with the first ending in the dominant key, were like those in the familiar version, so it would seem that Mason was responsible for the first half of the hymn tune as we know it. CREATION was set to Addison's hymn in *The Choral,* 1845, edited by I. B. Woodbury and B. F. Baker, but its form was quite different

59

from that in general use now. In 1848 the Haydn-Addison combination was included in *The National Psalmist,* edited by Mason and Webb. The tune, called HAYDN, had practically the same form as CREATION, with only slight rhythmic and harmonic differences. Obviously CREATION, as we know it, is a composite of various editors' versions.

Franz J. Haydn (1732–1809) started to work on *The Creation* when he was sixty-six years old. Of its composition he said: "Never was I so pious as when composing the 'Creation.' I knelt down every day and prayed God to strengthen me for my work." It met with success from the time of its first public performance in 1799, and rivaled Handel's *Messiah* in popularity. The beauty of its conception, the freshness, grace, and vitality of its music, the wonderfully imaginative and inventive instrumentation, make it a milestone in the history of the oratorio. Haydn's last public appearance was in 1808 at a performance of *The Creation* given in his honor, attended by a huge and notable crowd, including all the great Viennese musicians of the day. As he was carried into the hall and seated among the nobility, a flourish of trumpets and shouts of "long live Haydn" greeted him. When the passage "Let there be light" was sung, and thunderously applauded, Haydn was overcome with emotion, and lifting his hands upward exclaimed, "Not I — but a power from above created that." As people crowded around him for what they felt would be his last farewell, Beethoven bent down and kissed his hand and forehead. Haydn's innumerable works include over one hundred symphonies, eighty-three string quartets, much chamber music, songs, arias, cantatas, masses and other liturgical music, operas, and oratorios. His place in the history of music is unique, as is his contribution to the development of the classical sonata form and symphonic orchestration.

73 Angels Holy, High and Lowly

This hymn is a paraphrase of the *Benedicite,* an early canticle of the church. The canticle is based on verses from the Septuagint (the Greek version of the Old Testament) found in the apocryphal sections of the Book of Daniel, chapter 3, between verses 23 and 24, as the "Song of the Three Holy Children." The author of the paraphrase, John Stuart Blackie (1809–1895) was a classical scholar, professor of Latin at Marischal College, Aberdeen, and later professor of Greek at the University of Edinburgh. He published a volume of *Lyrical Poems,* 1860, and *Songs of Religion and Life,* 1876. He said of himself late in life, "I am rather a young old boy and I am one of the happiest creatures under the sun at this moment and my amusement is to sing songs." The year of his birth is memorable in that it was also the year that Alfred Tennyson, William Gladstone, Abraham Lincoln, Oliver Wendell Holmes, and Charles Darwin were born.

LLANHERNE   In 1926 this tune appeared in *School Worship,* published by the Congregational Union of England and Wales. It was composed by the music editor of the book, George T. Thalben-Ball (1896–   ) and named by him for the Vale of Llanherne in Cornwall where, in the village of St. Mawgan, his mother had played the organ. Dr. Thalben-Ball, born in Sydney,

Australia, has lived in England since 1901. At six he was given his first piano lessons. At fourteen his brilliant playing won him a scholarship at the Royal College of Music where in subsequent years he received several prizes for outstanding work. He had his first position as organist when he was fifteen, at sixteen became a fellow of the Royal College of Organists, at nineteen acting organist at the Temple Church in London, and in 1923 succeeded Walford Davies as organist, continuing in that post until the church was destroyed in an air raid in May, 1941. He resumed his duties as director in 1954 when the new church building was completed. His choir at the Temple is one of the finest in England.

Dr. Thalben-Ball, professor of organ at the Royal College of Music, an examiner of the Royal Schools of Music, curator-organist at Royal Albert Hall, consultant and advisor to the British Broadcasting Corporation (B.B.C.), and civic and university organist to the city of Birmingham, was a member of the committee that compiled the *B.B.C. Hymn Book,* 1951. In 1935 he was honored with the archbishop's D.Mus. degree. Early in his career he concertized as a pianist with great success, and later became well-known as an organ virtuoso, playing in Europe, Africa, Australia, and America. An outstanding member of the Royal College of Organists, he served as its president from 1948 to 1950. His compositions include organ, choral, and vocal music.

74 O How Glorious, Full of Wonder

One of two original hymns contributed to the present hymnal by Curtis Beach, this is a remarkably skillful and faithful paraphrase of Psalm 8. See No. 26 for comments on Beach.

IN BABILONE, a traditional Dutch melody, with three of its four phrases alike (AABA), was introduced into English hymnody through the *English Hymnal,* 1906, where it was set to an Ascension hymn, "See the conqueror mounts in triumph." It is from *Oude en Nieuwe Hollantse Boerenlities en Contradanseu,* c. 1710, a collection of old and new Dutch peasant songs and country dances, some of which were arranged in modern form by Julius Röntgen (1855–1932), distinguished Dutch pianist, conductor, composer, musicologist, editor, professor and director of the Amsterdam Conservatory (1914–1924), and friend of Liszt, Brahms, and Grieg. The present arrangement is from the *English Hymnal,* where it is credited to Prof. Röntgen.

75 Heaven and Earth, and Sea and Air

First published in his own hymnal, *Glaub- und Liebesübung,* 1680, this hymn of praise and thanksgiving by Joachim Neander appeared under the heading, "Rejoicing in God's Creation," with the note, "It is also a traveler's hymn by land and water." See No. 15 for comments on Neander.

GOTT SEI DANK (LÜBECK; PITTSBURGH) was set to the hymn "Gott sei Dank durch alle Welt" in Johann A. Freylinghausen's celebrated *Geistreiches Gesang Buch* (Spiritual Songbook), 1704, published in Halle, the center of the Pietistic movement. The tune, said to have secular roots, has gone through a number of changes. The version given here dates from a 1744 collection. The 1704 form, which follows, was used for two hymns in *The English Hymnal*, 1906. (Zahn 1230)

Gott sei Dank in al - ler Welt, der sein Wort be - stän-dig hält

und der Sün-der Trost und Rat zu uns her - ge - sen - det hat.

In *Old Church Psalmody,* 1847, the 1704 tune, shorn of its passing and dotted notes and harmonized by the editor, William H. Havergal, was called LÜBECK. Two bars of "hallelujah" were added. That version, minus the "hallelujahs," still appears in a number of English and American hymnals. The present form (1744) is found in hymnals of South Germany and Switzerland and also appeared with practically the same harmonies in *The Choir,* 1832, edited by Lowell Mason. It was named WATERBURY. The same form, arranged in three parts, was called PITTSBURGH in *Spiritual Songs for Social Worship,* 1832, edited by Thomas Hastings and Lowell Mason. In German usage the tune is associated not only with "Gott sei dank" and "Himmel, Erde, Luft and Meer" (the original of the present text) but also with "Walte, walte, nah und fern," the source of "Spread, O spread, thou mighty word."

After joining the ranks of the Pietists in 1691, Freylinghausen (1670–1739) served for twenty years as assistant to August H. Francke at St. George's in Glaucha, a suburb of Halle, declining all offers of other positions and accepting no salary. Francke (1663–1727), professor of theology, Greek, and Oriental languages at Halle, was also a preacher, and the organizing genius of Pietism. He founded two schools, an orphanage, printing press, publishing house, apothecary shops, a mission to the East Indies, and a Bible Society, all of which came to be known as the Francke institutions. In 1715 Francke was appointed pastor of St. Ulrich's church in Halle. Freylinghausen went with him, still as an assistant. After Francke's death Freylinghausen succeeded him as pastor and as director of the institutions. Under his administration they reached their fullest development. Freylinghausen was a singularly dedicated man and a very persuasive preacher, much beloved by those whom he served in a variety of capacities. In 1715 he married the only daughter of Francke, who said of his son-in-law that whereas his own sermons were like a waterspout which drenched the land but soon ran off again, Freylinghausen's were like a gentle, steady shower which penetrated to the depths of the soil. Francke was born in Lübeck, a fact which may account for one name of the tune.

See No. 17 for other comments on Freylinghausen.

76 How Gentle God's Commands

A close friend and great admirer of Isaac Watts as well as of Charles and John Wesley, Philip Doddridge (1702–1751) was for twenty-two years the minister of the Nonconformist chapel at Castle Hill, Northampton. His parishioners were poor, hard-working people, of whom he said, "I have not so much as a tea-table in my whole diocese, and but one hoop petticoat." There he also established his own academy, educating young men from England, Scotland, and Holland, most of whom became Independent (Congregational) ministers. He wrote more than four hundred hymns, none of which were published during his lifetime. Many of them were written to be sung following the sermons he preached. Only one copy was required since the words were lined out, that is, sung line by line by the precentor and the congregation. Doddridge was a man of wide learning and deep compassion. Always in poor health, he died of tuberculosis in Lisbon, Portugal, October 26, 1751, where he had gone for a rest and cure. The present hymn, based on I Peter 5:7, was published in Job Orton's *Hymns Founded on Various Texts in the Holy Scriptures,* 1755, a posthumous collection of Doddridge's hymns.

DENNIS appeared with Doddridge's hymn in *The Psaltery,* 1845, edited by Lowell Mason and George Webb. It was headed: "Arr. from H. G. Nägeli." Nägeli (1773–1836) was a Swiss music educator, composer, author, lecturer, and eminent music publisher of Zurich whose editions of Bach, Handel, Frescobaldi, and other masters were outstanding. He owned an autograph copy of *The Well-Tempered Clavichord* which he had procured from the daughter of K. P. E. Bach, and his edition of this work was finer than any that had preceded it and many that followed. A musical periodical started by him in 1803 published new piano works by contemporary composers, including the three Beethoven sonatas of Opus 31. He lectured in many towns in southern Germany on what would now be called music appreciation and founded a choral society, with branches throughout Switzerland, which did much to revive interest in choral singing. As a composer he is best known for his collections of songs, many of which are still popular in Switzerland. Lowell Mason was greatly influenced by Nägeli's writings on music education, and when in Europe in 1837 (after Nägeli's death) visited schools where his methods were being put into practice.

77 Be Still, My Soul

At the urging of her father, Jane L. Borthwick (1813–1897), together with her sister, Sarah, translated and published 122 German hymns, in four series, 1854, 1855, 1858, and 1862, under the title, *Hymns from the Land of Luther,* to which she contributed sixty-nine translations and her sister fifty-three. A devoted member of the Free Church of Scotland, she took an active interest in various missionary enterprises at home and abroad. This hymn first appeared in English in the second series of *Hymns from the Land of Luther,* 1855. It was written by Katharina von Schlegel, of whom little is known save that she was born on October 22, 1697, and seems to have been one of the ladies attached to the small ducal court at Cöthen, Germany. It originally contained six stanzas, five of which were translated by Miss Borthwick, and was first published in *Neue Sammlung Geistlicher Lieder,* Wernigerode, 1752.

FINLANDIA is an arrangement of the chorale-like theme in Jean Sibelius' tone poem "Finlandia," which had much to do with making him known outside his own country. It was one of the works he conducted at the Norfolk (Connecticut) Music Festival on his first visit to the United States in 1914. During that visit Yale University honored him with a Doctorate in Music with a citation that read in part:

> What Wagner did for the ancient German legends, Dr. Sibelius has, in his own magnificent way, done for the Finnish myths in Finland's national epos. He has translated the *Kalevala* into the international language of music.

"Finlandia" was composed when the Finnish people were chafing under the repressive measures of the Russian régime. On the night of Nov. 4, 1899, at the Swedish Theatre in Helsinki, a series of Historical Tableaux climaxed three days of festivities to aid the Press Pensions Fund. Known as the Press Celebrations and ostensibly fund-raising entertainments to help and honor the Finnish press, they were in fact demonstrations of intense patriotic feeling and rebelliousness against the Russian administration's increased restrictions on civil liberties. Sibelius' music for the final Tableau, No. VI — "Finland Awakes" — became one of his most popular, though not one of his most distinguished, works.

For the Finnish people "Finlandia" was a forceful expression of their love for their country and of their hopes for independence — hopes fulfilled in 1918. Sibelius told Karl Ekman that performance of "Finlandia" was forbidden in Finland during the years of unrest, and was not allowed in other parts of the Russian Empire under any name that in any way indicated its patriotic character. When he conducted the work in Reval and Riga in the summer of 1904 he called it "Impromptu." Harold E. Johnson, author of *Sibelius,* 1959, says that the work was performed in Helsinki in November 1901 as "Finlandia" and that while Finland was still a part of the Russian Empire it was available at local music stores under that name. When it was first performed by the Helsinki Philharmonic after its revision in 1900 it was called "Suomi," the generic name for Finland. Many of the themes in Sibelius' works are assumed to be folk melodies, but they originated with a man who, rooted and grounded in the folklore of his country, was able to create music which embodied the essential spirit and character of his people.

Sibelius (1865–1957), orphaned at an early age, was brought up by his grandparents and given a classical education which was intended to fit him for a legal career. But music had too strong a pull on him and after one semester of law study he began to study music intensively. He became Finland's greatest composer and the first to focus the attention of the world on his country's music. For forty years he received a liberal pension from his government which enabled him to devote all of his time and energies to composing as the spirit moved him, the only composer in the world to be so favored. Johnson says of him: "It must be clearly understood that in Finland, at least, Sibelius is far more than a great national composer. He is a national hero, a symbol of what a small nation can achieve, and thus it was inevitable that he should become a legend before his death." [5]

FINLANDIA appeared with the present text in *The Church Hymnary, Revised,* 1927. The present arrangement is a composite of the versions in the *Church Hymnary, The Hymnal,* 1933, and Sibelius' piano score of the work.

78 Hast Thou Not Known

A paraphrase of Isaiah 40:28–31 by Isaac Watts, the original of which appeared in his *Hymns and Spiritual Songs,* 1707 (beginning with the line, "Whence do our mournful thoughts arise?"), this hymn was radically revised in the draft of the Scottish *Translations and Paraphrases,* 1745, and was given its final form in the 1781 edition of this collection. See No. 1 for comments on Watts.

ST. MAGNUS (NOTTINGHAM) appeared anonymously in Henry Playford's *Divine Companion,* 1709, with "Let all the nations of the world, Their great Creator praise," a paraphrase of Psalm 117. It is traditionally ascribed to Jeremiah Clark (1670–1707), composer of several tunes in Playford's collection which had considerable influence on English and American hymnody because of the caliber of its music, composed by such men as Clark, Blow, and Croft.

Clark(e) started out as a chorister in the Chapel Royal under Dr. John Blow and in all likelihood sang at the coronation of James II in 1685. From 1692 to 1695 he was organist at Winchester College. In 1695 he was appointed organist of St. Paul's Cathedral and in 1703 master of the choristers. He and William Croft (No. 1), both students of Dr. Blow, were sworn in as gentlemen-extraordinary of the Chapel Royal in 1700, and in 1704 were appointed joint organists. Clark composed songs, anthems, hymn tunes, cantatas, music for harpsichord and for the theater. One of his songs was included in "The Beggar's Opera." The well-known "Trumpet Voluntary," attributed for many years to Henry Purcell, and arranged for orchestra by Sir Henry Wood, is now said to be Clark's "Prince of Denmark's March" which was published in *A Choice Collection of Ayres for the Harpsichord,* 1700. The "Trumpet Tune in D" is also said to be his (See *Musical Times,* October, 1953.) A gifted, sensitive musician, given to periods of despondency, Clark took his own life during one of these trying times, presumably over an unhappy love affair. In the *Yattendon Hymnal,* 1899, Robert Bridges included nine of Clark's tunes with the comments: "He seems to have been the inventor of the modern english Hymn-tune. His tunes are beautiful, and have the plaintive grace characteristic of his music and melancholy temperament. They are first in merit of their kind, as they were first in time; . . . their neglect is to be regretted." [6] Bridges did much to remedy this neglect as did Ralph Vaughan Williams who used six of Clark's tunes in *The English Hymnal.* The name ST. MAGNUS was given to this tune in 1762. It is frequently found with the name NOTTINGHAM.

79 The King of Love My Shepherd Is

Of the many paraphrases of Psalm 23 that have been written, this is one of the most popular and widely used. Sir Henry W. Baker (1821–1877) wrote the words for the 1868 Appendix of the epoch-making collection, *Hymns Ancient and Modern.* He took the lead in preparing and promoting this hymnal, notable for the high quality and comprehensiveness of its selections, and served as the chairman of the committee that compiled it, contributing several original hymns and a number of fine translations from the Latin. So successful was the book that it was published in several editions and sold more than sixty million copies between 1861, when it was first issued, and 1912. An able and skillful editor, Baker did not hesitate to alter the hymns sent in, so that one contributor was provoked into saying that H. A. and M. should be renamed "Hymns Asked for and Mutilated." However, most of his editorial changes have been accepted as improvements. A High Churchman, he was vicar of Monkland, near Leominster, from 1851 until his death. He published two devotional books for the people of his parish, *Family Prayers for the Use of those who have to work hard* and a *Daily Text Book.*

DOMINUS REGIT ME   The first three words of the Latin version of Psalm 23 (Psalm 22 in the Vulgate) were used by John Bacchus Dykes (1823–1876) as a name for this tune which he composed for Baker's hymn. Both were published in the Appendix to *Hymns Ancient and Modern,* 1868. Dykes, the best-known of the Victorian hymn tune writers and one of the most prolific, was the son of a banker (one of fourteen children), and grandson of a distinguished evangelical clergyman in whose church in Hull he sometimes assisted at the organ when he was only ten years old. During his undergraduate days at St. Catherine's, Cambridge, he studied music throughout his course and was active, along with William Thomson (later Lord Kelvin), in the Cambridge University Musical Society. After graduation he took holy orders, was ordained deacon in 1842, priest in 1848, minor canon of Durham Cathedral in 1845, and at the end of that year was appointed precentor, in sole charge of the choir and responsible for the religious instruction of the boys. His "spare" time was devoted to music, and it was during his years as precentor that he became known as a composer. Seven of his hymn tunes were included in the first edition of *Hymns Ancient and Modern,* 1861; in later editions the number rose to fifty-five. In 1861, the University of Durham conferred on him the Doctorate of Music in recognition of his gifts as musician and composer of church music. In 1862 he became vicar of St. Oswald's, Durham, where he remained for fourteen years, carrying a tremendous load single-handed in a rapidly growing parish. After his death it was said that few men had ever left such a mark on a parish as had Dykes on St. Oswald's. Unfortunately, it was during these years that Dykes, a High Churchman, came into conflict with the Bishop of Durham, a Low Churchman, which resulted in a prolonged dispute, finally carried to the Court of Queen's Bench, where Dykes lost the case. The strain of work in the parish and of this trying litigation told on his health, and resulted in a breakdown from which he never recovered. He published sermons, articles on theology and liturgics, and wrote anthems and service music, but his fame rests on his hymn tunes which number about three hundred.

80　The King of Love My Shepherd Is

See No. 79 for comments on the text.

ST. COLUMBA (ERIN), a traditional Irish melody, is named for St. Columba, (521–597), Irish saint who brought the Christian faith to Scotland. He left Ireland in 563 with twelve disciples on a mission to northern Britain, establishing himself first on the island of Iona in the Inner Hebrides. There he built a church and monastery which became the most famous center of Celtic Christianity in the Middle Ages. Iona has become familiar to many in recent years through the work of Sir George MacLeod who, in 1938, founded the Iona Community where ministers and laymen come together during the summer for study, worship, and work on a common task — the completion of the restoration of the Abbey and other buildings which have been in ruins since the Reformation. (See T. Ralph Morton, *The Iona Community Story*, 1957. Lutterworth, London.)

ST. COLUMBA is No. 1043 in *The Complete Collection of Irish Music as noted by George Petrie*, 1902, edited by Charles V. Stanford from the original manuscripts. It is printed there without words and without harmony and bears Petrie's caption, "Irish Hymn sung on the dedication of a Chapel — C. of Londonderry." ("Londonderry Air" was also in his collection.)

George Petrie (1790–1866), painter, writer, editor, best known as the first scientific investigator of Irish archaeology, thought that Irish melodies were the most beautiful national melodies in the world and collected them from his seventeenth until after his seventieth year. In the preface to his collection he said that he had "a passionate love of music, of melody especially" and that the indulgence of this passion had been "one of the great, if not the greatest, sources of happiness" in his life. His collection is the largest and most varied body of Irish folk music in existence, and his notes and comments on the melodies are of great value. The harmonization given here (except for the first chord in measure four) is from *The English Hymnal*, 1906, where ST. COLUMBA was set to the present hymn.

81　Through All the Changing Scenes

The first complete metrical psalter published in England, known familiarly as Sternhold and Hopkins, or the Old Version, appeared in 1562 and was largely the work of two Anglican clergymen, Thomas Sternhold (d. 1549) and John Hopkins (d. 1570 ?). One hundred thirty years later, in 1696, Nahum Tate (1652–1715) and Nicholas Brady (1659–1726), two Irishmen who spent most of their lives in England, published *A New Version of the Psalms of David, Fitted to the Tunes Used in Churches*, which gradually displaced the older one and came to be known as the New Version. That the acceptance of the latter was not achieved without a struggle is indicated by the remark of a bishop who replied on being asked what a drysalter was (that is, a dealer in dried and salted goods or canned foods), "Oh, Tate and Brady, of course." Although possessing only moderate abilities as a poet and as a playwright, Tate was made poet laureate in 1692 and royal historiographer in 1702.

Julian comments that he was reputed to be "a man of intemperate and improvident life." Brady, a loyal supporter of William III and later his chaplain, was the rector of several Anglican parishes and published a tragedy, *The Rape, or the Innocent Imposters*, 1692; a poetical translation of Vergil's *Aeneid*, 1726; and several volumes of sermons. Today the fame of Tate and Brady rests entirely on their collaboration in producing the New Version. This is one of the most enduring hymns from that collection. Based on Psalm 34, it originally contained eighteen stanzas.

WILTSHIRE, in a slightly different form, was composed by George Smart when he was nineteen years old and set to Psalm 48 (New Version) in *Divine Amusement*, c. 1795. (See *Musical Times*, July, 1907.) It was first associated with the present paraphrase of Psalm 34 in the revised edition of *Hymns Ancient and Modern*, 1875. Since then the combination of text and tune has become one of the most popular in England. During much of his long life Smart (1776–1867) served in the Chapel Royal as chorister, organist and composer. He was knighted in 1811 by the Lord Lieutenant of Ireland after conducting a series of concerts in Dublin. An eminently gifted conductor with unusual administrative ability, Smart was greatly in demand for large-scale performances and music festivals. One of the original members of the Philharmonic Society, he conducted forty-nine of its concerts between 1813 and 1844. In 1826 he became director of music at Covent Garden. The music for the coronations of William IV and Queen Victoria was arranged and conducted by him. Many singers came to him for coaching because of his knowledge of the Handelian traditions passed on to him by his father, who had seen Handel conduct.

It was Smart who introduced Beethoven's *Mount of Olives*, the *Battle Symphony*, and other works to England, and on March 21, 1825, conducted the first performance of the Ninth Symphony in London. This was the first time that it had been heard outside of Vienna. In the summer of 1825 Smart went to Germany with Charles Kemble who wanted to engage Weber to conduct *Oberon* at Covent Garden. Smart's main purpose was to meet Beethoven in order to learn from him the correct tempi and interpretation of various works, particularly the Ninth Symphony. He met Beethoven on three occasions, once as his invited guest at Baden, and gave a detailed account of these meetings in his journal. At the end of the Baden visit Smart gave Beethoven a diamond pin as a remembrance and Beethoven quickly wrote a short canon for his English visitor. Smart wrote glees, canons, much church music, and edited a number of works, including Gibbons' *First Set of Madrigals* and Handel's *Dettingen Te Deum*.

82 High in the Heavens, Eternal God

This is one of three paraphrases of Psalm 36 that Isaac Watts wrote for his *Psalms of David*, 1719. The original version contained six stanzas. See No. 1 for comments on Watts.

TRURO is an anonymous melody from Part II of Thomas Williams' *Psalmodia Evangelica*, 1789, a collection of psalm and hymn tunes for

"Churches, Chapels and Dissenting Meetings in England, Scotland and Ireland." It was set to "Now to the Lord a noble song" by Isaac Watts. Under the same name, with the same text, it was included in a number of nineteenth-century American collections. In Mason's collections it was attributed to Dr. Charles Burney, as it had been in England, but it has been shown that there is no valid foundation for that ascription. TRURO is described in *Songs of Praise Discussed* as a fine, springing tune, and an excellent specimen of its type in a familiar eighteenth-century idiom. It has appeared consistently with its present name throughout its long career.

83 If Thou but Suffer God to Guide Thee

Georg Neumark (1621–1681) was one of many individuals, especially in Germany, who suffered great hardships and deprivation as a result of the Thirty Years' War, 1618–1648. As a young man, while on his way to study law at the University of Königsberg, he was robbed by a band of brigands of all he possessed save a prayer book and a few coins hidden in his clothing. Forced to give up his plan to attend the university, he wandered from town to town in search of employment. Finally when he was almost destitute, he unexpectedly received a position as tutor in the home of a wealthy judge in Kiel. He was overjoyed at his good fortune, and later wrote, "Which good fortune coming suddenly, and as if fallen from heaven, greatly rejoiced me, and on that very day I composed to the honour of my beloved Lord the here and there well-known hymn 'Wer nur den lieben Gott lässt walten'; and had certainly cause enough to thank the Divine compassion for such unlooked for grace shown to me." Both the text and the tune were probably written at the same time in 1641. Neumark later graduated from the university and was eventually appointed court poet and librarian-registrar and keeper of the archives under Duke Wilhelm II of Saxe-Weimar. He published a collection of religious and secular songs in 1657, from which the present hymn was taken. He was totally blind the last year of his life. The translation is by Catherine Winkworth from her *Chorale Book for England*, 1863. See No. 2 for comments on Miss Winkworth.

NEUMARK (BREMEN), named for the composer, is best known under the title of the first line of his great hymn of trust "Wer nur den lieben Gott lasst walten," as in the accompanying example. (Zahn 2778)

In the Preface to *The Chorale Book for England*, 1863, a footnote on Neumark's hymn and tune reads, "The tune became so popular that within 100 years after its appearance no less than 400 hymns had been written to be sung to it." Bach used the melody in Cantatas 21, 27, 84, 93, 166, 179, 197, and in four organ movements: one in the Orgelbüchlein, two in the miscellaneous Preludes, No. 3 of the Schübler *Sechs Choräle*. There is one harmonization in the *Choralgesänge*. Mendelssohn used a 4/4 version of Neumark's melody for the chorale "To Thee, O Lord, I yield my spirit" in his oratorio *St. Paul*. (No. 9).

In Lowell Mason's *Boston Handel and Haydn Society Collection of Church Music*, 1828, the tune, in 4/4, was called WEIMAR; in his *Modern Psalmist*, 1839, AUGSBURG.

Wer nur den lie - ben Gott lässt wal - ten
Der wird ihn wun-der-lich er - hal - ten

und hof-fet auf ihn al - le - zeit, Wer Gott, dem Al - ler-
in al - ler Not und Trau-rig-keit.

höch-sten traut, der hat auf kei - nen Sand ge - baut.

84 The Lord's My Shepherd

Of several notable metrical psalters published in Scotland during the six-teenth and seventeenth centuries, the Scottish Psalter of 1650 (*The Psalms of David in Meeter*) holds a preeminent place. It is still in use and remains the only version officially authorized by the Church of Scotland. The culmination of a century of development, beginning with the version of 1564, the Scottish Psalter of 1650 ranks with the King James Version of the Bible and *The Book of Common Prayer* as a classic of Protestantism. This rendering of Psalm 23, of unknown authorship, is undoubtedly the most popular and beloved of all the paraphrases from this psalter.

CRIMOND There has been considerable controversy about the origin of this tune, one of the most popular tunes in the *Scottish Psalter* and the one to which Psalm 23 is now generally sung in Scotland. It was first printed with "Thou art the Way, the Truth, the Life" by G. W. Doane in *The Northern Psalter,* 1872. David Grant (1833–1893), who was named the composer of CRIMOND in the preface, the body of the book, and the index, was a successful Aberdeen business man who took great interest in music and psalmody and had some facility in harmonizing tunes. The harmonization given here is largely his. One of two original tunes contributed by Grant to *The Northern Psalter,* edited by his friend William Carnie, CRIMOND quickly became widely known and loved. In collections of tunes issued between 1872 and 1929, Grant continued to be listed as its composer. In 1911, eighteen years after Grant's death and three years after Carnie's, Miss Anna B. Irvine (then eighty-two years old) claimed that her sister Jessie Seymour Irvine (1836–1889) had written the melody of CRIMOND in 1871, and given it to David Grant to be harmonized, and that when Carnie printed it in *The Northern Psalter* he had mistakenly given Grant credit for the tune as well as for the harmonization. There were protests from two men who knew Carnie and Grant and had first-hand knowledge of the matter.

One had been precentor of the church in Crimond (a village in the north-east of Scotland) where Miss Irvine's father was minister for thirty years, the other had been associated with Carnie in the preparation of *The Northern Psalter*. Both men said that Miss Anna Irvine had confused CRIMOND with BALLANTYNE, a tune written by her sister and harmonized by Grant, and both insisted that Grant was the composer of CRIMOND. However, in the *Scottish Psalter*, 1929, the tune was assigned to Miss Jessie S. Irvine and this attribution has been quite generally accepted. In an article entitled "Authorship of the Psalm Tune 'Crimond'" published in the Edinburgh *Scotsman*, Nov. 19, 1960, Fenton Wyness presented all the known facts of the case summarized above, and questioned the justice of the attribution of the tune to Miss Irvine. At least there is no doubt about the tune's hold on people's affections. Its use, with a descant by W. David Ross, at the marriage service of Elizabeth II and Prince Philip, Duke of Edinburgh, in November 1947 helped to increase the popularity of both text and tune.

85 I to the Hills Will Lift Mine Eyes

This is another of the familiar paraphrases from the Scottish Psalter of 1650. Of unknown authorship, it is based on Psalm 121. See comments at No. 84.

DUNDEE The form of this tune differs from the original (No. 87) in its omission of the long notes at the beginning and end of each phrase. For comments on the tune see No. 87.

86 Our God, to Whom We Turn

Edward Grubb (1854–1939), a prominent English Quaker who edited the monthly periodical, *The British Friend*, for many years, wrote several books in the field of religion and was an ardent admirer of John Greenleaf Whittier. This hymn was included in a volume of poems he published in 1925, *The Light of Life: Hymns of Faith and Consolation*, in which he sought to turn men's attention from disillusionment with the world, following World War I, to God's unchanging being and eternal purposes.

STEADFAST This anonymous melody appeared in the following form in the 1648 Appendix to the *New Ordentlich Gesangbuch*, Hanover, 1646. (Zahn 5138) The asterisks indicate notes that were sharped in a Lüneburg chorale book of 1665, and in other later collections. The last four measures of the present form of the melody are from a 1690 Hamburg version which appeared with Johann Heermann's "O Gott, du frommer Gott." This version was used by Bach in his *Chorale Partita* by that name, a work consisting of nine variations on the tune, one for each stanza of the hymn, arranged for manuals alone. There is one harmonization of the melody, in a slightly different form, in Schemelli's *Gesanbuch*, 1736, with the text "Ich freue mich in dir."

Gross ist, O gro-sser Gott, die Not, so uns be-trof-fen;
das Un-recht ha-ben wir wie Was-ser ein-ge-sof-fen.

Doch ist das un-ser Trost: du bist voll Gü-tig-keit,

du nimmst die Stra-fe bin, wenn uns die Sünd ist leid.

The name STEADFAST, given to this chorale in *The Hymnal 1940,* helps to distinguish it from another well-known melody for "O Gott, du frommer Gott" harmonized by Bach. (See No. 198.)

87 God Moves in a Mysterious Way

Known as the greatest English poet of his age, William Cowper (1731–1800) was afflicted throughout his life by ill-health and a deep melancholy which drove him periodically to attempted suicide and insanity. His father, the Rev. John C. Cowper, was rector of the parish at Berkhampstead, Hertfordshire, and chaplain to George II; his mother, whom he idolized and who died when he was six years of age, was a descendant of John Donne. In the first school he attended he was bullied by an older boy, an experience which left a lasting mark on his sensitive spirit. Although he was made a barrister in 1754, he never practiced law, and his only source of income in his mature years was derived from a small inheritance and pension and the gifts of friends. He made his home in the family of the Reverend Morley Unwin, whose wife became his lifelong supporter and guardian, and he remained with the family until Mrs. Unwin's death in 1796. While residing in Olney, he became a close friend of the curate, Rev. John Newton (see No. 221), assisted him in the work of the parish, and eventually collaborated with him in the publication of *Olney Hymns,* 1779, one of the literary masterpieces in the history of hymnody. He contributed sixty-eight original hymns to this distinguished hymnal. The present hymn was first published anonymously in Newton's *Twenty-six Letters on Religious Subjects,* 1774, where it appeared under the subtitle, "Light shining out of Darkness." It was later credited to Cowper in *Olney Hymns* and has been described as the finest hymn on God's providence ever written. His collected works have appeared in many editions. Elizabeth Barrett Browning paid Cowper this tribute:

O Christians, at your cross of hope a hopeless hand was clinging:
O men, this man in brotherhood your weary paths beguiling,
Groaned inly while he taught you peace, and died while ye were
    smiling!
And now, what time you all may read through dimming tears his
    history,
How discord on the music fell and darkness on the glory, and
How when, one by one, sweet sounds and wandering lights departed,
He wore no less a loving face because so broken-hearted.

DUNDEE was one of the twelve common tunes in Andro Hart's Scottish Psalter, *The CL Psalmes of David . . . With their whole usuall Tunes, newly corrected and amended*, Edinburgh, 1615. For the first time, the four-line tunes were grouped together at the beginning and called Common, with the heading, "The XII Common Tunes, to the which all Psalmes of eight syllables in the first line, and six in the next may bee sung." This tune, known to English and Americans as DUNDEE, was called FRENCH TUNE in Hart's Psalter, and "French" it has been called ever since in Scottish usage, though no French source for it has as yet been found. When Ravenscroft printed the tune in 1621, he called it DUNDY TUNE, unfortunately, for the name DUNDIE had already been assigned in the Scottish Psalter to the tune known in England as WINDSOR, so that there has been confusion ever since. In some tune name indexes one finds "Dundee — French," "Dundee — Windsor," and happy the man who knows which is which! The form of DUNDEE has remained constant throughout its long history except for the omission of the gathering notes in some instances.

88   God Moves in a Mysterious Way

See No. 87 for comments on the text.

DUNDEE   This arrangement of DUNDEE with the melody in the tenor was made by Thomas Ravenscroft (c. 1592–c. 1635) for Psalm 36 in his *Whole Booke of Psalmes*, 1621, the most popular of the seventeenth-century books of tunes compiled for use with the Old Version, and the one that had the greatest influence on subsequent psalters. Ravenscroft gave place-names to the forty common tunes in the book, thus establishing the practice of naming tunes which had been initiated in a small way by Thomas Este. (See No. 146.) In preparing his psalter, in which all of the tunes were in four-part arrangements, Ravenscroft had the help of at least twenty-one musicians, including Morley, Tallis, Tomkins, Pierson, and Milton, who made settings for four-line tunes. Ravenscroft, himself, did the lion's share of the work, contributing forty-eight settings. He was a chorister in St. Paul's Cathedral, received a Bachelor of Music degree from Cambridge in his early teens, and became a teacher, composer, and editor. Ravenscroft's *Pammelia*, 1609, was the earliest collection of rounds and canons published in England. His Psalter was well known to the compilers of the *Bay Psalm Book*, 1640, for in their "Admonition" about the tunes to which the Psalms might be sung they wrote, "The verses of these psalmes may be reduced to six kinds, the first whereof may be sung in neere fourty common tunes; as they are collected, out of our chief musicians, by *Tho. Ravenscroft.*"

89 Lord of All Being, Throned Afar

One of Harvard's most distinguished graduates, Oliver Wendell Holmes (1809–1894) later returned to his alma mater as professor of anatomy in 1847, a position he held for thirty-five years. He was a brilliant lecturer and attained wide renown as a teacher. His greatest fame, however, derived from his writings. In 1857 he took the initiative in founding *The Atlantic Monthly,* which he named and to which he contributed a series of witty and delightful articles, under the captions, "The Autocrat of the Breakfast Table," "The Professor at the Breakfast Table," "The Poet at the Breakfast Table," and "Over the Teacups." He concluded the last essay of the second series in *The Atlantic Monthly* for December, 1859, with this hymn, which he called "A Sun-Day Hymn." His best-known single poems are "Old Ironsides," "The Chamber'd Nautilus," and "The Deacon's Masterpiece." Although he sided theologically with the Unitarians, he retained a devout, evangelical, religious faith and once confessed that he "believed more than some and less than others" and liked "those who believed more better than those who believed less." He was admired and beloved at home and abroad.

UFFINGHAM was set to Dr. Holmes' hymn in *The English Hymnal,* 1906, for which Ralph Vaughan Williams was music editor. It appeared originally in Playford's *Divine Companion,* 1701, with the heading, " 'An Evening Hymn' set by Mr. Jer. Clarke," and was arranged for two voices, "Cantus and Bassus."

> Sleep, downey Sleep, come close mine Eyes
> Tir'd with beholding Vanities.
> Welcome sweet sleep that driv'st away
> The toils and follies of the day.

With this text and called "Evening Hymn" it was included in collections compiled by Thomas Hastings, Lowell Mason, and other American editors. In American books the tune was altered rhythmically as it had been in Aaron Williams' *American Harmony or Universal Psalmodist,* 1771. Eric Routley says that UFFINGHAM was the first tune used with Bishop Ken's "Awake, my soul, and with the sun" (No. 32). In *Songs of Praise Discussed,* Archibald Jacob writes, "It is a beautiful tune in the best 17th-century manner, very smooth and 'vocal,' but deeply expressive; it is certainly one of Clarke's finest tunes." See No. 78 for comments on Clark.

90 Lord of All Being, Throned Afar

See No. 89 for comments on the text.

LOUVAN, composed by Virgil C. Taylor (1817–1891) appeared in his *Sacred Minstrel,* 1846, with Thomas Moore's words, "There's nothing bright above, below." Taylor, a Connecticut-born musician, much influenced by Thomas Hastings and Lowell Mason, taught in singing schools and institutes, served as organist and choirmaster in churches in Poughkeepsie, Brooklyn, New York, and Des Moines, Iowa, and edited several typical mid-nineteenth-century songbooks. In the *Pilgrim Hymnal* 1931, the upbeat of phrase one of LOUVAN was omitted for the sake of word accent, and in the 1958 edition, the upbeat before phrase three was omitted for the same reason.

91 The Man Who Once Has Found Abode

When the United Presbyterian Church of North America was organized in 1858, one of the first tasks undertaken was a revision of the famous Scottish Psalter of 1650, which had been in continuous use for over two hundred years. (See No. 84 for comments on the Scottish Psalter.) The work, completed in 1871, was known as the *United Presbyterian Book of Psalms, U.S.A.* This paraphrase of Psalm 91 by an anonymous author was taken from this collection.

TALLIS' CANON   See No. 56 for comments on the tune.

92 I Look to Thee in Every Need

One of the earliest American hymns, if not the first, to give expression to the close relationship between religious faith and physical and spiritual well-being, this hymn was written by Samuel Longfellow and published in his *Hymns of the Spirit*, 1864. Largely neglected in this country, it did not come into prominent use until after its appearance in W. Garrett Horder's *Worship Song*, 1905, and *The English Hymnal*, 1906, in England. See No. 42 for comments on Longfellow.

O JESU takes its name from the hymn, "O Jesu, warum legst du mir" to which it was set in Balthasar Reimann's *Sammlung alter und neuer Melodien Evangel. Lieder*, 1747, a collection of special interest to musicians because it included two of the few chorale melodies attributed to Bach. In 1729 J. B. Reimann (1702–1749) was appointed cantor and organist of a church in Hirschberg where a new organ by Roeder of Berlin had been installed. Some time later, after he had made a trip (financed by a noble patron) to Leipzig to meet Bach and hear him play, Reimann wrote in a letter, "This great artist received me amiably, and so enchanted me by his uncommon skill that I have never regretted the journey." From that time on Bach became his model. O JESU was set to Longfellow's hymn in the *English Hymnal*, 1906, the source of the present harmonization. Originally, Reimann's melody had a half-note at the beginning and end of each line. (Zahn 2368)

93 Guide Me, O Thou Great Jehovah

Often referred to as "the Sweet Singer of Wales," William Williams (1717–1791), the son of a prosperous Welsh farmer, intended originally to study medicine but decided instead to enter the ministry after hearing Howell Harris, a Calvinistic Methodist preacher, at Talgarth Churchyard. Ordained a deacon in the Church of England, he was later denied full ordination because of his evangelical views and his refusal to confine his preaching to his own parish, with the result that he became an itinerant evangelist of the Calvinistic Methodist Church, traveling on an average nearly three thousand miles a year throughout Wales and doing so for forty-five years. A forceful preacher, he also wrote more than eight hundred hymns in Welsh and one hundred in English and published a number of volumes, including a book of hymns, *Alleluia,* 1745, in which the present hymn first appeared. It has since been translated into at least seventy-five languages. Elvit Lewis said of him, "What Paul Gerhardt has been to Germany, what Isaac Watts has been to England, that and more has William Williams been to the little Principality of Wales."

Peter Williams, a Methodist minister in Wales, translated the first stanza of this hymn and the remaining two were done by Williams himself or possibly by his son.

CWM RHONDDA   The inspiration for this tune came to John Hughes (1873–1932) as he was attending a Sunday morning service at Salem Chapel (Baptist) in the village Llantwit Fardre, Pontypridd. Hughes, a lifelong member of this church, succeeded his father as deacon and precentor in it. His tune, CWM RHONDDA, composed for the 1907 anniversary services at Capel Rhondda, Pontypridd, soon became extremely popular throughout Wales. It is said that by 1930 it had been sung at no less than five thousand hymn festivals. It is sung fervently, with the present text, at football matches in Wales. In 1933 the tune was included in two English hymnals: the Revised *Fellowship Hymn Book* and *The Methodist Hymn Book.*

Hughes began working when he was twelve as a doorboy at Glyn Colliery. In later years he was employed by the Great Western Railway, became an official in its traffic department, and remained with the company until his death. He composed hymn tunes, anthems, Sunday school marches, but it is CWM RHONDDA which has made his name known. In *Hymns We Love,* 1954, Cecil Northcott says of the present combination of text and tune, "The hymn's imagery is well matched by the powerful glow of the tune 'Cwm Rhondda' which Wales has made the world sing to this great hymn." CWM (anglicized "coomb") means "low valley." Rhondda, an urban district in the center of the eastern division of the South Wales coalfield in Glamorganshire, comprises two valleys named after their respective rivers, Rhondda Faur and Rhondda Fach (the Great and Lesser Rhondda).

94   When All Thy Mercies, O My God

As he did with all his hymns, Joseph Addison first published this hymn in *The Spectator.* It appeared in the August 9, 1712 issue at the conclusion of an essay on "Gratitude." See No. 72 for comments on Addison.

TALLIS' ORDINAL   See. No. 18 for comments on this tune.

95 The Lord Will Come and Not Be Slow

Impelled by the stress of the Civil War in England, John Milton published in 1648, when he was forty years of age, *Nine of the Psalms done into Metre,* selecting Psalms 80 to 88. These were translations of the original, the Hebrew text appearing in the margins, with every English word not found in the original printed in italics. The present hymn is a cento from this work, based on lines taken from Psalms 82, 85, and 86, arranged probably by W. Garrett Horder and first published in his *Worship Song,* 1905. See No. 70 for comments on Milton.

YORK (THE STILT; SCOTCH STILT) This famous tune was first found among the Common Tunes (they could be used with any psalm in Common Meter, 8.6.8.6.) in Andro Hart's *The CL Psalmes of David,* 1615. It was named THE STILT. It came into English use and popularity through Ravenscroft's *Psalter,* 1621, where it was included in the "Northerne Tunes," called YORKE, assigned to four psalms and a "Prayer to the Holy Ghost," and recommended as being "proper for joyful ditties." The striding effect of this rather angular melody makes THE STILT an apt and picturesque name for it. In England it ran a close second to OLD HUNDREDTH in popularity. Sir John Hawkins wrote in his *History,* 1776, that the tune was so well known "that within memory half the nurses of England were used to sing it by way of lullaby; and the chimes of many country churches have played it six or eight times in twenty-four hours from time immemorial." YORK, one of thirteen tunes included in a 1698 edition of the *Bay Psalm Book* with music, was one of the few which continued to be sung by New Englanders in the days (c. 1700) when the number of psalm tunes known by some congregations was less than ten and singing in church reached an all-time low. The harmonization at No. 95 was made by John Milton, father of the poet and son of a staunch Catholic who disinherited him when he was found reading a Bible early in Queen Elizabeth's reign. He became a Protestant, and went to London where he eventually had a good deal of success as a scrivener and also as a musician, composing instrumental music, madrigals, anthems, and hymn tunes. One of his madrigals was included in *The Triumphes of Oriana,* 1601, a famous collection edited by Thomas Morley, in which all the madrigals were in praise of Queen Elizabeth and ended with "Long live fair Oriana," a name often applied to Elizabeth. The poet Milton referred to his father's musical ability in his poem "Ad Patrem." YORK was set to Milton's metrical psalm paraphrase in *The Congregational Hymnary,* 1916.

96 Whate'er My God Ordains Is Right

Following his graduation from the University of Jena in 1671, Samuel Rodigast (1649–1708) was appointed an adjunct, or instructor, of the philosophical faculty at the university. When his close friend, Severus Gastorius, cantor of one of Jena's Lutheran churches, fell seriously ill, Rodigast wrote these words to comfort and cheer him. Later, upon his recovery, Gastorius set them to music, to the present tune, WAS GOTT TUT, and frequently had them sung by his choir. The hymn first appeared in the Appendix in *Das*

Hannoverische Gesangbuch, 1676, beginning with the line, "Was Gott tut, das ist wohlgethan" ("What God does is rightly done"). Frederick III of Prussia requested that this hymn, his favorite, be sung at his funeral. Rodigast was made joint rector of the Greyfriars Gymnasium in Berlin in 1680, later becoming full rector, where he attained great fame as a scholar and where he remained until his death in 1708.

WAS GOTT TUT (BADEN; PACHELBEL)   All that is known of Severus Gastorius, cantor at Jena and composer of this melody, is included in the comments on the hymn which his friend Samuel Rodigast wrote for him. The earliest known form of WAS GOTT TUT is from a hymnbook published at Weimar in 1681. (See Zahn, Vol. VI, p. 577, No. 5.) There are numerous variants of the melody. Its present form is from a Nürnberg hymn and tune book of 1690. (Zahn 5629) WAS GOTT TUT was used by Bach in Cantatas 12, 69, 75, 98, 100, 144, and for the first of his *Drei Choräle zu Trauungen* ("Three Wedding Chorales"). A delightful and graceful chorale prelude for organ on WAS GOTT TUT by Johann P. Kellner (1705–1788), friend and admirer of Bach, was often played by Dr. Hugh Porter at weddings.

The tune name is from the first line of Rodigast's hymn. In some hymnals the chorale is called PACHELBEL because it was attributed to the distinguished organist and composer of that name by Karl Winterfeld. Zahn considered this ascription groundless and assigned the melody to Gastorius. WAS GOTT TUT, in a form much like that given here, was attributed to G. Gastorius and named ELBE in *The Seraph,* June, 1840, edited by Lowell Mason.

97   God of Our Life, Through All the Circling Years

Pastor for many years of the Shadyside Presbyterian Church in Pittsburgh, Hugh Thompson Kerr (1872–1950) was inspired to write these words for the fiftieth anniversary celebration of that great church in 1916. A Canadian by birth, Kerr served Presbyterian churches in Kansas and Illinois before going to Pittsburgh in 1913, and was the author of a number of religious books, including several fine collections of children's stories. He received many honorary degrees and in 1930 was elected Moderator of the General Assembly of the Presbyterian Church in the U.S.A.

SANDON, composed by Charles Henry Purday (1799–1885) for Cardinal Newman's hymn "Lead, kindly Light," was first published in Purday's *Church and Home Metrical Psalter and Hymnal,* 1860 and called "Landon" originally. Purday, who belonged to a family connected with music publishing in London, was at one time a vocalist of some reputation and was among those who sang at Queen Victoria's coronation. He lectured on musical subjects, was precentor (director of psalmody) at the Scottish Church, Crown Court, London, composed and edited sacred music, contributed articles to Grove's *Dictionary of Music,* and was an ardent advocate for revision of the laws pertaining to the copyright of musical publications. He was one of the first to recommend the use of program notes at concerts. In 1854 he published *Crown Court Psalmody* which contained "101 popular tunes and chants," maintaining that this number of tunes was enough for any book. In the introduction to one of his books is the following statement:

> If every family would take the pains to have their children taught to sing at sight, and use their tune-books at home, we should have no lack of good congregational singing in the church; and less complaint when the precentor, choir or organist introduces *new* tunes. Singing should be made a necessary part of the education of all classes, that everybody might be enabled to join in choral music, sacred and secular; and until such is really the case, we shall never have good congregational singing in our churches.

98 O Love of God, How Strong and True!

Adelaide Ann Procter (1825–1864) was the eldest daughter of Bryan Waller Procter, English barrister and author, who included among his close friends such literary notables as Charles Dickens, Leigh Hunt, and Charles Lamb. Showing early promise as a gifted poet, she sent several of her poems under the pseudonym "Mary Berwick" to Charles Dickens who published them in *Household Words*, which he edited. He assumed that they had been written by a governess in the Procter family. It was not until two years later, after several of her poems had appeared, that he discovered the real author. He later paid her the tribute, "Perfectly unselfish, swift to sympathize and eager to relieve, she wrought at such designs with a flushed earnestness that disregarded season, weather, time of day or night, food, rest." She published a volume of poems in 1858 and 1862, with the title *Legends and Lyrics, a Book of Verses*, from the first edition of which the present hymn was taken. She also wrote a number of popular songs, including "The Lost Chord."

WENTWORTH, composed for this hymn by Frederick C. Maker (1844–1927), was first published in the second series of *The Bristol Tune Book*, 1876, edited by Alfred Stone. Maker contributed several tunes to Stone's collections (1863, 1876, 1881), which were compiled with the hope that the tunes contained in them would be used with the hymns in nonconformist hymnals, which were customarily printed in word editions without any music. Maker was born in Bristol and spent his life there. He was organist in three different churches, one of them the Redland Park Congregational Church where he served as organist from 1882 to 1910. He was also accompanist for the Bristol Festival Choirs, which Alfred Stone directed, and was visiting professor of music at Clifton College for twenty years, and conductor of the Bristol Free Church Choir Association. This was a group of choirs united for special musical services through which much good music was introduced for use in the free churches. Although Maker composed anthems, cantatas, and piano pieces, he is remembered now only for his hymn tunes, the best known of which is REST, No. 341.

99 O Love of God, How Strong and True!

"The prince of Scottish hymn writers," Horatius Bonar (1808–1889) was an eloquent and forceful preacher as well as a distinguished theologian, scholar, and author. A student of Thomas Chalmers at the University of Edinburgh, he later followed Chalmers in withdrawing from the state church at the time of the Disruption in 1843 (a dispute over the question of patronage in which more than four hundred ministers left the Church of Scotland.) He played a leading part in forming the Free Church of Scotland, eventually becoming moderator of the General Assembly of that body and minister of the Chalmers Memorial Free Church in Edinburgh. He carried on a voluminous correspondence and produced on the average one devotional book a year. He was tireless in his devotion to his many duties. "One said of him that he was always visiting, another that he was always preaching, another that he was always writing, another that he was always praying." His earliest hymns were written for children, for whom he had a great affection. Most of his hymns — many of which are still in use in England, Scotland, and America — were dashed off rather hurriedly, not infrequently on trains, and were seldom revised, so that many are marred by imperfections. The best of them, however, rank with the finest.

The present hymn comes from Bonar's *Hymns of Faith and Hope,* 1861, second series.

EISENACH (MACH'S MIT MIR, GOTT; SCHEIN; LEIPSIC) The original form of the melody from which EISENACH is adapted, is given at No. 500. It was composed by Johann Hermann Schein (1586–1630) for a hymn of consolation which he wrote for the funeral of the wife of Caspar Werner, a masterbuilder and town councillor of Leipzig. It was published as a fly sheet in 1628, and was included in the 1645 edition of his *Cantional,* 1627, one of the major chorale collections of the baroque and one of his most important works. It contained old and new chorale melodies, harmonized in four, five, and six parts, for use in church. Schein contributed texts as well as tunes and harmonizations. In his settings one finds the flexible, irregular rhythms characteristic of the early chorale melodies.

The son of a Lutheran pastor, Schein was a chorister for four years in the chapel of the Elector of Saxony at Dresden, attended the Gymnasium at Schulpforta (see No. 54), studied law, theology, and philosophy at the University of Leipzig, and served for two years as music director at the court of Duke Johann Ernst of Saxe-Weimar. In 1615 (1616?) he succeeded Calvisius as cantor of St. Thomas' School in Leipzig, remaining there until his death. He was one of the most outstanding of Bach's predecessors and one of the first Lutheran composers to make use of the new techniques of the Italians. His sacred and secular works — including instrumental suites, compositions for organ based on chorales, songs, and a large number of varied choral works — made significant contributions to the development of German music, particularly in the field of chorale literature. The original form of this melody, in which the first phrase was repeated, appears in current German hymnals with "So jemand spricht: Ich liebe Gott" (Gellert) and "Mir nach, spricht Christus, unser Held" (Scheffler). Bach used the melody in the *St. John Passion* (No. 40) and in Cantatas 139 and 156.

Schein's melody, harmonized by Bach, was named BEER–SHEBA in Lowell Mason's *Modern Psalmist,* 1839. The same harmonization was named STUTTGART, LEIPSIC, and EISENACH in later English and American collections. Eisenach was Bach's birthplace. The present harmonization, which owes much to Bach, is from *Congregational Praise*, 1951.

100 O My Soul, Bless God, the Father

A remarkably faithful metrical version of Psalm 103, originally containing sixteen stanzas, this cento was first published in the *United Presbyterian Book of Psalms, U.S.A.*, 1871. See comments at No. 91.

STUTTGART is an adaptation of a melody set to "Sollt es gleich bisweilen scheinem" (Zahn 1353) from *Psalmodia Sacra*, a Lutheran hymnbook published at Gotha in 1715. It is generally attributed to Christian F. Witt (1660–1716), one of two editors of the book. In *Bach's Chorals, Part III, The Hymns and Hymn Melodies of the Organ Works*, 1921, Charles Sanford Terry has set forth convincingly his reasons for believing that Bach used the plan of *Psalmodia Sacra* as the model for his *Orgelbüchlein* ("Little Organ Book"), a collection of chorale preludes for use throughout the seasons of the church year. Witt, the son of Johann S. Witt, court organist at Altenburg, was given excellent music instruction in Vienna, Salzburg, and Nürnberg. In the latter city he was a pupil of G. K. Wecker with whom Pachelbel is thought to have studied. In 1686 he became court organist at Gotha and in 1713 Kapellmeister, directing with distinction until his death. He composed anthems, cantatas, works for orchestra, harpsichord, and organ, and wrote incidental music for dramatic presentations at court. His *Passacaglia* in D minor was mistakenly published as a work of J. S. Bach in Vol. 42 of the Bach-Gesellschaft edition.

Witt's tune was adapted to 8.7.8.7 meter and named STUTTGARD in William H. Havergal's *Old Church Psalmody*, 1847. His version of the melody came into American hymnody through *The National Psalmist*, 1848, edited by Lowell Mason and George Webb. The melody and harmonies were the same as in Old Church Psalmody but the rhythm was 3/2, much used by Mason and other editors of his time.

STUTTGART was set to "Earth has many a noble city" in *Hymns Ancient and Modern*, 1861, and was harmonized by Henry J. Gauntlett. The first half of the harmonization given here is Havergal's, the second half, Gauntlett's.

See No. 214 for comments on Havergal.

101 There's a Wideness in God's Mercy

Although his ancestors had been Huguenots for generations and he had been brought up in a strict Calvinistic home, Frederick William Faber (1814–1863) joined the Roman Catholic Church after coming under the influence of John Henry Newman at Oxford. For many years he served as the superior of the Brompton Oratory of St. Philip Neri in London, a religious society of secular priests. He published many devotional and theological works, mostly of a polemical nature, but he is best known today for his hymns, of which he wrote 150. They were written primarily to be read in private and were modeled after the hymns of Cowper, Newton, and Wesley so as to provide Catholics with devotional literature equal in merit and power to the hymns of Protestantism. Most of his hymns are too introspective, too emotional, or too explicitly theological to be suitable for general use. This hymn is a cento from a thirteen-stanza poem which appeared in his *Hymns,* 1862, but which had been published in shorter form in his *Oratory Hymns,* 1854, under the title "Come to Jesus."

IN BABILONE   See No. 74 for comments on this tune.

102   There's a Wideness in God's Mercy

See No. 101 for comments on the text.

WELLESLEY was written by a high-school senior. When Lizzie S. Tourjée (1858–1913) was asked to set a classmate's graduation hymn to music, she felt hopeless about the assignment. But her father, Dr. Eben Tourjée, founder of the New England Conservatory of Music (1867), encouraged her and suggested that she sit down at the piano with the words in front of her to see what musical ideas they might suggest. Thus WELLESLEY was evolved, and the hymn was sung at the end of the graduation exercises at the high school in Newton, Massachusetts, in 1877. Dr. Tourjée named his daughter's tune for the newly established college for women which she attended for one year (1877–1878), and included it in the *Hymnal of the Methodist Episcopal Church with Tunes,* 1878, for which he was one of the music editors. In that book "There's a wideness in God's mercy" was one of three texts printed on the page with WELLESLEY. After that, Faber's hymn and Miss Tourjée's tune appeared together in a number of hymnals, including some used at Wellesley College, and in *Tribute of Praise,* 1884, edited by Dr. Tourjée for use at the New England Conservatory.

Eben Tourjée (1834–1891), organist, choirmaster, teacher, administrator, was a man of remarkable initiative and ability, indefatigable in his efforts to further music education and to improve music in churches. In 1851, when he was seventeen, working in a music store and teaching in the schools of Fall River, Massachusetts, he organized and taught classes in piano, voice, and organ, thus introducing into America for the first time class instruction in applied music. He was the first president of the Music Teacher's National Association (1876), dean of the College of Music of Boston University, and director of the New England Conservatory of Music from its founding until his death.

103   Come, Thou Long-Expected Jesus

Charles Wesley first published this hymn in his *Hymns for the Nativity of our Lord,* 1744, in two eight-line stanzas. Surprisingly enough it was not included in the Wesleyan hymnals until 1875 but has since found its way into most Protestant books. See No. 43 for comments on Wesley.

STUTTGART   See No. 100 for comments on the tune.

104 Comfort, Comfort Ye My People

Court chaplain at Halle and later at Weissenfels, and at one time a member of the philosophical faculty at Wittenberg, Johann Olearius (1611–1684) wrote many hymns and compiled one of the most influential hymnals in Germany during the seventeenth century, *Geistliche Singe-Kunst,* Leipzig, 1671, containing 1,207 hymns, of which 302 were his own. This hymn, based on Isaiah 40:1–8, was written for St. John the Baptist's Day (June 24) and is especially suitable for Advent. The translation is by Catherine Winkworth from her *Chorale Book for England,* 1863. See No. 2 for comments on Miss Winkworth.

PSALM 42 (FREU DICH SEHR; BOURGEOIS) In the Genevan Psalter of 1551, this melody, composed or adapted by Louis Bourgeois (see No. 4) was set to Théodore de Bèze's version of Psalm 42, "As the hart panteth after the water brooks," and is still sung in France to a later version of that psalm. Translated into German by Ambrosius Lobwasser (1515–1585) it became "Wie nach einem Wasserquelle" and was set to PSALM 42 in his German Psalter published in 1573. This Psalter, which contained German translations of all the French psalm versions, set to the Genevan melodies, remained the standard for German Reformed churches until the middle of the seventeenth century and continued to be issued in new editions for two hundred years. The melody is known in Germany as FREU DICH SEHR, O MEINE SEELE, the first line of a burial hymn with which it appeared in 1627 and with which it has continued to be sung. Bach used it in Cantatas 13, 19, 25, 30, 39, 70, 194, sometimes in a 3/4 rhythm throughout, sometimes in 4/4 or 4/2. In Cantatas 19 and 70 the melody appears with "Freu dich sehr," in the other five with stanzas from five different hymns with which it was also associated. In the Anglo-Genevan Psalter, 1561, and in the Scottish Psalter, 1564, the melody was adapted to an L.M.D. version of Psalm 27, which required rather drastic changes. Its association with the present translation of Olearius' hymn dates from *The Chorale Book for England,* 1863 (see No. 15), where its original irregular rhythm was cast into a straight 4/4. The present harmonies are basically those found in Claude Goudimel's setting of the melody in 1565. (See No. 49.)

The tune TAPPNAH in Lowell Mason's *Modern Psalmist,* 1839, is a 4/2 version of PSALM 42.

105 Hail to the Lord's Anointed

Written by James Montgomery in 1821 for a Christmas service in a Moravian settlement in Yorkshire, England, this hymn, based on Psalm 72, was first published in its completed form in Dr. Adam Clarke's *Commentary on the Bible,* 1822, where it was included with a special note next to the psalm. A part of it had appeared earlier in the *Evangelical Magazine,* May, 1822, and a second completed version was printed at the close of the same year in the author's *Songs of Zion.* It has taken its place in many hymnals as one of the finest of all missionary hymns and is an excellent example of the blending of a fervent religious faith and a passion for social justice which so characterized Montgomery's life and work. See No. 25 for comments on Montgomery.

ROCKPORT was composed for this text by T. Tertius Noble (1867–1953) in 1938, at Rockport, Massachusetts, for *The Hymnal,* 1941. (Evangelical and Reformed.) Dr. Noble, who attained eminence on both sides of the Atlantic, was known to American church musicians not only as a composer but also as the distinguished and beloved organist and choirmaster of St. Thomas' Episcopal Church in New York City where he served from 1913 until his retirement in 1943. He established its Choir School in 1919. He was born in Bath, England, the youngest of twelve children. His father, an accomplished amateur musician, used to let him play the bass part of Bach's "Forty-eight Preludes and Fugues" on the piano while he played the upper parts. When he was twelve, and dissatisfied with school because music was ignored, he was allowed to go to Colchester where he became organist at All Saints Church and lived for three years in the home of the rector who held him to a rigorous schedule of practice and study. Advanced study followed at the Royal College of Music in London where he won a scholarship for three years. One of his teachers there was Charles V. Stanford (see No. 147) with whom he was associated for two years as assistant organist at Trinity College, Cambridge. For five years he was organist and choirmaster at Ely Cathedral, giving up that post in 1898 to fill a similar position at York Minster for fifteen years. In York he directed the York Musical Society, founded and directed the York Symphony, and revived the York Musical Festival after a lapse of seventy-five years. Honorary degrees were conferred on him by Columbia University, Trinity College, and the Archbishop of Canterbury. In 1932 a memorial window was installed in St. Thomas' Church to commemorate his fiftieth year as a church musician. He was a member of the Episcopal Hymnal Commission of 1916 and of the Joint Commission on Church Music until his retirement in 1943, when he settled in Rockport, long his summer home. His numerous compositions included anthems, services, hymn tunes, organ pieces, a comic opera, and works for orchestra. In 1943 he published *The Training of the Boy Choir.* Besides directing and playing at St. Thomas' he did much private teaching, and was a member of the faculty of the School of Sacred Music of Union Theological Seminary from 1931 to 1945. It would be difficult to name a church musician for whom young and old alike had greater admiration and affection, not only for his musical gifts but also for the warmth and charm of his personality and his integrity of spirit.

106 Hills of the North, Rejoice

Following graduation from Oxford, and after serving as examiner in the School of Jurisprudence, Charles Edward Oakley (1832–1865) became rector of Wickwar, Gloucestershire, in 1856, and rector of St. Paul's, Covent Garden, London, in 1863. Although he served the latter church for only two years before his untimely death, his parishioners placed a memorial in the church in his honor in which they paid moving tribute to his intellectual brilliance, devout spirit, and Christian character. This appears to be the only hymn he wrote. It was first published in Bishop T. V. French's *Hymns Adapted to the Christian Seasons*, 1870, and has since won its way into a number of modern hymnals by virtue of its poetic appeal and fresh missionary vision.

LITTLE CORNARD, named for the village in Suffolk, England, where its composer, Martin Shaw, spent his honeymoon, was written for these words in *Additional Tunes and Settings in use at St. Mary's, Primrose Hill,* 1915, the church to which Shaw went as organist in 1908 when Percy Dearmer was the vicar. Shaw (1875–1958), son of a well-known London organist and church musician, and brother of Geoffrey Shaw (see No. 445), studied at the Royal College of Music under Parry, Stanford, and Walford Davies, all of whom are represented in the *Pilgrim Hymnal*. His musical activities covered a wide field: conducting for Ellen Terry and Isadora Duncan in the theater; serving as organist and choir director of churches in London and as music director of the Guildhouse, London, and of the diocese of Chelmsford for ten years; working to revive interest in Purcell's music; composing extensively, arranging music, and editing a number of books for use in churches and schools. In the minds of church musicians his name is linked with those of Ralph Vaughan Williams and Percy Dearmer because of his collaboration with them in editing *Songs of Praise,* 1925, *The Oxford Book of Carols,* 1928, and *Songs of Praise, Enlarged,* 1931 — books which have had immeasurable influence in raising the level of music in church and school in England and America. Shaw, like Vaughan Williams, knew and set a high value on English folk music and through his arrangements did much to make it available and to promote its use. His own compositions show its influence. In 1932 the Archbishop of Canterbury conferred doctorate of music degrees on him and his brother.

107 Let All Mortal Flesh Keep Silence

This hymn, as used in the Eastern Orthodox Church, is sung at the beginning of the Liturgy of the Faithful as the bread and wine are brought into the sanctuary. Known as the Cherubic Hymn, it comes from the Liturgy of St. James of Jerusalem and dates back at least to the fifth century. It is especially appropriate for use in connection with the communion service. The present translation is by Gerard Moultrie (1829–1885), an Anglican clergyman, who wrote many hymns and poems, including a number of translations from Greek, Latin, and German sources. It was first published in *Lyra Eucharistica,* 1864.

PICARDY, the setting for these words in *The English Hymnal,* 1906, has appeared in an increasing number of American hymnbooks since its publication in *The New Hymnal* (Episcopal), 1918. An anthem composed by Gustav Holst on the text and the tune has become a favorite of choirs and has made the combination even more widely known. Both words and music draw forth a particularly sensitive response from children, who seem to feel at once the awe and mystery inherent in the text and invariably sing it with the mood proper to it. The melody is from Picardy, formerly a province of northern France, where it was sung traditionally to a "pious and poetic" legend about Jesus, who, dressed as a beggar, wanders from door to door asking for food and lodging. When he is hospitably received by a housewife whose husband had turned him away, a strange, wondrous light prompts her to ask if the moon is shining, whereupon he tells her that the light is the glow from her act of charity. She asks if he is Jesus Christ in disguise, and he replies that he is king of paradise, that she will die in three days and be with him there, and that her husband will burn in the fires of hell! The ballad, sometimes called "La parabole du mauvais riche" ("The parable of the sinful rich man,") sometimes "La ballade de Jésus-Christ," has some of the same awed awareness of Christ's presence that is given expression in the hymn. In *Sixty Folksongs of France,* Julien Tiersot says that this is one of the few songs of a religious nature (apart from carols) found among French folk songs. Jean B. Wekerlin, who included it in a group of "Chansons morales et mystiques," said that there is such a perfect union of feeling between the words and the music that it seems almost as if a trained musician had helped in its creation.

108 Wake, Awake, for Night Is Flying

Like so many of his hymns, this was written and composed by Philipp Nicolai during the time of a severe epidemic in which many of his parishioners lost their lives. The first stanza is drawn from the vision of Isaiah 52:8, while the second and third stanzas are based on the parable of the wise and foolish virgins, Matthew 25:1–13, and the song of the redeemed in the heavenly Jerusalem, Revelation 19:6–9. The hymn was first published in the Appendix to Nicolai's *Frewden-Spiegel des ewigen Lebens* ("Mirror of Joy of Life Eternal"), 1599. See No. 24 for additional comments on Nicolai. The translation, considerably altered, is by Catherine Winkworth from her *Lyra Germanica,* 1858. See No. 2 for comments on Miss Winkworth.

WACHET AUF Bach's Cantata No. 140 (see No. 24) in which this is the final chorale, remained in manuscript for over a hundred years, known to only a few individuals. Of this last movement William G. Whittaker says: "The cantata ends with the chorale in its unadorned form, harmonised in a simple and direct way quite unusual with Bach. Such treatment was the result of the unconscious sense of the fitness of things which produced masterly strokes of genius without effort." [7] Prof. Charles Sanford Terry's *Bach's Chorals,* which deals with the hymns and hymn melodies of the Passions and motets, the cantatas and motets, and the organ works, gives invaluable information on the sources of texts and tunes used by Bach. See No. 24 for further comments on WACHET AUF.

109 Watchman, Tell Us of the Night

Sir John Bowring (1792–1872), Member of Parliament, British Consul at Canton, and later Governor of Hong Kong, early in life displayed an amazing facility in acquiring languages, claiming eventually to know two hundred and to speak a hundred. His writings, published in thirty volumes, ranged over a wide variety of subjects, from the decimal system to poetry. Although he was a Unitarian, his hymns read as if they had been fashioned by an orthodox believer and have proved to be the most enduring things he wrote. This hymn, based on Isaiah 21:11–12, and first published in Bowring's Hymns, 1825, vividly recaptures the experience of an oriental traveler calling to the watchman on the ramparts for signs of day, and draws upon that image to convey a pilgrim's hopeful expectancy of the advent of Christ. Being in dialogue form, it is most suitable for antiphonal singing, which greatly enhances its effectiveness, the congregation singing the first and third lines, the choir responding by singing the second and fourth.

ABERYSTWYTH is the name of the town in Wales (a popular watering place on the west coast) in which this tune was composed by Joseph Parry (1841–1903) when he was professor of music at the University College there, an appointment he held from 1874 to 1879. Parry's life has many of the elements of a success story. He was born into a family with so little of this world's goods that before he was ten he had to leave school to work in the puddling furnaces of the iron works. In 1854 the family left Wales and emigrated to Danville, Pennsylvania, where at seventeen Parry had his first music lessons in classes conducted by fellow workmen. In 1863, his harmonization of a hymn tune won a prize in the Swansea Eisteddfod and attracted the attention of Brinley Richards, a Welsh musician of some reputation who was one of the adjudicators. Through his influence a fund was raised through contributions from Welshmen in the United States and abroad which enabled Parry to go to England for three years of study (1868–1871) at the Royal Academy of Music in London. He received a Bachelor of Music degree from Cambridge in 1871, and the Doctor of Music degree in 1878. After leaving Aberystwyth he directed a music school in Swansea for seven years, and in 1888 was appointed lecturer in music at University College of South Wales, Cardiff, where he remained until his death.

110 O Come, O Come, Emmanuel

Sometime prior to the ninth century it became customary in the Roman liturgy to chant or sing a brief versicle, or antiphon, before and after the Magnificat at vespers during the last week in Advent. There were seven antiphons sung on successive days, each beginning with "O" and centering on one of the titles ascribed to the Messiah in the Bible. Leonard Ellinwood comments that it was the custom in the Middle Ages for the principal officers of a monastery each to have a given "O" to sing on a particular day and then to provide a pittance or feast for the monks. Five of these antiphons were cast into a metrical form by an unknown author in the thirteenth century, who changed the order and added the refrain. This version first appeared in the Appendix to *Psalteriolum Cantionum Catholicarum*, Cologne, 1710, and was translated into English by John Mason Neale (1818–1866) in his *Mediaeval Hymns and Sequences*, 1851. The present hymn is based on

Neale's translation as it appeared in revised form in his *Hymnal Noted*, 1854. The last two stanzas were translated by Henry Sloane Coffin (1877–1954), distinguished American churchman and beloved president of Union Theological Seminary, in his *Hymns of the Kingdom of God*, 1910 (1916 edition).

Neale belongs among the immortals of hymnody. A brilliant classical scholar at Cambridge, he incurred the disfavor of his ecclesiastical superiors because of his High Church views and held only one appointment throughout his priestly career, that of Warden of Sackville College, East Grinstead, London, from 1846 to 1866. This was in reality an almshouse for indigent old men where his duties were more those of a caretaker than a chaplain and where his yearly salary never exceeded twenty-seven pounds. Yet, despite this lowly station and a continuous struggle against ill-health and penury, he did a prodigious amount of work and left a literary and spiritual legacy of unexcelled magnitude. His inspired translations of early Greek and Latin hymns, numbering more than two hundred, many of which owe their power and beauty more to his creative genius than to the originals, have never been surpassed and have seldom been equaled. Most of his translations and hymns appeared in the following notable collections: *Mediaeval Hymns and Sequences*, 1851; *The Hymnal Noted*, published in two parts, in 1852 and 1854; *Hymns of the Eastern Church*, 1862; *Hymns, chiefly Mediaeval, on the Joys and Glories of Paradise*, 1865; and *Sequences and Hymns and other Ecclesiastical Verses*, published after his death in 1866. He also published two small volumes of *Hymns for Children*, 1842; *Hymns for the Young*, 1844; *Carols for Christmastide*, 1853; and *Carols for Eastertide*, 1854. "Good King Wenceslas," an original work, was taken from *Carols for Christmastide*. It was typical of him that he never copyrighted any of his hymns, saying that he wished to cast his two mites into the Lord's treasury without thought of reward. Percy Dearmer rightly called him "the most learned hymnologist and liturgiologist of his time." [8]

One of Neale's signal achievements as a humanitarian was the founding of one of the first nursing homes in England, the Sisterhood of St. Margaret, which he accomplished against much opposition. Not limited to these attainments he also wrote *The History of the Holy Eastern Church*, 1847–1873, in five volumes, the completed work appearing posthumously; *A History of the so-called Jansenist Church in Holland*, 1858; and in collaboration with his friend R. F. Littledale, *A Commentary on the Psalms from primitive and mediaeval Writers*, 1874, in four volumes. Trinity College in Hartford conferred a D.D. degree upon him in absentia, prompting James Moffatt to comment, "His own church had no honors for him; even his D.D. came from America." [1]

The following inscription was placed on Neale's coffin at his request: J. M. Neale, miser et indigens sacerdos requiescens sub SIGNO THAU (J. M. Neale, poor and unworthy priest resting under the sign of the cross).

VENI EMMANUEL   Above the music for this hymn in Part II of the *Hymnal Noted*, 1854, is a quotation from Matthew: "They shall call his name Emmanuel, which being interpreted is, God with us." The melody is printed in plainsong notation on a four-line staff, with the heading "From a French

Missal in the National Library, Lisbon." Careful study of these missals has failed to disclose the source, and it is believed that Thomas Helmore (1811–1890) fashioned VENI EMMANUEL from phrases of plainsong settings of the *Kyrie* for Neale's translation. In *Accompanying Harmonies to the Hymnal Noted,* 1852, there is a harmonization of the melody by the Rev. S. S. Greatheed, with the free rhythm of the plainsong retained. Later, VENI EMMANUEL was cast into a measured rhythm as in the present form, although in some hymnals it still appears in the irregular rhythm with the type of plainsong accompaniment found in contemporary hymnals.

The *Hymnal Noted* (hymns with music) contained tunes selected and edited by Thomas Helmore for Neale's translations of Latin hymns. Both men, deeply involved in the Oxford Movement, hoped to revive and restore to use in the Church of England some of the office hymns and plainsong melodies which had been in use, particularly at Sarum (Salisbury) before the Reformation. Helmore became master of the choristers of the Chapel Royal in 1846, and one of the priests-in-ordinary the following year. He was the author and editor of a number of books on church music, particularly plainsong, and composed tunes for some of Neale's translations.

I I I   Of the Father's Love Begotten

Among the growing number of early Latin hymns set to plainsong melodies found in present-day hymnals, this is one of the most popular. It was written by Aurelius Clemens Prudentius (348–410), a native of northern Spain, who began his career as a lawyer and magistrate but at the age of fifty-seven entered a monastery where he devoted his talents to the writing of sacred poetry. While his poems were intended for personal, devotional use, they were freely drawn upon in medieval hymnaries and breviaries to provide some of the finest hymns and liturgical treasures of the Western Church. This hymn is a cento from one of his major works, *Cathemerinon,* from the section called *Hymnus omnis horae,* beginning "Corde natus ex Parentis, ante mundi exordium." A. S. Walpole said that it was Prudentius' intent in writing the poem that "at every hour of the day a believer should be mindful of Christ, who is the A and Ω, the beginning and the end." The refrain and the final stanza, taken from the last words of the full poem, were added later.

The translation of the hymn is jointly the work of John Mason Neale and Henry W. Baker. See Nos. 110 and 79 for comments on Neale and Baker respectively.

DIVINUM MYSTERIUM (CORDE NATUS)   is a plainsong melody found in various forms with the Latin hymn "Divinum Mysterium" in Italian, Bohemian, Gallican, and German manuscripts of the tenth to the fifteenth centuries. Technically speaking, the music was a Sanctus trope. Tropes consisted of words or phrases added to the authorized liturgical texts, with each syllable of the interpolation sung to one note of a florid (melismatic) passage of a plainsong setting, where originally a single vowel was vocalized. The following example of a tenth-century *Kyrie* and trope makes this clear.

Ky - ri - e - *

- e - le - - - - - - - i - son

Ky - ri - e fons bo - ni - ta - tis, Pa - ter in - ge - ni - te,

a quo bo - na cunc - ta pro - ce - dunt, e - le - - - - - - i - son.

Such kyries, called tropes or farsed, flourished and were sung in England and France up to the Reformation. The books containing tropes were called tropers. DIVINUM MYSTERIUM was introduced into English hymnody through the *Hymnal Noted,* 1854 (see No. 110), as the setting for Neale's translation of "Corde Natus ex Parentis." Its heading was "Evening Hymn from the Nativity till Epiphany." The source given for it, a thirteenth-century manuscript at Wolfenbüttel, has never been identified. It is thought that Thomas Helmore, music editor of the *Hymnal Noted,* took the melody from *Piae Cantiones,* 1582, where it was set to DIVINUM MYSTERIUM in a triple rhythm, the form in which it appears in English hymnals. The present harmonization was made by C. Winfred Douglas for *The Hymnal 1940.*

The terms plainsong, plain chant, Gregorian chant, refer to a vast body of remarkably beautiful music used in the liturgies of the Western Christian church. The Latin name, *Cantus planus,* was given to the chant in the thirteenth century to distinguish it from *Cantus figuratus* (melody adorned with another part) and *Cantus mensuratus* (measured song.) Plainsong is unaccompanied unison song, without a strictly measured rhythm, in one of the eight ecclesiastical or church modes. These differ from our major or minor scales (or modes) in the arrangement of the whole and half steps within the octave. For centuries these modes were the basis of secular as well as of sacred melodies. Modal melodies are disconcerting at first to those whose ears are accustomed to music in major or minor keys. The distinctive tonal flavor and the absence of a definite sense of key and of a regularly recurring accent may give the impression that plainsong wanders aimlessly, is formless and tuneless. But those who persist in listening to it and learning to sing it come to feel with Hugo Leichtentritt that "Gregorian chant is not only the most perfect expression of religious feeling in its time but one of the greatest achievements in music." [9]

112 Ah! Think Not the Lord Delayeth

One of the most creative and versatile churchmen in the field of worship and the arts during the first half of the twentieth century, Percy Dearmer (1867–1936) began his career as the curate of several small Anglican churches, and from 1901 to 1915 was the vicar of St. Mary the Virgin, Primrose Hill, London. He served as chaplain to the British Red Cross in Serbia during World War I and later was appointed professor of ecclesiastical art in King's College, London. The University of Oxford honored him with a Doctor of Divinity degree, and he was made canon of Westminster in 1931. He wrote and contributed to a number of significant books dealing with liturgics and social questions. He edited three notable and influential twentieth-century hymnals: *The English Hymnal*, 1906, with Ralph Vaughan Williams as music editor; *Songs of Praise*, 1925 and 1931; and *The Oxford Book of Carols*, 1931; the two latter in collaboration with Ralph Vaughan Williams and Martin Shaw. In cooperation with Archibald Jacob he also compiled the handbook, *Songs of Praise Discussed*, 1933. The present Advent hymn was written for *Songs of Praise*.

ALLES IST AN GOTTES SEGEN (EVANGELISTS; AUCTOR OMNIUM BONORUM) was suggested as an alternative tune for Percy Dearmer's Advent hymn in *Songs of Praise Enlarged*, 1931. It is said to be based on a melody in Johann B. König's *Harmonischer Lieder-Schatz*, 1738, one of the major chorale collections of the eighteenth century.

König (1691–1758) started out as a boy chorister in Frankfort-am-Main where he subsequently directed the music in two or three churches, taught singing, and in 1791 became choirmaster at St. Catherine's Church under Georg P. Telemann whom he later succeeded as music director of the church and of the city.

In four different hymnals the writer has found four different versions of this chorale melody. The form at No. 112, from Bach's *Choralgesänge* (on which the harmonization is based), seems distantly related to the melody in König's collection and also to one by Johann Löhner (1645–1705) who is listed as the composer in some books. (Zahn 3836)

113 Creator of the Stars of Night

This office hymn, originally beginning, "Conditor alme siderum," was sung during Advent at vespers in the daily services of the monasteries. It has sometimes been attributed to Ambrose but without foundation. The hymn is from a ninth-century manuscript found in Bern and was translated by John Mason Neale in his *Hymnal Noted*, 1852. See No. 110 for comments on Neale.

CONDITOR ALME (AMBROSE), the traditional plainsong universally associated with these words may be as old as the hymn with which it has been sung through the centuries. It is a fine example of a syllabic chant, with one note to each syllable of the text. In *The National Psalmist*, Boston, 1848, edited by Mason and Webb, this melody, named AMBROSE, in 4/2 with a long note at the beginning and end of each phrase, was given with the first stanza of the Latin hymn and the first of Charles Wesley's "My soul, inspired with sacred love." A footnote read:

This is called in some of the old service books, "The Ambrosian Advent Hymn." It is probably one of the oldest church tunes. The melody is within the compass of all voices, and "young men, and maidens; old men and children" may unite in singing it.

After the Reformation, CONDITOR ALME was sung by Protestants on the Continent with varied texts and with some melodic variants. It was set to Michael Weisse's "Kehrt euch zu mir, ihr liebe Leut" (Zahn 339) in *Ein New Gesengbuchlen*, 1531, edited by Weisse and printed in Bohemia, the first German hymnbook published for the Bohemian Brethren. Weisse (c. 1480–1534), born in Silesia, took priest's orders and was for a time a monk at Breslau. Deeply impressed by Luther's early writings, he left the monastery, sought refuge with the Bohemian Brethren at Leutomischel, Bohemia, was admitted as a priest at the Synod of Brandeis in 1531 and later served on their Select Council. Before that, however, he had been entrusted with important missions, one being the task of explaining the views of the Bohemian Brethren to Luther. He had great influence as a preacher and became the leader of the German communities of the Brethren at Landskron in Bohemia and Fulneck in Moravia. *Ein New Gesengbuchlen* contained original hymns by Weisse as well as his German translations of Latin and Bohemian hymns of the sixteenth and seventeenth centuries, and a number are still in use. In time CONDITOR ALME was associated with another of Weisse's hymns, "Lob sei dem allmächtigen Gott," used by Bach for the last of the Advent chorale preludes in the *Orgelbüchlein*. The first part of the melody appears also in a fughetta for manuals in the miscellaneous Preludes. There is no harmonization of the melody by Bach. CONDITOR ALME is given below in Weisse's 1531 version with "Lob sei dem . . ." which appeared with a different plainsong melody in *Ein New Gesengbuchlen*. (Zahn 308)

Lob sei dem all-mäch-ti - gen Gott, der un - ser sich er - bar-met hat,

ge-sandt sein al - ler - lieb-sten Sohn, aus ihm ge - born im höch-sten Thron.

With rhythmic modifications CONDITOR ALME was the basis for the setting of Bèze's version of Psalm 141 in the Genevan Psalter, 1562, and is still sung with Conrart's version of the same psalm. The name CREATOR ALME SIDERUM which appears with this melody in some books is from the first line of a revised version of the Latin hymn made in 1632 under the sponsorship of Pope Urban VIII. This version is given in *Liber Usualis*. CONDITOR ALME, an extremely simple melody, has a range of only six notes. The last six notes of the second and fourth phrases are identical.

114 Lift Up Your Heads, Ye Mighty Gates

Described by Julian as one of the most important of the early Prussian hymn writers, Georg Weissel (1590–1635), after studying at several universities, was appointed rector of the school at Friedland, near Domnau, but resigned after three years to complete his studies in theology at the University of Königsberg. He became pastor of the newly-built Altgrossgart Church in Königsberg at the age of thirty-three and remained there the rest of his life. Of some twenty hymns he wrote, this is the only one to have gained wide usage in English-speaking countries. Based on Psalm 24, it was intended to be sung on the first Sunday in Advent and was first published in his *Preussische Fest-Lieder,* Part I, 1642. The translation is by Catherine Winkworth from her *Lyra Germanica,* 1855. See No. 2 for comments on Miss Winkworth.

TRURO   See No. 82 for comments on TRURO.

115 On Jordan's Bank the Baptist's Cry

One of the few French poets whose hymns have found a place in English and American hymnals, Charles Coffin (1676–1749), eminent Latin scholar and churchman, was for a time rector of the University of Paris and later principal of the college at Beauvais. He wrote more than one hundred hymns, many of which were included in the Paris Breviary of 1736, a notable liturgical manual in the Roman Catholic Church containing psalms, prayers, scripture readings, hymns, and other devotional material for use in the Divine Office. See No. 59 and comments on the tune DIVA SERVATRIX, for further information on the Paris Breviary. He published in the same year his collection of hymns, *Hymni Sacri,* 1736, from which the present Advent hymn was taken, beginning in Latin, "Jordanis oras Praevia." His collected works appeared in two volumes in 1755. John Chandler (1806–1876), Anglican clergyman and gifted translator of early Latin hymns, included these lines in his *Hymns of the Primitive Church,* 1837, from which the English version has been taken. The alterations introduced by *Hymns Ancient and Modern* have been followed here.

WINCHESTER NEW   See No. 9 for comments on the tune.

116 Angels We Have Heard on High

Dating probably from the eighteenth century, this French carol was first published in *Nouveau recueil de cantiques,* 1855, beginning with the words, "Les anges dans nos campagnes." The translator is unknown. There are several English versions that have appeared in different hymnals, the present version being taken from the *Crown of Jesus,* 1862.

GLORIA is one of several names for this spirited tune with the refrain that brings special pleasure to adults as well as to children. The first half of the melody differs slightly in rhythm and cadences from its source, "Les anges dans nos campagnes," a French traditional carol of the eighteenth century.

The present text and harmonization, found in most carol collections in the United States, appeared in *Carols Old and Carols New,* 1916, edited by Charles L. Hutchins. No author, translator, or arranger is named with text or tune and only the second half of the refrain is given. However, in the same collection where the tune appears with "When the crimson sun had set," the refrain has twelve measures as at No. 116, and the Rev. S. S. Greatheed, English clergyman and musician who made some of the harmonizations for the *Hymnal Noted,* is listed as the arranger.

One finds almost as many forms of the melody as tune names, harmonizations, and texts. In the *Oxford Book of Carols,* 1928, the tune (in its traditional French form) was called IRIS and set to Montgomery's hymn "Angels from the realms of glory," which follows at No. 117.

117 Angels, From the Realms of Glory

As editor of *The Sheffield Iris,* James Montgomery included this poem, entitled "Nativity," in the Christmas Eve issue of his newspaper in 1816. It received little attention initially but after its appearance in his *Christian Psalmist,* 1825, where it was slightly revised, it soon became a great favorite. See No. 25 for further comments on Montgomery.

REGENT SQUARE   In the Church of Scotland, this tune is still sung with the hymn for which it was composed: "Glory be to God the Father," by Horatius Bonar. It was introduced into English hymnody along with LAN–CASHIRE (192), in *Psalms and Hymns for Divine Worship,* 1867, edited for the use of the English Presbyterian Church by Dr. James Hamilton, a "great champion of hymns," who named this tune for the Regent Square Church of which he was minister. REGENT SQUARE is found with Montgomery's Christmas hymn in most hymnals published in the United States but not in those of England and Scotland.

Henry Smart (1813–1879), a nephew of Sir George Smart (see No. 81) and son of a well-known violinist and piano manufacturer, declined the offer of a commission in the army and gave up law after four years of study so that he could follow the profession for which he had great aptitude and great enthusiasm. He did some study with William Kearns, a violinist prominent in English musical life in the mid-nineteenth century, but was largely self-taught. He became one of England's most eminent organists of the nineteenth century, distinguished not only as a performer, but in improvisation, service playing, composition and in the designing and installation of organs. While at the parish church in Blackburn he wrote an anthem for the tercentenary of the Reformation in England in 1835 which brought him favorable publicity. In 1836 he went to London and from then until his death served as organist and choirmaster successively in three prominent Anglican churches. During the last fifteen years of his life he was blind, but continued to play, compose, and even to supervise organ installations. A pension from the British government for his services to the cause of music was granted just a month before he died. Anthems, service music, hymn tunes, organ pieces, cantatas, operas, over two hundred part-songs (many of them for women's voices) were composed by him. Through his work as music editor of *The Chorale Book,* 1856, and *The Presbyterian Hymnal,* 1876, he exerted great influence on the harmonizations of hymn tunes in subsequent collections.

118 Break Forth, O Beauteous Heavenly Light

Crowned poet laureate in 1645 by Emperor Ferdinand III, Johann Rist (1607–1667) was a Lutheran pastor of many talents and interests. Although he had several opportunities to go to larger parishes and more important positions, he devoted most of his life to the people and the church in Wedel, on the Elbe River, near Hamburg, serving as both the pastor and the physician of the parish. His hymns, numbering approximately 680, were never sung in his home church during his lifetime but were widely used throughout the rest of Germany in both Protestant and Catholic communions. Despite the hardships and suffering he endured during the Thirty Years' War, he wrote a number of plays and secular poems, and became in addition an expert horticulturist. This Christmas hymn, based on Isaiah 9:2–7, was first published in his *Himlische Lieder,* 1641. The translation is from the version of Bach's *Christmas Oratorio* made by John Troutbeck (1832–1889), a translator for Novello, Ewer and Company, in London. He was chaplain and priest in ordinary to the queen, and compiled the *Westminster Abbey Hymn Book,* 1883.

ERMUNTRE DICH (SCHOP)   This chorale's most common name is derived from Johann Rist's hymn "Ermuntre dich, mein schwacher Geist" ("Bestir thyself, my feeble soul") of which stanza nine, "Brich an, O schönes Morgenlicht," is the source of the present translation. The melody, composed for the hymn by Johann Schop, was included in *Johann Risten Himlischer Lieder,* 1641, a collection of Rist's hymns for which Schop was music editor. It was in this book that Schop's music for "Werde munter, mein Gemüthe" ("Rouse thee up, my soul") first appeared — the chorale melody that has become familiar to many through its use with "Jesu, joy of man's desiring" in the setting from Bach's Cantata 147.

Rist, physician, pastor, and poet, and Schop, his fellow townsman, were intimate friends. In *Music in the Baroque Era,* Manfred Bukofzer speaks of these two men as being among those of the North German school whose collections of "sacred and secular miniature songs in very popular style" contributed to the literature of that period, which he calls the second great flowering in the history of the German song.

ERMUNTRE DICH was originally in triple meter. (Zahn 5741a) It appears in 6/4 in contemporary German hymnals. The present version, which differs melodically in the third phrase from the original, dates from Crüger's *Praxis pietatis melica,* 1648. It is the form in common use. In Bach's Cantatas 11 and 43, the melody is in 3/4; in the Christmas Oratorio (No. 12) it is in 4/4 with the harmonies used here. The melody also appeared with a figured bass by Bach in Schemelli's *Gesangbuch,* 1736.

Schop (c. 1590–1595–c. 1665–1667) was well known as an instrumentalist, skilled as violinist, lute player, trombonist, and cornettist. (*Zinke*) In

1615 he was in the court orchestra at Wolfenbüttel. From there he went (in 1615 or 1618) to the Danish court, remaining until 1619 when the plague struck. In Denmark he was renowned as a performer and teacher. Students came from all quarters to study with him. The historian, Johann Mattheson (1681–1764), spoke of him in the highest terms, saying that he was an artist without equal in his time and one of the finest violinists of the first half of the seventeenth century. After 1621 Schop held various posts in Hamburg — as violinist and organist to the town, later *Ratsmusikdirektor* and organist at St. James' Church. He composed much occasional music, suites (none extant), sacred concertos, instrumental music, and many chorale melodies.

119 As With Gladness Men of Old

The son of a well-known Bristol surgeon and author, William Chatterton Dix (1837–1898) combined a successful business career as manager of a marine insurance company in Glasgow with the career of a scholar and hymn writer. He published several volumes of poems and devotional works, including *Hymns of Love and Joy,* 1861; *Altar Songs, Verses on the Holy Eucharist,* 1867; *A Vision of All Saints,* 1871; *Seekers of a City,* 1878; and rendered a number of Greek and Abyssinian hymns and sequences into metrical form. This Epiphany hymn, written during an illness in 1860, prompted Sir Roundell Palmer (later Lord Selborne) to declare before a church congress at York in 1866 that he entertained great hopes for the future of British hymnody "when among its most recent fruits is a work so admirable in every respect as the Epiphany Hymn of Mr. Chatterton Dix."

DIX   See No. 66 for comments on the tune. The melody was named DIX for the author of this hymn.

120 Hark! The Herald Angels Sing

This hymn by Charles Wesley first appeared in his *Hymns and Sacred Poems,* 1739, and originally began with the lines, "Hark, how all the welkin rings, 'Glory to the King of kings.'" It was revised in the 1743 edition and then was published in its present and most common form in George Whitfield's *Collection* of 1753. It was one of five hymns included in the 1782 edition of the Supplement to the *New Version.* Julian has said of it that it is matched in popularity only by "Rock of Ages" and Bishop Ken's Morning and Evening hymns "and is excelled by none." See No. 43 for comments on Wesley.

MENDELSSOHN (BETHLEHEM; BERLIN; FESTGESANG)   It is said that this Christmas hymn is found in a greater number of old and new hymnbooks than any other of Charles Wesley's hymns, but it is probable that Mendelssohn's music has had much to do with its popularity even though the text had been in use for nearly 120 years before being set to the present tune in 1855. In that year this tune was adapted for Wesley's words by William H. Cummings (1831–1915) from Mendelssohn's *Festgesang*, Op. 68, for male voices and brass instruments, which was composed for and first sung at the Gutenberg Festival held at Leipzig in 1840 to celebrate the four hundredth anniversary of the invention of printing. The second movement of this work, "Vaterland in deinen Gauen," from which the hymn tune was adapted, extols Gutenberg. Cummings' adaptation is very close to the original. Several years before Cummings' use of the tune with Wesley's words, Mendelssohn wrote to his London publishers about an English translation of the *Festegesang* that was not entirely to his liking: "I must repeat the wish I already expressed in my letter to Mr. Bartholomew. I think there ought to be other words to No. 2. If the right ones are hit at, I am sure that piece will be liked very much by the singers and hearers, but it will *never* do to sacred words. . . . The words must express something gay and popular as the music tries to do it." Obviously, Cummings "hit at" the right words and nullified Mendelssohn's "never." The tune was published with Wesley's hymn in R. R. Chope's *Congregational Hymn and Tune Book*, 1857.

Cummings was singer, scholar, teacher, composer, editor, author. As a boy he sang in the choirs of St. Paul's Cathedral and the Temple Church, and in later years, after singing at Westminster Abbey and in the Chapel Royal, had a successful career as a tenor soloist in England, even filling engagements in the United States. He was noted for his singing of the principal tenor parts in Bach's Passions and other works. From 1879 to 1896 he was professor of singing at the Royal Academy of Music, and from 1896 to 1911 was principal of the Guildhall School of Music. He was one of the founders of the Purcell Society, editor of some of its publications, author of a biography of Purcell, and contributor to *Grove's Dictionary of Music*.

In his short life (1809–1847) Felix Mendelssohn was distinguished as a virtuoso pianist and organist, composer, conductor, and administrator, as well as linguist, artist, and master letter writer. He grew up with every material and cultural advantage in a family remarkable for the devotion of its members to one another and for their intellectual and artistic achievements. His father, Abraham Mendelssohn, a banker by profession, saw to it that his children made the most of their gifts and opportunities by holding them to a rigorous and demanding schedule of study. Felix's philosopher grandfather, Moses Mendelssohn (1729–1786), who was called the German Plato or the German Socrates after the publication of his *Phädon*, devoted much of his life to the emancipation of Jews in Germany. Through his German translation of the first five books of the Old Testament, the Psalms, and the Song of Solomon, they learned German and through its influence a new system of Jewish education was developed. A close friend of the German critic and dramatist, G. E. Lessing, he is considered to have been the model of the hero of Lessing's play *Nathan the Wise*.

Felix Mendelssohn's gifts as performer and composer were prodigious. At nine he performed publicly for the first time; from his twelfth year he composed in a variety of forms; at sixteen he wrote the *Octet* (Op. 20) for strings, at seventeen the matchless overture to *A Midsummer Night's Dream*. In 1833, when he was twenty-four, he conducted the Lower Rhine Festival so successfully that he was made the general musical director for the city of Düsseldorf; at twenty-six he was appointed director of the Gewandhaus concerts in Leipzig, the most coveted musical post in Germany. Under his direction the orchestra became the finest in Europe and attained worldwide distinction. In 1843 his dream of an academy of music in Leipzig became a reality with the founding of the Leipzig Conservatory which came to be the center of musical life not only of Germany but of other countries as well. He served as kapellmeister successively to the king of Saxony and the king of Prussia. When the latter, William IV, wanted to establish an academy of arts in Berlin, Mendelssohn was chosen to direct the music division, an appointment he accepted with misgivings and more from a sense of duty than from conviction. When plans for the academy failed to materialize, Mendelssohn was made director of the newly founded Domchor or Cathedral Choir in Berlin and put in charge of church music. He made ten trips to England where he was lionized as pianist, organist, composer, conductor, and was feted as a second Handel. His oratorio *Elijah,* one of the great oratorios in the history of that form, was first performed in England. Through piano and organ recitals, through orchestral and choral programs, he made known in Germany and England for the first time many of the works of Handel, Bach, Haydn, Mozart, and Beethoven, as well as music of his contemporaries. One of the great events in music history was his conducting of Bach's *St. Matthew Passion* in Berlin on March 11, 1829, one hundred years after its first performance by Bach in Leipzig (April 15, 1729). He was only twenty years old at the time and had never before conducted a large chorus and orchestra. This performance is generally considered to have given the initial and greatest impetus to the revival of Bach's music and to an awareness of his greatness as a composer.

121   From Heaven Above to Earth I Come

If Martin Luther (1483–1546) had contributed nothing more to the church than his hymns and discerning musical judgment, he would on that account alone deserve to be ranked among the great figures in Christian history. An accomplished musician himself, a skilled player on the flute and lute and possessing a fine tenor voice, he insisted that every minister be thoroughly trained in music, saying in his typically pungent way, "Those who have mastered this art are made of good stuff and are fit for any task." He also said: "I am strongly persuaded that after theology, there is no art that can be placed on a level with music; for besides theology, music is the only art capable of affording peace and joy of the heart, like that induced by the study of the science of divinity. A proof of this is that the devil, the originator of sorrowful anxieties and restless troubles, flees before the sound of music almost as much as before the Word of God." [1] Luther was largely responsible for restoring congregational singing and giving the hymn an important place in Christian worship, writing thirty-six hymns of his own in the vernacular. His adaptation of ancient plainsong melodies and secular songs created the German chorale which provided suceeding generations of German composers with some of their most inspiring themes. While extolling congregational singing, he also emphasized the role of the organist and choir, stressing high standards of musical excellence and freely drawing on all sources, Catholic or otherwise, for the music he employed, so long as it was of good quality. Of him, Philip Schaff said, "To Luther belongs the extraordinary merit of having given to the German people in their own tongue the Bible, the Catechism and the hymnbook, so that God might speak *directly* to them in His word, and that they might *directly* answer Him in their songs." [10]

This Christmas hymn, originally containing fifteen stanzas and based on a popular carol of the day, was written by Luther for his small son, Hans, for a Christmas Eve family celebration. The first few stanzas were sung by a man dressed as an angel, heralding the birth of Christ, and the next several stanzas were sung by the children in response to the angel's message, all joining in on the last stanza. The present version retains two of the stanzas sung by the herald, one sung by the children, and the doxology. The hymn first appeared in *Geistliche Lieder,* 1535, and the translation is from Catherine Winkworth's *Lyra Germanica,* 1855. See No. 2 for comments on Miss Winkworth.

VOM HIMMEL HOCH (ERFURT)   This anonymous tune, thought to have been adapted or composed by Luther, was set to his Christmas hymn in Schumann's *Geistliche Lieder,* 1539. It soon supplanted the melody of the popular pre-Reformation folk song "Aus fremden Landen komm ich her" ("From foreign lands I come") with which the words first appeared in 1535. (Zahn 344a) It has been said that no other hymn of Luther's is as simple and intimate in content and as folklike in structure as this one. The original melody follows. (Zahn 346)

Vom Him-mel hoch da komm ich her; ich bring
euch gu-te neu-e Mär, der gu-ten Mär bring
ich so viel, da-von ich sing'n und sa - gen will.

Bach used the chorale three times in his *Christmas Oratorio* (Nos. 9, 17, 23), and wrote several organ movements on it — one in the *Orgelbüchlein,* a fughetta, a fugue, an organ accompaniment for the melody, and the "Canonic Variations" — variations which Albert Schweitzer says are "full of Christmas joyousness and cheeriness." One of the best-known organ works of Johann Pachelbel (1653–1706), famous composer of Nürnberg, is based on this melody. For comments on Luther see No. 363.

122 God Rest You Merry, Gentlemen

Taken from a collection in the British Museum called the *Roxburghe Ballads,* Vol. III, c. 1770, this eighteenth-century Christmas carol is here given with the correct punctuation, that is, with the comma after "merry," so that the first line signifies, as it did originally, "God keep you merry," that is, cheerful, happy, tranquil.

In its traditional form, the carol contained eight stanzas.

GOD REST YOU MERRY was the first carol in the first series of *Christmas Carols New and Old,* 1871, edited by the Rev. H. R. Bramley and Dr. John Stainer. In his excellent Preface to the *Oxford Book of Carols,* 1928, Percy Dearmer says that the publication of this famous collection opened the second chapter in the nineteenth-century revival of Christmas carols and that Bramley and Stainer were mainly responsible for the restoration of the carol. As one looks through collection after collection of carols he realizes how many of Stainer's harmonizations are the accepted ones though not always credited to him. The present harmonization is one of those.

In the *Oxford Book of Carols* two tunes are given for these words. The tune used here is the version to which the carol has been sung in London from the eighteenth century on.

123 All My Heart This Night Rejoices

Appearing first in Johann Crüger's *Praxis pietatis melica,* 1653, with fifteen stanzas, this hymn by Paul Gerhardt has been described as "a glorious series of Christmas thoughts laid as a garland on the manger at Bethlehem." See No. 53 for comments on Gerhardt. It was freely translated by Catherine Winkworth in her *Lyra Germanica,* second series, 1858. See No. 2 for comments on Miss Winkworth.

WARUM SOLLT ICH (BONN; EBELING) The first name of this chorale melody by Ebeling is from Paul Gerhardt's hymn "Warum sollt' ich mich denn grämen" ("Why should sorrow so benumb me?") with which it was associated in a collection edited by the composer and published in 1666. The present hymn is a translation of another of Gerhardt's hymns, "Fröhlich soll mein Herze springen," which was set at first to a tune by Crüger but was later associated with "WARUM SOLLT ICH." The form of the melody given here is practically unchanged from the original, but that used by Bach in Motet No. 4 and in the *Christmas Oratorio* is quite different, taken from a 1713 collection edited by Daniel Vetter. There is one harmonization by Bach in the *Choralgesänge.*

Johann G. Ebeling (1637–1676), who wrote more than one hundred melodies for Gerhardt's hymns, was a prominent Lutheran musician of the seventeenth century. He succeeded Johann Crüger as cantor of St. Nicholas Church in Berlin, and was director of music at the College of St. Nicholas there. Later he became professor of music and cantor at the Carolinen Gymnasium at Stettin.

124 Bring a Torch, Jeannette, Isabella

Although some scholars attribute this delightful and sprightly French carol to Nicholas Saboly (1614–1675), a Provençal poet and musician, it is usually regarded as traditional. It was sung in Provence, France, at midnight on Christmas Eve. Families, carrying torches or candles, would join in processionals through the streets and greet each other with the words, "Jesus is come." It was a festive occasion, marked by the singing of carols, the ringing of bells, and the exchanging of greetings, and it recalls the ancient Jewish Festival of Lights, or Hanukkah. E. Cuthbert Nunn (1868–1914), to whom the translation is credited, was an English organist, composer, and conductor.

BRING A TORCH is an adaptation of the following melody written in 1672 by Marc-Antoine Charpentier (1634–1702) for the drinking song of Sganarelle in Molière's *Le Médecin malgré lui.*

The tune, with its original words, sung at a fast tempo with much gaiety, was heard in "Salut à Molière" given by the Théatre de France (Compagnie Renaud-Barrault) at the New York City Center in 1964. It is sung regularly in that company's performances of *Le Médecin malgré lui* in Paris, in a version that differs considerably from the original and is for the most part closer to the carol.

In Volume III of *Échos du temps passé,* J. B. Wekerlin gives the story of the composition of this song and prints the melody with the words for which it was composed. The tune itself became popular and in the course of time underwent melodic and rhythmic changes. It is now generally listed as a Provençal carol, sometimes attributed to Nicholas Saboly (1614–1675), poet-musician, organist and choirmaster of the Church of St. Pierre in Avignon, whose arrangements of Provençal Noëls have been sung for over two centuries. The present harmonization, as well as the translation, is largely that of E. Cuthbert Nunn.

Charpentier was, next to Lully, the most remarkable figure in French music of the middle baroque period, and musical collaborator with Molière after the latter's break with Lully. A pupil of Carissimi, he composed cantatas and other church music and established the oratorio in France, writing oratorios with Latin and French texts modeled on those of his teacher.

125 Good Christian Men, Rejoice

This early macaronic carol — that is, one combining Latin with another language, in this instance German and Latin — is a free translation by John Mason Neale of the old carol "In dulci jubilo" ("In sweet jubilation"). Tradition has it that the words were first sung by angels to Heinrich Suso (d. 1366), a Dominican monk and mystic, who was so enraptured that he joined the celestial host in "a heavenly dance." The earliest version, found in a Leipzig University manuscript (c. 1400), was first published in Klug's *Geistliche Lieder,* 1535. It first appeared in England in *Lyra Davidica,* a small collection of twenty-four hymns published anonymously in 1708, consisting largely of English translations from Latin and High German, and began with the lines:

> *In dulci jubilo*
> To the house of God we'll go.

John Mason Neale included the carol in his *Carols for Christmastide,* 1853, which he edited with Thomas Helmore. See No. 110 for comments on Neale.

IN DULCI JUBILO was first printed in Klug's *Geistliche Lieder,* in 1535, with the macaronic text from which the tune name is taken, but it probably originated in the fourteenth or early fifteenth century. It is said that the number of Catholic, Lutheran, and Bohemian hymnbooks which contained this carol in one form or another is too great to be counted. It was included in *Geystliche Lieder,* 1545, the last of the hymnbooks issued by Luther, with the third stanza somewhat altered in order to give it a Protestant cast. Originally this stanza was about the Virgin Mary. In current German hymnals one finds an all-German version, "Nun singet und seid froh," which appeared in 1646 and early in the nineteenth century displaced the Latin-German form. The Latin-English combination is given in *The Oxford Book of Carols,* No. 86. In *Piae Cantiones,* 1582, the text was given in Latin and Swedish.

Bach wrote two fine organ movements on IN DULCI JUBILO, one in the *Orgelbüchlein,* the other in the miscellaneous chorale Preludes. A list of twenty-five works for voice or organ in which the melody IN DULCI JUBILO has been used, is given in the Explanatory Notes at the end of G. R. Woodward's edition of *Piae Cantiones,* 1910.

Neale's version of the carol had News! News! after the third line — (Joy! Joy! Peace! Peace! in the other stanzas) — in order to fit what was thought by Thomas Helmore to be the correct form of the melody in *Piae Cantiones.* But in reading the old notation he had mistaken two short notes (the equivalent of two sixteenths at the end of measure six in the present version) for two long notes and thus added a measure of music, which did not belong there. This form of the text and melody, widely circulated through Bramley and Stainer's *Christmas Carols New and Old,* 1871, still appears in many collections. Fortunately it is simple to omit both words and music of the added measure. The present harmonization is based on Stainer's. (See No. 122.)

In *Church Music in History and Practice,* 1937, Winfred Douglas tells of the singing of this carol on Christmas Eve, 1741, under the leadership of

Count von Zinzendorf at the new Moravian mission in the settlement that became Bethlehem, Pennsylvania. There, four years later, it was sung simultaneously in thirteen languages with orchestral accompaniment. Douglas comments, "Surely the macaronic trend could go no further!" Tune and words of IN DULCI JUBILO appeared as follows in 1535. (Zahn 4947)

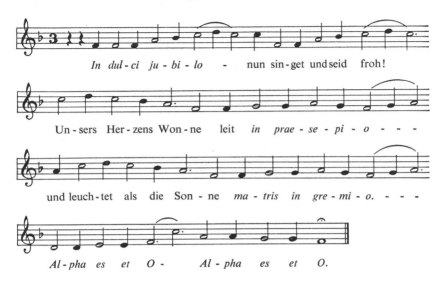

In dul-ci ju-bi-lo - nun sin-get undseid froh!

Un-sers Her-zens Won-ne leit *in prae-se-pi-o - - -*

und leuch-tet als die Son-ne *ma-tris in gre-mi-o. - - -*

Al-pha es et O - Al-pha es et O.

126 Brightest and Best of the Sons of the Morning

Although regarded as one of the finest of all of Bishop Heber's hymns, this Epiphany hymn was slow in winning approval, since many felt that the opening words bordered on star worship. While the phrase "the sons of the morning" is somewhat obscure, it may refer to angels, as would seem to be the case in Isaiah 14:12, and possibly also in Job 38:7. The hymn was first published in the *Christian Observer* for November, 1811, and was included in Heber's posthumous collection, *Hymns written and adapted to the Weekly Church Service of the Year,* 1827.

See No. 58 for comments on Heber.

MORNING STAR, part of an anthem written for use at the Gifford Hall Mission, Islington, London, was composed in 1892 by James (John) P. Harding (?–1911) amateur musician who was organist and choirmaster for thirty-five years at St. Andrew's Church in Islington and also served in the civil service for many years. He wrote anthems and part-songs, many of them for children's festivals at the mission, as well as secular songs for the musical association of the civil service.

Of Harding and his brother, W. Edmond Harding, also a benefactor of the mission, a friend wrote: "They lived glorious lives, seeking ever the material and spiritual well-being of the poor."

127 Christians, Awake, Salute the Happy Morn

John Byrom (1692–1763), after studying medicine, decided that his interests and talents lay elsewhere and so turned to literary pursuits. He devised and perfected a system of shorthand which he later taught to others with marked success. Parliament by a special act in 1742 authorized him to be the sole teacher of the system in England for twenty-one years. Among his pupils were John and Charles Wesley, the former making most of his entries in his famous journals and private papers in Byrom's shorthand. Byrom coined the phrase "Tweedledum and Tweedledee" in a popular epigram, referring to a dispute between friends of Handel and Bononcini as to their respective abilities as composers and meaning that the differences between them were so small as to be inconsequential. Many of his poems were first published in *The Spectator*. This hymn was written for his daughter, Dorothy, as a Christmas present in 1749. A facsimile copy of the first ten lines appeared in the *Musical Times*, 1902, carrying the heading "Christmas Day, For Dolly." Originally the hymn contained fifty-two lines. The full text is given in Erik Routley's *The English Carol*, 1959. It first appeared as a hymn in the ninth edition of *A Selection of Psalms and Hymns for Public and Private Use*, 1819, published by Thomas Cotterill and James Montgomery, and is especially appropriate for use on Christmas Day morning.

YORKSHIRE (STOCKPORT; WALWORTH)   In one of his notebooks Byrom (author of this hymn) wrote: "Christmas 1750. The singing men and boys with Mr. Wainwright came here and sang 'Christians, awake.'" ("Here" refers to Byrom's home in Manchester.) The hymn had been sung earlier in the day at the parish church in Stockport, six miles southeast of Manchester, where John Wainwright (c.1723–1768), composer of the tune, was organist. In 1767 he became "singing man" and organist at Manchester Collegiate Church, now the cathedral. Although he wrote the tune in 1749 or 1750, it was a long time before it and the words became generally known. The Rev. Caleb Ashworth, a Nonconformist preacher, named the tune MORTRAM (probably a misprint for Mottram, a village near Stockport) and set it to Psalm 50 in his *Collection*, c. 1760, the date of the tune's first publication. In Wainwright's own *Collection of Psalm-tunes, Anthems, Hymns*, 1766, he called it "Hymn for Christmas" but gave no name to the tune. Through the Rev. Ralph Harrison's *Sacred Harmony*, 1784, in which it was named STOCKPORT, the tune became widely known and found its way to the United States where it was included in many collections, usually for Watts' version of Psalm 50. In early nineteenth-century collections edited by Hastings, Mason, and Abner Jones, one finds this joyous tune set to the doleful words:

> Behold the Judge descends, his guards are nigh,
> Tempest and fire attend him down the sky.

It was named WALWORTH in American books. Benson says that it was the poet Montgomery who made a church hymn of the carol by arranging it for his friend Cotterill's *Selection of Psalms and Hymns*, 1819. Through the years, it had been sung in the north of England as one of the most popular

Christmas carols. There have been objections to the name YORKSHIRE which was given the tune in *Hymns Ancient and Modern*, 1861. The critics say that Wainwright was a Cheshire man who had nothing to do with Yorkshire. Perhaps the reason for the name is found in Davies Gilbert's *Some Ancient Christmas Carols*, 1823 (second edition), where the tune was printed with the following note: "Sent to the Editor from Yorkshire, since the preceding Carols were in the press." In *Studies of Familiar Hymns*, Second Series, 1923, Louis F. Benson comments:

> There are choir tunes, of delicate beauty, that one likes to listen to rather than to sing. And there are people's tunes that make one feel like joining in to swell the volume of sound. "Stockport" is just such a tune. It represents a period when people were getting tired of the old Psalm tunes . . . and church musicians were seeking a somewhat lighter and more cheerful type of tune. When one catches the spirit of its bluff heartiness and the swing of its melody it is still quite irresistible.[11]

128 In the Bleak Midwinter

The daughter of an Italian refugee who became professor of Latin at King's College, London, Christina Georgina Rossetti (1830–1894) was a gifted person with many talents. She wrote several volumes of poetry and a number of prose works. Because of her exceptionally fine features, she was selected by her noted brother, Dante Gabriel Rossetti, to sit as the model of the Virgin for his "Ecce Ancilla Domini." This Christmas poem, written possibly in 1872, was first used as a hymn in *The English Hymnal*, 1906, and vividly portrays the nativity scene as it might have taken place in England in the dead of winter rather than in the milder climate of Palestine. In giving a contemporary setting to the ancient story, Miss Rossetti achieved in poetry what the great medieval artists attained in their paintings.

CRANHAM   Christina Rossetti's poem was first set to music by Gustav Holst for *The English Hymnal*, 1906. Since then, words and music have taken their place alongside the best-loved traditional Christmas carols. The simplicity of the tune, in the A A B A form characteristic of many folk songs, seems to give perfect expression to the words.

Holst (1874–1934), whose great-grandfather came from Sweden to England around 1807, was one of England's leading composers of the twentieth century and a teacher of unusual gifts. Handicapped throughout life by defective eyesight and weak lungs and forced by neuritis to give up hopes of a career as a concert pianist, he never let those calamities deter him. A friend wrote to him, "I feel that the evil and scandal in the world must put its tail between its legs when it meets you." At seventeen he was organist and choir-director in a small church in the Cotswolds. At nineteen (1893) he entered the Royal College of Music where he stayed for five years, studying composition with Stanford and forming a lifelong friendship with Ralph Vaughan Williams. Holst also studied the trombone, and for a number of years made his living by playing it in theater orchestras and in pier bands at seaside resorts. In a lecture on "Gustav Holst: The Man and His Music," given at

Union Theological Seminary in May, 1957, Archibald T. Davison commented that this practical experience helped to give Holst a place among "the first orchestrators of this age." In 1898 Holst left the Royal College of Music to accept an appointment as first trombonist and coach with the Carl Rosa Opera Company, and later played with the Scottish orchestra.

From 1895 until his death Holst was musical director of St. Paul's, London's most aristocratic school for girls; from 1907 to 1924 was musical director at the Morley College for Working Men and Women; and from 1919 taught composition at the Royal College of Music. Every year the "Morleyites" and the girls from St. Paul's would join forces for a music festival, and the description of these festivals in Imogen Holst's biography of her father reveals his exceptional gifts for awakening enthusiasm for the best in music. During the war, when he was physically debarred from enlisting, he went to the Middle East under the auspices of the Y.M.C.A. to organize and direct musical activities for members of the armed forces. Percy Scholes, writing of Holst, says that he had power "from his village days, of communicating a love for the finest music to any body of men, women, or children with whom he might happen to meet."

In 1923 Holst conducted at the Musical Festival in Ann Arbor, Michigan, and in 1932 was lecturer in composition at Harvard for six months. That same year he conducted the Boston Symphony in three concerts featuring his own compositions. His compositions include choral and orchestral works, operas, anthems, many arrangements of carols and hymns. His love for folk music is shown in the number of arrangements he made of folk tunes, and its influence is apparent in his own music. One of Holst's maxims was: "A little learning is *not* a dangerous thing, as long as you know that it is only a little."

129 It Came Upon the Midnight Clear

One of the earliest American hymns to stress the social implications of the Christmas message, this hymn by Edward Hamilton Sears (1810–1876) quickly established itself as a favorite in this country and in England after its appearance in the *Christian Register,* Boston, in December, 1850. Although he devoted his entire ministry to serving Unitarian churches in Massachusetts, the greater part of it at Wayland, Sears was orthodox in his beliefs and is said to have been greatly influenced by Swedenborg. While others of his classmates at the Harvard Divinity School went on to large parishes and became well-known figures, he was content to remain in smaller churches, saying in later life, "I had no other ambition than to lead such a quiet pastorate as Goldsmith describes in the *Deserted Village."* He published several books during his lifetime, including *Regeneration,* 1853, *Foregleams of Immortality*, 1858, and *The Heart of Christ,* 1872, and was greatly admired by Elizabeth Barrett Browning. His name today is chiefly remembered because of this hymn.

CAROL   Richard Storrs Willis (1819–1900), composer of this tune, was the son of Nathaniel Willis, founder of *The Youth's Companion.* After graduation from Yale where he was active in student musical organizations he spent six years in Germany. He knew and studied with Mendelssohn and contributed a short but graphic description of him to the American edition of Lampadius' *Felix Mendelssohn-Bartholdy: Ein Denkmal für seine Freunde,* 1866. On his return from Germany, Willis was advised by Charles A. Dana to go into journalism, which he did, serving as music critic for the *New York Tribune, The Albion, The Musical Times,* later editing the latter and *The Musical World.* In 1856 he published *Our Church Music,* a practical handbook for pastors and musicians. CAROL is an adaptation of STUDY NO. 23, an original tune for "See Israel's gentle shepherd stand" in Willis' *Church Chorals and Choir Studies,* 1850, which contained arrangements of a good selection of chorales and psalm tunes as well as a number of original compositions. The first eight measures of the present hymn tune and a short coda constituted the "study" from which CAROL was taken. In a letter written in 1887, Willis said that while he was a vestryman of the Church of the Transfiguration ("The little church around the corner"), 1854–1861, he arranged this tune as a Christmas carol for "While shepherds watched their flocks by night." Later he gave a copy of the manuscript to Dr. Potter of Grace Church and found on his return from Europe in 1876 that it had been included in various collections. In some hymnals Uzziah Burnap is credited with the arrangement.

In English hymnals (which do not include CAROL) these words are set to NOEL, a traditional melody adapted and arranged by Arthur Sullivan.

130 Joy to the World! the Lord Is Come

Based on the last five lines of Psalm 98, this free paraphrase by Isaac Watts summons all nature to join in celebrating the birth of Christ. It was first published in Watts' *Psalms of David,* 1719, under the heading, "The Messiah's Coming and Kingdom." See No. 1 for comments on Watts.

ANTIOCH (COMFORT; HOLY TRIUMPH; MEDIA)   When James T. Lightwood, English hymnologist, asked the distinguished musician, Ebenezer Prout, about ANTIOCH's supposed Handelian ancestry, the latter said that he thought it was "very far from Handel." But certainly one can detect melodic snippets from the *Messiah* if he is willing to accept Lowell Mason's statement in his various collections that ANTIOCH is "from Handel." The first four notes of the tune are identical with those for the sopranos in the first measure of the chorus, "Lift up your heads, O ye gates"; and the music for the two short phrases "And heaven and nature sing" could have been taken from the introduction to the recitative "Comfort ye my people." The music for "And heaven and nature sing" was originally for sopranos and altos alone, in double thirds, a kind of passage that abounds in Mason's arrangements and in other books of the period. In America this tune is so indissolubly associated with Christmas that one never thinks of the hymn as being a paraphrase of Psalm 98. Originally text and tune had no particular Christmas significance. The combination does not appear in English hymnals.

131 Lo, How a Rose E'er Blooming

Of unknown authorship and uncertain origin, this Christmas or Twelfth Night carol, "Es ist ein' Ros' entsprungen," appears to have been current at the time of Luther and first appeared in print in a Catholic hymnal, *Speirischen Gesanbuch,* Cologne, 1599. In its complete version it related the events reported in the first two chapters of Luke and the second chapter of Matthew, giving special emphasis to the role of Mary in the nativity story. The rose tree was and is held in special regard throughout Germany and has continued to be widely employed as a symbol for Mary or for Christ. Theodore Baker, distinguished American scholar and music editor, is responsible for the translation. See No. 21 for comments on Baker. The hymn has also appeared in other translations as "A Great and Mighty Wonder," "I Know a Rose-tree Springing," "Behold a Branch Is Growing," and "The Noble Stem of Jesse."

EST IST EIN' ROS' (ROSA MYSTICA)   Michael Praetorius' familiar arrangement of this traditional German melody, first published in Vol. IV of *Musae Sionae,* 1609, was for many years considered to be only a choir number. Its slightly irregular rhythm seemed to make it difficult for congregational singing. Fortunately, the free rhythm, characteristic of most chorale and Genevan Psalter melodies in their original form, has come into more general use and no longer seems formidable to choirmasters or to congregations. In the Preface to *The English Hymnal,* 1906, Ralph Vaughan Williams says: "No attempt has been made to square the irregular times of some tunes. These irregularities are always easy to sing by ear — and this is the way in which a hymn melody should be learnt — so that choirmasters should not let the fear of what may appear to be irregular deter them from using many splendid and essentially congregational melodies." [12] The form of this melody is very simple — its first, second, and fourth phrases are identical, melodically, but the fourth is harmonized differently. The two measures for "It came, a flow'ret bright" provide the only melodic contrast. The German text for this carol may be found in the *Oxford Book of Carols,* No. 76. See No. 39 for comments on Praetorius.

132 O Come, All Ye Faithful

The probable author of this great Christmas hymn, John Francis Wade (c. 1711–1786), was an English layman who devoted most of his life to copying and selling manuscripts of plainsong and other early music. He lived and conducted his business at Douay, France, famous Catholic center to which many English Catholic refugees came following the abdication of James II in England. There are six extant manuscript copies of this text, all by Wade. The translation by Canon Frederick Oakeley (1802–1880), somewhat altered by later editors, is based on the Latin version used in England rather than that in use in France. Oakeley was associated with the Oxford Movement in its beginnings and later joined the Catholic Church. The hymn was first published in America in Benjamin Carr's *Musical Journal,* II, 1800.

ADESTE FIDELES (PORTUGUESE HYMN; OPORTO) Despite much research on the part of many people, nothing is known positively of the origin of the words or the tune of this celebrated Christmas hymn. Its authorship has been called a "tantalizing problem, much like a jigsaw puzzle." However, in *The Adeste Fideles; a study on its origin and development,* 1947, Dom John Stéphan describes in detail how his study of a fairly recently discovered small manuscript book which included ADESTE FIDELES convinced him that Wade was both author and composer, even though the title page was missing and there was no signature or date. Furthermore, he came to believe that this manuscript was Wade's first and original version of the hymn. He admits that his theory may be disproved, but states the case for Wade convincingly.

After the publication of ADESTE FIDELES in Part II of the *Essay on the Church Plain Chant,* 1782 (its first printed form, with no composer's name given), it became popular with Catholics and Protestants alike. In the six extant manuscript copies the tune is in triple time; in Samuel Webbe's copy it is in duple time, altered (Dom Stéphan suggests) with Wade's consent, and arranged for four parts. Erik Routley reminds us that the two most celebrated tunes taken over from Roman Catholic sources, ADESTE FIDELES and MELCOMBE, are from this 1782 collection (see No. 36). In all these manuscripts the melody in measure 12 skips down a third, as at No. 132. The refrain, in its present familiar arrangement, contains an example of a fuguing tune with the phrase for sopranos "O come, let us adore him" being repeated two measures later by the tenors. Such repeat tunes were popular in England and America in the late eighteenth and early nineteenth centuries.

PORTUGUESE HYMN, the name for this tune in many hymnals, has been the subject of much speculation. According to Vincent Novello (1781–1861), founder of the music publishing firm, Novello and Co., in 1811, the tune was so named by the Duke of Leeds when he introduced it at his Ancient Concerts after hearing it sung at the chapel of the Portuguese Embassy in London c. 1785.

Novello himself, in a collection he published in 1843, set the tune to a version of Psalm 100 calling it "Air by Reading, 1680," but nothing resembling it has been found in the works of either of the two English composers who bore that name. Dom Stéphan, noting that one of Wade's manuscripts was made for the use of the English College at Lisbon, suggests that "it may have spread to other choirs of the Portuguese capital, and gone from there to other countries." He also mentions and dismisses as unfounded the tune's supposed connection with one Portogallo. In early nineteenth-century American hymnbooks the tune was generally called PORTUGUESE HYMN, and often appeared with the words:

> The Lord is our shepherd, our guardian and guide,
> Whatever we want He will kindly provide.

In one of his hymnals Lowell Mason labels it "Romish Melody." Dom Stéphan comments on the fact that there is one form of this tune found in every hymnbook in the English language, that it is probably "one of the very few hymns that has found its place in every collection of Christian hymns," and that no attempt has been made to supplant the original tune with an alternative.

133 Adeste Fideles

The Latin original contained eight stanzas, of which this version retains stanzas one, seven, and eight from the English version. The original second stanza, not included here, began with the words, "Deum de Deo, Lumen de Lumine" ("God of God, Light of Light"). See No. 132 for comments on the English translation.

ADESTE FIDELES   See No. 132 for comments on the tune.

134 O Little Town of Bethlehem

Regarded by many as the foremost preacher America has produced, Phillips Brooks (1835–1893) wrote these words for the children in his Sunday school at Holy Trinity Church, Philadephia, in 1868, following a visit to Bethlehem and the Holy Land in 1866. First printed in leaflet form, this hymn, now so widely known and esteemed, was slow in gaining recognition. As a boy Brooks was taught to memorize new hymns and recite them for the benefit of his family each Sunday so that by the time he entered Harvard he is said to have known two hundred by heart. He intended originally to become a teacher and only turned to the ministry after proving to be a "conspicuous failure" in this role at Boston Latin School. Although Brooks never married he had a special fondness for children. He was an eloquent spokesman for orthodox Christianity during the Unitarian controversy, and was greatly admired and beloved in England as well as in this country. His volumes of sermons and his book *Lectures on Preaching,* based on a series of lectures he gave at Yale Divinity School in 1877, are regarded as classics. Oxford University conferred the Doctor of Divinity degree upon him in 1885, and a statue of him by Augustus Saint-Gaudens stands next to Trinity Church, Copley Square, Boston, where throngs of people came to hear him preach.

ST. LOUIS   Lewis N. Redner (1831–1908), composer of ST. LOUIS, the original tune for Phillips Brooks' Christmas hymn, was born and educated in Philadelphia. He was a highly successful real estate broker who devoted much time to church, Sunday school, and music, and served as organist in four Philadelphia churches. He was at Holy Trinity when Phillips Brooks was rector there. Well before Christmas, Redner was asked to provide music for Brooks' hymn, but a tune did not take shape in his mind until the middle of the night before the day on which it was to be sung. He jotted down the melody, and the next morning (December 27, 1868) sketched in the harmonies in time for the Christmas service of the Sunday school. Although tune and words were known and sung locally for many years, they did not appear in the *Hymnal* (Episcopal) until 1892. The tune was named ST.

LOUIS by the Rev. Dr. William Huntington, rector of All Saints' Church, Worcester, Massachusetts, in his Sunday school hymnbook, *The Church Porch*, 1874. Brooks' hymn was hardly known in England until it appeared in *The English Hymnal*, 1906, set to FOREST GREEN (No. 456), a traditional English melody harmonized by Ralph Vaughan Williams. It is the tune most often sung with the carol in Great Britain although CHRISTMAS CAROL by Walford Davies appears with it in several hymnals. Redner's tune does not appear in English hymnals.

135 O Jesu Sweet, O Jesu Mild

Valentin Thilo (1607–1662) was for twenty-eight years professor of rhetoric at the University of Königsberg, where he was elected dean of the philosophical faculty five times and twice served as rector of this outstanding educational institution later made famous by Immanuel Kant. He wrote a number of hymns for the great festivals of the church year. This poem, ascribed to Thilo, is his most widely known hymn. The translation is by E. Harold Geer (1886–1957), choirmaster and organist emeritus at Vassar College and editor of the *Hymnal for Colleges and Schools* (known as the Yale Hymnal), Yale University Press, New Haven, 1956.

O JESULEIN SÜSS   This melody, set to an Easter hymn, had the following form in a Roman Catholic hymnbook published at Cologne in 1623. (Bäumker, Vol. I, No. 279.) It was anonymous.

Ist dass der Leib Herr Je - su Christ, Der todt   im Grab ge-

le - gen ist,   Kom,kom, O   kom, kom jung und   alt, Kom schaw
          Al - le - lu - ia,   Al - le - lu - ia   Al - le-

die schö - ne Leibs Ge - stalt, Al - le - lu - ia,   Al - le - lu - ia.
lu - ia,   Al - le - lu - ia,   Al - le - lu - ia,   Al - le - lu - ia.

It appeared in two Protestant collections published in 1650; and from then on in both Protestant and Catholic hymnals with a variety of texts. It was set to "O Jesulein süss, O Jesulein mild" for the first time in the Görlitz *Tabulatur-Buch*, 1650, an important collection of one hundred chorales harmonized by Samuel Scheidt (1587–1654), one of the three celebrated "S's" of Germany: Schein, Scheidt, and Schütz. A pupil of the great Jan P. Sweelinck of Amsterdam, Scheidt was the best German organist of his time, renowned for his playing, his organ and vocal compositions, and for his contributions to the development of the art of organ playing and composition. The tune was given its present melodic and harmonic form by J. S. Bach who edited the music in G. C. Schemelli's *Musicalisches Gesang-Buch,* 1736, which contained spiritual songs and arias. In the preface to this collection of 954 melodies it was stated that they were "partly composed and partly improved in their figured basses by Herr J. S. Bach of Leipzig." In some German and American Lutheran hymnals, O JESULEIN SÜSS, with simpler harmonies, appears with a Pentecost (*Pfingsten*) hymn, "O heiliger Geist, O heiliger Gott." Other English translations associated with it are: "O Saviour sweet, O Saviour kind" and "O Little One sweet, O Little One kind." The correct English pronounciation of *Jesu* is Jē-sŭ, with a long *e* and the *u* as in *unite*. Too often the word is given its Latin pronunciation when sung in an English translation.

136 On This Day Earth Shall Ring

One of the most invaluable sources of medieval songs and carols, both sacred and secular, is the famous collection *Piae Cantiones* published in Griefswald, Sweden, in 1582, from which this hymn was taken. The collection was assembled and edited by a young Finnish student, Theodoric Petri, while studying at the University of Rostock. It contains Latin texts and plainsong tunes and other medieval music, from Swedish, German, Hussite, and other sources, dating from the tenth to the sixteenth centuries. Petri saw the need to preserve these great pre-Reformation and early Lutheran songs and carols for future generations. Had it not been for his great interest and careful scholarship, many of these treasures would have been irretrievably lost. In 1852, the British Minister in Stockholm, G. J. R. Gordon, was presented with a copy of this rare volume, and he brought it to London where it may now be seen in the British Museum. The present translation is by Jane Marion Joseph (c. 1894–1929), a gifted young English musician who studied under Gustav Holst. The word *ideo* means *therefore* and suggests that we sing our glorias at Christmas because of what God has done in Christ.

PERSONENT HODIE This delightfully square-cut traditional German tune, with its "steady, unflinching rhythm" and its stirring refrain, has been traced to a Mosburg gradual of 1360; its source is unknown. The Latin carol "Personent hodie," with which the melody appeared in *Piae Cantiones,* 1582, and in *The Oxford Book of Carols,* 1928, was probably a parody of an older German *cantio* in honor of St. Nicholas — "Intonent hodie," the words with which the music appeared in the 1360 gradual. In the Latin text the words of the refrain differ in each stanza; for instance, in stanza 1 they are: "et de vir, vir, vir, et de vir, vir, vir, et de virgineo ventre procreatus." These changes make the carol even more rousing than when *ideo* is repeated at the end of each stanza. The melody is in the Dorian mode (*d* to *d* on white notes of the piano), one of the eight church or ecclesiastical modes which dominated music for centuries and which have been brought into considerable use again by contemporary composers. Gustav Holst's arrangement of the tune adds greatly to the effectiveness of the carol. For comments on Holst, see No. 128.

137 Away in a Manger

Popularly known as "Luther's Cradle Hymn" and frequently attributed to him, this delightful carol is undoubtedly of American origin, probably coming from the pen of an anonymous Lutheran author in Pennsylvania during the nineteenth century. The scattered facts about the carol were brought together in a scholarly and interesting article by Richard S. Hill published in the December, 1945, issue of *Music Library Association Notes,* Second Series, III, No. 1, under the arresting title, "Not so far away in a Manger: forty-one settings of an American carol." A full account of Mr. Hill's research is given in Armin Haeussler's excellent handbook, *The Story of Our Hymns,* pages 158–161. The carol was first published in a collection authorized in 1885 by the General Council of the Evangelical Lutheran Church in North America, *Little children's book: for schools and families,* and is a favorite in the United States but is hardly known in Germany.

AWAY IN A MANGER   Although in the past this melody has been variously ascribed to Martin Luther, Carl Mueller, and James R. Murray, in recent years it has more often been captioned "Anonymous" because of the seeming impossibility of ascertaining its source. Sometimes one finds the words assigned to Luther, the music to Mueller. No one knows who this Mueller was. The connection of his name with the tune goes back to *Worship and Song,* 1921, published by the Pilgrim Press, but they have no information about him. Murray's claim to its composition rests on the appearance of his initials J. R. M. with it in *Dainty songs for little lads and lasses,* 1887, which he edited. The present harmonization is very close to Murray's. "Luther's Cradle Hymn" was the caption for the carol, with the additional parenthetical comment: "Composed by Martin Luther for his children, and still sung by German mothers to their little ones." In *The Hymnal 1940 Companion* it is suggested that it was probably Murray's heading that "spread the myth throughout the land" that this tune was Luther's. In a later collection (1888) Murray wrote over the tune: Music by J. R. M. Evidently others had been attributing the tune to Luther, the arrangement to Murray. In *The Story of Our Hymns,* 1952, Dr. Armin Haeussler states his conviction that the tune is without question by Murray but notes that "he has never been credited with being the composer except in his own collections." and adds "For this he has only himself to blame, since his very first edition gave the impression that Martin Luther composed the music." [13] Of the forty-one or more tunes associated with the carol, two besides AWAY IN A MANGER are rather well known. CRADLE SONG by W. J. Kirkpatrick (1838–1921), an American, is said to have taken the carol beyond the confines of America and is the tune sung with these words in Great Britain and Canada. There are many people in the United States who still prefer to sing the carol to the melody of "Flow Gently, sweet Afton" written in 1838 by J. S. Spilman.

138 Silent Night, Holy Night

First sung on Christmas Eve, 1818, in the village church in Oberndorf, Upper Austria, this familiar and beloved hymn was written by Joseph Mohr (1792–1848), assistant priest in St. Nicholas Church. Because of a breakdown in the organ, his efforts were inspired by the need to prepare a different Christmas Eve program from the one that had previously been planned. This hauntingly beautiful hymn was the result, sung originally to the accompaniment of a guitar. See comments below on the tune. It was heard by the man who repaired the organ and was carried by him to other Tyrolean towns, from whence it has gone around the world and "is sung as reverently in the Himalayas of India as in the Alps of Austria." Thanks to the careful research investigations of the Rev. Byron E. Underwood, rector of St. Ann's Episcopal Church, Revere, Massachusetts, the translator of this familiar version is now known to be Bishop John Freeman Young (1820–1885), distinguished American hymnologist and liturgiologist and second bishop of the Episcopal Diocese of Florida. His translation first appeared in John Hollister's *The Sunday-School Service and Tune Book,* 1863, and was later included in Young's posthumous collection, *Great Hymns of the Church,* 1887. A full account of Mr. Underwood's research is given in *The Hymn,* October, 1957, Volume 8, Number 4, pp. 123–130. Bishop Young's translation consists of stanzas one, six, and three of the original text.

STILLE NACHT   There are many different accounts of the origin of this carol, some of them highly fanciful and sentimental. According to the most reliable sources, Franz Gruber, acting organist at the Church of St. Nicholas in Oberndorf, where Mohr was assistant priest, wrote the tune for his words a few hours before the Christmas Eve service, 1818. Mohr, a tenor, sang the melody, Gruber sang bass and played his guitar. Gruber (1787–1863), the son of a linen weaver, was forced to learn his father's trade in spite of his desire to be a musician. He took organ lessons secretly, and when he substituted successfully for an organist who was ill, his father was reconciled to the idea of his continuing with music. He left the loom at eighteen, and became an apprentice to Georg Hartdobler, organist of the town church in Burghausen. Most of his life was spent in three towns — Arnsdorf, Oberndorf, Berndorf — in the vicinity of Salzburg, as schoolteacher and organist. From 1833 to 1863 he was choral director at Hallein. STILLE NACHT is the one tune by which he is known. Oddly enough, it does not appear in German Protestant or English hymnals nor in the *Oxford Book of Carols,* but is included in Catholic collections.

Karl Maraucher, the organ repair man from Zillerthal, had much to do with making the tune known, for after hearing it he passed it on to friends who were folk singers and included STILLE NACHT in their programs of Tyrolean songs at fairs and concerts throughout Austria and Germany. Although generally considered a Tyrolean folk song, STILLE NACHT was sometimes attributed to Michael Haydn, and in 1854 when the Royal Court Band in Berlin was trying to trace its source, an inquiry was sent to the Benedictine monastery of St. Peter's in Salzburg where Haydn had spent much time. Gruber's youngest son, Felix, a choirboy there, was told of the inquiry and passed it on to his father, whose letter telling of the composition of the tune is reproduced and translated in *Stille Nacht, Heilige Nacht,* 1933, by Melbert B. Cary, Jr., and his wife, Mary Flagler Cary, who give an account of their trip to Austria to learn about the carol's origin. The church in Oberndorf where STILLE NACHT was first sung, was swept away by the Salzach flood in 1899; but there is a new St. Nicholas Church in which a memorial plaque honors Mohr and Gruber, whose beloved carol is sung there every Christmas Eve.

139 Stille Nacht, Heilige Nacht

Although there are many versions of this hymn in German, and many variations in the text, this version is the one in most common use. It was a favorite of the great German contralto, Mme. Ernestine Schumann-Heink, who sang it as an encore at many of her concerts. The original manuscript has not been discovered and presumably has been lost. The hymn first appeared in a collection popularly known as the *Leipziger Gesanbuch,* 1838. See No. 138 for additional comments on the text.

STILLE NACHT   See No. 138 for comments on the tune.

140 What Child Is This, Who, Laid to Rest

These three stanzas were taken from a longer Christmas poem, "The Manger Throne," written by William C. Dix. See No. 119 for comments on Dix.

GREENSLEEVES   Here is a traditional English ballad tune that has been sung to so many different sets of words that it would be impossible to list them all. It was mentioned by Shakespeare and other writers of his time, to say nothing of the discussions of it in books about folk songs. Lady Green Sleeves, "an inconstant ladylove," seems to have given her name to the tune. Political ballads of the Cavaliers during the Civil War were sung to it; a song in *The Beggar's Opera,* "Since laws were made for every degree," was set to it; and even hymns "declaring the manifold benefites and blessings of God" were associated with a modified form of it. In Chappell's *Popular Music of the Olden Time,* 1855–1859, several pages are devoted to this tune and to the great variety of texts found with it. *The Oxford Book of Carols,* 1928, prints the tune with a carol for the New Year, "The old year now away is fled," with which it appeared in 1642. Some versions of the tune have a C sharp in measures one and five of the refrain. Except for the last chord in measures two, six, ten, and fourteen, the present harmonization is Stainer's. (See No. 122.)

141 The First Nowell

This traditional English carol, with the refrain given in the old English form, originally contained nine stanzas of which this is a cento of stanzas one, two, three, four, and six. The original Latin word *Natalis,* meaning birth or birthday, appears as *Noël* in French, *Natal* in Spanish, and *Natale* in Italian. The word *Nowell* is a joyous expression that was sung or shouted as a word of greeting to celebrate the birth of Christ. The carol was first published in Davies Gilbert's *Some Ancient Christmas Carols,* 1823, second edition.

THE FIRST NOWELL   The source of this tune, as of the text, is unknown. Percy Dearmer says that it is not later than the seventeenth century. There are those who think that it may have been a descant to an older tune that has been lost. Both text and tune as we know them appeared in William Sandys' *Christmas Carols, Ancient and Modern,* 1833. Sandys (1792–1874), a lawyer and musical amateur, did much to preserve traditional carols and to interest people in them. The present harmonization is from Bramley and Stainer's *Christmas Carols New and Old,* 1871. (See No. 122.) The tune is made up of three practically identical phrases. The only melodic contrast comes in the refrain with the third and fourth "Nowell," and the omission of two eighth notes leading up to "Born" in measure five.

142   Unto Us a Boy Is Born

First found in a fifteenth century manuscript in Trier, Germany, this Latin Christmas song, "Puer Nobis Nascitur," was translated into English in its present form by Percy Dearmer for *The Oxford Book of Carols,* 1928. See No. 112 for comments on Dearmer.

PUER NOBIS (OMEGA AND ALPHA) is the melody found with the Latin original of this German carol in a Trier manuscript of the fifteenth century. The large number of variants found with it, some in triple rhythm as at No. 144, attest its popularity and wide use. The harmonization given here is the first section of an arrangement made by Geoffrey Shaw for *The Oxford Book of Carols,* 1928, in which each of the five stanzas has a different setting. In *Songs of Praise, Enlarged,* 1931, the tune is named OMEGA AND ALPHA, obviously because of the words in stanza five. The first stanza of the Latin text which appeared with the melody in *Piae Cantiones,* 1582, the source of the present version, follows.

> Pu-er no-bis nas-citur,
> Rec-tor an-ge-lo-rum,
> In hoc mun-do pan-di-tur
> Do-mi-nus Do-mi-no-rum,
> Do-mi-nus Do-mi-no-rum.

143   We Three Kings of Orient Are

An outstanding figure in the Episcopal Church during the nineteenth century in the fields of church music and the liturgical arts, John Henry Hopkins, Jr. (1820–1891), was successively a reporter, law student, teacher, editor, and priest. He published several books, including *Carols, Hymns and*

Songs, 1863, from which this Epiphany hymn was taken, and he was the rector of churches in Plattsburg, New York, and Williamsport, Pennsylvania. While some have criticized this hymn, because of its vivid legendary imagery, the editors of *The Oxford Book of Carols* describes it as one of the most successful modern examples of a carol. It lends itself readily to dramatic presentations inasmuch as the first and last stanzas can be sung in concert by all three kings while the middle three stanzas can be sung as solos.

KINGS OF ORIENT   Both text and tune of this carol were written by Dr. John H. Hopkins, Jr., a native of Vermont, grandson of the second Episcopal bishop of that state, and the first instructor in music at General Theological Seminary in New York City, from which he was graduated in 1850. He was the founder of *The Church Journal* and its editor from 1853 to 1868. Because of the folk-song character of this melody, Hopkins has often been thought of as its arranger rather than as its composer. Its inclusion in the third series of Bramley and Stainer's *Christmas Carols New and Old,* 1871, and in *The Oxford Book of Carols,* 1928, shows how widely it has been known and sung in England. In *The Hymnal 1940* (No. 51) this carol is given as it appeared originally in Hopkins' *Carols, Hymns and Songs,* 1863. There the rhythm of the melody for "O" at the start of the refrain was ♩♪. The lengthening of those two notes dates from the Stainer version as do the E minor chords in measure five and nine. The mistaken dotted quarters for "perfect" in measures seventeen and eighteen of the refrain should be ♩♪.

144 What Star Is This, With Beams so Bright

Although much altered in its present translated form, this Epiphany hymn by Charles Coffin, originally beginning, "Quae stella sole pulchrior," retains much of its original charm and beauty. Now often found in modern French breviaries as the first vesper hymn in Epiphany, it first appeared in Coffin's collection of Latin poems, *Hymni Sacri,* 1736, and was translated into English in John Chandler's *Hymns of the Primitive Church,* 1837. See No. 115 for comments on Coffin and Chandler.

PUER NOBIS NASCITUR   The tune names of Nos. 142 and 144 show their close relationship; both stem from the same melody which appeared in a variety of forms with the words "Puer nobis nascitur" (Unto us a son is born). The earliest printing of this tune seems to have been in 1568; Zahn states that it is found in fifteenth-century manuscripts. Comments on the melody and on Praetorius may be found at No. 39. The harmonization given here is largely that of the Rev. George R. Woodward in *The Cowley Carol Book,* 1901, where it is set to "Geborn ist Gottes Sönelein" for which Praetorius adapted the melody in 1609. The harmonies in measures nine, ten, and eleven, however, are from *The English Hymnal,* 1906, where, although attributed to Woodward, they differ from his setting. Woodward (1848–1934) was clergyman, scholar, musician, editor, accomplished linguist whose *Songs of Syon* (1904–1910) made a unique contribution to English hymnody. Not intended "to compete with existing hymnals but only to supplement them," it is an invaluable source book. It includes plainsong melodies, metrical melodies from the thirteenth to the sixteenth centuries, Lutheran tunes, English and Scottish psalm tunes, French psalm tunes and canticles. Woodward himself provided translations for many fine tunes of unusual meters.

145 O Morning Star, How Fair and Bright

Known as the queen of chorales, this noble hymn by Philipp Nicolai was written during a period of intense suffering while a pestilence raged through Westphalia. First published in the Appendix to his *Frewden-Spiegel* ("Mirror of Joy"), 1599, it immediately established itself as a favorite in Germany and was frequently sung at weddings where it came to be regarded as almost an indispensable part of the service. Nicolai wrote it, initially with seven stanzas, in the space of a few hours, during a profoundly personal religious experience as he brooded over the distress around him and then thought of the consolations of the gospel. It is said that he refused to be disturbed while he worked on it, forgetting everything about him, even his midday meal. See No. 24 for further comments on Nicolai. The present translation, extensively altered, is taken from Catherine Winkworth's *Chorale Book for England*, 1863. See No. 2 for comments on Miss Winkworth. There are several other translations, including "How Bright Appears the Morning Star" and "How Brightly Shines the Morning Star."

WIE SCHÖN LEUCHTET (FRANKFORT) This deservedly renowned melody, called the queen of chorales and the golden chorale, first appeared with Nicolai's hymn in 1599 and is attributed to him although it was undoubtedly based on older material. The melody of "Jauchzet dem Herren, alle Land," a setting for Psalm 100 in a 1538 Strasbourg psalter was probably Nicolai's source, for whole sections of it are identical with phrases of the chorale. This in no way detracts from the majesty of his adaptation which follows. (Zahn 8359)

Wie schön leuch - tet der Mor - gen - stern, voll Gnad und Wahr - heit
Du Sohn Da - vids aus Ja - kobs Stamm, mein Kö - nig und mein

von dem Herrn, die sü - sse Wur - zel Jes - se! lieb-lich, freund-lich,
Bräu - ti- gam, hast mir mein Herz be - ses - sen,

schön und herr - lich, gross und ehr - lich, reich von Ga - ben, hoch und

sehr präch - tig   er - ha - ben.

In *Christian Singers of Germany* Catherine Winkworth wrote of this hymn: "So popular did it soon become, that its tune was often chimed by city chimes, lines and verses from it were printed by way of ornament on the common earthenware of the country, and it was invariably used at weddings and certain festivals." Since 1666 it has been associated with Paul Gerhardt's "Wie schön ists doch, Herr Jesu Christ," a hymn for weddings with which it still appears in German hymnals. Strangely enough, this chorale was also frequently sung around deathbeds. Bach used Nicolai's melody in Cantatas 1, 36, 37, 49, 61, 172, with varying texts, and in one of the miscellaneous Preludes for organ. There is one harmonization of it in the *Choralgesänge*. The present harmonization is from the Advent Cantata No. 36; several fermata and a few passing notes are omitted. Of many organ compositions based on this melody, the *Chorale Fantasia* by Dietrich Buxtehude (c. 1637–1707) is one of the most distinguished.

146 While Shepherds Watched Their Flocks

In publishing their famous collection *A Supplement to the New Version of the Psalms,* 1700, which contained sixteen hymns, Nahum Tate and Nicholas Brady hoped that the churches might thereby learn to sing something other than literalistic metrical versions of the psalms. This hymn by Tate, however, is the only one to have survived. It has been translated into Latin and many modern languages and has remained in use largely unaltered, as in this version. Perhaps one reason for its success, at least initially, is that it so faithfully paraphrases the text on which it is based, Luke 2:8–14. See No. 81 for comments on Tate.

WINCHESTER OLD   Although many Americans are accustomed to sing these words to CHRISTMAS (362), the association of WINCHESTER OLD with Tate's hymn goes back to *Hymns Ancient and Modern,* 1861, which revived the tune after two hundred years of neglect. In Este's *Whole Book of Psalmes,* 1592, it had appeared unnamed with a version of Psalm 84, "How pleasant is thy dwelling place," in a four-part setting by George Kirbye, one of ten eminent composers who harmonized the tunes in the book. It was one of four new Common Meter tunes that appeared for the first time. It was named WINCHESTER in Ravencroft's Psalter, 1621.

Thomas Este (Est, Easte, East), 1540?–1609, was a famous printer and music publisher, celebrated for the collections of Italian and English madrigals which he issued. Este's Psalter, which held the field for many years, was distinguished by the quality of its music and is credited with being the first in which distinctive names were given to tunes (three had place names) and voice parts were printed on opposite pages instead of in separate part-books.

WINCHESTER OLD seems to have been adapted from the second half of a melody for chapter eight of Christopher Tye's *Actes of the Apostles, Translated into Englyshe Metre,* 1553. It contained four-part settings composed by Tye for his own versifications of the early chapters of Acts. Tye's *Actes* were not written for use in church but to spread the knowledge of the "good and Godlye storyes of the lyves of Christ hys Appostles" with simplicity and tunefulness through music that was to be sung, or played on the lute. The eight-line, C.M.D. tunes which he wrote, served as a quarry out of which phrases were taken by later editors for some of the shorter four-line church tunes in Common Meter. (See No. 226 — WINDSOR.) Christopher Tye (c. 1500– c. 1572) was one of England's greatest sixteenth-century composers. Little is known of his early life. He had Mus.B. and Mus.D. degrees from Cambridge, was master of the choristers at Ely Cathedral and a gentleman of the Chapel Royal under Edward VI, Mary, and Elizabeth. In 1560 he was ordained a priest and gave up his musical positions. He is sometimes spoken of as the father of the anthem, because of his influence on the style and development of English church music. Although one of the masters of Tudor polyphony, he seems to have chosen deliberately to write music for the new church services that was direct, almost popular in character, and in the simpler musical style called for by the language and the liturgy of the new English *Book of Common Prayer.* Tye is said to have done more than any man to rescue church music from ruin after the dissolution of the monasteries by keeping it up in the cathedrals and at court and by giving in his music a model that was accepted and imitated by Elizabethan church musicians.

147 All Praise to Thee, for Thou, O King Divine

Based on Paul's famous exhortation to the Philippians, 2:5–11, this hymn by F. Bland Tucker (1895–   ) was written in 1938 and first appeared in *The Hymnal 1940.* Tucker was a member of the commission that prepared this hymnal and has served as rector of Episcopal churches in Virginia, Washington, D.C., and Georgia.

ENGELBERG is connected with Bishop How's hymn "For all the saints" (306) in a number of ways. It was composed for that text by Stanford for *Hymns Ancient and Modern,* 1904, which has retained it ever since with the composer's varied settings for different stanzas which add greatly to its effectiveness. Since 1906, SINE NOMINE (No. 306), composed by Ralph Vaughan Williams for the same text, has made its triumphant way into hymnal after hymnal, and was the tune Tucker had in mind when he wrote "All praise to Thee." ENGELBERG, the present setting for his hymn, was introduced into American hymnody through *The Hymnal 1940.*

Sir Charles V. Stanford (1852–1924), distinguished composer, conductor, organist, teacher, and author, was born in Dublin and educated at Cambridge and in Germany. Oxford and Cambridge universities conferred honorary music doctorates on him and in 1901 he was knighted. His output in all branches of composition was enormous and included church music, songs, chamber music, choral, organ, and orchestral works. For nearly forty years he was professor of music at Cambridge, where he did much to raise the standard of requirements for musical degrees. Greatly gifted as a teacher, he was appointed professor of composition at the Royal College of Music when it opened in 1883. Many of his pupils became notable musicians, among them Ralph Vaughan Williams, Gustav Holst, Walford Davies. He was an orchestral and choral conductor of great reputation abroad as well as in England. With Sir Hubert Parry he led in the renaissance of English music in the twentieth century, and was an energizing force in church music. Through his interest in and use of folk music, particularly of Irish melodies, he contributed to a new appreciation of it. His ashes are buried in Westminster Abbey under a stone bearing the simple phrase, "A great musician."

148 Forty Days and Forty Nights

Adapted from one of three Lenten poems by George Hunt Smyttan (1822–1870) and first published in *The Penny Post* for March, 1856, this hymn was considerably revised by the Reverend Francis Pott for his *Hymns Fitted to the Order of Common Prayer,* 1861. See No. 181 for comments on Pott. It has been further revised in the present version. The motif of the hymn provides a somewhat fitting commentary on Smyttan's life inasmuch as he died friendless and penniless while traveling abroad and was buried in a pauper's grave in Frankfort-am-Main. He served Anglican churches at Ellingham and Hawksworth, resigning from the latter charge in 1859, and published several volumes of verse, including *Thoughts in Verse for the Afflicted,* 1849.

HEINLEIN (AUS DER TIEFE) was one of three melodies bearing the initials M. H. in a Nürnberg hymnbook of 1676–1677, for the hymn "Aus der Tiefe rufe ich" ("Out of the depths I cry to thee") from which its second tune name is taken. Zahn attributes these melodies to Martin Herbst (1654–1681), a Lutheran pastor who was born in Nürnberg, studied philosophy and theology in Altdorf and Jena, became rector of the gymnasium and pastor of St. Andreas' Church in Eisleben in 1680, and died of the plague the following year at the age of twenty-seven. The name HEINLEIN was given the tune at a time when it was attributed by some to M. (P.?) Heinlein. The present form of the melody from *Hymns Ancient and Modern,* 1861, is slightly different from the original. Archibald Jacob comments in *Songs of Praise Discussed:* "This superbly solemn tune merits in every way the celebrity it has attained." In Vol. 40 of the Bach-Gesellschaft Edition of Bach's works, a chorale prelude on HEINLEIN, No. 3 of six "doubtful or incomplete" organ compositions, may be an early work of Bach and is the source of the harmonization of this melody in some hymnals. The tune appears in no other works of Bach.

149 I Know Not How That Bethlehem's Babe

Awarded first prize in a contest for a Christian hymn at Harvard University in 1910, this poem by Harry Webb Farrington (1879–1931) has made its way into a number of hymnals, and has been translated into Chinese and

Russian. Simple in form and yet rich in beauty and meaning, it was described by Prof. George Herbert Palmer as a perfect poem, even though Farrington wrote it in less than half an hour and did not regard it highly. He submitted it because he wanted to give modern expression in a skeptical age to the classic Christian faith in Christ. Born in the British West Indies, Farrington grew up in Baltimore as an orphan, having lost his parents in infancy. He did not know his last name until eventually some long-lost relatives were discovered in Williamsport, Pennsylvania. Ordained a minister in the Methodist Church, after receiving an M.A. degree in philosophy and education from Harvard, he was the pastor of several Methodist churches and became widely known as an authority in the field of public religious education as a result of his work with the Methodist Board of Sunday Schools. Because of his distinguished service among French troops as an athletic director during World War I, France conferred on him the title Maréchal des Logis Adjutant au Colonel, an honor that only one other person outside France had been given at the time, that being the king of Italy. By the time he returned to the United States after the war, he was popularly called the poilu poet.

Farrington published several volumes on Americana and collections of poems as well as twenty-nine hymns. This hymn was published in his *Rough and Brown,* 1921, under the title, "Our Christ."

BANGOR   Bangor, Maine, was named for this tune. Although some have labeled this statement a folk tale, the *Encyclopaedia Britannica* (eleventh edition) gives credence to it. When the village, known originally as Conduskeag and later as Sunbury, decided to petition for incorporation in 1791, it sent its first pastor, the Rev. Seth Noble, to Boston to carry out the negotiations. While waiting for a clerk to fill out the required forms, Noble hummed a favorite hymn tune to himself. When the clerk asked unexpectedly, "What's the name?" he replied, "Bangor"—and so the tune's name became the town's name.

BANGOR was set to Psalm 12 in William Tans'ur's *A Compleat Melody: or The Harmony of Sion,* 1735, with the heading, "Composed in Three parts, W. T." Since a similar phrase preceded fifty-nine other tunes, it is not known whether the editor composed them or made his own arrangements of existing tunes.

William Tans'ur (c. 1706–1783), was born in Dunchurch, Warwickshire, the son of a laborer of German descent, whose name Tanzer he spelled Tans'ur, for what reason no one knows. He was a composer and organist, editor of numerous books of psalm tunes and anthems, and the author of two books on music theory. From his early youth psalm singing was Tans'ur's favorite pursuit, and in later years he went from town to town, teaching music, conducting classes in psalmody, playing the organ in church, eventually settling down as a bookseller and music teacher. It is said that he did much to improve psalm singing in the Church of England. At least eleven editions of Tans'ur's *Compleat Melody* are known to have been published in America and selections from his collections made their way into many American tune books. BANGOR was included in most American collections of psalm and hymn tunes published in the late eighteenth and early nineteenth centuries.

150 O Love, How Deep, How Broad, How High

This anonymous fifteenth-century Latin hymn on the incarnation, originally containing twenty-three stanzas and beginning with the words "Apparuit benignitas," was translated by Benjamin Webb (1819–1885) for the *Hymnal Noted,* 1854. The hymn has sometimes, but wrongly, been attributed to Thomas à Kempis. The version given here has been considerably altered and begins with the second stanza of the original poem. Webb was a noted ecclesiological scholar and author and an intimate friend of John Mason Neale. During his tenure as vicar of St. Andrew's, Wells Street, London, where he remained twenty-three years, from 1862 to 1885, the church became renowned for the excellence of its music.

See No. 110 for comments on Neale.

DEUS TUORUM MILITUM, from a Grenoble antiphoner of 1753, is one of the French Church Melodies introduced into English hymnody by Ralph Vaughan Williams in *The English Hymnal,* 1906, where it was one of two settings for an anonymous Latin Office hymn for martyrs, "Deus tuorum militum" ("God, the portion, the crown and reward of Thy soldiers"). The tune appeared with its present words and harmonization in *The Hymnal 1940.* Its first four notes, which outline the major tonic chord, and its strong triple rhythm show how far removed from plainsong it was and how much it reflected the musical developments of the period in which it was written. The tune has a sweep and a directness that inspire full-hearted singing.

See Nos. 41 and 59 for further comments on French Church Melodies.

151 O Love, How Deep, How Broad, How High

See No. 150 for comments on the text.

DEO GRACIAS (AGINCOURT)   The two names by which this tune is known tell much of its history. It was the melody sung to a minstrel's ballad extolling the victory of King Henry V at the battle of Agincourt, 1415.

The Holinshed Chronicles tell us that when Henry entered London in triumph after the battle and saw gates and streets decorated with tapestries, and boys in artificial turrets singing verses in his honor, he ordered this pageantry to cease and commanded that "no ditties should be made or sung by Minstrels or others . . . for that he would whollie have the praise and thankes altogether given to God." This song survived the censorship. The rhythm of the third measure of each phrase of DEO GRACIAS, with its unexpected accent on the second beat, is one of the striking characteristics of this fine tune. In *Songs of Praise Discussed,* Archibald Jacob describes it as "a magnificently direct and stirring tune, with a vehement dignity, and a remarkable expression of triumphant pride." Its original form follows.

De - o gra - ci - as an - - - gli - - a, red - de pro vic - to - - - ri - - a.

Owre kynge went forth to nor-man - dy, With grace and myght of

chy - val - ry: Ther god for him wrought mer-velus - ly. Wher-fore eng-

londe may calle and cry De - - - - o gra - - ci - - as. De - - o gra-

ci - as an - - - gli - - - - a, red - de pro vic - to - - - - ri - - a.

152 We Would See Jesus; Lo! His Star Is Shining

The son, grandson, great-grandson and father of Protestant clergymen, John Edgar Park (1879–1956) was for nineteen years the minister of The Second Church in Newton (Congregational Christian), West Newton, Massachusetts, before he became president of Wheaton College, Norton, Massachusetts, a position in which he served for eighteen years. The author of many religious books and articles and the Lyman Beecher lecturer at the Yale Divinity School in 1936, he received many honors and was in great demand as a lecturer and preacher. He wrote this hymn for *Worship and Song,* 1913, published by Pilgrim Press. The first line was taken from another hymn, but the rest of the hymn was written by Park "for a hymn for youth and promise and sunshine . . . and an inner glimpse of the Young Man of Nazareth living and moving among us."

CUSHMAN was composed by the Rev. Herbert B. Turner (1852–1927) for Anna B. Warner's hymn "We would see Jesus, for the shadows lengthen" when he was editing *Hymns and Tunes for Schools,* 1907. At that time he was chaplain of Hampton Institute in Virginia, a position he held from 1892 to 1922. Educated at Amherst College, which honored him with a D.D. degree in 1905, and at Union Theological Seminary in New York City, he was ordained a Congregational minister in 1874. PSALM 80 (No. 168) is a suitable alternative tune for these words.

153 Lord, Who Throughout These Forty Days

Daughter of an Anglican clergyman, the Rev. W. H. Ibotson, and wife of the Rev. J. W. D. Hernamann, an inspector of schools, Claudia Frances Hernamann (1838–1898) displayed a lifelong interest in the religious training and nurture of children. She was the author of a number of books, several especially designed for children, and wrote many hymns, including translations from the Latin. This hymn, one of the few that seeks to encompass the whole of the Lenten story, was first published in her *Child's Book of Praise,* 1873. She died in Brussels, Belgium, October 10, 1898.

ST. FLAVIAN is adapted from the first half of an eight-line tune for Psalm 132 in *The Whole Booke of Psalmes,* 1562. This famous book, known variously as Sternhold and Hopkins, the Old Version, and Day's Psalter, dominated English hymnody for well over a century. It was printed by John Day (1552–1584), one of the earliest music printers and one to whom "both literature and typography are deeply indebted." An ardent advocate of the Reformation, he suffered imprisonment for his loyalty to its principles and for a time had to live abroad. In Ravenscroft's *Whole Booke of Psalmes,* 1621, the third note *e* was substituted for *c* in the original tune. The present form of the melody and harmony is from *Church Hymn Tunes,* 1853, edited by Richard Redhead whose name accounts for the tune's being called RED-HEAD NO. 29 in some hymnals. The tune has been called ST. FLAVIAN since the 1875 edition of *Hymns Ancient and Modern.*

154 O Thou Who Through This Holy Week

John Mason Neale wrote this Passiontide hymn for his *Hymns for Children,* 1842. He captioned the hymn, "For Monday, Tuesday, Wednesday and Thursday of Passion Week." See No. 110 for comments on Neale.

WALSALL, named for a town in Staffordshire, England, north of Birmingham, is an anonymous melody from William Anchors' *Choice Collection of Psalm Tunes,* c. 1721. Although in later eighteenth-century books it continued to be listed as anonymous, from about 1800 on it was frequently attributed to Henry Purcell in English and American hymnals. There seems to be no foundation for this ascription, though it seems to show high regard for the quality of the tune. It was included in many early nineteenth-century American collections and was one of the one hundred psalm tunes "such as are most used in churches of all denominations" in Joshua Leavitt's *Supplement* to the *Christian Lyre,* New York, 1831, where it appeared with the text "My God, the spring of all my joys." The harmonization at No. 154 is from *The English Hymnal,* 1906.

155 All Glory, Laud, and Honor

A leading intellectual in Charlemagne's court, Theodulph of Orléans (c. 760–c. 821) was bishop of Orleans from about 781 to 818 and became the king's first theologian after the death of Alcuin. He was accused later of conspiring against Louis I, the son and successor of Charlemagne, and spent the last few years of his life in prison, where he is said to have written this hymn. One story, undoubtedly legendary, recounts that Louis I, who was popularly known as Louis the Pious, heard the song while riding by the prison in which Theodulph was incarcerated at Angers and was so impressed that he set the saint free and restored him to his bishopric. In medieval times the hymn, which consisted of thirty-nine couplets, was sung on Psalm Sunday while the clergy and congregation marched in procession through the town streets, and it is still so used in some parts of England and France. The translation is by John Mason Neale as it appeared somewhat altered in the 1859 edition of *Hymns Ancient and Modern*. See No. 110 for comments on Neale.

ST. THEODULPH (VALET WILL ICH DIR GEBEN). Most English-speaking Protestants, hearing this tune, think instantly of Palm Sunday and its unique associations. It has no such connection in German usage. It was the second of two settings composed in 1613 by Melchior Teschner (1581–1635) for "Valet will ich dir geben" ("Farewell, I gladly bid thee"), a hymn of consolation in which "a pious heart bids farewell to this world" and looks ahead to the joys of heaven. The hymn was written in a time of pestilence by Valerius Herberger, pastor of the Lutheran church in Frau-stadt where Teschner was cantor for five years. This is the only tune by which Teschner is known. When it was set to the present text in *Hymns Ancient and Modern*, 1861, it was named ST. THEODULPH. Since its publication in 1615 it has been known in Germany as VALET WILL ICH DIR GEBEN. Like other chorale melodies it has had its share of alterations. Its original form follows. (Zahn 5404a)

Va - let will ich dir ge - ben, du ar - ge, fal - sche Welt;
dein sünd-lich bö - ses Le - ben durch - aus mir nicht ge - fällt.

Im Him - mel ist gut woh - nen, hin - auf steht mein Be - gier,

da wird Gott ehr - lich loh - nen dem, der ihm dient all - hier.

Teschner, born in Fraustadt, Silesia, served there as cantor and parish schoolmaster until 1614 when he became pastor of the Lutheran church in Oberprietschen, Posen, remaining there until his death. In Germany his tune is sung with several texts, frequently with Gerhardt's Advent hymn, "Wie soll ich dich empfangen?" ("O Lord, how shall I meet thee?"). Bach used the melody in the *St. John Passion* (No. 28), in Cantata 95 where it is in 3/4, and in two chorale preludes on "Valet will ich dir geben." The repetition of the first half of the tune as a refrain, found in some hymnals, goes back to *Hymns Ancient and Modern,* not to Teschner. Traditionally, the first stanza of Theodulph's "Gloria, laus, et honor" was sung after each stanza as it still is in Catholic churches. Monk followed this tradition when he arranged Teschner's tune for the words. When Neale's translation of the hymn appeared with its plainsong melody in the *Hymnal Noted* the repetition was indicated. That melody is given in the *Historical Companion to Hymns Ancient and Modern,* 1962. (No. 598)

156 Draw Nigh to Thy Jerusalem

The author of two devotional classics, *The Rule and Exercise of Holy Living,* 1650, and *The Rule and Exercise of Holy Dying,* 1651, Bishop Jeremy Taylor (1613–1667), who came from a humble family, rose to become chaplain to Archbishop Laud and Charles I and later bishop of Dromore and vice-chancellor of the University of Dublin. Because he remained a staunch Royalist during the Commonwealth period, he was imprisoned three times. This hymn — which originally began, "Lord come away! why dost thou stay?" — was appended to his famous book of devotions, *The Golden Grove,* 1655, in a Supplement entitled "Festival and Penitential Hymns."

WOODLANDS, a "bold, resolute" unison tune, was composed by Walter Greatorex (1877–1949) who was a chorister of King's College, Cambridge, from 1888 to 1893, assistant music master for ten years at Uppingham School (an English school founded in 1584, and brought to distinction by Edward Thring, headmaster from 1853 to 1887, who attached great importance to the study of music and art), and director of music at Gresham's School, Norfolk, from 1911. The tune set to the text of "Lift up your hearts!" (see No. 352) in the *Public School Hymn Book,* 1919, was named for one of the houses at Gresham's School.

157 In the Cross of Christ I Glory

Based on Galatians 6:14, which was also the text that inspired Isaac Watts to write "When I Survey the Wondrous Cross," this hymn by Sir John Bowring first appeared in his *Hymns,* 1825. The opening line was inscribed on his tombstone after his death in 1872. See No. 109 for comments on Bowring.

RATHBUN was composed by Ithamar Conkey (1815–1867) in 1849 when he was organist and choirmaster of the Central Baptist Church in Norwich, Connecticut. On a rainy Sunday of that year, according to an account in the *Norwich Bulletin* of June 24, 1907, only one member of the choir appeared for the morning service. After playing the prelude Conkey left the church, discouraged and disheartened. In the afternoon, while he was playing the piano, the words of "In the cross of Christ I glory" kept running through his head. The hymn had been suggested by his minister for use with a series of sermons on "The Words on the Cross." Conkey composed the present tune for the words, had it sung the following Sunday by the choir, and named it for Mrs. Beriah S. Rathbun, the leading soprano.

After leaving Norwich in 1850, Conkey had considerable success in New York City as a church and oratorio singer. He was bass soloist at Calvary Episcopal Church where H. W. Greatorex was organist and director of music. He was also a member of Grace Church choir, and from 1861 until his death was bass soloist and conductor of the quartet choir in the Madison Avenue Baptist church. He was born in Shutesbury, Massachusetts, and died in Elizabeth, New Jersey.

RATHBUN was first published in Henry W. Greatorex's *Collection of Psalm and Hymn Tunes,* 1851, with the text "Saviour, who thy flocks art feeding." In 1865 the tune appeared with Bowring's text and since then has become almost a proper for it, replacing a number of greatly varied tunes to which the hymn had been sung.

158 Go to Dark Gethsemane

James Montgomery wrote two versions of this hymn, one which appeared in Thomas Cotterill's *A Selection of Psalms and Hymns for Public Worship,* ninth edition, 1820, and another which was published in his own *Christian Psalmist,* 1825. The present version is a composite of these. See No. 25 for comments on Montgomery.

REDHEAD NO. 76 (PETRA; GETHSEMANE) Richard Redhead (1820–1901) English organist, choir director, composer and arranger of tunes, edited several books of church music which played an important part, on the musical side, in the Oxford Movement with which he was deeply sympathetic. From 1835 to 1864 he was organist and choirmaster at Margaret Chapel (later All Saints' Church), sometimes called the Tractarian Cathedral, where he and the Rev. Frederick Oakeley gave great attention to the music and the choir and established what have been called ultra-ritualistic services. His *Laudes Diurnae,* 1843, with a preface by Canon Oakeley, was the first Gregorian Psalter for use in the Anglican Church. For thirty years, 1864–1894, he was organist and choir director at the church of St. Mary Magdalene, Paddington, where his skill in training boys' voices and his sensitive service playing brought him considerable reputation. In *Church Hymn Tunes,* 1853, he selected, composed, and edited a number of tunes (many of them traditional and by other composers) to each of which he gave, not a name, but a Roman numeral. The present tune, LXXVI, was assigned to "Rock of Ages" and has been closely associated with it ever since in England. From this association comes its name PETRA, the Latin word for rock; and from its connection with the present hymn comes its third tune name, GETHSEMANE.

159 Alone Thou Goest Forth, O Lord

Famed in his time as a brilliant intellectual and teacher, Peter Abelard (1079–1142) ranks as one of the greatest and most colorful figures in Christian history. As a student of William of Champeaux he overcame his teacher in classroom debate and with the acuteness of his arguments forced him to modify his ultrarealist position. Appointed Lecturer in the Cathedral School at Notre Dame, Paris, he attracted students from all parts of Europe, including many future high-ranking members of the clergy. Called by some authorities the first of the modernists, he was a man of faith but also of reason, and his book *Sic et Non* ("Yes and No"), a compilation of real and apparent contradictions contained in the Scriptures and writings of the church fathers, did much to develop and promote the scholastic method. His tragic romance with Héloïse, beautiful and gifted niece of Canon Fulbert, and one of his pupils, aroused such opposition that he was attacked and emasculated by ruffians hired by Canon Fulbert. Just prior to this tragic event they had been secretly married, and a son had been born to them. Abelard subsequently entered the Abbey of St. Denis as a monk, where his fame as a teacher continued to grow, and Héloïse took the veil, eventually becoming head of a religious house for women which Abelard had originally founded as a hermitage and which he called the Paraclete. Their love letters have inspired many novels and plays. Near the end of his life, at the insistence of Bernard of Clairvaux he was tried and found guilty of heresy, and died while on his way to Rome to plead his innocence. His ashes with those of Héloïse lie buried in the Père-la-Chaise Cemetery in Paris. His gifts as a hymn writer were largely unknown until the nineteenth century when several of his poems were found in the Vatican, and others were later discovered in the Royal Library at Brussels. He wrote this hymn, originally beginning, "Solus ad victimam procedis, Domine," depicting the love and compassion of Christ, as an office hymn for Good Friday and included it in his *Hymnarius Paraclitensis,* 1129(?), which he prepared for use in Héloïse's Convent of the Paraclete. The free translation by F. Bland Tucker was made for *The Hymnal 1940.*

See No. 147 for comments on Tucker.

BANGOR   See No. 149 for comments on the tune.

160   Beneath the Cross of Jesus

Descended from a distinguished Scottish family, Elizabeth C. Clephane (1830–1869) was born in Edinburgh but spent most of her short life in Melrose, near Abbotsford, the home of Sir Walter Scott, where she was given the name Sunbeam because of her philanthropic work among the poor. Three years after her death two poems appeared anonymously in *The Family Treasury,* a popular religious magazine in Scotland at the time, under the general title "Breathings on the Border." The present hymn, later credited to her, is a selection of stanzas from the first of these poems and appeared with the editorial note that the "lines express the experiences, the hopes and the longings of a young Christian lately released."

ST. CHRISTOPHER was composed for these words by Frederick C. Maker (1844–1927) for the 1881 edition of the *Bristol Tune Book,* edited by Alfred Stone.

See No. 98 for comments on Maker.

161 Before the Cross of Jesus

After graduating from Amherst College and Yale Divinity School, Ferdinand Q. Blanchard (1876–   ) served Congregational churches in Southington, Connecticut, and East Orange, New Jersey, before becoming the minister of the Euclid Avenue Congregational Church in Cleveland, Ohio, where he remained for forty years. This hymn was written in 1928 for his congregation in Cleveland in order to provide the tune ST. CHRISTOPHER with words "which would have a modern appeal." A leader in his denomination and a vigorous exponent of providing greater educational opportunities for Negroes, Dr. Blanchard was Moderator of the General Council of the Congregational Christian Churches from 1942 to 1944 and has been active in the American Missionary Association and in the American Board of Commissioners for Foreign Missions. He has written many books as well as a number of hymns.

ST. CHRISTOPHER.   See No. 160 for comments on the tune.

162 When My Love to God Grows Weak

This is an instance of a hymn that has found its way into a number of hymnals as much by its usefulness as a Passiontide hymn as by its intrinsic worth. The author, John R. Wreford (1800–1881), wrote it for the Rev. J. R. Beard's *Collection of Hymns for Public and Private Worship,* 1837, an English compilation of hymns considered suitable for Unitarian worship, omitting all Trinitarian and Evangelical hymns. The books met with little success even among Unitarians, but this hymn gained general acceptance after Samuel Longfellow revised the words in his *Book of Hymns,* 1848. It is subjective without being unduly introspective, as is the case with some Passion hymns. Originally the first line began, "When my love to Christ grows cold." Wreford trained for the Unitarian ministry, but resigned his position as associate minister of the New Meeting, Birmingham, when his voice failed. He opened a school at Edgbaston after he left the ministry and spent the last years of his life in retirement at Bristol.

SONG 13 (CANTERBURY; SIMPLICITY; NORWICH; GIBBONS) is an adaptation of one of the sixteen songs composed by Orlando Gibbons (1583–1625) for George Wither's *Hymnes and Songs of the Church,* 1623, which Julian calls "the earliest attempt at an English hymnbook." It included a number of metrical paraphrases of Scripture. SONG 13 was the setting for one of these from the Song of Solomon, "O my love, how comely now." Like the other melodies in the book (from which all of Gibbons' hymn tunes are drawn) this was arranged for two parts, treble and bass.

The form of the melody at No. 162 is that used in the 1861 music edition of *Hymns Ancient and Modern* whose music editor, William Monk, set it to two texts, one of which, "Jesu, grant me this I pray," is found in several hymnals with Gibbons' original rhythm and harmony. Wither (1588–1667), poet and satirist, had a patent from King James I authorizing his book to be bound with all copies of the Old Version that were sold; but the Stationers'

Company — publishers of that noted book, who had a monopoly on its printing and wanted no rivals for it — opposed this patent and eventually had it revoked, so that Wither's hymns and Gibbons' tunes never had wide circulation and were neglected for generations. Robert Bridges' use of eight of Gibbons' tunes in the *Yattendon Hymnal*, 1899, and the *English Hymnal*'s inclusion of eleven, (five of which were set to two texts), brought these fine tunes into use in their authentic form. Five are included in the *Pilgrim Hymnal*.

Born into a family of musicians, of whom he became the most renowned, Gibbons was enrolled at twelve in the King's College Chapel choir at Cambridge, where his brother Edward was master of the choristers. At twenty-one he became organist of the Chapel Royal, a post he held for the rest of his life. In 1619 he was appointed one of the king's musicians for the virginals and in 1623 succeeded John Parsons as organist of Westminster Abbey. As a performer on the organ and virginals he was unrivaled. He received the Mus.B. degree from Cambridge in 1606 and in 1622 was honored with the D.Mus. by Oxford. His compositions include services, anthems, hymns, madrigals, and instrumental fancies (fantasies) which have been called incomparable masterpieces. All of his sacred music was written for the English rite, a fact which distinguishes him from all of his contemporaries. As senior organist at Westminster Abbey, Gibbons officiated at the funeral of King James I in March, 1625. Three months later he died of a stroke in Canterbury where he had gone with the Chapel Royal to attend Charles I at his reception for Queen Henrietta Maria whom he had married by proxy in Paris on May first. Gibbons' death occurred a week before the queen's arrival. He was buried in Canterbury Cathedral. In *The National Psalmist*, 1848, edited by Lowell Mason and George Webb, SONG 13, harmonized with the composer's original bass, was named GIBBONS as it had been in Havergal's *Old Church Psalmody*, 1847.

163 Ah, Holy Jesus, How Hast Thou Offended

In the opening words of *Either/Or*, Soren Kierkegaard defines a poet as "an unhappy being whose heart is torn by secret sufferings, but whose lips are so strangely formed that when the sighs and the cries escape them, they sound like beautiful music." That observation, born out of Kierkegaard's own experience as a writer, might fairly serve to describe Johann Heermann (1585–1647), Lutheran pastor and poet of Köben, in Silesia, although the situations of the two men were quite different. Afflicted with ill-health, Heermann also endured many grievous hardships during the Thirty Years' War, losing all his personal belongings on several occasions and barely escaping with his life. These ordeals only deepened his faith and led him to write some of his greatest hymns. Among them is this Passion hymn, "Herzliebster Jesu, was hast du verbrochen," based on a passage from the fifteenth-century Latin work, *Meditationes,* occasionally but incorrectly attributed to Augustine. The original author of the passage is now known to be Jean de Fëcamp (d. 1078). Heermann's hymn first appeared in his *Devoti musica cordis,* 1630, in fifteen stanzas and was translated into English by Robert Bridges in his *Yattendon Hymnal*, 1899. See No. 430 for comments on Bridges.

HERZLIEBSTER JESU Since 1640 this nobly expressive melody has been associated with Heermann's Passion hymn. Although parts of it are found in two earlier melodies, Bourgeois' setting of Psalm 23 (Zahn 3199) and a melody in Schein's *Cantional*, 1627 (Zahn 981), a study of these convinces one not so much of Crüger's indebtedness to them as of his own great melodic gifts and of his ability to create noble, strong tunes for congregational singing. Bach used the chorale in the *St. Matthew Passion* (Nos. 3,25,55), and in the *St. John Passion* (Nos. 7, 27). His version of the melody starts on an upbeat and includes passing notes not in the original. The present harmonization is from *The Chorale Book for England*, 1863. (See No. 15.) It differs in measures one, two, seven, and twelve from Crüger's setting of the melody in *Newes vollkömliches Gesangbuch*, 1640 (Zahn 983), which appears in *Hymnal for Colleges and Schools*, 1956, in *Christian Hymns*, 1963, and in the Historical Edition of *Hymns Ancient and Modern*, 1909. See No. 29 for comments on Crüger.

164 O Come and Mourn With Me Awhile

These lines were taken from a longer poem by Frederick William Faber in his collection *Jesus and Mary: or, Catholic Hymns for Singing and Reading,* 1849. Extensively revised, the second line originally read, "See, Mary calls us to her side." The refrain was changed from "Jesus, our Love, is crucified," to its present form. The words "Amor meus crucifixus est," on which Faber purportedly based his refrain, were written by Ignatius of Antioch (? – 107?) while on his way to Rome and a martyr's death. See No. 101 for comments on Faber.

ST. CROSS, written for Faber's hymn, was one of the seven tunes composed by John B. Dykes which appeared in the original musical edition of *Hymns Ancient and Modern*, 1861. See No. 79 for further comments on Dykes.

165 Sunset to Sunrise Changes Now

Sometimes called the first Christian hymn writer in that he wrote hymns of his own based neither on the psalms nor on the New Testament canticles, Clement of Alexandria (c. 170–c. 220) was for many years head of the famous catechetical school at Alexandria. He sought to bring all Greek learning and philosophy into the service of expounding Christian truth, and is known consequently as the father of Greek theology. On one occasion, Clement described his fellow Christians in these words: "We plough the fields praising; we sail the seas hymning." This hymn is taken from his *Exhortation to the Greeks,* one of the few evangelistic tracts to have survived from the earliest centuries of the church. Howard Chandler Robbins (1876–1952), professor of Pastoral Theology at General Theological Seminary in New York City before his retirement in 1941, translated and quoted this hymn in paraphrase form in his book *Preaching the Gospel,* 1939, based on lectures he gave in Philadelphia the previous year.

KEDRON was the setting for Dr. Robbins' paraphrase in *The Hymnal, 1940*. The tune was first published in Amos Pilsbury's *The United States' Sacred Harmony*, 1799, with the following stanza from Charles Wesley's hymn "Ye that pass by, behold the man."

> Thou man of grief remember me,
> Thou never canst thyself forget
> Thy last mysterious agony,
> Thy fainting pangs and bloody sweat.

Undoubtedly the first verse of John 18 accounts for the name of the tune: "When Jesus had spoken these words, he went forth with his disciples over the brook Cedron, where was a garden."

Pilsbury, whose book is one of the earliest known tune books to contain authentic folk hymns, was a singing master, active in Charleston, South Carolina. The composer of KEDRON is unknown. George Pullen Jackson includes it in a list of eighty of the most popular tunes of pre-Civil War days in the rural south. John Jacob Niles calls KEDRON "one of the most powerful tunes in all Shape-note music."

Shape-note hymnbooks, widely used in certain districts of the South for generations, are those in which the music is printed not in ordinary notation but according to systems which assign a note of a particular shape (such as circle, square, diamond, triangle) to a particular degree of the scale in order to facilitate the reading of music. These systems of notation stirred up controversy, but were taken up enthusiastically by publishers of songbooks and are still used in some areas of the South and West. Many of the tunes in the shape-note books have been traced to traditional folk songs from England, Scotland, and Ireland. A large number are modal (in one of the medieval modes) or in some form of the pentatonic (five-tone) or hexatonic (six-tone) scales, characteristic of music in certain stages the world over. The songs, frequently harmonized in only three parts, were always sung without accompaniment.

166 Jesus, in Thy Dying Woes

A member of the committee that compiled the most popular and widely sold of all English hymnals, *Hymns Ancient and Modern,* Thomas Benson Pollock (1836–1896) was an Anglican clergyman who spent half his life in religious work at St. Alban's Mission in Birmingham. Although he had many opportunities to go to wealthier parishes, he preferred to minister to the poor in Birmingham. His yearly stipend never exceeded £150 ($420). He wrote many hymns in the form of metrical litanies, of which this hymn based on Jesus' last words on the cross is a good example. It first appeared in his *Metrical Litanies for Special Services and General Use,* 1870. It is especially suitable for use on Good Friday.

SWEDISH LITANY, an anonymous melody, dated 1697, and set to the text "Ack, vad är dork livet här?" in the *Hemmets Koralbok,* 1819, appeared with the present litany in *The Hymnal 1940.*

133

167 Jesus, in Thy Dying Woes

See No. 166 for comments in the text.

TON–MÂN is the second half of a tune composed by David Evans in 1912 for a hymn by the Rev. E. Rees, found in *Cân a Moliant,* a collection of Welsh hymns published in 1917. It appeared with this text in *The Hymnal 1940.* See No. 38 for comments on David Evans.

168 Lord, Through This Holy Week

Following graduation from Keble College, Oxford, William Henry Draper (1855–1933) served successively as curate of St. Mary's, Shrewsbury; vicar of Alfreton; vicar of the Abbey Church, Shrewsbury; rector of Adel, Leeds; rural dean of Shrewsbury; Master of the Temple, London; and vicar of Axbridge. He published several books in the field of hymnody, notably translations of Latin and Greek hymns. Julian has said of his hymns, exceeding sixty in number, that they "are worthy, taken as a whole, to be published as a volume of sacred verse." This hymn by Draper was taken from his *Hymns for Holy Week,* 1898, consisting of six original hymns and seven translations.

PSALM 80   In *The Church Hymnary, Revised,* 1927, this beautiful melody was set to "O word of pity for our pardon pleading" (No. 173) for which it has been suggested as an alternative tune. It was the second setting for Psalm 80 in the Scottish Psalter of 1564, and was included in eight later Scottish psalters. In the great Scottish Psalter of 1635, PSALM 80 was harmonized in the irregular rhythm of its 1564 form, probably by the editor, Edward Millar, whom Charles I appointed master of the music in the Chapel Royal of Scotland, Edinburgh, in 1635. The present adaptation was made by James S. Anderson (1853–1945), Scottish musician and one of the committee of experts who edited the music of *The Church Hymnary, Revised,* 1927.

PSALM 80, formerly thought by some to be of Scottish origin, has been found in two fifteenth-century manuscripts (c. 1410, c. 1420) and in sixteenth-century Catholic and Protestant books with "Jesus Christus, nostra salus," a communion hymn often ascribed to John Hus. With these words it appeared as follows in *Piae Cantiones,* 1582.

Je - sus Chri - stus no - stra sa - lus, Quod re - cla - mat om - nis

ma - - lus, no-bis fu - i me-mo - ri - am de-dit in pa - nis ho - sti - am.

134

In *Songs of Syon,* 1910 (No. 141), George R. Woodward's English version of the Latin hymn is set to the melody as it appeared in a book edited by Johann Walther in 1524. There are four organ movements by Bach on Luther's "Jesus Christus, unser Heiland," two in Part III of the *Clavierübung,* two in the *Eighteen Chorales.* There is one harmonization in the *Choralgesänge.* Terry says the melody "appears to have been very dear to Bach."

169 My Song Is Love Unknown

Samuel Crossman (c. 1624–1684) was one of the first English authors before Isaac Watts to write hymns whose content was other than scriptural. After graduation from Cambridge in 1660, he identified himself with the Puritan cause and was ejected from the Anglican ministry, but later conformed and became one of the king's chaplains. This Passion hymn was published in his *The Young Man's Meditation,* a collection of sermons and poems, published in London in 1664, the year of the plague.

RHOSYMEDRE (LOVELY)   We are indebted to the editors of *Songs of Praise, Enlarged,* 1931, for the association of this beautiful Welsh melody with Crossman's poem. The tune is from *Original Sacred Music, Composed and Arranged by The Revd. John Edwards, B.A., Jesus College, Oxford,* c. 1840, the first of two such volumes. For some years the composer (1806–1885) was vicar of Rhosymedre, Ruabon, in North Wales. His name for this tune, LOVELY, appeared with it in the *English Hymnal,* 1906, the *Pilgrim Hymnal,* 1931, and in Ralph Vaughan Williams' *Three Preludes on Welsh Hymn Tunes.* In *Songs of Praise* it is called RHOSYMEDRE. The rhythm of the last two phrases is very different from that of the first two and sometimes takes people by surprise at the first hearing; after that, they are prepared for it and realize that this unexpected rhythmic variety gives the melody distinctiveness. Rhosymedre is the name of a small village in Anglesey, an insular northern county of Wales.

170 O Sacred Head, Now Wounded

Although considerably altered in transition, this hymn has grown rather than diminished in power and beauty through the centuries. It was written originally in Latin in the thirteenth century, possibly by Arnulf of Louvain (c. 1200–c. 1250), although some scholars attribute it to Bernard of Clairvaux (1091–1153). It consisted of seven parts, each of which was to be sung on a different day of the week, and each of which focused attention on some part of Christ's body as he hung upon the cross. In the seventeenth century Paul Gerhardt made a free translation of the entire hymn into German, the most popular part of which was the seventh section beginning, "O Haupt voll Blut und Wunden." This was the part addressed to Christ's face and originally read in the Latin, "Salve caput cruentatum." It is this section which forms the basis of the present hymn. See No. 53 for comments on Gerhardt.

James W. Alexander (1804–1859), scholar, teacher, and poet, long associated with Princeton University and later minister of the Fifth Avenue Presbyterian Church in New York City, translated stanzas 1, 2, 4, 5, 7–10 of Gerhardt's version into English in *The Christian Lyre,* 1830. His translation of all the stanzas first appeared in *Cantate Domino,* 1859, and two years later in his posthumous collection, *The Breaking Crucible, and other Translations* 1861. Numerous other translations exist in English and German. Philip Schaff has rightly observed: "This classical hymn has shown an imperishable vitality in passing from the Latin into the German, and from the German into the English, and proclaiming in three tongues, and in the name of three confessions, — the Catholic, the Lutheran, and the Reformed, — with equal effect, the dying love of our Saviour, and our boundless indebtedness to Him." [14] To that can be added the comment that it is the product of three different centuries and possibly three different countries, France, Germany, and the United States, thus making it the most ecumenical in origin of all hymns in popular use.

PASSION CHORALE (HERZLICH TUT MICH VERLANGEN; O HAUPT VOLL BLUT UND WUNDEN) This chorale brings to mind Bach, Holy Week (especially Good Friday), and the *St. Matthew Passion.* However, it is sung at other times and with other texts in German usage. Originally it was the music for a love song, "Mein G'müt ist mir verwirret, das macht ein Jungfrau zart" ("My peace of mind is shattered by a young maiden's charms") published in 1601 in Hassler's *Lustgarten neuer teutscher Gesäng* ("Pleasure garden of new German songs"). In 1613 the tune appeared with a hymn for the dying, "Herzlich thut mich verlangen" ("My heart is filled with longing") which gave it the name by which it is best known. In Crüger's *Praxis pietatis melica,* 1648, it was set to "Ach, Herr, mich armen Sünder" (with which it had been associated since 1620), and in the 1656 edition for the first time to Gerhardt's "O Haupt voll Blut und Wunden" ("O Head, all scarr'd and bleeding"). The Catholics adapted Hassler's tune for their hymn "Salve caput cruentatem." Since Hassler was a Catholic, the music of this chorale adds to its ecumenical character. Albert Schweitzer calls this the most important melody of Bach's *St. Matthew Passion* in which its use, five times, is central to and casts its mood over the whole work. Bach used the tune also in Cantatas 25, 135, 153, 161, twice in the *Christmas Oratorio* (Nos. 5 and 64, the first and the last chorales in the work), and in one chorale prelude for organ. There are two harmonizations of it in the *Choralgesänge.* In Brahms' *Eleven Chorale Preludes* for organ, Op. 122, there are two settings of "Herzlich tut mich verlangen." (Nos. 10 and 11.)

Eight stanzas of Dr. Alexander's translation of Gerhardt's hymn were first published in Vol. I of *The Christian Lyre,* New York, 1830, set to Hassler's melody arranged in two parts, soprano and bass. The chorale, named HOFWYL, had been "Furnished for the Lyre, by Mr. Kammerer, of New York, formerly Professor of Music at Hofwyl." (Hofwyl was an estate near Bern, Switzerland, on which the Swiss educator, Philipp E. Von Fellenberg had founded a famous school.) Lowell Mason used the melody in *The Choir,* 1833, and *The Seraph,* March, 1839, naming it RHINE in the former, MIZZAH in the latter.

Bach's genius and his inspired use of this chorale have tended to obscure the name and the fame of the creator of the melody, Hans Leo Hassler (1564–1612), the foremost composer in Germany around 1600 and one of the great masters of the early baroque. He was the most famous member of a well-known family of musicians of Nürnberg, and was noted as an organist as well as a composer. Hassler studied in Venice with Andrea Gabrieli whose nephew, Giovanni (a fellow student), became a lifelong friend. On his return to Germany he served for a number of years as private organist to Count Octavian Fugger in Augsburg, later as composer and organist at the imperial court in Prague for Emperor Rudolph II who knighted him, and subsequently as composer and organist at the Electoral Chapel in Dresden. He died in Frankfurt where he had gone with the Elector of Saxony for the imperial election. Hassler wrote much secular and sacred music including *Psalmen und Christliche Gesäng,* 1607, containing fifty-two settings of well-known chorale melodies in motet form, a work of importance musically and liturgically.

Hassler's song had the following form originally.

171   There Is a Green Hill Far Away

Recognized early in life as a gifted poet, due largely to the sacred verses she wrote for children, Cecil Frances Alexander (1818–1895) continued throughout her career to publish volumes of poetry, including four hundred hymns. Her best known work, *The Burial of Moses,* prompted Tennyson to comment that he wished he had written it. She was the daughter of Maj. John Humphreys of the Royal Marines and was born at Miltoun House, County Tyrone, Ireland. In 1805 she was happily married to William Alexander, a clergyman with literary talents to match her own, who later was to become archbishop of Armagh and primate of all Ireland. This catechetical hymn, written for her Sunday school class and intended to teach the meaning of the fourth article of the Apostles' Creed, "suffered under Pontius Pilate, was crucified, dead, and buried," first appeared in her *Hymns for Little Children,* 1848. She later reported that she was inspired to write the hymn because a small grassy hill she passed on her way to shop in Derry reminded her of Calvary.

HORSLEY   Since its appearance with these words in the Appendix to *Hymns Ancient and Modern,* 1868, this tune has been inseparably associated with Mrs. Alexander's hymn for children, and in many hymnals is the only setting for it. It was published originally in *Twenty-Four Psalm Tunes and Eight Chants, composed by William Horsley,* 1844. In spite of poverty, and ill treatment by the musician to whom he was apprenticed in his youth, Horsley (1774–1858) had a successful musical career. He composed and published collections of glees and canons, edited two volumes of psalm and hymn tunes, wrote works on theory, and served as organist of Ely Chapel, Holborn, Belgrave Chapel, and Charterhouse. He was an intimate friend of Mendelssohn, though thirty-five years his senior, and was one of the founders of the Philharmonic Society. For fifty-two years he was organist and teacher of psalmody at the Asylum for Female Orphans which had been founded in 1738 — the first institution of its kind — where training in music and singing was a regular part of the program. HORSLEY was written for the use of the children there.

172   There Is a Green Hill Far Away

See No. 171 for comments on the text.

MEDITATION was set to Isaac Watts' hymn "There is a land of pure delight," in *Original Tunes,* 1890, edited by John Henry Gower, composer of the tune. Although in a number of American hymnals MEDITATION is the only setting for these words, it does not appear in English hymnals. Gower (1855–1922), born in England, educated at Oxford (D.Mus. 1883), was organist and music master at Trent College, Nottingham, 1876–1887, and was active also as conductor and recitalist. In America he was identified with mining interests in Denver where he became organist successively of the Cathedral of St. John, the Central Presbyterian Church, and Unity Church. He was organist of the Church of the Epiphany in Chicago at the time of the

World's Fair (Columbian Exposition) in 1893. In his later life he became much interested in the psychical research of Sir Oliver Lodge and Sir Arthur Conan Doyle.

173 O Word of Pity, for Our Pardon Pleading

Written expressly for *Hymns Ancient and Modern,* 1904 edition, by Ada Rundall Greenaway (1861–1937), English author of children's verses and children's religious books, these lines were based on the text, "Father, forgive them for they know not what they do." The daughter of Gen. Thomas Greenaway, an officer in the Indian army, she was brought to England as a child and spent the rest of her life there, making her home in Guildford. Among her published works is a collection of verses, *A Book of Posies,* and a booklet for children, *The Story of a Father's Love.* Four of her hymns were included in the 1950 edition of *Hymns Ancient and Modern.*

ZU MEINEM HERRN Johann G. Schicht (1753–1823), composer of this fine chorale, is mentioned by Albert Schweitzer as one of the chief private collectors of Bach's manuscripts and as the person to whom credit is due for first publishing Bach's motets in 1803, through Breitkopf and Härtel, famous music publishers of Leipzig. Although Schicht had been trained as a pianist and organist, he studied law for a time, but gave it up when he was appointed pianist for Hiller's "Liebhaber-Konzerte" which later developed into the Gewandhaus concerts. In 1785 he succeeded Hiller as conductor, and held that post until 1810. After serving in several churches as organist and choirmaster, Schicht was appointed cantor of the Thomasschule (1810–1823), the post held by Bach from 1723 to 1750. ZU MEINEM HERRN was set to a German metrical version of Psalm 110 in the *Allgemeines Choral-Buch,* 1819, which contained 1,285 tunes, including 306 composed by Schicht, editor of the collection. He composed oratorios, church and chamber music, and edited the piano works of Clementi and Pleyel, but his most important work is his edition of the Bach motets. The present harmonization is by David Evans (see No. 38).

174 Throned Upon the Awful Tree

This Good Friday hymn by Canon John Ellerton was written in 1875 and was first published in *Hymns Ancient and Modern* in the same year. See No. 47 for comments on Ellerton.

ARFON was set to these words in *The English Hymnal,* 1906, with the heading "Welsh Hymn Melody," credit for the present form and harmonization being given to the Rev. Hugh Davies. The writer, who had known the tune only in connection with Ellerton's hymn for Good Friday, was puzzled at hearing it played as an organ solo in a quite different form, obviously not in the mood of Good Friday. She learned that it was named "Noël" and was based on a traditional French carol, "Joseph est bien marié." In the *Companion to Congregational Praise* (No. 772) Erik Routley gives as possible sources for the tune two forms of a Welsh folk tune, "Tros y Garreg" ("Over the Stone"), one of them dating from 1794. He mentions two French sources as well and concludes that at this point it seems impossible to determine the tune's origin. However, when one sees the music of "Joseph est bien marié" (from the Champagne, sixteenth century, with words by Henry IV's maître de chapelle) and its form in a 1760 collection of Noëls arranged for "le Clavecine et le Forte Piano" by Claude Balbastre, organist of St. Roch, Paris, he feels no doubt about where the tune came from but finds himself wondering how this rather gay, nimble carol tune became converted to the uses of hymnody.

The carol and the theme of the set of variations by Balbastre follow:

175 Ride on, Ride on in Majesty!

It is not often that a professor of poetry produces a hymn that has popular appeal as well as literary excellence, but this is one instance of that unusual combination. Henry Hart Milman (1791–1868), an Anglican clergyman, was professor of poetry at Oxford when he wrote this hymn, first published in Reginald Heber's posthumous *Hymns written and adapted to the Weekly Church Service of the Year,* 1827. Heber, referring to a hymnal he was preparing and for which he had solicited the help of several poets, wrote to Milman after reading the hymn, "A few more such [hymns] and I

140

shall neither need nor wait for the aid of Scott and Southey." Milman was appointed dean of St. Paul's Cathedral in 1848 where he initiated the great services under the dome. He was a successful playwright and wrote a standard work on the *History of Latin Christianity,* 1854. He is remembered today largely because of this Palm Sunday hymn.

ST. DROSTANE was composed by John B. Dykes for this text in R. R. Chope's *Congregational Hymn and Tune Book,* London, 1862, but did not come into general use until after its appearance in *Hymns Ancient and Modern,* 1875. It was named by Dykes for St. Drostane, a nephew of St. Columba (see No. 80) and the founder of at least two churches in Ireland and Christian settlements in Scotland. WINCHESTER NEW, the alternative tune suggested for this hymn, has been associated with it since its appearance in *Hymns Ancient and Modern,* 1861. See No. 79 for comments on Dykes.

176 Ride on, Ride on in Majesty!

See No. 175 for comments on the text.

THE KING'S MAJESTY   In reply to an inquiry about the origin of this tune, Graham George, its composer, wrote:

It originated as the result of a choir-practice before Palm Sunday in — I suppose — 1939, during which I had been thinking, 'Winchester New' [the tune often sung with these words.] is a fine tune, but it has nothing whatever to do with the 'tragic trumpets', as one might theatrically call them, of Palm Sunday. At breakfast the following morning I was enjoying my toast and marmalade when the first two lines of this tune sang themselves unbidden in my mind. This seemed too good to miss, so I went to my study, allowed the half-tune to complete itself — which it did with very little trouble — and there it was.

Since its inclusion in *The Hymnal 1940* THE KING'S MAJESTY has appeared in two English hymnals and in at least three other American books. The composer's arrangement of it as a hymn-anthem has been widely used by choirs. Its free rhythm and modal harmonies may seem strange at first to congregations accustomed to nineteenth-century tunes, but it is a fine, strong, unison tune which seems to reinforce and strengthen the impact of the words. To have the choir sing it as an anthem is a good way to introduce it to congregations.

Graham George (1912–), was born in England, came to Canada in 1928, studied organ with Alfred E. Whitehead, became a Fellow of the Canadian College of Organists and earned B.Mus. and D.Mus. degrees from Toronto University. From 1941 to 1945 he served with the Canadian Armed Forces overseas. Since 1946 he has been a member of the music faculty of Queen's University, Kingston, Ontario, and has served as organist and choirmaster of St. James Church, Kingston. His compositions include works for orchestra as well as for choir and organ.

177 When I Survey the Wondrous Cross

Acclaimed by Matthew Arnold as the finest hymn in the English language, these lines first appeared in Isaac Watts' *Hymns and Spiritual Songs,* 1707, Book III, in the section of hymns for the Lord's Supper. It was entitled "Crucifixion to the World by the Cross of Christ," and was based on Galatians 6:14. Robert Bridges has given it as his opinion that it "stands out at the head of the few English hymns which can be held to compare with the best old Latin hymns of the same measure." The second line of the first stanza originally read, "Where the young Prince of glory died."

See No. 1 for comments on Watts.

HAMBURG In the Preface to the *Boston Academy Collection of Music* (third edition), 1835–1836, Lowell Mason lists the types of music contained in it. The First Class includes "Gregorian Chants arranged as metrical tunes," with the comment "There is a beautiful simplicity in these chants which renders their performance peculiarly appropriate to religious purposes. Indeed, their devotional effect cannot be exceeded, and is but seldom equalled."

Some writers have been skeptical about HAMBURG being related to plainsong, even though Mason gave "Gregorian Chant" as its source, in the *Boston Handel and Haydn Society Collection of Church Music,* 1825. Perhaps even in his lifetime he was questioned about this, for in subsequent editions the headings become more explicit. In the *Boston Handel and Haydn Society Collection,* 1828, the heading was: "Gregorian Chant; 'Benedictus.' " In *The Psaltery,* 1845, he wrote: "This tune, now extensively used, was arranged from a Gregorian Chant by L. Mason, and first published in a metrical form in 1825." In a later collection the heading was "Arranged from the Gregorian Tone I by L. Mason."

Gregorian or Psalm Tones are the melodic formulas used for chanting the psalms; there are eight, one for each of the church modes.

The form of HAMBURG, given below as it appeared in the *Boston Handel and Haydn Society Collection,* 1828, with the text to which it was set, shows its close relationship to the Gregorian Tone I and its *f* termination.

Sing to   the Lord with   joy - ful   voice; Let ev'ry land his   name a - dore;

Let earth, with one u - nit - ed   voice, Re-sound his praise from shore to   shore.

142

178 'Tis Midnight, and on Olive's Brow

Having dropped out of school after the sixth grade, William Bingham Tappan (1794–1849) was apprenticed to a clockmaker in Boston, and thereafter largely educated himself. He became interested in the Sunday school movement and secured a position with the American Sunday School Union of Philadelphia in 1822, remaining with that organization until his death. He was licensed as a Congregational minister in 1840 and traveled extensively in the United States on behalf of the religious training of children. Among his books are *New England and Other Poems,* 1819; *Poems,* 1822; and *Gems of Sacred Poetry,* 1860. It was from the second of these that the present hymn was taken, with the title "Gethsemane."

OLIVE'S BROW was written for this hymn by William B. Bradbury (1816–1868) and published in *The Shawn,* 1853, which he edited in collaboration with George F. Root, composer of "Tramp, Tramp, Tramp," "The Battle Cry of Freedom," and other well-known Civil War songs. *The Shawn* was described by its editors as "a library of church music; embracing about one thousand pieces, consisting of psalm and hymn tunes adapted to every meter in use." Sales of Bradbury's numerous publications (there were fifty-nine between 1841 and 1867) ran into the millions. There was much criticism and belittling of Bradbury's "sugared American psalmody," but, as one writer comments, it met the needs of the time and seemed to feed the "infantile musical life of the country." Bradbury's tunes exemplify his belief that tunes for congregational singing should be "simple in their structure and very easy of execution." His Sunday school tunes appealed to young people and supplied evangelists with the earliest examples of the Gospel song.

Bradbury, a native of York, Maine, had never seen a piano or an organ until he went to Boston in 1830 and began his studies in harmony, organ, and voice. Lowell Mason, one of his teachers at the Boston Academy of Music, took a great interest in him and gave him teaching assignments in Maine and New Brunswick. He served as organist in churches in Boston and Brooklyn before becoming organist and choir director of the First Baptist Church in New York City in 1841. Free singing classes which he organized in a number of churches, and large-scale juvenile music festivals which he instituted and directed, led to the introduction of music into New York's public schools. With Lowell Mason and Thomas Hastings he took part in numerous musical conventions and normal institutes. He spent two years abroad (1847–1849), much of the time in Leipzig, studying with some of the finest teachers of the day. In 1854, with his brother and a German piano maker, he established the Bradbury Piano Company in New York City. It was merged with the Knabe firm in 1917.

Bradbury was active at a time when people in churches were crying out for something more lively and more popular in style than psalm tunes. Many of his hymns were written for religious social gatherings, not for church services. The quantity of his output was enormous — the quality of much of it poor. But some of his hymns such as WOODWORTH and HE LEADETH ME have continued in use and in their hold on people's affections, not only in America but in countries around the world where missionaries have taken them.

179 Were You There?

Fashioned in the crucible of suffering and hardship, the Negro spiritual is today widely recognized as one of America's finest contributions to hymnody. Where one might expect to encounter a spirit of bitterness and hate, this is entirely lacking and one finds instead a quality of deep melancholy, patient resignation, and quiet confidence that faith will be vindicated and right will prevail. The phrases and images, however simple and unpolished, have a deeply moving appeal in their scriptural character and emotional intensity. Margaret Just Butcher has written: "The spirituals, though ostensibly naïve and simple, are intrinsically profound. Underneath broken words, childlike imagery, and peasant simplicity lie an epic intensity and a tragic depth of religious emotion for which the only equal seems to be the spiritual experience of the Jews, the only analogue the Psalms. The spirituals stand as one of the great classic expressions of religious emotion." [15] These powerful religious songs were first brought to national and world attention through the concert tours of the "Jubilee Singers" of Fisk University, Nashville, Tennessee, from 1871 to 1878. Although George Pullen Jackson implies that this spiritual may have been derived from an earlier white version, most authorities credit it to the Negro people in slavery. First published in William E. Barton's *Old Plantation Hymns,* 1899, the original text concluded with these two triumphant lines, "Were you there when he rose from the dead?" and "Were you there when he ascended on high?"

WERE YOU THERE This moving Negro spiritual brings to mind the events of the Crucifixion with directness, simplicity, and poignancy. Dr. G. Wallace Woodworth of Harvard once told a group of church musicians that they should remember always that Negro spirituals are *spiritual* and should be sung with the dignity and deep religious feeling inherent in them, not as if they were popular music with religious words, and not in arrangements that should be called more properly "derangements" because of their distortion of the music and their violation of the spirit of the words. Except for one note in the last phrase, this melody is in the pentatonic mode. That one note for the last "you" in some miraculous way seems to direct the question to each individual and to make him feel personally involved in the Crucifixion, as if no centuries had intervened.

In Chapter fifteen of *White and Negro Spirituals,* 1943, George Pullen Jackson gives a tune comparative list of 116 white spirituals paired with Negro-sung variants. No. 106 is the white spiritual "Have you heard how they crucified our Lord" which, he says, came from the upper Cumberland region of Tennessee, where there were few Negroes. The melody and words are similar to those of the Negro spiritual but there is a marked difference between the quality of the two versions. The restraint and solemnity of "Were you there?" bring to mind James Weldon Johnson's comment that "if ignorant Negroes evolved such music . . . by listening to their masters sing gospel hymns, it does not detract from the achievement but magnifies it." [16]

180   Alleluia! Alleluia! Hearts to Heaven

The son of a scholarly clergyman, for whom he was named, and the nephew of the celebrated English poet, William Wordsworth, Christopher Wordsworth (1807–1885) was equally renowned in his own right. After a brilliant career at Cambridge in both classics and mathematics, eventually becoming a Fellow and classical lecturer and public orator at the university, he was successively headmaster of Harrow, one of England's finest preparatory schools, canon of Westminster Abbey, vicar of Stanford-in-the-Vale-cum-Goosey, Berkshire, where he served for nineteen years as a model parish priest, archdeacon at Westminster, and finally bishop of Lincoln, from which position he resigned one month before he died. Because most of his hymns were excessively didactic, inspired by his conviction that "it is the first duty of a hymn to teach sound doctrine, and thence to save souls," few have continued in popular use. The present Easter hymn, however, taken from his *The Holy Year,* 1862, containing hymns for every season and festival of the Christian year, is found in many hymnals today. The wording of several of the phrases has been altered. Many of his hymns were written on scraps of paper as he traveled about England. Of Bishop Wordsworth, Canon Ellerton once wrote: "He was a most holy, humble, loving, self-denying man. And the man is reflected in his verse. To read one of his best hymns is like looking into a plain face, without one striking feature, but with an irresistible charm of honesty, intelligence, and affection." [1]

WEISSE FLAGGEN is closely related to the following tune which appeared, with the words given below, in many German Roman Catholic hymnals after its publication in 1808. (Baümker lists nearly thirty, between 1808 and 1909, Vol. IV, No. 344.)

Hei-lig! ü-ber al-les hei - lig! hei - lig bist du
was du thust und willst ist hei - lig: hei - lig sey uns

un - ser Gott! Herr! du hast es uns ge - ge-ben,
dein Ge - bot. dass das gan - ze Er - den - le-ben

uns be - rei-te nach der Zeit ei - ne fro-he E - wig - keit.

145

The first three phrases of WEISSE FLAGGEN would seem to stem from an anonymous melody in a Catholic hymnal printed at Bamberg in 1732 with "Grosse Sorgen, Grosse Schmerzen." (Bäumker Vol. III, No. 185–I.) In another Catholic hymnal, *Tochter Sion*, Cologne, 1741, a variant of the melody was set to "Lasst die weissen Flaggen wehen," the hymn from which the present tune name was drawn. (Bäumker Vol. III, No. 185–II.) Bäumker thought that the melody very likely had its origin in a popular folk song.

181 Alleluia! The Strife Is O'er

John Mason Neale claimed that this Latin Easter hymn of unknown authorship, "Finita iam sunt praelia," goes back as far as the twelfth century, but it is now assumed to be of much later origin. The earliest appearance of the hymn was in a Jesuit publication in Cologne, *Symphonia Sirenum Selectarum*, 1695, from which source Francis Pott (1832–1909) translated it for his *Hymns Fitted to the Order of Common Prayer*, 1861. Pott served an Anglican church at Norhill, Bedfordshire, England, for twenty-five years until deafness compelled him to resign, following which he devoted the last eighteen years of his life to the improvement of hymnody and worship in the Church of England. He was a charter member of the committee that produced *Hymns Ancient and Modern*, 1861, and contributed significantly toward a wider use of early Christian hymns through his Latin and Syriac translations.

VICTORY was adapted from the first two phrases of a *Gloria Patri* in Palestrina's *Magnificat Tertii Toni*, published in 1591. The Alleluias and their music were added by William H. Monk who made the adaptation for the original music edition of *Hymns Ancient and Modern*, 1861. Some music editors, following the example of *The English Hymnal*, 1906, omit the introductory Alleluias which often get off to a poor start. Monk had made earlier use of the *Gloria* in a setting for Cosin's "Come, Holy Ghost" (No. 231) in *The Parish Choir*, 1851, but this was singularly dull. His second try was more effective and VICTORY has remained a favorite hymn tune for Easter.

Giovanni Pierluigi da Palestrina (c. 1525–1594), one of the greatest musical geniuses of all time and the foremost composer of the Roman Catholic Church, is known by the name of his birthplace, Palestrina, ancient Praenestes, a city twenty-three miles east of Rome. He had his early musical training in Rome, going there in 1534 as a choirboy. In 1544 he returned to his native town to be organist and choirmaster for the cathedral. When the bishop of Palestrina became Pope Julius III, he appointed Giovanni choirmaster at the Capella Giulia at St. Peter's. (1550) Palestrina's first book of masses was dedicated to the Pope who, in January 1555, made the composer one of the members of the Pontifical Choir. After the death of Pope Marcellus (Julius' successor who reigned for only two weeks), Pope Paul IV, a stern reformer, dismissed Palestrina and two other married singers from the choir, traditionally open only to single men in minor clerical orders. Within a short time Palestrina became choirmaster at St. John

Lateran, leaving it in 1561 for a similar post at Santa Maria Maggiore, continuing there for about seven years. From 1565 to 1571 he directed the music at a new Seminary in Rome where two of his sons were students. In the latter year he returned to the Capella Giulia as choirmaster, remaining there until his death. After the death of two gifted sons, two brothers, and his wife, Palestrina decided in 1580 to enter the priesthood; but early in 1581 he changed his mind and married the widow of a prosperous furrier and leather merchant whose business he and a partner carried on with considerable success for a number of years. Many of his greatest masterpieces were composed during the latter years of his life. His *Mass of Pope Marcellus* has been cited often as the work which staved off the possible banishment of polyphony from the services of the church because of the abuses that had become prevalent in the contrapuntal music of the time. This has proved to be a legend, but certainly this celebrated mass fulfilled the ideals called for by those who were seeking a purer form of liturgical music. The noble style of Palestrina's music became the model for his contemporaries and has continued to be studied by musicians who want to understand sixteenth-century ecclesiastical polyphony at its best. In perfection of technique and purity and depth of religious expression it has never been surpassed. The metal plate on Palestrina's coffin bore the inscription: Princeps Musicae — The Prince of Music. The bulk of his music was sacred. Two complete editions of his works have been published, each containing over thirty volumes of masses, motets, and other liturgical music, and some sacred and secular madrigals.

182 Christ the Lord Is Risen Today

Originally written with eleven stanzas, including fifty-five Alleluias (a Latin form of the Hebrew word *Hallelujah,* meaning "Praise the Lord"), this hymn by Charles Wesley first appeared in the Wesley brothers' *Hymns and Sacred Poems,* 1739, and was later published in altered form in Martin Madan's *Collection of Psalms and Hymns,* 1760, a famous volume that provided the nucleus of hymns of most English hymnals for a hundred years after its appearance. The present version uses stanzas one, four, the first half of stanza two and the last half of stanza three (as stanza three), and stanzas five and six of the original. See No. 43 for comments on Charles Wesley.

EASTER HYMN (WORGAN; EASTER MORN) This anonymous tune, set to the anonymous hymn "Jesus Christ is risen today" (No. 187) in *Lyra Davidica,* 1708, needs little comment, for all who sing it know its power to awaken and express the joy of the day with which it is associated. The original form of the melody, possibly composed for the words, was entitled "The Resurrection." After a series of modifications the tune reached its present form in the sixth edition of John Arnold's *Compleat Psalmodist,* 1749. In Thomas Butts' *Harmonia Sacra,* c. 1753?, EASTER HYMN was named CHRISTMAS DAY and set to Charles Wesley's "Hark, how all the welkin rings." This combination was printed in *Harmonia Sacra,* 1816, published at Andover, Massachusetts. In the same volume, "Christ the Lord is ris'n today"

147

was set to JUDAS MACCABAEUS (No. 192) which was named EASTER.

The compiler of *Lyra Davidica* wanted music with more movement and spirit than he found in the grave, slow-paced psalm tunes, with one note to a syllable. Lightwood comments that this unknown editor (probably of German descent) little knew what he was initiating when he introduced EASTER HYMN with its freer air and lively Alleluia passages in a style that was taken up later by the Methodists. In England, in 1850, there were those who wanted to go back to tunes of a strictly ecclesiastical character and who felt that EASTER HYMN was too florid, hence inappropriate for use in church. So The Cheadle Association for the Promotion of Church Music offered a prize for a musical setting of "Jesus Christ is risen to-day." It was won by William Monk, but his prize song, which was published in *Hymns Ancient and Modern,* 1861, never fulfilled its purpose and failed utterly to supplant EASTER HYMN.

183 Christ the Lord Is Risen Again

In the liturgical music of the Roman Catholic Church of the ninth century, there developed a new form of hymn differing from the office hymn known as the sequence, Latin words and paired phrases sung to a free-flowing melody coming at the end of the Alleluia between the gradual and the gospel. One of the earliest of these was the Easter sequence, "Victimae paschali laudes." Later, in the twelfth century in Germany, vernacular lines were interpolated between the Latin lines. From this practice came one of the earliest and most famous of German hymns, both text and tune, "Christ ist erstanden, von der Marter alle." This was a favorite with Luther, and he based one of his chorales on it, "Christ lag in Todesbanden." It was from the same source that Michael Weisse (c. 1488–1534) drew his inspiration for the present hymn, originally beginning, "Christ ist erstanden, von des Todes Banden." Weisse was one of many monks who left the Catholic Church as a result of Luther's writings. He became a preacher and leader among the Bohemian Brethren and edited their first hymnal, *Ein New Gesengbuchlen,* 1531, a collection containing 155 hymns, most if not all of which he translated from the Bohemian into German or wrote himself. Luther is reported to have said after reading through the volume, "It is the work of a good poet." The translation by Catherine Winkworth is from her *Lyra Germanica,* 1858, second series. See No. 2 for comments on Miss Winkworth.

CHRIST IST ERSTANDEN   The large number of variants of this distinctive pre-Reformation melody witness to its age, its extensive use, and its popularity. In some books it is referred to as a Gregorian melody, not older than the twelfth century. In others it is called a folk song. References to it in thirteenth century manuscripts show that it was well known by then.

Luther's "Christ lag in Todesbanden" was entitled: "The hymn, 'Christ ist erstanden' improved." Both are related, textually and musically, to the eleventh-century plainsong sequence "Victimae paschali." (See *The Hymnal 1940,* No. 97; *Liber Usualis,* p. 780.)

The earliest printing of the melody was in Peter (the Younger) Schöffer's

148

Liederbuch, Mainz, 1513, the first four-part song book of any kind published in Germany. Of the sixty-two songs contained in it, only two were sacred. CHRIST IST ERSTANDEN, one of these, was the *cantus firmus* of a motet for four voices. In 1531 the melody was published in Michael Weisse's *Ein New Gesengbuchlen* (see No. 113). It had no refrain. The present form is almost identical with that in Klug's *Geistliche Lieder, 1535*, except that the first nine measures were repeated with a second stanza before the refrain. Klug's version, with English and German words, harmonized by Hans L. Hassler, is given at No. 30 in *Cantate Domino, 1951*. The wide circulation of the hymn is indicated by its inclusion in *Goostly Psalmes and Spirituall Songes,* printed in England c. 1543, with Miles Coverdale's translation. Maurice Frost draws attention to its similarity to the following 1531 version in Weisse's book. (Zahn 1970)

Chris-tus ist er - stan - den von des To - des Ban - den, des freu-et sich der En-gel Schar sin - gend im Him - mel im - mer - dar: Hal - le - lu - ja!

Bach wrote one chorale prelude on the melody in the Easter section of the *Orgelbüchlein* and used the Refrain for the final Chorale in Cantata 66. There is one harmonization in the *Choralgesänge*. The melody should be sung with a consciousness of phrases rather than of measures, and with the freshness and vitality expressed in the words — more in the spirit of a carol. Luther said: "After a time one tires of singing all other hymns, but 'Christ ist erstanden' one can always sing again." In *English and Scottish Psalm and Hymn Tunes, 1953*, Maurice Frost gives five early versions of the melody, including that used by Coverdale. (No. 270, p. 315)

184 Good Christian Men Rejoice and Sing!

Cyril Alington (1872–1955) wrote this Easter hymn for *Songs of Praise,* 1925, and for the tune GELOBT SEI GOTT while he was headmaster of Eton. He was later dean of Durham, honorary Fellow of Trinity College, select preacher to Oxford University, and chaplain to the king. His publications were numerous and diverse, including works in theology as well as poems, essays, and novels.

GELOBT SEI GOTT (VULPIUS) appeared with Michael Weisse's Easter hymn "Gelobt sei Gott im höchsten Thron" in *Ein schön geistlich Gesangbuch,* 1609, edited by Melchior Vulpius (c. 1560–1616). The tune, attributed to him, is thought by some to have roots in an earlier source. In any case it was Vulpius' setting that made the melody widely known. In Germany it is still sung with Weisse's words. It was set to the present text in *Songs of Praise,* 1931. The Alleluias in the refrain are as Vulpius wrote them and as they are sung in Germany.

Vulpius, cantor at the Gymnasium in Weimar for many years, composed several fine chorales, made distinguished contrapuntal settings of existing melodies for five, six, seven, and eight voices, and edited a number of books, one of which included settings for Luther's hymns. Some of his works have come out in modern editions. Part of the charm of GELOBT SEI GOTT lies in the syncopation in measures seven and eleven.

185 Come, Ye Faithful, Raise the Strain

Sometimes called the last of the Fathers of the Greek Church and the greatest of her hymnodists, John of Damascus (c. 696–c. 754), whose Saracen name was Mansur, was educated by a captive Italian monk, Cosmas, and spent most of his life in the famous monastery of St. Sabas, near Jerusalem, overlooking the Dead Sea. A man of encyclopedic learning, he was the author of one of the theological classics of the Eastern Church, *The Fountain of Knowledge,* and vigorously defended the use of icons. His role in organizing the chants of the liturgy of the Eastern Church is often likened to the part Gregory the Great played in organizing the music of the Western Church. Both the Greek and Latin churches have canonized him. His most notable literary achievement consisted of six Greek canons to celebrate the festivals of Christmas, the Epiphany, Pentecost, Easter, St. Thomas' Sunday (also called Low Sunday or Little Easter), and Ascension Day. A Greek canon is a series of odes, usually eight in number, each of which is based generally on a biblical canticle and follows an acrostic pattern with the key word given at the beginning of the first ode. This ode for St. Thomas' Sunday, the Sunday after Easter, is based on the "Song of Moses," Exodus 15, and vividly compares and relates the deliverance effected by Moses with that effected by Christ. The translation is by John Mason Neale written to illustrate an article by him on "Greek Hymnology" in the *Christian Remembrancer* for April, 1859. It later appeared in his *Hymns of the Eastern Church,* 1862. See No. 110 for comments on Neale.

ST. KEVIN, composed by Arthur Sullivan (1842–1900) for Neale's translation in Joseph Barnby's *Hymnary,* 1872, was named for an Irish saint in the composer's *Church Hymns with Tunes,* 1874. Sullivan wrote fifty-six hymn tunes, edited two hymnals, played the organ in two London churches, wrote anthems, service music, oratorios, and cantatas that were widely acclaimed, and was the most popular and successful composer in England in his day. However, his lasting fame does not rest on his church music. As fewer and fewer people sing his hymn tunes and anthems, more and more continue to be captivated and enchanted by the music he wrote for Sir William S. Gilbert's operetta libretti. There is something ironic in the fact that many of Sullivan's friends and admirers wanted him to devote his time to the composition of works they considered more important than comic operas, — something in a serious vein: oratorios and symphonies which they said would do justice to his gifts and bring honor to English art. His contemporaries did not realize that through these wonderfully infectious, spontaneous creations, his genius was giving England unique distinction in a field in which he is unrivalled.

Sullivan, a child prodigy of extraordinary gifts, was the son of an Irish musician who became master of the band at the Royal Military College, Sandhurst, and later professor of brass band at Kneller Hall, the Royal Military School of Music. By the time Arthur was eight he could play most of the wind instruments in the band — first-hand experience that helps to explain his remarkable skill and inventiveness in orchestration. At twelve he became a chorister in the Chapel Royal, after singing for his audition with Sir George Smart (see No. 81) "With verdure clad" from Haydn's *Creation,* accompanying himself at the piano. His three years in the Chapel Royal, under the guidance of Thomas Helmore (No. 110), master of the choristers, gave him excellent musical training and familiarized him with much great choral music. At fourteen he entered the competition for the first Mendelssohn scholarship. He and Joseph Barnby, the youngest and the oldest of seventeen contestants, tied for first place, but in a second difficult trial Sullivan won, and spent one year at the Royal Academy of Music in London where he studied harmony and composition with John Goss. (No. 16) He did so well that the scholarship was extended for two years of intensive study in Leipzig. There he became aware for the first time of the greatness of such composers as Schubert, Schumann, and Wagner. His lessons in fugue and counterpoint with Hauptmann were given at the Thomasschule in the room where Bach had composed much of his music when he was cantor. Soon after Sullivan's return to England (he was under twenty), his incidental music for Shakespeare's *Tempest* was performed and met with tremendous success. From that time on, he went from triumph to triumph as composer, conductor, teacher. In 1867 he went to Vienna with Sir George Grove in search of Schubert manuscripts. Their trip was rewarded by discovery of the score of *Rosamunde.* For six years he was principal and teacher of composition at the National Training School for Music, the forerunner of the Royal College of Music. He was given honorary degrees by Oxford and Cambridge, made a Chevalier of the Legion of Honor, and knighted in 1883. During his lifetime Sullivan did much to further the cause of English music and musicians. His own music in the operettas, inimitable and unmistakably British, has become a national institution and one of England's choicest exports.

186 Come, Ye Faithful, Raise the Strain

See No. 185 for comments on the text.

AVE VIRGO VIRGINUM (GAUDEAMUS PARITER) This bright, cheerful, traditional German tune of the fourteenth or fifteenth century was set to Neale's translation in *The English Hymnal,* 1906, and from there has passed into a number of English and American hymnals. In 1544 it appeared with an Advent hymn, "Nun lasst uns zu dieser Frist," in a hymnbook of the Bohemian Brethren published at Nürnberg and edited by Johann Horn to whom the melody is sometimes attributed. It bore the heading, "Gaudeamus pariter omnes," the first line of an Advent hymn with which it was associated in fifteenth-century Bohemian collections. The melody, in the same form, was set to a Christmas hymn, "Lob sei Gott im höchsten Thron," in Leisentritt's *Catholicum Hymnologium Germanicum*, 1584, with a note indicating that it was the tune for "Ave virgo virginum," a *Marienlied* with which it was associated in western Germany. (See Bäumker, Vol. I, No. 32.) Some music editors have altered the rhythm in measure eleven in order to make it easier to sing. Actually, the rhythm, as it stands and as it appeared in Horn's and Leisentritt's collections, is not difficult to sing and gives variety and a delightful lilt to the melody. The fact that phrases one, two, and four are identical melodically and rhythmically, and that the tune moves by steps in phrase three, makes AVE VIRGO VIRGINUM simple to learn.

187 Jesus Christ Is Risen Today

Based on three German and Bohemian manuscripts of the fourteenth century, this Latin carol, "Surrexit Christus hodie," was introduced into English usage in a small but important collection, *Lyra Davidica, or a Collection of Divine Songs and Hymns, partly newly composed, partly translated from the High German and Latin Hymns; and set to easy and pleasant tunes,* London, 1708, which departed in its selection of both texts and tunes from the rigid psalmody prevailing at the time. The translator is unknown. The modern form of the hymn first appeared in John Arnold's *Compleat Psalmodist,* 1749, and it became popular by being included in a late Supplement to the *New Version,* c. 1816. The last stanza in the form of a doxology was written by Charles Wesley in his *Hymns and Sacred Poems,* 1740. Although considerably altered, it is often referred to as "the Easter Hymn par excellence."

LLANFAIR   See No. 19 for comments on the tune.

188 Joy Dawned Again on Easter Day

Originally sung at lauds from the Sunday after Easter to Ascension in the monastic offices, this early Latin hymn, "Claro paschali gaudio," is a cento of a longer poem, "Aurora lucis rutilat." It is one of the earliest hymns selected for use for a special season in the medieval breviary (a book containing the prayers, psalms, lessons, and hymns, for the canonical hours). The translation, slightly altered, is by John Mason Neale from his *Hymnal Noted,* 1852. See No. 110 for comments on Neale.

PUER NOBIS NASCITUR   See No. 144 for comments on the tune.

189 Lift Up Your Hearts, Ye People

This new Easter hymn by Leonard A. Parr (1880–   ) came into the *Pilgrim Hymnal* through a fortuitous circumstance. The words, printed in a Sunday calendar of the First Congregational Church of Ann Arbor, Michigan, where Dr. Parr served as minister for twenty years until his retirement in 1957, were enclosed in a personal letter from a parishioner to a member of the hymnal committee. Later when the parishioner was told that the committee had voted to include the hymn, he was quite surprised and somewhat chagrined, for he had not told Dr. Parr of his action. The happy ending came, however, in Dr. Parr's answer to a letter asking permission to use the hymn: "Of course, I graciously forgave him," wrote Dr. Parr, a recognized scholar in English literature and the author of many hymns. He served Congregational Churches in Iowa, Wisconsin, Michigan, and Illinois and was special lecturer in literature and drama at Ripon College, Wisconsin.

DU MEINE SEELE SINGE Since 1671 this melody has been sung in Germany with "Du meine Seele, singe," Paul Gerhardt's paraphrase of Psalm 146: "Praise ye the Lord. Praise the Lord, O my soul." In a collection of Gerhardt's hymns published in 1666 with musical settings by Johann Georg Ebeling (No. 123) it was set to "Merkt auf, merkt Himmel, Erde, Und du, O Meeresgrund." (Zahn 5490) The initials "J.G.E." were written above the melody in a 1682 edition of the collection. The 1666 version of the melody, irregular in rhythm, appears in two contemporary German hymnals. The present form is from the *Kirchengesangbuch* of the Evangelical and Reformed Church of the German-speaking Swiss, published in 1952.

190 Lift Up Your Hearts, Ye People

See No. 189 for comments on the text.

GREENLAND In Vol. I (1806) of Christian I. Latrobe's six-volume *Selection of Sacred Music from the Works of the most Eminent Composers of Germany and Italy*, 1806–1825, GREENLAND was said to be from one of Johann Michael Haydn's "Services for Country Churches" — evidently his *Deutschen-Kirchen-Messen*. It was one of twelve "selections" attributed to Haydn. Latrobe, a prominent English Moravian, studied music in Germany and throughout his life devoted much time to music in the church. Feeling that his fellow Englishmen were too exclusively devoted to Handel, he hoped to acquaint them, through his collection, with music of the German and Italian composers. This tune was published later in Benjamin Jacobs' *National Psalmody*, 1819, as SALZBURG, with a version of Psalm I. Its present name comes from its association in some hymnals with "From Greenland's icy mountains."

J. Michael Haydn (1737–1806) started out, as did his older brother, Franz Joseph, as a chorister at St. Stephen's in Vienna. His voice had a remarkable range of three octaves, and when Franz's voice changed, Michael replaced him in the solo parts. He studied violin and organ, and sometimes acted as deputy organist at St. Stephen's. He had no regular instruction in composition but taught himself, by copying the whole of Fux's celebrated book on counterpoint, *Gradus ad Parnassum*. In later years, Carl Maria von Weber was one of his distinguished pupils. In 1757 he became Kapellmeister at Grosswardein for the bishop, Count Firmian, whose uncle, Archbishop Sigismund of Salzburg, appointed him his music director and concert master in 1762. Haydn was extraordinarily attached to Salzburg and spent more than forty years of his life there, from 1777 as organist at the churches of the Holy Trinity and St. Peter. In December, 1800, when the French took Salzburg, he lost all his property. The Empress Maria Theresa, hearing of his plight, commissioned him to write a mass for which she paid him handsomely. He presented it to her in person, and directed its first performance at Laxenburg Palace with Maria Theresa herself singing the soprano arias. At this time Prince Esterhazy, Franz Joseph's patron, offered Michael the vice-capellmeistership of his chapel but the younger Haydn preferred to return to Salzburg. At one time when Haydn was ill and unable to write a commissioned work, Mozart, who was in Salzburg at the time, carried out the assignment for him, writing two duets for violin and viola. For practice in orchestration Mozart scored some of Haydn's sacred works and sent some of them to Baron van Swieten in Vienna, to make them better known. In one of his letters, he speaks of Haydn as an "excellent contrapuntist." Haydn composed quantities of music — over three hundred sacred works, more than one hundred for organ, orchestra, and instrumental groups. He was too modest to let them be published, perhaps because he felt overshadowed by his illustrious brother, who in turn, felt that Michael's sacred music was superior to his own.

191   O Sons and Daughters, Let Us Sing

As a preaching Franciscan friar in Paris, Jean Tisserand (d. 1494) wrote this joyous Easter hymn, "O filii et filiae," in the style of a folk carol with refrain. It was later found in a small booklet without title printed between 1518 and 1536. The booklet is now in the collection of the Bibliothèque Nationale in Paris. Tisserand founded an order for penitent women and is the probable author of a devotional work commemorating the martyrdom of some members of his order in Morocco in 1220. The translation, considerably altered, is by John Mason Neale in his *Mediaeval Hymns and Sequences,* 1851. See No. 110 for comments on Neale.

O FILII ET FILIAE, the traditional melody for these words, appeared in a variety of forms in seventeenth- and eighteenth-century Catholic collections. It is probably of French origin. Its earliest known printed form has been found with Latin words in *Airs sur les hymnes sacrez, odes et noels,* Paris, 1623, set in four parts. Bäumker (Vol. I, No. 292), gives the melody as found in a Jesuit publication, *Nord-Sterns Führers zur Seeligkeit,* 1671, with a German translation *"O Söhn'und Töchter Christenleut."* This melody is the refrain of a "Motet pour la fête de Pâques" in La Feillée's *Méthode du Plain-Chant,* Poitiers, 1777. The word *gai* above the first measure is a suggestion still valid for those who sing this joyful Easter carol. The first printing in America of "this happy dance of the spirit" was in Philadelphia in John Aiken's *Compilation of the Litanies and Vespers, Hymns and Anthems as they are sung in the Catholic Church,* 1787. In the *Sabbath Hymn and Tune Book,* 1859, for which Lowell Mason was music editor, O FILII ET FILIAE, minus the preliminary and concluding alleluias and with the first phrase repeated as a fourth, was assigned to four hymns and named

EASTER–TIDE. With the same name and form it was set to "O Christ! with each returning morn" in *The People's Tune-Book* published by Mason in 1860. A footnote read, "This tune, highly esteemed, has long been sung in the Romish Church." In the index it was listed as "Roman Melody." Several different forms of the melody and varied harmonizations of it are found in present-day hymnals. The Solesmes version with twelve stanzas in Latin appears on pages 1875–1876 in *Liber Usualis*. Winfred Douglas' 1918 harmonization of that version is given at No. 99 in *The Hymnal 1940*.

192 The Day of Resurrection

At the midnight service on Easter Eve, worshippers in the Eastern Churches carry unlighted tapers which, upon a signal, are all lighted, filling the church with a brilliant glow. This is the hymn sung at that point in the service and, according to John Mason Neale's account of such a service in Athens, it is accompanied by the sound of drums and trumpets in the surrounding countryside and the jubilant greeting, "Christos anesti" ("Christ is risen"). Written by John of Damascus, it is the first ode of his Easter canon, known popularly as the golden canon. See No. 185 for comments on John of Damascus. John Mason Neale freely translated the stanzas in his *Hymns of the Eastern Church*, 1862. See No. 110 for comments on Neale.

LANCASHIRE was composed in 1836 by Henry Smart for Bishop Heber's hymn, "From Greenland's icy mountains," which was to be sung at a missionary meeting in Blackburn, Lancashire, where he served as organist in the parish church from 1831–1836. Later it was printed on single sheets and circularized for use at Nonconformist gatherings but was not widely sung until after its publication in the English Presbyterian hymnbook, *Psalms and Hymns for Divine Worship*, 1867. In *Hymn Tunes and Their Story*, Lightwood comments on the fact that this tune has remained just as Smart wrote it, without any tinkering or revision. See No. 117 for comments on Smart.

193 Thine Is the Glory

Gaining international popularity almost overnight as a result of the enthusiastic reception it received at the First Assembly of the World Council of Churches in Amsterdam in 1948, this hymn by Edmond L. Budry (1854–1932), who was a pastor in Vevey, Switzerland, was first published in the *Y.M.C.A. Hymn Book*, Lausanne, 1904. It was translated from the French into English in 1923 by Richard Birch Hoyle (1875–1939), Baptist minister and scholar, who held several pastorates in England and taught in Western Theological Seminary in the United States from 1934 to 1936. It later appeared in *Cantate Domino*, 1925, the hymnal of the World's Student Christian Federation, and has since become a great favorite, especially at ecumenical gatherings and youth rallies. The original first line in French reads, "A toi la gloire, O Ressuscité."

JUDAS MACCABEUS is an adaptation of part of the chorus, "See, the conquering hero comes," from Handel's oratorio *Judas Maccabeus*, first performed in April, 1747. This particular chorus, however, was not sung on that occasion for it was not until 1751 that Handel transferred it from *Joshua,* written in 1748, to *Judas Maccabeus,* a shift that remained permanent. In Thomas Butts' *Harmonia Sacra,* c. 1760, this chorus, arranged for three parts and called EASTER was set to "Christ the Lord, is ris'n today," whereas the tune commonly sung with those words (No. 182) was assigned to "Hark, how all the welkin rings," originally the first line of "Hark! the herald angels sing." Both combinations were reprinted in *Harmonia Sacra,* 1816, Andover, Massachusetts, an American edition of Butt's London collections.

In the *Seraph* (February 1839), edited by Lowell Mason, "Christ the Lord is ris'n today" was set to this tune in an arrangement almost identical with that at No. 193. It was called MACCABEUS.

The genius of German-born George Frederick Handel (1685–1759), who became a British subject in 1726, needs no proclamation. In contrast with his great contemporary, Johann Sebastian Bach (see No. 24), he was widely traveled, was enthusiastically acclaimed in England and on the Continent in his lifetime, and at his death was buried with high honors in Westminster Abbey. Although in the minds of many he is most often associated with oratorio — especially the *Messiah* — he spent thirty-five years of his life composing operas and in that field easily excelled all his contemporaries. He had written some forty-six operas before he finally turned to oratorio because of the collapse of Italian opera in England. In the oratorios, his genius for dramatic music is evident and the monumental grandeur of his choruses has never been surpassed in the history of choral composition.

Discussing "the gigantic figure of Handel" in *Music, History and Ideas,* Hugo Leichtentritt writes: "Everything accomplished in oratorio in the two hundred years after Handel is most profoundly indebted to him. Haydn, Mozart, Beethoven, Mendelssohn, Brahms and Bruckner are his pupils in their choral art, and even these great artists have never surpassed their master." [9] Beethoven said, "Go and learn of him how to achieve great effects with simple means." And Haydn, who attended the last of the five Handel commemorations in Westminster Abbey in 1791, in which unprecedented numbers of singers and instrumentalists took part, wept when the "Hallelujah Chorus" was sung, and exclaimed, "He is the master of us all!" Haydn's own oratorios, "The Creation" and "The Seasons," owed much to his having heard Handel's works performed in England.

194 The Whole Bright World Rejoices Now

This traditional German carol which first appeared in a hymnal published in Cologne, *Auserlesene Catholische Geistliche Kirchengesäng,* 1623, was translated by Percy Dearmer for *The Oxford Book of Carols,* 1928. "Hilariter" is an exclamatory shout of joy and is related to the word hilarity, regarded as one of the early Christian virtues. See No. 112 for comments on Dearmer.

HILARITER, the Latin word for cheerfully or merrily, supplies the tune name and one of the refrains for this gay, Easter carol from Germany and reminds one of Percy Dearmer's definition that "carols are songs with a religious impulse that are simple, hilarious, popular and modern." It is a traditional melody in the Dorian mode, found in several seventeenth-century German Catholic hymnals with the words, "Die ganze Welt, Herr Jesu Christ." In *Sirenes Symphoniacae,* 1678, the tune was set to the Latin words, "Surrexit Christus hodie." The present arrangement by Martin Shaw (see No. 106) is from *The Oxford Book of Carols,* 1928.

195 All Hail the Power of Jesus' Name

A man of independent mind and volatile temper, Edward Perronet (1726–1792) came from a family of Huguenot refugees who had left Switzerland in 1680 for England. His father was vicar of Shoreham, Kent, for fifty years and enjoyed the friendship and esteem of Charles and John Wesley, eventually receiving the cognomen the Archbishop of Methodism. Edward was also intimately acquainted with the Wesleys, becoming for a time an itinerant Methodist preacher, although he later dissociated himself from the movement when the Wesleys took exception to his attacks on the Church of England. He was subsequently connected with several dissenting religious groups, finally taking charge of an Independent Chapel in Canterbury where he served as minister until his death on January 2, 1792. On one occasion, while Perronet was still in the good graces of the Wesleys, John Wesley, seeing him in his congregation, announced that the young man would preach at the service the following morning. Feeling that he could not properly decline and yet not wanting to preach in the presence of the great evangelist, Perronet prefaced his sermon with the comment: "I am compelled by the respect I have for Mr. Wesley to occupy his place. I am entirely inadequate to the task; but, for all that, I will give you the best sermon that has ever been delivered." Whereupon, he read the Sermon on the Mount in its entirety without comment and concluded the service. Although he was a man of considerable talent, he is remembered today chiefly because he wrote this hymn. Consisting originally of eight stanzas, the first of which appeared in the November,

157

1779, issue of the *Gospel Magazine* and the remaining seven in the April, 1780, issue, the hymn has been considerably revised and improved by later editors. The version now most frequently employed comes from John Rippon's *Selection of Hymns from the best authors*, 1787, in which the familiar last stanza was added, "O that, with yonder sacred throng." John Rippon (1751–1836) was one of the most prominent Baptist ministers of his time and served the Carter's Lane Church in London for sixty-five years. He championed the use of Watts' hymns and is reported to have accumulated a small fortune through the wide sale of his published collections.

CORONATION is the only eighteenth-century American hymn tune still in general use. It was composed for Perronet's text by Oliver Holden (1765–1844). The little pipe organ at which it was composed is still preserved in the Old State House in Boston. CORONATION was published in *The Union Harmony,* 1793, one of several psalm and hymn tune collections compiled by Holden. *The Massachusetts Compiler,* 1795, a collection of tunes which he helped to edit, has been called "the most progressive work on Psalmody which appeared in America before 1800." Holden left his birthplace, Shirley, for Charlestown when he was twenty years old, and found much to do as a carpenter in helping to rebuild this city which had been burned by the British after the Battle of Bunker Hill. Building operations and real estate transactions were highly successful and profitable. His great interest in music found an outlet in leading and directing singing schools and choirs, writing music, compiling tune books, and selling music as a sideline in the general store he owned and ran. A generous as well as prosperous citizen, he gave the land for the site of a Baptist Church and later built, practically unaided, the Puritan Church where he preached from 1818 to 1833. After the death of William Billings, Holden was the most popular American composer of psalm and hymn tunes.

196 All Hail the Power of Jesus' Name

See No. 195 for comments on the text.

MILES LANE, the tune to which these words are sung in England, is the only one by which its composer, William Shrubsole (1760–1806), is known. A native of Canterbury, he was a chorister in the Cathedral from 1770–1777 and also studied organ there. MILES LANE, written when he was nineteen years old, was first published (anonymously) in the *Gospel Magazine,* November, 1779, with the first stanza of Perronet's hymn. In 1780 the tune, named MILES'S LANE and credited to Shrubsole, appeared in *A Collection of Psalm Tunes* edited by the Rev. Stephen Addington, minister of Miles' Lane Meeting House, London. Originally it was for three parts, alto, tenor, and bass, with each part coming in separately and successively on "crown him" before joining forces at the end. In this form it appeared in a number of early nineteenth-century American collections.

In 1782, Shrubsole, an Anglican, was appointed organist of Bangor Cathedral, but because of difficulties with the dean and chapter, due to his sympathies with Dissenters and Methodists and his attendance at some of their meetings, he was dismissed. He went to London, sang alto in the Drury Lane Theatre and at Westminster Abbey, taught music, and in 1784 became organist of the Spa Fields Chapel, a post he retained until his death. This was one of sixty-four (or more) chapels established and maintained by Lady Huntingdon (1707–1791), English religious leader, who was active in the Wesley revival and founder of a sect of Calvinistic Methodists who became known as "The Countess of Huntingdon's Connexion."

Shrubsole met Perronet in Canterbury when the latter was pastor of a small Independent Chapel there. They became close friends. Perronet appointed Shrubsole one of the executors of his will and left him some property because of (in the words of the will) "the fine disinterested affection he has ever shown me from our first acquaintance . . . even when a proverb of reproach, cast off by all my relatives, disinherited unjustly and left to sink or swim." Millar Patrick writes: "The wedding of the hymn of the one with the tune of the other perpetuates the memory of this friendship." A phrase of MILES LANE was carved on Shrubsole's tombstone at Bunhill Fields, London.

197 At the Name of Jesus

Although displaying talent as a hymn writer at the age of seventeen, it was not until she reached the age of forty and underwent a prolonged period of illness and suffering that Caroline Noel (1817–1877) produced her finest works, *The Name of Jesus, and Other Verses for the Sick and Lonely*, 1861, later enlarged and changed to *The Name of Jesus and Other Poems*, 1870. This hymn, written as a processional for Ascension Day and based on Philippians 2:5–11, was taken from the second of these volumes. An invalid the last twenty-five years of her life, she wrote her hymns to bring consolation to others in their suffering. She was the daughter of an Anglican clergyman and hymn writer, the Honorable Gerard Thomas Noel, and lies buried at his side near the Abbey Church of Romsey where he had been vicar.

KING'S WESTON was composed for this Ascension Day processional hymn by Ralph Vaughan Williams for *Songs of Praise*, 1925. It is a strong tune which seems austere at first but lays hold of one with new power at each hearing. When one knows it well he feels that there is a kind of inevitability about the flow of the melody with its gradual rise in pitch to the first note of measure thirteen which gives a sense of arrival and climax. The *b* natural in measure eleven, the only *b* in the melody, gives the flavor of the Dorian mode. The reversal in measures thirteen and fourteen of the rhythmic pattern ♩♩♩♩ established through repetition in measures 1,3,5,7,9, and 11, is arresting and a masterly touch. The simple diatonic harmonies and the fine bass line are worthy of notice.

"King's Weston is a country house on the River Avon near Bristol, England, noted for its beautiful park." (R. G. McCutchan, in *Hymn Tune Names*.)

See No. 306 for comments on Vaughan Williams.

198 Christ Is the World's True Light

Combining the Christological hope with a modern missionary perspective, this hymn by Canon George Wallace Briggs (1875–1959) first appeared in *Songs of Praise,* 1931, to which he contributed sixteen original hymns and six hymn tunes. Prior to his appointment as canon of Worcester Cathedral in 1934, he served as a chaplain in the Royal Navy, vicar of St. Andrew's, Norwich, rector of Loughborough College, and canon of Leicester Cathedral. By means of his published volumes of prayers and hymns, especially *The Daily Service,* 1936, he exerted a marked influence on the worship services in English schools. One of his prayers was read on the occasion of the historic meeting of President Franklin Delano Roosevelt and Prime Minister Winston Churchill on board H.M.S. *Prince of Wales,* August 10, 1941, when the Atlantic Charter was adopted.

O GOTT, DU FROMMER GOTT is named DARMSTADT in some English and American hymnals, probably because the present form of the melody is closer to a version found in a hymnbook published at Darmstadt in 1698 than to the original in Ahasuerus Fritsch's collection, *Himmels-Lust und Welt-Unlust,* 1679, published at Jena. The tune was called ROCH-ESTER in Mercer's *Church Psalter and Hymn Book,* 1854. It is often attributed to Fritsch (1629–1701) who, after a childhood spent in the upheavals and distress of the Thirty Years' War and in spite of poverty, managed by dint of hard work and sacrifice to attain distinction as author, educator, editor, and statesman. The family of a young nobleman of Rudolstadt, whom he tutored, did much to help advance his career. In 1661 he received a Doctor of Laws degree (LL.D.) from the University of Jena, later becoming its chancellor as well as the president of the consistory of Rudolstadt. Bach used this splendid tune in Cantatas 45, 64, 94, 128, 129, and in the unfinished Cantata "Ehre sei Gott in der Höhe." The present harmonization is from the last movement of Cantata 45. The German tune name is from the first line of Johann Heermann's hymn, "O Gott, du frommer Gott" ("O God, thou faithful God") with which the melody appeared in some collections. Heermann's hymn was also sung with two other tunes (Nos. 86 and 252) both of which appear in Bach's works. See Nos. 24, 233, and 281 for comments on Bach.

199 Crown Him With Many Crowns

Even though he was trained as an Anglican and wrote a polemical volume against the Roman Church, *The Roman Empire under Constantine the Great,* 1829, Matthew Bridges (1800–1894) later became a Catholic under the influence of John Henry Newman and the Oxford Movement. He devoted his life to producing literary works in the fields of poetry and history and spent his later years in Canada where he died in Quebec on October 6, 1894. The first, second, and fourth stanzas of the present hymn were taken from his *Hymns of the Heart,* 1851 edition (originally these were stanzas one, three, and five of his six-stanza hymn); stanza three was taken from Godfrey Thring's *Hymns and Sacred Lyrics,* 1874. Godfrey Thring (1823–1903) was an Anglican clergyman who published several volumes of hymns, one of which, *A Church of England Hymn Book*, 1880, was adjudged to have set a higher literary standard than any other hymnbook of its time.

DIADEMATA was one of three hymn tunes composed by Sir George Elvey (1816–1893), and was printed for the first time in the Appendix to *Hymns Ancient and Modern*, 1868. It was written for Matthew Bridges' hymn which obviously inspired the tune name DIADEMATA, the Greek word for crowns. Elvey, born in Canterbury, had his first musical training as a chorister in the cathedral choir there. When his voice changed he went to Oxford to study organ with his brother, Stephen Elvey, organist at New College and choragus of the University. Subsequently, he studied at the Royal Academy of Music and at Oxford where he received his Bachelor and Doctor degrees in music. Before he was seventeen Elvy was a skilled organist, and at nineteen was appointed organist and master of the boys at St. George's Chapel, Windsor, where he remained for forty-seven years. In this position he had to provide music for a variety of important events of state. In 1871 he was knighted by Queen Victoria. He composed anthems, service music, oratorios, but is known chiefly for his hymn tunes, two or three of which appear in most hymnals. He was buried outside the west front of St. George's Chapel where he had directed the music for so many years.

200 The Head That Once Was Crowned With Thorns

Intending originally to become a lawyer, Thomas Kelly (1769–1854) decided instead to enter the church after coming under the influence of the Evangelical movement. He was Episcopally ordained in 1792 but speedily incurred the displeasure of his superior, the Archbishop of Dublin, as a result of his "methodistical" activities. Forbidden to preach in the diocese, he left the Established Church and founded a sect of his own, no longer in existence, and built churches with his own funds at Athy, Portarlington, Wexford, and other Irish towns. A man of genius as well as of wealth, he published a volume of hymns, *Hymns on Various Passages of Scripture*, 1804, that came out in several editions and eventually contained 765 selections. The present hymn is from the 1820 edition of Kelly's *Hymns*. He later published a companion volume that included a number of original tunes, several of which were in unusual and distinctive meters. He was known both as a brilliant preacher and as a friend of the poor and oppressed, and one such admirer is said to have encouraged his wife during a difficult time, "Hould up, Bridget! There's always Misther Kelly to pull us out of the bog afther we've sunk for the last time."

ST. MAGNUS See No. 78 for comments on the tune.

201 The King Shall Come When Morning Dawns

Of unknown Greek origin, this hymn is a good example of the emphasis placed on light and redemption in the worship of the Eastern Church. Translated by John Brownlie (1857–1925), it first appeared in his *Hymns from the East,* 1907. Educated at Glasgow University and the Free Church College, he served first as junior minister and then senior minister of the Free Church, Portpatrick, Wigtownshire, Scotland. Later, because of his great interest in education, he was made chairman of the governors of Stanraer High School. His translations of early Latin and Greek hymns constitute a major contribution to the hymnody of the church. These were published in his *Hymns of the Early Church,* 1896; *Hymns from East and West,* 1898; *Hymns of the Greek Church,* 1900 to 1906 (four series); and *Hymns from the East,* 1907. He also wrote a helpful commentary, *Hymns and Hymn Writers of the Church Hymnary,* 1899, for the Scottish hymnal.

ST. STEPHEN (NAYLAND; NEWINGTON)   In 1789 William Jones (1726–1800), English clergyman, published *Ten Church Pieces for the Organ, with Four Anthems in Score, composed for the use of the church of Nayland in Suffolk and published for its benefit,* a book that brought him considerable reputation. "St. Stephen's Tune" was on the last page of his collection, set to Thomas Sternhold's version of Psalm 23, "My Shepherd is the living Lord." With a few harmonic changes and the name "Nayland Tune" it was also included at the end of Jones' last published work, *A Morning and Evening Service,* 1795, which was performed before the king in St. George's Chapel, Windsor, and in three cathedral churches. This clergyman-composer, a lineal descendant of Col. John Jones — brother-in-law of Oliver Cromwell, and one of those who signed the death warrant of Charles I — observed every January 30 as a day of fasting and humiliation for the sin of his ancestor. Educated at Charterhouse and University College, Oxford, ordained in 1751, elected a Fellow of the Royal Society in 1775, Jones was a person of varied and great accomplishments and one of the most prominent and influential churchmen of his day. He came to be known as Jones of Nayland after being appointed perpetual curate of Nayland, Suffolk, in 1777. A proficient musician, he once said that music was the delight of his soul and he was master of it. His concern for music in the church is of particular interest because he lived at a time when the Anglican church was almost entirely immune to the musical changes going on in the Nonconformist churches. His writings, published in twelve volumes in 1801, included *A Treatise on the Art of Music,* 1784 (quite a remarkable work for the time), as well as books on theology, the Bible, and natural science.

202 Jesus Shall Reign Where'er the Sun

Often referred to as the first great missionary hymn written in English, this hymn by Isaac Watts is from his *Psalms of David,* 1719, and constitutes the second half of his free paraphrase of Psalm 92, under the heading, "Christ's Kingdom among the Gentiles." It is given here in unaltered form save that three stanzas have been omitted. This affords a vivid illustration of how freely and radically Watts altered the psalms in order to "Christianize" them. See No. 1 for comments on Watts.

DUKE STREET (WINDLE, ST. HELENS)   The three names for this strong tune tell nearly all that is known of the man to whom it is ascribed:

John Hatton, who lived on Duke Street in the township of Windle in the district of St. Helens. It is thought that he was born in Warrington because he was referred to as John of Warrington, and it is known that he died in 1793 because his funeral sermon was preached in the Presbyterian Church of St. Helens on December 13, of that year. DUKE STREET first appeared in *A Select Collection of Psalm and Hymn Tunes . . . By the late Henry Boyd, Teacher of Psalmody,* Glasgow, 1793. It was headed "Addison's 19th Psalm," known now as "The spacious firmament on high." (72) No composer's name was given, but in William Dixon's *Euphonia,* c. 1805, published in Liverpool, it was called DUKE STREET and ascribed to Hatton. The quality of this tune is such that it enhances any text with which it is sung. Dr. Archibald T. Davison used it for five texts in *The Harvard University Hymn Book,* 1926. It would seem to fulfill the requirement for a classic (mentioned in the Preface to the *Pilgrim Hymnal,* 1958) as "a work of art over which the destroying hand of time is powerless."

DUKE STREET is a wonderfully compact tune: diatonic, within the range of an octave, with no melodic repetition, predominantly stepwise but with enough skips to give it variety, and with a different rhythmic pattern in each of its four phrases.

203 Look, Ye Saints, the Sight Is Glorious

This hymn by Thomas Kelly, inspired by Revelations 7:9–15, is from the third edition of his *Hymns on Various Passages of Scripture,* 1809. See No. 200 for comments on Kelly.

CORONAE obviously derives its name from the refrain of Thomas Kelly's hymn to which it was set in Tucker's *Hymnal with Tunes Old and New,* 1872. Its composer, William H. Monk (1823–1889) is best known for EVENTIDE (209) and for his contribution to hymnody as music editor of the epoch-making *Hymns Ancient and Modern,* 1861, often referred to in its early days as Monk's Book. He contributed nearly fifty tunes to its various editions, but few of them survive. It was he who suggested its apt title which describes so succinctly its eclectic character. Monk served as organist in various London churches before becoming organist and choirmaster at St. Matthias, Stoke Newington, where he remained from 1852 until his death, directing a volunteer choir in daily choral services which he established, and doing much to promote wholehearted congregational singing. He served successively as choir director (1847), organist (1849), and professor of vocal music (1874) at King's College, London, where he was associated with John Hullah (who did much to popularize sightsinging and music education in England). Monk was also professor of music at the School for the Indigent Blind (1851), at the National Training School for Music (1876) — the school which became the Royal College of Music — and at Bedford College, London. In addition to this teaching, he composed hymn tunes, anthems, and service music, edited collections of psalm and hymn tunes (three of which were for the Church of Scotland), and lectured on music in London, Manchester, and Edinburgh. In 1882 he was given an honorary Doctor of Music degree by Durham University. He was interested in the types of music advocated by the Oxford Movement, and was one of the founders of *The Parish Choir,* its musical periodical, which he edited for eleven years. Monk wrote only one musical setting for secular words. A man of deep religious conviction, his greatest concern in connection with church music was that it should be a fit vehicle for worship and contribute to its enrichment.

204 Rejoice, the Lord Is King

Taken from Charles Wesley's *Hymns for our Lord's Resurrection,* 1746, the words probably were prompted by the Pauline text, "Rejoice in the Lord always: and again I say, Rejoice" (Philippians 4:4). See No. 43 for comments on Wesley.

DARWALL'S 148th   See No. 23 for comments on the tune.

205 Hail the Day That Sees Him Rise

This is an instance of a hymn that has been considerably improved by means of additions and revisions. The original words, written by Charles Wesley, first appeared as a "Hymn for Ascension Day" in the Wesley brothers' *Hymns and Sacred Poems,* 1739. G. C. White added the alleluias in his *Hymns and Introits,* 1852. Thomas Cotterill (1779–1823), an Anglican clergyman who sought to introduce the singing of hymns into the worship of the Established Church, extensively altered the words in his *A Selection of Psalms and Hymns for Public and Private Use,* 1820 edition. The eighth edition of this hymnal, published in 1819 in collaboration with James Montgomery, aroused such opposition in Cotterill's congregation in Sheffield on the part of those who wanted to sing only metrical psalms that a diocesan court action ensued and the Archbishop of York felt called upon to intervene. The latter judiciously offered to sanction a new version if the old one was withdrawn, and this was done and accepted. The later volume was widely used but the earlier one exerted a greater influence, prompting John Julian to remark that it "did more than any other collection in the Church of England to mould the hymn-books of the next period." Wesley's first stanza originally read:

> Hail the day that sees Him rise,
> Ravished from our wishful eyes!
> Christ, awhile to mortals given,
> Re-ascends his native heaven.

See No. 43 for comments on Wesley.

GWALCHMAI   See No. 65 for comments on this tune.

206 Ye Servants of God, Your Master Proclaim

Given as the first selection in the section entitled "Hymns to be sung in Tumult" from Charles Wesley's *Hymns for Times of Trouble and Persecution,*

1744, this hymn has become an enduring favorite. The collection was published at a time of strife and intolerance in England's affairs when the people known as Methodists were persecuted for their beliefs and practices. See No. 43 for comments on Wesley.

HANOVER (ST. GEORGE'S; ST. MICHAEL'S; OLD 104th) is the musical setting in most English hymnals for "O worship the King" (No. 6), Robert Grant's hymn based on Psalm 104. Oddly enough, its first five notes are identical with the first five of LYONS to which those words are most often sung in America. At its first appearance in the sixth edition of *A Supplement to the New Version of the Psalms*, 1708, HANOVER was set to Psalm 67, "Our God bless us all with mercy and love," with no tune name or composer's name given, and was headed "A New Tune to the 149th Psalm of the New Version and the 104th Psalm of the Old." One of its names, OLD 104th, indicates its frequent use with the Old Version of that psalm which had the same meter as the present hymn: 10.10.11.11. Though William Croft has been named as the composer, it has never been proved conclusively that he wrote it. As in the case of ST. ANNE (No. 1) which also was introduced in the 1708 *Supplement*, HANOVER is ascribed to Croft because it is generally assumed that he had a major part in editing this collection. However, the main reason for the ascription to him stems from *The People's Music Book*, 1844, where, in the body of the book, the tune was called OLD 104th and attributed to Handel, but in the Index was credited to Croft with a note that this tune "has been ascertained to be the composition of Dr. Croft, by satisfactory evidence, since the page in which it is contained was printed." In late eighteenth- and nineteenth-century tune books HANOVER was often attributed to Handel, but since he did not come to England until 1810, two years after its first appearance, and since during his lifetime and immediately afterwards it was never assigned to him, the ascription seems to be unfounded. In early nineteenth-century American collections the tune was called ST. MICHAEL'S and attributed to Handel, and was often set to "O praise ye the Lord, prepare your glad voice." The *Handbook to the Church Hymnary*, 1927, characterizes Croft's tunes as "of importance historically, as they are the earliest examples of the English psalm-tune as distinguished from the Genevan; they require quicker singing, and the glorious rhythmical impulse of HANOVER and its triple measure marked at once a distinct originality." [21] See No. 1 for comments on Croft.

207 I Greet Thee, Who My Sure Redeemer Art

Although scholars and churchmen disagree as to whether John Calvin (1509–1564) wrote this hymn or whether it can even be attributed to him, the words in their emphasis on man's dependence on divine grace and omnipotence breathe the bracing air of Geneva. Originally beginning with the line, "Je Te salue, mon certain Redempteur," the hymn first appeared in the 1545 edition of the French Psalter, of which Calvin was the editor. Contrary to much popular opinion, Calvin placed a high valuation on music and actively encouraged congregational singing in all the Reformed churches. He also took the lead in encouraging the teaching of psalm paraphrases to children as a way of introducing these into the churches. It was his perceptive genius that enlisted the services of Clément Marot and Théodore de Bèze in translating the psalms into metrical form and that set Louis Bourgeois to work at providing the music for the Genevan psalters, the sources of some of the most magnificent tunes in the church's musical heritage. The psalters that emanated from Geneva under his leadership have had a wide and enduring significance. The English translation of this hymn was first published in Philip Schaff's *Christ in Song,* 1868, where it is credited to "Mrs. Prof. H. B. Smith." It is generally believed that she was Elizabeth Lee Smith (1817–1898), gifted wife of Henry Boynton Smith, a professor at Union Theological Seminary, New York City, and daughter of President William Allen of Bowdoin College.

SONG 24   In Wither's *Hymnes and Songs of the Church,* 1623, SONG 24 was the setting for the following paraphrase of Lamentations 1:1.

> How sad and solitary now (alas,)
> Is that well-peopled Citie come to be!
> Which once so great among the Nations was,
> And, oh how widdow-like appeareth she!
> She rule of all the Provinces hath had;
> And now her selfe is tributary made.

The soprano and bass of SONG 24 are Gibbons'; the inner parts are those found in *The English Hymnal,* 1906. This melody, which one writer calls solemn, another grave, is in the Dorian mode and seems to draw beautiful texts to it. See No. 162 for comments on Gibbons.

208 Dear Master, in Whose Life I See

Following an early conversion experience, John Hunter (1848–1917) determined to become a Christian minister. Since his lack of formal education precluded his seeking ordination in the Church of Scotland, he sought and was granted admission to Nothingham Congregational Institute and eventually, after further studies, became one of the outstanding Congregational preachers in the British Isles. He was for two notable periods, 1887–1901 and 1904–1913, pastor of the great Trinity Congregational Church in Glasgow and effected a marked improvement in the worship of the free churches by his teaching and example and by means of his *Devotional Services for Public Worship,* 1886. Appearing originally in "The Monthly Calendar" of Trinity Church, this hymn was later included in Hunter's collection, *Hymns of Faith and Life,* 1896.

O JESU CHRISTE, WAHRES LICHT, an anonymous German melody, is named here for the first line of Johann Heermann's hymn, "O Jesu Christe, wahres Licht" ("O Jesus Christ, our true light"), with which it came to be associated soon after its first appearance in a Nürnberg hymnbook of 1676 with Martin Behm's "O Jesu Christ, mein's Lebens Licht" ("O Jesus Christ, my life's light"). (Zahn 535) Both texts appear with the tune in old and contemporary German hymnals. In one hymnal published in the United States (*The Lutheran Hymnal*, 1941) the use of this melody with five hymns would seem to be indicative of its popularity. It is most often listed as "O Jesu Christ, mein's Lebens Licht," but the present name helps to distinguish it from the melody at No. 67 which was also associated with Behm's hymn. In some books "Herr" takes the place of "O" in both texts.

209 Abide With Me

Two widely held views are found concerning the origin of this hymn. One maintains that Henry Lyte wrote the words in 1820 following a visit to a dying friend, William Augustus Le Hunte, during which the latter continued to repeat the phrase "abide with me." The second contends that the lines were written after the last service Lyte conducted for his small congregation of fisher folk at Lower Brixham, Devon, September 4, 1847, when he knew that he probably did not have long to live. In a letter to "Julia," probably his daughter-in-law, Eleanor Julia Bolton, dated August 25, 1847, he included this hymn and referred to it as "my latest effusion," which would place the time of its composition during the summer of the year he died. The point is that it was written not as an evening hymn, as is commonly thought, but as a hymn for the close of life. However, it is often sung at important football matches in England and Wales. Henry Ward Beecher's *Plymouth Collection of Hymns and Tunes for the Use of Christian Congregations*, 1855, first introduced it to America. See No. 16 for further comments on Lyte.

EVENTIDE   There are two conflicting accounts of the composition of this well-known tune. According to one, it was written at the close of a meeting of the committee that compiled the original edition of *Hymns Ancient and Modern*, and was completed in ten minutes in spite of the fact that one of Monk's associates was playing a *Fantasia* by Thalberg on the piano a few feet away. According to Monk's widow, EVENTIDE was written at a time of great sorrow, after she and her husband had been watching "the glories of the setting sun." After its appearance in *Hymns Ancient and Modern*, 1861, the tune displaced two others that had been associated with the words, one of which, by Lyte himself, may be seen in H. Augustine Smith's *Lyric Religion*. There can be no doubt that the tune had much to do with making "Abide with me" one of the best-known and best-loved hymns of English-speaking peoples. With the discontinuance of evening services in many churches, EVENTIDE is not sung much any more, and in the minds of many has become almost exclusively associated with funerals instead of with a "contemplative prayer on the transitoriness of human life, the need of the soul for God, and the hope of a life to come."

Americans are always surprised when they learn that Lyte's hymn is sung at *the* great football match of the year in England. How this came about is told by Cecil Northcott in *Hymns We Love*, 1955. The Cup Tie is one of the great national sporting events in Great Britain when the two football teams which have "fought their way through the cup games of the year meet for a decisive battle." While waiting for the game to start the huge crowd in the stadium sings. One year when "Alexander's ragtime band" was assigned a place on the program, the manager, Sir F. J. Wall, "felt impelled by a mysterious power" to run his pen through the title and write beneath it that "Abide with me" was to be sung instead. Northcott concludes, "Thus started the annual custom which links Lyte's hymn with a great football occasion, and to hear a hundred thousand voices singing it in the open air is a tribute to the popular significance of the hymn." [17] In the words of Erik Routley, " 'Abide with me' brings God down into the milling crowds at Wembley."

210 Jesus, Lover of My Soul

It is surprising to note that this hymn which many now regard as the finest hymn Charles Wesley ever wrote was excluded from the official Methodist hymnal until nine years after his death, largely because of his brother's opposition to its use in public worship. Many of his followers felt that it was too intensely intimate although the Church of England hymnals had long included it. Few hymns have been more extensively revised, but it is given here as Wesley wrote it with the exception that two stanzas have been omitted and the vocative "Jesu" has been changed to "Jesus." Many stories are told about the origin of this hymn — that the words were inspired by a dove that had flown to Wesley for protection against a hawk, or a seabird that had taken refuge in his room from a storm, or his own escape from a mob. They are purely legendary. He wrote these lines shortly after his conversion in 1738 and published them in the Wesley brothers' *Hymns and Sacred Poems,* 1740, with the heading "In time of Prayer and Temptation," later changed to "In Temptation." One of the remarkable features of the hymn and one of its great strengths is the simplicity of the text. Of the 137 words used in these stanzas, 109 are monosyllables. See No. 43 for further comments on Wesley.

MARTYN, one of numerous settings for Wesley's hymn which R. G. McCutchan says "has worn out several generations of tunes," was composed in 1834 by Simeon B. Marsh while he was riding horseback from Amsterdam to Johnston, New York, on his weekly round of teaching at singing schools in that area. The tune was written originally for John Newton's Easter hymn, "Mary to her Saviour's tomb," with which it continued to appear in many nineteenth century collections after its publication with that text in Thomas Hastings' *Musical Miscellany,* I, 1836. It was set to Wesley's hymn in *Temple Melodies,* 1851, edited by Darius E. Jones. In a few years the combination of text and tune appeared in a number of books.

Marsh (1798–1875) was born in Sherburne, New York, where his parents had settled after giving up their home in Wethersfield, Connecticut. When only seven he was singing in a choir, at sixteen he had his first regular instruction in music, and at twenty was teaching in a singing school. In 1818 he met Thomas Hastings who encouraged him in his musical pursuits and became a lifelong friend. Marsh founded and edited two newspapers — *The Intelligencer* in Amsterdam, and *The Sherburne News* in his home town — and for thirty years taught music classes, conducted singing schools, and worked with choirs and congregations in churches of the Albany Presbytery. For thirteen years he taught music to children, free of charge, at Schenectady, New York. After 1859 he returned to Sherburne, taught voice, piano, and violin, and was active in the Presbyterian Church as Sunday school superintendent for six years and director of the choir for three. A son, John Butler Marsh, became professor of organ and voice at Elmira Female College.

MARTYN should be played at a deliberate, firm tempo with a conscious effort to smooth out the rhythm by giving all the notes their full value and an even touch (instead of playing the half notes heavily and the quarters lightly). In this way it can be given something of the character of a simple chant.

211 Jesus, Lover of My Soul

See No. 210 for comments on the text.

ABERYSTWYTH, composed by Joseph Parry, was set to another text in a Welsh hymn collection published in 1879, and later was associated with Charles Wesley's hymn in the composer's cantata *Ceridwen*. See No. 109 for comments on Parry.

212 Blessed Jesus, at Thy Word

After graduating from Leipzig University with the degree M.A., in 1643, Tobias Clausnitzer (c. 1619–1684) was appointed a chaplain in the Swedish army and in that office was called upon to preach the thanksgiving sermon in the famous St. Thomas Church, Leipzig, on the accession of Christina as queen of Sweden in 1645. He also preached the sermon at the field service held by General Wrangel's army at Weiden, in the Upper Palatinate, January, 1649, following the signing of the Peace of Westphalia which brought the Thirty Years' War to an end. Appointed pastor in Weiden in 1649, he remained there the last thirty-five years of his life during which time he also served as a member of the consistory and inspector of the district. This hymn, one of three by Clausnitzer which have survived, was first found in a German hymnal, *Altdorffisches Gesang-Büchlein*, 1663, as a Sunday hymn for use before the sermon and originally began, "Liebster Jesu, wir sind hier." It was translated in its present form by Catherine Winkworth in her *Lyra Germanica*, Second Series, 1858. See No. 2 for comments on Miss Winkworth.

LIEBSTER JESU (NUREMBERG; DESSAU) is adapted from a melody, composed by Johann Rudolf Ahle (1625–1673) for one of his four hundred sacred arias, "Ja, er ist's, das Heil der Welt," included in a collection published by him in 1664. In the Darmstadt *Cantional*, 1687, the following reconstruction of Ahle's melody appeared with Clausnitzer's hymn. (Zahn 3498b)

169

Lieb - ster Je - su, wir sind hier, dich und dein Wort an-zu-hö - ren;
len - ke Sin-nen und Be - gier zu den sü - ssen Him-mels-leh-ren,

dass die Her-zen von der Er-den ganz zu dir ge - zo - gen wer-den.

Several variants of the melody appear in later collections. There are five short organ movements by Bach on LIEBSTER JESU, two in the *Orgelbüchlein,* three in the miscellaneous Preludes, and there is one harmonization in the *Choralgesänge.* The present arrangement was made by George H. Palmer for *Songs of Syon,* 1910.

Ahle has the distinction of being the first and perhaps the only German organist and composer to be made mayor of a city — Mühlhausen, where he was born and in his later years took an active and prominent part in public affairs and in its musical life. He was one of the best-educated musicians of his time. After completing his studies at the universities of Göttingen and Erfurt, he remained in the latter city as cantor of St. Andreas Church and director of its school of music until 1649 when he returned to Mühlhausen to become organist of St. Blasius Church, a post that had been filled by a succession of gifted musicians. In 1654 he was elected to the City Council, and in 1661 became mayor. His compositions were numerous and varied, including cantatas, hymn tunes, arias, and organ compositions. Ahle was eager to reform and enliven German church music, but his efforts to do so sometimes met with opposition from the ecclesiastical authorities, who looked with suspicion and disfavor on some of his music which showed the influence of the Italian school in its ornate melodies and strongly marked rhythm. His son, Johann Georg, who succeeded him at St. Blasius, was the immediate predecessor of J. S. Bach who came to Mühlhausen in 1707, and remained for one year. In nineteenth-century American collections, LIEB–STER JESU was called NUREMBERG and was used with a variety of texts.

213 Jesus, Savior, Pilot Me

Appearing initially in *The Sailors' Magazine,* March 3, 1871, this hymn was first sung in public at the Broadway Congregational Church in New York City (then called Broadway Tabernacle) on May 10, 1880, at an anniversary service of The American Seamen's Friend Society. It is a favorite hymn of seamen around the world and has been described by Frank Scribner as one of those hymns which "has had greatness sung into it because of its rich associations and meanings." Edward Hopper (1818–1888) was minister of the Church of Sea and Land in New York City when he wrote these lines and was undoubtedly inspired to do so because of the many sailors who attended the services in that church. He also served Presbyterian churches in Greenville, New York, and Sag Harbor on Long Island.

PILOT, written for these words and inseparable from them, was first published in *The Baptist Praise Book,* 1871. Since then it has continued to appear in most denominational hymnals of the United States and was included in *The Baptist Hymn Book,* 1962, published in London. As a young man, the composer of the tune, John Edgar Gould (1822–1875), son of Capt. Horace Gould of Bangor, Maine, had much interest in music and in composing tunes. By the time he was thirty and established in a music store on Broadway in New York City, he had published four books of songs, two of them in collaboration with Edward L. White. After his marriage, Gould moved to Philadelphia where he became partner in a flourishing retail piano and music business with William G. Fischer, composer of the tune for "I love to tell the story." (No. 317) Gould's widow wrote in 1914 that PILOT was the last tune her husband composed and that he played it on his piano the night before sailing for Europe and northern Africa in an effort to regain his health. He died suddenly in Algiers on March 4, 1875.

214 Blest Are the Pure in Heart

This is a composite hymn. In 1819, John Keble wrote a seventeen-stanza poem based on the Beatitudes and celebrating the Feast of the Purification of the Blessed Virgin Mary. In 1827, he published the poem in *The Christian Year.* William J. Hall (1793–1861) selected the first and last stanzas of this poem, added two stanzas of his own, the second and fourth of the present version, and in 1836 published them in his *Psalms and Hymns adapted to the Services of the Church of England,* more familiarly known as the Miter Hymn Book because of a bishop's miter on the cover. This form was approved by Keble and has since become the established version. Hall, a Church of England clergyman, was for many years editor of the *Christian Remembrancer,* later becoming sole proprietor. See No. 36 for comments on Keble.

FRANCONIA is an adaptation of a melody which appeared in J. B. König's *Harmonischer Liederschatz,* 1738. (Zahn 2207) William H. Havergal (1793–1870) abridged and altered the original melody for a Short Meter text in *Old Church Psalmody,* which he published in 1847. In his version each line of the music started and ended with a long note. Havergal, educated at Oxford and ordained in 1816, was an Anglican clergyman dedicated and unremitting in his efforts to effect reform in English church music which was then in a low state. In 1829, the year in which he was made rector of Astley, Worcestershire, he was in a serious carriage accident which resulted in permanent injury to his sight and necessitated his retiring from active service in the church. During these years of retirement he devoted time and energy to the study of music and psalmody and published a number of hymn tunes, anthems, chants, and services. In 1842, when able to resume his ministerial duties, he became rector of St. Nicholas Church, Worcester. He was made an honorary canon of Worcester Cathedral in 1845. In *Musical Letters from Abroad*, 1852, Lowell Mason described in detail a service which he attended at St. Nicholas Church and said of the rector: "He only devotes odds and ends of his time to music, and never writes music when he is able to write sermons. . . . He has many curious and valuable old books of psalmody and is now himself writing, as he can find time, some historical notice of the 'Old Hundredth Psalm Tune.'"

Havergal left St. Nicholas in 1860 because of his health, spent the next seven years in a country vicarage, and retired from all parish work in 1867. His studies and his concern for the improvement of psalmody prompted him to issue in 1844 a reprint of Ravenscroft's *Whole Booke of Psalmes*, published in 1621, the date which, in his opinion, marked the zenith of those times when psalmody was best understood. *Old Church Psalmody* was described by his daughter, Frances Havergal the hymn writer, as "a fountain from which editors of subsequent collections have drawn — either at first or second hand — and the original guide to many valuable tune-sources, both English and foreign." The book not only "drew attention to the classical school of English ecclesiastical music" but also introduced a number of German chorale melodies. Its influence on English and American hymnody was considerable. Besides books of sermons, songs, carols, and rounds, Havergal published *A History of the Old Hundredth Psalm Tune, with specimens*, 1854, and *A Hundred Psalm and Hymn Tunes*, 1859, all of which he composed. See No. 112 for comments on König.

215 Lead, Kindly Light

These familiar lines of John Henry Newman (1801–1890) were written in 1833 while he was becalmed at sea on his way to Marseilles following his first visit to Italy. He had been seriously ill in Sicily and was longing to get home to England. He also faced a religious conflict in his own life prompted by his dissatisfaction with the Church of England, in which he had been ordained in 1824. It was in these circumstances that he set down these words for his own comfort and guidance. They first appeared in *The British Magazine*, February, 1833, and later in *Lyra Apostolica*, 1836. Although never intended for use as a hymn, they quickly made their way into many collections. Upon his return to England, Newman became a leading figure in the Oxford Movement which sought to reform and renew the church by returning to the high liturgical practices of earlier ages. After a prolonged inner struggle, he was received into the Roman Church in 1845, but despite his fame and brilliance he was never given responsibilities commensurate with his abilities and was never fully trusted by the communion he called his spiritual home. The greater part of his adult life was spent in semiseclusion in the Oratory of St. Philip Neri in Birmingham, a religious society of secular priests. From 1854 to 1858 he served as rector of the newly established Dublin Catholic University, during which period he wrote one of the notable educational classics of all time, *The Idea of a University*. Following a scathing attack on his religious sincerity by Charles Kingsley, he published what many regard as the finest autobiography in the English language, *Apologia pro Vita Sua* (Apology for His Life). His single greatest literary work is *The Dream of Gerontius,* 1865–1866. In 1879, after years of neglect, Rome elevated him to the College of Cardinals and belatedly honored him for his achievements. In *Handbook to the Church Hymnary,* James Moffatt summarizes his life in these words: "He leaves the memory of a religious poet of slender but high achievement, a master of the purest and most melodious English prose, a spiritual force of almost the first magnitude, albeit misdirected and largely wasted, a great Englishman, and a great saint." [1]

LUX BENIGNA   In *The English Hymn,* 1915, Louis F. Benson wrote: "A hymn has no mission until an acceptable musical setting is found. This finds illustration in Newman's 'Lead, kindly Light,' which was written in 1833, but whose popularity began only when Dykes' 'Lux Benigna' was set to it in the Appendix of 1868 [to *Hymns Ancient and Modern*]; a fact of which the Cardinal was well aware." In his biography of Dykes, J. T. Fowler quotes the following from the Rev. George Huntington, cousin of the composer:

> "I had been paying Cardinal Newman a visit . . . . I happened to mention his well-known hymn 'Lead, kindly Light.' . . . I ventured to say, 'It must be a great pleasure to you to know that you have written a hymn treasured wherever English-speaking Christians are to be found'; . . . He was silent for some moments, and then said with emotion, 'Yes, deeply thankful, and more than thankful'; then, after another pause, 'But you see it is not the Hymn, but the *Tune,* that has gained the popularity! The Tune is Dykes', and Dr. Dykes was a great Master!' "

Fowler continues: "Dykes' friends remember his telling them that the tune . . . came into his head while walking through the Strand, in London . . . . Thus the hymn, inspired while the poet was becalmed on the still water of the Mediterranean Sea, became wedded to the melody rising from the heart of the musician, as he walked through the noisy, crowded thoroughfare of the great city."

Dykes' tune first appeared as ST. OSWALD in *Psalms and Hymns for the Church, School, and Home,* 1867, in a form slightly different from the present one. See No. 79 for comments on Dykes.

216   Lead, Kindly Light

See No. 215 for comments on the text.

For comments on SANDON, the oldest surviving tune for Newman's hymn, see No. 97.

217   Lord of All Hopefulness

Jan Struther submitted these lines, written to celebrate the round of each day, to the editors of *Songs of Praise,* 1931, to which she contributed eleven other hymns. The hymn was written expressly for SLANE so as to insure the inclusion of this tune in the collection. As is true of all her poetic works, the words have a quality of literary excellence and refreshing contemporaneity. See No. 42 for further comments on Miss Struther.

SLANE is given as the traditional melody for the song "With my love on the road" in Patrick W. Joyce's *Old Irish Folk Music and Songs*, 1909. It was adapted and arranged by David Evans for "Be Thou my vision" (391) in *The Church Hymnary*, 1927, and appeared with the present text in *Songs of Praise*, Enlarged Edition, 1931, in an arrangement by Martin Shaw. Although SLANE has the rather wide compass characteristic of Irish tunes and no repetition in its four phrases, the melody is easy to learn and its singular attractiveness places it high in people's affections. Slane is a hill some ten miles from Tara in County Meath where St. Patrick is said to have challenged the authority of the pagan High-king, Loigaire (who reigned from 428 to 467), by lighting the paschal fire on Easter eve. This was done in defiance of the ruling that none could be kindled until the royal fire on the hill of Tara had been lit to symbolize the return of spring and light after the winter's darkness. It was this paschal fire (so the story goes) that caused the angry king to gallop to Slane to discover who had dared to break the law of the pagan gods. After the encounter with Loigaire, Patrick was given permission to preach the word of God wherever he would.

218 O Jesus, I Have Promised

This is the rare instance of a hymn written by a father for the confirmation of his children. John Ernest Bode (1816–1874), at one time rector of Westwell, Oxfordshire, and later of Castle Camps, Cambridgeshire, and Bampton Lecturer in 1855, wrote these words when his daughter and two sons were confirmed. They first appeared in print in a leaflet published in 1868 by the Society for the Promotion of Christian Knowledge, with the title "A Hymn for the Newly Confirmed," and later were included in the Appendix to *Psalms and Hymns*, 1869, published by the same society. Although he was the author of two volumes of verse containing many hymns, this is his only hymn to have achieved lasting fame.

ANGEL'S STORY was written for Emily H. Miller's hymn "I love to hear the story which angel voices tell," in *The Methodist Sunday School Tune-Book*, London, 1881, with which it appears in *The Church Hymnary, Revised*, 1927. Arthur H. Mann (1850–1929), composer of the tune, was born in Norwich and started out as a chorister in the cathedral there, sometimes even assisting at the organ, being able at eight to play the cathedral service. The story is told that he had such an overdose of singing under the direction of Dr. Zechariah Buck, who was noted for his extraordinary skill in training boys, that when his voice changed he vowed that he would never sing again — and he never did. It was probably this rigorous training, however, that helped make Mann an expert and uncommonly fine choir director, himself. In 1871 he became a Fellow of the Royal College of Organists, subsequently studying at New College, Oxford, and receiving the B.Mus. degree in 1874 and the D.Mus. in 1882. He directed the music in three parish churches before his appointment in 1876 as organist of King's College, Cambridge, where he did outstanding work for fifty-three years. In 1897 he became organist of the university and was granted an honorory M.A. in 1910. For a number of years he was head of the music at the Leys School in Cambridge. He was a recognized authority on Handel and with Ebenezer Prout shared in the discovery at the Foundling Hospital, in 1894, of the original wind parts for the *Messiah*. He gave a performance later that year with a reconstructed score. He composed anthems, organ pieces, and service music, was music editor of *The Church of England Hymnal,* 1895, brought out an edition of Tallis' famous forty-part motet "Spem in alium," and was an ardent collector of early hymnbooks.

219 O Thou Great Friend

Cast originally in the form of a sonnet and subsequently altered for use as a hymn, these lines by Theodore Parker (1810–1860) were first published in A. P. Putnam's *Singers and Songs of the Liberal Faith,* 1875, Boston, a collection of hymns and poems of American Unitarians. Despite the author's broad theological views, the lines are consonant with a high Christology. The son of a New England farmer, Parker studied at Harvard and was ordained as a Unitarian minister in 1837. He vigorously opposed slavery and preached and lectured widely on social and political issues. Spending most of his ministry in Boston, he is credited with the words, "Democracy is direct self-government, over all the people, by all the people, and for all the people," which are said to have provided Lincoln with the idea for the familiar closing lines of his Gettysburg Address.

FFIGYSBREN (CLÔD), a Welsh hymn melody first printed in R. Mills' *Caniadau Seion,* 1840, was set to Theodore Parker's hymn in *Hymns for Worship,* New York, 1939. FFIGYSBREN is starkly simple in melody, rhythm, harmony, and form, but this character gives an impression of elemental strength and conviction, particularly when the tune is sung rather slowly. *Ffigysbren* and *clod* are the Welsh words, respectively, for "fig tree" and "praise."

220 We Bear the Strain of Earthly Care

Combining a warm evangelical faith with a broad liberal outlook, Ozora Stearns Davis (1866–1931) was from 1909 to 1920 the beloved and distinguished president of The Chicago Theological Seminary. Educated at Dartmouth College and Hartford Theological Seminary, he served as the pastor of several Congregational churches in New England during his early ministry and was later elected to the highest office in his denomination, Moderator of the National Council of the Congregational Churches, holding this office from 1927 to 1929. Toward the end of his life when he knew that he had an incurable disease, he continued to inspire all who knew him with his confident and radiant spirit. He wrote this hymn in 1909 at his summer home at Lake Sunapee, New Hampshire, for the convention of the National Congregational Brotherhood, which was held that fall in Minneapolis, Minnesota. He also wrote "At Length There Dawns the Glorious Day," for the same occasion.

HERMON, composed by Jeremiah Clarke (c. 1670–1707), was the setting for "An Hymn for Easter" in the 1709 edition of Henry Playford's *Divine Companion*. Its original form follows:

If An-gels sung a   Sav - iour's   Birth, on that Aus-pi-cious morn;   we

well may I - mi - tate their mirth, now he a-gain is born,   now   he a - gain is born.

The present abridged form of the melody is from the *Scottish Psalter*. The tune in its entirety appeared in two early nineteenth-century New England collections. It was called UXBRIDGE in *The Columbian Sacred Harmonist,* 1808, two of whose three editors — Oliver Shaw of Dedham and Amos Albee of Medfield — were teachers and friends of Lowell Mason. In an American edition of Thomas Butts' *Harmonia Sacra,* published at Andover, Massachusetts, in 1816, the melody was called COMPARISON.

See No. 78 for comments on Clarke. See No. 294 for comments on Thomas Butts' *Harmonia Sacra.*

221   How Sweet the Name of Jesus Sounds

After years spent at sea, beginning at the age of eleven, during which time he was alternately a midshipman, deserter from the British Navy, and master of a slave ship, John Newton (1725–1807) turned from his dissolute life and by means of rigorous study prepared himself for ordination in the Church of England. Appointed to the curacy of Olney, Buckinghamshire, where he remained sixteen years, he formed a friendship with the poet, William Cowper, which led them to collaborate in producing a memorable volume, *Olney Hymns,* 1779, containing 280 hymns by Newton and sixty-eight by Cowper. See No. 87 for comments on Cowper. The present hymn, entitled "The Name of Jesus," was taken from this collection and was based on a line from The Song of Solomon 1:3, "thy name is as ointment poured forth." Transferred to St. Mary Woolnoth, London, in 1780, Newton continued to preach until the end of his life to large and appreciative congregations even when poor eyesight made it necessary for a servant to lead him into the pulpit. Princeton University, then the College of New Jersey, honored him with a Doctor of

Divinity degree in 1792. His epitaph, which he wrote the year he died, sums up the story of his life:

John Newton, Clerk
Once an infidel and libertine,
A servant of slaves in Africa:
Was by the rich mercy of our Lord and Saviour, Jesus Christ,
Preserved, restored, pardoned,
And appointed to preach the Faith
He had laboured long to destroy.
Near sixteen years at Olney in Bucks;
And twenty-seven years in this church.

ST. PETER was set originally to a version of Psalm 118, "Far better 'tis to trust in God" in Reinagle's *Original Psalm Tunes, for Voice and Pianoforte*, c. 1836, arranged as a solo melody with piano accompaniment. The composer reset it for the present text in the original edition of *Hymns Ancient and Modern*, 1861.

English-born Alexander R. Reinagle (1799–1877) belonged to a musical family of Austrian descent. In 1762, his grandfather, who is thought to have been born near Vienna, was appointed trumpeter to the king, presumably in Edinburgh where he was then established. His uncle, Alexander Reinagle, a friend of K. P. E. Bach, came to the United States in 1786 and had a distinguished career as conductor, composer, teacher, singer, pianist, and theatrical manager in Philadelphia and Baltimore, and is credited with introducing four-hand music to America. His father, Joseph, a well-known cellist in Edinburgh and conductor of the orchestra in St. Cecilia's Hall for a time, left Edinburgh for London, played violin and viola in various orchestras, took part in the Handel commemoration of 1784, and in 1796 was associated with Salomon in the concerts conducted by Haydn, who became his friend and helped him with some of his compositions. He settled eventually in Oxford, and was the first music teacher of his son, who served from 1822 to 1853 as organist at the church of St. Peter in the East (hence the tune name) and was also prominent as teacher, composer, editor of two books of psalm tunes, and compiler of several books of instruction for violin and cello.

222 Jesus, Priceless Treasure

Educated at the University of Königsberg, the only institution of higher learning in Germany that remained intact through the ordeals of the Thirty Years' War (1618–1648), Johann Franck (1618–1677) was first advocate and councillor and then burgomaster in his home town of Guben, eventually being appointed deputy to the Landtag (Diet) of Lower Lusatia in 1671. His fame today, however, rests on his gifts as a poet rather than his abilities as a lawyer. His hymns numbering 110 are characterized by an intense fervor and unaffected simplicity. In *Handbook to the Church Hymnary*, James Moffatt said of him, "He marks the transition from the objective form of church song prevalent till his time, to the more individual and mystical type: his leading idea is the union of the soul with its Saviour." [1] In this he followed

177

Paul Gerhardt. See No. 53 for comments on Gerhardt. This hymn, modeled on a German love song, "Flora meine Freude, meiner Seele Weide," and regarded by some Lutherans as too emotional for congregational use, was first published in the 1653 edition of Johann Crüger's *Praxis pietatis melica.* It has been translated into many languages, and Peter the Great is said to have had a Russian version made in 1724. The present English version has been taken from Catherine Winkworth's *Chorale Book for England,* 1863. See No. 2 for comments on Miss Winkworth.

JESU MEINE FREUDE (literally, "Jesu, my joy"), one of the most beautiful of all chorale melodies, appeared with Franck's hymn in *Praxis pietatis melica,* 1563, edited by Johann Crüger to whom it is attributed. Parts of it seem to be adapted from older traditional material. Crüger's melody (Zahn 8032) follows:

Je - su, mei-ne Freu-de, mei-nes Her-zens Wei - de, Je - su, mei - ne Zier!
Ach wie lang, ach lan-ge ist dem Her-zen ban - ge und ver-langt nach dir!

Got - tes Lamm, mein Bräu-ti-gam, au - sser dir soll mir auf Er - den

nichts sonst lie - bers wer - den.

The first two measures of this melody are almost identical with a phrase that appears three times in "Kyrie, Gott Vater in Ewigkeit," 1541, which was sung to an adaptation of the Latin plainsong "Kyrie fons bonitatis." (See notes on No. 111, and *Liber Usualis.*) That adaptation, first printed with other words in the *Teutsch Kirchenamt,* 1525, is given in *Bach's Chorals,* Part III, by Charles Sanford Terry. One cannot play Bach's harmonization of "Kyrie, Gott Vater in Ewigkeit" in the *Choralgesänge* without thinking of JESU MEINE FREUDE in the phrases "gross ist dein Barmherzigkeit," "bist in dem höchsten Thron," and "dass wir am letzten End'." In "Johann Crüger: On the Tercentenary of His Death," (*Response,* Vol. IV, No. 11, 1962), Dr. Walter E. Buszin writes:

A careful analysis of Crüger's chorale melodies reflects that he was influenced strongly by others and that he knowingly took over traits and musical phrases found in the compositions of other composers. We must not forget that prior to the nineteenth century composers did not stress originality as we stress it today. Musical phrases and even entire movements and melodies were considered common property which might be shared and used by all.[18]

Bach made use of the chorale in Cantatas 12, 64, 81, 87; in two organ movements — one in the *Orgelbüchlein* and one (for manuals only) in the miscellaneous Preludes — and in "Jesu meine Freude," which has been called the most beautiful and the most intimate of his motets. The melody appears in six movements of this work which Albert Schweitzer calls Bach's "sermon upon life and death" and which Spitta says embodies "the germ of Protestant Christianity."

There are a number of variants of the melody — Bach uses three, one of which is attributed to him. The present harmonization, from *The Hymnal 1940*, is derived largely from Bach.

For further comments on Crüger see Nos. 29 and 241.

223 O for a Thousand Tongues to Sing

On the first anniversary of his conversion experience which had taken place on Sunday, May 21, 1738, Charles Wesley wrote an eighteen-stanza hymn to commemorate the event. This hymn, originally beginning with the line "Glory to God, and praise and love," was first published in the Wesley brothers' *Hymns and Sacred Songs*, 1740. R. Conyers in his *Psalms and Hymns*, 1767, reduced the hymn in length and placed the first stanza last and the seventh stanza first, making it begin with the familiar opening line, "O for a thousand tongues to sing." This is the version now most commonly used although the number of stanzas varies in different hymnals. The words are as Charles Wesley wrote them except that John Wesley changed "dear" to "great" in the second line of the present first stanza. Peter Böhler, the Moravian missionary who was instrumental in Wesley's spiritual change, is credited with suggesting the main theme of the hymn with a remark he made when Wesley consulted him about praising Christ, "Had I a thousand tongues, I would praise Him with them all."

Since 1780, beginning with *A Collection of Hymns for the use of the People called Methodists*, this song of praise is often found as the first hymn in the Methodist hymnals.

See No. 43 for additional comments on Charles Wesley.

AZMON (GASTON; DENFIELD), a tune of German extraction, was brought into American hymnody by Lowell Mason in his *Modern Psalmist*, 1839, where it was in straight 4/4, set to "Come, let us lift our joyful eyes," and listed as a melody of Gläser. In his *Carmina Sacra*, 1841, it appeared with the same words but in 3/2, as given here.

The composer of AZMON, Carl G. Gläser (1784–1829), was a student at the Thomasschule in Leipzig when Johann A. Hiller was its director. He studied piano and violin, took up law for a time at Leipzig University, but eventually made music his profession and settled in Barmen where he taught piano, violin, and voice, directed choirs, published chorales, school songs, and piano music, and also became a music dealer.

Lowell Mason's name for the tune, AZMON, is the Hebrew word for "fortress" and was the name of an unidentified place on the border of Judah mentioned in Numbers 34:4, 5.

224 O Lord and Master of Us All

Although he disclaimed being a hymn writer, John Greenleaf Whittier (1807–1892), the Quaker poet, is credited with more than fifty hymns, most of which are found in present-day hymnals and consist of centos from his poems. "I am not a hymn-writer," he once said, "for the good reason that I know nothing of music. Only a very few of my pieces were written for singing. A good hymn is the best use to which poetry can be devoted, but I do not claim that I have succeeded in composing one." He is also reported to have said that the Quakers' emphasis on silence had taken all the "sing" out of them. Born on a farm in Haverhill, Massachusetts, and starting out as a village shoemaker, he chanced to hear an itinerant Scottish peddler sing some of Robert Burns' songs and was so stirred that he bought a copy of the bard's poems. This inspired him to compose verses of his own, some of which his sister sent to William Lloyd Garrison who, recognizing their merit, sought out the young man and prevailed upon him to enter the field of journalism. Subsequently, he contributed to and published magazines and newspapers in Boston, Hartford, Philadelphia, and Washington and became a leading figure in the abolition movement, as well as one of America's best-known poets. A lifelong member of the Society of Friends, he continued to dress and speak in the plain manner of the Quakers to the end of his days. The present hymn is a selection from his poem "Our Master," originally containing thirty-eight stanzas and first published in his *The Tent on the Beach, and Other Poems,* 1867, from which the hymn "Immortal Love, Forever Full" was also taken (No. 230).

WALSALL (READING) appeared with these words in *The English Hymnal,* 1906. See No. 154 for comments on the tune.

225 Jesus, the Very Thought of Thee

Though this hymn has often been attributed to Bernard of Clairvaux (1091–1153), more recent scholarship inclines to the view that it is from the pen of an unknown author of the twelfth century. The original Latin poem, "Jesu dulcis memoria," consisting of forty-two stanzas, was first found in manuscript form in England and presumably was carried from there to France and then to Sicily and Germany. The intensely devout character of the poem is in keeping both with Bernard's spirit and with medieval piety. Edward Caswall is responsible for the translation which appeared first in his *Lyra Catholica,* 1849. See No. 35 for comments on Caswall. In David Livingston's diary, this entry is found referring to the original Latin version of this poem: "That hymn of St. Bernard, on the name of Christ, although in what might be termed dog-Latin, pleases me so; it rings in my ears as I wander across the wide, wide wilderness." Another cento from the same poem is given at No. 290.

ST. AGNES, composed for these words, was first published in Grey's *Hymnal for Use in the English Church,* 1866. The sentiment of the hymn may have inspired Dykes to name the tune for the young Roman girl,

Christian by birth, who was martyred on January 21, 304, at the age of thirteen, during the reign of Diocletian. She was sentenced to death because of her refusal to marry a young nobleman, to whom she said: "I am already engaged to one — to him alone I keep my troth." In the Catholic church she is venerated as the patron saint of young girls. The name Agnes is from *hagnos,* the Greek word for "chaste." See No. 79 for comments on Dykes.

226 Jesus, the Very Thought of Thee

See No. 225 for comments on the text.

WINDSOR (DUNDEE; ETON), one of the Common Tunes in Andro Hart's Scottish Psalter, 1615, was called DUNDIE TUNE there, and has been known as DUNDEE ever since in Scotland. (See No. 85.) In "The Cotter's Saturday Night," Robert Burns pictures the family seated around the fire, after the "cheerfu' supper," listening while the father reads from the Bible, and then joining in a psalm of worship, when

> They chant their artless notes in simple guise,
> They tune their hearts, by far the noblest aim;
> Perhaps 'Dundee's' wild-warbling measures rise,
> Or plaintive 'Martyrs,' worthy of the name;

WINDSOR, in all probability adapted from chapter iii of Tye's *Actes of the Apostles* (see No. 146), first appeared as a psalm tune in Damon's *Booke of Musicke,* 1591, arranged in four parts for Psalm 116. In Este's Psalter, 1592, it was set to the same Psalm, harmonized by George Kirbye. It had no name in that edition but in three subsequent issues was called SUFFOLK TUNE. In Ravenscroft's Psalter, 1621, it was named WINDSOR or EATON, and was listed in the index among the English tunes and set to Psalms 62, 85, and 108. In *Grove's Dictionary,* under the heading "Windsor," are several forms of the tune from various psalters as well as the text and music of chapter iii of Tye's *Actes.* This tune was well known to early settlers in New England. It was assigned to Psalms 15 and 131 in Ainsworth's Psalter brought to Plymouth by the Pilgrims, and was one of the thirteen tunes in the ninth edition (1698) of the *Bay Psalm Book.* WINDSOR was one of the tunes that continued in use in the years around 1700 when some New England congregations had a repertoire of only five or ten tunes. In "Notes on Certain Tunes" in *Old Church Psalmody,* 1847, William H. Havergal wrote:

> Dundee is older than "Windsor" or "Eaton" as the name of this noble tune. The Scotch claim it as a national tune. Burns believed it to be such. Another poet said of it, "Could I, when being carried to my grave, wake up just to hear what tune would be sung at it, I should like it to be 'Dundee,' or, as we call it, 'Windsor.' "

Lowell Mason included much of the foregoing statement as a footnote to WINDSOR in *The National Psalmist,* 1848.

227 Fairest Lord Jesus

An oft-repeated legend relates that this hymn was sung by German knights of the twelfth century on their way to the Holy Land, from whence it derives its popular name, the Crusader's Hymn. Unfortunately, there is no historical support for this romantic tradition. The words can be traced back no further than 1662 to a manuscript bearing that date and found in Münster, and were first published in the *Münster Gesangbuch,* 1677. Subsequently, in much altered form, they appeared in *Schlesische Volkslieder,* Leipzig, 1842, a collection edited jointly by August Heinrich Hoffmann von Fallersleben (1798–1874), noted German poet and philologist (and author of the words, "Deutschland, Deutschland über alles"), and Ernst Friedrich Richter (1808–1879), director of the famous choir school at St. Thomas' Church in Leipzig. They appeared later in an anonymous English translation in Richard Storrs Willis' *Church Chorals and Choir Studies,* 1850. Since that time the hymn has established itself as a great favorite, especially in the United States.

SCHÖNSTER HERR JESU (CRUSADER'S HYMN; ST. ELISABETH; ASCALON). The names given here for this popular folk melody (sung by Catholics and Protestants alike) are as varied as the accounts of its origin. SCHÖNSTER HERR JESU, the most valid of the four, is from the first line of the German hymn with which it appeared in *Schlesische Volkslieder,* 1842. In his preface to the book, Richter, cantor of the Thomasschule in Leipzig from 1868 to 1879, praised the musical ability of the Silesians and described their tunes as "simple in their melodic sequence, rhythm and modulation" — qualities exemplified in SCHÖNSTER HERR JESU.

The tune was called CRUSADER'S HYMN and bore the heading "Melody of the Twelfth Century" in Richard S. Willis' *Church Chorals and Choir Studies,* 1850, which introduced it to the United States. In the same year it was circulated in England in leaflet form and described in *Evangelical Christendom,* an English journal, as "an unexpected treasure . . . discovered in 1850 in the guise of a Crusader's Hymn. It was found in Westphalia . . . and according to the traditional text by which it was accompanied, this hymn used to be sung by the German Pilgrims on their way to Jerusalem."

Franz Liszt's use of the melody for the middle section of the "Crusader's March" and in the instrumental interlude of Part VI of his oratorio *Die Legende von der heiligen Elisabeth,* 1862, helped to corroborate its supposed connection with the Crusades and obviously supplied the name ST. ELISA– BETH which appears with it in some hymnals. Liszt said that he had been given the melody of this old pilgrim song from the Crusades by a cantor named Gottschlag.

In England the tune, named ASCALON, was set to Isaac Watts' version of Psalm 122, "How pleased and blest was I," in the second edition of the *Congregational Psalmodist,* 1861. This combination of text and tune continues in *Congregational Praise,* 1951, and *The Baptist Hymn Book,* 1962, two English hymnals. Ascalon, the name of a fortified city on the coast of Palestine that was besieged often during the Crusades, must have been given to the tune by someone who believed in its legendary origin in those times.

In Lutheran hymnals published in the United States, the tune appears with Dr. Joseph A. Seiss' English translation of the hymn which begins with the line "Beautiful Saviour." The last phrase of the tune as set to that text differs slightly from the form given here. In Armin Haeussler's *The Story of Our Hymns*, 1952, (No. 182) there is a facsimile of the original printing of SCHÖNSTER HERR JESU in *Schlesische Volkslieder*, 1842. The harmonies given here are, with two exceptions, from Willis' arrangement. An entirely different tune, also named SCHÖNSTER HERR JESU, appeared with stanzas one and three of the present text in the Catholic hymnal published at Münster in 1677. It is given as an alternative tune for these words in *The Hymnal 1940, The Hymnbook*, 1955 (Presbyterian), and the *Hymnal for Colleges and Schools*, 1956.

SCHÖNSTER HERR JESU was played as the casket bearing the body of President John F. Kennedy was carried out of the Capitol on November 25, 1963.

228 Love Divine, All Loves Excelling

First published in a pamphlet by Charles Wesley with the unusual title, *Hymns for those that seek and those that have Redemption in the Blood of Jesus Christ*, 1747, this hymn was later included in John Wesley's *Collection of Hymns*, 1780, with the original second stanza omitted, beginning "Breathe, O breathe thy loving spirit." F. Luke Wiseman has said that the hymn was suggested by the "Song of Venus" from Dryden's play, *King Arthur*, which contained the opening lines:

> Fairest Isle, all Isles excelling,
> Seat of Pleasures and of Loves;
> Venus here will choose her Dwelling
> And forsake her Cyprian Groves.

The phrase "lost in wonder, love, and praise" is identical with the last phrase of the first stanza of Joseph Addison's poem "When All Thy Mercies, O My God" (see No. 94). See Nos. 9 and 43 respectively for comments on John and Charles Wesley.

BEECHER (ZUNDEL; LOVE DIVINE), written for these words and published in *Christian Heart Songs*, 1870, was named for Henry Ward Beecher with whom John Zundel was associated over a period of twenty-eight years. Zundel (1815–1882), born and educated in Germany, spent seven years in St. Petersburg (Leningrad) as music teacher, organist of St. Anne's Lutheran Church, and bandmaster of the Imperial Horse Guards before coming to the United States in 1847. After serving as organist in the First Unitarian Church, Brooklyn, and in St. George's Church, New York City, he went in 1850 to Plymouth Congregational Church in Brooklyn where he and Beecher (who had become its minister in 1847) became intimate friends and associates. Although Beecher was neither musician nor hymn writer, he believed in the importance of congregational singing, and he was determined to build it up in his church. He had able support from Zundel, and their collaboration was so successful that the common expression

"We're going to hear Henry Ward Beecher" became the more inclusive "We're going to hear Beecher and Zundel," for the spirited singing in the church was almost as much of an attraction as the preaching.

When Beecher came to Plymouth Church, singing was largely a function of the choir or quartette, a condition prevalent in many churches of the time and one which probably prompted Beecher's comment that "a choir should not sing *for* a congregation, but incite them to sing, and lead the way." Those in the pews had the words of the hymns, but no music. To remedy this state of affairs, Beecher, with the help of his musician brother, Charles, and of his organist, Zundel, prepared *The Plymouth Collection of Hymns and Tunes,* 1855, which had a tremendous sale and influence, aroused much criticism and controversy, and according to one writer "changed the face of congregational song." Beecher selected hymns from a wide variety of denominations, including the Roman Catholic, and in order to encourage singing, had the tune printed at the top of the page, with the words printed in two columns in the space below, an arrangement that had been tried in *Temple Melodies,* 1851, and became a model for subsequent editors. Louis F. Benson points out that this innovation was not an unmixed blessing, for some of the hymns did not fit the music, some were included merely as filler, and some were grievously abridged in order to get them on the page. One tune often served for nine hymns. Zundel contributed twenty-eight tunes to this collection. He also edited other collections and wrote books of instruction for melodeon and organ, and a *Treatise on Harmony.* His stay at Plymouth Church was interrupted by three retirements and three returns. After his final retirement in 1878 he was organist for a few months at Central Methodist Episcopal Church in Detroit, Michigan, before returning to Germany, where he died in 1882.

229 Join All the Glorious Names

Consisting originally of twelve stanzas, of which the present version is a cento of stanzas one, two, nine, and eleven, this hymn by Isaac Watts was first published in his *Hymns and Spiritual Songs,* 1707. Although this hymn on "The Offices of Christ" is not found in many hymnals, it is one of the most impressive and exalted hymns that Watts ever wrote. See No. 1 for comments on Watts.

CROFT'S 136th (CROFT'S 148th) The joining of Croft's tune with Watts' hymn by the editors of *Congregational Praise,* 1951, seems to be a perfect fit. In the *Companion to Congregational Praise,* 1953, Erik Routley says that "it is by no means improbable that these words of Watts were sung to it from the beginning." In England the tune attained great popularity in the eighteenth century through its use with paraphrases of Psalms 136 and 148. In American hymnody it has had little use. Thompson Stone, music editor of the *Pilgrim Hymnal,* 1931, gave it wider circulation by including it with a version of Psalm 19, "The glory of the Lord." Its first appearance was in the second edition of Playford's *Divine Companion,* 1707, arranged for "Cantus & Bassus." See No. 1 for comments on Croft.

230 Immortal Love, Forever Full

This is another favorite hymn based on a poem by John Greenleaf Whittier. The poem, "Our Master," was included in his *Tent on the Beach, and Other Poems*, 1867, and consisted of thirty-eight stanzas. The present version is comprised of stanzas one, two, five, thirteen, fourteen, and fifteen. In response to a comment that he could never have been a Puritan or a Calvinist, the Quaker poet is said to have replied: "Nay, thee are right! the world is much too beautiful, and God much too good. I never was of that mind."

See No. 224 for additional comments on Whittier and for another well-known hymn based on the same poem.

SERENITY The word *serenity* seems incongruous for anything connected with the Irish composer, William Vincent Wallace (1812–1865), whose love song "The winds that waft my sighs to thee" was the source of this hymn tune. The son of a bandmaster and skillful bassoonist, Wallace was a professional musician at fifteen, playing violin in a Dublin theater orchestra, and was also skilled as pianist, organist, and clarinetist. For a year he was organist at the Roman Catholic Cathedral in Thurles, Ireland, and professor of music at the Ursuline Convent there. Hearing Paganini in Dublin in 1831 inspired him to practice to such good effect that in later years he became known as a virtuoso on three continents. In 1835, worn out after four years of conducting, composing, and performing in Dublin, he set out for Australia. At the start he engaged in sheep ranching, but later resumed his playing, opened a music school in Sydney, and ran a music store for a time. In 1838, when he left Sydney, he was referred to in one paper as "the Australian Paganini." Travels in New Zealand, the South Seas, India, South America, Mexico, and the United States, were filled with concerts, honors, and narrow escapes from death in a variety of situations that make his life history something of a thriller. In 1844 he gave concerts in Holland and Germany, in 1845 made his debut in London. There, an introduction to the dramatist Fitzball launched his career in the field of opera. He composed the music for Fitzball's *Maritana* which had tremendous success in London, received an ovation in Vienna in 1848, and had many revivals in England. Five other operas composed by Wallace were produced and published during his lifetime. A commission from the Paris Opera in 1848 had to be given up because of threatened blindness. A long voyage and several months in Brazil restored his health and vision and enabled him to have another highly successful concert tour in South, Central, and North America.

Following his return to England in 1853, Wallace spent several years in Germany composing operas and piano music which had great vogue; but in 1864 he had to give up all work because of ill health, and went to France, where he died. His funeral in London was attended by some of the most famous musicians and men of letters of that time.

The first section of Wallace's song was made into a hymn tune by Uzziah C. Burnap (1834–1900), Brooklyn organist and music editor of *Hymns of the Church with Tunes*, 1869. (Dutch Reformed) He set his adaptation to three hymns, one of which, "The Lord's my shepherd, I'll not want," may have suggested SERENITY as the tune name. The tune had its present rhythmic pattern in *The Hymnal of the Methodist Episcopal Church with Tunes,* 1878. In this form it appeared with the present text in *The Hymnal of the Reformed Church,* 1920, and since then has been associated with these words in many hymnals published in the United States.

231 Come, Holy Ghost, Our Souls Inspire

Of this hymn John Julian has said that it "has taken deeper hold of the Western Church than any other mediaeval hymn, the *Te Deum* alone excepted." Known universally as the "Veni Creator Spiritus," it dates from the ninth century and has often been attributed to Rhabanus Maurus (776–856), Archbishop of Mainz, although his authorship has never been definitely ascertained. It was used early as an office hymn to commemorate the outpouring of the Holy Spirit on Whitsunday and for that reason has also been a favorite at ordinations since the eleventh century. The singing of it, at least in medieval times, was frequently accompanied by the ringing of bells and the use of incense, candles, and the finest of vestments. Luther held it in high regard. It is the only hymn officially designated for use in the *Book of Common Prayer,* one version appearing in the 1549 edition and a second, namely this one, in the 1662 edition. The latter version, the translation of John Cosin (1594–1672) and taken from his *Collection of Private Devotions in the Practice of the Ancient Church,* 1627, has been handed down without alteration and is the oldest English translation in the *Pilgrim Hymnal.* Cosin was vice-chancellor of the University of Cambridge and dean of Peterborough when the Long Parliament under Puritan influence deprived him of his benefices. Following a stay of eighteen years in France, he returned to England after the Restoration and was appointed bishop of Durham where he remained the last twelve years of his life.

Recognized as a liturgical authority, Bishop Cosin took a leading part in the revision of the *Book of Common Prayer* of 1662.

DAS WALT GOTT VATER (VETTER) was one of four melodies which appeared for the first time in Part II of *Musicalische Kirch- und Hauss-Ergötzlichkeit,* Leipzig, 1713, edited by Daniel Vetter. He may have composed all of these new tunes but laid claim only to this one, the setting for Martin Böhm's hymn "Das walt' Gott Vater und Gott Sohn." The one harmonization of the melody in Bach's *Choralgesänge* is the basis for the present arrangement. Little is known of Vetter (? –c. 1721) except that he was born in Breslau and studied with Werner Fabricius, organist and composer, whom he succeeded in 1679 as organist of St. Nicholas church in Leipzig. In a chapter on the state of music in Leipzig just before Bach went there in 1723 as cantor of the Thomasschule, Philipp Spitta says in his biography of Bach: "There were no remarkable musicians there at the time; the only one, besides Kuhnau, who had done anything important in his own branch of art was Daniel Vetter . . . as organist to the church of St. Nicholas." See Zahn 673 for the original melody.

186

232 Spirit of God, Descend Upon My Heart

Admired in his day as a distinguished literary figure, George Croly (1780–1860) was equally famous as a preacher of conservative views. Following graduation from Trinity College, Dublin, and after ministering in Ireland, he retired from parish work and made his home in London where he engaged in a wide variety of literary pursuits. His book, *Salathiel,* based on the legend of the Wandering Jew, created something of a sensation when it was published. Strongly opposed to the liberal tendencies of his time, he accepted appointment to one of the poorer churches in London, St. Stephen's, Walbrook, which had been closed for a century, and by his vigorous preaching and denunciation of liberalism attracted large congregations. Beloved by his people, he prepared a collection for use in his church, *Psalms and Hymns for Public Worship,* 1854, containing twenty-five psalms, fifty hymns, and six longer poems; of which ten psalms, twelve hymns, and the poems were initialed by Croly and presumably came from his hand. The collection was issued in only one edition, and unfortunately most of the copies were destroyed in a fire. The present hymn, based on Galatians 5:25, "If we live in the Spirit, let us also walk in the Spirit," was not included in his *Psalms and Hymns* but first appeared in Charles Roger's *Lyra Britannica,* 1867. Croly fell dead while taking a walk one day in Holborn shortly after his eightieth birthday.

MORECAMBE, named HELLESPONT originally, was composed by Frederick C. Atkinson for "Abide with me" and printed on a leaflet in 1870. It has become closely associated with the present text in a number of hymnals published in the United States, but does not appear in current English hymnals. Atkinson (1841–1897), born in Norwich, was a chorister in the cathedral there under the famous Dr. Zechariah Buck (see No. 218) whom he assisted as organist and choirmaster from 1849 to 1860, before going to Cambridge for his Mus.B. degree. He served as organist and choirmaster in two Anglican churches in Bradford, returned to Norwich as organist and choirmaster of the cathedral from 1881 to 1885, and then went to St. Mary's Parish Church in Lewisham. Morecambe is listed in *Hymn Tune Names* as a well-known watering place on Morecambe Bay in western England, not a great distance from Bradford.

233 Breathe on Me, Breath of God

James Moffatt wrote of Edwin Hatch (1835–1899), "Profound as his learning was, his published sermons show that his piety was as simple and unaffected as a child's." [1] After a brilliant career at Oxford, Hatch took orders in the Church of England and ministered for a time in an east-end parish in London. Appointed professor of classics at Trinity College, Quebec, in 1859, he later returned to England and held several appointments at Oxford, including that of university reader in ecclesiastical history. He was the Bampton and Grinfield Lecturer in 1880 and the Hibbert Lecturer in 1888. Adolph Harnack who translated his Bampton lectures into German tendered him this compliment: "He was a glorious man, whose loss I shall never cease to mourn." The present hymn is the best of the few hymns he wrote and was first published in a leaflet, "Between Doubt and Prayer," 1878; it was later published posthumously in his *Towards Fields of Light,* 1890.

POTSDAM   This simple, attractive hymn tune, adapted from the theme of the E-major Fugue in Book II of Bach's *Well-Tempered Clavichord,* was undoubtedly named for Bach's famous visit to Frederick the Great at Potsdam in May, 1747, the last journey he made. Bach's son, Karl Philipp Emmanuel, had been appointed kapellmeister and accompanist to the king in 1740, a position he held for twenty-seven years. According to another son, Wilhelm Friedemann, who accompanied his father on the journey, the king was about to play a flute concerto at his daily evening concert of chamber music when an officer brought him a list of strangers who had arrived. Glancing at the list, Frederick announced to his fellow musicians, "Gentlemen, old Bach has come" — and Bach, who had gone to his son's quarters, was commanded to come to the castle at once, even before he could change his traveling clothes for the black coat of the cantor. The king gave up his flute playing for the evening and asked Bach to try several of his Silbermann fortepianos (pianofortes) which were situated in different rooms of the castle. Accompanied by the musicians, they went from room to room and Bach played improvisations on each instrument. At one point in the tour of inspection Frederick played a theme on one of the claviers and asked Bach to develop a fugue on it. The skill of his improvisation astonished the king and whetted his appetite for more. The following evening he summoned Bach to the palace and asked to hear a fugue in six parts. Supplying his own subject Bach improvised brilliantly, to the amazement of all. Two months after his return to Leipzig he sent the king a "Musical Offering" (*Musikalisches Opfer*) consisting of elaborate contrapuntal compositions which he had worked out on the king's theme. In the dedication of the work he said that his improvisation at Potsdam had not done justice to the excellence of the theme. (For further comments on Bach, see No. 281.)

In his biography *J. S. Bach,* 1905, Albert Schweitzer recalls that the musicologist Robert Eitner, upon being detained in Potsdam one rainy afternoon in 1873, went to the castle and discovered one of the Silbermann instruments in Frederick the Great's rooms. Schweitzer comments, "We thus still possess one of the claviers upon which old Bach played to old Fritz."

POTSDAM was set to three hymns in the Church of England hymnal, *Church Psalter and Hymn Book,* 1854, with an arrangement and harmonization by the organist — a Mr. Phillips — of St. George's, Sheffield.

234 Breathe on Me, Breath of God

See No. 233 for comments on the text.

TRENTHAM, written originally for Sir Henry W. Baker's hymn "O perfect life of Love," was published in 1894 in the composer's collection *Fifty Sacred Leaflets.* Robert Jackson (1842–1914), English organist, teacher, composer of anthems, hymn tunes, and songs, studied at the Royal Academy of Music and was the recipient of one of its silver medals. For some time he was organist and choirmaster of St. Mark's Church, Grosvenor Square, London, but in 1868 returned to Oldham, Lancashire, his birthplace, to succeed his father who had been organist and choirmaster of St. Peter's Church for forty-eight years. Father and son served this church for a combined term of ninety-four years — something of a record. TRENTHAM was included by request as a second tune for these words.

235 Come, Holy Spirit, God and Lord!

In his busy career Luther found time to issue four hymnbooks as well as to give assistance in the preparation of several others. The first of these, *Geystliche Gesangk Buchleyn,* Wittenberg, 1524, containing thirty-two German hymns of which twenty-four were by Luther, was compiled in collaboration with Johann Walther, cantor at the palace of Frederick the Wise at Torgau. It was Luther's wish that the school children should be taught the hymns first, so that they in turn might teach them to the congregation, since the children learned new things more readily than adults. In the preface to this collection, Luther declared, "I am not of the opinion that all arts are to be cast down and destroyed on account of the Gospel, as some fanatics protest; on the other hand I would gladly see all the arts, especially music, in the service of Him who has given and created them." The four prefaces Luther wrote for his four hymnals provide an excellent summary of his views on the importance of congregational singing and the theological principles undergirding Christian hymnody. The present hymn, originally beginning, "Komm, Heiliger Geist, Herre Gott!" is from his first hymnbook and the translation is by Catherine Winkworth in her *Lyra Germanica,* First Series, 1855. See No. 2 for comments on Miss Winkworth. See No. 121 for additional comments on Luther.

DAS NEUGEBORNE KINDELEIN (JENA) Unlike many chorale melodies, this one has continued in its original form. It was composed by Melchior Vulpius for Cyriacus Schneegass' Christmas hymn "Das neugeborne Kindelein" ("The new-born Child") and was first published in *Ein schön geistlich Gesangbuch,* Jena, 1609, a collection edited by the composer. (Zahn 491) Bach used the melody in four of the five movements of Cantata No. 122 ("Das neugeborne Kindelein") in which the present arrangement is the concluding chorale. See No. 184 for comments on Vulpius.

236 Life of Ages, Richly Poured

Born at Salem, Massachusetts, and a graduate of Harvard University and Harvard Divinity School, Samuel Johnson (1822–1882) was a man of wide learning and spiritual sensitivity. Although he has often been regarded as a Unitarian, he never formally affiliated with any denominational group. In 1853 he formed a Free Church at Lynn, Massachusetts, which he served for seventeen years. Throughout his ministry he was a vigorous champion of human rights and a formidable opponent of slavery. The author of many essays on religious, political, and literary subjects, he also wrote a major work on *Oriental Religions, and their Relation to Universal Religion*, 1872, and an important treatise on *The Worship of Jesus in its Past and Present Aspects*, 1868. In collaboration with Samuel Longfellow, he published two significant hymnals, *A Book of Hymns*, 1846, and *Hymns of the Spirit*, 1864, the first of which they prepared while students at Harvard Divinity School. The present hymn is from the latter collection and is especially appropriate for use at interfaith services and on national holidays.

BUCKLAND (the name of a village not far from Oxford) has been associated with these words since the publication of Dr. G. S. Barrett's *Congregational Church Hymnal*, 1887, for which Dr. E. J. Hopkins was musical consultant. (See No. 60.) The tune, composed by Dr. Leighton G. Hayne (1835–1883) was first published in *The Merton Tune Book: a Collection of Hymn Tunes used in the Church of St. John Baptist, Oxford*, 1863, of which he was music editor. He was curate at St. John Baptist from 1864 to 1866. Educated at Eton, and at Queen's College, Oxford, he received a B.Mus. degree in 1856, a D.Mus. in 1860. He was ordained deacon in 1861, priest in 1862, and in 1863 was appointed coryphaeus (conductor of the chorus) of Oxford and public examiner in the school of music. From 1860 to 1866 he was precentor of Queen's College, and from 1868 to 1871 organist and succentor at Eton. When he succeeded his father as rector of Mistley, Essex, and vicar of Bradfield, a large five-manual organ he had built in the music room at Eton was divided between the two churches. In *The English Hymnal*, 1906, BUCKLAND was the setting for the children's hymn, "Loving Shepherd of thy sheep."

237 Send Down Thy Truth, O God

Edward Rowland Sill (1841–1887) wrote these lines at the close of the war between the states to counteract the bitter enmity between the North and the South. Written in the form of a prayer, "For the outpouring of the Holy Spirit," the poem first appeared in Sill's *The Hermitage*, 1867. It was included in *The Pilgrim Hymnal*, 1904. Born at Windsor, Connecticut, Sill was educated at Yale, and for several years (1874–1882) taught English literature at the University of California. His two best-known poems are "The Fool's Prayer" and "Opportunity."

ST. MICHAEL (OLD 134TH; GENEVA 101) is derived from a melody composed or adapted by Louis Bourgeois for Marot's version of Psalm 101 in the Genevan Psalter, 1551. Douen called the original melody one of the best in the Genevan Psalter. In the Anglo-Genevan Psalter, 1561 (*Foure Score and Seven Psalmes*), it was adapted to a Short Meter version of Psalm 134, and was one of the few four-line tunes in early psalters. First known in England as OLD 134TH, the tune had a number of variants in subsequent English and Scottish psalters. After 1595 it passed out of circulation and owes its second life in English hymnody to William Crotch (1775–1847) who adapted it for use in his *Psalm Tunes,* 1836, giving the last phrase its present melodic form, omitting the gathering notes, and naming the tune ST. MICHAEL. In Germany the tune was taken over from the Genevan Psalter without change for Lobwasser's translation of Psalm 101 in his psalter of 1573. (Zahn 919) Crotch, represented in the *Pilgrim Hymnal* by ST. MICHAEL and one chant (560), was so precocious as a child that many predicted he would be a second Mozart. When he was scarcely more than two he could play "God save the King," with a bass of his own invention, on an organ which his music-loving father, a master carpenter, had built. At four the boy gave daily recitals in London, at seven, played violin and piano, at eleven was a pupil assistant at King's and Trinity colleges, Cambridge, at fourteen had an oratorio performed, at fifteen was organist of Christ Church, Oxford, at twenty-two a professor of music there, and at twenty-four had his doctorate. He was the first principal of the Royal Academy of Music at the time of its establishment in 1822, retaining the post for ten years. Although the extraordinary promise of his youth was not fulfilled, he had a notable career as teacher, lecturer, composer of anthems, chants, service music, pieces for organ and piano, and writer on theoretical subjects.

238 Come, Gracious Spirit, Heavenly Dove

Simon Browne (1680–1732), a contemporary of Isaac Watts and like him the minister of a leading Independent Church in Old Jewry, London, wrote these words patterned on Watts' hymn, "Come, Holy Spirit, Heavenly Dove" (No. 240). Consisting originally of seven stanzas and considerably revised over the years, the hymn was first published in Browne's *Hymns and Spiritual Songs . . . designed as a Supplement to Dr. Watts,* 1720. In his later years, Browne suffered from strange mental aberrations, believing that he had "no more sense than a parrot," that he was a "mere beast," and that God had "annihilated in him the thinking substance," all of which may have been induced by the shock of killing a highwayman who attempted to rob him and by the sudden death of his wife and son. Despite these delusions, his literary output continued undiminished and comprised some twenty volumes, including translations of classical authors, children's books, apologetics, and a dictionary. Toplady said of him, "Instead of having no soul, he wrote and reasoned and prayed as if he had two."

MENDON, an anonymous German melody, was included in a number of early nineteenth-century American tunebooks with a variety of texts. In the fifth edition of the *New-York Selection of Sacred Music,* 1822, edited by Francis D. Allen, it was called GERMAN AIR and set to Watts' "Far from my thoughts, vain world, be gone." With the same name and text it appeared in Reed's *Musical Monitor,* 1824, and Samuel Dyer's *New Selection of Sacred Music,* 1825. Lowell Mason set the melody to "Loud swell the pealing organ's notes" in *The Choir,* 1833, and named it MENDON. The present harmonization, largely Mason's, is from his *Modern Psalmist,* 1839, and *Sabbath Hymn and Tune Book,* 1859.

239 Come Down, O Love Divine

Little is known of the life of Bianco da Siena beyond the report that in 1367 he joined a religious order of unordained men which followed the rule of St. Augustine, and that he lived for some years in Venice and probably died there in 1434. His hymns were gathered together in a collection entitled *Laudi Spirituali*, edited by Telesforo Bini and published at Lucca in 1851. The phrase "Laudi Spirituali" ("Spiritual Songs") refers to hymns written in the language of the people in Italy during the thirteenth and fourteenth centuries in response to popular demand, a demand that was to become more widespread in the Reformation. The present hymn is a cento from the original poem of sixty lines, "Discendi, Amor santo," and was translated by Richard F. Littledale (1833–1890), Anglican clergyman and scholar, in his *People's Hymnal*, 1867. In *Hymns and Human Life*, Erik Routley says that Littledale "produced a number of undistinguished translations and one of priceless beauty, 'Come down, O Love divine,' from the Italian of Bianco of Siena."

DOWN AMPNEY, composed for this hymn by Ralph Vaughan Williams (1872–1958), was first published in *The English Hymnal*, 1906, and named for his birthplace in Gloucestershire, where his father was vicar of Christ Church. His paternal grandfather and great-grandfather were lawyers of distinction; his mother, a descendant of Josiah Wedgewood, was a niece of Charles Darwin. After his father's death in 1875, the family moved to Leith Hill Place, Surrey, the estate of his grandfather, Josiah Wedgewood III. He had early instruction in piano, theory, and violin, and continued to study music privately during five years at a preparatory school in Rottingdean and later at Charterhouse. His piano teacher at Rottingdean introduced him to Bach's music, a revelation to the boy. He described this event as one of the landmarks in his musical education. From 1890 to 1892 he studied at the Royal College of Music, and in 1892 entered Trinity College, Cambridge, from which he received degrees in arts and music, and the Mus.D. in 1901. When he returned to the Royal College of Music in 1895 for further study, he formed the friendship with Gustav Holst which had far-reaching effect on the music of both men. For nearly forty years (Holst died in 1934) they met at least once a week for what they called field days, when they would spend a whole day or an afternoon examining and criticizing each other's compositions with utter freedom. Vaughan Williams' first and only position as a church organist was at St. Barnabas, South Lambeth, from 1895 to 1898. Besides playing for services and directing the choir, he gave recitals and conducted a choral and orchestral society which he organized in connection with the church. In 1897 he studied for several months with Max Bruch in Berlin. After returning to London he gave up the position at St. Barnabas in order to devote his time to composition.

In 1904 Vaughan Williams was asked by Percy Dearmer, then a complete stranger to him, to edit the music of a new hymnal. He was told that the work would take about two months and require of each editor the outlay of five pounds. After some hesitation on the ground that he knew nothing about hymnbooks, he accepted the assignment. The work took two years, and expenses for the musical side alone cost him two hundred and fifty pounds. In his *Musical Autobiography,* 1910, he wrote: "I know now that two years of close association with some of the best (as well as some of the worst) tunes in the world was a better musical education than any amount of sonatas and fugues." *The English Hymnal,* 1906, is one of the most significant books in the history of English hymnody. For nearly sixty years it has supplied music editors of English and American hymnals with some of their finest tunes and arrangements and has had enormous influence in raising the level of musical taste in churches. Its musical excellence reflects Vaughan Williams' conviction that the choice of tunes for congregational singing is "a moral rather than a musical issue." In the preface he wrote: "It ought no longer to be true anywhere that the most exalted moments of a church-goer's week are associated with music that would not be tolerated in any place of secular entertainment." One of the notable features of *The English Hymnal* was its inclusion of a large number of English folk tunes, many from secular sources. Vaughan Williams, one of the great collectors and arrangers of English folk songs, made use of them in a variety of ways and assimilated their idiom into his own music. He, more than any other individual, is responsible for the wide use of folk tunes in modern English and American hymnody. In 1908 he studied for three months in Paris with Ravel, working chiefly on problems of orchestration. Between 1907 and 1914, performances of several of his works established his reputation as a composer of marked originality.

At the outbreak of World War I, when he was nearly forty-two, Vaughan Williams enlisted as an orderly in the Royal Army Medical Corps. After three years with an ambulance unit in England, France, and Salonika, he volunteered for service in the Royal Garrison Artillery, was commissioned in 1918, and served in France until the end of the war. In 1919 Oxford honored him with a D.Mus. degree; in 1920 he was appointed professor of composition at the Royal College of Music, and conductor of the Bach Choir. Each succeeding year brought new commissions, new recognition, new honors. In 1935 he was awarded the Order of Merit by King George V. During World War II he contributed time, energy, and funds to various relief projects, organized musical activities and concerts for service men, began to write music for films, composed a variety of works, a number of them for amateurs. He did much to encourage participation by amateur choral and instrumental groups in competition festivals and set new standards for the music to be performed. For over fifty years he was the guiding spirit of the Leith Hill Musical Festival, taking part in its programs as composer, conductor, and organizer. His career as a composer covers sixty-five years. In that time he wrote nine symphonies, miscellaneous orchestral works, operas, a large number of choral works, songs, incidental music for plays and films, chamber music, and three preludes for organ on Welsh hymn tunes. With Martin Shaw he edited the music of *The Oxford Book of Carols,* 1928, and *Songs of Praise,* 1925, 1931. He made visits to the United States in 1922, 1932, and 1954. At the time of his death on August 26, 1958, he was the foremost composer in England, beloved at home and abroad, respected and admired as a great musician and a great man.

See No. 128 for comments on Gustav Holst.

240 Come, Holy Spirit, Heavenly Dove

Appearing under the heading, "Breathing after the Holy Spirit: or, Fervency of Devotion Desired," this hymn by Isaac Watts is from his *Hymns and Spiritual Songs,* 1707. The original contained five stanzas, of which the present version retains stanzas one, three, and five. There are approximately twenty different forms of the text in common use. John Wesley objected to the second stanza on the ground that it overstressed man's frailty, and he modified the fourth stanza because he thought it referred to God in too familiar terms. The stanzas given here are unaltered. See No. 1 for comments on Watts.

ST. AGNES See No. 225 for comments on the tune.

241 Spirit Divine, Attend Our Prayers

The son of a Congregational lay preacher and watchmaker, Andrew Reed (1787–1862) entered the Congregational ministry in 1811 and was appointed pastor of New Road Chapel, St. George's-in-the-East, London, where he had been brought up and was a member. His ministry was so successful that a larger edifice became necessary in 1831, and the church was renamed Wycliffe Chapel. He remained as its pastor until he retired in 1861. A brilliant organizer and an ardent humanitarian as well as an effective preacher, he was largely instrumental in founding six outstanding benevolent institutions in London. Most of them were devoted to helping needy children, and the cost of building them exceeded a half million dollars. In 1817, Reed published a *Supplement* to Watts' hymns. It was enlarged in 1825 and published as *The Hymn Book* in 1842, and included twenty-one of his own hymns and twenty of his wife's. These appeared anonymously in *The Hymn Book,* but their names were given in the *Wycliffe Supplement,* 1872. Yale conferred an honorary degree of Doctor of Divinity on him while he was visiting Congregational churches in the United States in 1834. In response to a request by his son that he write an autobiography, he replied: "I was born yesterday, and I shall die tomorrow, and I must not spend today in telling what I have done, but in doing what I may for Him who has done all for me." The present hymn, originally containing seven stanzas, was first sung on Good Friday, 1829, at a special service "for Solemn Prayer and Humiliation" called by the London Board of Congregational Ministers "to promote, by the divine blessing, a revival of religion in the British churches." As Reed first wrote it, each of the middle stanzas began with a metaphorical address to the Holy Spirit, invoking his presence as light, fire, dew, dove, and wind.

NUN DANKET ALL' (GRÄFENBERG; ST. MARY MAGDALENE), attributed to Johann Crüger, appeared in the second edition of *Praxis pietatis melica,* 1647, set to Paul Gerhardt's hymn "Nun danket all und bringet Ehr." (Zahn 207) The first six measures of NUN DANKET ALL' seem to have been derived directly from the first part of the setting for Psalm 89 in the 1562 Genevan Psalter. Its last six notes are like the last six of the melody for Psalm 75 in the same psalter. Parts of both tunes are related to the melody for Psalm 118, RENDEZ A DIEU. (No. 282) All three Genevan tunes were included in Lobwasser's Psalter published in 1573 for the German Reformed Church. Dr. Walter E. Buszin has said that "a significant influence was exerted on Crüger by Claude Goudimel" and that "certain traits found in the melodies of Crüger will be found also in the melodies of the Genevan Psalter." William Havergal wrote in the Preface to *Old Church Psalmody,* 1847:

> It may be taken as an indisputable fact, that in earlier times little or no account was made of the authorship of the tunes themselves. What chiefly was regarded, was the *harmonizing* of the tunes; or, as the phrase of the day expressed it, the *"composing them into parts";* for writers of the olden times used the term *"compose,"* in its Latin sense, not as meaning to make or frame a melody, but to *"put together"* certain parts which would harmonize with that melody.

Whatever the sources on which Crüger may have drawn, he certainly created a splendid tune. In *Hymns Ancient and Modern,* 1861, a version of NUN DANKET ALL' with its rhythm regularized and its melody altered was called ST. MARY MAGDALENE. See Nos. 29 and 222 for comments on Crüger.

242 Holy Spirit, Truth Divine

Samuel Longfellow wrote this hymn with the heading "Prayer for Inspiration" for *Hymns of the Spirit,* 1864, a Unitarian collection which he edited in collaboration with Samuel Johnson. See No. 46 for comments on Longfellow.

MERCY (GOTTSCHALK; LAST HOPE) was adapted from Louis Moreau Gottschalk's widely popular and sentimental piano piece, "The Last Hope," by Dr. Edwin P. Parker. (See No. 405.) Gottschalk (1829–1869), celebrated in his day as pianist and composer, was born in New Orleans, the son of an English Jew of German descent and a Creole mother of aristocratic French background. He had a spectacular and colorful career as virtuoso and composer, a career which had no connection with religious music or hymnody. A child prodigy with a remarkable ear and facility for playing and reading music, at seven he substituted at the last minute for the organist of the Cathedral of St. Louis in New Orleans, and by the time he was twelve had outdistanced his teacher and was sent to Paris for study. When he appeared at the Paris Conservatoire to take the entrance examinations, Zimmerman, director of the piano classes, would not even give him an audition, remarking that "America is only a country of steam engines." Ten years later Gottschalk sat at the side of Zimmerman as one of the judges at the auditions.

In a highly successful concert tour on the Continent (he went to Spain at the invitation of the queen) Gottschalk introduced many of his own compositions which met with great enthusiasm. The first American musician to be received and acclaimed on the Continent on an equal footing with European virtuosi, he was ranked with Liszt and Thalberg. When he returned to the United States after eleven years abroad, he was accorded the kind of reception usually reserved for foreign artists. His New York début in 1853 created almost as much of a sensation as had Jenny Lind's, and P. T. Barnum, who had arranged the "Swedish Nightingale's" first American tour, offered Gottschalk a contract for twenty thousand dollars a year, plus all expenses — an offer which his father would not let him accept. After six years of comparative retirement in the West Indies, he resumed his concertizing under the management of Max Strakosch, brother-in-law and manager of Adelina Patti.

Gottschalk traveled extensively in the United States, Cuba, Mexico, and South America as composer, pianist, conductor, often directing huge festivals of his own works. He died of yellow fever in Rio de Janeiro where he had gone to take part in one of these festivals. His reputation as a composer suffered badly from such vapid and sentimental pieces as "The Last Hope" and "The Dying Poet." He knew they were inferior but reminded his critics that "it is only mediocrity that pays" — and he had to make a living! His importance in American musical history is due to the originality of his earlier compositions, many of which, based on Creole rhythms and melodies, captured the flavor and spirit of the music which he had heard as a child. Many of these compositions have been played in recent years with great success.

243 Holy Spirit, Truth Divine

See No. 242 for comments on the text.

VIENNA (RAVENNA), composed by Justin Heinrich Knecht (1752–1817), organist, composer, conductor, theorist, was first published in *Vollständige Sammlung . . . Choralmelodien für das neue Wirtembergische Landgesangbuch*, Stuttgart, 1799. To this collection of four-part settings of chorales, edited by him and J. F. Christmann, he contributed ninety-seven melodies. Knecht, a native of Biberach, Württemberg, had a classical education at the college of the convent in Esslingen where he also learned to play a number of orchestral instruments and continued to study organ, sometimes substituting for his teacher (organist of the convent) who introduced him to the works of Bach, Telemann, and Handel. For a time he was professor of literature in Biberach, but gave up that position in 1792 to become organist and musical director of the town. He was a pioneer in the use of program notes, which he introduced in 1790 for his orchestral concerts. In 1807 he was appointed director of the court and theater orchestra in Stuttgart, resigning after two years because of criticism, intrigue, and the realization that he did not have the proper qualifications for the post. The rest of his life was spent in Biberach. Knecht's contemporaries regarded him as one of the best musicians of the day. As an organist he had only one rival, Abt Vogler, whose playing, musical theories, and system of harmony he admired greatly. Vogler, in turn, admired Knecht's compositions and played on the organ his *Le Portrait musical de la nature, ou grande Simphonie* for fifteen instruments, a work that has interest for musicians because its program or outline of movements anticipated that of Beethoven's *Pastorale Symphony* and was even thought, by some, to be its model. The list of Knecht's compositions takes up four columns in Eitner's *Quellen-Lexikon*, but his compositions lacked vitality and originality, and today he is known only through a few chorale melodies. The present harmonization of VIENNA (except for one chord) is from Havergal's *Old Church Psalmody*, 1847.

244 O Holy Spirit, Enter In

Like Paul Gerhardt and many other prominent seventeenth-century poets and hymn writers, Michael Schirmer (1606–1673) endured great hardships and much suffering as a result of the Thirty Years' War. In addition, he had to contend with poor health and prolonged periods of melancholy and to see his wife and two children precede him in death. Although he expected and deserved to be named head of the Greyfriars Gymnasium at Berlin, where he labored most of his life, he was repeatedly passed over, partly due to a weak constitution, and had to remain content with the positions of subrector and conrector. Despite these disappointments and difficulties, he was the author of several scholarly works and poems, including a number of hymns. The latter, five in all, were contributed to Johann Crüger's two notable collections, *Neues vollkömmliches Gesangbuch*, 1640, and *Praxis pietatis melica*, 1648. The present hymn, from the first of these volumes, was originally a poem of seven ten-line stanzas of which Catherine Winkworth translated five stanzas in her *Chorale Book for England*, 1863. Stanzas one and three are given here. See No. 2 for comments on Miss Winkworth.

WIE SCHÖN LEUCHTET appeared in this form in *The Chorale Book for England*, 1863. See No. 145 for comments on the melody.

245 Gracious Spirit, Dwell With Me

Frail in body, unattractive in appearance, little appreciated and often maligned, Thomas Toke Lynch (1818–1871) was one of the saintliest and most gifted ministers of his time. Although the congregations he served in London remained small — the last of them met at Mornington Chapel, an Independent (Congregational) Church — he attracted a select group of thoughtful people by the spiritual force and originality of his preaching. Upon the publication in 1855 of his collection, *The Rivulet: Hymns for Heart and Voice*, he was subjected to considerable abuse, one critic going so far as to describe its contents as "crude, disjointed, unmeaning, un-Christian, ill-rhymed rubbish." A heated controversy ensued within Congregational and other Nonconformist circles, and churches were divided into opposing factions as a result. Through it all Lynch maintained his composure, commenting with typical grace: "The air will be all the clearer for this storm. We must conquer our foes by suffering them to crucify us rather than by threatening them with crucifixion." Nevertheless, as he was a sensitive person, the controversy adversely affected his health and undoubtedly hastened his death. Lynch was a musician as well as a poet and composed tunes for twenty-five of his hymns, one of which he was heard to sing during his last illness to the words, "Guide me, O thou great Jehovah." The present hymn first appeared in *The Rivulet* and includes all but the third and fourth stanzas of the original poem.

REDHEAD NO. 76   See No. 158 for comments on the tune.

246 Come, Thou Almighty King

Appearing shortly after the publication of the British national anthem, "God save Our Lord the King," (the original version), in *Harmonica Anglicana*, 1743 (?), this hymn was first found in a leaflet bound in with the sixth, eighth, and ninth editions of George Whitfield's hymn collection. The leaflet contained two hymns, one by Charles Wesley, bearing the title "The Backslider" and beginning "Jesus, let thy pitying eye," and this anonymous hymn, entitled "An Hymn to the Trinity." The author may have withheld his name since the hymn was obviously an imitation of the national anthem and was sung to the same tune. The stanzas follow the classical Trinitarian formula in their sequence and include no less than seven names for God: King, Father, Ancient of Days, Word, Spirit, Comforter, and One in Three. One of the interesting features of the hymn is the author's use of the intimate form of address in the first three stanzas and the impersonal third person singular in the last stanza. The story is told of a group of British soldiers breaking into a church service on Long Island one Sunday morning during the American Revolution and ordering the startled worshippers to rise and sing the British national anthem. The congregation proved equal to the occasion by singing the right tune but substituting the words of this hymn!

ITALIAN HYMN (TRINITY; MOSCOW).   Here is a tune that since 1769 has been sung with the text for which it was written. In *Hymn Tunes and their Story*, James T. Lightwood, English hymnologist, credits "this fine tune to the spend-thrift habits of an eighteenth-century violinist." He says that the Italian virtuoso, Felice de Giardini, at a time of great financial distress, was persuaded by the Rev. Martin Madan to write some hymn tunes for a collection Madan was preparing for the use of the Lock Hospital in London, of which he was chaplain. (See No. 25.) Knowing that Giardini would be too proud to accept a gift of money outright, Madan offered to pay him well for the tunes. ITALIAN HYMN, one of four that were composed as a result of this offer, appeared in the *Lock Collection* with the caption: "Hymn to the Trinity. Set by F. G." Giardini (1716–1796), had his first musical training as a chorister in Milan Cathedral, but returned to his birthplace, Turin, for violin study with Giovanni B. Somis, a celebrated teacher who had studied with Corelli and Vivaldi. Giardini's gifts brought him into prominence early, and by the time he reached England in 1750 his reputation as a virtuoso had been established on the Continent. Charles Burney, English historian, who was present at his first public performance in London and came to know him well, wrote that his arrival in London, formed "a memorable aera in the instrumental Music of this kingdom," and spoke also of Giardini's superior gifts as a harpsichordist. He was the first violin virtuoso to be heard in London, and had enormous influence for over thirty years as soloist, leader of the Italian Opera, impresario, teacher of singing and violin, and composer of sorts. In 1784, he went to Italy with the British Ambassador to the Sardinian court, but returned to England after five years, thinking that he could take up his musical career where he had left off, only to discover that others had succeeded to his place. After three years he went to Russia in hopes of finding new opportunities and a warmer welcome, but met with no success and died in Moscow in "poverty, disappointment and distress."

247 Holy God, We Praise Thy Name

A popular German version of the "Te Deum," this hymn first appeared in the *Katholisches Gesangbuch,* Vienna, 1774. Four years later it was included in altered form in Ignaz Franz's collection of the same name and has therefore often been attributed to him. The original author however is unknown. Franz (1719–1790) was a Catholic priest in Breslau, Germany, who published several books, most of them hymnals. One of the latter was a collection of tunes and included several German chorales. The translator, Clarence Walworth (1820–1900), was born in Plattsburg, New York, and studied at General Theological Seminary in New York City. In 1845 he joined the Roman Catholic Church and helped found the order of Paulist Fathers. He served as rector of St. Mary's Roman Catholic Church in Albany, New York, the last thirty-four years of his life, in the final ten of which he was blind.

GROSSER GOTT, WIR LOBEN DICH ("Mighty God, we praise thee"), the tune for a German metrical version of the "Te Deum," had the following form in the *Katholisches Gesangbuch,* published in Vienna between 1774 and 1780, at the request of Empress Maria Theresa. Catholic authorities objected to the secular character of many of the tunes in this collection, but GROSSER GOTT was one of two that passed muster. Its source is unknown. (Bäumker, Vol. III, No. 219, I.)

Gros-ser Gott, wir lo - ben dich, Herr wir prei - sen dei - ne Stär - ke:
Vor dir neigt die Er - de sich, Und be -wun - dert dei - ne Wer - ke.

Wie du warst vor al - ler Zeit, So bleibst du in E - wig-keit.

The present form of the melody (Zahn 3495) is from J. G. Schicht's *Choral-Buch,* 1819 (see No. 173) which brought it into German Protestant usage. The heartiness and fervor with which this hymn is sung by Catholics and Protestants alike in Germany, suggests that it would be an excellent hymn for interfaith services in this country. It is the first hymn in *Cantate Domino,* hymnal of the World's Student Christian Federation, and is included in the

French hymnbook *Louange et Prière* with the words, "Grand Dieu, nous te bénissons." There are several variants of the melody. In Thomas Hastings' *Manhattan Collection,* 1838, this tune in a form close to the 1774 version was arranged by him, named HALLE, and set to his evening hymn "Now from labor and from care," with which it appeared in several other collections.

In Roman Catholic churches in the United States, GROSSER GOTT is one of the best-loved hymns often sung at the close of solemn services and festival celebrations. It was played as President Kennedy's casket was carried out of St. Matthew's Cathedral, Washington, D.C., after the requiem mass which preceded the funeral procession to Arlington Cemetery on Nov. 25, 1963. And it was sung by the huge crowd at Yankee Stadium, New York City, as Pope Paul VI was leaving after his historic celebration of the mass on October 4, 1965.

GROSSER GOTT WIR LOBEN DICH is the source of the tune Hursley. (See tune commentary at No. 50.)

248   O God, Thou Art the Father

St. Columba (c. 521–597) was one of the first and greatest missionaries to Scotland. Born of a noble family in Ireland, he was forced to leave his homeland, presumably because of a dispute of obscure character, and settled with twelve companions on the island of Iona off the west coast of Scotland. From this base he launched a vigorous and successsful evangelistic campaign on the mainland. He and his followers established religious houses throughout the country and won many converts to the Christian faith. Many legends have attached themselves to his name. Credited with writing sacred poetry in both Latin and Gaelic, he wrote a hymn called "Altus" as a hymn of praise to God for his works in creation. When it was criticized because it said nothing about redemption, he wrote a second hymn, "Christus Redemptor gentium" ("Christ is the world's Redeemer") which corrected the deficiency. The latter is the source of the present hymn.

On the occasion of the fourteen-hundredth anniversary of Columba's death, Duncan Macgregor (1854–1923), a Scottish minister and liturgiological scholar, published *St. Columba, A Record and a Tribute,* 1897, which included the present translation of the hymn in the section called "Offices for the Commemoration of St. Columba."

Iona today is the vital center of a remarkable religious community under the inspired leadership of George MacLeod. See the tune commentary at No. 80 for further comments on Columbia.

DURROW, a traditional Irish melody associated with "Captain Thomson," a sea song from County Limerick, was the setting for the present text in *The Church Hymnary,* 1927, harmonized by David Evans. DURROW is a hexatonic (six-tone) melody. The sixth degree of the scale, A flat, does not appear in it. There is much repetition. The wide range of DURROW, the skips down from *b* flat to *g* and from *f* to *d*, the repeated notes at the end of phrases two and four, give the melody a distinctive quality which is most apparent when the tune is sung without accompaniment.

See No. 38 for comments on David Evans.

249 Ancient of Days, Who Sittest Throned in Glory

Occasioned by the bicentenary celebration of the granting of the city charter of Albany, New York, in 1886, the first city in America to be so chartered, this hymn by Bishop Doane was first sung in the Episcopal Cathedral there. Beginning with the line from Daniel 7:9, referring to God as the "Ancient of days," each succeeding stanza of the hymn opens with an ascription to the Father, Son, and Holy Ghost, and concludes with an address to the Triune God. (See No. 438 for another American bicentenary hymn.) William Croswell Doane (1832–1913) was the first bishop of the diocese of Albany and was an influential leader in his denomination. Active in civic as well as religious affairs, he was respected by countless numbers of people within and outside the church. He served as chairman of the commission that prepared the *Hymnal,* 1892, of the Protestant Episcopal Church.

ANCIENT OF DAYS was composed in 1886 for Bishop Doane's bicentenary hymn by J. Albert Jeffery (1855–1929), his organist at All Saints' Cathedral in Albany, New York, and was first published in the Episcopal *Hymnal* of 1892. When Jeffery was fourteen years old, he succeeded his father as organist of St. Andrew's in Plymouth, England, where he was born. His first music lessons with his father were followed by study with Liszt in Weimar and with Carl Reinecke at the Leipzig Conservatory which gave him an honorary doctorate at his graduation. He also studied in Paris. When he came to America in 1876, he settled in Albany, organized a choral society, and became director of music at St. Agnes' School, founded by Bishop Doane. In 1887, St. Stephen's College in Annandale, New York, granted him a D.Mus. degree. He left Albany in 1893, was organist at First Presbyterian Church in Yonkers, New York, and then went on to Boston where he taught piano at the New England Conservatory of Music from around 1900 until his death in 1929. For a time, he was organist at the North Cambridge Universalist Church.

250 We All Believe in One True God

A metrical form of the Apostles' Creed, considerably revised in translation, this hymn by Tobias Clausnitzer made its first appearance in the *Culmbach-Bayreuth Gesangbuch,* 1668. It is a simplification of Luther's paraphrase of the Apostles' Creed, with the same title. See No. 212 for comments on Clausnitzer. Catherine Winkworth translated it in her *Chorale Book for England,* 1863. See No. 2 for comments on Miss Winkworth.

WIR GLAUBEN ALL' AN EINEN GOTT, an anonymous melody, was set to Clausnitzer's metrical paraphrase of the Apostles' Creed in the Darmstadt *Kirchengesangbuch,* 1699. (Zahn 4000) The present form of the melody, from Hiller's 1793 collection, appeared with Miss Winkworth's translation in *The Chorale Book for England,* 1863. (See No. 15.) Bach used the melody only once, in a chorale prelude for organ which Albert Schweitzer includes among Bach's "admittedly youthful works."

251 Holy, Holy, Holy! Lord God Almighty

Described by John Julian as a "splendid metrical paraphrase of Revelation 4:8–11," this hymn by Bishop Heber was written for Trinity Sunday but is now sung throughout the year. It was the poet Tennyson's favorite hymn, and was sung at his funeral in Westminster Abbey, April 12, 1892. Both the Unitarians and Christian Scientists included it in their official hymnals, although they substituted the last line of the second stanza for the last lines of the first and fourth stanzas, both of which refer to the Trinity. Appearing first in Heber's *A Selection of Psalms and Hymns for the Parish Church of Banbury,* third edition, 1826, the year of his death, it was published posthumously a year later in his *Hymns written and adapted to the Weekly Church Service of the Year,* 1827. Jeremiah Reeves said of this hymn, "The lines suggest cathedral heights and spaces, the spirit of worship described in Milton's 'At a Solemn Music,' or expressed in the Psalm, 'Lift up your heads, O ye gates!' "

See No. 58 for comments on Heber.

NICAEA, composed for Bishop Heber's hymn by John B. Dykes, was one of seven of his tunes included in the first music edition of *Hymns Ancient and Modern,* 1861. Erik Routley has called it the noblest of Dykes's tunes and says that "on the strength of it alone Dykes earns immortality in the annals of hymnody," while Leonard Ellinwood comments on the fact that since Dykes composed it not a note of either tune or harmony of NICAEA has been altered. Undoubtedly, the tune has had much to do with the popularity of the hymn. For many worshippers in the United States it has been the morning hymn of praise *par excellence.* Dykes' name for the tune recalls the city in Asia Minor where the famous church council, convened by Constantine in 325 A.D., formulated the Nicene Creed in which the doctrine of the Trinity was defined. Some hymnologists have noted reminiscences of WACHET AUF (No. 24) in NICAEA, and also of TRINITY, a tune by John Hopkins published with Heber's words in an 1850 English collection. Its first phrase follows:

NICAEA has much in common with the setting composed for Heber's text in 1850 by Lowell Mason and published in *Cantica Laudis,* 1850, edited by Mason and Webb. There is no way of knowing whether Dykes ever saw or heard Mason's setting. The similarities between it and NICAEA may be purely coincidental. During an extended trip abroad in 1852 and 1853 Mason spent considerable time in England. In a letter dated September 2, 1852, he told of his pleasure in giving two courses to music and school teachers at the Home and Colonial School, and at the Birkbeck School, in London. In October of the same year he wrote of having lectured on psalmody in several churches.

See No. 79 for comments on Dykes.

252 O Word of God Incarnate

William Walsham How (1823–1897) was known widely and affectionately as the poor man's bishop, the people's bishop, and the children's bishop. Respected and loved by all classes, he cared little for ecclesiastical preferments and is reported to have declined the bishopric of Manchester without even bothering to tell his family, and he later refused the same post at Durham, a position which would have more than doubled his salary. As suffragan bishop of Bedford, he devoted most of his time to the poor and downtrodden in the depressed areas of East London. Engraved on his pastoral staff was the saying of St. Bernard, *Pasce verbo, pasce vita* (Feed with the word, feed with the life). Ecumenical in outlook, he collaborated with the Rev. Thomas Baker Morell, a Congregational minister, in compiling *Psalms and Hymns,* 1854, from the Supplement of which (1867) the present hymn was taken. He also joined with Sir Arthur Sullivan in producing *Church Hymns,* 1871, for many years the chief rival of *Hymns Ancient and Modern* as the most popular English hymnal. James Moffat has rightly observed that "modern hymnody owes to him some of its richest treasures," [1] of which one could mention, "For All the Saints" (Nos. 306 and 307), "O Jesus, Thou Art Standing" (No. 329), and "We Give Thee But Thine Own" (No. 535).

MUNICH (KÖNIGSBERG) is an adaptation of the quartet, "Cast thy burden upon the Lord" from Mendelssohn's *Elijah,* 1846 (Part I, No. 15). The soprano of the quartet is a recasting of a chorale melody from a Meinigen hymnbook of 1693, set there to Johann Heermann's "O Gott du frommer Gott" ("O God, thou faithful God") with which it appeared in *The Chorale Book for England,* 1863. The early form of the melody, with slight variants, still appears in some present-day hymnals published in Germany and the United States, among them *The Hymnal* (Evangelical and Reformed), 1941; *The Lutheran Hymnal,* 1941; *Common Service Book with Hymnal* (United Lutheran Church in America), 1917.

Johannes Zahn traced parts of the melody to a book of psalm tunes published at Regensburg in 1675 and remarked on the wide use of the hymn and melody which, originating in the south of Germany, had spread to all parts of the country by the nineteenth century. Bach used the melody, with some modifications, in Cantatas 24 and 71. In the *Choralgesänge* there is one harmonization of it — the third tune used by Bach with Heermann's text. (See Nos. 86 and 198.)

Two years after the first performance of ELIJAH in Birmingham, the quartet was adapted to a C.M.D. text in *The National Psalmist,* 1848, edited by Lowell Mason and George Webb. Mendelssohn's harmonies and the holds at the end of each two-measure phrase were there but the form of the melody was essentially that of MUNICH. It was called ELIJAH.

In the majority of hymnals published in the United States MUNICH is now the accepted setting for "O Word of God incarnate." This combination of text and tune is not found in contemporary English hymnals. MUNICH was set to Bishop How's hymn in the *Irish Hymnal,* Dublin, 1874, edited by Sir Robert Prescott Stewart, and *The Plymouth Hymnal,* Boston, 1893, edited by Lyman Abbott.

253 Book of Books, Our Peoples' Strength

Published first in *Songs of Praise,* 1925, this hymn by Percy Dearmer was written for the tune LIEBSTER JESU, "to express the modern appreciation of the Bible." See No. 112 for comments on Dearmer.

LIEBSTER JESU was the setting for these words in *Songs of Praise,* 1925. See No. 212 for comments on the tune.

254 Break Thou the Bread of Life

This is one of seven hymns written by Miss Lathbury in the summer of 1877 at the request of Bishop John H. Vincent for use at Chautauqua. Although often selected as a communion hymn, it was intended to be sung with the scriptures in mind, the "bread of life" referring to the Word of God. Another of her hymns written in 1877 has remained in popular use, "Day Is Dying in the West." See No. 45 for comments on Miss Lathbury.

BREAD OF LIFE was composed for Miss Lathbury's hymn about the Bible by William F. Sherwin in 1877, at the request of Bishop John H. Vincent, founder of the Chautauqua Institution. In *Lyric Religion,* 1931, H. Augustine Smith wrote of Sherwin: "He was all that was lovable and witty and devout. Such a genial personality won for him a great host of warm friends."
See No. 31 for further comments on Sherwin.

255 Most Perfect Is the Law of God

This faithful paraphrase of verses 7–9 and 14 of Psalm 19 is by an unknown author. It first appeared in *The Psalter* of 1912 which was a twentieth-century version of the Scottish Psalter of 1650, prepared by a joint committee representing nine Presbyterian and Reformed denominational groups in the United States.

STRACATHRO is one of the best of the newer type of psalm tune that originated in England and Scotland in the eighteenth and early nineteenth centuries. Its range and contour show the influence of the Evangelical Revival which brought new life not only into religion but into hymnody as well, and introduced tunes with considerable rhythmic and melodic variety in a style markedly different from that of the classic syllabic psalm tune. STRACATHRO was composed by Charles Hutcheson (1792–1860), Glasgow merchant, who was a skilled amateur musician with a good voice, refined taste, and a deep interest in psalmody. It was published in *Christian Vespers,* 1832, a collection of psalm tunes compiled and arranged by him. In *Four Centuries of Scottish Psalmody,* 1949, Millar Patrick mentions STRA–CATHRO as one of the few tunes produced at that time which survived and found a secure place in peoples' affections. He comments also on the fact that it is one of several Scottish hymn tunes which use a six-tone (hexatonic) scale. The fourth note of the scale does not appear in this melody.

The daughter of a close friend of Hutcheson's said that after the tune had been sung for the first time at St. George's Church in Glasgow, it took hold at once and became a great favorite. It was named by the composer for the estate which his friend Sir James Campbell purchased just at the time of the tune's publication. See No. 445 for comments on Geoffrey Shaw.

256 Lamp of Our Feet, Whereby We Trace

A Quaker all his days, Bernard Barton (1784–1849) was educated at a Society of Friends school at Ipswich and worked as a clerk in a bank in Woodbridge, England, for the last forty years of his life. According to one report, "So punctual and methodical was he that as he returned from the office each midday, the housewives knew it was the correct time to put their potatoes into the water as he passed their doors, and they liked to watch him as, meeting a friend, he stopped to offer a pinch of snuff or tell a good story from Boswell." He knew Edward Fitzgerald, translator of *The Rubáiyat of Omar Khayyám,* and counted Charles Lamb, Lord Byron, Sir Walter Scott, and Robert Southey within his circle of friends. He was the author of eight volumes of verse. The present hymn is a cento from a poem entitled "The Bible" in his *Reliquary,* 1836.

NUN DANKET ALL' (GRÄFENBERG)   See No. 241 for comments on this tune.

257 The Heavens Declare Thy Glory, Lord

Entitled "The Book of Nature and of Scripture compared," this paraphrase of Psalm 19 by Isaac Watts appeared first in his *Psalms of David,* 1719. See No. 1 for comments on Watts.

UXBRIDGE, one of Lowell Mason's original hymn tunes, was set to Isaac Watts' version of Psalm 19 in *The Modern Psalmist,* 1839. It had appeared in earlier collections edited by Mason and others with different texts and with a slightly different melodic form in the first measure. In *Lowell Mason: An Appreciation of his Life and Work,* 1941, Henry Lowell Mason says that his father had two cardinal principles to which congregational tunes for the church should conform: "First, they should be such that all could sing them, their melodies should not exceed the limits of the average range of the human voice; and secondly, they should be the complement of the verses to which they were set, thus strengthening the meaning and the significance of the hymns themselves." [19] Uxbridge is the name of an ancient borough in England and of a town in Massachusetts. Lowell Mason (1792–1872) was a descendant of English-born Robert Mason who landed at Salem, Massachusetts, in 1630. His eldest son, Thomas, settled in Medfield in 1653. There, six generations later, Lowell was born and spent the first twenty years of his life. His grandfather, a Harvard graduate in 1742, was a schoolmaster, a teacher in singing schools, and a selectman of the town. His father taught school in the family homestead for several years, was a merchant and manufacturer of straw goods, an inventor of sorts, town clerk for nineteen years, town treasurer, and a member of the legislature. He played the cello and sang in the church choir for over twenty years. Lowell's interest in music was apparent to all; he spent much time learning to play whatever instruments were available, bought books of instruction, attended a singing school when he was thirteen, played clarinet in the Medfield band, taught in singing schools in neighboring communities, and at sixteen began to direct the church choir. A Medfield historian has said that it was his common practice to play the flute or clarinet on the steps of the meeting house on summer evenings to the delight of those who gathered around him.

In 1812 Mason and two Medfield friends set out with horse and wagon for Savannah, Georgia. His parents hoped that this venture would result in his becoming something more practical and more promising than a musician. For the first few years in Savannah he worked in a dry goods business. In 1817 at the time of his marriage to Abigail Adams of Westboro, Massachusetts, he was a member of the firm Stebbins and Mason, which added musical instruments to its merchandise in 1818. For seven or eight years he was a teller in the Planter's Bank. In his spare time he studied harmony and composition with F. L. Abel, a well-schooled German musician, and began assembling, arranging, composing, and harmonizing tunes for what became in 1822 *The Boston Handel and Haydn Society Collection of Church Music* which went through twenty-two editions and was the first of more than sixty publications which he edited. It was modeled on Gardiner's *Sacred Melodies,* 1812–1815, and contained a number of its texts and tunes. In the first edition of the book Mason's name did not appear. Speaking of this in later years he said: "I was then a bank officer in Savannah, and did not wish to be known as a musical man, as I had not the least thought of ever making music a profession." His collection set the Handel and Haydn Society on its feet financially and helped to establish it as "one of the characteristic institutions of Boston" which "initiated a purer and healthier taste for music in New England." It also brought fame to Mason and resulted in his choice of music as a career. In Savannah he organized singing schools, had classes for instruction in sacred music, arranged and directed concerts of music from oratorios, and helped organize an interdenominational Sabbath school and served as its superintendent; he also formed a Sunday school teachers association, helped found the Savannah Missionary Society, was on the Board of Health, was secretary, treasurer, and librarian of the library, and a charter member of the First Presbyterian Church — activities which show the initiative, imagination, and executive ability of this public-spirited man of varied interests and stupendous energies. From 1820 to 1827 he was the official organist of the Independent Presbyterian Church with a salary of twenty-five dollars a month. Before 1820 he had served without pay. At the dedication of the church in 1819, President James Monroe with members of his Cabinet and dignitaries from the Army and Navy were in the congregation. They were in town for the launching of the steamboat *Savannah* on its maiden voyage across the Atlantic.

In 1827 Mason left Savannah for Boston to direct the music in three churches. He was to serve each, successively, for six months at a salary of two thousand dollars a year. The plan was not practicable, Mason was released from the contract, returned to banking for a time, and later became director of the choir at the Bowdoin Street Church where Lyman Beecher, father of Henry Ward Beecher and Harriet Beecher Stowe, was minister. During his fourteen years there the choir became nationally known and drew many visitors to the church. For five years Mason was president and conductor of the Handel and Haydn Society, resigning in 1832 in order to have more time for teaching music, especially to children. In 1833, with George Webb and a group of influential Bostonians, he founded the Boston Academy of Music which played an important part in the musical life of the city until 1847. One of its principal objectives was to secure music instruction for children in the public schools. For more than six years Mason taught hundreds of children without remuneration, presented them in concerts and demonstrations, and finally succeeded in having music introduced into the curriculum of the Boston public schools. When the City Council failed to appropriate funds for music teachers, Mason volunteered to teach in one school for a year without salary. He supplied the necessary books and materials as well. At the end of the year his goal was won and public school music was established in Boston. Seeing the need for teacher training he organized classes, institutes, and conventions which were forerunners of normal schools, workshops, and music festivals. He was an ardent advocate of Pestalozzi's educational principles, lectured on them in England and America, and based his own methods on them. Through his teaching and publications he had enormous influence on the musical life of schools and churches throughout the country.

Mason was a born leader with exceptional gifts as a teacher and great personal magnetism. Horace Mann said that he would walk fifty miles if he had to, just to hear Mason teach. In 1855 New York University granted him an honorary doctorate in music, the second of its kind to be conferred in the United States. The last years of his life were spent in Orange, New Jersey. His fine library, containing eight hundred manuscripts and seven hundred volumes pertaining to hymnology, is at Yale University in the library of the School of Music.

258 Lord, Thy Word Abideth

Bearing the caption, "Thy word is a lantern unto my feet, and a light unto my paths" (Psalm 119:105), this hymn by Henry Williams Baker was written for the original edition of *Hymns Ancient and Modern,* 1861, of which Baker was the editor. See No. 79 for comments on Baker.

RAVENSHAW   The English name of this short tune gives no hint of its ancestry. It was the setting for these words in *Hymns Ancient and Modern,* 1861, adapted by William H. Monk from a medieval melody first printed in *Ein New Gesengbuchlen,* 1531, the earliest German hymnbook of the Bohemian Brethren, edited by Michael Weisse. He set it to his hymn "Menschenkind, merk eben" (Zahn 3294) but indicated that the melody was traditionally associated with "Ave Hierarchia," an Advent hymn in Catholic collections.

Got - tes Sohn ist kom-men uns al - len zu from - men hie auf die-

se Er - den in ar-men Ge - ber - - - den, dass er uns

von Sün - de frei - et und ent - bün - - de.

In 1544 the tune appeared in another hymnbook of the Brethren with Johann Horn's Christmas hymn, "Gottes Sohn ist kommen," and in a German collection with "Gott, durch deine Güte." In the *Orgelbüchlein* Bach gives the first lines of both of these hymns as the heading for one of his most charming canonic preludes, and also uses the melody for a fughetta and prelude among the miscellaneous Preludes. There is one harmonization of the melody in the *Choralgesänge*. "Gottes Sohn ist kommen" still appears with Weisse's melody in present-day German hymnals and in Lutheran books published in the United States. The melody, set to German words, continued in use among Protestants and Catholics. (Bäumker Vol. I, No. 7) It is given with "Ave Hierarchia" in the notes on RAVENSHAW in the Historical Edition of *Hymns Ancient and Modern*, 1909. See Nos. 113 and 183 for comments on Weisse.

259 We Limit Not the Truth of God

George Rawson (1807–1889), a Congregational layman and solicitor of Leeds, England, was moved to write these lines in remembrance of John Robinson's farewell speech to the Pilgrims as they departed by ship from Leyden for England and the New World. Edward Winslow, one of the founders and leaders of Plymouth Colony, in his memoirs recalled the scene in these words: "We were now ere long to part asunder; and the Lord knoweth whether ever he should live to see our faces again. But whether the Lord had appointed it or not; he charged us, before God and His blessed angels, to follow him no further than he followed Christ: and if God should reveal anything to us by any other instrument of His, to be as ready to receive it, as ever we were to receive any truth by his ministry. For he was very confident that the Lord had more truth and light yet to break forth out of His holy word." The hymn first appeared in *Psalms, Hymns and Passages of Scripture for Christian Worship*, 1853, popularly known as the Leeds Hymn Book, which Rawson helped prepare in collaboration with several Congregational ministers. Other of his hymns were later published in *Hymns, Verses and Chants*, 1876, and *Songs of Spiritual Thought*, 1885.

OLD 22ND The use of this tune with three hymns in the *Pilgrim Hymnal* shows how greatly the music editors admired it. OLD 22ND adds distinction to any text with which it is sung. In the Anglo-Genevan Psalter, 1556, it was the setting for Psalm 16; in the psalters of John Day (1563), Thomas Este (1592), and Richard Allison (1599) it was associated with Psalm 22. Thomas Morley harmonized it in four parts for Ravenscroft's Psalter (1621) in which it was set to Psalm 38 and was listed in the index as one of the English tunes "imitating the High-Dutch, Italian, French and Netherlandish Tones." It dropped out of use in England early in the seventeenth century but was one of the fine tunes brought back into circulation by *The English Hymnal*, 1906, the source of the harmonization given here.

260 The Church's One Foundation

As were many of the hymns of Ambrose centuries earlier, this hymn by Samuel J. Stone (1839–1900) was called forth by a doctrinal dispute. In 1866 Bishop John William Colenso of South Africa wrote a book in which he questioned the historicity of some of the Old Testament stories. His advanced views were severely criticized by other churchmen with the result that Bishop Gray of Cape Town deposed him as a dangerous teacher. Although Stone was only twenty-seven years of age, he was so stirred by the controversy that he published a series of twelve hymns based on the Apostles' Creed in defense of Bishop Gray's position, giving it the title *Lyra Fidelium*. The present hymn was inspired by the ninth article, "I believe in . . . the holy Catholic Church, the communion of saints." Containing originally seven stanzas, it was later expanded into ten stanzas for use as a processional in Salisbury Cathedral. It became so popular that at the Lambeth Conference in 1888 it was sung as the opening hymn at each of the impressive services at Canterbury Cathedral, Westminster Abbey, and St. Paul's Cathedral. In the Appendix to *Hymns Ancient and Modern*, 1868, it was reduced to five stanzas, and this shortened form has become the normative one, though with the third stanza often omitted, as in this version.

> Though with a scornful wonder
>   Men see her sore opprest,
> By schisms rent asunder,
>   By heresies distrest:
> Yet saints their watch are keeping,
>   Their cry goes up, "How long?"
> And soon the night of weeping
>   Shall be the morn of song.

John Julian described Stone's hymns as "strongly outspoken utterances of a manly faith, where dogma, prayer, and praise are interwoven with much skill. Usually the keynote of his song is Hope." Stone, an Anglican clergyman, later became rector of All-Hallows-on-the-Wall, London, and served on the committee that prepared the 1909 edition of *Hymns Ancient and Modern*.

AURELIA Although at the present time this tune can hardly be thought of apart from "The Church's one foundation," it was introduced into English hymnody as the setting for "Jerusalem the golden" in *A Selection of Psalms and Hymns* edited by the Rev. Charles Kemble and S. S. Wesley, 1864, and was set to the same text by the composer in his *European Psalmist,* 1872. This association is recalled in the tune's name (derived from *aurum,* Latin for "gold") which was suggested by Wesley's wife. AURELIA was assigned to two hymns published in the Appendix to *Hymns Ancient and Modern,* 1868, one of them being the present text for which it has become almost a proper. When it was selected as one of the hymns to be sung at the service of thanksgiving for the recovery from illness of the Prince of Wales (Edward VII), held in St. Paul's Cathedral on February 27, 1872, Dr. Henry Gauntlett issued a circular in which he objected strenuously to the use of music which he called "secular twaddle." He found it difficult to understand why AURELIA should have been chosen in preference to Teschner's "All glory, laud and honor" which was in the same book. His protests were unavailing.

Samuel Sebastian Wesley (1810–1876), the greatest musical genius of the Wesley family, was the grandson of Charles Wesley, the great-nephew of John Wesley, and the son of Samuel Wesley whose love for Bach accounts for his son's middle name. For eight years he was one of the choristers of the Chapel Royal, at sixteen he had his first appointment as church organist, and during his lifetime served in five parish churches and four cathedrals: Hereford, Exeter, Winchester, and Gloucester. In 1839 he was granted the B.Mus. and D.Mus. degrees by Oxford. In 1850 he became professor of organ at the Royal Academy of Music. He was a passionate and outspoken champion of reforms in church music at a time when conditions in the cathedrals and churches must have been trying for musicians even less sensitive and less gifted.

That Wesley was a memorable and remarkable character is evident from any account of his life. His passion for fishing was such that he is said to have accepted or rejected a new post depending upon the fishing advantages of the district. An assistant related that on one occasion when he and Wesley were on their way to the dedication of a new organ, Wesley noticed the apparently fine fishing in a river they had to cross; whereupon he sent the assistant on to play the opening number on the instrument, instructing him to say that Wesley himself was unavoidably detained. He was the finest organist of his day, renowned for his improvisations. His service music, particularly the anthems which he composed for the Church of England, place him in the highest ranks of nineteenth-century English church musicians. In *English Cathedral Music,* 1941, Edmund H. Fellowes says that Wesley "stands out as the greatest English church musician between Purcell and Stanford." Belated official recognition of his genius and of his service to the cause of church music in England came three years before his death when Queen Victoria granted him a yearly pension of one hundred pounds. The following unidentified comment appears in the *Handbook to the Church Hymnary:*

> Wesley was a great Englishman. In that word lies perhaps the secret of much of his appeal. He was above all English. In his downrightness, his humours, (using the word in its old sense), his blend of kindliness and wrongheadedness, and his love of outdoor life, no less than in his music, he bore the stamp of the country that produced him.

261 City of God, How Broad and Far

This is another of the hymns taken from *Hymns of the Spirit,* 1864, which Samuel Johnson edited in collaboration with Samuel Longfellow. Johnson wrote this hymn in 1860 while minister of the Free Church in Lynn, Massachusetts. It has become a great favorite in England since Percy Dearmer introduced it in *The English Hymnal,* 1906, so much so that it was sung at the consecration of the Liverpool Cathedral on July 19, 1924. See No. 236 for comments on Johnson.

RICHMOND (HAWEIS; SPA FIELDS CHAPEL) introduces us to another gentleman associated with the Countess of Huntingdon (see No. 196). It was written by Thomas Haweis for his hymn "O Thou from whom all goodness flows," first published in the ninth edition of *Carmino Christo,* c. 1792, a collection of hymns and tunes which he compiled and which, in time, came to be a companion book to and was often bound with Lady Huntingdon's *Select Collection of Hymns* used in her chapels. The tune, named for the composer's friend, Leigh Richmond, rector of Turvey, had the following form originally, and is one of the best examples of a typical eighteenth century English hymn tune, with its rather florid melody in triple time and the repetitions of part of the text.

O thou from whom all good - ness flows, I lift my heart to thee;

In all my sor - rows, con - flicts, woes, Dear Lord, re-mem-ber me, re-

mem - ber me, re - mem-ber me, Dear Lord, re - mem - ber me.

Haweis (1734–1820), a native of Redruth, Cornwall, apprenticed for a time to a surgeon and apothecary, decided to study for Holy Orders and attended Christ Church and Magdalen colleges at Oxford, without, however, taking a degree. Ordained in 1757, he was appointed chaplain to the earl of Peterborough, and later became curate at St. Mary Magdalene, Oxford, from which he was dismissed because of Methodist leanings. After a period as assistant to Martin Madan at Lock Hospital (see No. 25) he became rector of All Saints, Aldwinkle, Northamptonshire, remaining there until his death. In 1768 he became chaplain at Lady Huntingdon's chapel in Bath — he is said to have been the most musical of all her chaplains — and later her trustee, executor, manager of her chapels, and of the college she established in Trevecca, Wales, for the training of ministers of the Connexion. It was moved to Cheshunt, Hertfordshire in 1792, transferred to Cambridge in 1905, and was noted for the number of men it sent to foreign missions. Haweis was a friend and correspondent of John Newton, a pioneer in the foreign mission movement, and was one of the first to welcome the formation of an interdenominational missionary society.

262 Forgive, O Lord, Our Severing Ways

Although derived in large part from Whittier's poetry, this is a composite work. The last three stanzas come from Whittier's poem, "Amidst these glorious works of thine," written in 1864 for the dedication of the church of which Thomas Starr King, prominent Unitarian preacher and author, was the minister, the House of Worship in San Francisco. The first stanza is of unknown origin. See No. 224 for comments on Whittier.

O MENSCH SIEH; BOHEMIA, the setting for these words in *The Hymnal* (Presbyterian), 1933, is another melody from the Bohemian Brethren, published in one of their hymnals in 1566, possibly at Prague, with a text by Michael Weisse (see 113). The caption "Stabat Mater" indicated its earlier association with that famous thirteenth-century Latin hymn which grew out of the Franciscan movement and in 1727 was admitted officially to the Roman Missal as one of the sequences. This association of the melody is reflected in the *English Hymnal*, 1906, and in *Songs of Praise*, 1925, where it was set to a hymn for Good Friday or Easter Eve, in a straight 3/1 meter. The following comments on the rich hymnody which grew up in the fifteenth century among the followers of John Huss are from *The Handbook to the Hymnal*, 1935:

> The foundations for congregational song were laid by these people before the Reformation in Germany and Switzerland. . . . From the first, the Bohemian Brethren were deeply concerned about congregational song. . . . They encouraged the writing of sacred verse and music that would appeal to the artisan class, young people, and schools of mastersingers which flourished in Germany in the fourteenth, fifteenth, and sixteenth centuries. Secular folk songs were appropriated by the Brethren, and many of these, because of their beauty, have come down the centuries to enrich the worship of today.[20]

263 Christ Is Made the Sure Foundation

Of unknown authorship, this early medieval hymn, dating from the seventh century and based on I Peter 2:4–6, Ephesians 2:20–22, and Revelation 21, is the classic hymn for use at the dedication of a church. In the oldest extant manuscripts it is listed as the proper office hymn to be sung at dedication festivals. Originally divided into two parts, the first four stanzas, beginning "Urbs beata Hierusalem" ("Blessed city, heavenly Salem"), emphasize the vision of the heavenly Jerusalem descending to earth; and the last five stanzas, beginning "Angularis fundamentum lapis Christus missus est" ("Christ is made the sure foundation"), emphasize and invoke God's continued blessing upon his church. Described by Archbishop Trench, noted Anglican clergyman and author, as a "rugged but fine old hymn," it was translated by John Mason Neale in his *Mediaeval Hymns and Sequences*, 1851. The version given here has been considerably revised. See No. 110 for comments on Neale.

REGENT SQUARE   See No. 117 for comments on the tune.

264   O Where Are Kings and Empires Now

While a student at General Theological Seminary, Chelsea Square, in New York City, Arthur Cleveland Coxe (1818–1896) wrote a ballad on which this hymn was based. The ballad, "Chelsea," first appeared in *The Churchman*, 1839, and a year later was published in his *Christian Ballads*. It began with the lines:

> When old Canute the Dane
>   Was merry England's king;
> A thousand years agone, and more,
>   As ancient rymours sing,
> His boat was rowing down the Ouse,
>   At eve, one summer day,
> Where Ely's tall cathedral peered
>   Above the glassy way.

Coxe likened the singing King Canute heard as his boat was rowed past Ely Cathedral to the singing heard on the Hudson River "from Chelsea's student train" in New York City. The present cento, found in most American hymnals, consists of the first half of stanza six, the second half of stanza eight, and stanza seven, the latter being divided into two parts. These have all been extensively altered. Theodore Dwight Woolsey, president of Yale University from 1846 to 1871, in an address to the General Conference of the Evangelical Alliance in 1873 in New York City, dealing with the skepticism prevailing at the time, had the sudden inspiration to quote the first stanza of this hymn. There was a moment's pause, and then, as the aptness of the words came home to his listeners, there was a spontaneous burst of applause which lasted for several minutes. Coxe was rector of several prominent Episcopal churches and later became Bishop of the Western Diocese of New York. As a member of the hymnal committee of his denomination from 1869 to 1871 he refused to allow his hymns to be included in the hymnal of his own church.

ST. ANNE   See No. 1 for comments on the tune.

265   O God, Within Whose Sight

After years spent in business involving travel in Europe and the United States, William A. Dunkerley (1852–1941) turned to writing, using the pseudonym John Oxenham, and was so successful that he devoted the rest of his life to this calling. He derived his nom de plume from one of the leading characters in Charles Kingsley's *Westward Ho!,* a copy of which had been given him by his Sunday school teacher in a Congregational Church in Manchester. The author of many books, including novels and volumes of prose and poetry, Oxenham was a man of deep religious faith and sensitivity. He exerted a tremendous influence upon Christian intellectuals before and during World War II through his editorship of *The Christian News-Letter,* published in Great Britain. From 1882 to 1890 he published an English version of the *Detroit Free Press* in London. He carried on an extensive correspondence with people all over the world and received this tribute from a minister: "Forgive me if I say I feel drawn to a man who writes poems and novels that have the fresh air of God blowing all about them — a none too common quality in 20th century literature." This hymn was first published in his *Bees in Amber* in 1913 under the title "Liberty, Equality, Fraternity."

SERUG   In searching for some clue as to the origin of this tune which was in only three out of twenty-four hymnals consulted, the writer was led to look in some of Lowell Mason's collections and found it in his *Modern Psalmist,* 1839, set to "Praise ye Jehovah's name." An asterisk next to its name in the Index of Tunes led to the following explanation in the Preface:

> Every tune to the name of which a star (*) is annexed in either of the indexes at the end of the volume, has either been arranged, adapted or composed for this work, or taken from other recent works of the Editor, and is therefore property.

Except for four chords, Mason's harmonization was the same as that in the present arrangement from S. S. Wesley's *European Psalmist,* 1872, a large collection of hymns, chants, and short anthems from British and foreign sources. In it no source was given for the melody which was set to "Thou whose almighty word." The fact that Serug is a name mentioned in Genesis 11:20 and Luke 3:35, made it seem likelier than ever that this tune originated with Mason, who had a faculty for attaching unusual names, many of them Biblical, to melodies in his collections. In *The Choir,* 1832, an anonymous tune, OAKHAM, which starts out with three measures that are identical with the first three of SERUG, was suggested for a hymn in *Church Psalmody,* 1831, a collection of hymns and psalm versions edited by Mason and David Greene. With the discovery in *The National Psalmist,* 1848, of another anonymous tune, ZAMORA, which is the same melodically and harmonically as SERUG, except for its first three measures, the writer feels reasonably certain that Mason composed the present tune. It has continued in use principally because of the dearth of tunes in 6.6.4.6.6.6.4. — the meter of AMERICA, ITALIAN HYMN, and Mason's OLIVET.

266 One Holy Church of God Appears

This is another of Samuel Longfellow's hymns that appeared initially in *Hymns of the Spirit,* 1864. It was given the title, "The Church Universal," and conveys a breadth of vision akin to many of Paul's letters to the early church. See No. 46 for comments on Longfellow.

ST. JAMES has remained substantially unchanged since its first appearance anonymously in *Select Psalms and Hymns for the use of the Parish Church and Tabernacle of St. James's,* 1697. Lightwood says that this collection was one of the first in England to be compiled for a particular place of worship. In the sixth edition of the *Supplement to the New Version,* 1708 (see No. 1), ST. JAMES was assigned to Psalm 19 and also recommended as the tune for "While shepherds watched their flock by night." It was still anonymous as it continued to be in successive editions of the *Supplement.* However, in Phil Hart's *Melodies Proper to be Sung,* c. 1716, it was attributed to R. Courteville about whose life and activities there is considerable uncertainty. There may have been three Raphael Courtevilles. The composer of ST. JAMES (born not later than 1675 or 1676), son of Raphael I, a gentleman of the Chapel Royal in the reigns of Charles I and Charles II, was one of the choristers of the Chapel. On September 7, 1691, he was appointed the first organist of St. James's, Westminster (now St. James's, Piccadilly), to which Queen Mary had given an organ from the Chapel Royal earlier in the year. If the records of the church are correct, Courteville continued in this post for eighty-one years, until his death in 1772. Some, doubting the possibility of this, have thought that a son of the same name succeeded him in 1735, but this comment has been quoted: "So prolonged a tenure is not impossible, as one Charles Bridgman was organist of All Saints', Hertford, for eighty-one years, having been appointed at thirteen, and dying at ninety-five; A. H. Brown also began his career as an organist at eleven and continued it till he died at ninety-six." [21]

After 1752 Courteville seems to have neglected his duties to such an extent that he was warned more than once of possible dismissal. An assistant was appointed, and did virtually all the work. Apparently Courteville held the position long after he was able to carry out its responsibilities acceptably. He composed secular songs, six sonatas for two flutes, and was one of the musicians who provided music for Part III of D'Urfey's *Don Quixote,* 1695.

267 Glorious Things of Thee Are Spoken

Based on Psalm 87 and Isaiah 33:20–21 for its main themes and bearing the title "Zion, or the City of God," this hymn by John Newton was first published in *Olney Hymns,* 1779, which he edited jointly with William Cowper. It originally contained five stanzas, but the last two have been omitted in this version. This is undoubtedly the finest hymn Newton wrote and is found in most hymnals. See No. 221 for comments on Newton.

AUSTRIAN HYMN   During his two extended visits to England (1791–1792, 1794–1795), Haydn was deeply moved by the spirited singing of "God save the King" and expressed regret that his own people had no such national anthem. After his return to Vienna, when events of the Napoleonic wars were causing great uneasiness, tension, and hardship, Haydn felt more than ever his countrymen's need for a patriotic hymn. He told his friend Baron van Swieten of his concern, the baron communicated his wishes to the imperial chancellor, Count von Saurau, who, in turn, commissioned the poet Leopold Haschka, to write words for a national hymn. In January, 1797, Haydn set the words to music, arriving at the present form of the tune after making many sketches which are now preserved in the Vienna National Library. On February 12, 1797, the birthday of the emperor, "Gott, erhalte Franz, den Kaiser" was sung in all the theaters in Vienna and in the provinces. The hymn kindled tremendous enthusiasm and built up and strengthened morale at a crucial time. It became the most popular of all Haydn's songs as well as his own favorite tune and did more than anything else to increase his popularity among his own people. Franz II, the last of the Holy Roman Emperors, showed his appreciation by giving the composer a gold box decorated with the royal portrait. On May 26, 1809, when the French were bombarding Vienna, Haydn called his household together, asked to be carried to the piano, and played this hymn three times with great emotion and solemnity. Five days later he died. The slow movement of his "Emperor Quartet" ("Kaiserquartett"), Op. 76, No. 3, consists of four variations on the Austrian Hymn, in each of which the melody is given to a different instrument.

The first use of Haydn's melody as a hymn tune was in England about 1802. It may have been sung before that with "Praise the Lord, ye heav'ns adore Him" (No. 13). In Germany its earliest use as a hymn tune was with "Christen! singt mit frohem Herzen" in a Catholic hymnal printed at Breslau in 1804. (Bäumker Vol. IV, No. 313) In early nineteenth-century American collections AUSTRIAN HYMN appeared with a variety of texts, forms, and names.

AUSTRIAN HYMN was made use of in a novel way by music-loving William Gardiner, the English hosiery manufacturer. (See No. 6.) He asked Johann P. Salomon, the impresario, to take a gift to the composer when he went to Vienna in 1804. The following letter, written by Gardiner on August 10, 1804, accompanied the gift:

Sir, —

For the many hours of delight which your musical compositions have afforded me, I am emboldened (though a stranger) to beg your acceptance of the enclosed small present, wrought in my manufactory at Leicester. It is no more than six pairs of cotton stockings, in which is worked that immortal air "God preserve the Emperor Francis," with a few quotations from your great and original productions. Let not the sense I have of your genius be measured by the insignificance of the gift; but please to consider it as a mark of the great esteem I bear to him who has imparted so much pleasure and delight to the musical world.

Among other quotations woven into the stockings were parts of "My mother bids me bind my hair," also the bass solo from the Terzetto (No. 19) in *The Creation,* in which "th' immense Leviathan" is mentioned, and the "Andante" from the *Surprise Symphony.*

The first phrase of AUSTRIA is said by some to have originated in a Croatian folk song; by others, to be traceable to certain compositions used in the Catholic church. It has been claimed that other parts of the melody are also highly derivative. Haydn, however, composed it as a hymn tune, and

216

Eric Routley observes that as such it "stands as one of the very few examples of a first-class hymn-tune written by a symphonic composer of the front rank."

268 Lord, We Thank Thee for Our Brothers

This hymn by Roger K. Powell (1914–   ) was written for a Union Thanksgiving Service in 1948 as a "prayer of thanksgiving for one of the greatest blessings of the Christian life: the fact that there are others like us who share both the enjoyment and the cost of the Christian movement." At the time he wrote it, Mr. Powell was minister of the Baptist Church in Camillus, New York. He is presently the registrar at Colgate Rochester Divinity School in Rochester, New York. The hymn has become a favorite at ecumenical youth rallies and was sung at many interchurch meetings throughout the country in preparation for the first meeting of the National Council of Churches in 1952.

AUSTRIAN HYMN   See No. 267 for comments on the tune.

269 I Love Thy Kingdom, Lord

Timothy Dwight (1752–1817) was one of New England's most illustrious sons. A precocious child, reading the Bible with ease at the age of four and graduating with the highest honors from Yale when he was only seventeen, he was successively a grammar-school teacher, tutor, chaplain in the Revolutionary Army (where he gained the esteem of George Washington), legislator, Congregational pastor, and president of Yale. In the latter office he effected a religious revival that changed the attitude of many students not only at Yale, but at Dartmouth, Amherst, and Williams. His frank chapel talks and sermons on "Theology Explained and Defended" won a new respect for the truth and relevance of the Christian faith. In addition to his duties as president he taught classes in ethics, metaphysics, logic, theology, literature, and oratory and served as the college chaplain. Because of his strenuous study habits as a child, when he studied much by candlelight, he injured his eyes with the result that for the last forty years of his life he was unable to read for more than fifteen minutes at a time. Nevertheless, he continued to do a prodigious amount of reading and writing. One of his students said of him:

> I never knew a man who took so deep an interest in everything — the best mode of cultivating a cabbage, as well as the phenomena of the heavens, or the employment of angels. He was as pleased to talk with lowly people as with lofty ones — his kitchen servant, the college janitor, blacksmiths, hostlers, boatmen, ploughmen; he drew from them what they best knew, and he well paid them in kind for what they gave.

In addition to his other attainments, he was the foremost hymnologist of his time. At the invitation of the General Association of Connecticut he revised and completed Watts' *Psalms of David,* adding thirty-three of his own hymns and paraphrases, which proved so successful that it was used extensively in both Congregational and Presbyterian churches in Connecticut. The volume was known familiarly as Dwight's Watts. The present hymn, the only one that has survived from this collection, is perhaps the oldest hymn written by an American that has remained in continuous use.

ST. THOMAS   This bright, sturdy tune has been sung on both sides of the Atlantic for nearly two hundred years and still shows no sign of wear. It is one of the best Short Meter tunes, a good one to remember as a model of its kind. It appears with Dwight's hymn in a large number of American hymnals. ST. THOMAS is a shortened version of HOLBORN, set to Charles Wesley's "Soldiers of Christ arise" in the 1763 edition of Aaron Williams' *The Universal Psalmist*. Since it bore the note "never before printed" it may well have been Williams' own composition. The shortened form appeared in Williams' *New Universal Psalmist,* 1770, set to "Great is the Lord our God," a version of Psalm 48. The original tune appeared in *The American Harmony or Universal Psalmodist,* printed and sold by Daniel Bayley at Newbury-Port, Massachusetts, in 1771.

Aaron Williams (1731–1776) seems to have spent much of his life in London, as a music engraver, teacher of music and psalmody, compiler and publisher of psalm tune collections, and clerk of the London Wall Scots Church. His books supplied American editors with a number of tunes.

270   Built on the Rock

In a century when religious unbelief was increasingly common and skepticism held the field, Denmark produced two redoubtable champions of the Christian faith in Nicholai Frederik Severin Grundtvig (1783–1872) and Sören Kierkegaard (1813–1855). Although they held sharply differing views and openly ridiculed one another's interpretation of Christianity, they effected, each in his own way, a marked change in the religious climate of their time and in succeeding decades. If Kierkegaard is better known and more influential today with his emphasis on the radically existential character of faith, it was Grundtvig who was the more famous and who made the greater impact during their lifetimes. The son of a Lutheran pastor, he came under the influence of rationalism at the University of Copenhagen and graduated from that institution "without spirit and without faith." As a teacher of history, however, he was finally convinced of the truth of Christianity's claims, and this, coupled with the spiritual torpor to which skepticism seemed to lead, prompted him to return to the church. Ordained in 1811, he soon gained recognition as an eloquent and forceful preacher and drew large congregations to his services. Because of his interest in raising the educational standard of his people, he founded folk schools in Rödding and other cities which proved so popular that they were copied in Sweden, Norway, and Finland and earned for him the title "the father of the public school in Scandinavia." In addition to these activities he did an immense amount of writing, including several volumes of poetry and a large body of hymns. The latter are characterized by a strong emphasis on the Word of God and the

218

Holy Spirit and an uncompromising doctrinal forthrightness. Of all the hymns he wrote the present one is the most popular. It first appeared in *Sang-Värk til den Danske Kirke,* 1837. It was translated into English by Carl Döving (1867–1937), noted Norwegian hymnologist, and was first published in English in *The Lutheran Hymnary,* 1913.

KIRKEN DEN ER ET, one of the best-loved hymns of the Norwegians, was written for these words in 1840. It was the first hymn tune composed by Ludvig Mathias Lindeman (1812–1887), the most gifted member of a family of musicians whose ancestors, probably from Germany, established themselves in Norway in the eighteenth century. His father, Ole Andreas Lindeman, made a name for himself as a pianist in the last decade of the eighteenth century, touring with great success in Denmark as soloist in Mozart concertos. He was organist of the cathedral in Trondheim for fifty-seven years. Ludvig studied piano, organ, and theory with his father, and in his early years assisted him in his work, but his thoughts of a career centered around theology rather than music, and after completing a liberal arts course, he entered the seminary in Christiania (Oslo) in 1833. Theological studies did not absorb all of his time, however, and from 1833 to 1840 he played cello in the Christiania theater orchestra and frequently substituted for his brother Jacob, organist of Our Saviour's Church. He succeeded to this position in 1840 and retained it until his death. He was the outstanding organ virtuoso of his day in Norway and by invitation played several recitals in Albert Hall, London, when the new organ was installed in 1871. Although he gave up theology for music, he continued his association with the Seminary as a professor of singing and church music. With his son, Peter, he founded a school in 1883 which became the Musikkonservatoriet, the only music college in Oslo.

Through his teaching, writings, and compositions, Lindeman did much to raise the general level of music appreciation in Norway. His compositions were numerous: hymn tunes, songs, choral and instrumental works; sonatas, fugues, and fantasias for organ; and chamber music. He is remembered chiefly for his collections of folk music, for his hymn tunes, and his revision of the Lutheran hymnbook. (His father had edited a chorale book in 1835.) Even though there were musicians in Norway who were highly critical of what Ludvig Lindeman did to the old chorales rhythmically and harmonically, there was no question about the impetus he gave to a revival of interest in them and to the singing of them; and there was general agreement that through his hymn tunes and the books of chorales which he edited he brought new life and vitality into the music of the churches. At his funeral it was said that he had taught the Norwegian people to sing. His folk-song collections provided later composers with a store of beautiful melodies on which to draw. Between 1840 and 1867 he collected nearly two thousand melodies, six hundred of which were published in his lifetime, many in his monumental three-volume *Older and Newer Mountain Melodies,* published between 1853 and 1867. KIRKEN DEN ER ET GAMMELT HUS means literally, "Church it is an old house." The tune is in the Dorian mode, and like a number of Lindeman's original melodies has some of the character of a folk song as well as the depth and strength of the majestic chorales he loved.

271 We Come Unto Our Father's God

Barred from Oxford because of his Unitarian upbringing and his refusal to subscribe to the Thirty-nine Articles of the Church of England, Thomas H. Gill (1819–1906) studied on his own in history and theology and devoted his life to literary pursuits. He is credited with nearly two hundred hymns and several volumes of poetry and historical works. Later in life he turned from Unitarianism and associated himself with the Evangelical wing of the Established Church. W. Garrett Horder explained the change in these words: "Delight in the divine songs of Watts was his earliest intellectual enjoyment, and in after years the contrast between their native force and fulness and their . . . dwindled presentation . . . in Unitarian hymn-books, began that estrangement from his hereditary faith which gradually became complete." The present hymn, based on the first verse of Psalm 90, was taken from Gill's *The Golden Chain of Praise*, 1869, which included this notation: "The birthday of this hymn, November 22, 1868 (St. Cecilia's Day) was almost the most delightful day of my life. Its production employed the whole day and was a prolonged rapture."

NUN FREUT EUCH (ES IST GEWISSLICH AN DER ZEIT; LUTHER'S HYMN; MONMOUTH; ALTORF) The first three names of this chorale outline its history. In 1535 it was the setting in Joseph Klug's *Geistliche Lieder* for one of Luther's most famous hymns, "Nun freut euch, lieben Christen gmein" ("Dear Christians, one and all rejoice") which he entitled "A Christian hymn . . . setting forth the unspeakable grace of God, and the true faith." It "went from end to end of the country like a flash of lightning preparing the path for the Gospel." In 1565 Tileman Hesshusius wrote: "I do not doubt that through this one hymn . . . many hundreds of Christians have been brought to the true faith, who before could not endure the name of Luther." In *Etlich Christliche Lyeder*, Wittenberg (1523 or 1524), the first German Evangelical hymnbook, Luther's hymn was set to the following tune with which it is still sung and to which the name NUN FREUT EUCH properly belongs. (Zahn 4427)

Nun freut euch, lie-ben Chri-sten gmein, und last uns fröh-lich sprin-gen,   lasst Gott
dass wir ge-trost und all in ein   mit Lust und Lie-be sin - gen,

an uns ge-wen-det hat und sei-ne gro-sse Wun-der-that; gar teur hat ers er-wor-ben.

After 1586 the present tune became the accepted setting for "Es ist gewisslich an der Zeit" (" 'Tis sure that awful day will come"), Bartholomaeus Ringwaldt's revision of an earlier German paraphrase of the *Dies Irae* which was sung much during the Thirty Years' War when thoughts of impending doom were rife. In many hymnals the tune is called ES IST GEWISSLICH. Its connection with the last judgment carried over into English and American hymnody. In nineteenth-century American collections it was often set to "In robes of judgment, lo, He comes" and "Great God, what do I see and hear!" The latter text appeared with it in *The Christian Lyre,* 1831, *The English Hymnal,* 1906, and in a large number of books published between those dates. The tradition that NUN FREUT EUCH was Luther's adaptation of a secular melody which he heard sung by a traveling artisan accounts for its names LUTHER and LUTHER'S MELODY in English and American hymnals. Lowell Mason consistently called this melody MONMOUTH in his collections.

Bach used the melody for one of the miscellaneous Preludes for organ with the double title "Nun freut euch" and "Es ist gewisslich." In his *Christmas Oratorio* it is the setting for "Ich steh an deiner Krippen hier" ("Beside thy cradle, Lord, I stand"). (No. 59) There is one harmonization in the *Choralgesänge.* Doom and thanksgiving, the two widely divergent moods associated with NUN FREUT EUCH come into play in a marvelous way in Bach's Advent Cantata No. 70 where the trumpet plays this melody throughout a bass recitative which pictures first the desolation of the end of the world and then the joy of the future life made possible through Christ's Passion. Bach was not the only one to use the trumpet in connection with NUN FREUT EUCH. In *Hymn-Tunes and Their Story,* 1923, James T. Lightwood tells of the great popularity of the tune in England during the nineteenth century, partly because of an arrangement for solo voice with trumpet obbligato made by C. F. Baumgarten, organist at the Lutheran Chapel in London. His arrangement was particularly popular in country churches where the trumpeter would be concealed in the gallery or roof so that when the trumpet tones were suddenly heard, coming apparently from nowhere, the effect was such as to "arouse the most hardened sinners in the parish."

272 Blest Be the Tie That Binds

While pastor of the small Baptist church at Wainsgate, Yorkshire, John Fawcett was invited to become the minister of Carter's Lane Chapel in London, a much wealthier and larger parish. Having accepted the call and having actually packed his belongings in several wagons for the journey, he decided at the last minute, in response to the earnest entreaties of his devoted people and his wife, to remain at Wainsgate. It was this experience, according to popular accounts, which prompted him to write this hymn, published ten years later in his collection, *Hymns adapted to the Circumstances of Public Worship and Private Devotion,* 1782. See No. 63 for additional comments on Fawcett.

DENNIS   See No. 76 for comments on the tune.

273 Blest Be the Tie That Binds

See No. 272 for comments on the text.

BOYLSTON, composed by Lowell Mason, was set to "Our days are as the grass" in *The Choir*, 1832. It seems to have "the spirit of devotion, vitality, and the strength of simplicity and enduring qualities" which Henry Lowell Mason gave as characteristics of his father's tunes. It was named either for a town in Massachusetts or a street in Boston — no one really knows. See No. 257 for comments on Mason.

274 How Lovely Are Thy Dwellings Fair

First published in *Nine of the Psalms done into metre*, 1648, this paraphrase of Psalm 84 by John Milton was later included in his *Poems . . . both English and Latin*, 1673. Consisting originally of twelve stanzas, the present version has stanzas one, five, seven, and twelve. See No. 70 for comments on Milton.

BISHOPTHORPE (ST. PAUL'S; CHARMOUTH), which Dr. Millar Patrick describes as "a captivating tune, with a fine melodic contour and a bright grace of spirit impossible to resist," first appeared in *Select Portions of the Portions of the Psalms of David for the use of Parish-Churches* (date unknown, but a second edition was printed in 1786). With slight changes, marked *Cantabile* and named "Bishop Thorpe," it was ascribed to Jeremiah Clark (c. 1670–1707) and set to five different psalms in Dr. Edward Miller's *The Psalms of David, for the use of Parish Churches*, 1790. (One may see this version in the *Historical Companion to Hymns Ancient and Modern*, 1962, at No. 43.) The tune was called ST. PAUL'S in a 1774 English collection, and appeared with that name, in two versions, in the *Yattendon Hymnal*, 1899. In the *English Hymnal*, 1906, BISHOPTHORPE was the setting for Whittier's "Immortal Love, forever full."

275 Eternal Ruler of the Ceaseless Round

This hymn by John W. Chadwick (1840–1904) was written for the graduation service at the Harvard Divinity School, on June 19, 1864. That was the summer when Grant and Lee were locked in mortal combat in the Civil War and when the skies were ominous with strife and hate. Undoubtedly, it was with this in mind and with a desire to counteract the bitter enmity prevailing on both sides of the struggle that Chadwick wrote these lines. Following graduation, he was called to the Second Unitarian Church in Brooklyn, New York, and remained there the rest of his life, achieving fame as an eloquent preacher and a poet of distinction. Among his volumes of verse was *A Book of Poems*, 1876, which included the present hymn. The latter was introduced into English usage by W. Garrett Horder in his *Congregational Hymns*, 1884.

SONG I   This noble tune was set to Chadwick's text in *The English Hymnal*, 1906, for which Ralph Vaughan Williams was music editor. In Wither's *Hymnes and Songs of the Church*, 1623, the melody, captioned "Song I The First Song of Moses," was set to this paraphrase of Exodus 15:1, 2:

Now shall the praises of the Lord be sung;
For, Hee a most renownèd Triumph wonne:
Both Horse and Man into the Sea he flung:
And then together there both overthrowne.
The Lord is He, whose strength doth make me strong;
And he is my salvation, and my Song;
My God, for whom I will a house prepare;
My Fathers God, whose prayse I will declare.

The last two phrases of the music were repeated. The treble and bass at No. 275 are Gibbons'; the inner parts are from *The English Hymnal*. See No. 162 for comments on Gibbons.

276 Unto Thy Temple, Lord, We Come

After learning the blacksmith trade in England, Robert Collyer (1823–1912) came to America and settled in Shoemakersville, Pennsylvania, where he ran a blacksmith shop and conducted services as a licensed Methodist preacher. Although he had only four years of schooling, he educated himself by extensive reading and later entered the Unitarian ministry. The present hymn was written in 1859 for the dedication services of Unity Church (Unitarian) in Chicago, of which he was the first pastor. It was one of the churches later destroyed in the great fire of 1871. The hymn originally began:

> With thankful hearts, O God, we come
> To a new temple built for Thee.

In the spring of 1866 Collyer became minister of the Church of the Messiah in Chicago, which had been dedicated that year. He and his congregation were forced to vacate the new building as a result of the devastation caused in the surrounding area by the 1871 fire. Another new church, the Second Church of the Messiah, was built some distance away and was dedicated on November 16, 1873. For this ceremony Collyer wrote a dedication hymn which began with the words, "O Lord, our God, when storm and flame." He remained with his people through the difficult days of rebuilding the city and became a forceful preacher, author, and civic leader. In 1879 he was called to the Church of the Messiah (Unitarian) in New York City and remained there until he retired. *Harper's Monthly* published an extended account of his life in its May, 1874, issue.

EISENACH   See No. 99 for comments on the tune.

277 Jesus, Friend, So Kind and Gentle

Following his graduation in 1907 from Queen's Park College in London, the city of his birth, Philip E. Gregory (1886–   ) came to the United States and was ordained in 1909. After serving Congregational churches in South Dakota, Wisconsin, Minnesota, and Illinois, during which time he was elected to a number of positions of leadership in his denomination, he became the minister of the Neighborhood Congregational Church in Laguna Beach, California, where he had a notable pastorate for ten years before his retirement in 1956. In a letter to Dr. Ruth E. Messenger, research consultant to the committee that prepared the *Pilgrim Hymnal* and editor of *The Hymn*, he explained the origin of this hymn in these words: "The main reason for writing it was the lamentable paucity of children's hymns in our church hymnal. On a particular Sunday I was to baptize a number of children and I wanted that part of the service to have a worship value with congregational participation. I looked in vain in the hymnbook for a children's hymn which might be used as a processional and recessional as the parents brought their children to the baptismal font and returned again to the Narthex. Failing to find such a hymn, I wrote this one."

SICILIAN MARINERS   See No. 63 for comments on the time, which was the setting for this baptism hymn in *The Hymnbook,* 1955.

278   Lord Jesus Christ, Our Lord Most Dear

Written originally as a cradle song, this hymn by Heinrich von Laufenburg (c. 1400–c. 1458), first discovered in a Strassburg manuscript of 1429, was translated by Catherine Winkworth in her *Christian Singers of Germany,* 1869. This is the first stanza of the original five-stanza hymn, of which Miss Winkworth translated the first three. Laufenburg was connected with churches in Switzerland and Germany and during the last fifteen years of his life was a monk in the monastery of the Knights of St. John in Strassburg. He did a prodigious amount of writing, including many hymns modeled on the texts of secular songs and tunes and usually dedicated to the Virgin. He has been called one of the fathers of German vernacular hymnody. See No. 2 for comments on Miss Winkworth.

VOM HIMMEL HOCH   See No. 121 for comments on this tune.

279   Blessed Jesus, Here Are We

This hymn by Benjamin Schmolck (1672–1737) was written for his collection *Heilige Flammen der Himmlischgesinnten Seele,* 1706, third edition, and bore the caption, "Seasonable Reflections of the Sponsors on their way with the child to Baptism." This is the first stanza of the seven-stanza hymn originally beginning "Liebster Jesu, wir sind hier." Schmolck is credited with having written more than one thousand hymns, many of which are still popular in Germany. As a Lutheran pastor in Schweidnitz, a predominantly Catholic center, he labored under severe restrictions and was allowed under the terms of the Peace of Westphalia to have no more than two ministerial colleagues to serve a district of thirty-six villages. Nevertheless, he was a popular preacher and despite poor health and eyesight carried on a vigorous and successful ministry. The present translation is by C. Winfred Douglas (1867–1944). See No. 371, notes on ST. DUNSTAN'S, for comments on Douglas.

LIEBSTER JESU   See No. 212 for comments on this tune.

280   Be Known to Us in Breaking Bread

Based on the familiar incident of Jesus' post-resurrection appearance to two disciples on the road to Emmaus (Luke 24:30–31), this communion hymn by James Montgomery was first published in his *Christian Psalmist*, 1825, entitled "The Family Table." It is suitable for use both at the celebration of the Lord's Supper and as a family grace. See No. 25 for comments on Montgomery.

ST. FLAVIAN   See No. 153 for comments on this tune.

281   Bread of Heaven, on Thee We Feed

Josiah Conder (1789–1855), one of the leading Congregational laymen of his day, edited the first official hymnal of The Congregational Union of England and Wales, *The Congregational Hymn Book, a Supplement to Dr. Watt's Psalms and Hymns*, 1836, which contained fifty-six of his own hymns. He owned and edited the *Eclectic Review* for twenty years and also edited *The Patriot*, a newspaper devoted to furthering the cause of Nonconformity. Among many other works, he also prepared an edition of Bunyan's *Pilgrim's Progress*, with a life of the author, in 1838. The present hymn, entitled "For the Eucharist," is from his *Star in the East, with other Poems*, 1824, and is derived from John 6:51–54 and 15:1. John Julian said of Conder's hymns: "His finest hymns are marked by much elevation of thought expressed in language combining both force and beauty. . . . The outcome of a deeply spiritual mind, they deal chiefly with the enduring elements of religion."

NICHT SO TRAURIG, the setting for this Communion hymn in *Songs of Praise*, 1925, is one of the few chorales composed by J. S. Bach. It was one of two hundred melodies ready for inclusion in the second edition of Schemelli's *Gesangbuch,* which was never published. (See No. 135.) Its name is from the first line of Paul Gerhardt's fifteen-stanza hymn "Nicht so traurig, nicht so sehr," published in Crüger's *Praxis pietatis melica*, Berlin, 1647, set there to another melody which is still in use. The use of NICHT SO TRAURIG as an anthem for a communion service, with the first stanza sung in unison, the second in parts, would be an effective way of introducing it to a congregation.

Johann Sebastian Bach (1685–1750) was born in Eisenach, a town distinguished for its musical heritage and steeped in memories of St. Elizabeth, the minnesingers, and Martin Luther. In the Wartburg, overlooking Eisenach, Luther had been hidden from his enemies after the Diet of Worms, in 1521, and there finished his translation of the New Testament. Bach had

225

his elementary education in the classical school which Luther attended for three years and, like him, was a member of the school choir which sang at the St. Georgenkirche. Bach's father, a town musician, taught him to play the violin and viola. After the death of both parents in his tenth year, Sebastian went to live with his oldest brother, a pupil of Pachelbel and organist of St. Michael's Church in Ohrdruf. From him he learned to play the organ and clavier. The education and musical training which he received during five years in Ohrdruf were crucial for his development as a church musician. At fifteen he set out on foot for Lüneburg to earn his living as a chorister and continue his academic studies at the convent school of St. Michael. Three years there put him in touch with a wealth of musical resources, with traditions which made lavish use of music in church, and with George Böhm who had considerable influence on his early compositions. From Lüneburg he made trips on foot to Hamburg, thirty miles north, to hear the Dutch organist, Johann A. Reinken, and to the ducal court at Celle, sixty miles south, where he was introduced to French music and French instrumental techniques. When appointed organist of the New Church at Arnstadt, in 1703, he was "precociously equipped at every point" for the career ahead of him.

In 1705 Bach asked for a month's leave of absence in order to hear Dietrich Buxtehude in Lübeck and attend his *Abendmusiken*. What he heard was such a revelation that he stayed for nearly four months. On his return to Arnstadt he was reproved by the consistory for his long absence and for accompanying the chorales with variations and ornaments which confused the congregation; but he stayed on until 1707. After a year at St. Blasius Church in Mühlhausen, he became court organist and chamber musician (concertmaster in 1714) to Duke Wilhelm Ernst at Weimar. During nine years there he achieved fame as the foremost organist of his time, composed the majority of his great organ works, and a number of cantatas. Charles Sanford Terry has said that even if Bach's career had ended in 1717 the works of his Weimar years would place him among the immortals. From 1717 to 1723 he was director of music for Prince Leopold at Cöthen where he composed matchless instrumental music: orchestral suites, concertos for harpsichord and violin, sonatas for solo instruments, the Brandenburg concertos, and some of his best-known works for clavier including the first book of *The Well-Tempered Clavier*. In 1723 he became cantor of the Thomasschule in Leipzig after two better-known musicians had declined the post. For twenty-seven years, in spite of difficulties with the rector, the consistory, and the town council, Bach composed music which has never been surpassed: five cycles of cantatas for the church year, the *Magnificat*, the *Christmas Oratorio,* the *St. John Passion,* the *St. Matthew Passion,* the Mass in B Minor, *The Art of Fugue,* the *Goldberg Variations,* motets, and works for organ and clavier.

The magnitude of Bach's output is staggering. He composed in nearly every form then known, except opera, and created masterpieces in them all. "With every form he touched he said the last word." Curt Sachs has written of Bach: "He was the colossal summit of hundreds of years of musical energy."

For further comments on Bach, see Nos. 24 and 233.

282 Bread of the World, in Mercy Broken

Written to be sung before the observance of the Lord's Supper, this hymn by Reginald Heber first appeared in his posthumous collection *Hymns written and adapted to the Weekly Church Service of the Year,* 1827. It is found in most hymnals in unaltered form as given here. See No. 58 for comments on Heber.

RENDEZ À DIEU (GENEVA 118; NAVARRE) is one more of the tunes composed or adapted by Louis Bourgeois which gave such unique musical distinction to the Genevan Psalter. If he had written no other hymn tune than this, he would have enriched the hymnody of the Protestant church immeasurably. Douen says that almost all of the most beautiful and most original melodies belong to the first period of the Psalter when Bourgeois was responsible for its music. RENDEZ À DIEU was set to Marot's version of Psalm 118 ("Oh give thanks unto the Lord") in the 1543 edition. Measures four, five, and six of the melody were less attractive originally, but were revised by Bourgeois in 1551. This tune, which was also the setting for Psalms 66 and 98, was taken over by Lobwasser for the same psalms in his German Psalter, 1573. Whoever edited the 1564–1565 Scottish Psalter must have recognized the beauty of the tune, for it appeared in its original form with John Craig's version of Psalm 118, "Give to the Lord all praise and honor." Commenting on the intrinsic quality of the Genevan Psalter, Waldo Selden Pratt wrote in his *The Music of the French Psalter of 1562*: "Its texts were made by but two poets and its tunes mostly compiled or composed by but one musician — all these being experts. The result was a remarkable unity and intensity, so great that much of it persists unchanged to the present day." [22]

It would seem that credit for the combination of text and tune at No. 282 should go to the Sheffield clergyman, William Mercer, in whose *Church Psalter and Hymn Book*, 1854, Bourgeois' tune was named NAVARRE and set to the present text.

The original form follows.

Ren-dez à Dieu lou-ange et gloi - re,   Car il est be - nin et clé-ment,

Qui plus est, sa bon - té no-toi - re   Du - re per-pe - tu - el - le - ment.

Qu'Is - ra - el or - es se re-cor-de   De chan-ter so - len - nel -le - ment

Que sa gran-de mi - se - ri-cor-de   Du - re per - pe - tu - el - le - ment.

Archibald Jacobs says of RENDEZ À DIEU in *Songs of Praise Discussed:*

This lovely and impressive tune is, in some ways, the finest of all the early psalm-tunes; it is perfectly proportioned; it begins with a phrase of remarkable expressiveness, and continues with others as significant as they are logically consistent, while the beauty of the change of rhythm in the downward scale of the 5th line is extraordinary; . . . of its kind it is unsurpassed." [8]

283 Bread of the World, in Mercy Broken

See No. 282 for comments on the text.

EUCHARISTIC HYMN, the setting in a large number of American hymnals for Bishop Heber's hymn, was composed for it by the Rev. John Sebastian Bach Hodges (1830–1915) and first published in his *Book of Common Praise*, 1868. He was born in Bristol, England, came to the United States in 1845, and was educated at Columbia University (B.A. 1850, M.A. 1853) and at General Theological Seminary (1854) in New York City. In 1867 he received an honorary S.T.D. from Racine College. After ordination he served as an assistant at Trinity Church, Pittsburgh, taught for three years at Nashota House, Wisconsin, and served at the Church of the Holy Communion in Chicago; he became rector of Grace Church, Newark, New Jersey, in 1860, and in 1870 went to St. Paul's, Baltimore, where he remained as rector for thirty-five years. There he abolished the mixed choir of men and women, built up an outstanding choir of men and boys, and established the first choir school in the United States. He composed a large number of hymn tunes and anthems; compiled the *Book of Common Praise*, 1868, and a collection of *Hymn Tunes*, revised edition, 1903; helped in the revision of the *Hymnal*, 1874, and was a member of the Joint Commission on the Hymnal which prepared the 1892 edition.

284 According to Thy Gracious Word

Inspired by the words, "this do in remembrance of me" (Luke 22:19), this hymn comes from James Montgomery's *Christian Psalmist*, 1825. Stanzas three and four have been omitted here from the original six-stanza hymn. See No. 25 for comments on Montgomery.

BANGOR   See No. 149 for comments on this tune.

285 According to Thy Gracious Word

See No. 284 for comments on the text.

MARTYRDOM (FENWICK; AVON), one of the finest psalm tunes, is another of the melodies dear to Scottish hearts. Like STRACATHRO (No. 255) it is in a six-note scale: the seventh degree does not appear in the melody and the fourth only once so that it is largely pentatonic, like many Scottish tunes. Composed in the latter part of the eighteenth century, it was originally in common time, in a two-part arrangement for melody and bass, printed on single sheets for the use of teachers in psalmody classes. In 1825 it appeared in R. A. Smith's *Sacred Music Sung at St. George's Church, Edinburgh,* in triple time, harmonized "by Mr. Smith" and called "Old Scottish Melody." Two years later it appeared in a Glasgow collection, *The Seraph,* in triple time, with a footnote stating that "the above tune 'Fenwick' or 'Martyrdom' and by some called 'Drumclog,' was composed by Mr. Hugh Wilson, a native of Fenwick." In litigation which resulted from Smith's claim that the tune was an "Old Scottish Melody," there was abundant evidence to prove that Wilson was its composer. There are still some who believe that Wilson adapted the melody from a Scottish folk song. A mid-nineteenth-century writer in *The Psalmodist* said: "I well remember the day it [MARTYRDOM] was first sung in St. George's, Edinburgh, for Dr. Thomson then said to me, 'O, man! I could not sing for weeping.'" It has been suggested that the name MARTYRDOM was given this tune by someone who assumed that the name FENWICK referred to James Fenwick, martyred Covenanter.

Hugh Wilson (1764–1824), who is known by this one tune, was born in Fenwick, Ayrshire, educated in the village school, and apprenticed to his father, a shoemaker. He taught reading, writing, arithmetic, and music to supplement his income, and also found time to study mathematics and allied subjects with such good results that in later years he had an important job as draughtsman and calculator for the owner of mills in Pollockshaws and Duntocher, towns near Glasgow. His hobby was making sundials — one of which (it is said) may still be seen in Fenwick. He composed a number of hymn tunes, was for a time leader of psalmody in the Fenwick church, and in Duntocher became manager of the Secession Church (now the United Presbyterian) and was one of the two founders of the first Sunday school there. In *The Church Hymnary,* MARTYRDOM appears in common time, the original form of the melody.

286 Come, Risen Lord

Canon Briggs wrote this communion hymn for *Songs of Praise,* 1931, basing it upon the disciples' request at Emmaus (Luke 24:28 ff.). For another hymn on the same passage see No. 280. One of its significant and unique aspects as a communion hymn is that Christ is recognized as the host. Originally, the first stanza ended with the words, "In thine own sacrament of bread and wine." Percy Dearmer prevailed upon Briggs to allow him to alter this to "In this our sacrament of bread and wine," a change which Briggs later regretted. See No. 198 for comments on Briggs.

SURSUM CORDA, composed by Alfred Morton Smith (1879–   ) for "'Lift up your hearts!' We lift them, Lord, to thee" (No. 352), was first published in *The Hymnal 1940* which also included two other tunes by him. He was born in Jenkintown, Pennsylvania, attended the University of Pennsylvania and the Philadelphia Divinity School (B.D., 1905; S.T.B., 1911) and after a short time at St. Peter's Church, Philadelphia, went to California as assistant at St. Luke's, Long Beach. From 1906 to 1916 he was at St. Matthias' Church, Los Angeles, and for two years was in the City Mission there. During World War I he served as an army chaplain in France and Germany. He was on the staff of the Episcopal City Mission of Philadelphia from 1919 to 1954, serving also as chaplain of Eastern State Penitentiary and Sleighton Farm School. He assisted at St. Clement's Church, 1920–1928, was chaplain of the Valley Forge Military Academy for two years, and associate priest of St. Elizabeth's Church from 1930 to 1933. He retired to Jenkintown in 1954, moving later to "Druim Moir," the Houston Foundation's home for retired clergy at Chestnut Hill.

Smith had no musical training until his adult years. One of his friends, the Rev. Herbert B. Satcher, says: "Melodies used to come to him, but he didn't quite know what to do with them, so he embarked on a course of study in harmony and counterpoint with Frederick M. Schlieder, who came to Philadelphia every week from New York to meet a group of pupils. This he continued for four years. He studied the 'cello with Bertrand Austin, a well-known teacher and performer of Philadelphia, and became sufficiently proficient to play in the Old York Road Symphony Orchestra. He is surprised at the apparent success of SURSUM CORDA and particularly delighted that the B.B.C. requested to use it in their hymnal."

287 Here, O My Lord, I See Thee Face to Face

At the request of his older brother, Dr. John James Bonar, minister of St. Andrew's Free Church, Greenock, Scotland, Horatius Bonar wrote this communion hymn. It was first printed in the calendar of his brother's church for the first Sunday in October, 1855, and later appeared in *Hymns of Faith and Hope,* 1857, under the heading, "This do in remembrance of me." The present arrangement uses the first five stanzas, without alteration, in the order in which they were written. The original hymn had ten stanzas. See No. 99 for comments on Bonar.

LANGRAN was written originally for "Abide with me" by James Langran (1835–1909) and printed in leaflet form in 1861. Two years later it was published with the same text and named EVENSONG in John Foster's *Psalms and Hymns,* 1863. In English and Scottish hymnals that include this tune, it is named ST. AGNES. Langran, a pupil of John B. Calkin (No. 296) and of Sir John F. Bridge, served in two small churches before being appointed organist of the parish church in Tottenham, a position he retained from 1870 until his death. He also taught music at St. Katherine's Training College for Schoolmistresses in Tottenham, then a suburb of London, where he spent all but three years of his life. His first job, gained through a competition in which there were fifty-three candidates, was in a church where there was a one-manual organ, a choir composed of a few elderly ladies from a nearby almshouse, and a half dozen school children. In his second post at Holy Trinity Church in Tottenham his choir consisted of eight school girls and a few ladies and gentlemen from the neighborhood. Fortunately at his Sunday evening services he had the help of three choristers from St. Paul's Cathedral. He is said to have had the ability to get much, musically, out of inadequate instruments and from unpromising choir material — a feat that all organist-choirmasters can appreciate. During over fifty years as organist, he never missed a service through illness. There must have been patience and persistence in his character for he did not get his B.Mus. degree from Oxford until he was forty-nine years old. Langran composed and published about fifty hymn tunes, a Morning and an Evening Service, and was music editor of *The New Mitre Hymnal,* 1875.

288 Let Us Break Bread Together

Combining a deeply reverent spirit with an exalted view of the sacramental elements, this communion hymn is another example of the power and beauty of the Negro spirituals. As is true of all the spirituals, the original author is unknown. See No. 179 for further comments on these great religious songs of the American Negro people.

LET US BREAK BREAD   The words and music of this spiritual speak for themselves with simplicity and profundity. The refrain reminds us of the publican's prayer, commended by Jesus (Luke 18:13), and of the age-old petition, "Kyrie eleison" — "Lord have mercy" — which has been a part of the Communion Service in the Eastern Church since the fifth century, and of the Western Church since the sixth.

289 Father, We Thank Thee Who Hast Planted

One of the early Christian classics is the *Didache* ("The Teaching of the Twelve Apostles"), a brief church manual written approximately in the second century and containing ethical admonitions and directions relating to baptism, fasts, prayers, and the Lord's Supper. The present hymn is a metrical paraphrase of some of the short traditional prayers found in this volume. F. Bland Tucker translated the Greek hymn into English for *The Hymnal 1940* (Episcopal). See No. 147 for comments on Tucker.

RENDEZ À DIEU   See No. 282 for comments on this tune.

290 Jesus, Thou Joy of Loving Hearts

Of the two well-known hymns derived from "Jesu dulcis memoria," a medieval religious poem of the twelfth century (see No. 225 for comments on the source and the second hymn), this cento was arranged and translated by Ray Palmer (1808–1887). It is made up of stanzas four, three, twenty-four, and ten of the original forty-two stanzas and first appeared in English in the *Sabbath Hymn Book,* 1858, edited by Edwards Amasa Park, Austin Phelps, and Lowell Mason. Palmer, the son of a judge, was born in Little Compton, Rhode Island, and when thirteen years of age went to Boston where he worked for a time as clerk in a dry-goods store. It was during this period that he came under the influence of Dr. Sereno Edwards Dwight of Park Street Congregational Church and decided to become a minister. Later he attended Phillips Academy, Andover, Massachusetts, for three years, and graduated from Yale in 1830. Before beginning his theological studies in New Haven, he taught for a year at a select school for young ladies in New York City. Palmer served Congregational churches in Bath, Maine, and Albany, New York, each for fifteen years, and later was corresponding secretary of the American Congregational Union with offices in New York City.

FEDERAL STREET was brought to light by Lowell Mason when he was conducting a music class in Salem, Massachusetts, in 1834, and asked if anyone in the group had tried his hand at composition. Henry Kemble Oliver (1800–1885) presented this tune which he had jotted down in 1832. It was published in Mason's *Boston Academy Collection of Church Music* in 1836. In 1872, at the great Peace Jubilee in Boston, Oliver conducted some twenty thousand people as they sang FEDERAL STREET to his words, "Hail gentle peace."

Oliver was born in Beverly, Massachusetts. His long life was filled with varied and productive activities impressive in their outreach and in what they show of his character and abilities. From childhood on, music had a strong hold on him and remained a lifelong and primary interest in spite of the fact that because of his father's objections he did not make it his profession. He studied at Boston Latin School and Phillips Academy, Andover, spent two years at Harvard, and graduated from Dartmouth in 1818. In 1862 Harvard granted him B.A. and M.A. degrees and included his name in the class of 1818. In 1883 Dartmouth gave him an honorary Doctor of Music degree. He taught school for twenty-four years in Salem and was one of seven members of a committee that drew up plans for an organization which was the forerunner of the National Education Association.

From 1844 to 1848 Oliver was adjutant general of the Massachusetts Militia and was commonly referred to as General Oliver. At the time of the Mexican War he raised the only volunteer regiment to go to Mexico from New England. For ten years, 1848–1858, he was superintendent of the Atlantic Cotton Mills in Lawrence, and showed his concern for the employees by helping to establish a library, presenting free concerts and lectures, and bettering the physical set-up of the plant. From 1860 to 1865 he was state treasurer. The crowning work of his life was the organization and development of the Massachusetts Bureau of Statistics of Labor, a pioneer institution of its kind; he was its first head and directed it from 1869 to 1873 when he retired to Salem where he was mayor from 1877 to 1880. He founded the Salem Oratorio Society, the Salem Glee Club, and the Mozart Association, of which he was also president, organist, and director.

For over thirty years, Oliver was active as a church organist even though his first musical training as a ten-year-old chorister was in the Park Street Church in Boston, a church known for its conservatism and for its opposition to the use of an organ in church, "using flute, bassoon, and violoncello as a godly substitute for the more varied, and therefore more sinful, instrument." He was organist at St. Peter's in Salem for two years, at the Barton

Square Church for two years, at North Church (Unitarian), of which he was a member, for twenty years, and at the Unitarian Church in Lawrence for twelve. His former home in Salem is now a prized historic landmark.

291 Lord, Enthroned in Heavenly Splendor

The first two stanzas of this hymn were written by George Bourne (1840–1925) and were privately printed by the author in 1874 as part of a six-stanza post-communion hymn for use in the chapel of Chardstock College, England. It was one of seven such hymns written by Bourne for use in the chapel. At the time, he was headmaster of the school, having previously served as curate of Sandford-on-Thames. The college was later moved to St. Edmund's, Salisbury, where it is presently located, and in 1886 Bourne was made warden of the school. The third stanza is taken from a three-stanza hymn which appeared as Part II of this hymn in *Songs of Praise*, 1931, revised edition, and was credited to B.R. In *Songs of Praise Discussed*, 1933, the identity of B.R. is revealed as Percy Dearmer, the editor, in the commentary on the hymn, "Lord of health, thou life within us." Dearmer in his self-effacing and sometimes eccentric ways often used a pseudonym or initials instead of his name.

See No. 112 for comments on Dearmer.

BRYN CALFARIA has been called "a piece of real Celtic rock" by Erik Routley. Anyone who has heard it sung by Welshmen knows what power and grandeur it has. A Welsh friend has said that it would be heresy and unthinkable for a Welshman to sing this particular tune to English words. Those who do not know Welsh, however, are grateful that the tune was set to the present text in the *English Hymnal*, 1906. BRYN CALFARIA means "hill of Calvary." There seems to be no adequate translation of the hymn for which the tune was written, "Gwaed y groes sy'n codi fynny," words touching and deep about Jesus and the cross, intense in their evangelical fervor. There is such a close connection between the mood and thought of the words and the music that for Welshmen, at least, their association is indissoluble. It is said that at times of tragedy in Wales, as in the case of a mine disaster when members of miners' families go to the pit to see if their kinfolk are safe, the singing of this hymn brings special strength and comfort to them.

William Owen (1814–1893), composer of BRYN CALFARIA, was born in Bangor, Carnarvonshire, Wales, where his father worked in the celebrated Penrhyn slate quarries. Those who heard him sing in the quarries and elsewhere when he was growing up, predicted that he would make a name for himself as a musician. At eighteen he wrote his first tune, a setting for a popular hymn. He was criticized sharply for this boldness and counseled to write *new* tunes for *new* hymns, counsel which shows how strongly the Welsh feel about preserving traditional combinations of tunes and words. One English hymnologist says that Owen's melodies are so uniquely fitted to the words for which they were written that it is hard for Welshmen to separate them. BRYN CALFARIA was published in Vol. II of *Y Perl Cerddorol* (The Pearl of Music) which contained anthems and hymn tunes composed by Owen. The Welsh sing this tune with inimitable intensity of feeling and with great flexibility of rhythm.

292 And Now, O Father, Mindful of the Love

William Bright (1824–1901), both as a student and later as a scholar, fulfilled the promise of his name. Winning many honors in his student days at Oxford, he was appointed Regius Professor of Ecclesiastical History and canon of Christ Church, Oxford, at the age of forty-four. He was the author of many scholarly books, among them *Ancient Collects and Other Prayers, selected for devotional use from various Rituals*, 1857 (second edition, 1862); *History of the Church from the Edict of Milan to the Council of Chalcedon*, 1860; *Chapters of Early English Church History*, 1877; and *Hymns and Other Poems*, 1866 (revised and enlarged, 1874). Many of the new prayers in the 1928 revision of the *Book of Common Prayer* were taken from his *Ancient Collects*. Several authorities have claimed that he was the equal of Cranmer in writing collects. This communion hymn was first published in *The Monthly Packet*, October, 1873, and was included in the 1875 edition of *Hymns Ancient and Modern*. H. Scott Holland wrote in *Personal Studies*, "It is worth living to have left behind one such hymn which will be sung by unnumbered generations."

SONG I was the setting for Bright's hymn in *The English Hymnal*, 1906. For comments on this tune see No. 275. For comments on Gibbons see No. 162.

In many hymnals William H. Monk's UNDE ET MEMORES is the setting for these words. When one of the minister members of the Pilgrim Hymnal Committee presented this hymn for consideration, he stipulated that Gibbons' SONG I should be the only setting for such a splendid text. It might well be used as an anthem.

293 Come, Labor On

Drawn undoubtedly from the New Testament passages likening the winning of souls to the harvesting of grain, this hymn for church workers was written by Jane Borthwick in her *Thoughts for Thoughtful Hours*, 1859. In its original form it consisted of seven six-line stanzas. She later rewrote it, in its present form, in her *Thoughtful Hours*, 1863. Stanzas three, four, and seven have been omitted here. See No. 77 for comments on Miss Borthwick.

ORA LABORA, composed for these words by T. Tertius Noble was first published in *The New Hymnal*, 1918. Dr. Noble once wrote that he was "a great believer in tunes which are wholesome and masculine." See No. 105 for comments on Dr. Noble.

294 Eternal God, Whose Power Upholds

This hymn by Henry Hallam Tweedy (1868–1953) was awarded first prize in a contest for modern missionary hymns sponsored by The Hymn Society of America from November, 1928, to June, 1929, in which more than one thousand entries were submitted. It has made its way into most contemporary hymnals. It was first sung at the Riverdale Presbyterian Church, New York City, on May 30, 1930. Tweedy was Professor of Practical Theology at the Yale Divinity School from 1909 to 1937 and was greatly in demand as a preacher and speaker. Despite a Vandyke beard and a somewhat formal manner, he was exceedingly popular with preparatory school boys and college students. His influence on twentieth-century American hymnody has been considerable, and the hymnal he edited, *Christian Worship and Praise*, 1939, was a widely used collection in its time.

HALIFAX   In the spring of 1748 Handel composed *Susanna* which is more a choral opera than an oratorio, intended for the concert hall, not for use in church. After four performances of the work at Covent Garden in 1749 the aria "Ask if yon damask rose be sweet" became popular, was adapted to numerous texts, and arranged for a variety of instruments. It appeared as HALIFAX in *Harmonia Sacra or A Choice Collection of Psalm and Hymn Tunes* published some years before 1761 (all editions were undated) by Thomas Butts who was a good friend of both Charles and John Wesley and accompanied them on some of their travels. His collection was a handsome book, one of the best examples of music engraving of the time and was much used by the Methodists. It contained texts and tunes from a variety of sources and a large number of adaptations from popular songs and from Handel's and Arne's oratorios. The English hymnologist, James T. Lightwood, felt that these adaptations provided "a sure indication as to what were some of the most popular airs of the period."

HALIFAX, with the text chosen for it by Thomas Butts, was in the American edition of *Harmonia Sacra* published at Andover, Massachusetts, in 1816. The present arrangement and harmonization was made by Winfred Douglas for *The Hymnal 1940*.

See No. 193 for comments on Handel.

295   Christ for the World We Sing!

As a Congregational pastor attending the Ohio State Convention of the Young Men's Christian Association in Cleveland in 1869, Samuel Wolcott (1813–1886) was impressed with the motto placed over the stage, "Christ for the world, and the world for Christ." Walking home from one of the sessions and thinking about these words, he was stirred to write this hymn. It has been sung for many years at the beginning of each semester at Yankton College, Yankton, South Dakota. Wolcott intended to devote his life working as a missionary in Syria, but poor health made it necessary for him to change his plans. After serving Congregational churches in Providence, Rhode Island, Chicago, Illinois, and Cleveland, Ohio, he was for several years the secretary of the Ohio Home Missionary Society. Although he did not write his first hymn until he was fifty-six years of age, he wrote more than two hundred hymns during the last seventeen years of his life, most of which have not continued in use.

ITALIAN HYMN   See No. 246 for comments on the tune.

296 Fling Out the Banner

George Washington Doane (1799–1859) wrote this hymn in 1848 at the request of the girls at St. Mary's Hall, Burlington, New Jersey, for a flag-raising service. He founded this school as well as Burlington College, a training school for young men planning to enter the ministry. The hymn was first published in *Verses for 1851 in Commemoration of the Third Jubilee of the S.P.G.*, and has been one of the most popular and widely sung missionary hymns of the last century.

Ordained in 1821 in Christ Church, New York City, Doane was successively assistant minister of Trinity Church, New York, professor of rhetoric and belles lettres in Washington (later Trinity) College, Hartford, Connecticut, assistant to the rector and subsequently rector of Trinity Church, Boston, Massachusetts, and finally bishop of New Jersey. A man of tremendous energy and zeal, he greatly increased and strengthened the churches of his diocese and gave vigorous support to the cause of missions, often being referred to as the missionary bishop of America. He was responsible for the first American edition of Keble's *Christian Year*, 1834, and took an active part in furthering the interests of the Oxford Movement. Many of his hymns were printed in his *Songs of the Way*, 1824.

Doane's son, also a bishop, William Croswell Doane, wrote the well-known hymn, "Ancient of Days, who sittest throned in glory." (See comments at No. 249.)

WALTHAM (DOANE; CAMDEN), an English hymn tune which does not appear in English hymnals, was composed by John Baptiste Calkin (1827–1905), English organist and composer, who at twenty went to Dublin as organist, precentor, and choirmaster of St. Columba College, Ruthfarnham, for seven productive and successful years. Later he returned to London and served in Woburn Chapel, Camden Road Chapel, and St. Thomas Church in Camden Town, London. He was professor at the Guildhall School of Music, taught also at Croydon Conservatory, was on the council of Trinity College, and was a Fellow of the Royal College of Organists. He wrote anthems, service music, and hymn tunes.

297 O God, Above the Drifting Years

These lines by John Wright Buckham (1864–1945) were written for the fiftieth anniversary celebration of the Pacific School of Religion, Berkeley, California, in 1916 and were first sung on Founder's Day for that occasion. They were later included in *The Pilgrim Hymnal*, 1931. After serving Congregational churches in New England, Buckham was a faculty member of the Pacific School of Religion for thirty-four years and became distinguished in the field of the philosophy of religion.

Another hymn, similar in character and also written for an anniversary celebration, is Leonard Bacon's "O God, beneath thy guiding hand." (See No. 438 for comments on Bacon.)

DUKE STREET   See No. 202 for comments on the tune.

298 God Is Working His Purpose Out

Appearing first in leaflet form, this hymn was written in 1894 by Arthur Campbell Ainger (1841–1919) and was inspired by the line, "For the earth shall be filled with the knowledge of the glory of the Lord, as the waters cover the sea" (Habakkuk 2:14). Educated at Eton and Trinity College, Cambridge, Ainger returned to Eton as an assistant master and remained there throughout his active career. He was described as "one of the most distinguished and useful of Eton masters, a man of clear head, controlling character, wide accomplishments, a fine and *habile* scholar of the old school, with a remarkable memory, an incisive speaker, a good critic, fertile in suggestion, complete in execution. . . . He set no punishments, and his justice, courtesy and unruffled good humor won the respect and admiration of the boys." [1] He was the author of *Carmen Etonense*, 1901; *Eton Songs*, 1901; and the popular *Vale* (which were set to music by Sir Joseph Barnby); and in collaboration with H. G. Winkle, an *English-Latin Verse Dictionary*. He died at Eton on October 26, 1919.

PURPOSE, written by Martin Shaw especially for the present text, was first published in the enlarged edition of *Songs of Praise*, 1931. The music with its steady, resolute, on-going rhythm and its melodic climax in the refrain, heightens the effect of the words. People have often sung this hymn without being aware of the canon between the melody and the bass. See No. 106 for comments on Martin Shaw.

299 O Spirit of the Living God

James Montgomery wrote this hymn "to be sung at the Public Meeting of the Auxiliary Missionary Society for the West Riding of Yorkshire, in Salem Chapel, Leeds, June 4, 1823." It was later included in his *Christian Psalmist*, 1825. The original hymn had six stanzas of which the present version uses one, three, four, and five.

See No. 25 for comments on Montgomery.

MELCOMBE   See No. 36 for comments on the tune.

300 Rise Up, O Men of God!

Among church laymen in America this hymn by William Pierson Merrill (1867–1954) is a great favorite. It is included in every major denominational hymnal in this country as well as in several hymnbooks in England and Canada and is also found in many other collections. Merrill was prompted to write it after reading a stirring article by Gerald Stanley Lee on "The Church of the Strong Men." At the time he was traveling by steamer on Lake Michigan to his church in Chicago and the lines came to him "almost without conscious thought or effort." The hymn first appeared in the Presbyterian *Con-*

tinent, XLII, February 16, 1911, for the Brotherhood Movement. The University of Wales *Student Hymnal,* 1923, altered the third stanza to read:

> Her strength shall make your spirit strong,
> Her service make you great.

Merrill however preferred his own original version, saying, "How can the Church be made great without the service of men of God? It is not a Platonic entity, independent of human collaboration." After serving Presbyterian churches in Philadelphia and Chicago, he was pastor of the Brick Presbyterian Church in New York City from 1911 to 1938 and attained fame as a forceful preacher, an authority on hymnology, and a champion of worthy civic causes.

FESTAL SONG   Published in 1894 as the setting for "Awake and sing the song," by William Hammond in *The Hymnal Revised and Enlarged* (Protestant Episcopal), FESTAL SONG was first associated with Dr. Merrill's hymn in the *Pilgrim Hymnal,* 1912. Since then it has displaced most of the twelve tunes which appeared with the hymn between 1912 and 1930, being the setting in sixteen out of twenty American hymnals consulted.

The composer of the tune, William Henry Walter (1825–1893), born in Newark, New Jersey, played the organ as a boy, first at a Presbyterian church, then at Grace Episcopal Church, in Newark. He studied with Edward Hodges and became organist successively of St. John's Chapel, St. Paul's Chapel, and Trinity Chapel, in New York City, remaining in the last post until 1869. In 1865 he was appointed organist of Columbia University, which had given him a Doctor of Music degree the year before. He composed anthems, hymn tunes, service music, compiled and edited collections of church music, and during Hodges' illness helped in the publication of several of his works.

301   Jesus, With Thy Church Abide

Based on a litany of the church written by Thomas B. Pollock, this hymn is largely from his *Litany Appendix,* 1871, a supplement to his *Metrical Litanies for Special Services and General Use,* 1870. The litany consisted of eighteen stanzas in metrical form and was revised and enlarged to twenty stanzas in *Hymns Ancient and Modern,* 1875. The present hymn is a cento of these two versions, stanzas one, two, and four being stanzas one, ten, and nine of the first version and stanzas three and five being stanzas sixteen and eighteen of the second version. See No. 166 for comments on Pollock.

VIENNA   See No. 243 for comments on the tune.

302   O Zion, Haste, Thy Mission High Fulfilling

As the author of more than forty hymns and poems, all of which she wrote for *The Churchman,* New York, and *The Living Church,* Chicago, published by The Protestant Episcopal Church, Mary Ann (Mrs. John) Thomson

(1834–1923) had four of her hymns appear in *The Church Hymnal*, 1894, including this one. She described the origin of this hymn in these words:

> I wrote the greater part of the hymn, "O Sion, Haste," in the year 1868. I had written many hymns before, and one night, while I was sitting up with one of my children who was ill with typhoid fever, I thought I should like to write a Missionary hymn to the tune of the hymn, "Hark, hark, my soul, angelic songs are swelling," as I was fond of that tune, but as I could not then get a refrain I liked, I left the hymn unfinished and about three years later I finished it by writing the refrain which now forms part of it.

She was born in London but spent most of her life in Philadelphia where her husband was the first librarian of The Free Library of Philadelphia.

TIDINGS (ANGELIC SONGS), the setting for this missionary hymn in a large number of hymnals published in the United States, was composed by James Walch in 1875 or 1876 for Frederick Faber's "Hark, hark my soul! angelic songs are swelling," the source of its alternative name. Faber's hymn had appeared earlier with two tunes, one by John B. Dykes, one by Henry Smart. Which of these Mrs. Thomson had in mind when she wrote "O Zion, haste," is not known. It was set to TIDINGS in *The Church Hymnal* (Episcopal) 1894, and gradually came to be associated almost exclusively with it in American hymnody. It seems reasonable to assume that Walch's tune has continued in use because of its connection with the present hymn; it does not appear in English hymnals.

Walch (1837–1901), born near Bolton, Lancashire, studied music with his father and with Henry Smart (No. 192). From 1851 to 1871 he served successively as organist in Duke's Alley Congregational Church, Walmsley Church, St. George's Parish, and from 1870 to 1874 was conductor of the Bolton Philharmonic Society. From 1877 he was a music dealer in Barrow-in-Furness and honorary organist of the parish church there.

303 Creation's Lord, We Give Thee Thanks

William DeWitt Hyde (1858–1917) began his career as a Congregational minister serving the Congregational Church in Paterson, New Jersey, for two years. Prior to that he attended and graduated from Phillips Academy, Exeter, New Hampshire, Harvard University, and Andover Theological Seminary. In 1885, when he was twenty-eight years of age, he was called to the presidency of Bowdoin College, a position he held until his death on June 29, 1917. As an educator, scholar, author, and religious leader he significantly influenced his own and succeeding generations. The present hymn was first published in the *Outlook*, LXXIV (May, 1903), with the title "The Strenuous Life," and originally began, "O Lord, we most of all give thanks." It first appeared in its present altered form in *Unity Hymns and Carols*, 1911, edited by William C. Gannet, J. V. Blake, and Frederick Lucian Hosmer.

RAMWOLD, one of the tunes submitted anonymously for the present text which was circularized by the Pilgrim Hymnal Committee among a number of church musicians, was composed by Richard Warner (1908–), a native of Medina, Ohio, and currently head of the department of music at Kent State University, Kent, Ohio. He did his undergraduate work at the Cincinnati Conservatory of Music (B.S.), graduate work at Columbia University (M.M.), and at the Eastman School of Music at the University of Rochester (Ph.D.). Before going to Kent State, Dr. Warner taught music successively at Centre College of Kentucky, Berea College, and the Eastman School of Music, and served as organist-choirmaster of Christ Church (Episcopal), Glendale, Ohio, and of St. Paul's Church (Episcopal), Rochester, New York. Active in the American Guild of Organists, he was a former dean of the Rochester chapter and has given illustrated lectures for various chapters on choral and organ music suitable for church weddings. More than fifty of his anthems and organ compositions have been published. A number of the anthems are settings of hymn tunes; several were composed for texts written by his wife, Katherine Root Warner. He has had special interest in composing anthem settings on fine hymn tunes for youth choirs, and in making better music available for the wedding service. One of his hymn tunes was the winner in the tenth Herbert Memorial Psalm Tune Competition, 1952. He has given the following account of the naming of this tune:

> At the time RAMWOLD was written, my wife was working on a study of an early codex involving Abbot Ramwold of Germany in the 10th century. (A study for her master's thesis in library science.) Since my initials R W dominated the name, it appealed to me, and I chose it for the hymn-tune title.

304 Rejoice, O People, in the Mounting Years

This triumphant hymn by Albert F. Bayly (1901–), originally written for the Triple Jubilee of the London Missionary Society, was published in the Northumbrian Triple Jubilee booklet, *Faith's Transcendent Dower*, 1945. A third stanza was added later on the occasion of the 750th anniversary of Lichfield Cathedral where the hymn received wide recognition and use. Bayly trained as a shipwright at the Royal Dockyard School, Portsmouth, but later decided to study at Mansfield College, Oxford, and become a Congregational minister. He is at present pastor of Eccleston Congregational Church, St. Helens, Lancashire. His hymns have appeared in English periodicals and have been published by the London Missionary Society.

YORKSHIRE   See No. 127 for comments on the tune.

305 The Morning Light Is Breaking

Stirred by the missionary letters of Adoniram Judson describing his work in Burma, Samuel Francis Smith (1808–1895) was inspired to write this hymn while a first-year student at Andover Theological Seminary in 1832. It was the same year in which he wrote the words for which he is now chiefly remembered, "My country, 'tis of thee." Following graduation from Andover, he was pastor of the Baptist Church in Waterville, Maine, for eight years, and during the same time taught modern languages at Waterville College (now Colby College). It is said that he knew at least fifteen languages and at the age of eighty-six was beginning the study of Russian. From 1842 to 1854 he served the Baptist Church at Newton Centre, Massachusetts, resigning after twelve years to become the editorial secretary of the American Baptist Missionary Union. He was the author of many books and approximately one hundred hymns, and in 1843, in collaboration with Baron Stowe, published *The Psalmist*, the most popular Baptist collection of its time. On the occasion of his eightieth birthday, one of his Harvard classmates, Oliver Wendell Holmes, sent him a tribute in the form of a poem with these lines:

> Time wrecks the proudest piles we raise,
> The towers, the domes, the temples fall,
> The fortress crumbles and decays, —
> One breath of song outlasts them all.

The present hymn was first given to Lowell Mason and Thomas Hastings who included it in their *Spiritual Songs for Social Worship*, 1833. It has since been translated into many languages and sung in many parts of the world.

WEBB (MORNING LIGHT; GOODWIN), a tune which has gone round the world, was written originally for a secular song, " 'Tis dawn, the lark is singing," on board the ship that was carrying its composer to America. It was first published in *The Odeon*, 1837, a collection of "Secular Melodies . . . for Adult Singing Schools and for Social Music Parties" edited by Webb and Lowell Mason. The book was named, probably, for the unused theater in Boston where some of the classes of the Boston Academy were held in the early days of its existence. Webb's melody was first used as a hymn tune in the *Wesleyan Psalmist*, Boston, 1842, a little pocket-size book issued for use at "Camp meetings . . . prayer meetings and other occasions of social devotion." Its Methodist editor, M. L. Scudder, set the tune to "The Morning light is breaking," and named it "Millennial Dawn." Text and tune soon became popular and appeared in numerous other collections with a variety of names. Mason and Webb called it GOODWIN in their publications; Bradbury and Root named it WEBB in *The Shawm*, 1853; some editors labeled it MORNING LIGHT, the name which appears with it in English hymnals.

George Webb (1803–1887), born near Salisbury, was the son of a prosperous landowner who had a great love for music but no training in it. Webb's mother gave him his first music lessons. Later, at a Salisbury boarding school whose headmaster was the son of a former principal of the Royal Academy of Music, he received a good musical education and learned to play the piano and violin. At sixteen he returned to his home, gave some consideration to the ministry, but finally decided on music as a career. He went to Falmouth to study organ and for a time was organist in a church there. In 1830 he booked passage on a ship bound for New York but was persuaded by the captain of another ship, sailing for Boston, to change his destination — a providential switch. Soon after his arrival in Boston he was appointed organist of the Old South Church and remained there for forty years. He and Lowell Mason became close friends and associates, both being founders of the

Boston Academy of Music where Webb directed the secular music and vocal studies. He was a fine voice teacher and organist and was famous as a choral and orchestral conductor. In 1840 he was president of the Boston Handel and Haydn Society and from 1840 to 1843 was its conductor. With Mason he edited a number of collections of sacred and secular music, and on his own issued several books including two on vocal techniques. At Mason's invitation he moved to Orange, New Jersey, in 1870.

Webb was a Swedenborgian. He became a member of the Boston Society of the New Jerusalem in 1835, was its first organist and director of music (1835–1870), and served the national organization in the musical supervision of its liturgical service book in 1836 and the complete revisions in 1854 and 1876. He became organist of its New York church (founded in 1859) when he left Boston.

306 For All the Saints

First published in Earl Nelson's *Hymn for Saints' Day, and Other Hymns,* 1864, this magnificent hymn by Bishop William W. How is an enduring favorite in all English-speaking lands. In its original form it contained eleven stanzas, of which the present version is a cento of stanzas one, two, six, seven, and eight. Bishop How initially began the hymn with "thy saints" in the first line but later changed this to "the saints." See No. 252 for comments on Bishop How.

Earl Nelson was the son of Thomas Bolton, nephew of the famous Admiral Viscount Nelson, whose name he assumed when he succeeded to the title. He was active in the Home Reunion Society and in collaboration with John Keble edited the *Salisbury Hymn-Book,* 1857, which was later revised and published as *The Sarum Hymnal,* 1868.

SINE NOMINE, one of the finest and most stirring hymn tunes of the twentieth century, was written for Bishop How's words by Ralph Vaughan Williams and was first published in *The English Hymnal,* 1906, of which he was music editor. In *The Story of Our Hymns,* Armin Haeussler calls SINE NOMINE the perfect setting for these words and comments further, "The accents in the music coincide with those in the text, and the melody and harmonization move forward with the strides of a victorious faith."

See No. 239 for comments on Ralph Vaughan Williams.

307 For All the Saints

See No. 306 for comments on the text.

SARUM, composed for these words by Joseph Barnby, was the accepted tune for Bishop How's hymn until SINE NOMINE by Ralph Vaughan Williams appeared in 1906. Since then SARUM has taken second place in most hymnals and has even disappeared from some.

See No. 35 for comments on Joseph Barnby.

308 For the Brave of Every Race

As in Thomas Gray's "Elegy" and in Ben Sirach's tribute to men of the past (Ecclesiasticus 44:1–16), this hymn by Canon George W. Briggs extols those who served their day valiantly and selflessly but who have since been largely forgotten. It was written in 1920 for Loughborough College, a small technical school in England before World War I which during and after the war grew in size and importance and attracted students from all parts of the world. Canon Briggs' lines have been adopted as the college hymn. The first line originally began, "For thy saints unknown to fame." It was altered to its present form in *Songs of Praise,* 1925. See No. 198 for comments on Briggs.

SALZBURG   See No. 69 for comments on the tune.

309 Jerusalem the Golden

Although his name is familiar to every student of church history, Bernard of Cluny is a figure about whom little is known. Beyond the fact that he was a monk at Cluny under Peter the Venerable during the twelfth century and wrote one of the greatest medieval poems, practically nothing is known of his life. His fame rests entirely upon his poem, "De Contemptu Mundi" ("On the Contemptibleness of the World"), consisting of 2,966 lines and written in one of the most difficult meters, dactylic hexameter, with each line broken into three parts and rhymed both at the end of the second and fourth feet and at the end of each pair of lines. The first two lines read as follows:

> Hora novissima   tempora pessima   sunt, vigilemus
> Ecce minaciter   imminet arbiter   ille supremus.

After completing the poem Bernard wrote, "Unless the Spirit of wisdom and understanding had flowed in upon me, I could not have put together so long a work in so difficult a meter." The poem itself is at once a scathing attack on the evils of the age, including the moral laxity among the clergy, and an intensely vivid portrayal of the bliss and peace of heaven. John Mason Neale's translation, consisting of the first 218 lines, appeared in his *Rhythm of Bernard de Morlaix, Monk of Cluny, on the Celestial Country,* 1858. Although his translation does not follow the original meter but is cast instead in one of the simplest meters, it retains to a remarkable degree the beauty and meaning of the Latin. Neale comments, "As a contrast to the misery and pollution of earth, the poem opens with a description of the peace and glory of heaven of such rare beauty as not easily to be matched by any medieval composition on the same subject." See No. 110 for comments on Neale.

EWING (ST. BEDE'S) is the only hymn tune its composer ever wrote and the only music by which he is known. After a rehearsal of the Aberdeen Harmonic Choir which met to sing madrigals and anthems, one of the most active and enthusiastic members went up to William Carnie, its distinguished director, to say that he had written a hymn tune which he would like to have the choir try and offered to pass out the voice parts. This was the debut of

EWING which has had a long and popular career in England and America. It was first set to "For thee, O dear, dear country," Part IV of Bernard of Cluny's hymn, and published in Grey's *Manual of Psalm and Hymn Tunes,* 1857. In *Hymns Ancient and Modern,* 1861, it appeared with the present text and has been associated with it ever since. The rhythm of the tune, originally 3/2, was changed to 4/2 by William H. Monk without the consent of the composer who was out of the country at the time. Dr. John M. Neale, whose translation was set to EWING, wrote in 1861: "I have so often been asked to what tune the words of Bernard may be sung, that I may mention that of Mr. Ewing, the earliest written, the best known, and with children the most popular; no small proof in my estimation of the goodness of church music."

Alexander Ewing (1830–1895) studied law for a time at Marischal College in Aberdeen where his father, Dr. Alexander Ewing, lectured on surgery. When he found that he had no real bent for a legal career he went to Heidelberg to study music and German. Although he never became a professional musician, he was an excellent pianist, could play the violin, cello, and cornet, and was a gifted linguist. He took a major part in the activities of the Haydn Society of Aberdeen, another group directed by Carnie who did notable service for the cause of psalmody in Scotland. During the Crimean War, Ewing joined the commissariat department of the army, was stationed at Constantinople, attained the rank of lieutenant colonel, and served later in South Australia and China. In 1867, a year after his return to England, he married Juliana Horatia Gatty, who, like her mother, was noted for the charming stories she wrote for children. She was the sister of Alfred Scott-Gatty, composer of many popular songs and of the hymn tune WELWYN (411). On the Sunday after Ewing's death (July 11, 1895), the one tune by which he is now known was sung at most of the churches in Taunton where he had lived since 1883. It was sung also at his funeral.

310 O What Their Joy and Their Glory Must Be

In his celebrated Introduction to the Historical Edition of *Hymns Ancient and Modern,* 1909, Walter H. Frere said that this hymn "deserves attention for its origin as well as for its merits. It was a feat that few smaller men would have cared to attempt, to produce a whole hymnal off the reel; but Abelard did this in his *Hymnus Paraclitensis,* written for the Nunnery of Heloïsa; and this history gives the familiar hymn a special interest." Abelard's notable volume contained ninety-three hymns, all of which he wrote himself. This one, intended to be sung at Saturday vespers, originally had seven stanzas, of which the present version uses stanzas one, two, five, and seven. See No. 159 for comments on Abelard. The translation is by John Mason Neale in *Hymnal Noted,* 1851. See No. 110 for comments on Neale.

O QUANTA QUALIA (REGNATOR ORBIS), the second of two settings for this hymn in *The Hymnal Noted,* 1854, bore the heading, "Melody from La Feillée." It was not an ancient plainsong but one of the French Church Melodies that came into use in the latter half of the seventeenth century. (See No. 41.) We are told that Thomas Helmore, musical editor of *The Hymnal*

Noted had a copy of Aynès' 1808 edition of LaFeillée's *Méthode du Plain-Chant* which contained a number of hymn melodies not included in earlier editions. O QUANTA QUALIA is from a Paris antiphoner of 1681 where it was set to "Fumant Sabaeis," a hymn on the purification of the Virgin Mary. Aynès made slight alterations in the melody when he set it to J. B. Santeuil's hymn, "Regnator orbis summus et Arbiter" which accounts for the tune name REGNATOR ORBIS found with it in English hymnals. In *Accompanying Harmonies to the Hymnal Noted*, 1858, there were two harmonizations of the melody by the Rev. S. S. Greatheed. The first of these is the source of much of the present harmonization.

311 Ten Thousand Times Ten Thousand

Henry Alford (1810–1871), dean of Canterbury Cathedral from 1857 until his death was one of the ablest and most influential biblical scholars of the nineteenth century. His commentary on the Greek New Testament, published in four volumes between 1844 and 1861, was for many years the standard work in its field and introduced English readers for the first time to the advanced views of German exegetical scholarship. An indefatigable worker, in addition to his biblical studies and churchly duties, he published several volumes on English literature, wrote much poetry, and distinguished himself in hymnology. His contribution to hymnody consisted of both original hymns and translations, most of which appeared in *Psalms and Hymns*, 1844, *Year of Praise*, 1867, and *Poetical Works*, 1868. He was ecumenically minded and maintained close and friendly relations with Nonconformists. His lifelong wish to visit the Holy Land was never realized, but his confident spirit inspired the lovely inscription on his tombstone: *Deversorium viatoris proficiscentis Hierosolyman* ("The inn of a pilgrim traveling to Jerusalem"). The first three stanzas of the present hymn were first printed in the magazine *Good Words*, VIII (March, 1867), and were also included in his *Year of Praise*. The fourth stanza was added in F. R. Pickersgill's and Alford's *The Lord's Prayer Illustrated*, 1870, and the entire hymn was sung at Alford's funeral the following year.

ALFORD, composed for this text by John B. Dykes, was first published in the revised edition of *Hymns Ancient and Modern*, 1875. It was Dykes who named the tune for the author of the hymn. In a letter to Mrs. Dykes after her husband's death, Sir Henry Baker, one of the original members and first chairman of the committee that compiled *Hymns Ancient and Modern*, 1861, wrote: "We are going to sing *only his* tunes to every hymn all next Sunday, and the 'Dies Irae' after Evensong *for him;* followed by 'Ten thousand times ten thousand.' "

See No. 79 for comments on Dykes.

312 Jerusalem, My Happy Home

The earliest source of this hymn, consisting originally of twenty-six stanzas, is a late sixteenth- or early seventeenth-century manuscript in the British Museum, entitled "A Song Mad by F. B. P. to the tune of Diana." Although various attempts have been made to ascertain who "F. B. P." might be, the authorship remains unknown. In his *Dictionary of Hymnology,* John Julian concludes, after a careful survey, that both this hymn and a similar one by W. Prid, "O mother dear, Jerusalem," are based on a passage in an earlier sixteenth-century translation of the volume known to us as *The Meditations of St. Augustine (Liber Meditationum),* and says of this volume, "At the time of the Reformation, Roman Catholic and Protestant alike vied in translations of it, in whole or in part." The present hymn and "O mother dear, Jerusalem," were drawn upon frequently and extensively by seventeenth-century hymn writers. These later versions often appeared as broadsides (a large sheet of paper printed on one side), because this was an inexpensive and convenient way to distribute them at a time when hymns were beginning to become popular in England. In all their forms, but especially in their original versions, there is an intense longing to be released from earthly bonds and received into the joys of the heavenly Jerusalem. Leonard Ellinwood in *The Hymnal 1940 Companion,* 1951 edition, has said of this hymn, "Here is sacred folk literature at its very finest, coming at a time when the singing of English congregations was limited to the metrical paraphrases of the Psalms." [14]

LAND OF REST, harmonized by Annabel Morris Buchanan (1888–), is the first of two settings for these words in *The Hymnal 1940.* In her book *Folk Hymns of America,* 1938, Mrs. Buchanan says that it is a variant of a traditional tune of Scottish or North England origin. She first heard it from her grandmother who brought it to Texas from South Carolina by way of Tennessee. It was sung to the words:

> O Land of rest, for thee I sigh
> When will the moment come
> When I shall lay my armor by
> And dwell in peace at home?

Many forms of the tune, with sacred and secular words, have been found by Mrs. Buchanan and other folk song specialists. It has been widely sung in the Appalachian region. Similarities between LAND OF REST and "Swing low, sweet chariot" have been noted. The Negro spiritual is a pentatonic melody, LAND OF REST is hexatonic with a strong pentatonic flavor. The fourth degree of the scale (B flat) appears only twice.

Annabel Morris was born in Groesbeck, Texas. She graduated from the Landon Conservatory of Music in Dallas in 1907, attended the Guilmant Organ School in New York City, and studied privately with Emil Liebling, William C. Carl, John Powell and others. For eight years she taught music in Oklahoma and Texas, and for three years at Stonewall Jackson College in Abingdon, Va., before her marriage in 1912 to John Preston Buchanan. She has done distinguished work in the field of Anglo-American folk music and American hymnody. At the first International Music Congress in America, at New York City in September 1939, she gave a lecture on "Modal and Melodic Structure in our Anglo-American Folk Music," which was published later by the American Musicological Society. Mrs. Buchanan was cofounder of the Virginia State Choral Festival, cofounder and director of the White Top Music Festival and Conference (1931–1941) and president of the Virginia Federation of Music Clubs, 1927–1930.

313 My God, I Love Thee

The earliest known source of this seventeenth-century hymn is Joannes Nadasi's *Pretiosae Occupationes Morientium,* 1657, where it began with the line, "Non me movet, Domine, ad amandum te." A Spanish version in the form of a sonnet appeared five years later, "No me muene, mi Dios, para querere." It reappeared in Latin in a Cologne book, *Caeleste Palmetum,* 1669, from which source Edward Caswall translated it into English in his *Lyra Catholica,* 1849. The claim that St. Francis Xavier (1506–1552) wrote this hymn is purely conjectural and is belied by the evidence. It is fortunate that Caswall apparently was not aware that the hymn was not originally by Xavier. Had he been, it is unlikely that he would have gone to the bother of translating it, one of the finest things he did, since the Latin poem he used was not especially noteworthy. The poem began:

> O Deus ego amo te,
> Nec amo te ut salves me.

St. Francis Xavier was one of the original seven members of the Society of Jesus, founded by Loyola at the Church of St. Mary on Montmartre in Paris in 1534. He became one of the great missionary figures of the Roman Catholic Church, winning many converts in the Far East, where he finally died of a fever on the Island of St. John off the coast of Kwang-tung, China, on December 2, 1552.

See No. 35 for comments on Caswall.

ABBEY, named "Abbay Tune," was one of the twelve Common Tunes grouped together in a separate section in Andro Hart's *The CL. Psalmes of David,* 1615, discussed at No. 87. This was its first appearance in a Scottish psalter. In 1621 it was included in Ravenscroft's *Whole Booke of Psalmes,* classed as a Scottish tune. Millar Patrick says that throughout a century these twelve Common Tunes constituted the church's entire repertory and "gathered to themselves an inviolable sanctity not far short of that which in ancient days invested the sacred Ark" (*Four Centuries of Scottish Psalmody,* 1941). He attributes this monopoly of the twelve tunes to the Scots' characteristic resistance to change, for generations a "persistent habit in Scottish religious practice" which kept any new tune from entering the church, although there was a revival of interest in music outside. He comments:

> The common people had for centuries been excluded by the musicians from any share in the Church's praise; but once they got hold of the easy, straight-forward Common Tunes, they reversed the situation: they assumed the mastery, and would permit the singing of nothing else. They did not know it, but this was their revenge for the wrong done to generations of their forefathers: they closed, locked, and barred the door of the church against any innovation upon the new and narrow musical tradition which their resolute ignorance imposed upon the Church.[23]

It might be added that resistance to change characterizes many congregations other than the Scottish.

314 Lord Jesus, Think on Me

Although he continued to lead the life of a wealthy country squire after his appointment as a bishop in the church, Synesius of Cyrene (c. 375–430) surprisingly met most of the conditions required of the ideal prelate as outlined in I Timothy 3:2–7. Born of wealthy parents, he was early attracted to Neoplatonism and devoted much of his time to philosophy, books, and "the chase." Popularly elected to be the Bishop of Ptolemais in 409 or 410, a few years after his conversion to Christianity, he accepted the office with some reluctance and gained renown more for his cultural interests than his religious zeal. Charles Kingsley wrote a charming sketch of him in his *Hypatia*, 1853. Synesius' ten odes, the last of which forms the basis of this hymn, were described by C. S. Phillips as "of great interest and beauty in their presentation of Christian devotion as seen through the eyes of a Platonist philosopher," (*Hymnody Past and Present*, 1937). The translation by Allen W. Chatfield (1808–1896) in his *Songs and Hymns of the Earliest Greek Christian Poets*, 1876, was depicted by him "as a paraphrase or amplification, rather than an exact translation of the original." His version gives a more somber cast to Synesius' thought than the original Greek lines. Chatfield was for nearly fifty years vicar of Much-Marcle, Herefordshire, and achieved recognition in his time by his translations into Greek in various metres of the litany, the "Te Deum," and other parts of the Anglican liturgy.

SOUTHWELL   In "Noyes' Fludde" Benjamin Britten makes telling use of this hymn and tune which have been associated at least since their appearance together in *The English Hymnal*, 1906. SOUTHWELL, one of three tunes by that name and one of the earliest Short Meter tunes in English hymnody, was set to Psalm 45 in *The Psalmes of David in English meter, with Notes of foure parts set unto them by Guilielmo Daman*, 1579.

In Ravenscroft's Psalter, 1621, this tune was named SOUTHWELL, listed among the "Northerne Tunes," harmonized by Martin Peirson, B. of M. (Bachelar of Musicke), and set to Psalms 50, 70, and 134. It was in the Dorian mode, as it had been in Daman's Psalter. Lowell Mason included SOUTHWELL in *The National Psalmist*, 1848, and in later collections, using the form in which it appeared in Havergal's *Old Church Psalmody*, 1847, with a long note at the beginning of each phrase and with the melody in the natural minor mode as in the present version. Daman's 1579 setting of SOUTHWELL is given in the *Historical Companion to Hymns Ancient and Modern*, 1962.

315 Come Unto Me, Ye Weary

In describing the circumstances that surrounded the writing of this hymn, William Dix said in a letter to Mr. F. A. Jones, author of *Famous Hymns and Their Authors*, 1902:

> I was ill and depressed at the time, and it was almost to idle away the hours that I wrote the hymn. I had been ill for many weeks, and felt weary and faint, and the hymn really expresses the languidness of body

from which I was suffering at the time. Soon after its completion I recovered, and I always look back to that hymn as the turning point in my illness.

It was first published in *The People's Hymnal*, 1867, edited by Dr. R. E. Littledale. See No. 119 for comments on Dix.

WHITFORD was one of two settings for this hymn in *The Church Hymnary, Revised,* 1927. Its composer, John Ambrose Lloyd (1815–1874), born in Mold, Flintshire, in North Wales, was the son of a Baptist minister. When he was fifteen he moved to Liverpool where his brother lived and there he composed his first hymn tune. In later years he traveled for a business firm. Though largely self-taught he became an influential and well-known musician, was one of the founders of the Liverpool Welsh Choral Union, and frequently acted as adjudicator at the National Eisteddfod of Wales and at provincial eisteddfodau as well. He composed many hymn tunes, a number of anthems, and three cantatas, one of which, *The Prayer of Habakkuk*, is said to be the first work of its kind published in Wales. He published two collections of hymn tunes, *Casgliad o Donau*, 1843, and *Aberth Moliant*, 1873.

316 God of Earth and Sea and Heaven

This modern hymn on stewardship by Frank L. Edwards (1898–   ) is remarkable not only for its rich use of biblical language and imagery but also for the way in which it follows the sequence of the biblical drama, beginning with creation, continuing with the prophetic tradition, and closing with the Christian revelation and the response of discipleship. Published here for the first time in a hymnal, it appeared earlier as a fly sheet, in which form it was widely used by Edwards in his stewardship schools conducted for ministers and laymen. Ordained as a Congregational minister following graduation from Yale Divinity School, Edwards served churches successively in Highland, Illinois, Brookfield Center, Connecticut, and Tuckahoe, Sherburne, Watertown, and Buffalo, New York, before becoming Minister of Stewardship and Missions for the New York Congregational Christian Conference in 1947. He was later called to be the Midwest director of the Church Building and Loan Fund Campaign of his denomination and went from that position to become the superintendent of the Congregational and Christian Conference of Illinois in 1953. He retired in 1960 because of poor health, and has served since then as Consulting Minister of Stewardship of the Florida Conference of the United Church of Christ. He has been described by his successor in Illinois, Clarence F. McCall, Jr., as "a sensitive prophet in the churches" who has "challenged communities, ministers and laymen to examine the nature and meaning of Christian stewardship."

LLANSANNAN, an anonymous Welsh melody from John A. Lloyd's *Aberth Moliant*, 1873 (see No. 315), was harmonized for *The Church Hymnary, Revised,* 1927, by David Evans. It is a strong, rugged tune, with three of its four phrases identical melodically, except for the first note in the first measure of the last phrase. The harmonies of phrases one and two are the same. The *e* flat in the soprano, and the two *a* flat major chords in measure thirteen, seem to establish the destination of the upward-moving third phrase and provide a welcome contrast to the prevailing C minor tonality. The last two chords in measure fourteen also provide some variety. See No. 38 for comments on David Evans.

3l7 I Love to Tell the Story

Arabella Katherine Hankey (1834–1911), known more familiarly as Kate Hankey to her friends and admirers, belongs to a notable company of outstanding nineteenth-century English women. Born into a family of means — her father was a successful banker — she early displayed a great interest in religious work. As a member of the Clapham Sect, a small but influential body of evangelicals of which William Wilberforce was the leading figure, she did the unheard-of thing of starting a Bible class for working girls in London which, while it remained small in numbers, had a strong and lasting influence on all who attended. She later started a second class for girls from well-to-do families with similar results. Several of those who participated became dedicated religious workers. As a result of a trip to South Africa, where she had gone to nurse and bring home an invalid brother and where she was required to travel much of the way by oxcart, her interest in Christian missions was quickened to the point where she decided to turn over all the proceeds from her writings to this cause. In 1866 she wrote a long poem on the life of Jesus. It was divided into two parts, the first of which was entitled "The Story Wanted" and from which one of her best-known hymns was taken, "Tell me the old, old Story." The present hymn was taken from the second part, bearing the title "The Story Told." It was published in P. P. Bliss' *Gospel Songs*, 1874, and gained international fame through the evangelistic campaigns of Dwight L. Moody and Ira D. Sankey.

HANKEY (I LOVE TO TELL THE STORY; EATON SQUARE), was first published in *Joyful Songs*, 1869, a pamphlet issued by the Methodist Episcopal Book Room, Philadelphia. The composer of the tune, William Gustavus Fischer (1835–1912), was of German descent, born in Baltimore. It is said that even as a boy of eight he was often asked to start the singing in the German church which his family attended. For some years he worked in Philadelphia as a bookbinder, studying music in his spare time and managing to get a reasonably good background in harmony, piano, and organ. The singing schools, institutes, and conventions directed by Lowell Mason and Thomas Hastings influenced him greatly. He wrote more than two hundred gospel hymns but, unlike Mason and Hastings, never compiled any collections. He taught piano and voice, was professor of music at Girard College in Philadelphia from 1858 to 1868, led choral groups, and was much in demand as a conductor at conventions and revival meetings. At one Moody and Sankey gathering in 1876 he directed a chorus of one thousand voices, and in 1881 at the bicentennial celebration of the landing of William Penn led a large chorus of Welsh singers. Shortly before his death when he was attending an international Sunday school convention in Philadelphia, Fischer was introduced to the large assembly by John Wanamaker, well-known businessman, Sunday school superintendent, and member of President Benjamin Harrison's Cabinet. After the introduction the huge crowd sang the present tune as a tribute to its composer. With John E. Gould as a partner (see No. 213) Fischer established a flourishing retail piano business and music store in Philadelphia. It is possible that HANKEY was first published in a leaflet put out by this company at a time when dealers in musical merchandise were accustomed to issue small collections of gospel songs by way of advertising. The refrain of HANKEY was added by Fischer.

318 Draw Thou My Soul, O Christ

Following the death of her father, a New England sea captain, Lucy Larcom (1826–1893) moved to Lowell, Massachusetts, with her mother and family and began working in a mill there at an early age. In those days the "Lowell factory system" was renowned as a desirable place for girls to work and attracted young women from well-to-do families. Far from being thought of as a social liability it was regarded as a social asset to be so employed. The first magazine written exclusively by women in this country, the *Lowell Offering,* was published by the Improvement Circle, a factory women's organization in Lowell. Miss Larcom frequently contributed poems to the journal and was thereby brought to the attention of John Greenleaf Whittier who became interested in her literary gifts and remained a lifelong friend. After pursuing her education and graduating from Monticello Female Seminary, Alton, Illinois, she returned to Massachusetts and taught in advanced schools and continued her studies at Wheaton Seminary, Norton. Because of poor health she retired from teaching and devoted her full time to writing. She edited several volumes of poetry in collaboration with Whittier and published a number of works of her own, including *Childhood Songs,* 1875; *Wild Roses of Cape Ann,* 1881; *Poetical Works,* 1885; and *Beckonings,* 1886, her compilation of excerpts from the writings of the world's great religious thinkers. The present hymn is taken from her book *At the Beautiful Gate,* 1892, a compilation of her own poems.

ST. EDMUND (FATHERLAND; PILGRIMAGE) was set to Thomas R. Taylor's hymn "We are but strangers here, heaven is our home" in *The Hymnary,* 1872 — a circumstance which accounts for the two alternative tune names. See No. 185 for comments on Arthur Sullivan.

319 Just As I Am, Without One Plea

Despite being invalided the last fifty years of her life and having to endure almost constant pain, Charlotte Elliott (1789-1871) was both a radiant person and a creative and dedicated hymn writer. Born at Clapham, England, the home also of Katherine Hankey (see No. 317), she began at an early age to write poems in a humorous vein and was interested in music and painting. However, after meeting César Malan, the Genevan evangelist, who paid a visit to her father in 1822, she devoted all her time and energies to religious and humanitarian interests. She wrote the present hymn in 1834 while residing at Westfield Lodge, Brighton. Her brother, the Rev. Henry V. Elliott, had arranged a bazaar for the purpose of raising funds to build a much-needed college in the town. Not able to attend or help in any direct way, Miss Elliott, oppressed by feelings of uselessness, finally penned these lines to relieve her distraught mind and overcome her sense of futility. They appeared in her *Invalid's Hymn Book,* 1836, which had been compiled in an earlier edition by Miss Kiernan of Dublin but which Miss Elliott re-edited and re-published, adding thirty-two of her own hymns. This hymn was a great favorite of William Wordsworth's daughter, Dora, and has been translated into many languages. More than a thousand letters were found among Miss Elliott's belongings thanking her for this hymn. Among her other works are *Hours of Sorrow Cheered and Comforted,* 1836; *Hymns for a Week,* 1839; and *Thoughts in Verse on Sacred Subjects,* 1869. She is credited with having written more than 150 hymns.

WOODWORTH, the best-known and most widely used setting for Miss Elliott's hymn in the United States, was not associated with it originally. When first published in the *Mendelssohn Collection,* 1849, edited by Thomas Hastings and William Bradbury, WOODWORTH was set to "The God of love will sure indulge, the flowing tear, the heaving sigh" which continued to appear with it in subsequent Bradbury publications. In the *Mendelssohn Collection* "Just as I am" was set to a trite anonymous tune. Two tunes composed by Bradbury for the hymn and published in later collections, were of no consequence, but at least they did fit the original meter of the text: 8.8.8.6. When he set WOODWORTH to it in his *Eclectic Tune Book,* 1860, he altered the meter to 8.8.8.8. (Long Meter) by the simple expedient of repeating "I come" at the end of each stanza — a repetition not found in English hymnals. The combination of tune and text took hold and eliminated a number of other settings. Undoubtedly the inclusion of WOOD–WORTH with the present hymn in the collections of *Gospel Hymns and sacred Songs* (1875–1891) used by Moody and Sankey at their meetings, had much to do with its extensive use. ELLIOT, composed by Lowell Mason for "Just as I am" and published in *The Sabbath Hymn and Tune Book,* 1859, is given below. It fits the original meter of the hymn.

320 Just As I Am, Without One Plea

See No. 319 for comments on the text.

ST. CRISPIN was composed by George J. Elvey for these words and first published in E. H. Thorne's *Selection of Psalm and Hymn Tunes*, 1863. See No. 199 for comments on Elvey.

321 My God, Accept My Heart This Day

In 1848, the year in which he followed John Henry Newman into the Roman Catholic Church, Matthew Bridges wrote this confirmation hymn. It was published that same year in his *Hymns of the Heart* and has since appeared in many denominational hymnals. The words make it equally suitable as a stewardship hymn or for use in the communion service and reception of new members. The first line bears a strong resemblance to the motto of John Calvin as found on a sixteenth-century seal, *Cor meum velut mactatum domino in sacrificium offero* ("My heart I offer as a sacrifice devoted to God.") See No. 199 for comments on Bridges.

ST. STEPHEN See No. 201 for comments on William Jones.

322 Jesus Calls Us, O'er the Tumult

Based on Matthew 4:18–20 and written for St. Andrew's Day, 1852, this hymn by Mrs. Cecil F. Alexander is found in almost every modern hymnal. It was first published by the Society for the Promotion of Christian Knowledge in Tract No. 15, *Hymns for Public Worship*, 1852, and has been adopted by the Brotherhood of St. Andrew of The Protestant Episcopal Church in the United States and by the Church of England in Canada as their brotherhood hymn. The version given here is the original as Mrs. Alexander first wrote it. See No. 171 for comments on Mrs. Alexander.

GALILEE is an instance of a hymn tune written by an Englishman that has found no place in English hymnody but is included in most denominational hymnals published in the United States. It is not known when it was composed for these words, but it appeared with them in the *Congregational Church Hymnal*, 1887, edited by George S. Barrett and E. J. Hopkins.

William H. Jude, (1851–1922) started out as organist for a charitable institution, the Blue Coat Hospital in Liverpool. After 1889 he was organist for the Stretford Town Hall near Manchester. He had great interest in the music of Purcell, lectured on it as well as on other musical subjects, and was one of the first to go to Australia as a lecture-recitalist.

323 Jesus Calls Us, O'er the Tumult

See No. 322 for comments on the text.

GOTT DES HIMMELS (SILESIA; WALTHAM) introduces Heinrich Albert (1604–1651), a nephew of the great Heinrich Schütz, and a poet, organist, and composer of distinction in his own right. After a period of study with Schütz in Dresden, Albert yielded to his parents' insistence that he become a lawyer and for a time studied law at the University of Leipzig, only to give it up for music. Both the text and tune of "Gott des Himmels und der Erden" ("God, thou Lord of heaven and earth") were by Albert, published in Part V of his *Arien oder Melodyen* (1638–1650) a famous eight-volume collection of sacred and secular music to which he contributed texts as well as tunes. In *Music in the Baroque Era*, Manfred Bukofzer speaks of Albert as a leader in the North German School in the development of the *continuo lied* (song with chordal accompaniment) in "the second great flowering of German song" and says that his songs were sung all over Germany. He has also been called the father of the German Lied. Paul Henry Lang comments that Albert "gave the Lied the place it has occupied ever since in German music," and that "other composers wrote songs among other works, but Heinrich Albert was a song composer pure and simple [who] composed a great variety of songs: simple folk-song-like pieces, more pretentious arias, and in particular, deeply felt spiritual songs." [24] His collections were so popular that they sold rapidly and were even surreptitiously published under another name. In 1627 when Albert was on his way to Warsaw with a peace delegation, he was seized as a prisoner of war by the Swedes and was not released until 1628, when he settled in Königsberg, becoming organist of the cathedral in 1631.

Bach used the melody of GOTT DES HIMMELS only once, for the concluding chorale of Part 5 of the *Christmas Oratorio*. The present harmonization is derived from it. Albert's melody (Zahn 3614a) in its original form, in triple measure, is given with an English translation of his hymn in *Songs of Praise*, 1931, *Congregational Praise*, 1951, and *The Harvard University Hymn Book*, 1964. His original harmonization is given in *Songs of Syon*, 1910.

324 O Thou to Whose All-Searching Sight

Nicolaus Ludwig von Zinzendorf (1700–1760) in his life and religious motivation bears a striking resemblance to Leo Tolstoy. Born into a wealthy noble family, he was brought up by a pious aunt and his grandmother and devoted his life and substance to religious and charitable works and enterprises. After studying at the universities of Halle and Wittenberg, he traveled through Europe and while visiting at Düsseldorf saw a picture of Christ with the inscription, "This have I done for thee. What doest thou for Me?" which was the turning point of his life. In 1722 he bought a large estate in Saxony and began to settle in one part of it the persecuted descendants of the Moravian Brethren. Known as Herrnhut, it became a great Moravian center from which missionaries were sent out to all parts of the world. Zinzendorf himself went on many missionary journeys, including visits to Holland, England, Scotland, and the American colonies. John Wesley visited Herrnhut in 1738 and was so impressed by the singing and the religious fervor of the community that he was led to write in his diary, "Oh, when shall this Christianity cover the earth as the waters cover the sea!" Zinzendorf died a poor man but he left behind a strong, unified company of followers and a rich spiritual legacy. Although he wrote over two thousand hymns, few have remained in use. The present hymn was first published in the Leipzig *Sammlung geistlicher und lieblicher Lieder*, 1725, and later in the Moravian *Gesang-Buch der Gemeine in Herrn-Huth*, 1741. It was translated by John Wesley in the Wesley brothers' *Psalms and Hymns*, 1738. See No. 9 for comments on Wesley.

GRACE CHURCH (NAPLES; HAWEIS) is one of seven melodies attributed to Ignaz Pleyel (1757–1831) in Vol. II of Gardiner's *Sacred Melodies*, 1815, where it was set to "Father of mercies! God of love." Lowell Mason's adaptation of the tune, named NAPLES, appeared in his *Boston Handel and Haydn Society Collection*, 1822, and was taken into other nineteenth-century American books. In *Music of the Church*, 1828, edited by Jonathan Wainwright, rector of Grace Church, New York City, the melody, in practically its present form, was set to "Almighty Father bless the word" and named GRACE CHURCH. Mr. Gear, organist of Grace Church, was mentioned in the preface as one of the gentlemen who "improved the work by their suggestions and by several of their own compositions." The present harmonization is basically Gardiner's.

Pleyel, born near Vienna, was the twenty-fourth child of a village schoolmaster and "a lady of high degree" who was disinherited by her family for marrying beneath her rank. She died at the birth of this child. He studied violin and piano in Vienna, and at fifteen became a protégé of Count Erdödy, a Hungarian nobleman, who placed him with Haydn as student and boarder, an arrangement that continued for five years. Haydn spoke of Pleyel as his favorite pupil and dedicated the six quartets of Op. 2 to him. In 1777, after being appointed kapellmeister to his patron, Pleyel was given a leave of absence and sufficient funds for a long period of study in Italy. He was made assistant director of music at Strasbourg Cathedral in 1783, director in 1789. Two years later he was invited to conduct the Professional Concerts in London as a rival attraction to Haydn who was conducting Salomon's concerts. Any hoped-for rivalry or hostility between the two conductors never materialized — Pleyel included one of Haydn's symphonies at his first concert (which Haydn attended) and the two musicians remained fast friends. Upon his return to Strasbourg, Pleyel was classed as an aristocrat and traitor and, according to one account, narrowly escaped the guillotine. For a week he was put under guard and ordered to write music for a poem extolling the ideals of the revolution. He left Strasbourg in 1795, settled in Paris as a music dealer, and in 1807 established the piano firm, Pleyel et Cie. Chopin made his Paris debut in the rooms of the Pleyel firm. Pleyel composed an enormous amount of instrumental music, but it was superficial and imitative and has not endured.

325 Lord Christ, When First Thou Cams't

As one of the editors of *Songs of Praise*, 1931, Dean Dwelly of Liverpool Cathedral invited Walter Russell Bowie (1882–   ) to write a hymn that would be a modern counterpart to the "Dies Irae" (a celebrated thirteenth-century poem by Thomas of Celano which is sung in the Roman Catholic Church at the mass for the dead). The present hymn is the result, which Dr. Bowie described as "an effort to express both the solemnity and inspiration of the thought of Christ coming into our modern world in judgement." After graduating from Harvard University with Phi Beta Kappa honors and from Virginia Theological Seminary, Dr. Bowie first served two Episcopal churches in Virginia before becoming rector of Grace Episcopal Church, New York City, where he remained for sixteen memorable years. Following that, he was professor of practical theology and dean of students at Union Theological Seminary, New York, from 1939 to 1950. He later taught at his theological alma mater and has lectured at General Theological Seminary in New York City, at Yale Divinity School in New Haven, Connecticut, and at Seabury-Western Divinity School in Evanston, Illinois. His ecumenical and scholarly activities included membership on the Commission on Faith and Order of the World Council of Churches and the committee which prepared the Revised Standard Version of the Bible. A churchman of sensitive and vigorous social concern, he has published many books including *The Master, A Life of Christ*, 1928; *On Being Alive*, 1931; *The Story of the Bible*, 1934; *Great Men of the Bible*, 1937; and *Lift Up Your Hearts*, 1939. Although his hymns are few in number, they are all of high quality and are to be found in English as well as in American hymnals.

MIT FREUDEN ZART (BOHEMIAN BRETHREN) Dr. Bowie's hymn was set to this tune in *The Hymnal 1940*. See No. 20 for comments on the music.

326 Thou Didst Leave Thy Throne

First sung from leaflets in the church of which her father was the Rector, St. Mark's Parish, Brighton, England, this hymn by Emily E. S. Elliott (1836–1897) was later printed in the *Church Missionary Juvenile Instructor*, 1870, of which Miss Elliott was the editor for six years, and in her *Chimes for Daily Service*, 1880. The latter was divided into two parts, the second of which was printed separately as a compilation of forty-eight hymns with the title, *Under the Pillow*. It was intended for use by patients in hospitals and by invalids and was so designed that it could be slipped under the pillow. Most of

256

her hymns were first sung in St. Mark's Church and were published in her two major collections, *Chimes for Consecration,* 1873, and *Chimes for Daily Service,* 1880. The present hymn is based on the incident described in Luke 2:7, "there was no room for them in the inn." Miss Elliott was the niece of Charlotte Elliott (see No. 319).

MARGARET (ELLIOTT) was composed for these words and named MARGARET by the Rev. Timothy R. Matthews (1826–1910), English clergyman, organist, and composer, whose simple, melodious hymn tunes brought him considerable renown. It was first published in *Children's Hymns and Tunes,* 1876. When Matthews was asked by William W. How to furnish six tunes for *The Children's Hymn Book,* 1881, he composed and sent off the requested number in twenty-four hours! Matthews was the son of the Rev. T. R. Matthews who was referred to as "my noble preacher" in one of the letters of Edward Fitzgerald, poet-translator of *The Rubáiyát of Omar Khayyám.* When Matthews was a private tutor in the family of the Rev. Lord Wriothesley Russell, canon of Windsor, he became acquainted with George Elvey (199), later studied with him, and the two became lifelong friends. After graduation from Cambridge, Matthews was ordained in 1853 and served in only two parishes over a period of fifty-four years: from 1853 to 1859 at St. Mary's Nottingham, and from 1859 to 1907 at North Coates in the marshes of Lincolnshire where he was in charge of a small, run-down parish. Church life was at a low ebb when he went there, the church itself was in a dilapidated state and the place isolated and depressing. Matthews did much to improve conditions in the parish, and through his writings encouraged fellow clergymen to take a more active interest in the music of the local parish churches. A great lover of trees, Matthews planted many around the church and school in his parish. His love for gardening prompted him to remark to a friend, "When my time comes, I hope I shall find a garden awaiting me." He wrote over one hundred hymn tunes, morning and evening services, edited collections of tunes and the first series of *The Village Organist,* 1877.

327 Savior, Like a Shepherd Lead Us

As the compiler of *Hymns for the Young,* 1836, where this hymn first appeared, Dorothy Ann Thrupp (1779–1847) is usually credited with these words, although they were given without authorship. James Moffatt suggests that they may have been written by Henry F. Lyte (see No. 16).

Miss Thrupp contributed several children's hymns to the Rev. W. Carus Wilson's *Friendly Visitor* and *Children's Friend,* under the nom de plume "Iota," and to Mrs. Herbert Mayo's *Selection of Hymns and Poetry for the Use of Infant Schools and Nurseries,* 1846, third edition, which she signed D. A. T. She was born in London and lived there all her life.

BRADBURY, named for its composer, was written for Miss Thrupp's text and published in *Oriola,* 1859, one of numerous collections of Sunday school songs compiled by Bradbury. ("Jesus loves me," a pentatonic melody, was one of his most popular tunes for children.) The repetition of the last line of the present hymn as a refrain, typical of Bradbury's tunes, is not part of the original poem.

The fact that a number of Bradbury's melodies for children passed into hymnody for adults substantiates the insight inherent in John Calvin's plan to have children learn to sing the Psalm versions written for the Protestants in Geneva in order that through their singing the adults might learn the music. In *The English Hymn* Louis Benson has said that it was the tunes in Sunday school books edited by Bradbury, Root, Lowry, and others of their time which helped "in developing a taste in the young for the lighter type of religious song" and "furnished the evangelists with the earliest examples of what are now known as Gospel Hymns." See No. 178 for comments on Bradbury.

328 The Lord Is Rich and Merciful

This has been taken from Thomas T. Lynch's *The Rivulet,* third edition, 1868, where it was given the heading, "Have Faith in God." Each line begins with an affirmation about God and then is followed by an appropriate religious response — come, trust, learn. See No. 245 for comments on Lynch.

SHEPHERDS' PIPES   This tune and its title have an unusual origin. Every year since their marriage in 1949, the Rev. and Mrs. William Gay's Christmas greeting to friends has been an original Christmas song. In 1952 it was a carol about "The shepherds' pipes on Bethl'hem's height." Mrs. Gay writes:

> We take turns writing either words or music first. In 1952 it was time for the music to be first. This tune "dropped out of the blue" one evening while I was at the piano. Bill said, "Sounds like shepherd pipes," and ran for the Bible dictionary to see if such were used by the shepherds in Palestine. The words came quickly for him.

Annabeth McClelland Gay (1925–   ) was born in Ottawa, Illinois, where her father was pastor of the Presbyterian Church for thirty-four years. After graduation from Knox College, 1947 (B.M.E.) she attended the School of Sacred Music of Union Theological Seminary in New York, receiving an M.S.M. in 1949, the year in which her husband, the Rev. William Gay, was granted his B.D. at the Seminary. They have served Congregational-Christian churches, in Jefferson, Ohio, three rural churches in Brown county, and since 1958 have been at Pleasant Hill, Ohio. Mrs. Gay has directed children's choirs, the music in vacation church schools, has conducted several festivals, and has been active in leading hymn-singing sessions of the Ohio Women's Fellowship of Congregational Christian Churches.

SHEPHERDS' PIPES was one of the new tunes submitted anonymously to the Pilgrim Hymnal Committee, and set by it to the present text.

329 O Jesus, Thou Art Standing

Based on Revelation 3:20 ("Behold, I stand at the door, and knock"), this hymn by William W. How was written in 1867 and was printed the same year in the Supplement to *Psalms and Hymns,* edited by How and Thomas Baker Morrell. Although some authors have proposed that the hymn was inspired by Holman Hunt's painting "Light of the World," which was shown in 1854 and now hangs in Keble College, Oxford, How attributed the source of his inspiration to Jean Ingelow's poem, "Brothers, and a Sermon," which he read in 1867 and which prompted him to write: "The pathos of the verses impressed me very forcibly at the time. I read them over and over again, and finally, closing the book, I scribbled on an old scrap of paper my first idea of the verses beginning, 'O Jesus, Thou art standing.' I altered them a good deal subsequently, but I am fortunate in being able to say that after the hymn left my hands it was never revised or altered in any way." See No. 252 for comments on How.

ST. HILDA (ST. EDITH; BARTON)   The first four measures of this tune are from a melody written in 1793 by Justin H. Knecht for "Der niedern Menschheit Hülle" which was included in *Vollständige Sammlung . . . Choralmelodien,* 1799, edited by him and Johann F. Christmann. In the Appendix to *Hymns Ancient and Modern,* 1868, Knecht's tune in its entirety was set to John M. Neale's hymn "O happy band of pilgrims" with which it still appears in some English hymnals, named KNECHT, KOCHER, or BARTON.

Using the first half of Knecht's melody for an opening phrase, Edward Husband (1843–1908), an English clergyman, composed ST. HILDA in 1871. It was set to Bishop How's hymn in *The Hymnal with Tunes Old and New,* 1872, edited by the "pioneer exemplar of the ideals of the Oxford Movement" in the United States, John Ireland Tucker, rector of the Church of the Holy Cross in Troy, New York. In *The Church Hymnal,* 1879, edited by Rev. Charles L. Hutchins, the tune was set to the same hymn but was called ST. EDITH. Husband, who became vicar of St. Michael and All Angels' in Folkestone in 1878, had considerable interest in music, played the organ, composed hymn tunes and an Evening Service, lectured on church music, published *The Mission Hymnal,* 1874, edited *Supplemental Tunes to Popular Hymns,* 1882, and an *Appendix for use at the Church of S. Michael and All Angels,* 1885. His tune ST. HILDA does not appear in English hymnals. See No. 243 for comments on Knecht.

330   One Who Is All Unfit to Count

Narayan Vaman Tilak (1862–1919) ranks as the greatest Christian hymn writer of India. Born into a Hindu family of wealth and prominence, he became dissatisfied with Hinduism and after years of study and searching finally turned to Christianity in 1894. A scholar, poet, ardent patriot, and social reformer, he served for twenty-one years at the American Marathi Mission at Ahmednagar, teaching, doing social work, and preaching. During this time, he wrote many hymns for the Marathi Christian Church, all of which are marked by a moving simplicity and an intense devotion to Christ. Near the end of his remarkable career he began an eleven-volume work on the life of Christ but was able to complete only one volume before his untimely death. In

1917 he gave up all means of support to begin a new movement of evangelism called "God's Durbar," intended to unite all mankind in "a real universal family, to be known as real friends of men and real patriots through whom the world gains once more a vision of the Lord Jesus Christ." The translation of Tilak's hymn is by Nicol Macnicol (1870–1952), a distinguished missionary who spent many years in India under the auspices of the United Free Church of Scotland. The hymn first appeared in translated form in *The Indian Interpreter* and was later included in J. C. Winslow's *Narayan Vaman Tilak, the Christian Poet of Maharashtra,* second edition, 1930.

WIGTOWN, the setting for Tilak's moving poem in *The Church Hymnary, Revised,* 1927, was introduced to the United States in *The Hymnal,* 1933 (Presbyterian). One of the thirty-one Common Tunes in the great Scottish Psalter of 1635 (see No. 168), it seems to be of Scottish origin. Its expressiveness, its beauty and distinctiveness of form (no repetition of phrases), set it off from the other more typical Common Tunes. Wigtown is a royal burgh and the county town of Wigtownshire, Scotland, on the western shore of Wigtown Bay — the name comes from the Scandinavian *vik,* bay. The acts against nonconformity were stringently enforced in Wigtown — field preaching was a capital crime, attendance at conventicles, treason. A veritable reign of terror caused many to flee in order to escape persecution. Margaret MacLachlan, a widow aged sixty-three, and Margaret Wilson, eighteen, were two covenanting martyrs who were tied to stakes in the sands of Wigtown Bay and drowned in the rising tide. On a hill outside the town, an obelisk known as Martyrs' Memorial, was erected in 1858 to the memory of these women and three men who were hanged without trial. The tune name thus is a reminder of those days in which many died for their religious convictions. The following arrangement of WIGTOWN is from the Scottish Psalter of 1635. The melody is in the tenor.

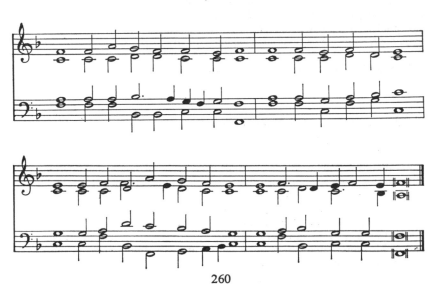

331 Savior, Thy Dying Love

Sylvanus Dryden Phelps (1816–1895) is remembered today chiefly because he was the father of William Lyon Phelps, renowned author and professor of English literature at Yale University, and because he wrote this hymn. The hymn first appeared in 1862 in *The Watchman and Reflector,* a Baptist journal of which Phelps was the editor, and was later included in Robert Lowry's *Pure Gold,* 1871, a compilation of gospel songs and hymns. On Phelps' seventieth birthday, Dr. Lowry sent a note with these words: "It is worth living seventy years even if nothing comes of it but one such hymn as 'Savior, Thy dying love.'. . . Happy is the man who can produce one song which the world will keep on singing after its author shall have passed away." Phelps was the pastor of First Baptist Church in New Haven, Connecticut, for twenty-eight years and published many prose works and volumes of poetry. His *Holy Land, with Glimpses of Europe and Egypt, a Year's Tour,* 1862, was widely read and passed through nine editions in twenty-five years.

SOMETHING FOR JESUS Robert Lowry (1826–1899), the Baptist minister who wrote this hymn tune, once said that he would rather preach to a responsive, appreciative congregation than write a hymn — yet, as R. G. McCutchan comments, "His songs have helped millions, his sermons reached only a few thousands."

The career of Dr. Lowry, a native of Philadelphia, was closely bound up with Bucknell University where he did his undergraduate and graduate work and later served as Crozer Professor of Rhetoric, a member of the Board of Curators, and chancellor from 1876 to 1882. The university gave him an honorary D.D. in 1875. He served as pastor in Baptist churches of West Chester and Lewisburg, Pennsylvania, New York City, Brooklyn, and Plainfield, New Jersey. He went to Plainfield in 1876 and remained in the community until his death. For several years he was president of the New Jersey Baptist Sunday School Convention and for two years moderator of the East New Jersey Baptist Association.

332 Lord, Thy Mercy Now Entreating

A lifelong friend of Henry Smart, the noted English composer and organist, Mary Ann Sidebotham (1833–1913) was an accomplished musician and pianist. Most of her life was spent with her brother, the vicar of St. Thomas-on-the-Bourne, Surrey, serving as his housekeeper and the organist of the church. As the musical editor of *The Children's Hymn-Book,* 1881, she composed several of the tunes and the words of this hymn, but she would not allow her name to appear on the title page. Most of her contributions simply bore the initials M.A.S. *The Bird's Nest,* a collection of fifty songs for children, contained many of her tunes. She died on the Isle of Wight in 1913.

RINGE RECHT (ELLERKER; BATTY) was set to this hymn in *The Hymnary,* 1930, of the United Church of Canada. The tune is William H. Monk's adaptation of an eighteenth-century Moravian melody first published in Johann Thommen's large collection of hymns and tunes, *Erbaulicher Mu-*

sicalischer Christen-Schatz, 1745. It was set to the German hymn "Ringe recht wenn Gottes Gnade" ("Strive aright when God doth call thee") with which it still appears in German hymnals. The Thommen version was rather florid; the present form is closer to that found in Johann C. Kühnau's *Choralgesänge*, 1786. Monk used the tune for "Sweet the moments, rich in blessing" in *Hymns Ancient and Modern*, 1861, where it was called BATTY. See No. 203 for comments on Monk.

333 Father Almighty, Bless Us with Thy Blessing

Of unknown origin, this hymn first appeared in the *Berwick Hymnal*, 1886, an independent collection of hymns compiled by the Rev. A. W. Oxford, vicar of St. Luke's Church in London. It derived its name from the street on which the church was located.

INTEGER VITAE (FLEMMING) won a place for its composer in *Grove's Dictionary of Music*, where the work from which it was adapted is called an excellent setting of Horace's Ode XXII, "Integer Vitae." Composed for male voices by Dr. Friedrich F. Flemming (1778–1813), it has been a favorite among students in schools and universities of Germany and England.

Flemming was born in Neuhausen, Saxony, studied medicine in Wittenberg, Jena, Vienna, and Trieste and established a successful practice in Berlin. There he was active in the musical life of the city, a musician by avocation who composed many part-songs for the *Liedertafel* (a group of men who met together to sing) founded in 1808 by Carl F. Zelter, friend of Goethe, teacher of Mendelssohn and champion of Bach. Dr. Flemming's tune appeared in three nineteenth-century Catholic hymnals of Germany with the text "Danket dem Schöpfer" (Bäumker, Vol. IV, No. 341) and was also adapted to the secular text "Hier in des Abends traulich ernster Stille." In a number of song collections printed in the United States this tune is given with the first two stanzas of Horace's Ode in an extremely free, anonymous English translation.

334 Father, in Thy Mysterious Presence

Taken from *A Book of Hymns for Public and Private Devotion*, 1846, edited jointly by Samuel Johnson and Samuel Longfellow, this hymn by Johnson reflects his deeply fervent and even mystical religious faith. The lines recall a portion of Paul's sermon on Mars Hill, Acts 17:27. See No. 236 for comments on Johnson.

DONNE SECOURS (GENEVA 12), one of the finest tunes composed or adapted by Louis Bourgeois, was the setting for Marot's version of Psalm 12, "Donne secours, Seigneur, il en est heure," in the Genevan Psalter of 1551, replacing one that had been in use since 1542. It has been described as "nobly impressive" and "widely celebrated," and is included by Douen in his list of the most beautiful and most original melodies of the Psalter. It is in the Dorian mode. DONNE SECOURS was used for Psalm 12 in the complete Psalter (1573) prepared by Ambrosius Lobwasser for use in the Reformed Church of Germany. (Zahn 900) After 1779 the tune was taken into Lutheran use. In Ainsworth's Psalter, used by the Pilgrims at Plymouth, the tune, with one note less in the first and third phrases, was set to Psalms 3 and 86. See Nos. 4 and 282 for comments on Genevan Psalters.

335   What a Friend We Have in Jesus

Joseph Scriven (1820–1886) belongs to that company of saints whose intense devotion borders on the eccentric. Crushed by his fiancée's drowning in Ireland on the eve of their wedding, he sought consolation in communion with Christ. At the age of twenty-five he emigrated to Canada and settled in Port Hope, Ontario, where he endeavored to live according to the precepts of the Sermon on the Mount. He lived most of his life in the homes of others, accepting the lodgings offered by friends and neighbors, and spent much of his time doing menial chores for the sick and handicapped. He wrote this hymn to comfort his mother in a time of sorrow, never intending that it should receive public attention. A friend came upon it while sitting by Scriven's bedside during the latter's last illness. When asked by another friend whether he had written it, Scriven replied, "The Lord and I did it between us." Written about 1855, it probably was first published in Horace L. Hastings' *Social Hymns, Original and Selected,* 1865, where it appeared anonymously. It was substituted at the last minute for another hymn in Ira D. Sankey's and Philip P. Bliss's famous collection, *Gospel Hymns and Sacred Songs,* 1875, prompting Sankey to remark later that "the last hymn that went into the book became one of the first in favor." Scriven died by drowning near Port Hope on October 10, 1886.

ERIE (WHAT A FRIEND; CONVERSE) has carried Joseph Scriven's hymn to the far corners of the earth. It was first published in *Silver Wings,* 1870, a small book of Sunday school hymns obviously compiled by the composer, Charles C. Converse (1832–1918), although his name appears with only one hymn. His liking for noms de plume is evident in *Silver Wings.* Thirteen tunes, including ERIE, are by Karl Reden, twelve by C. O. Nevers, nine by E. C. Revons, the last two names plainly concocted from the letters of his own last name. These three names appear again and again in his collections.

Converse, born in Warren, Massachusetts, was a descendant of one of the early settlers of Woburn, Massachusetts. After a thorough education in English and the classics in the United States, he studied philosophy, law, and music in Germany, where he had as teachers the most eminent musicians at the Leipzig Conservatory, and became a friend of Liszt and Spohr. He returned to America in 1859, and in 1861 graduated from the law school at Albany University. He practiced law in Erie, Pennsylvania, from 1875 until his retirement to Highwood, New Jersey, where he died. His activities were even more numerous than his names: lawyer, judge, a partner in the Burdett Organ Company, composer, editor, inventor, philologist, writer.

Converse composed songs, hymn tunes, oratorios, chamber music, and symphonic works. (Only ERIE survives.) His concert overture "Hail Columbia," the only symphonic work by an American played at the great Peace Jubilee in Boston, 1872, was also performed at the Columbian Exposition in Chicago under Theodore Thomas' direction, and a Christmas overture was conducted by Walter Damrosch. One biographical account states that Sterndale Bennett was so impressed by a five-voice fugue which Converse had written that he offered him an honorary Mus.D. degree from Cambridge University — an offer which he declined. It has been said that ERIE has "most of the merits without the disadvantages of the gospel song." For many years this hymn was sung in the annual services of Negro Spirituals at St. George's Church in New York City, under the direction of George Kemmer. It was one of the favorite hymns of Harry Burleigh, distinguished Negro baritone of that church, and was sung at his funeral in 1949.

336 O Thou By Whom We Come to God

This is a cento of two hymns by James Montgomery. The first stanza is the final stanza of his hymn "Prayer is the soul's sincere desire," which he wrote at the request of Edward Bickersteth for the 1819 edition of the latter's *Treatise on Prayer*. The other stanzas are stanzas two, three, four, and seven respectively of his hymn, "Lord, teach us how to pray aright," which first appeared in published form in the eighth edition of Thomas Cotterill's *Selection of Psalms and Hymns*, 1819. Both hymns were written in 1818 for use in the Nonconformist Sunday schools in Sheffield, England, and were printed on a broadsheet with two other hymns on prayer. See No. 25 for comments on Montgomery.

SONG 67 (ST. MATTHIAS) appeared in George Wither's *Hymnes and Songs of the Church*, 1623, set to a metrical version of Acts I:26. (See No. 162.)

> When one among the Twelve there was,
>   That did thy Grace abuse;
> Thou left'st him, Lord, and in his place,
>   Did'st just Matthias chuse.

Since Gibbons had supplied the music for Wither's book it was assumed that he had composed SONG 67 until it was discovered that the tune had appeared with Psalm 1 in Edmund Prys' Welsh psalter, *Llyfr y Psalmau*, 1621, two years before the publication of *Hymnes and Songs*. This has raised questions as to Gibbons' composition of the tune, particularly since it is more typical of traditional psalm tunes than of his music. Erik Routley says, "It is an excellent tune, but not on either external or internal evidence ascribable to the great English madrigalist." He thinks, rather, that Gibbons included it "so that a good tune might not be lost to circulation." Like several other first-rate tunes, SONG 67 is strictly diatonic and within the compass of an octave.

337 Give to the Winds Thy Fears

Originally written as a twelve-stanza hymn in two parts, with eight lines to each stanza, this hymn of assurance and hope by Paul Gerhardt, beginning "Befiehl du deine Wege," is based on Luther's translation of Psalm 37:5, each stanza beginning with a word from the latter's version. It was first printed in the 1653 edition of Johann Crüger's *Praxis pietatis melica*. See No. 53 for comments on Gerhardt. John Wesley translated the hymn into English in his *Hymns and Sacred Poems,* 1739, and reduced it to eight stanzas of eight lines each with the first line reading, "Commit thou all thy griefs." The present version is taken from Wesley's translation, somewhat rearranged and altered. See No. 9 for comments on Wesley.

ICH HALTE TREULICH STILL ("I remain ever faithful") is from Schemelli's *Musicalisches Gesangbuch* (Musical Songbook), 1736, for which Bach was the music editor. This book was modeled on Freylinghausen's *Geistreiches Gesangbuch,* 1704, but the hymns in it were neither pietistic nor sectarian in spirit and the collection as a whole contained "whatever was good from any quarter . . . and the recognized treasures from among the old hymns" (Spitta). (See No. 135.) Although there is no way of proving that Bach wrote this particular song, Spitta includes it among those melodies which seem to him to bear "the unmistakable impress of Bach's style." [25] Several other authorities agree with him. In writing of these melodies, which were sacred arias or devotional songs intended primarily for use at home rather than in church, Albert Schweitzer says: "Their peculiar loveliness comes from the fact that they are the work of an artist brought up on the German chorale, writing under the influence of the formally perfect Italian melodic form."

ICH HALTE TREULICH STILL was named BACH in *The Bristol Tune Book,* 1876, and was printed on the same page with another S.M.D. tune for which "Give to the winds thy fears" was the heading. It may well be that this collection was responsible for the present combination of tune and words.

338 Give to the Winds Thy Fears

See No. 337 for comments on the text.

ST. BRIDE (ST. BRIDGET; ALL SAINTS; BRIDGEPORT) was set to the New Version of Psalm 130, "From lowest depths of woe," in William Riley's *Parochial Harmony. . . . A Collection of Psalm Tunes in three and four parts,* 1762, which the English hymnologist James T. Lightwood describes as "the only church tune-book of importance issued during the second half of the 18th century." Riley, director of music at the Asylum or House of Refuge for Female Orphans at Westminster Bridge, and a teacher of psalmody, objected to the type of music being popularized by the Methodist Revival and made every effort to train children and adults in the "appreciation and use of a sounder type of religious music" and to reform the method of singing psalm tunes in the churches.

Samuel Howard (?1710–1782), composer of ST. BRIDE, had his first musical training as a chorister of the Chapel Royal under Dr. Croft (No. 1) and studied later with J. C. Pepusch, learned theorist and composer, who was Handel's predecessor as organist and composer to the Duke of Chandos. Howard graduated from Cambridge with the degree Mus.D., in 1769, and served as organist of St. Clement Danes and of St. Bride's, Fleet Street. His compositions for the church and the theater, cantatas and instrumental works, were popular in his day. He assisted William Boyce in compiling the important collection, *Cathedral Music.* Since its first appearance, ST. BRIDE has had wide and continuous use in England and America. It was called BRIDGEPORT in Thomas Hastings' *Musical Reader,* 1817, set to the same version of Psalm 130 with which it appeared in 1762.

339 All My Hope on God is Founded

This hymn by Joachim Neander was intended to be sung as a "grace after meat." Based on I Timothy 6:17, it was first published in Neander's *Glaub- und Liebesübung,* 1680, which appeared in the year of his death. See No. 15 for comments on Neander. The translation by Robert Bridges is more a free paraphrase than a strict rendering of the original into English. One of the marks of Bridges' genius was that he could take a great work and enhance it in the process of translation by his changes and additions. See No. 430 for comments on Bridges.

MEINE HOFFNUNG ("My Hope") was the setting for Joachim Neander's hymn "Meine Hoffnung steht feste" in his *Glaub- und Liebesübung,* 1680. (See No. 3.) There he indicated that it was a melody already known, but gave no source for it. Words and tune appear together in *The Chorale Book for England,* 1863, and in the *Yattendon Hymnal,* 1899. A tune quite similar to MEINE HOFFNUNG was used by Bach in the sixth movement of Cantata No. 40 with the second stanza of Paul Gerhardt's hymn "Schwing' dich auf zu deinem Gott." During the eighteenth century the melody was used extensively in Germany and among German colonists in America with "Auf ihr Christen, Christi Glieder" ("Rise, ye children of salvation"), the best-known hymn of Justus Falckner (1672–1723) who came from Germany to Philadelphia in 1700 and was the first Lutheran clergyman ordained in America. In *Three Centuries of American Hymnody,* 1940, Henry Wilder Foote tells of Falckner's ordination in 1703 for which friends "provided music with viols, hautboys, trumpets and kettledrums, and a small organ," and says that "this appears to be the earliest definite record of the use of an organ in any church in the colonies on the North Atlantic coast."

340 They Cast Their Nets in Galilee

Inspired by the incident describing the calling of Simon and Andrew, James and John (Mark 1:16–20), this is the only known hymn based on this text. William Alexander Percy (1885–1942) wrote it for his volume of collected poems, *Enzio's Kingdom, and Other Poems,* 1924, under the heading of "His Peace." Percy was the son of a United States senator from Mississippi, LeRoy Percy, and practiced law with his father for a time in Greenville, Mississippi. He later distinguished himself in relief work and in military service in Europe during World War I. Returning to Greenville after the war, he settled on the family plantation and continued to write poetry. A year before he died he published an autobiography, *Lanterns on the Levee; Recollections of a Planter's Son*, 1941.

GEORGETOWN, composed in 1941 for this hymn, was named for Georgetown Parish, D.C., where the composer's friend, F. Bland Tucker (No. 147), was rector of St. John's Church.

David McK. Williams (1887–   ) was born in Carnarvonshire, Wales, but grew up in Denver, Colorado, where his family moved when he was three months old. As a boy he was a chorister in the Cathedral of St. John in the Wilderness, at thirteen became organist and choirmaster of St. Peter's Church, Denver, and in 1908 went to New York City, serving as organist of Grace Church Chapel and studying with Clement Gale. During the years 1911–1914 he was in Paris studying with D'Indy, Vierne, and Widor, and on his return to the United States was appointed organist of the Church of the Holy Communion in New York City, remaining there until 1916 when he went overseas with the Royal Canadian Artillery. In 1920 he returned to the Church of the Holy Communion for six months then became organist and choirmaster of St. Bartholomew's Church in New York City where he stayed until his retirement in 1947. There he built up an extraordinarily fine musical program that drew crowds not only from the city but from all over the country. He taught organ and composition privately, and also at the School of Sacred Music of Union Theological Seminary and at the Julliard School of Music. He was a Fellow of the American Guild of Organists and a member of the Joint Commission on Church Music and the Joint Commission on Revision of the Hymnal of the Protestant Episcopal Church. His anthems, services, and descants are still widely used. No verbal account of the man or his musical services at St. Bartholomew's can do justice to him or them. When this engaging, witty, exceptionally gifted musician retired there was regret on all sides, and an irreparable gap was left in the musical life of the city.

341 Dear Lord and Father of Mankind

In his poem, "The Brewing of Soma," published in 1872, John Greenleaf Whittier describes the ritual practice of a sect in India that sought to achieve communion with deity by means of an intoxicating drink made from the Soma plant. One stanza reads:

> "Drink, mortals, what the gods have sent,
> Forget your long annoy."
> So sang the priests. From tent to tent
> The Soma's sacred madness went,
> A storm of drunken joy.

In contrast to such pagan practices, which he contends have their modern counterparts, he then goes on in the latter part of the poem to depict the real spirit of true worship. The last six stanzas of this seventeen-stanza poem, omitting stanza fifteen, comprise the present hymn. W. Garrett Horder was the first to use these lines as a hymn in his *Worship Song*, 1884. See No. 224 for comments on Whittier.

REST (ELTON), probably the best known of Frederick C. Maker's hymn tunes, was composed for these words in *The Congregational Church Hymnal*, 1887, edited by the Rev. G. S. Barrett and E. J. Hopkins. See No. 98 for comments on Maker.

342 I Need Thee Every Hour

This hymn by Annie Sherwood Hawks (1835–1918), written for the meeting of the National Baptist Sunday School Association in Cincinnati, Ohio, in November, 1872, was a great favorite in America during the last part of the nineteenth century, especially in the revival meetings of Moody and Sankey. It is still found in most modern hymnals. Miss Hawks said of the hymn that it "was wafted out to the world on the wings of love and joy, rather than under the stress of a great personal sorrow, with which it has so often been associated in the minds of those who sing it. I remember well the morning . . . when in the midst of the daily cares of my home . . . I was so filled with the sense of nearness to the Master that, wondering how one would live without Him either in joy or pain, these words, 'I need Thee every hour,' were ushered into my mind, the thought at once taking full posession of me." Born in Hoosick, New York, Miss Hawks lived most of her life in Brooklyn where she was an active member of Hanson Place Baptist Church. The hymn was first published in *The Royal Diadem: songs for the Sunday School*, 1873, compiled by Robert Lowry and W. H. Doane.

NEED was composed for Mrs. Hawks' hymn by the Rev. Robert Lowry, who for eight years was pastor of the Brooklyn church which she attended. The refrain was added by the composer with the author's consent. It was first published in *The Royal Diadem*, 1873. There are two settings for this hymn in the French hymnal *Louange et Prière* under the title "J'ai soif de ta présence." The first tune given for it is PASSION CHORALE (No. 170), the second is NEED. See No. 331 for comments on Lowry.

343 In Heavenly Love Abiding

Because of her desire to read the poetry of the Old Testament in the original language, Anna Laetitia Waring (1823–1910) mastered Hebrew as a young girl and daily read the Psalter throughout her life. Raised in the Society of Friends, she was attracted to the Church of England because of its sacraments and joined that communion in 1842. She was a person of simple faith and infectious good humor and devoted much of her time in later years to visiting prisoners in Bristol jails and in helping ex-convicts through the Discharged Prisoners' Aid Society. Most of her hymns, including the present one, were first published in her *Hymns and Meditations*, 1850, which appeared in several editions. The distinguished Unitarian leader, James Martineau, was a close friend and acknowledged that he owed her "a long-standing spiritual obligation."

NYLAND, a Finnish folk melody arranged by David Evans, was set to these words in *The Church Hymnary Revised*, 1927. It was named for a Finnish province by Millar Patrick, a member of the Revision committee and joint editor with James Moffatt of the *Handbook to the Church Hymnary*, 1935. NYLAND was first included in the hymnal of the Finnish Evangelical Lutheran Church in 1909. In 1908, Pastor Immanuel Colliander and others who were interested in introducing Finnish folk melodies into their hymnody, had issued two booklets of forty tunes each, entitled "New Religious Compositions." NYLAND was one of twenty-nine of these tunes which were adopted by the state church in 1909. It is said to have come from Kuortane, a small village in Etalapohjanmaa (South Ostrobothnia). It has the A A B A form characteristic of many folk songs. See No. 38 for comments on Evans.

344 Lead Us, Heavenly Father, Lead Us

Although he was a prominent and successful architect and surveyor in London, James Edmeston (1791–1867) is remembered today chiefly because of his hymns. For many years it was his practice to write a hymn a week for his family which he read at Sunday morning devotions. He is credited with having written more than two thousand hymns. He was devoted to children and often visited the London Orphan Asylum, which provided him with the inspiration for many of his hymns. These appeared in several of his publications, including *Sacred Lyrics*, 1821, *Infant Breathings*, 1846, and *Sacred Poetry*, 1848. His grandfather was a minister in the Congregational Church, and Edmeston was raised in that communion but later joined the Church of England, eventually becoming a warden of St. Barnabas' Church, Homerton, a post which he held for many years. The present hymn, "written for the children of the London Orphan Asylum," first apeared in the second set of his *Sacred Lyrics*, 1821, and is typical of the simple, childlike quality of most of his works.

DULCE CARMEN (ALLELUIA DULCE CARMEN; TANTUM ERGO; CORINTH; WEBBE; WALPOLE; ORIEL)   This tune's association with John M. Neale's English translation of the medieval Latin hymn "Alleluia dulce carmen" ("Alleluia, song of sweetness") accounts for its most familiar name. In Part II of *An Essay on the Church Plain Chant*, 1782, a Roman Catholic collection which contained "several Anthems, Litanies, Proses, and Hymns, as they are sung in the Public Chapels at London," this melody, headed "The Hymn at Benediction," was one of the settings for "Tantum ergo sacramentum," stanza five of St. Thomas Aquinas' "Pange, lingua gloriosi corporis mysterium" ("Of the glorious body telling, O my tongue, its mysteries sing"). The music was anonymous and was arranged in two parts and printed in plainsong notation. In Samuel Webbe's *Collection of Motetts or Antiphons,* 1792, the tune, in modern notation, was still anonymous, so it is not known whether Webbe composed it or adapted it from an older melody. The present harmonization of DULCE CARMEN (except for the last three chords in measure seven, which are from the *English Hymnal*) is William Monk's from *Hymns Ancient and Modern,* 1861. There the tune, named BENEDICTION or ALLELUIA DULCE CARMEN, was set to Neale's translation and mistakenly attributed to Michael Haydn. In a number of nineteenth-century American collections this melody, with the first eight measures repeated, is called WALPOLE, the name given it in Lowell Mason's *Boston Handel and Haydn Society Collection of Church Music,* 1822, where it was set to "May the grace of Christ our Saviour." In some hymnals the omission of the passing notes in measure seven (as in Monk's version) is a detriment to the tune. See No. 36 for comments on Webbe.

345 Rejoice, Ye Pure in Heart

Edward H. Plumptre (1821–1891) was renowned in his day as a distinguished Anglican scholar, lecturer, and preacher. After holding such important positions as chaplain of King's College, London, dean of Queen's College, Oxford, prebendary of St. Paul's Cathedral, professor of New Testament Exegesis at King's College, and rector of Pluckley, Kent, he was appointed dean of Wells Cathedral, an office which he held the last ten years of his life. He was a member of the Old Testament Company of Revisers of the Bible and published many notable works, including a biography of Bishop Ken, translations of Sophocles, Aeschylus, and Dante, and two volumes of poetry. John Julian said of him: "As a writer of sacred poetry he ranks very high. His hymns are elegant in style, fervent in spirit and broad in treatment. . . . The rhythm of his verse has a special attraction for musicians, its poetry for the cultured and its stately simplicity for the devout and earnest-minded." Plumptre (pronounced Plum-ter) wrote this hymn for the annual choir festival at Peterborough Cathedral in May, 1865, and included it in the second edition of his *Lazarus and other Poems.* It first appeared in a hymnal in the 1868 Appendix to *Hymns Ancient and Modern,* and has been widely used as a processional and recessional hymn. Originally containing eleven stanzas, the present version includes stanzas one, two, six, seven, eight, and eleven.

MARION, composed by Arthur H. Messiter (1834–1916), is the only setting for these words in the majority of denominational hymnals in the United States. In *The Hymnal 1940,* however, it yielded first place to CARLISLE (see No. 25). The tune was named by the composer for his mother. Messiter, born and educated in England, came to the United States in 1863, sang for a time as a volunteer in the choir of Trinity Church, New York City, then served successively as organist of four churches in Philadelphia. In 1866 he was appointed organist and choirmaster of Trinity Church and remained there for thirty-one years, retiring in 1897. In *Our Hymnody,* R. G. McCutchan gives the following amusing comment which appeared in a New York musical paper at the time of Messiter's appointment: "We hear that the authorities of Trinity Church have appointed an organist from Philadelphia. We suppose that at the next vacancy they will try Coney Island." Evidently at that time the City of Brotherly Love did not have the high musical rating among all New Yorkers that it has now. The singing of Messiter's choir of men and boys, and the quality of music used in services at Trinity, all in the best English Cathedral tradition, set a new high standard for church music and "went far toward counteracting the pernicious influence of the 'quartet choirs.'" (*Hymnal 1940 Companion*) The musical edition of the Episcopal Hymnal of 1893 was Messiter's work; he also edited a *Psalter*, 1889, *The Choir Office-Book*, 1891, composed some anthems, and wrote *A History of the Choir and Music of Trinity Church*, New York, 1906.

346   Come, Let Us Join with Faithful Souls

As the minister of the Unitarian Christian Church of Wandsworth, London, from 1883 to 1920, William George Tarrant (1853–1928) was a leading Unitarian figure in England for nearly half a century. He was the editor of *The Inquirer*, a weekly Unitarian paper, a post he held from 1887 to 1897 and from 1918 to 1927. In addition to his pastoral and journalistic duties, he was keenly interested in hymnody and wrote many hymns, both texts and tunes. Most of these were published in his collection, *Songs Devout*, 1912, and in *The Inquirer*. The present hymn first appeared in a small Supplement to the *Essex Hall Hymnal*, 1892. He also wrote *The Story and Significance of the Unitarian Movement*, 1910, and three devotional manuals.

AZMON   See No. 223 for comments on the tune.

347   Lord, As to Thy Dear Cross

Born into a wealthy family, John Hampden Gurney (1802–1862) began his career by studying law but changed his mind and decided instead to enter the ministry. Following his ordination he was made curate of John Wycliffe's former church in Lutterworth and served also as chaplain of the poor-law Union there. Although many attractive offers were extended to him to move to more prominent and lucrative positions, he declined all such invitations, preferring to remain with the poorer people of his parish. Eventually, after serving in Lutterworth for seventeen years, he accepted a call to become rector of St. Mary's, Bryanstone Square, Marylebone, London, and in 1857 became prebendary of St. Paul's Cathedral. An active supporter of the Society for the Promotion of Christian Knowledge and the Religious Tract Society, he compiled and contributed to two well-known volumes, *A Collection of Hymns for Public Worship*, 1838, and *Psalms and Hymns for Public Worship*, 1851, referred to respectively as the Lutterworth Collection and the Marylebone Collection. The present hymn, originally containing six stanzas, is from the first volume. Gurney died in London in 1862.

ST. BERNARD'S roots are in a tune set to one of the *Marienlieder* (songs in praise of the Virgin Mary) in *Neues . . . Kirchen- und Hauss-Gesang der . . . Tochter Sion*, 1741, a Roman Catholic collection of over two hundred German and Latin hymns edited by H. Lindenborn. In two later Catholic hymnals (1767, 1847) the melody had a more subdued form. Both versions are given on page 193 of the *Historical Companion to Hymns Ancient and Modern,* 1962. It is believed that ST. BERNARD was derived from the latter version by John Richardson (1816–1879) for his *Easy Hymn Tunes . . . adapted for Catholic Schools,* c. 1851. In that book it was set to "Jesus the very thought of Thee" and headed "Hymn of St. Bernard." Richardson, educated at the Catholic school in Preston, his birthplace, attracted considerable attention as a boy because of his fine alto voice, and at thirteen was engaged as principal alto singer at St. Nicholas Catholic Chapel in Liverpool. Later he was apprenticed to a housepainter and decorator, but quit that trade at the expiration of his apprenticeship. When nineteen, he became organist of St. Mary's Catholic Church in Liverpool, and in 1837 returned to St. Nicholas' Chapel as organist, a post he held for over twenty years. He taught music privately and at St. Edward's College in Liverpool for thirteen years, and was prominent in the musical life of that city. One of his pupils, the famous English organist, W. T. Best, spoke highly of his ability as organist and teacher. Richardson composed several pieces at the request of Cardinal Newman and was honored by Pope Pius IX for his service to Catholic churches.

348 My Faith Looks Up to Thee

Written in 1830 when he was only twenty-two years of age, this is the first and finest hymn Ray Palmer wrote. The familiar lines are not connected with any dramatic incident but simply were born in the heart of a young man of unspoiled faith. Palmer later said: "I gave form to what I felt, by writing with little effort, the stanzas. I recollect I wrote them with very tender emotion and ended the last lines with tears." At the time, he was teaching in a select school in New York City, having shortly before graduated from Yale College (1830). A year later, on a street in Boston, he met Lowell Mason who informed him that he was publishing a hymnal and invited him to submit some hymns. The two friends stepped into a store and Palmer made a copy of the words of this hymn for Mason's collection. The hymn was first published in the notable collection, *Spiritual Songs for Social Worship,* 1831, edited by Lowell Mason and Thomas Hastings, and has since been translated into many languages, including Arabic, Chinese, Tahitian, Tamil, and Marathi. See No. 290 for comments on Palmer.

OLIVET   Lowell Mason, who composed OLIVET as a setting for Ray Palmer's first hymn, said to him, "Mr. Palmer, you may live many years, and do many good things, but I think you will be best known to posterity as the author of 'My faith looks up to Thee.'"

The tune, set to Palmer's words, was first published in Spiritual *Songs for Social Worship,* 1831, a collection described by its editors as "devotional songs for use of families and social religious meetings." In the Preface the editors wrote: "In the larger and more dignified assemblies, psalmody will continue to hold its appropriate place; but for social and private uses, something is needed which is more familiar, more melodious, and more easy of execution." They hoped that these songs would counteract the baneful effect of the "insipid, frivolous, vulgar, and profane melodies" which were being used in revival meetings. Although the book was not intended for church use, some Congregational and Presbyterian churches introduced it into prayer meetings and other services and familiarity with its hymns and tunes increased the demand for them in authorized hymnals. In later publications OLIVET was given its present form and harmonization. This was one of two tunes by Mason included in *The English Hymnal,* 1906. See No. 257 for comments on Mason.

349 O for a Closer Walk With God

These lines by William Cowper were written while his great friend and benefactress, Mrs. Mary Unwin, lay critically ill. After finishing the hymn on December 9, 1769, he sent it the following day to another friend with this message, "I began to compose the verses yesterday morning before daybreak but fell asleep at the end of the first two lines: when I awakened again, the third and fourth were whispered to my heart in a way which I have often experienced." The hymn first appeared in William Conyers' *Collection of Psalms and Hymns,* 1772, and was included in the famous *Olney Hymns,* 1779, compiled in collaboration with John Newton, where it bore the caption, "Walking with God" (Genesis 5:24, "and Enoch walked with God"). See No. 87 for comments on Cowper and the *Olney Hymns.*

CAITHNESS, named for a county in the extreme northeast of Scotland, was one of the thirty-one Common Tunes in the Scottish Psalter of 1635. Cowper's hymn was set to CAITHNESS in *The English Hymnal,* 1906. Since then the combination has appeared in a number of English and American hymnals.

350 O for a Closer Walk With God

See No. 349 for comments on the text.

BEATITUDO was written for "How bright these glorious spirits shine" in the revised edition of *Hymns Ancient and Modern,* 1875. See No. 79 for comments on John B. Dykes.

351 Nearer, My God, to Thee

Few hymns during the past one hundred years have had a more universal appeal than this one by Sarah Flower Adams (1805–1848). It was a favorite of Queen Victoria, Edward VII, William McKinley, and Theodore Roosevelt, among others, and has been translated into many languages. As a member of the South Place Religious Society (Unitarian) in London, Mrs. Adams was asked by her minister, the Rev. William Johnson Fox, to contribute some hymns to a collection he was preparing for use in his chapel. She responded by writing thirteen hymns for his *Hymns and Anthems,* 1840–1841, and her equally gifted sister, Eliza, who served as the music editor, composed sixty-nine of the 150 tunes. Among these thirteen hymns was "Nearer, My God, to Thee," which is based on the account of Jacob's dream at Bethel in Genesis 28:10–22. It speedily made its way across the ocean and appeared in hymnals compiled by James Freeman Clarke, Samuel Longfellow, and Henry Ward Beecher. Mrs. Adams aspired to be an actress, displaying considerable talent in her appearance as Lady Macbeth in 1837 at the Richmond Theatre, but her delicate constitution forced her to give up the stage. Instead, she turned her attention to literary endeavors, producing two major works, *Vivia Perpetua,* 1841, a dramatic poem in five acts, and *The Flock at the Fountain,* 1845, a catechism for children with hymns interspersed. Neither of these has continued in use. She was a close friend of Robert Browning and was admired by Leigh Hunt for her intellectual and poetic gifts. She died of tuberculosis on August 11, 1848, having contracted the disease while nursing her sister who succumbed to the same illness twenty months earlier.

BETHANY   In 1868 Lowell Mason gave a friend the following account of the composing of this hymn tune:

> When we were compiling the collection known as the *Sabbath Hymn and Tune Book,* they [his associates, Edwards A. Park and Austin Phelps, of Andover Theological Seminary] applied to me for a musical setting for the hymn, "Nearer, my God, to Thee." The metre was irregular. But one night some time after, lying awake in the dark, eyes wide open, through the stillness of the house the melody came to me, and the next morning I wrote down the notes of Bethany.

In the Second Series of *Studies of Familiar Hymns,* 1923, Louis F. Benson says of the hymn: "Henry Ward Beecher . . . included it in the *Plymouth Collection,* 1855. But what started the hymn on its free course in America was the tune BETHANY. . . . And when the hymn, set to this taking tune, appeared in 1859 in the wonderfully successful *Sabbath Hymn and Tune Book . . .* its general use became assured." [11] In *Church Music in History and Practice,* Winfred Douglas wrote:

> Probably I should not now feel so intense an interest in the Hymns of the Church if my Presbyterian father had not, out of his poverty, provided a Hymnal for each of his children. My mother's Hymnal, Lowell Mason's fine *Sabbath Hymn and Tune Book,* is beside me, as I write. [26]

352 Lift Up Your Hearts!

The familiar *Sursum Corda* (Lift up your hearts), taken from the introduction to the canon of the mass in the Roman liturgy, was the inspiration for this hymn. Henry Montagu Butler (1833–1918) wrote it for the boys at Harrow while he was headmaster of that famous school. It appeared first in the *Harrow School Hymn Book,* 1881, and subsequently was included in *The Public School Hymn Book,* 1903, and *The English Hymnal,* 1906. Percy Dearmer thought it a "little heavy for schoolboys" but added that "its fine moral passion makes it too good to be missed by adults." Butler served as headmaster at Harrow for twenty-six years and later became dean of Gloucester Cathedral and master of Trinity College, Cambridge. In 1889 he was appointed vice-chancellor of Cambridge University. His published works include *Ten Great and Good Men* (biographical), *Some Leisure Hours of a Long Life* (essays), and several books of sermons.

WOODLANDS   See No. 156 for comments on the tune.

353   Lord, I Want to Be a Christian

This is another instance of the grace and simplicity, the beauty and emotional intensity, of the Negro spirituals. See No. 179 for further comments on these religious folk songs of the American Negro.

I WANT TO BE A CHRISTIAN is one of a large number of Negro spirituals in the pentatonic mode. It can be played on the black keys of the piano, starting on *g* flat, or in any major key by starting on the tonic and omitting the fourth and seventh degrees of the scale. In some collections the second stanza reads: "I don't want to be like Judas in my heart"; and in many the refrain is "in-a my heart." The writer has seen a restless, unruly group of children transformed by the singing of this spiritual. Something of its simple, deep longing and its sincerity touched them, as it touches all who know it. It would be a fine hymn for a service of confirmation. In the Preface to *The Book of American Negro Spirituals*, James Weldon Johnson says that the spirituals voice all the cardinal virtues of Christianity — patience, forbearance, love, faith, and hope. "The Negro took complete refuge in Christianity," he says, "and the Spirituals were literally forged of sorrow in the heat of religious fervor." [16]

354   Who Trusts in God, a Strong Abode

Joachim Magdeburg (c. 1525–after 1587) was a Lutheran pastor who suffered many disappointments and hardships because of his strict adherence to Luther's teachings. A close friend and follower of Matthias Flacius Illyricus, he was opposed to Melancthon's views and held that many of Luther's adherents really falsified his doctrines. He was often banished and dispossessed, and on one occasion his house was burned. Nothing is known of the latter part of his life. The first stanza of the present hymn, originally beginning, "Wer Gott vertraut, hat wohl gebaut," has much in common with "Ein' feste Burg ist unser Gott," and was first published in his *Christliche und tröstliche Tischgesänge, mit vier Stimmen,* Erfurt, 1572. The second and third stanzas first appeared in Sethus Calvisius' *Harmoni Cantionum ecclesiasticarum,* Leipzig, 1597. The hymn was freely translated by Benjamin H. Kennedy (1804–1889), brilliant English classical scholar, in his *Hymnologia Christiana,* London, 1863, and was considerably altered by William W. How in *Psalms and Hymns,* 1864. This hymn is found in surprisingly few modern hymnals. See No. 252 for comments on How.

WAS MEIN GOTT WILL (ST. LUKE'S)   This is not the tune which appeared originally with Joachim Magdeburg's "Wer Gott vertraut, hat wohl gebaut" in *Christliche und tröstliche Tischgesänge,* 1572, which he edited. In that collection his one-stanza hymn, for use on Saturday evening, was set to a longer melody which he may have composed. (Zahn 8207a) There is one harmonization of it in Bach's *Choralgesänge.* The present tune, attributed to Claude de Sermisy (c. 1490–1562), was also in Magdeburg's book set to "Was mein Gott will, das g'scheh allzeit" (What my God wills is always best), the hymn with which it has had long and continuous association in German hymnody. It was the setting for the secular song "Il me souffit de tous mes maulx" in *Trente et quatre chansons musicales,* Paris, c. 1529, published by Pierre Attaingnant, the first French music printer. (Words and music are given on pages eleven and twelve in *Bach's Chorals,* Part I, by Charles S. Terry.) The melody appeared with a Flemish version of Psalm 140 in a collection printed at Antwerp in 1540. Sermisy was an accomplished singer and composer and was noted for his chansons. From 1508 to 1561 he served in various capacities at the royal musical establishments in Paris under Louis XII, Francis I, and Henri II.

Bach used WAS MEIN GOTT WILL in Cantatas 65, 72, 92, 103, 111, 144, and in the St. Matthew Passion, No. 31. In Cantata 92 the melody is used in five movements. In Cantatas 65, 92, and 103 it is associated with stanzas from two of Paul Gerhard's hymns. In German hymnody WAS MEIN GOTT WILL is the accepted setting for Magdeburg's "Wer Gott vertraut, hat wohl gebaut" as well as for the hymn from which its name is derived. It appears in contemporary German hymnals with the rhythmic freedom of its early form.

355 Who Trusts in God, a Strong Abode

See No. 354 for comments on the text.

BISHOPGARTH   At the request of the Prince of Wales who wanted a new hymn and tune to be sung in churches of the British Empire at home and abroad on June 20, 1897 — the Diamond Jubilee which marked the sixtieth anniversary of Queen Victoria's accession to the throne — Bishop William W. How wrote "O King of Kings, whose reign of old," for which Arthur Sullivan composed this tune. It was Sullivan's suggestion that any profits from the hymn and tune go to the Prince of Wales' Hospital Fund. Sullivan named the tune for the bishop's residence in Wakefield, where Dr. How went in 1888 as the first bishop of that diocese. "Garth" means yard, croft, or enclosed field near a house. See No. 185 for comments on Sullivan.

356 Make Me a Captive, Lord

Despite defective eyesight throughout his life, George Matheson (1842–1906) was one of the most learned and creative Scottish churchmen of the nineteenth century. Following graduation from Glasgow University with first honors in classics, logic, and philosophy, he was ordained in 1866 and became the assistant to Dr. J. R. Macduff in the Sandyford Church, Glasgow. Two years later he began an eighteen-year ministry at the Innellan Church, Argyllshire, a popular seaside resort area near the mouth of the River Clyde, where he gained recognition as a brilliant preacher and distinguished author. His first theological work, *Aids to the Study of German Theology,* 1874, established his reputation as a front-rank scholar. In 1886 he was called to St. Bernard's Parish Church, Edinburgh, with a communicant membership of two thousand, where he remained for thirteen notable years, exercising a marked influence on all who heard him, finally retiring due to ill health. As gifted as he was as a preacher and scholar, he was equally noted as a warm-hearted pastor and as a writer of devotional literature. Much of his success is to be credited to his faithful sister who learned Hebrew, Greek, and Latin to help him in his studies and who was his constant companion, guiding him on his daily rounds. Between his retirement from the ministry and his sudden death in 1906, he wrote more than a score of books. As he grew older his works took on an increasingly devotional character. The present hymn is from his *Sacred Songs,* 1890, where it appears under the title "Christian Freedom." Based on Ephesians 3:1 ("I Paul, the prisoner of Jesus Christ for you Gentiles"), it conveys with poetic truth and power the Christian paradox of losing life and thereby finding it.

LLANLLYFNI   Two Welshmen of rather unusual background are responsible for this fine tune. The melody is attributed to John Jones (1797–1857), a man endowed with "a personality of almost formidable strength." He had no formal schooling, learned to read at home, had some music instruction from a local harper, worked on roads and in the quarries as a young boy, and later became manager and one of the proprietors of a quarry at Tal-y-sarn. He received lessons from the famous Evan Evans, a Welsh Nonconformist divine, and in time became a lay preacher. In 1829 he decided to go into the ministry, was ordained in the Welsh Calvinistic Methodist church and became one of the most powerful preachers ever known in Wales, often speaking to thousands in open-air meetings. In spite of his scant schooling he acquired a great fund of knowledge, was an independent thinker of great vitality and, in the words of Millar Patrick, "more than anyone else was instrumental in breaking the tyranny of the hyper-Calvinists." He was an excellent musician with a deep voice of unusual range which added greatly to his powers as an orator. He was buried in Llanllyfni where a monument was erected to his memory. The name "Llanllyfni," made up of llan (church) and Llyfni, a small stream in Wales, means literally, "Church by Llyfni."

David Jenkins (1848–1915), arranger of the tune, had a meager education, was apprenticed to a tailor but left that trade for music, studying largely on his own until he became a pupil of Dr. Joseph Parry. (109) When he received his Mus.B. degree from Cambridge in 1878 he was in first place on the list of successful candidates for that degree. In 1899 he was appointed lecturer in music at University College, Aberystwyth, and later professor of music and head of the department. For many years he was precentor to the English Presbyterian Church at Aberystwyth. As competitor, and later as judge, he was a prominent figure at national and provincial Eisteddfodau. His compositions were numerous: songs, anthems, cantatas, oratorios, hymn tunes. It is said that more of his works were performed at the National Eisteddfod than those of any other composer.

LLANLLYFNI, the setting for Matheson's hymn in *The Church Hymnary, Revised,* 1927, has had wide use in the United States since its inclusion with these words in *The Hymnal,* 1933. (Presbyterian) Unlike many Welsh tunes, LLANLLYFNI has no repeated phrases. It is a fine tune of great strength and breadth and is an excellent setting for the words.

357 Strong Son of God, Immortal Love

As poet laureate of England for nearly half a century, Alfred, Lord Tennyson (1809–1892) has been called "the most entirely and typically English of any great poet since Shakespeare — more so even than Browning." One of his most intimate friends at Trinity College, Cambridge, was Arthur Hallam whose unexpected and untimely death in 1833 plunged him into prolonged and inconsolable grief. Seventeen years later, in 1850 (the year in which he married Miss Emily Sellwood, of whom he said, "The peace of God came into my life when I married her"), he published a long poem, *In Memoriam,* in tribute to his friend. The poem began with a prologue from which the present hymn has been taken, consisting of stanzas one, three, four, five, six, and seven. Among his many famous works are *Poems,* 1842, in two volumes; *Maud,* 1855; *Idylls of the King,* 1859; and *Harold,* 1876. He was elevated to the peerage in 1884, an honor that won universal acclaim. A man of refined tastes and restrained temperament, he is said to have spent an entire evening with a close friend, sitting by the fireside while they smoked their pipes without exchanging a word, and finally to have broken the silence by remarking as his friend left, "Thank you for a delightful evening!" An impressive list of other great figures came upon the scene in the year of his birth, including Abraham Lincoln, William Gladstone, Charles Darwin, Edgar Allen Poe, Frédéric Chopin, Felix Mendelssohn, and Oliver Wendell Holmes. Tennyson died at Aldworth, October 6, 1892, and was buried in Westminster Abbey.

ROCKINGHAM (MAYHEW) had its source in a tune called "Tunbridge" which was set to a hymn of Charles Wesley's in Aaron Williams' *Second Supplement* to the 1783 edition of *Psalmody in Miniature.* Its original form follows.

All ye that pass by, to Je - sus draw nigh. To you is i

noth-ing that Je - sus should die? Your ran-som and peace, your

sure-ty He is, Come see if there ev - er was sor-row like His.

In a copy of this "curious little tune-book" owned by Edward Miller (1731–1807) he wrote under "Tunbridge," "Would make a good long M.[eter]." In *The Psalms of David for the Use of Parish Churches,* 1790, which he edited, the tune, adapted to Long Meter and used seven times, had the heading "Part of the melody taken from a hymn-tune." Miller named it ROCKING–HAM for the Marquis of Rockingham, a patron and friend and twice prime minister of Great Britain.

Miller, the son of a stonemason, ran away from home in order to study music, became a skilled player of the German flute (transverse), and played in Handel's orchestra. Before going to Cambridge he studied with Charles Burney, the eminent musician and historian. In 1756 he was appointed organist of Doncaster Parish Church and retained the post until his death fifty-one years later. His Mus.D. degree from Cambridge was granted in 1786. A man of literary as well as musical attainments, he wrote on antiquarian subjects, published "The History and Antiquities of Doncaster" (1804), was the author of a treatise on harmony and composition and of articles on psalmody, edited a number of collections of psalm tunes, composed solos for the German flute, sonatas for the harpsichord, and wrote a book of "Easy Instructions" for the harpsichord which went through sixteen editions. He was zealous in his efforts to raise the standards of church music. Erik Routley says, "In his works he provides music for the three great sources of eighteenth-century hymnody — the psalms, Wesley and Watts."

ROCKINGHAM has had long association in English and American hymnody with Watts' "When I survey the wondrous cross" which first appeared with it in 1833. In Scotland it is known as COMMUNION because of long use with Paraphrase 35 (Matthew 26:26–29), " 'Twas on that night when doomed to know," which is used as a Communion hymn. In Lowell Mason's collections this tune is called MAYHEW.

358 Rock of Ages

Despite its later wide popularity, this hymn by Augustus M. Toplady (1740–1778) was largely overlooked for nearly half a century after it was written in 1776. The critical appraisals it has received have been as diverse as they have been pronounced. Described by John Hudson as "a medley of confused images, and accumulated, if not misapplied metaphors," it prompted Professor Saintsbury to exclaim, "Every word, every syllable, in this really great poem has its place and meaning," and led Oliver Wendell Holmes to refer to it as "the Protestant *Dies Irae*." Of its author, Dr. A. B. Gossart wrote: "He is no poet or inspired singer. He climbs no heights. He sounds no depths. He has mere vanishing gleams of imaginative light. His greatness is the greatness of goodness. He is a fervent preacher, not a bard." Yet, Earl Selborne solemnly declared, "Few writers of hymns had higher gifts than

Augustus Montague Toplady, author of 'Rock of Ages,' known to everybody, and by some esteemed the finest [hymn] in the English language." Perhaps the clue to the secret of its success and to its author's renown is revealed in Percy Dearmer's discerning comment that "a hymn may become popular by some heart-piercing quality which overrides its faults." That quality in Toplady's hymn may best be defined by the firm conviction, expressed in every line, that in God alone as he is known in Christ can man find forgiveness and an abiding security. The hymn first appeared at the conclusion of a rather strange and remarkable article by Toplady in the *Gospel Magazine* for March, 1776, in which he drew a comparison between the size of the National Debt and the enormity of man's sins, contending that neither could ever be paid off by human effort alone. The first two lines of stanza one and the fifth and sixth lines of stanza three were published in an earlier edition of the magazine in October, 1775, and the entire hymn was printed with the heading, "A living and dying Prayer for the Holiest Believer in the World." The only alteration, found in most hymnals, is in the last stanza, where the second line has been changed from "When my eye-strings break in death" to the present version.

Toplady was ordained in the Church of England and served as the vicar of the parish church in Broadhenbury, Devonshire, until the inclement climate affected his health and forced him to leave. Following that, for a short time he was the preacher at a chapel in Leicester Fields, London. An ardent Calvinist, he vigorously opposed John Wesley and his views, causing the latter to remark, "Mr. Augustus Toplady I know well; but I do not fight with chimney-sweepers." On one occasion, after a particularly heated exchange, Toplady retorted: "I do not expect to be treated by Mr. John Wesley with the candour of a gentleman or the meekness of a Christian; but I wish him, for his reputation's sake, to write and act with the honesty of a heathen." This unfortunate controversy has now been largely and happily forgotten and the better qualities of both men are what are remembered today. Much of Toplady's rancor undoubtedly can be attributed to poor health, caused by tuberculosis, which ended his life when he was only thirty-eight years of age.

TOPLADY (ROCK OF AGES; DEVOTION), the best-known of Thomas Hastings' tunes, composed in 1830 for this hymn, was one of the new melodies in *Spiritual Songs for Social Worship*, edited by Hastings and Lowell Mason. (See No. 348.) It was called ROCK OF AGES, the name which continued to appear with it in Hastings' books. The rhythm was altered and the tune named TOPLADY in Mason's *Sabbath Hymn and Tune Book*, 1859.

Thomas Hastings (1784–1872), chief pioneer in the development of choral singing and instruction in New York State, and the leading Presbyterian Church musician of his day, was born in Washington, Connecticut. When he was twelve his family moved by sleigh and ox sledge to Oneida County, New York, then frontier country. He taught himself the rudiments of music by studying a six-penny pamphlet and a treatise on music which his brother bought at an auction. At eighteen he was leading the village choir and beginning to make collections of hymns and tunes. After 1806 he taught in village schools, singing schools, and was a successful teacher of psalmody in Troy, Albany, and other eastern New York towns. After settling in Utica he took an active part in the Oneida County Handel and Burney Society for which he compiled his first publication, *The Utica Collection.* In 1816 it was combined with Warriner's *Springfield Collection,* 1813, and given the title *Musica Sacra.* This went through many editions and was popular for a quarter of a century.

From 1823 to 1832 Hastings edited *The Western Recorder,* a weekly periodical through which he expressed his views on religion and music. His *Dissertation on Musical Taste,* written in 1822, was widely read for a generation. In 1832 he was called to New York City by twelve Presbyterian churches to lead in the training of their choirs and to help them raise the standards of church music in the city. This joint enterprise continued for nearly a year. He lived and worked in New York until his death, serving for many years as choirmaster of the Bleecker Street Presbyterian Church, collaborating with Lowell Mason and William Bradbury in institutes and conventions, and continuing with conspicuous success as editor, lecturer, composer, author, choral conductor. New York University granted him an honorary Doctor of Music degree in 1858. Through his writings and through his activities he insisted on higher standards of "text, tune and performance" in church music, always stressing his belief that music in church was not for aesthetic purposes but for the furtherance of the gospel and the deepening of devotion, at all times subordinate to religion.

359 Rock of Ages

See No. 358 for comments on the text.

REDHEAD NO. 76   See No. 158 for comments on the tune.

360 Within the Maddening Maze of Things

This is a cento from John Greenleaf Whittier's poem "The Eternal Goodness," comprising stanzas eleven, eighteen, twenty, nineteen, and sixteen in that order. The poem began with the lines:

> O friends! with whom my feet have trod
> The quiet aisles of prayer.

As with so many of his best-known poems, it first appeared in *The Tent on the Beach, and other Poems,* 1867, from which several of his finest hymns have been taken. See No. 224 for comments on Whittier.

SONG 67   See No. 336 for comments on the tune.

361 Have Faith in God

After graduating from New College, London, Bryn Austin Rees (1911–) served Congregational churches at Sawbridgeworth, Hertfordshire, Ipswich, and Felixstone, Suffolk, and Muswell Hill, London. He was called to be the minister of the Woodford Green Congregational Church, Essex, in 1962. The present hymn was submitted in manuscript form to the committee that prepared *Congregational Praise*, 1951, where it first appeared in print.

SOUTHWELL   See No. 314 for comments on the tune.

362 Awake, My Soul, Stretch Every Nerve

As were many of his hymns, this hymn by Philip Doddridge was written to be sung following one of his sermons. Based on Philippians 3:12–14, it was given the title "Pressing on in the Christian Race" and was published posthumously in Doddridge's *Hymns, founded on various texts in the Holy Scriptures,* 1755, edited by Job Orton. Dr. Charles S. Robinson, American Presbyterian minister in New York State during the last half of the nineteenth century, who published many volumes of sermons and collections of hymns and tunes, remarked that the hymn is a "matchless challenge — ringing like a trumpeter's note to start the athletes." One of its particular strengths is its many scriptural allusions: Philippians 3:13–14, I Corinthians 9:24, Hebrews 12:1, II Timothy 4:8, and Revelation 4:10. All but the fourth stanza have been included in the present version, and these appear without alteration.

See No. 76 for further comments on Doddridge.

CHRISTMAS (SANDFORD; LUNENBERG; HARLEIGH) is adapted from the closing aria of Act II of Handel's opera *Siroe,* first performed in London in Feb. 1728, little more than a month after *The Beggar's Opera* had opened. Writing of *Siroe* in his *General History of Music,* Charles Burney said: "The final air of this act 'Non vi piacque, ingiusti Dei' is one of the most elegant, beautiful, and pathetic, in all Handel's works." The first part of the aria and its closing phrase were used for the hymn tune.

In J. H. Hewitt's *Harmonia Sacra,* Boston, 1812, and in several of Lowell Mason's collections, this tune is set to Doddridge's hymn, attributed to Handel, and called CHRISTMAS, a name said to have been given it because of its association with "While shepherds watched their flocks by night." In Weyman's *Melodia Sacra,* Dublin, 1815, it was called SANDFORD and set to a version of Psalm 132. The tune was named HARLEIGH and associated with "I asked them whence their vict'ry came?" in Thomas Hastings' *Musica Sacra,* 1817, and Joshua Leavitt's *Christian Lyre,* 1831.

See No. 193 for further comments on Handel.

363 A Mighty Fortress Is Our God

Described by James Moffatt as the "greatest hymn of the greatest man in the greatest period in German history," [1] this hymn by Martin Luther, based on Psalm 46, has been translated into nearly two hundred languages with more than sixty different English versions extant. Miles Coverdale was the first to translate it into English in his *Goostly Psalmes and Spiritualle Songes,* 1543–46, the first stanza reading as follows:

Oure God is a defence and towre
A good armour and good weapen,
He hath been ever oure helpe and sucoure
In all the troubles that we have ben in.
Therefore wyl we never drede
For any wonderous dede
By water or by londe
In hilles or the sea-sonde.
Our God hath them al i his hond.

It was not widely known or used in English-speaking countries, however, until the middle of the nineteenth century. The most popular version in England today is that by Thomas Carlyle ("A safe stronghold our God is still"), who said of it, "There is something in it like the sound of Alpine avalanches or the first murmur of earthquakes in the very vastness of which dissonance a higher unison is revealed to us." The present version is by Frederick H. Hedge (1805–1890), Unitarian minister and professor of ecclesiastical history at Harvard University and later professor of German at the same institution, and is from *Hymns for the Church of Christ,* 1853, of which he was co-editor. The hymn first appeared, according to the latest German research, in Michael Blum's *Enchiridion geistlicher gesenge und Psalmen,* Leipzig, 1528–29, and was probably inspired either by the historic meeting that took place at the Diet of Spires in 1529, which gave rise to the word *Protestant,* or by the persecutions that swept over southern Germany in 1527. Its success in Germany was immediate, and it quickly spread to other lands where Luther's teachings had taken root. Gustavus Adolphus had it sung by his entire army before the Battle of Leipzig, and Frederick the Great called it "God Almighty's grenadier march." The original first line "Ein feste Burg ist unser Gott," is appropriately inscribed on the monument to Luther in Wittenburg. Percy Dearmer calls it "the true national hymn of Germany." See No. 121 for comments on Luther.

EIN FESTE BURG   Tune and words of this great hymn are indissoluble and, like their creator, tower above the centuries. Schweitzer thinks that the melody is "woven out of Gregorian reminiscences" and says that "the recognition of this fact deprives the melody of none of its beauty and Luther of none of the credit for it; it really takes considerable talent to create an organic unity out of fragments." [27] (Albert Schweitzer, *J. S. Bach,* 1905) In an article in *Jahrbuch für Liturgik und Hymnologie,* 1960, Ursula Aarburg points out that four of Luther's hymn melodies (including EIN FESTE BURG and VON HIMMEL HOCH) seem to be related to a twelfth-century troubadour song. (The last two measures of these tunes are alike, and there are other melodic similarities.) Whatever the claims may be as to probable sources of this famous tune, they do not detract from the power and stirring quality of Luther's musical setting for his matchless hymn which has nerved, comforted, and uplifted generations of Christians. EIN FESTE BURG had the following form in a hymnbook published at Nürnberg in 1531 and in the second edition of Joseph Klug's *Geistliche Lieder,* 1535. (Zahn 7377a) This form of the melody is given at No. 219 in *Hymnal for Colleges and Schools,* 1956.

Ein fe - ste Burg ist un - ser Gott, ein gu - te Wehr und Waf - fen;
er hilft uns frei aus al - ler Not, die uns jetzt hat be - trof - fen.

Der alt bö - se Feind mit Ernst ers jetzt meint, gross Macht und

viel List sein grau-sam Rü-stung ist; auf Erd ist nicht seins Glei - chen.

There are many forms of the chorale melody and many harmonizations. The 4/4 version may have come from König's 1738 collection. (See No. 112.) Bach used EIN FESTE BURG in four movements of his Reformation festival Cantata No. 80 and in one chorale prelude for organ. There are two harmonizations of it in the *Choralgesänge*. The chorale, used again and again by composers, appears in the last movement of Mendelssohn's *Reformation Symphony* and in Meyerbeer's opera *Les Huguenots*. EIN FESTE BURG was sung by the Huguenots during the fearful persecutions between 1560 and 1572 when many died "joyfully as martyrs with this hymn upon their lips." In *Music, History and Ideas*, 1938, Hugo Leichtentritt writes:

One of Luther's immortal accomplishments is the Protestant chorale. . . . Since his intention was to make the common people in the churches sing the chorale tunes, he made them as plain and as popular as possible. At the same time he knew how to give them a dignified spiritual character, with no trace of vulgarity, of cheap popularity, emptiness or insignificance. . . . The melodies were new only in part; a number of them were taken over from the Ambrosian hymns of the Catholic Church, from medieval sequences, from Gregorian chant, and from German popular songs. Luther did not simply copy these old melodies; he changed them and adapted them to their new purposes with eminent insight and skill.[9]

It seems providential that one of the greatest figures in church history should have been endowed, as Luther was, with more than ordinary musical capacities and sensitivity. His knowledge of music was not by hearsay but from first-hand experience as a performer on the lute and the flute, as an amateur composer, as a well-schooled singer, and as a highly perceptive listener whose understanding of the merits and texture of music would have done credit to a professional. His much-quoted comment that Josquin des Près, his favorite composer, was "a master of the notes; others were mastered by them" is an instance of his keen judgment and his understanding and love of polyphonic music. Luther's frequent allusions to the power of music to drive away the devil should delight the musical therapists:

> I am not ashamed to confess publicly that next to theology there is no art which is the equal of music, for she alone, after theology, can do what otherwise only theology can accomplish, namely, quiet and cheer up the soul of man, which is clear evidence that the devil, the originator of depressing worries and troubled thoughts, flees from the voice of music just as he flees from the words of theology.

Luther knew the power of music in helping to shape the religion of people. His opponents knew it too. One wrote: "The whole people is singing itself into this Lutheran doctrine." His hymns penetrated into places where his other writings were excluded. In the foreword to Georg Rhau's *Symphoniae Iucundae,* 1538, he wrote:

> I truly desire that all Christians would love and regard as worthy the lovely gift of music, which is a precious, worthy and costly treasure given mankind by God. . . . Next to the Word of God, the noble art of music is the greatest treasure in this world.

See No. 121 for further comments on Luther.

364 Christian, Dost Thou See Them

John Mason Neale credited St. Andrew of Crete (c. 660–c. 732) with this hymn in his *Hymns of the Eastern Church,* 1862, from which the present translation was taken. The hymn appeared with the Greek incipit, "οὐ γὰρ Βλέπεις τοὺς ταράττοντας," and the caption, "Stichera for the Second Week of the Great Fast." (A stichera is a long hymn of loosely connected stanzas frequently found in Greek service books.) However, since no Greek hymn has been found from which the translation could come, many scholars regard this as an original work by Neale, based possibly on a line from some unknown Greek poem. Several alterations have been made, including a change in the second line of the first stanza, which originally read, "How the troops of Midian prowl and prowl around." Dr. C. S. Robinson said of this hymn: "It is one of the most vivid and dramatic presentations of our positions as Christians in the midst of an array of evil forces ever on the watch to overcome our resistance. A vigilance that never relaxes is our only safeguard; and as long as life lasts it is bound to be a struggle." St. Andrew of Crete, a native of Damascus, entered the monastery of St. Saba on the outskirts of Jerusalem at the age of fifteen. He was later made archbishop of Crete and was the author of many hymns, some of which are still sung in the Greek Church. He died on the island of Hierissus, near Mitylene, about 732.

See No. 110 for further comments on Neale.

ST. ANDREW OF CRETE was composed for this text and first published in the Appendix to the *Hymns Ancient and Modern,* 1868. See No. 79 for comments on Dykes.

365 Faith of Our Fathers

Shortly after joining the Roman Catholic Church, Frederick Faber published a collection of hymns, *Jesus and Mary; or, Catholic Hymns, for singing and reading,* 1849, which contained several of his own works. Among them was this hymn, which appeared in two versions, one for England and one for Ireland. The third stanza in the latter read as follows, and one should bear in mind that Ireland was predominantly a Catholic country:

> Faith of our fathers! Mary's prayers
> Shall keep our country fast to thee;
> And through the truth that comes from God,
> O we shall prosper and be free!

The same stanza in the version for England read:

> Faith of our fathers! Mary's prayers
> Shall win our country back to thee;
> And through the truth that comes from God,
> England shall then indeed be free.

It is the latter version that has been altered and adapted for use by Protestants. One of the earliest versions appeared in the Unitarian collection, *Hymns for the Church of Christ,* 1853, prompting John Julian to comment that "the hymn is regularly sung by Unitarians on the one hand, and by Roman Catholics on the other, as a metrical embodiment of their history and aspirations." Armin Haeussler has described it as "one of the great hymns of the entire Church." See No. 101 for comments on Faber.

ST. CATHERINE (TYNEMOUTH; FINBAR; PRINCE)   The tune, as well as the text, of this hymn has a Roman Catholic background. It was composed by Henri F. Hemy and first published in his *Crown of Jesus Music,* 1864, as the setting for a hymn to St. Catherine. It required only sixteen measures of music — the last eight measures which carry the refrain were added by James K. Walton (1821–1905) when he adapted Hemy's melody for use in his *Plainsong Music for the Holy Communion Office,* 1874.

Henri F. Hemy (1818–1888), born in Newcastle-on-Tyne, of German parents, was a Roman Catholic musician who served for many years as organist of St. Andrew's Roman Catholic church in Newcastle. He was also professor of music at Tynemouth, and taught singing and piano at St. Cuthbert's College, Ushaw, Durham. *The Crown of Jesus Music,* which was in four parts and contained Latin hymns, chants, masses, service music, and very little original music, was widely used in Catholic churches.

366 God of Grace and God of Glory

This stirring hymn by Harry Emerson Fosdick (1878–   ) was written in the summer of 1930 while he was vacationing at his home in Boothbay Harbor, Maine, for use at the dedication of Riverside Church in New York City, of which he was the minister. It was first sung at the opening service on October 5, 1930, and again at the dedication service on February 8, 1931, and has since become one of the most popular hymns by a modern author. More requests were received by the hymnal committee for this hymn to be included in the new *Pilgrim Hymnal* than for any other twentieth-century hymn. Dr. Fosdick was pastor of the First Baptist Church, Montclair, New Jersey, from 1904 to 1914, during which time he also taught homiletics at Union Theological Seminary in New York City. From 1915 until 1946 he was professor of practical theology at Union and, in the same period, served successively as the associate minister and preacher of the First Presbyterian Church (1919–1926) and minister of Park Avenue Baptist Church and Riverside Church (1926–1946), all in New York City. He was forced to resign from the first of these churches because of his pronounced liberal views. At this point John D. Rockefeller, Jr., invited him to become the pastor of the Park Avenue Church. At first Dr. Fosdick declined, saying that Mr. Rockefeller was "too wealthy," to which the latter replied, "Do you think more people will criticize you on account of my wealth than will criticize me on account of your heresy?" After laying down certain conditions, including the provision that a new church be built in "a less swank district," Dr. Fosdick accepted, and shortly thereafter Riverside Church was built. Preaching to enormous congregations and reaching millions of others by means of his radio broadcasts and many books, he became one of the most influential twentieth-century interpreters of religious belief and thought in America. Among his numerous and significant publications, in addition to several volumes of sermons, are *The Meaning of Prayer,* 1915; *The Modern Use of the Bible,* 1924; *A Guide to Understanding the Bible,* 1938; *On Being a Real Person,* 1938; and *The Living of These Days* (an autobiography), 1956.

CWM RHONDDA Dr. Fosdick's hymn was written with REGENT SQUARE (No. 117) in mind and fits it perfectly. That tune requires no repetition of the last line, and still appears with the words in some hymnals, notably *Hymnal for Colleges and Schools,* 1956. In reply to an inquiry about the setting of this hymn to CWM RHONDDA, Dr. Fosdick wrote: "My secretary has already written you the answer to your question about my hymn's divorce from 'Regent Square' and re-marriage to 'Cwm Rhondda.' The Methodists did it! And both here and abroad they are being followed."
See No. 93 for further comments on the tune.

367 Fight the Good Fight

Written for the nineteenth Sunday after Trinity, this hymn by John S. B. Monsell was based on I Timothy 6:12 ("Fight the good fight of faith, lay hold on eternal life") and first appeared in his *Hymns of Love and Praise for the Church's Year,* 1863. The lines also recall other scriptural texts, namely II Timothy 4:7–8; I Corinthians 9:24 and 26; and Ephesians 3:13. See No. 31 for comments on Monsell.

PENTECOST was given its name by William Boyd (1847–1928) who composed it for the classic Whitsuntide hymn "Veni Creator Spiritus" — "Come, Holy Ghost, our souls inspire" (No. 575) — at the request of his friend, Sabine Baring-Gould (51, 382) who wanted a simple tune for these words so that a group of Yorkshire colliers could sing them at a Whitsuntide meeting. Boyd, who was seventeen when he wrote the tune, said: "I walked, talked, slept and ate with the words, and at last evolved the tune which I naturally named Pentecost." This was in 1864. In 1868 the tune appeared with "Veni Creator" (571) in *Thirty-two Hymn Tunes composed by Members of the University of Oxford*. Arthur Sullivan was responsible for setting PEN–TECOST to "Fight the good fight" with which it is most often sung in the United States. (English hymnals assign other tunes to these words.) Boyd's account of Sullivan's use of the tune was given in the *Musical Times* XLIX (1908), 786–8. Part of his comment follows:

> One day, as I was walking along Regent Street, I felt a slap on my back, and turning round I saw my dear old friend Arthur Sullivan. "My dear Billy" he said, "I've seen a tune of yours which I must have." (He was then editing *Church Hymns*.) "All right," I said, "Send me a cheque and I agree." No copy of the book, much less a proof was sent to me, and when I saw the tune I was horrified to find that Sullivan had assigned it to "Fight the good fight"! We had a regular fisticuffs about it, but judging from the favour with which the tune has been received, I feel that Sullivan was right in so mating words and music." [28]

Boyd was born in Montego Bay, Jamaica, and had his early schooling at Hurstpierpont in England where Sabine Baring-Gould was his tutor. In later years when Baring-Gould was in Iceland he wrote frequently to Boyd and jotted down tunes that he had heard during his travels, three of which the pupil harmonized for his former tutor's book, *Iceland, Its Scenes and Sagas*, 1863. Boyd attended St. Edmund Hall and was organ scholar at Worcester College, Oxford, playing also at Trinity and Pembroke. After ordination he served for five years as rector of a church in Sussex and for twenty-five years as vicar of All Saints', Norfolk Square, London, retiring in 1918.

PENTECOST was sung to these words at the funeral service for Sir Winston Churchill at St. Paul's Cathedral, January 30, 1965.

368 Father, Hear the Prayer We Offer

Appearing originally in *Tiffany's Monthly*, 1859, as "Father, hear the prayer I offer," under the heading "Aspiration," this hymn by Mrs. Love Willis (1824–1908) was included in *Hymns of the Spirit*, 1864, edited by Samuel Johnson and Samuel Longfellow, in considerably altered form. It later appeared in two English collections, Horder's *Worship Song*, 1905, and *The English Hymnal*, 1906. Mrs. Willis was described by Erik Routley as "the only woman writer from America who has given us a famous hymn," exclusive of the "revivalist writers." She and her husband, Frederick L. H. Willis, a physician, made their home in Rochester, New York, and later in Glenora, Seneca Lake.

REGENSBURG is an abridged form of Johann Crüger's melody for Johann Franck's hymn "Herr, ich habe missgehandelt" (Lord, I have sinned and gone astray). Tune and words, inseparable in German usage, were published in Crüger's *Geistliche Kirchen-Melodien*, 1649. They were included in *The Chorale Book for England*, 1863, and may be seen at No. 326 in *The Lutheran Hymnal*, 1941 (Concordia) with Catherine Winkworth's English translation. The version of the melody given here is from *Louange et Prière*, 1957, where it is set to "Seigneur, tu donnes ta grâce." In German hymnals the name of the tune is the first line of Franck's hymn. REGENSBURG, the name given this altered version by the editors of the *Pilgrim Hymnal*, recalls the city in Bavaria where Crüger studied music with Paul Homberger, a pupil of Giovanni Gabrieli. There are two harmonizations of the melody in the *Choralgesänge* of Bach. See No. 29 for comments on Crüger.

369 God's Glory is a Wondrous Thing

Taken from Frederick Faber's *Hymns*, 1862, this hymn appeared with the title, "The Right Must Win." It consisted originally of nineteen stanzas, of which the present version is a cento of stanzas fifteen, eleven, twelve, thirteen, and nineteen, in that order. See No. 101 for comments on Faber.

HUMMEL The composer of this tune was one of the first thoroughly grounded musicians from abroad to settle in the United States. Heinrich C. Zeuner (1795–1875) was a native of Eisleben, the town where Luther was born and died. Before coming to America in 1824 (?1830) he had studied in Erfurt and Frankfurt-am-Main, had had works published and had been a court musician. In Boston he was organist of the Park St. Church for thirty years and of the Handel and Haydn Society from 1830 to 1837, and was its president for one year. In 1854 he went to Philadelphia and served as organist successively in St. Anne's Episcopal Church and the Arch Street Presbyterian Church. He was a highstrung, nervous, sensitive, intolerant person, and left one church precipitately, never to return, because he was questioned after a service about a rather elaborate fugue he had improvised. His last years were spent in Camden, in obscurity and isolation, clouded by periods of increasing depression which ended with suicide.

HUMMEL may have been named by Zeuner for the pianist who lived and studied with Mozart for two years and succeeded Haydn as Kapellmeister to Prince Esterhazy. Tradition has it that Zeuner studied with him. The tune was published in *The American Harp*, 1832, a collection of "new and original church tunes" all but five of which were composed by Zeuner. HUM–MEL was set to Faber's hymn in the *Harvard University Hymn Book*, 1926.

370 He Leadeth Me, O Blessed Thought

Joseph H. Gilmore (1834–1918), prominent Baptist minister and teacher, wrote these words following a midweek service he conducted at the First Baptist Church in Philadelphia in 1863. He had been invited to lecture on Psalm 23 in the church and later was taken to the home of Deacon Thomas Wattson. "During the conversation," as he recalled sometime afterward, "the blessedness of God's leadership so grew upon me that I took out my pencil, wrote the hymn just as it stands today, handed it to my wife, and thought no more of it. She sent it, without my knowledge, to the *Watchman and Reflector,* and there it first appeared in print. Three years later I went to Rochester, New York, to preach for the Second Baptist Church. President Anderson took me to their place of worship on the day after my arrival, and, on entering the chapel, I took up a hymnbook, thinking, 'I wonder what they sing!' The book opened at 'He Leadeth Me,' and that was the first time I knew that my hymn had found a place among the songs of the church." Dr. Gilmore was professor of logic, rhetoric, and English literature at the University of Rochester from 1868 until his retirement about 1911. The hymn is sung in all parts of the world and has been translated into many languages.

HE LEADETH ME   William B. Bradbury saw Dr. Gilmore's hymn in *The Watchman and Reflector,* composed the present tune for it, and published it in *The Golden Censer,* 1864, one of his numerous collections of Sunday school hymns and tunes. In the Preface he tells of his determination that "his best talents as a composer should be devoted to the Sabbath School cause." Commenting on the contents of the book he wrote:

> More than the usual number of scripture themes will here be found, while the most popular and appropriate modern feature, the ever-recurring "Refrain" and "Chorus," sung as children only *can* sing them, tend to fasten like "a nail in a sure place" the sentiment of the hymns.

In those words we have the explanation for the refrain in HE LEADETH ME and in many other Bradbury tunes. Three fermatas in Bradbury's arrangement have been omitted here. The harmonization is his throughout. See No. 178 for further comments on Bradbury.

371 He Who Would Valiant Be

In Part II of *Pilgrim's Progress,* published in 1684, following the conversation between Great-Heart and Valiant-for-Truth, this hymn is given as a summing up of all that John Bunyan (1628–1688) had been attempting to say in his great story. It is likely that he intended it to be sung inasmuch as it is cast in metrical form and inasmuch as Bunyan championed the singing of hymns in congregational worship. The hymn was modified for use in *The English Hymnal,* 1906, and in that revised form has been included in most modern hymnals. The first stanza originally read:

> Who would true Valour see,
>   Let him come hither;
> One here will Constant be,
>   Come Wind, come Weather.
> There's no Discouragement,
> Shall make him once Relent,
> His first avow'd Intent,
>   To be a Pilgrim.

This was the first hymn sung at Sir Winston Churchill's funeral in St. Paul's Cathedral, London, on January 30, 1965.

Bunyan was the son of a tinker (an itinerant mender of pots and pans), but unlike most children of such fathers, who traveled from place to place selling their services and wares, he grew up in one town, Bedford, where he attended the village school and learned to read and write. After passing through a period of emotional and religious crises, he joined the Baptist Church in Bedford and shortly thereafter was called to be the preacher, following the death of the minister. His fiery sermons drew large congregations but also got him into trouble with the government. He was arrested and sentenced to three months' imprisonment; but because he would not promise to refrain from preaching, he was incarcerated for twelve years. During this time he made and sold tagged laces to support his four children, his wife having died just prior to his imprisonment, and he wrote several books, including an autobiography that now ranks as a classic, *Grace Abounding to the Chief of Sinners,* 1666. Released in 1672 as a result of the Declaration of Indulgence, he returned to his preaching, but was again put in jail three years later when the Declaration was revoked. It was at this time that he began his famous work, *Pilgrim's Progress,* Part I, which appeared in 1678. Most of his other books and tracts, almost sixty in number, were written while he was in prison. He died in London of pneumonia as a result of catching a cold while traveling in the rain to help a friend, and was buried in Bunhill Fields. So highly esteemed was he among Independents (or Nonconformists) that he was affectionately known as Bishop Bunyan.

ST. DUNSTAN'S   Anne Woodward Douglas, widow of the composer of this fine tune, has given the following account of its origin:

> The tune, St. Dunstan's, was written in 1917 especially for Bunyan's words. From the time of his little boyhood Winfred Douglas was fascinated and excited by *The Pilgrim's Progress,* and he felt these words demanded a tune of strength and vigor. It was written on the train between Peekskill and New York, while he was living in St. Dunstan's Cottage, at St. Mary's School in Peekskill when he was acting as choir master of the Community of St. Mary and traveling to New York City several times a week to lecture in the Seminary.

Charles Winfred Douglas (1867–1944), priest, musician, scholar, poet, translator, editor, liturgiologist, explorer, lecturer, outstanding authority on plainsong and church music, made distinctive and unique contributions in a number of fields. He was born in Oswego, New York, the son of school-teaching parents (his father was superintendent of schools in Oswego) in whose home books and music played a large part. As a boy he showed more than usual interest in music, borrowed theory books and musical biographies from the library, copied music for a choirmaster and thus earned organ lessons and occasional opportunities to practice on the organ in the Presbyterian church. At sixteen, after the death of his father, he went to work in order to supplement the family income. He became organist of the Presbyterian church, worked in a hardware store, and also in a thermometer factory. At Syracuse University he continued to earn his way, clerking in a music store, singing in the choir of St. Paul's Episcopal Cathedral (his first contact with the Episcopal Church) serving as assistant organist at the cathedral and as choirmaster of St. Paul's Mission. He also assisted in the music department of the university as accompanist, and sang and played frequently in churches in Oswego, Marcellus, and at a mission on the Onondaga Indian Reservation. In 1891 he received the Bachelor of Music degree from Syracuse and during the following academic year remained in the music department as assistant instructor in vocal music. His duties at St. Paul's had deepened his interest in the church and before his graduation he was accepted as a candidate for Holy Orders. In 1892 he served as organist at the Church of Zion and St. Timothy in New York City, staying until the spring of 1893. He returned in the summer to St. Andrew's Divinity School, Syracuse, was ordained deacon in October, 1893, and on his return to New York City served as curate at the Church of the Redeemer, with responsibility for the music, and also taught at St. John's parochial school. One night he was found lying unconscious near the organ on which he had been practicing, and after several weeks in the hospital, went to Denver to build up his strength and remained there three years as minor canon at St. John's Cathedral. In 1896 he married Dr. Mary Josepha Williams, a physician, whose family had spent many summers camping in the area of Evergreen, Colorado, where in later years the Mission of the Transfiguration was established on property provided by the Douglases. (Mrs. Douglas died in 1938. He married again in 1940.)

Canon Douglas was ordained to the priesthood at the little mission in Evergreen in August, 1899. The following years were divided between Denver and New York with frequent stops in Chicago, Fond du Lac, and Kenosha, Wisconsin, lecturing, teaching, and taking part in a variety of musical activities. During several trips abroad he studied plainsong with the Benedictines of Solesmes who were then temporarily established on the Isle of Wight. The teaching of plainsong, which he began in 1906 at the convent of the Community of St. Mary (Protestant Episcopal) in Kenosha, Wisconsin, remained a paramount interest for the rest of his life. Through lectures, teaching, and publications he did more than any one person in America to break down the prejudice against the singing of plainsong in Protestant churches and to make it available for choirs and congregations. He stands out as one of the great figures in the history of American church music. He was music editor of the *New Hymnal* (Episcopal), 1918, and of *The Hymnal 1940,* one of the outstanding books in the history of American hymnody. The lectures he delivered at Seabury-Western Theological Seminary were published in 1937 as *Church Music in History and Practice,* a classic, revised by Leonard Ellinwood in 1962.

372 How Firm a Foundation

Although written in England by an unknown English author, this hymn has had its greatest success in the United States. It first appeared in John Rippon's *A selection of Hymns from the best authors, intended as an Appendix to Dr. Watts's Psalms and Hymns,* 1787, where it was simply attributed to "K." Various proposals have been made as to who "K" might have been but the most plausible seems to be that of John Julian who held that the letter referred to Robert Keen, precentor in Rippon's church in London. See No. 195 for comments on Rippon. The hymn is based on several scriptural texts, most notably II Timothy 2:19, Isaiah 43:12, and Hebrews 13:5. It was a favorite hymn of both Theodore Roosevelt and Robert E. Lee and was sung at their funeral services.

ADESTE FIDELES (PORTUGUESE HYMN) The association of "How firm a foundation" with ADESTE FIDELES is peculiar to American hymnody and may date from *Temple Melodies,* 1851, edited by Darius E. Jones (1815–1881). Darius Jones was a business man who became associated with Lowell Mason and George Webb in editing *The Choral Advocate,* a monthly musical journal, and subsequently edited *The Congregational Herald* in Chicago. He felt called to the ministry and was ordained in 1858. He served in the Iowa General Association and for four years was connected with Iowa College — later Grinnell. When he was directing the music at the Plymouth Church in Brooklyn, Henry Ward Beecher asked him to compile a hymnal which would contain both words and music so that the congregation would sing. Those in the pews had only the words of the psalm versions and hymns, with no music, and gradually they had found it easy to let the choir take full responsibility for the singing. One of the new features of *Temple Melodies* was the printing of the hymns on the same pages with the tunes to which they were to be sung, a format which became the norm in subsequent hymnals.

ADESTE FIDELES had been included in many American tune books before 1851 with a variety of texts. "How firm a foundation," set to this tune, was Gen. Robert E. Lee's favorite hymn, and was sung at his funeral. This hymn did not gain a foothold in the Church of England nor among Wesleyans or Presbyterians of Great Britain; it was sung to some extent by Congregationalists, but mostly by Baptists. In the English hymnals which contain it there is no repetition of the last line, and the musical settings are generally in triple time. See No. 132 for further comments on the tune.

373 God is My Strong Salvation

This is another fine example of James Montgomery's skill in distilling the essence of a psalm by means of a free paraphrase. Based on Psalm 27, it was first published in his *Songs of Zion,* 1822. See No. 25 for comments on Montgomery.

MEIN LEBEN (CHRISTUS DER IST MEIN LEBEN; BREMEN; CHRIST IS MY LIFE; VULPIUS; PHUVAH) is another fine melody by Melchior Vulpius from *Ein schön geistlich Gesangbuch,* 1609, in which it was set to the funeral hymn "Christus, der ist mein Leben." There are two harmonizations of this tune in Bach's *Choralgesänge,* one in 3/4 of rare beauty. In the first part of the opening chorale chorus of Cantata 95, "Christus der ist mein Leben," Bach uses Vulpius' melody. The present version of the melody, slightly different from the original, is that used by Bach, from Crüger's *Praxis pietatis melica* 1662. A number of German hymnals, and some Lutheran hymnals published in the United States, use the original form of the melody with the hymn for which it was the setting in 1609. (Zahn 132)

Chri-stus, der ist mein Le-ben, Ster-ben ist mein Ge-winn;

dem thu ich mich er-ge-ben, mit Fried fahr ich da-hin.

In order to use MEIN LEBEN with Common Meter as well as with 7.6.7.6. some editors have substituted two quarter notes for the half notes in measures 2 and 6. This C.M. form appears in several of Lowell Mason's collections with the strange name PHUVAH. Above the music in his *Cantica Laudis,* 1850, Mason wrote: *"One of the best German tunes."* Both form and name of the melody were taken over by editors of other American collections. See No. 184 for comments on Vulpius.

374 In the Hour of Trial

Derived from Jesus' word to Peter, "I have prayed for thee, that thy faith fail not" (Luke 22:32), this hymn by James Montgomery was written on October 13, 1834, but was not published until 1853 with the appearance of Montgomery's last collection, *Original Hymns for Public, Private, and Social Devotion.* It was extensively altered by Mrs. Frances A. Hutton (1811–1877) in *Supplement and Litanies,* edited by her husband, Henry Wollaston Hutton. The second line of the first stanza originally read, "Jesus, pray for me," but this was criticized as being unscriptural, despite the text on which it was based and other scriptural references, notably John 17:9. Montgomery later changed it to "Jesus, stand by me." Godfrey Thring, in *The Church of England Hymnbook,* revised edition 1882, is responsible for its present form. See No. 25 for comments on Montgomery.

PENITENCE (LANE) Dissatisfaction on the part of an organist-choirmaster prompted the writing of this tune. One Sunday morning when Spencer Lane (1843–1903) was given the list of hymns to be sung at the evening service of St. James' Church in Woonsocket, Rhode Island, he found one set to a tune he did not like. While his wife prepared dinner he composed PEN–ITENCE, had it sung at the evening service, and afterwards was asked by Bishop Clarke of Rhode Island where this particular tune had come from. When Lane told him that it was his own composition the bishop said, "That will make you famous." At the suggestion of the rector the tune was sent to Dr. Charles L. Hutchins who included it in *The Church Hymnal,* 1879, as the third tune for the present text. Lane, who was born in Tilton, New Hampshire, left school at the outbreak of the Civil War to enlist in the Union Army and served for more than three years. After study at the New England Conservatory of Music he taught voice and instrumental music in New York City. He opened a music store in Woonsocket, Rhode Island, and for thirteen years was organist and choirmaster of St. James' church there. Later he directed the music in churches in Monson, Massachusetts, and Richmond, Virginia, and at All Saints' Church, Baltimore, for seven years. He was a member of a music firm in that city until his death.

375 Lead On, O King Eternal

On the occasion of his graduation from Andover Theological Seminary in 1888, Ernest Warburton Shurtleff (1862–1917) was asked by his classmates to write an appropriate hymn. He obliged by writing these words, which met with instant success and were published that same year in his *Hymns of the Faith*. Subsequently he held three important pastorates in California, Massachusetts, and Minnesota. In 1905 he founded the American Church in Frankfurt, Germany, and the following year began a significant work among American students at the Academy Vitti in Paris, where he served as the director of student activities and remained until his death in 1917. Although he published several volumes of poems, his lasting fame rests upon this hymn.

LANCASHIRE is the favored setting for these words in the majority of hymnals published in the United States. See No. 192 for comments on the tune.

376 Lead Us, O Father

Entitled "Prayer for Guidance," this hymn by William H. Burleigh (1812–1871) was written sometime prior to 1859. The original source is often given as *Lyra Sacra Americana*, 1868, an English collection of American hymns edited by C. D. Cleveland, but it appeared earlier in *The New Congregational Hymn Book*, 1859, and may have been published before that date. Burleigh, a descendant on his mother's side of Governor William Bradford of Plymouth Plantation, was a Unitarian and an ardent abolitionist. After working as a printer and journalist in Pittsburgh, he became the editor of *The Christian Freeman*, an antislavery paper published in Hartford, Connecticut. From 1849 to 1855 he was associated with the New York State Temperance Society, and lived in Syracuse and Albany. The last fifteen years of his life were spent in Brooklyn, New York, where he served as the harbor master of New York City. For some time his wife was the minister of the Unitarian Church in Brooklyn, Connecticut. She later wrote his biography, to which she added several of his poems. His hymns, often marked by an underlying quality of melancholy, are more known and used in England than in America, due largely to the wide popularity of *Lyra Sacra Americana*.

LANGRAN See No. 287 for comments on the tune. The present harmonization differs slightly from the original.

377 Lift Thy Head, O Zion, Weeping

Like so many of the German chorales and the Negro spirituals, this hymn came out of an experience of intense suffering. In 1674, during a period of ruthless persecution of Protestants by Jesuits and the wealthy classes in Hungary, forty-one Protestant (mostly Reformed) ministers, after refusing to renounce their faith, were sold as galley slaves and condemned to be chained to oars on ships that plied their trade between Trieste and Naples. Among these unfortunate prisoners was Karoly Jeszensky, who wrote this hymn, now known as the "Hymn of the Hungarian Galley Slaves," while enduring this servitude. It was sung as he and his fellow prisoners pulled at the oars in their backbreaking task. In its cadenced lines and music, one can almost feel the measured movements of the rowers and the sweep of the oars. Eventually news of their brutal treatment became known in Europe and brought vigorous protests. When they were finally released in 1676, as a result of the intervention of the Dutch ambassador at Vienna and the payment of a huge sum of money, the hymn was sung to celebrate their emancipation, and it has since become, in Armin Haeussler's words, "the 'Ein feste Burg' of all Hungarian Protestants." The present translation was made in 1938 by William Toth (1905–1963) who was pastor of the Evangelical and Reformed Church of South Norwalk, Connecticut, at the time. He was professor of history and archeology at Franklin and Marshall College, Lancaster, Pennsylvania, from 1946 until his resignation in 1963, shortly before he died.

MAGYAR   The name of this anonymous melody was suggested by Dr. William Toth, translator of the hymn. In a letter to Dr. J. P. Meyer, chairman of the committee that edited *The Hymnal*, 1941, he wrote: "If HUNGARIAN GALLEY SLAVES is too cumbersome . . . I would suggest MAGYAR REFORMATUS, meaning 'Hungarian Reformed,' or MAGYAR MARTYR, or simply MAGYAR. Magyar means Hungarian." There are only two rhythmic patterns in MAGYAR: (a) ♩♪ ♩♩ | ♩♩♩ | 𝅝 | (b) ♩♪♩♩ | ♩♩ | 𝅝 | The melody is tightly knit, with considerable repetition and imitation. Its first three measures supply the basic thematic material. A time signature of 3/1 would be fitting for this tune and would keep it from sounding piecemeal.

378 Lord of Our Life, and God of Our Salvation

Toward the close of the Thirty Years' War (1618–1648), Matthäus Appelles von Löwenstern (1594–1648) wrote a "Sapphic Ode: for spiritual and temporal peace." "Christe, du Beistand deiner Kreuzgemeine," which vividly described the perils faced by the church and bravely affirmed the supremacy of God. It was first published in *Geistliche Kirchen- und Hauss-Musik*, Breslau, 1644. Three hundred years later Philip Pusey (1799–1855), brother of Dr. Edward B. Pusey, renowned leader of the Oxford Movement, and a man of wide learning and great culture in his own right, wrote this free paraphrase of von Löwenstern's ode. It was published in A. R. Reinagle's *Psalm and Hymn Tunes*, 1840. In writing to his brother, Philip Pusey commented on this hymn: "It refers to the state of the Church — that is to say, the Church of England in 1834 — assailed from without, enfeebled and distracted within, but on the eve of a great awakening." Both the original and the paraphrase, therefore, seem to have come from similar circumstances, although Percy Dearmer in *Songs of Praise Discussed,* 1933, takes exception to this, arguing that in 1834 the Church was in a position of strength rather than weakness. Löwenstern was the son of a saddler and was recognized both for his business ability and musical talent. He wrote approximately thirty hymns, set to his own melodies, and served as music director in the courts of Ferdinand II and his son, Ferdinand III, the latter of whom raised him to the nobility.

ISTE CONFESSOR (ROUEN)   In *The English Hymnal,* 1906, two different French Church melodies are named ISTE CONFESSOR. The present tune is the second of these: ISTE CONFESSOR (2). The source given for it, "Rouen Church Melody," accounts for its alternative name. However, in *The French Diocesan Hymns and their Melodies,* 1954, Cyril E. Pocknee has said that this is a mistaken ascription and that the tune is from a Poitiers antiphoner of 1746, where it was set to the traditional eighth-century Latin hymn for a confessor, "Iste Confessor Domini sacratus" ("This confessor of the Lord"). In the 1777 edition of LaFeillée's *Méthode* (see No. 41) which is dedicated to the bishop of Poitiers, this is the only melody to bear the caption "Hymne." The editor says that he has included it in order to show the difference between it and the older chants. See No. 59 for comments on French Church Melodies.

379   Lord of Our Life, and God of Our Salvation

See No. 378 for comments on the text.

CLOISTERS was composed for this hymn by Sir Joseph Barnby and published in the Appendix to *Hymns Ancient and Modern,* 1868. See No. 35 for comments on Barnby.

380   March on, O Soul, With Strength

George Thomas Coster (1835–1912) wrote this stirring hymn, based on Judges 5:21 as given in the American Revised Version ("O my soul, march on with strength"), in 1897, during a period of ill-health and while he was without a pastorate. Ordained as a Congregational minister in England, he suffered all his life with a weak constitution and often had to resign a charge because of the need to rest and recuperate. Nevertheless, he was an effective pastor and engaged in a wide range of useful and successful activities. He founded a Hospital for Poor Sick Children in Hull, now Victoria Hospital, and was instrumental in establishing the Guild of Brave Poor Things, an organization designed to help the blind and crippled to help themselves. He also took the lead in having shelters built in London for cold and hungry cabmen. He published several volumes of poetry and other works. This hymn first appeared in an American hymnal, the *Pilgrim Hymnal*, in 1904.

ARTHUR'S SEAT, the setting for "Hark, hark the notes of joy" in Roswell D. Hitchcock's *Hymns and Songs of Praise*, 1874, was headed: "Arranged from John Goss, 1800–   ." The music editors of this hymnal were John Knowles Paine (1837–1906), professor of music and chapel organist at Harvard University for twenty years, the first incumbent of a chair of music in an American university, and Uzziah C. Burnap (1834–1900), New York merchant, prolific composer and organist of the Church on the Heights in Brooklyn (see No. 230). ARTHUR'S SEAT appeared with the present text in the *Pilgrim Hymnal*, 1904.

Geographicaly speaking, Arthur's Seat is a hill overlooking Edinburgh, named, it is believed, for the British King Arthur who is said to have watched from its heights the defeat of the Picts by his followers. It is not known why the name of this hill came to be associated with the present tune.

381 My Faith, It Is an Oaken Staff

Taken from Thomas Toke Lynch's *The Rivulet*, 1855, this has been called the "best of his hymns" by K. L. Parry in the *Companion to Congregational Praise*, 1953. It was strangely overlooked until its appearance in *Congregational Praise*, 1951. See No. 245 for comments on Lynch.

THE STAFF OF FAITH   There are only six measures of melody to learn in this Swiss folk tune: the first, second, and fourth phrases are identical, the third phrase is made up of a repeated two-measure figure. The tune, with these words, was introduced into English usage through the *Fellowship Hymn Book*, 1910.

382 Onward, Christian Soldiers

As curate of the church in Horbury, Sabine Baring-Gould was responsible for the mission at Horbury Bridge, a short distance away. It was the custom there for the children to march in procession from one village to another during Whitsuntide with cross and banners "going on before." This hymn was written so that the children might sing as they marched. It met with instant success and has remained an enduring favorite. Thirty years after writing it Baring-Gould commented: "It was written in great haste, and I am afraid some of the rhymes are faulty. Certainly, nothing has surprised me more than its popularity." It was first published in *The Church Times*, October 15, 1864, and was later included in the 1868 Supplement to *Hymns Ancient and Modern*. A story is told of a bishop on one occasion ordering the cross to be left behind as a procession was about to get under way in one of his churches. In whimsical retaliation the choristers were heard to sing at the end of each chorus, "Left behind the door" in place of the original words. Percy Dearmer has said that "Baring-Gould was thinking of his happily united children when he wrote in verse three, 'We are not divided,' " and not of the church universal. Two stanzas have been omitted. See No. 51 for further comments on Baring-Gould.

ST. GERTRUDE was named for Mrs. Gertrude Clay-Ker-Seymer, in whose home at Hanford, Dorsetshire, Sullivan was a guest when he composed this tune for Baring-Gould's text. In a letter to the *Musical Times* of July, 1902, Mrs. Clay-Ker-Seymer wrote of Sullivan being a frequent guest in her home, often for weeks at a time, and of singing ST. GERTRUDE in the private chapel attached to the house, with Sir Arthur playing the harmonium. There is little doubt that the tune is largely responsible for the fame and popularity of the hymn. *The Hymnary,* 1872, edited by Joseph Barnby, was the first hymnal to include ST. GERTRUDE, a year after its first appearance in the *Musical Times* of December, 1871. The first tune to which these words were sung by the children of Horbury Bridge mission was ST. ALBAN (or HAYDN), an arrangement of the slow movement of Haydn's *Symphony in D,* No. 15. (see *The English Hymnal,* 1906, No. 643.) See No. 185 for comments on Sullivan.

383 Forward Through the Ages

Among the gifted Unitarian hymn writers that America has produced, Frederick Lucian Hosmer (1840–1929) deserves to be placed in the first rank. He served both Congregational and Unitarian churches in Massachusetts, Illinois, Ohio, Missouri, and California, and because of his scholarly interests in hymnody was invited to give a series of lectures on the subject at the Harvard Divinity School in 1908. He wrote the present hymn in 1908 and included it in the 1918 edition of *The Thought of God in Hymns and Poems,* which he edited jointly with William C. Gannet and which contained 56 of his own hymns. These are more poetic and literary than biblical and evangelical, and they reflect the growing social concern within the churches of his time.

ST. GERTRUDE. See No. 382 for comments on the tune.

384 Soldiers of Christ, Arise

Based on Ephesians 6:10–18, with the title, "The Whole Armour of God," this hymn by Charles Wesley consisted originally of sixteen eight-line stanzas and first appeared in the Wesley brothers' *Hymns and Sacred Poems,* 1749. "The mastered simplicity of this," said Percy Dearmer, "its faultless technique, its sagacity in the use of imperfect rhymes, are signs of high accomplishment." [8] William Thomas Stead noted that it was "as inspiring as the blast of a bugle." See No. 43 for comments on Wesley.

DIADEMATA The use of this tune with the present hymn is peculiar to American hymnody and less general than might be supposed by those to whom the combination seems indissoluble. In most English hymnals and in a number of those published in the United States DIADEMATA appears only with "Crown Him with many crowns" for which it was written. In some books Wesley's hymn is set to an eight-measure tune. See No. 199 for comments on DIADEMATA.

385 Stand up, Stand up for Jesus

George Duffield (1818–1888) came from a distinguished Presbyterian family and perpetuated that heritage in his own ministry, serving Presbyterian churches in New York, Pennsylvania, Illinois, and Michigan. Among his intimate friends was a young Episcopal clergyman, Dudley Atkins Tyng, rector of the Church of the Epiphany in Philadelphia. In 1858, during the time that religious revivals were sweeping the country, Tyng preached one Sunday to a congregation of over five thousand young men in Jaynes' Hall. The following Wednesday he was severely injured in an accident in which he lost his arm. He died in the hospital shortly afterwards with this parting message for the young men attending the revival: "Tell them to stand up for Jesus." Duffield preached to an immense congregation the following Sunday on the text "Stand therefore, having your loins girt about with truth, and having on the breastplate of righteousness" (Ephesians 6:14), and concluded his sermon with the words of this hymn written in tribute to his colleague and friend. First published in flyleaf form for Sunday school children, the hymn later appeared in a Baptist newspaper and then successively in garbled form in the *Church Psalmist,* 1858, and in its present form in *Lyra Sacra Americana,* 1868. It has been translated into many languages and has been sung in all parts of the world. Duffield wrote in a letter dated May 29, 1883, "I knew young Tyng as one of the noblest, bravest, *manliest* men I ever met."

WEBB (MORNING LIGHT; GOODWIN) The first association of this tune with the present words — an association which has become universal — seems to have been in William B. Bradbury's *Golden Chain of Sabbath School Melodies,* 1861. On one page in this small collection "The morning light is breaking" was printed with the present tune. On the opposite page the words of "Stand up, stand up for Jesus" and two other hymns were printed with the caption "Hymns to the tune 'Webb.' " Evidently this suggested combination spread like wildfire and in time carried the tune and the words to all parts of the world. It is another instance of the influence of Bradbury's Sunday school publications. (See No. 319.) See No. 305 for further comments on WEBB.

386 Lighten the Darkness

The somber background that characterizes this hymn is a reflection of the life of Frances Mary Owen (1842–1883) whose untimely death at an early age ended the career of a talented author. The wife of the Rev. Albert Owen, assistant master at Cheltenham College, she actively engaged in philanthropic work and wrote several books, including *John Keats: A Study; Soldier and Patriot: A Life of George Washington;* and *Essays and Poems.* The present hymn first appeared anonymously in *Trefoil, Verses by Three,* 1868.

SONG 24 was the setting for Mrs. Owen's poem in *The English Hymnal,* 1906, and in the Enlarged Edition of *Songs of Praise,* 1931. See No. 207 for further comments on WEBB.

387 Through the Night of Doubt and Sorrow

Idolized by the people of Denmark during his lifetime, Bernard Severin Ingemann (1789–1862) was both a scholar and a popular writer whose historical novels, modeled after those by Sir Walter Scott, were enormously successful. In his youth he helped defend Copenhagen against the English during the Napoleonic Wars, and as a result of this experience he was an intense patriot all his life. In 1822, following a period of foreign study and travel, he was appointed lector of Danish language and literature at the Academy of Sorö, in a quiet cathedral town on the island of Zeeland, where he remained for forty years until his death in 1862. His children's stories were almost as widely read and as much beloved as those by Hans Christian Anderson. In addition, he wrote many poems and hymns and edited the official church hymnal, *Nyt Tillaeg til Evangelisk-christelig, Psalmebog,* Copenhagen, 1859, in which the present hymn first appeared. It was written in 1825 and originally began, "Ggjennem Nat og Traengsel." The translation is by Sabine Baring-Gould and was first published in *The People's Hymnal,* 1867, edited by Richard F. Littledale. See No. 51 for comments on Baring-Gould. On the occasion of his seventieth birthday Ingemann was given a beautiful golden horn engraved with figures from his poems and presented to him by the school children of Denmark whose half-penny contributions had made the gift possible.

ST. ASAPH is associated with the present text only in hymnals of the United States. Musical settings for it in Canada and England are varied and include tunes of Dykes, Parry, and Martin Shaw. ST. ASAPH was composed in 1872 for a hymn of thanksgiving for the recovery of the Prince of Wales (Edward VII) from a long and severe attack of typhoid fever. Many hymns and anthems were composed for services of thanksgiving and rejoicing which were held throughout the United Kingdom on February 7, 1872.

William S. Bambridge (1842–1923) was born in New Zealand but lived in England from the time he was six years old. For a year he was a chorister at St. George's, Windsor; at ten he was appointed organist of Clewer Church. He studied music at the Royal Academy of Music, was a Fellow of the Royal College of Organists, and received the Bachelor of Music degree from Oxford in 1872. From 1864 to 1911 he served as organist and choirmaster of Marlborough College, Wiltshire, and as conductor of the college and Marlborough choral societies. He was active in civic affairs as a member of the Marlborough town council for forty years and as mayor for two terms. For many years he was Masonic grand organist in England.

388 The Son of God Goes Forth to War

This militant hymn by Bishop Heber, written for St. Stephen's Day, the day after Christmas, was first published posthumously in his *Hymns written and adapted to the Weekly Church Service of the Year,* 1827. Reference to St. Stephen, the first Christian martyr, is made in the second stanza. It has remained unaltered since it was written. See No. 58 for comments on Heber.

ALL SAINTS NEW   With vested choirs in the chancels of liturgical and free churches an accepted part of the American scene, it comes as a surprise to read of the bitter opposition that met Henry Cutler's innovations as an organist-choirmaster a hundred years ago. A native of Boston, Cutler (1824–1902) had his early schooling and musical training there, studying later in Frankfurt, Germany, and traveling extensively in England where he fell under the spell of the cathedral services and familiarized himself with the details of the liturgical practices and ideals of the Oxford Movement. Back in Boston he served as organist and choirmaster of Grace Church before going to the Church of the Advent, one of the pioneers of the Oxford Movement in this country. The choir of men and boys which he organized there was distinguished for its singing and was one of the first vested choirs in the United States.

In 1858 when Cutler went to Trinity Church in New York City as organist and choirmaster there were two women, ten boys, and seven men in the choir. The women, the last to sing in the choir at Trinity, were dismissed a few months after his arrival, and within the first year Cutler succeeded in moving the choir from the gallery to the chancel, in having psalms chanted, and in having some parts of the service sung. Surplices were presented to the choir in 1859, but it took the Prince of Wales to put them into service! In *The History of the Choir and Music of Trinity Church,* 1906, Arthur H. Messiter (345) gives the following details of how and when this was accomplished:

> We come now to the interesting event of the introduction of choir vestments; this matter, which had so long been agitating the minds of Vestry, congregation and choir, was happily settled by the visit of the Prince of Wales. When His Royal Highness notified his intention of attending service at Trinity Church, it was deemed most proper that the service should be carried out in a manner worthy of the occasion, which certainly called for the vestments as used in the Church of England. To prevent any possible awkwardness on the occasion, the choir wore their surplices on the previous Sunday, October 7. [1860] On the first Sunday when the choir was vested, two reports were heard during the second lesson, and a musket ball fell in one of the pews without hurting anyone. Whether this was simply an accident or a hostile demonstration was never discovered.[29]

Cutler remained at Trinity until two weeks after the Easter service in 1865. At that time he set out on a concert tour with three members of the Trinity choir, and when his absence was discussed by the rector and the vestry, it was decided that his appointment as organist should be terminated on June 30, for "absence without leave." After this unexpected turn of events Cutler served in churches in Brooklyn, Providence, Philadelphia, and Troy before his retirement in 1885, after which he returned to Boston. In 1864 Columbia University honored him with a Doctor of Music degree. Cutler wrote anthems, service music, organ music, and published *The Trinity Psalter*, 1864, and *Trinity Anthems*, 1865.

ALL SAINTS NEW was set to these words and first published in *The Hymnal with Tunes Old and New*, 1872, edited by the Rev. J. Ireland Tucker.

389 O God of Bethel, by Whose Hand

Among hymns of a composite character, this is one of the finest. The original version was a paraphrase of Genesis 28:20–22 by Philip Doddridge. It was slightly changed in the Scottish *Translations and Paraphrases*, 1745, and considerably revised by John Logan (1748–1788), onetime Scottish preacher who left the ministry because of intemperate habits. He included the hymn in his *Poems*, 1781, and claimed it as his own. That same year a revised edition of the *Translations and Paraphrases* was published with a version of the hymn as it is largely known today. James Moffatt has said that it "holds a place in the affections of all Scotsmen second only to 'The Lord's my Shepherd, I'll not want.' " See No. 76 for comments on Doddridge.

DUNDEE   See No. 87 for comments on the tune.

390 As Pants the Hart

Consisting originally of thirteen stanzas, of which the present version uses stanzas one, two, and twelve, this free paraphrase of Psalm 42 is from Tate and Brady's *New Version of the Psalms of David*, 1696. See comments at No. 81.

MARTYRDOM   See No. 285 for comments on the tune.

391 Be Thou My Vision

Dating from approximately the eighth century, this old Irish poem, originally beginning, "Rob tu mo bhoile, a Comdi cride," was translated into English prose by Mary E. Byrne (1880–1931) in the journal, *Erin*, Volume II, 1905. This prose version was put into verse form by Eleanor H. Hull (1860–1935) in her *Poem Book of the Gael*, 1912. The quaint and picturesque phrases are typical of early Irish poems. Miss Byrne, a graduate of the National University of Ireland, was a leading contributor to the *Old and Mid-Irish Dictionary*, and received the Chancellor's Gold Medal in the Royal University for her brilliant treatise on *England in the Age of Chaucer*. Miss Hull was the founder and honorary secretary of the Irish Text Society and onetime president of the Irish Literary Society of London. Through her many activities and books on Irish literature and history she was instrumental in promoting a reawakened interest in early Gaelic culture.

SLANE   See No. 217 for comments on the tune, which was set to these words in *The Church Hymnary Revised*, 1927.

392   Father in Heaven, Who Lovest All

Born in Bombay, India, Rudyard Kipling (1865–1936) received his higher education at the United Services College, Westward Ho, North Devonshire, England. After graduation he returned to India, and at age seventeen became assistant editor of *The Civil and Military Gazette* in Lahore, where his father was curator of the art museum. Many of his first stories appeared in this publication and in *The Pioneer*, of which he was also the assistant editor. These brought him early fame. In 1892 he married Caroline Starr Balestier, an American, and established a home near Brattleboro, Vermont, where he resided for four years before settling in England. A prolific and brilliant author, he wrote stories, poems, novels, children's books, histories, and journalistic pieces. Several of his works now rank as classics, among them *The Light That Failed*, 1890; *The Jungle Book*, 1894; *Second Jungle Book*, 1895; *Captains Courageous*, 1897; *Plain Tales from the Hills*, 1898; *Kim*, 1901; *Just-So Stories*, 1902; and *Puck of Pook's Hill*, 1906. The Nobel Prize for Literature was appropriately awarded him in 1907. James Moffatt described him as "the unofficial Poet Laureate of the Empire, . . . and in his highest moments, as in *Recessional* and *The Children's Song*, a singer of the faith that has made Britain great." [1] The present hymn was written as a patriotic song for English schoolboys in *Puck of Pook's Hill*, with the title "The Children's Hymn."

SAXBY was the setting for Kipling's poem in the *Pilgrim Hymnal*, 1931. It was written for John Keble's "Sun of my soul" in connection with a prize competition for a new setting of that hymn. SAXBY was awarded fourth place. It was subsequently published in the composer's *Twenty-four Hymn Tunes*, 1867. Saxby is a small town in the Midlands of England. For comments on the Rev. Timothy R. Matthews, composer of the tune, see No. 326.

393   God Be in My Head

First found in a *Book of Hours*, 1514 (a collection of prayers in manuscript form for use at designated times during the day), and later included in the *Sarum Primer* of 1558 (a prayer book used in Salisbury, England), this hauntingly beautiful hymn appeared in many sixteenth-century books of devotion as a prayer to be said before the daily offices. It was first published as a hymn in *The Oxford Hymn Book*, 1908.

LYTLINGTON, one of two settings in the *Pilgrim Hymnal* for this text, was composed for it by Sir Sydney H. Nicholson (1875–1947), organist, composer, educator, whose influence on English hymnody and church music has been great. He was educated at Rugby and at New College, Oxford (M.A. and D.Mus.), at the Royal College of Music, and in Frankfurt, Germany. As organist he served at Carlisle Cathedral, Manchester Cathedral (1908–1918), and at Westminster Abbey (1918–1927) where he did much to raise the level of the choral work and organized and directed the Westminster Abbey Special Choir in performances of oratorios, motets, and anthems from the great periods of church music. As chairman of the Church Music Society he campaigned vigorously for the improvement of music in parish churches and in 1927 resigned his post at the Abbey in order to devote his time and energies to St. Nicholas College, Chislehurst, the center for the School of English Church Music which he founded and directed for many years. As its warden and in its interests he traveled far and wide, speaking, interviewing ministers and organists, visiting churches not only in England but in Australia, New Zealand, and Canada. In 1945 the College became the Royal School of Church Music with quarters first at Canterbury and from 1954 at Addington Palace, Croydon. In 1938 Nicholson was knighted for his outstanding service to church music. He edited the music for the 1916 Supplement to *Hymns Ancient and Modern* continuing as chief musical advisor for the Revised Edition until his death. He composed hymn-tunes, service music, cantatas, and operettas and published *Quires and Places where they sing,* 1932, *Boys' Choirs,* 1922, and with George L. H. Gardner edited *A Manual of English Church Music,* 1923.

LYTLINGTON, published for the first time in the 1928 edition of *The Winchester Hymn Supplement,* was named for the house in which Sir Sydney Nicholson lived when he was organist at Westminster Abbey. Known as Lytlington Tower, it was said to be the home of a former Abbot of Westminster called Lytlington.

394 Heart and Mind, Possessions, Lord

Born in the city of Ahmednagar, near Bombay, India, Krishnarao Rathnaji Sangle (1834–1908) received much of his early education from Christian missionaries, although he came from a Hindu family. Largely as a result of this training, and despite the strong opposition of his parents and especially his older brother, he was baptized on January 1, 1860, in Ahmednagar by the Rev. S. B. Fairbanks and devoted the rest of his life to evangelism and teaching, eventually becoming headmaster of the Girls' School in his home city. It was said of him that he became a Christian "not because he hoped to gain earthly comfort and benefits from the missionaries, but because he fully recognized Christ as his Saviour." Skilled in English and Sanskrit, he was also a poet and musician as well as an excellent weaver and gardener. He wrote approximately 1,050 hymns and poems, many of which were included in the *Upasanasangit,* the Marathi Christian hymnal. The translation is by Alden H. Clark (1878–1960), distinguished Congregational missionary in India for nearly thirty years. Founder of the famous Nagpada Neighborhood House in Bombay, Clark later returned to Boston to serve The American Board of Commissioners for Foreign Missions as candidate secretary and then as secretary for India, Ceylon, the Philippines, Spain, and Mexico.

305

TANA MANA DHANA (MARATHI) is an authentic Indian hymn set to its native tune. A director of religious education once told the writer that this was the favorite hymn of the children and young people she had taught in a Daily Vacation Bible School. The first visual impression of the melody may seem to spell difficulty, but it is a simple chant with quite a bit of repetition as will be seen from the following analysis.

When TANA MANA DHANA is sung in India the following lines are repeated:

> Heart and mind, possessions, Lord, I offer unto thee;
> All these were thine, Lord; thou didst give them all to me.
> Plans and my thoughts and everything I ever do

Mrs. Ross Cannon, daughter of Dr. Alden Clark, translator of the hymn, has given the following information about it:

> This hymn is sung with many verses in all the Marathi churches and also with many variations. The hymn books have only the words in many places, and the Bhajan band, or instruments used in leading music, create variations, as in all folk music. We heard a variation of it used in Vadala near Ahmednagar in Maharashtra in the sturdy Christian church there, with a Bhajan band playing and leading the singing, with an Indian congregation of 250, most of them seated on the floor, children in the front. . . . There might be six or seven players, all seated on the floor of course, with drums, cymbals, castanets, pipe, tabla, etc. . . . The Indians love to sing in church, at work, or in a village hut at evening.

The phrase "Tana, mana, dhana" means "Heart, mind, possessions" in the language spoken in Marathi, an area of the State of Maharashtra of which

Bombay is now the capital. This particular song belongs to the Christian community in the Marathi Mission, the first mission of the American Board to be established anywhere in the world. It was founded in Western India in 1813. The Marathi churches are indigenous Indian churches, formerly related to the Congregational Mission but now part of the United Church of Northern India. TANA MANA DHANA should be played quietly and not too quickly, with a regular, even flow, as legato as possible, with particular attention to the words and musical phrases. It can be played in octaves in both hands if more support is needed. Children find this pentatonic melody easy to play on the black notes of the piano, starting on G flat. The adaptation of the melody to English words was made by Marion Chute, a missionary, Mrs. Clark, and Mrs. Cannon.

395 Behold Us, Lord, A Little Space

Percy Dearmer has said of this hymn that it is "one of the earliest hymns in which science and art are mentioned and are recognized as part of God's work." [8] Written by Canon Ellerton for a midday service in a London church, it was first published in *Church Hymns,* 1871, and later appeared in his *Hymns, Original and Translated,* 1888, with the heading, "Midday: for a city church." See No. 47 for comments on Ellerton.

DUNFERMLINE, one of the twelve Common Tunes in Andro Hart's *The CL Psalmes of David,* 1615 (see Nos. 87, 330), passed into English usage through Ravenscroft's Psalter, 1621, where it was set to Psalms 36 and 89, classified as a Scottish tune and named DUMFERMELING. It is a simple tune within the compass of seven notes. Its last phrase is like that of ST. FLAVIAN and the second and fourth phrases of DUNDEE. In *Four Centuries of Scottish Psalmody,* Millar Patrick says, "DUNFERMLINE is almost certainly the work of 'good and meike John Angus,' one of the conventual brethren of Dunfermline Abbey, and sometime precentor there, who accepted the Reformation." The history of Dunfermline (Gaelic for "the fort on the crooked linn") in Fifeshire, Scotland, goes back to a remote period. Celtic monks had an establishment there and the foundations of the Benedictine priory (later raised to the rank of an abbey) were laid in 1075. This abbey is one of the most important remains in Scotland and, with the exception of Iona, is said to have received more of Caledonia's royal dead than any other place in the kingdom.

DUNFERMLINE is not new to American hymnody. In *The Psaltery,* 1845, edited by Lowell Mason, it was in 4/4 time, as in the present version, with simple diatonic harmonies and the name DUMFERLINE. In *The National Psalmist,* 1848, it was in 4/2 and had a long note at the beginning and end of each phrase as in Hart's book and Ravenscroft's Psalter. The name was spelled DUNFERMLINE. In this form it appeared in some of Mason's later collections. A footnote to the tune in *The People's Tune Book,* 1860, reads: "This is one of the finest Scotch tunes; from the time of John Knox it has often been sung, we doubt not, to the words to which it is here set, being the Scottish Version of the 23rd Psalm." In another book Mason called

307

it an "admirable old tune" and included it in a list "consisting mostly of such tunes as, having been long and thoroughly tried and proved, are known to be good, ay, among the very best."

396 Fill Thou My Life, O Lord

Entitled "Life's Praise," this hymn by Horatius Bonar is from his *Hymns of Faith and Hope,* third series, 1866. See No. 99 for comments on Bonar.

WIGTOWN   See No. 330 for comments on the tune.

397 Lord, Speak to Me, That I May Speak

Printed originally in leaflet form, with the title "Worker's Prayer," and based on the Pauline text, "None of us liveth to himself" (Romans 14:7), this hymn by Frances R. Havergal (1836–1879), youngest child of Rev. William H. Havergal (see tune commentary, No. 214) is a fitting commentary on her life. Because of delicate health, she was forced to conserve her energies and restrict her activities. Nevertheless, despite this handicap, her accomplishments were numerous and varied. At the age of seven, she began to write verses, and her poems soon appeared in *Good Words* and other religious journals. She mastered several modern languages as well as Hebrew and Greek and also composed music. Following an intense religious experience as a young girl, of which she later wrote that "earth and heaven seemed brighter from that moment," she gave herself unstintingly to helping others, so far as her strength allowed. Much sought after for her counsel, which she gave without reservation and which often drained her frail constitution, she expressed the hope on one occasion that "the angels would have orders to let her alone a bit when she first got to heaven." James Moffat said of her that she "disclosed a remarkable Christian character, exhibiting all the beauty, freshness and charm of that life of complete and happy consecration which was the chief subject of her song." [1]

CANONBURY   See No. 46 for comments on the tune.

398 Hope of the World

This hymn by Georgia Harkness (1891–   ) was inspired by the Second General Assembly of the World Council of Churches which met in Evanston, Illinios, in the summer of 1954 and which had as its theme the Christian hope. It was published that same year by The Hymn Society of America in *Eleven New Ecumenical Hymns.* Following graduation from Cornell and Boston universities, from which institutions she received the A.B. and Ph.D. degrees respectively, Dr. Harkness taught courses in religion and philosophy at Elmira and Mount Holyoke colleges. Ordained as a Methodist minister in 1926, she was professor of applied theology at the Garrett Biblical Institute in Evanston, Illinois, from 1939 to 1950, and subsequently taught at the

Pacific School of Religion in Berkeley, California. Awarded many honors, she is the author of numerous books, including *Prayer and the Common Life*, 1948; *The Modern Rival of Christian Faith*, 1952; *The Sources of Western Morality*, 1954; *Christian Ethics*, 1957; and *The Providence of God*, 1960. She is also a poet and hymn writer, and has been active in the ecumenical movement.

DONNE SECOURS (GENEVA 12)   See No. 334 for comments on the tune.

399   O Love That Wilt Not Let Me Go

George Matheson said of this hymn, which he wrote while serving as the minister of the church in Innellan, Argyllshire, Scotland: "It was composed with extreme rapidity; it seemed to me that its construction occupied only a few minutes, and I felt myself rather in the position of one who was being dictated to than of an original artist. I was suffering from extreme mental stress and the hymn was the fruit of that pain." He later explained that the phrase "blossoms red" was meant to describe the new life that emerges out of sacrifice, of the rebirth that comes by losing oneself. The hymn first appeared in *Life and Work; the record of the Church of Scotland*, January, 1883, and was included in *The Scottish Hymnal*, 1885. See No. 356 for comments on Matheson.

ST. MARGARET   Albert Lister Peace (1849–1912) composed this well-known setting for Matheson's hymn while serving as music editor of *The Scottish Hymnal*, 1885. As no tune in the unusual meter of the text was available at the time, the Hymnal Committee asked Peace to compose one especially for it. "After reading it over carefully," he said, "I wrote the music straight off, and may say that the ink of the first note was hardly dry when I had finished the tune."

As a child, Peace was extremely precocious. When only four or five years old he could name accurately any note or combination of notes that he heard; and at nine he was made organist of the parish church of Holmfirth, Yorkshire, the first of a number of Anglican and Nonconformist churches that he served. In 1866 he went to Trinity Congregational Church in Glasgow and in 1879 to Glasgow Cathedral, remaining there until 1897. At that time he won, by competition, the post of organist of St. George's Hall, Liverpool, succeeding W. T. Best, and retaining the position until his death. He received the degrees Bachelor of Music (1870) and Doctor of Music (1875) from Oxford, and in 1886 was named a Fellow of the Royal College of Organists. In 1865 the Church of Scotland lifted its ban on the use of organs in public worship. During the next twenty-five years two thirds of the organs built in Scotland were opened by Peace whose remarkable technique and brilliant pedaling brought him much renown. Dr. A. K. H. Boyd of St. Andrews has been quoted as saying that when he preached in the cathedral he "dared not give out the hymn, 'Peace, perfect peace,' lest the organist should take it as a personal compliment." Peace edited the music of four books for the Church of Scotland.

400 More Love to Thee, O Christ

Displaying exceptional poetic gifts as a young girl, Elizabeth P. Prentiss (1818–1878) became a regular contributor to *The Youth's Companion,* a popular American magazine for children and young people with high literary standards, when she was only sixteen years of age. In 1845, after teaching school in Portland, Maine, Ipswich, Massachusetts, and Richmond, Virginia, she married Dr. George L. Prentiss, prominent Presbyterian minister, who later became professor of homiletics and polity at Union Theological Seminary in New York City. Despite poor health, she wrote several volumes of poems, hymns, and other works, including a religious best-seller, *Stepping Heavenward,* 1869, which sold nearly one hundred thousand copies. In his biography of his wife, *Life and Letters,* Dr. Prentiss made this comment:

> The hymn, "More Love to Thee, O Christ," belongs probably as far back as the year 1856. Like most of her hymns, it is simply a prayer put into the form of verse. She wrote it so hastily that the last stanza was left incomplete, one line having to be added in pencil when it was printed. She did not show it, not even to her husband, until many years after it was written; and she wondered not a little that, when published, it met with so much favor.

Printed initially in leaflet form, it appeared the following year in William Howard Doane's *Songs of Devotion,* 1870, and has since been translated into many languages, including Chinese. It was sung by her friends at the side of her grave when she was buried in August, 1878.

MORE LOVE TO THEE is one of over 2,200 tunes composed by William H. Doane (1832–1915), industrialist, inventor, and compiler of more than forty collections of hymns and tunes. A number of these were edited in collaboration with the Rev. Robert Lowry. (331) Music was a major interest throughout his life. In his teens he became a skilled flutist, learned to play the double bass and harmonium, and in later years had some theoretical training. For two years he conducted the Norwich [Connecticut] Harmonic Society. The quantity of his tunes, however, is not matched by quality. "Rescue the perishing" and "Safe in the arms of Jesus," two of many settings he wrote for Fanny Crosby's hymns, were among the best-known of his vast output of gospel-type songs that had tremendous sales. Doane, born in Preston, Connecticut, started out in his father's cotton mills as clerk and accountant, subsequently serving in the latter capacity for the J. A. Fay Company, a large woodworking firm with plants in Norwich, Chicago, and Cincinnati. He invented some of the machinery used in the wood-working factories and after a series of promotions became president of the company with headquarters in Cincinnati. A man of considerable wealth, he gave generous support to churches, missions, the Y.M.C.A., the Y.W.C.A., and to evangelistic enterprises. He was a devoted and active member of the Baptist Church, served for twenty-five years as superintendent of the Sunday school in Auburn, Ohio, and gave the endowment for the library at Denison University, which honored him with a Doctor of Music degree in 1875. He was music editor for *The Baptist Hymnal,* 1883.

401 | Teach Me, My God and King

Admired by Sir Henry Walton, John Donne, Isaak Walton, and Lord Bacon, all of whom were his intimate friends, George Herbert (1593–1632) exemplified in a remarkable way the saintly type of parson later described in Oliver Goldsmith's *The Vicar of Wakefield.* Following a brilliant career at Trinity College, Cambridge, he enjoyed for a time the favor of James I as one of his courtiers. After the king's death in 1625, however, he took holy orders and in 1630 became rector of Bremerton, near Salisbury. He remained there the last three years of his short life and won the esteem of all who knew him for his poetic and homiletical gifts and the Christlike quality of his life. His major literary work, *The Temple,* which he completed just three weeks before he died of tuberculosis, is a collection of devotional poems and hymns, marked by their "homely imagery and quaint humour." John Wesley selected forty-seven pieces from *The Temple* for his various collections of hymns and sacred poems. The present hymn is from this work, entitled "The Elixir," and derives much of its meaning and imagery from medieval alchemy. The "famous stone" mentioned in the last stanza refers to the so-called philosophers' stone by means of which alchemists hoped to change base metals into gold. Herbert uses this imagery to describe the miraculous transformation of human nature by divine action. An accomplished musician, he often sang his hymns as he played on the lute or viol.

MORNINGTON was set to Herbert's poem in *The Harvard University Hymn Book,* 1926, and in the *Pilgrim Hymnal,* 1931. It is an adaptation of a chant composed c. 1760 by Garrett Wellesley (Wesley), the first Earl of Mornington (1735–1781). The chant was first published as a Short Meter tune in the Rev. W. E. Miller's *David's Harp,* 1805, the book in which ADESTE FIDELES was introduced to English Methodists. Wellesley's chant and the hymn tune adapted from it were included in Lowell Mason's collections and in other nineteenth-century American tune books. The composer of MORNINGTON was a gifted musician who learned without much assistance to play the violin, harpsichord, and organ, to improvise, and to compose. He was educated at Trinity College, Dublin (B.A. 1754, M.A. 1757), which granted him an honorary Doctor of Music degree in 1764 and appointed him its first professor of music. He is known chiefly as a composer of madrigals and glees although he also wrote some church music.

Garrett Wellesley's family, a distinguished one, was related to the English Wesley family of Methodist fame. He was the son of Richard Colley, first Baron Mornington who took the name of Wesley when he succeeded to the estates of an earlier Garrett Wesley after Charles Wesley, the hymn writer, had declined to become the adopted heir of his Irish kinsman. In 1758 the composer of MORNINGTON succeeded his father as Baron Mornington and in 1760 was advanced in the peerage and granted the titles of Viscount Wellesley of Dangan Castle and Earl of Mornington. Three of his sons attained great distinction. One of them, Arthur Wellesley, the first Duke of Wellington, became the most influential personality in Europe after the victory at Waterloo. When living in London Lord Mornington used to breakfast once a week with Charles Wesley and then spend the morning playing and discussing music with his two precocious sons, Charles and Samuel. Frequently he took part in the series of private subscription concerts which these two young musicians planned and gave in their father's home before fashionable and distinguished audiences.

The biographical sketch of the Earl of Mornington in *The Oxford Companion to Music* ends with the following:

> Like his more famous son, the hero of Waterloo, he was a man of cool courage, for he is reputed to have been the first member of the British aristocracy who dared to walk through the London streets openly and unashamedly carrying a violin case.

402 Jesus, Where'er Thy People Meet

During the time that William Cowper and John Newton lived and worked together in Olney, England, it was decided to move the prayer meeting they conducted into a larger place. John Newton wrote in a letter to a friend, "We are going to remove our prayer-meeting to the great room in the Great House [an empty mansion at Olney belonging to Lord Dartmouth]. It is a noble place, with a parlour behind it, and holds one hundred and thirty people conveniently." The present hymn was written for the opening service by Cowper, who undoubtedly was thinking of this move when he included the line, "Thy former mercies here renew." Newton also provided a new hymn for the occasion, "Great shepherd of thy people, hear." Both hymns were published in Book II of *Olney Hymns,* 1779. See No. 87 for comments on Cowper and No. 221 for comments on Newton.

FEDERAL STREET   See No. 290 for comments on the tune.

403 Those Who Love and Those Who Labor

This hymn is a paraphrase of various sayings attributed to Jesus as recorded in the *Agrapha,* a collection of first or second century Greek texts purporting to be the words of Jesus but which were not included in the New Testament. These sayings were found among the Oxyrhynchus papyri discovered in 1897 by Bernard P. Grenfell and Arthur S. Hunt, English classical scholars and Egyptologists. The paraphrase is by Geoffrey Dearmer (1893–), son of the illustrious Percy Dearmer and a gifted literary figure in his own right. He has written several volumes of poems, a drama entitled *St. Paul* and a number of hymns. This hymn first appeared in *Songs of Praise,* 1931.

ALTA TRINITA BEATA   In his *General History of Music,* 1782, Charles Burney wrote that the most ancient melodies he could find in Italy which had been set originally to Italian words were in a manuscript collection of *Laudi spirituali* preserved at the Magliabecchi Library in Florence. In his chapter on "The State of Music to 1450," he printed "Alla Trinità," an early fourteenth-century hymn of praise to the Trinity, in plainsong notation and also in his own two-part measured version. The latter is the source of the present tune. His form of the melody, although supposedly a faithful transcript of that in the manuscript, was considerably simplified and contained much of his own invention. Archibald Jacob says in *Songs of Praise Discussed:* "As it stands . . . the tune, from a purely musical point of view, is a very good one; Burney's ability as a musician was considerable, and the present melody, though evidence of his habitual negligence as an historian, is an excellent instance of his high capacity as a composer." [8] It became popular in England and was included in many hymn collections under the name FLORENCE.

The *Laudi Spirituali* were nonliturgical, popular, devotional songs set to vernacular texts which were often interspersed with Latin phrases. St. Francis who played an important part in the development of Italian poetry, is said to have composed some of these religious poems which were sung to simple melodies founded on plainchant and influenced by popular folk songs. The *laudi* were sung by *Compagnie de' Laudesi* (or *Laudisti*), groups first organized at Florence in 1310 which continued to play an important part in the religious life of the people for centuries. They were also sung and widely disseminated by the fanatical brotherhoods of flagellants in the thirteenth and fourteenth centuries who used them in regular song meetings and in their processions as they wandered through Italy inflicting punishment on themselves and each other in penance for their sins.

Because Burney misread the first word of the manuscript from which he adapted this tune, it is mistakenly named ALLA TRINITA BEATA in some books. The first phrase of this tune is practically the same as that of Lowell Mason's HAMBURG (177). Perhaps both are related to the same Gregorian tone.

404 Take My Life and Let It Be

Translated into many languages and included in most hymnals, this hymn by Frances Havergal had its origins in a prayer meeting at Areley House, England, on February 4, 1874. She later described the experience in a letter:

> There were ten persons in the house, some unconverted and long prayed for, some converted but not rejoicing Christians. He gave me the prayer 'Lord give me *all* in this house!' And He just *did*. Before I left the house every one had got a blessing. The last night of my visit . . . I was too happy to sleep, and passed most of the night in praise and renewal of my own consecration; and these little couplets formed themselves and chimed in my heart one after the other, till they finished with *"Ever, Only, ALL for Thee!"*

The hymn was first published, according to Armin Haeussler, in the Appendix of Snepp's *Songs of Grace and Glory,* 1874, and appeared later in Miss Havergal's *Loyal Responses,* 1878. See No. 397 for further comments on Miss Havergal.

VIENNA (KNECHT)   Three years before this tune appeared with its present harmonization in Havergal's *Old Church Psalmody,* London, 1847, it was included in *The Psalmodist,* Cincinnati, 1844, edited by Thomas Hastings and William Bradbury. Named FLEETWOOD, it was set to "Bread of heaven on Thee we feed." The harmonization was simple and in good taste. The second note of the melody in measure five was the lowered seventh of the scale as in Knecht's original version. (Zahn 1238) See No. 243 for comments on Knecht.

405 Master, No Offering Costly and Sweet

As the minister of Center Church (Congregational), Hartford, Connecticut, for fifty years, Edwin Pond Parker (1836–1925) was known as a poet and a musician as well as a preacher and a pastor. Born in Castine, Maine, he was educated at Bowdoin College and Bangor Theological Seminary. He retained a lifelong interest in hymnody, editing several collections of hymns and writing approximately two hundred hymns of his own. He wrote the present hymn as the summation and conclusion of one of his sermons. It was first published in *The Christian Hymnal,* 1889.

LOVE'S OFFERING was composed in 1888 by the author of the present hymn when he was pastor of the Center Congregational Church, Hartford, Connecticut, and director of its music as well. In addition to preaching, writing, and editing, Dr. Parker composed anthems for his choir, settings for some of his hymns, and adapted a number of tunes from the works of various composers. MERCY (No. 242) is one of his arrangements.

406 Forth in Thy Name, O Lord, I Go

Called by K. L. Parry "one of the greatest of all hymns of Christian service," this hymn was written by Charles Wesley for Christians to sing before going to work. It first appeared in the Wesley brothers' *Hymns and Sacred Poems,* 1749, with the title, "For Believers Before Work." The original third stanza, omitted here, read:

> Preserve me from my calling's snare,
> And hide my simple heart above,
> Above the thorns of choking care,
> The gilded baits of worldly love.

See No. 43 for comments on Wesley.

MORNING HYMN   See No. 32 for comments on the tune.

407 O Light That Knew No Dawn

Gregory Nazianzen (c. 329–389) was one of the three famous Cappodocian theologians (the others being Basil the Great and Gregory of Nyssa) who successfully resisted the ideas of Arianism, a school of thought which taught that Jesus was not truly God and truly man but an intermediate being. In his boyhood, his saintly mother, Nonna, daily read the Bible to him and exerted a lasting influence on his life. She was also largely responsible for converting his father to Christianity. The father later was appointed bishop of Nazianzus. After studying at Alexandria and Athens, where he first came to know his brilliant colleague and friend, Basil the Great, Gregory was baptized and ordained a priest by his father and later became bishop of Sasima. His stay there was not a happy one, and he moved to Constantinople, where he achieved fame as a theologian. Torn throughout his career between leading an active or a contemplative life, he finally retired to Nazianzus and later to Arizanzus, where he spent his time writing devotional poetry. The present hymn is a cento from his "Hymn to Christ." It was translated by John Brownlie (1857–1925), noted Free Church minister and classical scholar in Scotland, in his *Hymns of the Greek Church*, 1900. Brownlie later revised the third stanza as given here for *The Church Hymnary*, 1927.

HAREWOOD, composed by Samuel S. Wesley, was the setting for "Rejoice, the Lord is King!" in Hackett's *National Psalmist*, 1839. It appeared with the present text in *The Church Hymnary, Revised*, 1927. See No. 260 for comments on Wesley.

408 I Sought the Lord, and Afterward I Knew

Of unknown authorship, this hymn, according to Charles L. Atkins, first appeared in *Holy Songs, Carols and Sacred Ballads*, 1889, published in Boston. It was included later in the *Pilgrim Hymnal*, 1904. Some scholars have attributed it to Jean Ingelow (1820–1897), talented English poet, but it has not been found in her collected works. The second stanza recalls the incident of Peter walking on the sea (Matthew 14: 22–32).

GENEVAN PSALM 22 was set to this hymn in *The Harvard University Hymn Book*, 1926. Its beauty enhances the words, which appear in some hymnals with quite inferior tunes. GENEVAN PSALM 22 is the first half of the melody for Marot's version of Psalm 22 in the 1542 Genevan Psalter: "Mon Dieu, mon Dieu, pourquoi m'as-tu laissé?" Douen ascribes it to Bourgeois. The four phrases which comprise the present tune have remained unchanged since 1542. See Nos. 4 and 282 for comments on Bourgeois and the Genevan psalters. See No. 578 for another setting.

409 Jesus, Thou Divine Companion

Derived from an earlier narrative poem, *The Toiling of Felix*, which he wrote in 1898, this "Hymn of Labor" by Henry van Dyke was written in 1909 and first appeared in *Hymns of the Kingdom of God*, 1910, edited by Henry Sloane Coffin and Ambrose White Vernon. It is one of the finest hymns on the dignity of work that has ever been written. See No. 8 for comments on van Dyke.

PLEADING SAVIOR (SALTASH), an anonymous American melody described as "an old camp-meeting tune, popular on the American frontier," appeared in Vol. I of *The Christian Lyre*, 1831, set to John Leland's "Now the Saviour standeth pleading." It is a pentatonic melody in AABA form. Like the majority of tunes in *The Christian Lyre*, it was set in only two parts, treble and bass. Some melodies did not have a second part. Joshua Leavitt (1794–1873), editor of the collection, said in its preface, "The *religious* effect of a hymn is heightened by having all sing the air only." The present harmonization, from *The English Hymnal*, 1906, was set to the present text in *The Hymnal 1940* with the directive, "Somewhat slowly." In March, 1830, Leavitt started publication of *The Evangelist*, a weekly paper concerned with temperance, antislavery, and religious revivals, and in October of that year began to print specimen hymns and tunes for a revival hymnbook to be issued in monthly installments. The first six parts appeared as Vol. I of *The Christian Lyre* in April, 1831. Vol. II and a supplement of "more than one hundred Psalm tunes such as are most used in churches of all denominations" were issued before the end of the year. The book was an immediate success; by 1842 twenty-six editions had been issued. There was considerable criticism of it because Leavitt had used popular, secular melodies for some of the hymns, but his collection contained a number of very good tunes. One of its important contributions to American hymnody was "O sacred head, now wounded" set to the PASSION CHORALE. (See No. 170.)

Leavitt, born in Heath, Massachusetts, graduated from Yale at twenty. For a time he was preceptor at Wethersfield Academy, then studied law and practiced at Heath and in Putney, Vermont, before returning to Yale in 1823. He completed the two-year divinity course in one year. After ordination in 1825 he served as minister of the Congregational Church in Stratford, Connecticut, for three years, leaving in 1828 for New York City to be secretary of the Seamen's Friend Society and editor of the *Sailor's Magazine*. He founded sailors' missions in several cities, was one of the first lecturers of the American Temperance Society, and a member of the executive committee of the New York Anti-Slavery Society. After the depression of 1837 he moved to Boston where he crusaded for the causes of temperance, cheap postage, and free trade. In 1848, on the advice of his friend John Greenleaf Whittier, he returned to New York as assistant editor of *The Independent*, remaining with it as office editor until his death.

410 O Brother Man, Fold to Thy Heart

In his disdain for purely formal and ritualistic worship, John Greenleaf Whittier wrote a fifteen-stanza poem in 1848, entitled "Worship," which included the stanzas:

> The pagan's myths through marble lips are spoken,
> And ghosts of old beliefs still flit and moan
> Round fane and altar overthrown and broken,
> O'er tree-grown barrow and gray ring of stone.

He asks no taper lights, on high surrounding
The priestly altar and the saintly grave,
No dolorous chant nor organ music sounding,
No incense clouding up the twilight nave.

Under its title the poem had the familiar text, "Pure religion and undefiled before God and the Father is this, To visit the fatherless and widows in their affliction, and to keep himself unspotted from the world" (James 1:27). The present hymn comprises the last three stanzas of this poem and expresses the essential beliefs of the poet's Quaker faith. The poem was first published in his *Labor and Other Poems*, 1850. See No. 224 for comments on Whittier.

INTERCESSOR was composed for "O word of pity, for our pardon pleading," in *Hymns Ancient and Modern*, 1904, to which Charles Hubert Hastings Parry (1848–1918) contributed a number of tunes. It was set to the Whittier text in *Songs of Praise*, 1925. Since then the combination has appeared in a number of English and American hymnals.

Parry, the son of Thomas Gambier Parry, distinguished amateur painter and art patron, began writing chants when he was eight or nine and by the time he was sixteen had tried his hand at songs, instrumental music, and every kind of Anglican church music. During his years at Twyford School, near Winchester, he was deeply impressed by the work of Samuel S. Wesley, organist of the cathedral. (See No. 260.) At Eton he was outstanding as musician and athlete, and before finishing his course there had earned a B.Mus. degree from Oxford. Sports and academic studies were his major interests at Exeter College, Oxford, but he took part in a variety of music activities. He received his B.A. in 1870, spent three years with Lloyd's of London, but gave up business for a musical career in 1874. In 1883 he was appointed professor of composition and lecturer in musical history at the Royal College of Music and in 1894 became its director, succeeding Sir George Grove with whom he had collaborated as assistant editor of the *Dictionary of Music and Musicians*. He was given honorary doctorates in music by Cambridge, Oxford, Durham, and Dublin universities, was knighted in 1898, and in 1902 was made a baronet at the coronation of Edward VII. In 1900 he succeeded Sir John Stainer as professor of music at Oxford, remaining there until 1908. Of his many compositions, "Blest Pair of Sirens," for double choir and orchestra, is considered the finest. He was also the author of a number of books on music and musicians.

411 Lord God of Hosts, Whose Purpose

The words of this virile hymn were written by Shepherd Knapp (1873–1946) in 1907 for a meeting of the Men's Association of The Brick Presbyterian Church in New York City. At the time he was serving as the assistant pastor. He was called later to be the minister of Central Congregational Church, Worcester, Massachusetts, where he remained for twenty-eight years. Among the books he wrote are *On the Edge of the Storm*, 1921; *Old Joe and other Vesper Stories*, 1922; and *The Liberated Bible: the Old Testa-*

ment, 1941. An honorary Doctor of Divinity degree was conferred on him in 1912 by New York University.

WELWYN seems to be the only hymn tune by which Sir Alfred Scott-Gatty (1847–1918) is known. His major interest was heraldry but he was a successful amateur musician with a flair for composing songs of a sentimental, light nature which attained great popularity. For many of these he wrote words as well as music. He also composed a number of songs and musical plays for children. He held a number of heraldic offices and was knighted in 1904 at the time of his appointment as Garter Principal King-of-Arms by the College of Heralds. WELWYN was first published in Part IV of *Arundel Hymns.* 1900, a collection of Roman Catholic hymns edited by the Duke of Norfolk and the composer's uncle, Charles T. Gatty. The present form of the tune, from *The English Hymnal,* 1906, differs rhythmically from the original in several measures. The changes are an improvement.

412   O Master Workman of the Race

Shortly before leaving for a brief vacation at his summer camp in the Adirondack Mountains in the spring of 1912, Jay Thomas Stocking (1870–1936) was asked by Pilgrim Press in Boston to write a new hymn for the revised edition of the *Pilgrim Hymnal* that was soon to be published. The inspiration for this hymn came not long afterward as he watched some carpenters at work in the camp. He later described the experience in these words: "The figure of the carpenter, as applied to Jesus, flashed on me as never before, and I sat down and wrote the hymn, almost, if not quite, in the exact form in which it now appears." Stocking, a graduate of Amherst College and Yale Divinity School, was an ordained Congregational minister and held several important pastorates in New England, New Jersey, Missouri, and Washington, D.C. He was elected in 1934 to the highest office in his denomination, Moderator of the General Council of the Congregational Christian Churches, and was a member of the Commission on International Justice and Good Will of the Federal Council of Churches. Active in many religious and cultural bodies and affairs, he was also noted for his literary skills and especially for his children's stories. He died a few months after being called to First Congregational Church, Newton Centre, Massachusetts.

KINGSFOLD, a traditional English melody, arranged by Ralph Vaughan Williams and named by him for a village in Surrey where he heard a variant of it, was set to Horatius Bonar's hymn, "I heard the voice of Jesus say," in *The English Hymnal,* 1906. It has been found in many places in a variety of forms, with a number of texts. The source of KINGSFOLD is a version of a melody noted by Alfred J. Hipkins in Westminster and included in *English County Songs,* 1893, edited by Lucy E. Broadwood and J. A. Fuller Maitland. In that collection the tune was given with an accompaniment arranged by Fuller Maitland which was quite different in style and harmonization from the present four-part arrangement. Hipkins heard the melody without words, but the name "Lazarus" by which it was known seemed to indicate its common usage with "Dives and Lazarus," the ballad to which it was set in

English County Songs. The tune was sung also to a ballad-carol about Job and Lazarus, "Come all you worthy Christian men," with which it appears at No. 60 in *The Oxford Book of Carols,* harmonized by Martin Shaw. In *Songs of Praise Discussed* Archibald Jacob describes KINGSFOLD as "a modal tune of great dignity and significance, very characteristic of a large class of the folk-tunes which have been collected during the last forty odd years." It is in A A B A form, in the Aeolian mode, within the compass of an octave, *d* to *d.* There is much repetition in KINGSFOLD but the alternation of *d* and *e* as the final note of the phrases and of the D major and E minor chords in the cadences, and the melodic and tonal contrast in measures nine and ten provide the necessary variety. The tune never seems monotonous.

413 Son of God, Eternal Savior

After graduating from Trinity Hall, Cambridge, Somerset C. Lowry (1855–1932) was ordained in 1879 and became curate at Doncaster, Yorkshire. He was later vicar at North Holmwood, Surrey; at St. Augustine, Bournemouth; and at St. Bartholomew's, Southsea. The author of approximately sixty hymns, he also published several devotional books, including *The Work of the Holy Spirit,* 1894, and a collection of *Hymns and Spiritual Songs.* The present hymn, entitled "For Unity," was first published in the February, 1894, issue of *Good Will,* and was included in the *Christian Social Union Hymn Book,* 1895.

WEISSE FLAGGEN   See No. 180 for comments on the tune.

414 In Christ There Is No East or West

This hymn by John Oxenham was written in 1908 for a great missionary pageant, The Pageant of Darkness and Light, which was presented in London as one feature in a month-long exhibition and celebration of Christian missions. The exhibition was sponsored by the London Missionary Society and had as its theme, "The Orient in London." Oxenham wrote the entire script and planned the scenes for the pageant, which met with great success and was performed for several succeeding years in England and America. The most enduring part of the pageant is undoubtedly this hymn. Recalling St. Paul's words, "There is neither Jew nor Greek, there is neither slave nor free, there is neither male nor female: for you are all one in Christ Jesus" (Galatians 3:28), it also reminds one of Kipling's more assertively humanistic lines:

Oh, East is East, and West is West, and never the twain shall meet,
Till Earth and Sky stand presently at God's great Judgment Seat.
But there is neither East nor West, Border, nor Breed, nor Birth,
When two strong men stand face to face, though they come from the
    ends of the earth!

The hymn first appeared in Oxenham's *Bees in Amber,* 1913, and is now found in most hymnals. See No. 265 for comments on Oxenham.

ST. PETER   See No. 221 for comments on the tune.

415 In Christ There Is No East or West

See No. 414 for comments on the text.

McKEE The grandson of a Maryland slave adapted a Negro spiritual for these words and named the tune for the Rev. Elmer M. McKee, rector of St. George's Protestant Episcopal Church on Stuyvesant Square in New York City (1936–1946), where the composer was baritone soloist for fifty-two years. McKEE was set to the present text in *The Hymnal 1940*.

As a boy, Harry T. Burleigh (1866–1949), a native of Erie, Pennsylvania, earned money by running errands, selling papers, working as a houseboy and as a street lamplighter. In the summers he worked as a deck steward on Great Lakes passenger ships and for one season as a wine boy at a Saratoga Springs hotel where he became acquainted with Victor Herbert, cellist in the hotel orchestra. His first choir experience was at St. Paul's Cathedral, Erie. In 1892 he borrowed money to go to New York City and was granted a scholarship at the National Conservatory of Music, then under the direction of Anton Dvořák. Since only tuition was covered by the scholarship, Burleigh worked as janitor and handy man to pay for his living expenses during his four years at the school. He played bass viol and tympani in the Conservatory orchestra and taught there for three years. Dvořák, who was very much interested in national types of music, loved to hear Burleigh sing the songs of his people and would ask him to sing them over and over. It was Burleigh's conviction that themes in Dvořák's "New World Symphony" showed the influence of these Negro melodies.

From 1892 to 1894 Burleigh sang in the choir of St. Philip's Protestant Episcopal Church in Harlem. When he heard of a vacancy in the choir at St. George's church in 1894 he applied for an audition (the only Negro among sixty applicants). He won the position and held it until his retirement in 1946. He was the first Negro to apply for a place in St. George's choir. One of the vestrymen of the church, J. Pierpont Morgan, in whose home Burleigh often sang, stipulated in his will that the Negro baritone be asked to sing the spiritual "Calvary" at his funeral.

From 1900 to 1925 Burleigh was in the choir of Temple Emanu-El in New York City, the first Negro to sing with that group. During the summers of 1901–1914, when Booker T. Washington was in the North to raise funds for Tuskegee Institute, he took Burleigh with him to Lake Mohonk, Poland Springs, and the White Mountains. On these trips Burleigh sang spirituals to his own piano accompaniments. In 1908 he sang at two command performances before King Edward VII. He was known internationally as a composer of original songs, arranger of Negro spirituals, and distinguished soloist. He often said that too much stress was laid on nationalism in music. He felt that the emphasis should be, rather, on the power of music to strengthen international understanding.

From 1911 until his retirement Burleigh was a music editor for G. Ricordi and Company, publishers. He was a charter member of the American Society of Composers, Authors and Publishers (A.S.C.A.P.), the recipient of an honorary Master of Science degree from Atlanta University and of a Doctor of Music degree from Howard University. The National Association for the

Advancement of Colored People awarded him the Spingarn Medal in 1917 for the highest achievement during 1916 by an American citizen of African descent. In 1930 he was one of seven Negroes to receive a William E. Harmon award for distinguished achievement. Roland Hayes and Marian Anderson were among the many Negro musicians who received encouragement and help from this man who "for half a century and more was the standard-bearer of Negro music."

In *The Hymnal 1940* the direction *With dignity* is given for McKEE, printed there in 4/2. One sometimes hears this tune played too quickly and in a rather trivial style. The one B flat in the melody gives it the flavor of the Mixolydian mode.

McKEE was adapted from "The Angels changed my name," a Negro spiritual published in the 1884 edition of *Jubilee Songs,* compiled by Theodore F. Seward and George White.

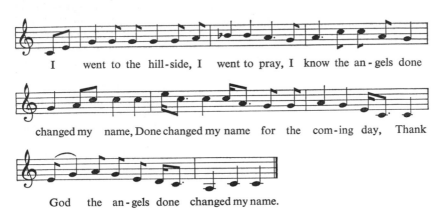

The following is from the foreword which Harry T. Burleigh wrote for all the Negro spirituals he arranged:

> The plantation songs known as "spirituals" are the spontaneous outbursts of intense religious fervor, and had their origin chiefly in camp meetings, revivals and other religious exercises.
>
> They were never "composed," but sprang into life, ready made, from the white heat of religious fervor . . . as the simple, ecstatic utterance of wholly untutored minds. . . .
>
> Success in singing these Folk Songs is primarily dependent upon deep spiritual feeling. The voice is not nearly so important as the spirit; . . . Their worth is weakened unless they are done impressively, for through all these songs there breathes a hope, a faith in the ultimate justice and brotherhood of man. The cadences of sorrow invariably turn to joy, and the message is ever manifest that eventually deliverance from all that hinders and oppresses the soul will come, and man — every man — will be free. (By permission of the Publisher, Franco Colombo, Inc.)

For further comments on Negro spirituals see Nos. 179, 353, and 428.

416 Christian, Rise and Act Thy Creed

First published in the *Pilgrim Hymnal*, 1904, so far as can be ascertained, this hymn does not appear in any other major denominational hymnal. It was written by Francis Albert Rollo Russell (1849–1914), English writer on scientific subjects and a Fellow of the Royal Meteorological Society. His hymns were published in his *Break of Day*, 1893. W. Garrett Horder included three of them in his *Hymns Supplemental to Existing Collections*, 1894.

INNOCENTS   See No. 33 for comments on the tune.

417 The Day of the Lord Is at Hand

Described as "a joyous knight-errant of God, thirsting for labour and strife," Charles Kingsley (1819–1875) was one of the pioneer leaders in the social gospel movement. As a boy he witnessed the Bristol Riots in 1831, and as a result became a lifelong champion of the oppressed. Following graduation from Magdalene College, Cambridge, he was ordained in 1842 and became curate, and later rector, of Eversley, Hampshire. At this time he came under the influence of John Frederick Denison Maurice and helped found the Christian Socialist Movement. Because of his radical views he was accused of being a revolutionary and was prohibited from preaching for a time by the bishop of London. After disproving the charges, he was appointed chaplain in ordinary to the queen and, in 1860, professor of modern history at Cambridge. He was later named a canon of Chester and, two years before he died, canon of Westminster. His two novels of social protest, *Yeast*, 1848, and *Alton Locke*, 1850, and his major historical novels, *Hypatia*, 1853, and *Westward Ho!*, 1855, established him as a front-rank English author. In his controversy with John Henry Newman, leading protagonist of the Oxford Movement, he evoked one of the greatest autobiographies ever written, *Apologia pro Vita Sua*, 1864, Newman's brilliant and unrestrained defense of his defection to Rome. Despite the bitter conflicts in which he engaged, Kingsley maintained an irenic spirit and refused to vilify those who opposed him. Matthew Arnold said of him after his death: "He was the most generous man I have ever known; the most forward to praise what he thought good, the most willing to admire, the most free from all thought of himself in praising and admiring, the most incapable of being made ill-natured or even indifferent by having to support ill-natured attacks himself." The present hymn, which vividly and dramatically recaptures the fervor of those who initiated the modern movement of Christian social reform, is from Kingsley's *Andromeda and other Poems*, 1858.

REMEMBER THE POOR   This adaptation of a traditional Irish melody from the *Irish Hymnal*, Dublin, 1919, was the setting for Kingsley's words in *Songs of Praise*, 1925. In Petrie's *Collection of Irish Melodies* (see No. 80) "Remember the poor" was the caption for the melody; no words were given for it.

REMEMBER THE POOR has the A A B A form characteristic of many folk songs. It should be played at a rather deliberate tempo, no faster than seventy-six to a quarter. The irregular meter presents some difficulties at first; but once the tune is known well, it becomes easy to adjust the words to it. In *Songs of Praise Discussed* Archibald Jacob calls it "a very fine, dignified tune," and says that it is "extremely characteristic of a large class of Irish folk-tunes, both in rhythm and in the general lay-out of the melody." [8] In view of Charles Kingsley's concern for the underprivileged, it seems particularly apt that these words of his should be set to a tune named REMEMBER THE POOR.

418 O Master, Let Me Walk with Thee

Among the churchmen in America who played leading roles in awakening the churches to their social responsibilities, Washington Gladden (1836–1918) ranks with Walter Rauschenbusch as one of the most influential. Ordained in 1860, he held pastorates in New York and Massachusetts before beginning his long and notable ministry in First Congregational Church, Columbus, Ohio. His forthright preaching and writing attracted nationwide attention and helped to shape the thinking of an entire generation. The three dominant interests of his life were social justice, higher biblical criticism, and Christian unity, all of which he did much to advance. The author of thirty-two books with a diversity of subjects ranging from *Working Men and Their Employers,* 1876, to *Art and Morality,* 1897, he summed up his creed in these words, taken from one of his last works, *Recollections,* 1906:

> Because the Christian life is the noblest life; because it is more blessed to give than to receive, and better to minister than to be ministered unto; because the good of life is not found in separating yourself from your fellows, but by identifying yourself with them — therefore, let us be Christians. If the Church would dare to preach and practice the things which Jesus Christ commanded, she would soon regain her lost power.

He wrote the present hymn not as a hymn but as a poem, with the caption "Walking with God," for the devotional section in *Sunday Afternoon,* III, 1879, a religious magazine he edited. He later described how it became a hymn: "Dr. Charles H. Richards found the poem . . . and made a hymn of it by omitting the second stanza, which was not suitable for devotional purposes. It had no liturgical purpose and no theological significance, but it was an honest cry of human need, of the need of divine companionship." It was published the following year in Dr. Richards' *Songs of Christian Praise,* 1880, and has become one of the most widely used and beloved hymns in this country.

MARYTON, composed for "Sun of my soul" by a clergyman of the Church of England, was Washington Gladden's choice for this hymn. It is said that he granted permission for its use only on condition that it be sung to MARYTON which was first published with Keble's hymn in *Church Hymns with Tunes,* 1874, edited by Arthur Sullivan. After receiving his B.A. and M.A. degrees from Balliol College, Oxford, Henry Percy Smith (1825–

1898) took holy orders and for two years was curate to Charles Kingsley at Eversley. He became perpetual curate of St. Michael's, York Town, Farnborough, Surrey (1851–1868), vicar of Great Barnton, Suffolk (1868–1882), chaplain of Christ Church, Cannes, France (1882–1895), and canon of the Cathedral of Gibraltar in 1892.

419 Thou God of All, Whose Spirit Moves

After graduating from Harvard University in 1902, summa cum laude and Phi Beta Kappa and receiving a Bachelor of Sacred Theology degree two years later from the same institution, John Haynes Holmes (1879–1964) was ordained as a Unitarian minister and called to the Church of the Messiah (Unitarian) in New York City. He remained there for forty-two years, until his retirement in 1949, achieving national recognition as a preacher, lecturer, author, hymn writer, and social reformer. Both Holmes and the church left the Unitarian denomination in 1919 to become nonsectarian, the church changing its name to The Community Church of New York. An ardent pacifist and a great admirer of Gandhi, he was active before his retirement in the American Civil Liberties Union and received the Gottheil medal for distinguished service to the Jews. Many institutions of higher learning conferred honorary degrees upon him. Among his numerous books are *The Revolutionary Function of a Modern Church,* 1912; *Religion for Today,* 1917; *Is Violence the Way Out?,* 1920; *The Sensible Man's View of Religion,* 1933; *The Affirmation of Immortality,* 1947; *My Gandhi,* 1953; and *I Speak for Myself,* 1959. His volume of *Collected Hymns* was published in 1960. The present hymn was among several that Holmes sent to the hymnal committee preparing the *Pilgrim Hymnal* in response to its request for new hymns dealing with social justice. This was its first appearance in a major Protestant hymnal, indeed in any hymnal. In his *Collected Hymns,* Holmes added this comment preceding the hymn: "This hymn is unused, which is a pity, for it is perhaps the best among my hymns on the theme of brotherhood. Record and recollection seem to agree that it is a late hymn, probably written after World War II." [30]

OLD 22ND   See No. 259 for comments on the tune.

420 O Holy City, Seen of John

In speaking of this modern counterpart to the vision of a heavenly Jerusalem as seen by John of Patmos in Revelations 21 and 22, Walter Russell Bowie, its author, has said:

> It was written at the request of Dr. Henry S. Coffin, who wanted some new hymns that would express the convictions that our hope of the Kingdom of God is not alone some far-off eschatological possibility but in its beginnings, at least, may be prepared for here on our actual earth. It is in this sense that it would differ from the mood of "O mother dear, Jerusalem."

It was first published in *Hymns of the Kingdom of God*, 1910, edited by Henry Sloane Coffin and Ambrose White Vernon. See No. 325 for comments on Bowie.

MORNING SONG   See No. 34 for comments on the tune.

421   We Thank Thee, Lord, Thy Paths of Service

For a period of more than ten years, Calvin Weis Laufer (1874–1938) met for luncheon once a week with his close friend and colleague, Dr. Herbert H. Field, pastor of the Flatbush Presbyterian Church in Brooklyn. At the time, Laufer was field secretary of the Board of Publication and Sabbath School Work of the Presbyterian Church, U.S.A. Following one such meal in the fall of 1919, when their thoughts and conversation had turned to the need and opportunities for Christian service, Laufer conceived the idea of writing a hymn appropriate to this theme, emphasizing the truth that communion with God and compassion for one's fellow men are inseparable. The present hymn is the result, each stanza of which celebrates the close tie between divine vision and human service. Sung at many summer conferences the following year, it was first published in *The Century Hymnal*, 1921. Laufer graduated from Union Theological Seminary in 1900 and ministered to Presbyterian churches in New York and New Jersey for fourteen years. He then served his denomination with distinction in various capacities as a national officer the remaining twenty-five years of his life. Endowed with talent as a musician, author, and educator, he wrote several books, supervised the publication of a number of hymnals, and was assistant editor of *The Hymnal*, 1933 (Presbyterian), and associate editor of the *Handbook to The Hymnal*, 1955.

FIELD   There is no record that Calvin Laufer, the composer of this tune, had any formal musical education. His son, Edward B. Laufer, says in a letter: "He was raised on a farm and probably received his early musical training from some local teacher. . . . His training was undoubtedly a composite of minor local teaching and some self-teaching." Dr. Laufer has been quoted as saying: "I began to play at service before I was ten and succeeded my father at the organ before I was sixteen." He earned his way through Franklin and Marshall College by giving music lessons and serving as organist of the college chapel and in a church as well. He harmonized his own tunes and made arrangements and harmonizations of existing tunes for the various publications which he edited. In 1925 Dr. Laufer became assistant editor for musical publications of the Board of Christian Education of the Presbyterian Church in the United States and prepared *When a Little Child Wants to Sing, Primary Music and Worship, The Junior Church School Hymnal,* and *The Church School Hymnal for Youth.* FIELD was one of five of his tunes included in *The Hymnal*, 1933. Throughout his life he was concerned about the relationship of music to worship and was deeply interested in hymnody and the "development of more appreciative hymn-singing in churches." He wrote in the Preface to *Hymn Lore:* "To live with hymns and make them one's own is the only sure way of appreciating their literary beauty and spiritual power."

422 When Through the Whirl of Wheels

Beloved by those who had known him as a chaplain in the first World War and admired for the fresh originality and vigor of his preaching, Geoffrey A. Studdert-Kennedy wrote this hymn for the Industrial Christian Fellowship, a movement aimed at achieving a greater measure of justice for the working man. First published in leaflet form, it later appeared in *The Unutterable Beauty,* 1927, a volume of his collected poetry. No other modern hymn matches it in its vivid fusion of scenes drawn from industrial life and the vision of an eschatological hope. See No. 34 for comments on Studdert-Kennedy.

LOMBARD STREET was composed for these words by an English musician, Frederick George Russell (1867–1929), a great admirer of Studdert-Kennedy. The tune appeared with the present text in *Songs of Praise,* 1925. After receiving his B.A. and Mus.B. degrees from London University, Russell served for thirty years as organist and choirmaster of St. Edmund the King and Martyr, Lombard Street, and for many years as master and director of music at Haberdashers' Aske's School where he had been a student. He wrote musical settings for a number of Studdert-Kennedy's poems, composed school songs, hymn tunes, church music, and piano pieces. In *Songs of Praise* the suggestion for the tempo of LOMBARD STREET is "slow."

423 Where Cross the Crowded Ways of Life

When *The Methodist Hymnal,* 1905, was in process of preparation, Caleb T. Winchester, a member of the editorial committee and a professor at Wesleyan University in Middletown, Connecticut, invited Frank Mason North (1850–1935) to write a missionary hymn for the new book. The latter demurred at first, saying that he was not a hymn writer, but he finally agreed to try. A short time later, as he was preparing a sermon on the text, "Go ye therefore into the highways, and as many as ye shall find, bid to the marriage" (Matthew 22:9), his attention was drawn to the American Revised Version which reads, "Go ye therefore unto the partings of the highways." It was this which suggested the first line, "Where cross the crowded ways of life," and gave him the idea of writing a missionary hymn for the city. The rest of the lines came easily, especially since North was deeply interested in the role of the church in urban life. First published in *The Christian City,* June 1903, the monthly newsletter of the New York City Missionary and Church Extension Society of the Methodist Episcopal Church, the hymn was included in *The Methodist Hymnal,* 1905, and is universally recognized as one of the finest hymns of its kind. After serving Methodist churches in New York and Connecticut, North was for the rest of his life a denominational executive in missionary work. He played a leading role in the formation of the Federal Council of Churches of Christ in America, and was its president from 1916 to 1920. Although he wrote several hymns, this is the only one to remain in use.

GERMANY (WALTON; FULDA; MELCHISEDEC) is another tune from Gardiner's *Sacred Melodies* (see Nos. 5 and 324) where it was headed

"Subject from Beethoven." In *Music and Friends,* 1838, Gardiner admitted that the tune was "somewhere in the works of Beethoven, but where I cannot point out." No convincing source in Beethoven's works has been found although Leonard Ellinwood's suggestion in *The Hymnal 1940 Companion* that the beginning and end of GERMANY might be from the *Allegretto ma non troppo* movement of his *Piano Trio,* Op. 70, No. 2, has merit. Some have noted the resemblance of the first phrase to the four-measure introduction to the aria "O Isis und Osiris" from the second act of Mozart's *Magic Flute,* and others think that it may be a German folk song. Whatever its source, the tune has had long and wide use. The association of GERMANY with North's hymn has been so widespread in American hymnody that it seems to be almost a proper for it. In English hymnals the tune is called FULDA or WAL–TON. The present harmonies are Gardiner's. See No. 5 for comments on Gardiner.

424 Hail the Glorious Golden City

As founder of The New York Society for Ethical Culture in 1876, Felix Adler (1851–1933) established himself as one of the foremost exponents of a nontheistic religious faith in this country. Born in Germany, he was brought to New York as a small child and graduated from Columbia University in 1870. In connection with his work with the Ethical Culture Society, he started the first free kindergarten in New York City and the first child study society in the United States. For many years he was Chairman of the National Child Labor Committee. In 1902 Columbia appointed him professor of political and social ethics, and in the academic year of 1908–1909 he was the Roosevelt professor at the University of Berlin. Oxford University invited him to give the Hibbert lectures in 1923. His major published works are *Creed and Deed,* 1877, *An Ethical Philosophy of Life,* 1918, and *The Reconstruction of the Spiritual Ideal,* 1923. He wrote this hymn in 1878 for use in the Sunday morning service of the Society for Ethical Culture, and it was first recited on that occasion by a daughter of one of the members. It is probably the most lyrical expression of the humanistic vision of "a new heaven and a new earth" that has been written, certainly in hymnic form. The last phrase almost brings the author to affirm an otherworldly hope.

LLANSANNAN   See No. 316 for comments on the tune.

425 Men, Whose Boast It Is

Although he had an undistinguished academic career at Harvard University as a student and failed as a practicing lawyer, James Russell Lowell (1819–1891) became one of the most widely known and respected leaders and literary figures of the nineteenth century. Upon discovering that his talents lay in writing, he rose rapidly in his chosen field and was appointed Smith professor of modern languages at Harvard in 1855, succeeding Henry Wadsworth Longfellow. From 1857 to 1862 he was the first editor of *The*

Atlantic Monthly and subsequently joined Charles Eliot Norton in publishing *The North American Review* for nine years, both journals notable for their high literary standards. An intense patriot and humanitarian, Lowell strongly opposed slavery and the annexation of the Southwest Territory in the Mexican War. He further distinguished himself and promoted his country's interests as Minister to Spain, 1877–1880, and Ambassador to Great Britain, 1880–1885. Best known for his poems, from which several hymns have been fashioned, he also wrote many books, including the epic *The Vision of Sir Launfal,* 1848; *The Biglow Papers,* 1846–1848 and 1867; and *Political Essays,* 1888. The present hymn, taken from his *Poems,* 1844, was first written as stanzas to be sung at the Anti-Slavery Society picnic in Dedham, Massachusetts, held on August 1, 1843, to mark the anniversary of the emancipation of the slaves in the West Indies.

IVES (GREENWOOD; BEULAH) This tune, of American origin, was restored to circulation by *The English Hymnal,* 1906, and set to Lowell's hymn in *Songs of Praise,* 1925. In both books the source given for it was the *Plymouth Collection* (U.S.A.), 1855, where it was named IVES and attributed to E. Ives, Jr. The tune was first published in *The Beethoven Collection of Sacred Music,* 1844, set to Montgomery's "Who are these in bright array?" the hymn found with it in a number of nineteenth-century American collections. Elam Ives, Jr. (1802–1864) was one of three editors of *The Beethoven Collection.* The other two were Henry C. Timm and A. Alpers, musicians closely connected with the Philharmonic Society of New York in its early days. In Ives' *Mozart Collection,* 1846, the present tune was named GREENWOOD. It is reminiscent of the Irish air for "The Ministrel Boy" and, like it, is in AABA form.

Ives was born, and died, in Hamden, Connecticut. Nothing is known of his general education or musical background. Apparently he started teaching in his early twenties, first near Hamden, later in Hartford, remaining there until 1830. With Deodatus Dutton, Jr., he edited *American Psalmody,* Hartford, 1829, which went through several editions. In 1830 he went to Philadelphia where he was active as teacher, author, editor, and for four years was principal of the Philadelphia Seminary. He moved to New York in 1830 and is thought to have lived there until a year or two before his death. Ives Academy of Music where "Singing, Playing, and the science of Harmony and Composition" were taught "in a thorough manner" was advertised on the back of *One Hundred Songs, Original and Selected,* published by Ives in the 1840's. In the American Musical Directory, 1861, he was listed as a teacher of piano, violin, and singing. During the summer of 1830, Ives and the educator, William C. Woodbridge, trained a choir of children at Hartford, basing their methods on Pestalozzi's educational theories which Woodbridge had seen practiced in Swiss and German schools. Ives's *American Elementary Singing Book,* 1831, "was probably the first music book written in America advocating the Pestalozzian principles," and it is quite possible that it was Woodbridge's account of Ives's application of these precepts to music teaching that led Lowell Mason to experiment with them. (See Robert W. John, "Elam Ives and the Pestalozzian Theory of Music Education," *Journal of Research in Music Education,* VIII, 1960, pp. 45–50.)

In 1831 Ives and Mason edited the *Juvenile Lyre,* described by Mason as "the first school song book published in this country." From May 1838 to June 1839, Ives served as editor of *The Music Review and Record of Musical Science, Literature, and Intelligence,* a periodical launched by a group of professional musicians in New York City. The collections he edited and his teaching received high praise from the famous music critic, John S. Dwight, in *The Harbinger,* published by the Transcendentalists at Brook Farm. When this journal was edited in New York, Ives was the only professional musician to contribute to its columns. In the music division of the New York Public Library there is a pamphlet (Drexel No. 880) describing the "Very Extensive, Rare and Valuable Musical Library, The entire Professional Library of Mr. E. Ives, Jr.," which was sold at auction in New York City on March 12 and 13, 1851. The items as listed in the catalog would seem to indicate that Ives was a person of considerable learning with a wide range of interests. One unusual feature of his *Mozart Collection* was the inclusion of four chorales harmonized by Johann Sebastian Bach.

426 The Voice of God Is Calling

Like John Henry Newman's "Lead, Kindly Light," this great hymn by John Haynes Holmes was written at sea while the author was returning from a trip abroad. In the Introduction to his *Collected Hymns,* 1960, he described the experience in these words:

> In September, 1913, I was returning on the S.S. *Laconia* to America, after a summer of delightful travel in England, Scotland, and Wales. Before leaving on this trip, I had promised a committee of the Young People's Religious Union (Unitarian), in charge of a convention in the fall, to write a special hymn adapted and dedicated to the occasion; and here I was on a swift ship headed for New York, and not a line of my hymn written. I had tried my hand at composition several times without result, except failure. Then suddenly, there came within me a veritable explosion of energy. In a few days I was listening to my words sung by a chorus of voices, fresh and lifted up.[30]

Based on Isaiah 6:8, the hymn was first published in the *New Hymn and Tune Book,* 1914, and was included in the *Pilgrim Hymnal,* 1931. It has been translated into German, Spanish, and Japanese. See No. 419 for comments on Holmes.

MEIRIONYDD has been attributed to William Lloyd (1786–1852). It was named BERTH in a manuscript book of tunes which he owned. It may be his own composition or his arrangement of a traditional Welsh hymn melody. The present form of the tune is from *Caniadau Seion,* 1840. Lloyd, thought to have been a farmer and cattle drover, was a self-educated man and an amateur musician with a fine voice and considerable knowledge of music. During frequent trips to England he made a point of attending church services in order to hear the congregational singing which impressed him greatly. He did much in Wales to further the cause of music. His home was a center for those whom he taught and for those who enjoyed singing together. In the parishes and districts of Lleyn he conducted music classes and singing meetings. MEIRIONYDD, pronounced Mer'-i-on-eth, is the Welsh name for Merioneth, a county south of Carnarvon, where Lloyd lived and died.

Those who play this splendid tune should give full value to the first two notes of phrases one, two, and four. They are sometimes played as if they were written ♪. ♪, a practice which deprives the music of much of its strength and individuality.

427 We Are Living, We Are Dwelling

These stirring lines by Arthur Cleveland Coxe were written in 1840 during a period of national stress, a few years before the outbreak of the Mexican War, when the author was only twenty-two years of age. James Russell Lowell's "The Present Crisis" was inspired by the same critical times (see No. 441). Later generations were to refer to these years as the golden age of American literature. The hymn first appeared under the title "Watchwords" in *Athanasion . . . also miscellaneous poems,* 1842. See No. 264 for comments on Coxe.

BLAENHAFEN, a traditional Welsh melody, was the setting for these words in the Presbyterian *Hymnal,* 1933. In *University Hymns,* published in 1931 by the Yale University Press, the tune was called BLAENHAFEN. There seems to be no available information about its source or its name. The rhythmic motif ♩. ♪ ♩ which appears three times in each phrase gives the melody individuality as well as an air of dogged resolution and earnestness well suited to the text. The tune is in the familiar AABA form. It should be played with deliberateness and with care not to shorten the eighth notes or hurry the dotted quarters.

428 When Israel was in Egypt's Land

Of unknown origin and authorship, this Negro spiritual belongs among the many great folk songs of the Negro people that emerged during the period of slavery. In the present struggle for freedom, justice, and social equality, music and singing have again become important and spontaneous forms of expression. Martin Luther King, Jr., president of the Southern Christian Leadership Conference, has declared: "The freedom songs are playing a strong and vital role in our struggle. They give the people new courage and a sense of unity. I think they keep alive a faith, a radiant hope, in the future, particularly in our most trying hours." (*The New York Times,* Monday, August 20, 1962.)

GO DOWN MOSES is a fine example of the type of spiritual in which the leading lines were sung by one voice followed by the response of a group and then by a true refrain or chorus. In his preface to the first *Book of American Negro Spirituals,* 1925, James Weldon Johnson says of "Go down,

Moses": "There is not a nobler theme in the whole musical literature of the world. If the Negro had voiced himself in only that one song, it would have been evidence of his nobility of soul." [16]

See Nos. 353 and 415 for further comments on Negro spirituals.

429 Eternal Father, Strong to Save

Written for travelers at sea, this hymn is known in the United States as the Navy Hymn, and is sung regularly at the United States Naval Academy at Annapolis. There is a beautiful version in *Nouveau Libre Cantique* (the hymnal of the French Navy) which ends with the refrain:

> Vois nos pleurs, entends nos sanglots,
> Pour ceux en péril sur les flots.

William Whiting (1825–1878) wrote the hymn in 1860, and it was considerably revised by the compilers of *Hymns Ancient and Modern,* 1861. The present version with slight modifications is from the Appendix to *Psalms and Hymns,* 1869, as revised by the author himself. Sir Evelyn Wood made the discerning comment, "It is much used by those at sea, and when the wind blows hard, by those on land." As the favorite hymn of Franklin Delano Roosevelt, it was sung at his funeral at Hyde Park, New York, April 14, 1945. It was also played at the funeral services for John Fitzgerald Kennedy on November 25, 1963. Whiting was a Londoner by birth and served for twenty years as master of the Winchester College Choristers' School. He is remembered today chiefly for this one hymn.

MELITA, composed for these words, was one of seven tunes by John B. Dykes included in *Hymns Ancient and Modern,* 1861. It was named for the island on which Paul landed after being shipwrecked (Acts 28:1), now known as Malta, the largest of the Maltese Islands situated in the Mediterranean between Europe and Africa. The hymn was played by the Navy Band as President John F. Kennedy's casket was carried up the east front steps of the Capitol on November 25, 1963.

MELITA is sometimes played at too rapid a tempo with a sense of pushing ahead at the ends of phrases. Originally there was a fermata over the third note in measures four and eight, as in measure twelve. In *The Hymnal 1940* these notes are printed as half notes. See No. 79 for comments on Dykes.

430 Rejoice, O Land, in God Thy Might

Beginning his career as a physician, Robert Seymour Bridges (1844–1930) gave up his medical practice in 1882 as well as his position as casualty physician at St. Bartholomew's Hospital, London, and physician at the Great Northern Hospital, to devote his talents to literature, music, and hymnody. At the time, he had already been recognized as an exceptionally gifted poet. Establishing his home in the Berkshire village of Yattendon, he was put in charge of the local church choir and immediately set to work to improve the quality of the hymns and congregational singing. This led to the publication of his notable and handsome collection, *The Yattendon Hymnal*, 1899, containing one hundred hymns, for which he selected and matched texts and tunes. No less than forty-four of the hymns were either written, adapted, or translated by him. James Moffatt has described the collection as "easily the most distinguished of individual contributions to modern hymnody." [1] and Percy Dearmer has referred to Bridges' hymns as "the advance-guard of a movement which will lead the Englishman of the future to read hymn-books for the poetry that is in them." The present hymn, first published in *The Yattendon Hymnal*, was written in 1897, the year of the Diamond Jubilee of Queen Victoria. Bridges published a number of volumes of poetry and other literary works and an oratorio, all distinguished by their quality of excellence. He was named poet laureate in 1913 in recognition of his great contribution to English letters.

WAREHAM, a well-known and deservedly popular eighteenth-century psalm tune found in most English and American hymnals, has been praised as one of the best congregational tunes ever written. It is a fluent melody, moving in step-wise progression except for one skip in the second measure. With the heading "For the holy Sacrament," and set to Psalm 36, WARE–HAM was published in 1738 in William Knapp's *Sett of New Psalm Tunes and Anthems in Four Parts*.

Not much is known about Knapp (1698–1768), composer of this melody. The records of the parish church in Wareham, Dorsetshire, where he was born, were destroyed by fire in 1762. It is believed that he was of German descent and that he served as organist in Wareham and also at St. James' parish church in Poole, a neighboring town where he was parish clerk for thirty-nine years. Knapp's services and those of George Savage, sexton at St. James', prompted one H. Price, a fellow townsman, to contribute the following to the London Magazine in 1742:

> From pounce and paper, ink and pen,
>   Save me, O Lord, I pray;
> From Pope and Swift and such-like men,
>   And Cibber's annual lay;
> From doctors' bills and lawyers' fees,
>   From ague, gout and trap;
> And what is ten times worse than these,
>   George Savage and Will Knapp.

In the *Yattendon Hymnal* the present hymn was set to TALLIS' CANON but in *The English Hymnal*, 1906, to WAREHAM, a combination now found in a number of hymnals in England and America. Knapp's melody has been known in America at least since 1771. In that year it appeared in *The American Harmony: or Royal Melody Complete*, compiled by William Tans'ur and published at Newbury-Port, Massachusetts, by Daniel Bayley. In a form close to the original, without text, it was called ALL–SAINTS, the name found with it in numerous American collections.

431 God of Our Fathers, Known of Old

This well-known poem by Rudyard Kipling was written for Queen Victoria's Diamond Jubilee in 1897 at the request of the *Times,* London. He later remarked:

> That poem gave me more trouble than anything I ever wrote. I had promised the *Times* a poem for the Jubilee, and when it became due I had written nothing that had satisfied me. The *Times* began to want the poem badly, and sent letter after letter asking for it. I made many more attempts, but no further progress. Finally the *Times* began sending me telegrams. So I shut myself up in a room with the determination to stay there until I had written a Jubilee poem. Sitting down with all my previous attempts before me, I searched through those dozens of sketches, till at last I found just one line I liked. That was "Lest we forget." Round these words "The Recessional" was written.

It appeared in the *Times* of July 17, 1897, and was included in his *The Five Nations,* 1903, as "Recessional." The stern warning against the perils of a self-righteous imperialism, made acutely specific by the allusions to the jubilee procession and naval review in the second and third stanzas, caused a national furor that brought both praise and cries of outrage. It is now universally recognized as one of the greatest national poems ever written. See No. 392 for comments on Kipling.

FOLKINGHAM, selected for these words by Ralph Vaughan Williams, editor of *The English Hymnal,* 1906, is from *A Supplement to the New Version of the Psalms,* 1708, where it was described as a new tune and set to a metrical version of the Lord's Prayer. It is a tune of great dignity and breadth. The oftener it is sung with Kipling's words, the finer it seems as a setting for them. Its last six measures give new force to the refrain. The harmonization given here is from *The English Hymnal.*

432 God of the Nations, Who from Dawn of Days

Originally published in *The Survey,* January, 1914, under the title, "One Hundred Hymns of Brotherhood and Aspiration," this hymn by W. Russell Bowie first appeared in a hymnal in *Social Hymns of Brotherhood and Aspiration,* 1914, published by A. S. Barnes and Company. It is another fine example of the author's ability to combine a flawless literary style with a profoundly biblical social concern. It has not been included in any other major denominational hymnal. See No. 325 for comments on Bowie.

TOULON consists of four of the five phrases of the tune for Psalm 124 in the Genevan Psalter of 1551 which is given in its full and original form at No. 451. The third phrase has been omitted, the rhythm of the last phrase has been altered, and *g* in measure eight has been substituted for *e.* In *The National Psalmist,* 1848, edited by Lowell Mason and George Webb, the tune MONTAGUE is the same as TOULON except for two notes. See No. 451 for further comments on the tune.

433 God of Our Fathers, Whose Almighty Hand

On the occasion of the centennial celebration of the Declaration of Independence, Daniel Crane Roberts (1841–1907), then rector of St. Thomas' Episcopal Church in Brandon, Vermont, wrote these stirring words for use during the festivities there. He later sent them anonymously to the commission preparing a new hymnal for The Protestant Episcopal Church, and they were accepted for inclusion in *The Hymnal*, 1894. Two members of the commission selected this hymn to be sung at the centennial of the adoption of the Constitution of the United States held in New York City in 1887. After graduating from Kenyon College, Gambier, Ohio, in 1857, and serving as a private in the Civil War, Roberts was ordained a deacon in 1865 and a priest the following year. For the last twenty-nine years of his life he was the vicar of St. Paul's Episcopal Church in Concord, New Hampshire, where he died on October 31, 1907. In an autobiographical letter he said of himself: "My personal history is of little account. . . . I remain a country Parson, known only within my own small world." His hymn has brought him wide and probably lasting recognition.

NATIONAL HYMN   By request, the musical editors restored to this tune the introductory trumpet figure which had been omitted in the 1931 *Pilgrim Hymnal, The Hymnal 1940,* and the *Hymnal for Schools and Colleges,* 1956. Too often the trumpet interludes dominate to such an extent that worshippers hardly think of the words they are singing and the music is cheapened. Organists should remember that a little trumpet goes a long way.

George W. Warren (1828–1902) composed NATIONAL HYMN for this text (then anonymous) after it had been selected as the hymn for New York City's centennial celebration of the adoption of the Constitution of the United States. Warren, a native of Albany and a graduate of Racine College which granted him an honorary doctorate in music, was largely a self-taught musician. He served as organist at St. Peter's and St. Paul's in Albany; at Holy Trinity, Brooklyn; and at St. Thomas' in New York City from 1870 to 1900. He composed anthems, cantatas, service music, and published *Warren's Hymns and Tunes as Sung at St. Thomas' Church,* 1888. His compositions, though popular at the time, have not endured.

434 God Send Us Men Whose Aim 'Twill Be

As a leading member of the Society of Friends in England and a gifted hymn writer, Frederick John Gillman (1866–1949) served as one of the editors of the Society's hymnal *The Fellowship Hymnbook,* 1910 (revised edition, 1933). The present hymn first appeared in this collection. Gillman was active in the work of the Hymn Society of England and the National Adult School Union. His book *The Evolution of the English Hymn,* 1927, is a recognized and highly regarded work in its field.

MELROSE, the setting for this text in the 1931 *Pilgrim Hymnal* was retained at the request of those familiar with it. The simple, sturdy melody DAS WALT' GOTT VATER, is suggested as an alternative tune. See No. 98 for comments on Frederick C. Maker, the composer of MELROSE.

435 Judge Eternal, Throned in Splendor

Educated at Eton and Balliol College, Oxford, Henry Scott Holland (1847–1918) became one of England's great preachers and social reformers. Among the important positions he held were select preacher at Oxford, 1879–1880, and 1894–1896; canon of St. Paul's Cathedral, 1884–1910, and precentor, 1886–1910; Romanes lecturer at Oxford, 1908; regius professor of divinity at Oxford, 1910–1918. Because of his deep concern about social problems, he helped found the Christian Social Union and edited its official monthly journal *The Commonwealth* from its inception in 1896 until his death. Five of his books were composed of articles that he had written for this publication. A skilled musician, he raised the musical standards of the services at St. Paul's and helped edit *The English Hymnal,* 1906. The only hymn he wrote is the present one which was first published in *The Commonwealth,* July, 1902, and was included in *The English Hymnal.* It reflects his two major interests, social reform and mission. A memorial tablet in his honor in Christ Church Cathedral in Oxford bears the words: *Invisibilem tanquam videns Deum, Regnum Ejus coeleste fide inconcussa, spe vivida, caritate hilari, nunquam non in terra praestruebat"* ("As beholding God Invisible, he was unceasingly founding on earth His Heavenly Kingdom, in unshaken faith, lively hope, joyous love").

RHUDDLAN, in the present arrangement, was set to Holland's hymn in *The English Hymnal,* 1906, and *Songs of Praise,* 1925. It is a traditional Welsh melody, found in Edward Jones' *Musical Relicks of the Welsh Bards,* 1794. The original Welsh title of the tune, "Dewch i'r Frwydr" (Come to Battle) indicates its rather martial character. RHUDDLAN is set to Harry Emerson Fosdick's hymn, "God of grace and God of glory" in three English hymnals: *The Fellowship Hymnal,* 1933, *Congregational Praise,* 1953, and *The Baptist Hymn Book,* 1962. This was one of more than sixty Welsh folk tunes arranged for voices, violin, and piano (or harp) by Franz J. Haydn for George Thomson, Edinburgh publisher, between 1799 and 1805.

Rhuddlan, a small village located near the mouth of the river Clwyd in Flintshire, North Wales, was once a seaport of considerable importance, a place linked with stirring episodes in Welsh and English history. The name (pronounced "Rithlan"), made up of "rhudd" meaning red, and "glan" meaning shore, was apparently given to the town because of the reddish color of the banks of the river on which it is situated.

436 O God of Earth and Altar

Few men during the first half of the twentieth century aroused more diverse reactions than Gilbert Keith Chesterton (1874–1936). George Bernard Shaw called him a colossal genius, and others regarded him as an intolerant medievalist. His trenchant pen and tongue, spilling over with provocative ideas and paradoxes, made him one of the most brilliant journalists of his day. A militant foe of almost everything modern and an ardent converted Catholic, he argued for a return to the guild system of the medieval period as the cure for the ills of an industrial society. He was intensely religious and his book *Orthodoxy,* 1908, was both a scintillating defense of the Christian faith and a scathing attack on secularism. So prodigious were his energies that he was able to dictate 13,000 to 14,000 words a week while meeting a schedule of lectures that would have floored an ordinary man. He is best known in the United States for his delightful series of *Father Brown* detective stories extolling the wit and perspicacity of a droll Catholic priest. Originally published in Henry Scott Holland's magazine, *The Commonwealth,* the present hymn was later included in *The English Hymnal,* 1906.

LLANGLOFFAN, a Welsh hymn melody, was set to Chesterton's hymn in *The Hymnal,* 1933, (Presbyterian). The present harmonization is from *The English Hymnal,* 1906. The origin of the tune is unknown. It was included in the Rev. D. Evans' *Hymnau a Thonau* ("Hymns and Tunes"), 1865. Erik Routley calls LLANGLOFFAN sturdy and describes it as "one of those tunes which give the lie to the superstition that tunes in minor modes are mournful."

437   My Country, 'Tis of Thee

This most popular of all our national hymns was written by Samuel Francis Smith in 1832 while he was a first-year student at Andover Theological Seminary in Andover, Massachusetts. Having been given a number of German song books by Lowell Mason with the request that he translate the texts into English, Smith was particularly impressed with one of the tunes, now known as AMERICA, set to the words "Gott segne Sachsenland" (God bless our Saxon land"). It was this which provided him with his inspiration and he later said:

I instantly felt the impulse to write a patriotic hymn of my own, adapted to the tune. Picking up a scrap of waste paper which lay near me, I wrote at once, probably within half an hour, the hymn "America" as it is now known everywhere. The whole hymn stands today as it stood on the bit of waste paper.

It was first sung in the Park Street Congregational Church, Boston, Massachusetts, July 4, 1832, at the Independence Day services held by the Boston Sabbath School Union under the direction of Lowell Mason. In his book, *Baptist Hymn Writers and Their Hymns,* 1888, Henry S. Burrage wrote of this hymn that it "soon became popular in children's celebrations, patriotic meetings, thanksgivings, and having come into general use in this country, it has traveled round the globe, and is everywhere known as the American national hymn." See No. 305 for further comments on Smith.

AMERICA (NATIONAL ANTHEM)   It is curious that the melody for the British national anthem which had been sung by colonists in New England before and after the American Revolution with a variety of words, should have come into general use in the United States by way of a German patriotic hymn found in a German hymnbook. Obviously, the young Samuel Smith was not one of those Americans who knew the tune, although in 1831, the year before he wrote "My country 'tis of thee," it appeared in Volume

II of *The Christian Lyre,* named CREATION and set to two hymns. Its inclusion in that collection would seem to indicate that it was a well-known tune.

In spite of research on the part of a number of people for more than two centuries, nothing is known definitely of the origin of AMERICA which Percy Scholes said "must be the best-known tune in the world," basing his statement on its use throughout the British Commonwealth of Nations, in the United States, and in a number of other countries. Among various compositions which scholars have thought might have some rhythmic or melodic connection with the tune are a medieval plainsong, an "Ayre" by John Bull, a Scottish carol, an English ballad, two instrumental pieces, and a catch of Purcell's. The latter, printed in 1685, seems convincing evidence that the tune was well known by then. It has been attributed to Henry Carey, Jack Oswald, Lully, and Handel; and it has been said that it was written for and sung in the Catholic chapel of King James II. The earliest printed versions of the tune with the words "God save the King" were in *Thesaurus Musicus* (c. 1744, 1745) and *The Gentleman's Magazine,* 1745, the period from which its popularity dates.

Hearing "God save the King" sung in England inspired Haydn to write the AUSTRIAN HYMN (see No. 267). Other composers also admired it and made use of it. Weber used it in his cantata "Kampf und Sieg," in his "Jubel Overture," and made two four-part settings of it for voices. Beethoven, who wrote in his diary, "I must show the English what a blessing they have in 'God save the King,'" introduced it into his *Battle Symphony,* wrote a set of seven variations on it for piano, and made an arrangement of it for solo and chorus with piano, violin, and cello accompaniment. Brahms used it in his "Triumphlied."

In "The Boys," written by Oliver Wendell Holmes in 1859 for the thirtieth reunion of his class at Harvard, are the following lines about Smith, who was one of his classmates:

> And there's a nice youngster of excellent pith:
> Fate tried to conceal him by naming him Smith;
> But he shouted a song for the brave and the free —
> Just read on his medal, "My country" — "Of thee."

438 O God, Beneath Thy Guiding Hand

Born in the trading post of Fort Detroit (now Detroit, Michigan), the son of missionaries to the Indians, Leonard Bacon (1802–1881) spent the early years of his life on the frontier and then went east to live with his uncle in Hartford, Connecticut. After graduating from Yale University and Andover Theological Seminary, he was ordained and installed as pastor of Center Church, New Haven, Connecticut, in 1825, where he remained for forty-one years. He helped found *The Independent* in 1848, which has been called the most influential religious publication in America in the last half of the nineteenth century. An eloquent preacher and a formidable debater, Bacon played a leading part in the antislavery struggle. During the last fifteen years of his life he taught theology, church polity, and American church history at the Yale Divinity School. He retained a lifelong interest in hymnology, beginning with his student days in seminary where in 1823 he edited an important tract entitled *Hymns and Sacred Songs for the Monthly Concert*. Bacon wrote the present hymn in 1838 for the bicentennial celebration of the founding of New Haven, Connecticut. He revised and included it in *Psalms and Hymns for Christian Use and Worship*, 1845, of which he was one of the editors.

DUKE STREET   See No. 202 for comments on the tune.

439   Not Alone for Mighty Empire

At a Union Thanksgiving Service in Chicago, probably in 1909, Jenkin Lloyd Jones, a Unitarian minister, offered a prayer which emphasized the spiritual blessings bestowed upon America. William Pierson Merrill, then minister of the Sixth Presbyterian Church of Chicago, was present and was so impressed with the prayer that he went home and, as he later said, "wrote a rather diffusive hymn about it and later made it over into the present one." It first appeared in 1911 in *The Continent*, a Presbyterian paper published in Chicago. Howard Chandler Robbins has described this as one of the greatest national hymns in the English language. See No. 300 for further comments on Merrill.

AUSTRIAN HYMN   See No. 267 for comments on the tune.

440   O Beautiful for Spacious Skies

Katherine Lee Bates (1859–1929), author of this hymn, developed from a shy, nearsighted, small-town, New England girl, "always hiding away with a book," into an English instructor and later head of the English department at Wellesley College. Thinks to the rigid frugality and interested generosity of her eldest brother, then having only a clerk's meager salary, she was able to obtain her A.B. from Wellesley, entering that college when it was only a year old. Sabbaticals and summer vacations took her abroad a number of times, but the summer of 1893 found her in the West for the first time, at a Colorado Springs summer school, lecturing on English religious drama. One morning, as she watched the sunrise from the summit of Pikes Peak, she was so enraptured over "the expanse of mountain ranges and sea-like sweep of plains" that in the evening she wrote the first version of this famous patriotic hymn. The present and revised version was first printed in the *Boston Evening Transcript*, November 19, 1904. En route to Colorado, Miss Bates visited the Chicago World's Fair, and later reported in the *Journal* of the National Education Association that the fair's White City appealed so strongly to patriotic feeling that it was largely responsible for at least the last stanza of the hymn. "It was with this quickened and deepened sense of America," she wrote, "that we went on, my New England eyes delighting in the wind-waved gold of the vast wheat fields."

Commenting on this hymn again in 1928 Miss Bates said, "All through these years requests have come to use the song in one way or another. . . .

I am only too glad to give it free as my own slight gift to my country." She did not accede to requests to add a stanza expressing international brotherhood, although she longed for world brotherhood and United States membership in the League of Nations. She felt the song was long enough and had been written for one special purpose, and suggested instead that when singing the first stanza "you think of 'From sea to shining sea,' as applying from the Pacific to the Atlantic, around the other way, and all the states between, and that will include all the nations and all the people from sea to shining sea." Miss Bates was honored by doctorates from Middlebury, Oberlin, and Wellesley colleges and was the author or editor of about two dozen books. She collected her poems in 1911 under the title, *America the Beautiful*. Orbiting the earth in the summer of 1960, Echo I, the United States communications balloon satellite, served as the dramatic relay for this, the first song, indeed the first music, ever to be projected to and returned from outer space.

MATERNA, composed by Samuel A. Ward for "O mother dear, Jerusalem" (whence its name) and first published with that text in the *Parish Choir* for July 12, 1888, was included in Charles L. Hutchins' musical edition of the Protestant Episcopal *Hymnal,* 1894. It is said that Ward composed and jotted down the tune on his cuff as he was crossing New York harbor after a day's outing at Coney Island, then a fashionable resort. An employee of the prosperous retail music business founded by Ward in 1878 said that MATERNA was first sung in 1882 by a choir of two hundred men and boys in Grace Church, Newark, New Jersey. Ward, a native of Newark and the son of a shoemaker, is said to have studied harmony in New York City and to have played for a time at the Collegiate Church of St. Nicholas, perhaps as a substitute. The records of that church contain no reference to him. After serving in various Newark churches he became organist and choirmaster of Grace Church in 1880. The Orpheus Club which he founded and directed was a highly respected musical organization of its day. After Ward's death, his widow received a request from the president of the Massachusetts Agricultural College to use the tune MATERNA as a setting for "America the beautiful." During World War I the combination became popular and MATERNA is now the accepted setting for Miss Bates' hymn, although some sixty other tunes have been used with it. A plaque on the exterior wall of the parish house of Grace Church, Broad and Walnut Streets, Newark, reads:

> 1847–1903   Samuel Augustus Ward for many years organist and choirmaster of this Church. In 1882 he composed the tune "Materna" for the hymn "O Mother Dear Jerusalem." In 1912 this composition was adapted to "America the Beautiful" by Katherine Lee Bates and gained for him national distinction. Founder and director of the Orpheus Club, 1889–1900. Erected in his memory by the Schoolmen's Club, assisted by the public-school pupils of Newark, New Jersey, May 17, 1934.

441   Once to Every Man and Nation

To express his strong opposition to the war with Mexico in 1845, which he considered to be an unjust aggression and which he felt would result in extending the institution of slavery, James Russell Lowell wrote a poem, "The Present Crisis," consisting of ninety lines, condemning the action of his country. It was later published in his *Poems,* 1844. W. Garrett Horder selected sixteen of the lines to form a hymn for his *Hymns, Supplemental to Existing Collections,* 1894, and later included them in his *Worship Song,* 1905. The original lines were rearranged and considerably altered, and, in order to fit the meter, one line was omitted in each stanza. By this skillful editing, Horder transformed a great poem into a great national hymn. See No. 425 for comments on Lowell.

EBENEZER (TON–Y–BOTEL) People whose knowledge of hymn tunes is slight are often able to call this Welsh melody by name and even tell its history. The baseless but romantic legend of its having been found sealed in a bottle that was washed ashore on the Welsh coast has captivated them as it did those who first heard the story from a young English singer. After this young man had sung the tune for a group of friends, he was asked where it came from, and on the spur of the moment and in jest he made up the name and the tune-in-the-bottle story, which they believed. Like the tune, the tale was given wide and enthusiastic circulation. When it was first published in a Welsh hymnal, *Llawlyfr Moliant,* 1890, it was called EBENEZER, the name given it in most English collections. The tune, composed by Thomas J. Williams (1869–1944), Welsh organist and choirmaster, pupil of Dr. David Evans (No. 38), was used originally in the second movement of a memorial anthem "Golen yn y Glyn" ("Light in the Valley"). Williams was no more than twenty-one years old when he wrote the tune. *The English Hymnal,* 1906, is said to have introduced the melody into English hymnody, but not with Lowell's words; they were set to HYFRYDOL in that collection. In the United States EBENEZER has become a proper for Lowell's poem. It is an extremely effective tune, very simple in its form (AABA), built almost entirely on the motif in the first measure and restricted in its range to seven notes. Erik Routley calls it one of the noblest and most striking examples of modern Welsh hymnody and speaks of its majestic stride.

442 Thou Judge By Whom Each Empire Fell

These lines were written by Percy Dearmer "in the attempt to express what is felt to be the truth about the idea of judgment, and also because there were not enough hymns to carry the great tunes in this meter." [8] (*Songs of Praise Discussed*) The hymn first appeared in *Songs of Praise,* 1925. See No. 112 for comments on Dearmer.

NUN FREUT EUCH was the setting for this hymn in *Songs of Praise,* 1925. See No. 271 for comments on the tune.

443 Mine Eyes Have Seen the Glory

In December of 1861, six months after the start of the Civil War, the poet and social reformer Julia Ward Howe (1819–1910) heard Union troops singing "John Brown's Body" in Washington, D.C. Its stirring tune prompted James Freeman Clarke to suggest that she write more fitting words for it, which she did before the next daybreak. *The Atlantic Monthly,* February, 1862, printed them under the title, "The Battle Hymn of the Republic." Mrs. Howe, one of America's outstanding women, was a pioneer in woman suffrage and an ardent abolitionist. On public platforms and in Unitarian and other pulpits she was a strong and persuasive speaker. In 1870 she proposed that women should organize themselves to end wars. She was the author of three volumes of verse as well as books on social issues and a biography of Margaret Fuller. Her husband, Samuel Gridley Howe, was also a remarkable idealist who as a youth fought in the Greek Civil War and devoted the rest of his life to helping the blind, the dumb, and the mentally ill.

This hymn was sung at Sir Winston Churchill's funeral on January 30, 1965, in St. Paul's Cathedral, London, at his request and in homage to the honorary citizenship granted him by the United States of America in 1963.

BATTLE HYMN OF THE REPUBLIC   The source of the "John Brown tune" which inspired Mrs. Howe's great poem is unknown, although since the 1880's, when it was probably the best-known tune in America, it has been attributed in many books to William Steffe, a Philadelphian, who died in 1911. In an article which appeared in the *Grand Army Scout and Soldier's Mail,* Philadelphia, November, 1883, it was stated that Steffe claimed the tune as his own, saying that he had written it in 1855 or 1856 for some verses starting "Say, bummers, will you meet us" and later had set it to a song of welcome with which the Goodwill Engine Company of Philadelphia greeted the Liberty Fire Company of Baltimore. Brander Matthews made use of this information in his "Songs of the War," published in the *Century Magazine,* August, 1887, and thus gave considerable circulation to Steffe's story. In *Glory, Glory Hallelujah! The Story of "John Brown's Body" and the "Battle Hymn of the Republic,"* 1960 (C. J. Krehbiel Company, Cincinnati), Boyd B. Stutler calls the Steffe claim a myth and confirms the general opinion that the source of the tune, like that of many folk tunes, may never be known.

BATTLE HYMN OF THE REPUBLIC was sung in the south in Negro churches and by firemen long before the Civil War according to Louis Elson who discusses it in *National Music of America,* 1900. It was associated with the camp-meeting song "Say, brothers, will you meet us" which was a favorite at revival meetings. Both Elson and Stutler tell of the tune's being popularized by men of the Second Battalion, Boston Light Infantry, Massachusetts Volunteer Militia, familiarly known as "The Tigers." They had learned the camp-meeting song originally from a group of singers in their unit but early in the war began to improvise words about one of their number, Sergeant John Brown of Boston, a good-natured Scotsman who was the object of much bantering on their part because of his name. Later when some of his group joined the Twelfth Massachusetts Volunteer Infantry commanded by Col. Fletcher Webster, son of Daniel Webster, they took the John Brown song with them and came to be known as the "Hallelujah Regiment" after their march up Broadway in New York City on July 24, 1861. Their singing on that occasion created tremendous enthusiasm, and news of the song spread rapidly. On August 9, 1861 a writer in the Chicago *Tribune* said: "It is a queer medley but the soldiers like it and sing it with great energy to an old camp meeting melody. The Virginians will think that John Brown is worshipped as a Northern hero, in spite of all denials, if even Fletcher Webster's Boston troops sing such a song as this. So on all hands providence seems to be involving slavery with the war, notwithstanding the most sincere efforts of patriotism and statesmanship to keep the constitutional lines distinct." To the Northerners there was only one John Brown, the man who had led the raid on Harper's Ferry, and the Scottish soldier whose name had inspired the words in the beginning was forgotten. He was drowned crossing the Rappahannock River on June 6, 1862. The use of the song by troops and civilians in the North made it "the mighty war song that roared its way from first to last through all the four years of the Civil War." Elson calls the tune "one of the best marching melodies in existence." It has been sung and marched to not only in the United States with a great variety of words but in nearly all parts of the world in one form or another.

Mrs. Howe's words transformed the song into a minor national anthem. As a matter of fact, during his presidency Theodore Roosevelt tried to have it authorized as *the* national anthem. For Americans the present tune and words are inseparable. In some English hymnals the words are set to tunes by Walford Davies and Martin Shaw, settings which may seem strange to those for whom the "John Brown Tune" and Mrs. Howe's words and the Civil War are all one piece.

444   O Day of God, Draw Nigh

This modern hymn, with its decidedly this-world conception of the Last Judgment was written in 1937 by Robert B. Y. Scott (1899–   ) for a hymn sheet of the Fellowship for a Christian Social Order. It was later published in *Hymns for Worship,* 1939. Scott was ordained as a minister of the United Church of Canada in 1926 and from 1931 to 1955 taught Old Testament at United Theological College, McGill University, Montreal. During World War II he served as honorary flight lieutenant and chaplain of the Royal Canadian Air Force. Since 1955 he has been professor of religion at Princeton University. Active all his life in the cause of social reform, he has published two significant books in this field, *The Relevance of the Prophets,* 1944, and *Towards the Christian Revolution,* 1936, the latter as joint author with Gregory Vlastos.

ST. MICHAEL   See No. 237 for comments on the tune.

445   Father Eternal, Ruler of Creation

Equally noted as a book illustrator, novelist, poet, and dramatist, Laurence Housman (1865–1959) has been called England's most censored playwright. He achieved overnight fame and created a sensation with *An English-woman's Love Letters,* 1900, published anonymously, which the public thought genuine and which some critics attributed to Queen Victoria. More than eighty books have come from his pen, including several religious plays. His play *Victoria Regina,* which was banned from the English stage, had a successful run on Broadway during the 1935–1936 season with Helen Hayes in the leading role. Confirmed as an Anglican, Housman was attracted to Roman Catholicism for a time, but in later years, because of his pacifist convictions, he was drawn to the Society of Friends. He wrote the present hymn in 1919 at the request of H. R. L. Sheppard, rector of St. Martin's-in-the-Fields, London, for the Life and Liberty Movement, a group formed after World War I to promote international peace. It was first published in a hymnal in *Songs of Praise,* 1925. A friend said of him, "Laurence Housman has the heart of compassion for the little ones of the earth, the dumb and helpless, that ought to be, but is not always, an essential part of poetry. His is the true Franciscan spirit."

LANGHAM, written for these words in 1919 by Geoffrey T. Shaw (1879–1943), was first sung at a mass meeting of the Life and Liberty Movement (dedicated to the cause of international peace) at Queen's Hall, London. Shaw shared many of the interests of his older brother Martin (see No. 106) and like him played an important part in helping to raise the standard of music in schools and churches, and to encourage wider interest in good music. This he did as composer, teacher, editor, senior inspector of music in schools in London, and chairman of the school music subcommittee of the British Broadcasting Company. His early musical education was as a chorister at St. Paul's Cathedral; later, as organ scholar at Caius College, Cambridge. From 1902 to 1910 he was music master at Gresham's School, Holt; in 1920 he succeeded his brother as organist of St. Mary's, Primrose Hill. He was a well-known adjudicator at music festivals. He composed songs for use in schools, hymn tunes, edited a number of sacred and secular collections, and was one of the major contributors to *Songs of Praise. The Descant Hymn-Tune Book* (in two volumes), edited by Shaw, contains sixty-nine descants written by him for well-known hymn tunes. In 1932 the Archbishop of Canterbury conferred the Doctor of Music degree on both Martin and Geoffrey Shaw.

446 God the Omnipotent

The first two stanzas of this hymn are from a hymn written by Henry F. Chorley (1808–1872) in 1842, beginning with the line, "God the All-Terrible! King, who ordainest." Based on the Russian national anthem and set to the tune RUSSIA, Chorley's hymn was first published in John Hullah's *Part Music,* 1842, with the title "In Time of War." In 1870, a few days before the crucial Battle of Sedan in the Franco-German War, John Ellerton, following Chorley's example, wrote a hymn, "God, the Almighty One, wisely ordaining," from which the last two stanzas of the present hymn are derived. These verses were brought together in their present form, with considerable alterations and revisions, in R. Brown-Borthwick's *Select Hymns for Church and Home,* 1871. The opening line, "God the Omnipotent," originally written for the second stanza of Chorley's hymn, was first used to begin the hymn in

Hymns of the Spirit, 1864. Chorley, a prolific author and a friend and admirer of Charles Dickens, wrote musical and literary reviews for *The Athenaeum* in London for thirty-five years, and served as music critic for *The Times* the last few years of his life. See No. 47 for comments on Ellerton.

RUSSIAN HYMN (RUSSIA) has been sung in the United States at least since 1844 when it appeared with "Let me with light and truth be blessed" in *The Beethoven Collection,* New York. The form of the melody was substantially the same as that given here. In 1845 the melody was set to "God the all-terrible" in the Mason and Webb collection, *The Psaltery.* RUSSIAN HYMN was composed in 1833 by Alexis F. Lvov (1799–1870) by order of Czar Nicholas I who wanted something to supplant the British tune GOD SAVE THE KING which had been sung with Russian words as a national anthem. In his memoirs Lvov says:

> One night, on returning to my quarters at a very late hour, I composed and wrote out the tune of the hymn on the spur of the moment. Next day I went to Joukovsky and asked him to suggest some words; . . . The Emperor expressed a desire to hear it, and came on November 23, 1833, to the Court Chapel, accompanied by the Empress and the Grand-Duke Michael. I had assembled the whole choir and it was supported by two orchestras.

> The sovereign ordered the hymn to be played over several times, and asked to hear it sung without accompaniment, then he had it played by each orchestra in turn and finally with the united body of performers. His Majesty then said to me in French: "It is really superb," and there and then he commanded Count Benkendorff to inform the Minister of War that the hymn was adopted for the army. . . . The first public performance took place on December 11, at the Grand Theatre, Moscow.

Lvov (Lwoff, Lwow), born in Reval, Esthonia, was the son of the musician who in 1825 had succeeded Bortniansky as director of the choir of the Russian Imperial Court Chapel at St. Petersburg. In 1837, the son succeeded his father, retiring from the army in which he had been adjutant to the czar and in high favor with him. Lwow was an excellent violinist and a fine quartet player. Besides his activities as a violinist, he composed instrumental music and operas, edited a collection of ritual chants for the liturgical year of the Greek Orthodox Church, and composed a considerable amount of church music. In 1867 he retired from his various posts because of deafness. Now he is remembered for this one tune. Tchaikovsky used it in his *1812 Overture* along with the "Marseillaise."

447   O God of Love, O King of Peace

Bearing the heading, "The Lord shall give his people the blessing of peace," this hymn by Henry Williams Baker was written for the original edition of *Hymns Ancient and Modern,* 1861, as a hymn for use in time of war. See No. 79 for comments on Baker.

HESPERUS (WHITBURN; QUEBEC; ELIM), composed in 1854 by Henry Baker (1835–1910) when he was a student, was first associated (without his knowledge) with "Sun of my soul" through being submitted as an anonymous tune by one "S.C.C." to the London *Penny Post* in 1861 or 1862. There had been prolonged correspondence in that paper's columns about a suitable setting for Keble's hymn and evidently some friend of Baker's who was familiar with the tune had sent it in. The *Post* commended it as very suitable for Keble's hymn but nothing more seems to have been heard of it until 1866 when at the suggestion of John B. Dykes (see No. 79) it was published in Rev. John Grey's *Hymnal for Use in the English Church with accompanying Tunes,* set to "Sun of my soul" and named WHITBURN. It was given the name HESPERUS by Baker when it was published in Bickersteth's *Hymnal Companion to the Book of Common Prayer,* 1871. Baker, the son of an English clergyman who became chancellor of the diocese of Durham, was a civil engineer by profession and spent many years in India engaged in railway construction work. Always much interested in music and with talent for it, he was encouraged by his friend John B. Dykes to study it seriously, and in 1867 received his Bachelor of Music degree from Exeter College, Oxford. Several of his hymn tunes were included in W. Garrett Horder's *Worship Song,* 1905.

448 Thy Kingdom Come, O Lord

Two hymns with the same opening words, "Thy Kingdom come" were written by Frederick L. Hosmer in 1891, the other being, "Thy Kingdom come! on bended knee." Both are based on the second petition of the Lord's Prayer and both emphasize world concord and peace. The present hymn remained unpublished until 1904, when it appeared in the *Hymn and Tune Book,* a Unitarian collection, under the title, "The Prophecy Sublime." It is especially fitting for use at peace rallies and interfaith gatherings. See No. 383 for comments on Hosmer.

ST. CECILIA, named for the patron saint of music, was composed for Horatius Bonar's hymn "Thy way, not mine, O Lord" in *The Merton Tune Book,* 1863. See No. 236 for comments on the composer, Leighton G. Hayne.

449 Let There Be Light, Lord God of Hosts

Described by Armin Haeussler as one of the greatest lay missionaries ever produced by the church, William Merrill Vories (1880–   ) went to Japan in 1905 under the auspices of the International Young Men's Christian Association and founded a nondenominational Christian mission in the predominantly Buddhist province of Omi-Hachiman. Under his inspired leadership it has grown into one of the most successful and influential Christian enterprises in the Far East. Believing that the church must reach out into all areas of life, Vories established kindergarten schools, a hospital, and various business ventures, as well as one of the finest architectural firms in Japan. Much of the support for his work has come from the sale of American products in Japan and China, the profits of which have all been turned over to the mission. The story of the Omi Mission is told in his book, *A Mustard Seed in Japan,* 1911. He said of his work that its aim was "to demonstrate here the fact that loyalty to the vision of the Kingdom of God can overcome all obstacles of race, social systems, and personal prejudices and make possible a community of brothers and sisters in Christ — which is *the only Church* that He is apt to recognize, since it was such unity that he prayed for, 'in order that the World may believe.' "

Vories wrote the present hymn in 1908 in response to the increasing threat of German militarism. It was published by the American Peace Society in its *Advocate of Peace,* Vol. 71, No. 2, February, 1909.

ELTON is one of two tunes by that name in Lowell Mason's collections, the earlier one in Short Meter being included in *The Choir,* 1833; *The Boston Academy Collection,* 1835; and *The Modern Psalmist,* 1841. The Long Meter tune under consideration is from *The Hallelujah,* 1854, in which it appeared in B flat with its present harmonies, without any text. See No. 257 for comments on Mason.

450 These Things Shall Be

Despite ill health all his life, John Symonds (1840–1893) was an exceptionally active and enterprising person. After a brilliant record at Harrow and at Balliol College, Oxford, he was elected a Fellow at Magdalen College. Because of a tubercular condition, brought on partly by overwork, he finally gave up his studies and plans to become a lawyer and moved to Switzerland, where he built a home in the highlands at Davos Platz. There he entertained a growing circle of friends, engaged in scholarly pursuits, interested himself in the welfare of the Swiss people, and produced several notable books, including *Renaissance in Italy,* 1875–1886 (his magnum opus in six volumes); *Introduction to the Study of Dante,* 1872; *Studies of the Greek Poets,* 1873–1876; *Our Life in the Swiss Highlands,* 1891. He also published translations of the autobiographies of Benvenuto Cellini and Count Carlo Gozzi and of the sonnets of Michelangelo and Campanella. He contracted a chill in Rome, where he had gone to recover from fatigue and a personal bereavement, and died there on April 19, 1893. The present hymn is a cento from a fifteen-stanza poem, "A Vista," taken from his *New and Old: A Volume of Verse,* 1880. His daughter has said that it "was probably thrown off hurriedly during some moments of deep longing, a longing for the betterment of the people . . . which his study of Whitman and his own later life among a prosperous and democratic people helped so much to foster." Occasionally the word *inarmed* has been changed to *unarmed* in the third stanza on the assumption that it was a misprint, but Symonds wrote it that way, meaning "arm in arm." The hymn was a favorite among soldiers during World War I.

TRURO   See No. 82 for comments on the tune.

451 Turn Back, O Man, Forswear Thy Foolish Ways

Clifford Bax (1886–1962) began his career as a painter but later turned to literary pursuits and attained distinction as an English playwright and poet. His first play to be produced was *The Poetasters of Ispahan,* 1912. Many of his later plays were given musical settings, among them *Midsummer Madness,* 1924, *Mr. Pepys,* 1926, and *Waterloo Leave,* 1928, the latter two being set to music by Martin Shaw. In addition to his plays he published poems, essays, and a volume of memoirs, *Inland Far,* 1925. He informed Armin Haeussler in 1945 that he had become a Buddhist. At the request of Gustav Holst, he wrote this hymn in 1916 for the tune OLD 124TH, which Holst later used in a special setting for chorus and orchestra. First published in the League of Arts' *Motherland Song Book,* 1919, and later in Bax's *Farewell, My Muse,* 1932, the hymn has become a favorite at peace services and gatherings.

OLD 124TH, one of the best-known of all psalm tunes, was composed or adapted by Louis Bourgeois for Psalm 124 in the 1551 Genevan Psalter. Its first phrase is almost identical with that of the plainsong melody for "Jesu, corona Virginum." It was the proper for Psalm 126 in English, Scottish, and German psalters. Ainsworth assigned it to eight psalms in his 1612 Psalter, used by the Pilgrims. It appears with various forms and names in American collections. Lowell Mason called it MONTAGUE.

OLD 124TH is associated in Geneva with the *Escalade* (scaling of the wall) of 1602 when the Duke of Savoy's treacherous schemes to attack and gain possession of Geneva, called the Protestant Rome, were foiled by the bravery of its citizens. In gratitude for their deliverance they crowded into the cathedral where Bèze, then eighty-three years old, bade them sing the 124th Psalm which Genevans have sung ever since on the anniversary of this victory.

The English form of OLD 124TH differs rhythmically in lines two and three from the French form given below with Bèze's version of the psalm. The melody has been transposed from C, its original key.

Or peut bien dire Is - ra - el main-te - nant, Si le Sei-gneur pour nous point

n'eust es - té, Si le Sei-gneur nos-tre droict n'eust por-té Quand tout le

monde à grand fu-reur ve-nant Pour nous meur-trir des-sus nous s'est jet - té.

452 Lord, Save Thy World

The present hymnal is the first to include this hymn. It was taken from *Rejoice, O People*, 1951, a privately published collection of hymns and poems by Albert F. Bayly. See No. 304 for comments on Bayly.

UFFINGHAM   See No. 89 for comments on the tune.

453 Ring Out, Wild Bells

These lines are from Alfred Tennyson's poem, *In Memoriam*, 1850, Part CVI, stanzas one, two, three, six, and eight. They provide an interesting contrast to Edgar Allen Poe's equally famous lines from his poem, "The Bells." Tennyson hears a profoundly more religious note in the sound of the bells than Poe, who is primarily enchanted with their tonal qualities and varied effects. See No. 357 for comments on Tennyson.

DEUS TUORUM MILITUM, the setting for Tennyson's words in *Songs of Praise*, 1925, seems uniquely fitting for them with its clear, ringing melody and its strong rhythmic movement. See No. 150 for comments on the tune.

454 Great God, We Sing That Mighty Hand

As were all his hymns, this hymn by Philip Doddridge was first sung from a fly sheet by his congregation following one of his sermons. It was first published posthumously in Job Orton's edition of Doddridge's *Hymns Founded on Various Texts in the Holy Scriptures*, 1755, under the heading, "Help obtained from God, Acts xxvi: 22. For the New Year." See No. 76 for comments on Doddridge.

TRURO   See No. 82 for comments on the tune.

455 'Tis Winter Now; the Fallen Snow

This is one of the few hymns that extol the beauty and subtle radiance of winter. Another hymn of like quality is "All beautiful the march of days" (No. 456). For contrast, see Christina Rossetti's hymn, "In the bleak midwinter" (No. 128). Written by Samuel Longfellow, it is from his *Hymns of the Spirit*, 1864, which he edited jointly with Samuel Johnson. See No. 46 for comments on Longfellow.

DANBY, a traditional English ballad tune, appeared with Longfellow's hymn in *The English Hymnal*, 1906, and in *Songs of Praise*, 1925, 1931, harmonized differently in both books by Ralph Vaughan Williams. The present harmonization is from *Songs of Praise*. A comparison of the two arrangements shows that in the later book Vaughan Williams shifted from a major to a modal conception of the melody. The earlier setting was in four parts.

His arrangement of this beautiful melody can be spoiled if it is played in the square-cut style of a typical hymn tune. It looks simple, but practice is necessary in order to play DANBY as its mood deserves — smoothly, with the quarter notes in the three voices moving evenly and concurrently, and with the melody brought out.

456 All Beautiful the March of Days

Asked by her minister to write a "Winter Hymn," Frances Whitmarsh Wile (1878–1939) complied by writing these words. At the time she was an active member of the First Unitarian Church in Rochester, New York, of which the Rev. William Channing Gannett was the minister. The hymn was included in Dr. Gannett's revised hymnal, *Unity Hymns and Carols,* 1911, and has since found its way into many American books. The quiet mood and reverent spirit of the lines recall the pastoral charm of John Greenleaf Whittier's "Snowbound." Mrs. Wile was largely self-educated and spent most of her life in Rochester, where she engaged in civic affairs, championed woman's rights, and frequently contributed her poems to the local newspapers. Her husband, Abram J. Wile, was a teacher and served for a time as the secretary of the Young Men's Hebrew Association in Rochester. In her later years, Mrs. Wile became interested in theosophy and devoted much of her time to this religious and philosophical cult.

FOREST GREEN, another English folk tune (see 455) introduced by Ralph Vaughan Williams in *The English Hymnal,* 1906, was set in that book to "O little town of Bethlehem," an association which has become well-known through its inclusion in a number of English and some American hymnals and in the *Oxford Book of Carols,* 1928. The tune is an arrangement of "The Ploughboy's Dream," a Sussex tune noted by Vaughan Williams at Forest Green, Surrey, in 1903. Each phrase of the song starts with a quarter note. In Vaughan Williams' arrangement, the upbeat to the fourth phrase is a half note, a slight change which makes a great difference and adds a distinctiveness that one misses when all phrases begin in the same way.

457 The Summer Days Are Come Again

Intended to be sung in the open air at a "Summer Rural Gathering," this hymn by Samuel Longfellow has been considerably revised to make it suitable for regular church use. Originally containing three eight-line stanzas, each of which began with the line, "The sweet June days are come again," it was first printed in *A Book of Hymns and Tunes for the Sunday School,* 1860. In its present revised form, with the original first stanza omitted, it was included in *The English Hymnal,* 1906. See No. 46 for comments on Longfellow.

FOREST GREEN   See No. 456 for comments on the tune.

458 Praise to God, Your Praises Bring

Known as a gifted poet and hymn writer, William Channing Gannett (1840–1923) was the minister of the First Unitarian Church in Rochester, New York, from 1889 to 1908. In collaboration with Frederick L. Hosmer, he edited an important collection, *The Thought of God in Hymns and Poems,* 1885, of which Louis F. Benson said: "The beauty and devoutness of their work at once commended it to all religious minds, and it has already become a source book for editors of all religious persuasions." They published a second series in 1894.

Gannett wrote this hymn in 1872 for a harvest festival in St. Paul, Minnesota, where he was serving as the minister of a Unitarian church. It was first published in the 1885 edition of *The Thought of God in Hymns and Poems.* The first and last lines originally read, "Praise to God and thanksgiving" and "Praise and love and thanksgiving."

SAVANNAH (HERRNHUT), an anonymous melody, has been found in a manuscript collection of chorales (c. 1735–1744) used by the Moravians at Herrnhut, Saxony, their headquarters in Germany. On the second page of the collection is the statement that this is the first and oldest *Choralbuch* of the Brethren (*Brüdergemeine*) and that it was compiled by Tobias Friedrich, the first organist at Herrnhut. SAVANNAH was one of the German melodies included in John Wesley's *Collection of Tunes . . . As they are commonly Sung at the Foundery,* 1742, the first Methodist tune book. (See No. 9.) In this, its first printing in England, the tune was called HERRNHUT. Wesley named it SAVANNAH in two later collections, possibly because he heard it sung by the Moravians who were on the ship that carried him and his brother Charles to Savannah, Georgia, in 1735, when they went as missionaries of the Church of England to Oglethorpe's newly established colony. Still later he named the tune IRENE for the ship on which a group of Moravians sailed from London to America in 1742. Before sailing "some of them ascended the gallery of St. Paul's, and in full view of the wide panorama of the city, sang to this tune a hymn of intercession to God for the teeming population below them."

SAVANNAH appeared in eighteenth-century German chorale books (Zahn 1256), in English collections used by Methodists and Moravians, and after 1816 in a number of American tunebooks. Lowell Mason called it SUMMER, EDYFIELD, or LATROBE. Its inclusion in *The English Hymnal,* 1906 — the source of the present harmonization — seems to have restored it to circulation in England and America.

459 With Songs and Honors Sounding Loud

This free paraphrase of Psalm 147 is from Isaac Watts' *Psalms of David,* 1719. Originally consisting of eight four-line stanzas, the present hymn is a cento of stanzas one, two, four, five, seven, and eight. The omitted sixth stanza reads:

When from his dreadful stores on high
He pours the rattling hail,
The wretch that dares this God defy,
Shall find his courage fail.

See No. 1 for comments on Watts.

ELLACOMBE   See No. 68 for comments on the tune.

460   We Plow the Fields and Scatter

The son of a Lutheran pastor, Matthias Claudius (1740–1815) intended to enter the ministry, but the rationalistic influences he encountered at Jena University turned him to the law and journalism instead. He edited *Der Wandsbecker Bothe* ("The Wandsbeck Messenger") for several years and, as a result of his association with Goethe and other freethinkers, found himself estranged from his early religious heritage. A severe illness in 1777 was the means of restoring his faith, and his later writings were marked by a rugged piety. In *Poets and Poetry of Europe,* 1845, Henry Wadsworth Longfellow said of Claudius: "None of his poems are used in the churches. They exercised, nevertheless, a great influence on the religious life of the country by their strong, primitive, and sympathetic Christian feeling." In 1782 he wrote a delightful account of a harvest festival held in the home of a farmer in North Germany, "Paul Erdmann's Feast," which included a seventeen-stanza "Peasants' Song," each stanza of which ended with a refrain. The song reappeared in shortened form, stanzas three to ten, in a book published in 1800 for use in the common schools in Hanover, and as a result it became immensely popular throughout Germany. Jane M. Campbell (1817–1878), the daughter of an Anglican clergyman in London and a remarkably able and successful music teacher of children, recast and translated the "Peasants' Song" into English for Charles S. Bere's *Garland of Songs,* 1861. She also translated a number of other German hymns for his *Children's Choral Book,* 1869, and published *A Handbook for Singers,* a textbook of musical exercises which she had used in her work with children in her father's parish.

WIR PFLÜGEN (DRESDEN; CLAUDIUS) was not the tune which Claudius heard sung to his words originally, but it was set to stanzas three to ten of his poem in the second edition of a German school songbook, *Lieder für Volksschulen,* 1800. No composer's name appeared with the tune in this collection but in Lindner's *Jugenfreund,* 1812, it was ascribed to Johann Abraham Peter Schulz (1747–1800). It became popular throughout Germany and in 1854 appeared with an English translation in the *Bible Class Magazine,* November, 1854, and with Miss Campbell's paraphrase in *Garland of Songs,* 1861.

Schulz's father, a Lüneberg baker, wanted him to become a minister. But the boy loved music, and his organ and clavecin lessons with a fellow townsman who told him about music in Berlin and about the great teacher and composer, Johann Philipp Kirnberger, in particular, fired him with the determination to be a musician. At fifteen he ran away from home, penniless, went

351

straight to Berlin and succeeded in persuading Kirnberger to accept him as a pupil. Schulz must have been a gifted and worthy student, for in 1768 he left Berlin and traveled for five years in Germany, France, and Italy in the entourage of the Polish Princess Sapieha. During these years he heard much music, met many musicians, including Haydn, and learned much. From 1776 to 1780 he directed the music in the French theater in Berlin; in 1780 he became Kapellmeister to Prince Henry of Prussia and from 1787 to 1795 filled a similar post at the court of the king of Denmark in Copenhagen. He composed operas, instrumental works, and much church music, but his fame rests on his collections of sacred and secular German songs published between 1785 and 1790.

WIR PFLÜGEN ("We plow") was published in the United States fourteen years before its first appearance in England. In the January, 1840, issue of *The Seraph,* a monthly publication of selected and original church music, edited by Lowell Mason from August 1838 to July 1840, Schulz's tune appeared with "Words translated from the German, for the Seraph." It was labeled HYMN, with the first line of the translation given for a title: "We plough the fertile meadows." No composer's name was given. Except for four notes the melody was identical with the present version.

461 Come, Ye Thankful People, Come

Several versions of this magnificent harvest hymn were published by Henry Alford, the author. The first appeared in his *Psalms and Hymns,* 1844, and eight years later was republished in revised form in his *Poetical Works.* Because he did not approve of the changes made in the text in other versions, most notably in the version published in *Hymns Ancient and Modern,* 1861, he issued a final authorized text in the 1865 edition of his *Poetical Works,* which included only the present four stanzas under the heading, "After Harvest." Although the hymn is a great favorite at harvest festivals in England and at Thanksgiving services in the United States, the harvest to which it alludes in the last three stanzas is the final consummation of history as depicted in Jesus' explanation of the parable of the wheat and the tares (Matthew 13:36–43). In the author's final revised form of 1865 it is primarily an eschatological hymn. See No. 311 for comments on Alford.

ST. GEORGE'S WINDSOR was written for James Montgomery's hymn "Hark! the song of jubilee" and was first published in E. H. Thorne's *Selection of Psalm and Hymn-Tunes,* 1858. Its association with the present text dates from *Hymns Ancient and Modern,* 1861. WINDSOR in the tune name is a reminder of the composer's long term of service (forty-seven years) at St. George's Chapel, Windsor, and also distinguishes it from at least three other English hymn tunes named ST. GEORGE. This is one of the Victorian tunes which C. Winfred Douglas described as excellent. It abounds in the rhythmic figure ♩ ♪ ♩ ♩ a favorite of Victorian hymn tune composers. By playing this tune at a rather deliberate tempo and by giving full value to the dotted quarters and eighths, organists and pianists can keep it from sounding trivial. See No. 199 for comments on George J. Elvey.

462 Come, Ye Thankful People, Come

This radically revised version of Henry Alford's hymn (see No. 461) includes lines by Anna Laetitia Aiken Barbauld and several unknown authors. The changes ostensibly were prompted by the desire to make this exclusively a harvest festival hymn without any eschatological overtones. See No. 464 for comments on Mrs. Barbauld.

ST. GEORGE'S WINDSOR   See No. 461 for comments on the tune.

463 Praise, O Praise Our God and King

Based on John Milton's paraphrase of Psalm 136 ("Let us with a gladsome mind," No. 70), this hymn by Henry Baker was written for *Hymns Ancient and Modern*, 1861, of which he was the editor. Consisting initially of eight stanzas, the present hymn includes stanzas one, four, six, and eight.
See No. 79 for comments on Baker.

MONKLAND was arranged for this hymn of praise by John Wilkes (1785–1869), organist at the Monkland church of which Sir Henry W. Baker was vicar. Wilkes had taken the melody from *Hymn Tunes of the United Brethren*, 1824, a collection in which nearly all of the tunes were arrangements of German chorales. The editor of the book was John Lees, organist of the Moravian church at Leominster, about three miles from Monkland. Since no composer's name appeared with the tune there has been considerable speculation as to its source. Miss Frances Blandford of Bristol, England, foreign consultant for the Moravian Music Foundation may have solved the mystery. In going through the archives of the Moravian Church in London she came upon two autographed manuscript volumes of hymn tunes, one of which was inscribed *A Collection of Hymn Tunes chiefly composed for private amusement by John Antes*. MONKLAND, in the following form, and as it had appeared in Lees' book, was included in both volumes and may very well be an original composition of Antes.

John Antes (1740–1811), born in Frederick, Pennsylvania, where the Moravians had a preaching mission, was one of eleven children of Heinrich Antes (1704–1755) who came to America in the eighteenth century and was one of the most influential of the early German settlers in Pennsylvania. In 1741, acting as agent for the Moravians, he bought the 500-acre tract of land on which Bethlehem was established, and in 1752 made a long and difficult journey to North Carolina with the group of Moravians who purchased a hundred thousand acres for the settlement known as Wachovia, of which Salem, founded in 1766, became the center. Young Antes' early academic and musical education was received in his own home, in a school for boys which his father had established there. When he was twelve he entered the boys' school in Bethlehem, which was noted throughout the colonies for the quality of its curriculum and teaching. Antes' musical interests and mechanical aptitudes and inventiveness led him to experiment with making stringed instruments. He is said to have made a cello, viola, and violin, but only the last-named is still in existence in the Museum of the Moravian Historical Society at Nazareth, Pennsylvania, one of the earliest specimens of an American-made violin. In 1764 Antes was "called for service" at Herrnhut, Saxony, the international headquarters of the Moravians. After a year there he was apprenticed to a watchmaker in Neuwied for four years. In two biographical accounts he is referred to as a mechanic and watchmaker. On the day of his ordination as a Moravian minister (1769) he left London for a twelve-year term as a missionary in Egypt, the first American missionary to that country. It was a time of great political unrest, and Antes' last two years in Egypt were spent in convalescing from the effects of being stripped and beaten by order of the Turk, Osman Bey, whose repeated demands for money he resisted in spite of intensified lashings which nearly killed him. His constitution was weakened by the torture and imprisonment. During his recovery from this ordeal he wrote three trios for two violins and cello — the earliest chamber works composed by an American-born musician, and said to be the only secular music he wrote. In 1781 Antes left Egypt, spent some time in Germany, and in 1783 went to Fulneck, England, where he was made warden (treasurer) of the Moravian congregation, a position which he held for nearly twenty-five years. While in England, Antes composed a number of choral works for four voices and instruments, and some chorales. These works establish him as one of the finest early American composers of sacred music. With Antes, however, music was always an avocation; as with other Moravian composers, his duties as a minister were his primary concern.

464 Praise to God, Immortal Praise

Of the six hymns Anna Laetitia Aiken Barbauld (1743–1825) wrote for *Hymns for Public Worship,* 1772, a collection published by William Enfield, an English Presbyterian minister, this has been by far the most popular. Extensively altered and abbreviated, the original hymn had nine stanzas and was titled. "Praise to God in Prosperity and Adversity." In its altered form all references to adversity have been omitted. Lines from this hymn are included in an earlier hymn (see No. 462). Anna Barbauld's father, a Dissenting minister and scholar, encouraged her throughout her life to engage in academic pursuits. As a girl she studied with Philip Doddridge, and later wrote several works in collaboration with her brother. She is credited with approximately twenty original hymns. Her *Hymns in Prose for Children,* 1781, received wide and long-continued use and was translated into several languages, including French, Spanish, and Italian. Her husband, Rochemont Barbauld, was a descendant of a French Protestant family and became a Dissenting minister in England.

DIX See No. 66 for comments on the tune.

465   O Perfect Love

This wedding hymn by Dorothy Frances Gurney (1858–1932) was written for the marriage of her sister to Hugh Redmayne at Ambleside, England, in 1883. Her sister had complained that no words suitable for use at a wedding had been written for her favorite tune, STRENGTH AND STAY, composed by John B. Dykes, whereupon Mrs. Gurney wrote these words in the space of fifteen minutes. She said later: "The writing of it was no effort whatever after the initial idea had come to me of the two-fold aspect of perfect union, love and life, and I have always felt that God helped me to write it." Mrs. Gurney's father, the Rev. Frederick George Blomfield, and her grandfather, Bishop Blomfield were both Anglican clergymen; and her husband, Gerald Gurney, an actor in his early career, was later ordained in the Church of England. Both she and her husband eventually joined the Roman Catholic Church. The author of three volumes of verse, including *A Little Book of Quiet,* she is best known for this hymn and the lines from her poem "God's Garden":

> The kiss of the sun for pardon,
> The song of the birds for mirth:
> One is nearer God's heart in a garden
> Than anywhere else on earth.

O PERFECT LOVE (SANDRINGHAM) is from an anthem setting of these words, composed by Sir Joseph Barnby for the marriage of the Duke of Fife to Princess Louise of Wales, sister of George V, on July 27, 1889. See No. 35 for comments on the composer.

466   Our Father, By Whose Name

In recognition of the need for some new hymns on the family, F. Bland Tucker wrote this hymn in 1939 for *The Hymnal 1940,* the authorized hymnal of The Protestant Episcopal Church in the United States. At the time, he was a member of the editorial committee. Each stanza begins in the form of a prayer addressed to a Person of the Trinity — Father, Son (Christ), and Holy Spirit. See No. 147 for comments on Tucker.

RHOSYMEDRE was the setting for this text in *The Hymnal 1940.* See No. 169 for comments on the tune.

467   Father, to Thee We Look in All Our Sorrow

Frederick L. Hosmer wrote this hymn in 1881 after a beloved member of his congregation had died. He was then the minister of the Church of Unity

(Unitarian) in Cleveland, Ohio. It was first published in *The Thought of God in Hymns and Poems,* 1885, which he edited jointly with William C. Gannett. See No. 383 for comments on Hosmer.

L'OMNIPOTENT (GENEVA 110), adapted or composed by Louis Bourgeois for Psalm 110 in the 1551 Genevan Psalter, was the setting for Hosmer's hymn in *The English Hymnal,* 1906, and *Songs of Praise,* 1925. The tune, given below in its original form, replaced an earlier setting (1542) for the same psalm. Waldo Selden Pratt in *The Music of the French Psalter of 1562,* 1939, comments on the predominantly stepwise progression of this melody. In the Scottish Psalter of 1564 it was slightly altered to fit a 10.10.-10.10. version of Psalm 110 by John Craig, a Scotsman who had been a Dominican monk and had fled to Rome, found a copy of Calvin's *Institutes* in the library at Bologna, and eventually adopted the Reformed faith. L'OMNIPOTENT was taken over into Lobwasser's German Psalter for Psalm 110, "Der Herr zu meinem Herren hat gesprochen" (Zahn 901), and after 1778 passed into Lutheran use.

See No. 4 for comments on Bourgeois and the French Psalter.

468 God of the Living, in Whose Eyes

Originally written for his *Hymns for Schools and Bible Classes,* 1859, this hymn by John Ellerton was revised and enlarged by him in 1867, in which form it appeared in several hymnals, including *Church Hymns,* 1871. It was later included in his own compilation, *Hymns, Original and Translated,* 1888. The hymn was sung at his funeral on June 20, 1893. See No. 47 for comments on Ellerton.

GOTTLOB, ES GEHT (WEISSE)   Scholars do not agree about the source of this chorale melody. Some, including Spitta, assign it to Bach without qualification; others think it might possibly be his, others that it is his adaptation of an older tune. Its first appearance in its present form was in the second edition of Bach's *Choralgesänge,* 1769. Bach's harmonization of the melody was for Christian Weise's burial hymn, "Gottlob, es geht nunmehr zum Ende," the first line of which Drinker translates "Thanks be to God, my end is near me." The meter of the German hymn required two notes ($\quarternote\ \eighthnote$) in measures four and twelve. (Zahn 2855) In *The Harvard University Hymn Book,* 1926, this chorale was set to four fine texts, one of which is given at No. 542. The present hymn would be an excellent choice for Armistice Day or Memorial Day services; the category in which it was placed should not limit its wider uses.

469   O Lord of Life, Where'er They Be

This hymn by Frederick L. Hosmer was written in 1888 for the Easter service in the Church of Unity, Cleveland, Ohio, of which he was the minister. It was first printed in the *Chicago Unity* and later in *The Thoughts of God in Hymns and Poems,* second series, 1894. See No. 383 for comments on Hosmer.

GELOBT SEI GOTT was the setting for these words in the *Church Hymnary, Revised,* 1927. See No. 184 for comments on the tune, harmonized by Henry G. Ley.

470   God of the Prophets

In October, 1884, on the occasion of the centenary of the New Brunswick Theological Seminary (Reformed), New Brunswick, New Jersey, Denis Wortman (1835–1922), a graduate of the class of 1860, sent this hymn to his alma mater as an expression of gratitude. Entitled "Prayer for Young Ministers," it was accompanied by the message: "May I take the liberty of sending you the enclosed verses; a very humble attempt to express the prayer that our Class of 1860, and indeed all loyal sons of New Brunswick Seminary, lift to God at this unusual anniversary, for His blessing upon her and all who go forth from her instructions." Wortman served Reformed churches in Brooklyn, Philadelphia, Schenectady, Fort Plain, and Saugerties, New York, and was later appointed Secretary of Ministerial Relief for his denomination, a position he held for seventeen years, and in 1901 he was elected president of the General Synod of the Reformed Church in America. Union College, Schenectady, conferred the Doctor of Divinity and Doctor of Humane Letters degrees upon him. He was the author of *Reliques of the Christ,* 1888, and *The Divine Processional,* 1903.

TOULON   See No. 432 for comments on the tune.

471   Lord of True Light, We Gratefully Adore Thee

During the time that he was the minister of the Congregational Church in Summertown, Oxford, England, 1936–1949, Henry Roberts Moxley

(1881–   ) published a collection of his own hymns, *The Coming, and Other Hymns,* 1948, in which this hymn appeared. It was also included that same year in a small book of *Popular Hymns,* issued by Independent Press. Moxley was a graduate of Cheshunt College, Cambridge, and following his ordination as a Congregational minister served churches in Essex, Kent, Sheffield, and Oxford, retiring in 1949.

WELWYN   See No. 411 for comments on the tune.

472   Lord, Thou Hast Known Our Joy

Ordained as a Congregational minister in Springfield, Vermont, July 2, 1885, Charles Smith Mills (1861–1942) served Congregational churches in Vermont, Massachusetts, Ohio, Missouri, and New Jersey before becoming the General Secretary of the Board of Ministerial Relief and the Pilgrim Memorial Fund of the Congregational churches in 1920. His wide knowledge and understanding of finance made him an invaluable member of the pension and relief agencies of his denomination and led many individuals and institutions to seek his counsel and guidance. He was a member of the Committee of Nineteen on Polity that played a major role in shaping the organizational structures of modern Congregationalism prior to the formation of the United Church of Christ. His books include *The Pilgrim Church and the Republic,* 1907, *Christian Ethics and Social Problems,* 1908, and *The Strategy of the Church in the Crisis of the World,* 1917. This dedicatory hymn which first appeared in the *Pilgrim Hymnal,* 1931, is apparently the only hymn he wrote.

ITALIAN HYMN   See No. 246 for comments on the tune.

473   O Lord, Almighty God, Thy Works

When the Pilgrims landed at Plymouth in 1620, it is reported that they "worshipped God with prayer and the singing of psalms." The book from which they probably sang was Henry Ainsworth's Psalter (*The Booke of Psalmes: Englished both in Prose and Metre,* 1612), which they brought with them from Holland, and which Longfellow describes in *The Courtship of Miles Standish* as the book that John Alden found Priscilla reading when he called:

> Open wide on her lap lay the well-worn psalm-book of Ainsworth,
> Printed in Amsterdam, the words and the music together,
> Rough-hewn, angular notes, like stones in the walls of a churchyard,
> Darkened and overhung by the running vine of the verses.

Twenty years later, the Congregationalists who settled in the Massachusetts Bay Colony produced their own psalter, the Bay Psalm Book (*The Whole Booke of Psalmes Faithfully Translated into English Metre,* 1640), which was the first book published in English on the North American continent. In the concluding words of the Preface, the editors defended their literalistic and rather wooden rendition by saying:

> If therefore the verses are not alwayes so smooth and elegant as some may desire or expect; let them consider that Gods Altar needs not our pollishings: Ex. 20. for we have respected rather a plaine translation, than to smooth our verses with the sweetness of any paraphrase, and soe have attended Conscience rather than Elegance, fidelity rather than poetry, in translating the hebrew words into english language, and Davids poetry into english meetre; that soe wee may sing in Sion the Lords songs of prayse according to his owne will; untill hee take us from hence, and wipe away all our teares, & bid us enter into our masters joye to sing eternall Halleluiahs.

Printed by Stephen Day in Cambridge, it appeared in twenty-seven editions and held uncontested sway in the New England colonies for a hundred years. It was also reprinted in several other editions abroad and used extensively in England and Scotland. Beginning with the second edition, published in 1647 in England, hymns began to appear in the back pages. The present hymn, known popularly at the time as "The Song of Moses and the Lamb" (Revelation 15:3–4), was one of a number of "hymns and spiritual songs" found in the third edition of 1651, edited by President Dunster of Harvard College. It undoubtedly existed in some form at an earlier date, possibly as a fly sheet or as a manuscript, and was well known to the colonists. This is the hymn that closed the first great council of Congregational churches in New England, the Cambridge Synod of 1648, and that was similarly used in recent years at meetings of The General Council of Congregational Christian Churches.

YORK   See No. 95 for comments on the tune.

474   O Lord, Almighty God, Thy Works

See No. 473 for comments on the text.

YORK   In Ravenscroft's Psalter, 1621, Simon Stubbs' harmonization of this "Northerne Tune" with the melody in the tenor — *Faux-bourdon* as at No. 5 — was set to Psalm 115 and to the anonymous Common Meter version of Psalm 100, "In God the Lord be glad and light," from the Sternhold and Hopkins Psalter. Stubbs' only other contribution to Ravenscroft's Psalter was a harmonization of the Scottish tune MARTYRS which appeared with six Psalms (39, 75, 92, 99, 118, 147) and "A Thankes-giving" included in *The Hymnes Evangelicall, and songs Spirituall* which followed the Psalms. All that seems to be known about Stubbs is that he lived in the late sixteenth and early seventeenth centuries and was a composer of church music.

475   O Lord of Hosts, Whose Glory Fills

Consisting initially of six stanzas, of which the last two stanzas have been omitted here, this hymn by John Mason Neale is from his *Hymns for the*

Young, 1844. This volume of original poems was intended as a sequel to his earlier work, *Hymnes for Children*, 1843. Altogether he wrote sixty-one hymns for these two volumes, the first of his published works. See No. 110 for comments on Neale.

WAREHAM   See No. 430 for comments on the tune.

476 Now Praise We Great and Famous Men

Based on the familiar lines from Ecclesiasticus 44:1–7, extolling faithful men of earlier generations, this hymn by William G. Tarrant is taken from his *Songs of the Devout*, 1912. Ecclesiasticus ("the church book") was used by the early church fathers as a text in teaching catechumens and is included as a canonical book in the Douay Bible. See No. 346 for comments on Tarrant.

ACH GOTT UND HERR, an anonymous melody, appeared with a penitential hymn, "Ach Gott und Herr, wie gross und schwer" (Alas! my God! my sins are great), in *As hymnodus sacer*, Leipzig, 1625. (See No. 67.)

Ach Gott und Herr,   wie gross   und schwer sind mein be-gang-ne Sün-den!

da ist nie-mand, der hel-fen kann, in die - ser Welt   zu fin-den.

In 1655 a version in major appeared in Christoph Peter's *Andachts Zymbeln,* Freiberg. (Zahn 2051)

Bach used the major form in the concluding chorale of Cantata 48 and in two of three miscellaneous Preludes on the melody; in the third he used a form close to the 1625 version. There is one harmonization in the *Choralgesänge*.

477 Founded on Thee, Our Only Lord

Best known for his hymn, "My country, 'tis of thee" (No. 437), Samuel Francis Smith probably wrote this hymn for use at the dedication service of the Roslindale Baptist Church in Boston, June 17, 1889, although in a letter he indicated that it was written in 1894 for "a young man's social union in Boston." With its scriptural allusions to the figure of a rock upon which the faith of the church rests, it is especially suitable as a dedicatory hymn. See No. 305 for comments on Smith.

MENDON See No. 238 for comments on the tune.

478 All Things Bright and Beautiful

Of the several hymns Cecil F. Alexander wrote to illustrate various clauses in The Apostles' Creed, this is the first, based on the words, "Maker of heaven and earth," and on Genesis 1:31, "And God saw every thing that he had made, and, behold, it was very good." As with her other hymns of a similar character, it is from her *Hymns for Little Children,* 1848. Three stanzas have been omitted, including the third, the latter because it introduces a note somewhat at variance with the best of contemporary Christian thought:

> The rich man in his castle,
> The poor man at his gate;
> God made them high or lowly,
> And ordered their estate.

See No. 171 for comments on Mrs. Alexander.

ROYAL OAK, an English traditional melody, was arranged for these words by Martin Shaw (No. 106) and first published in 1915. The tune, known as "The Twenty-ninth of May," was sung on Charles II's thirtieth birthday, May 29, 1660, the day on which he entered London after his restoration. It is given below in a 1667 version which appeared in William Chappell's *Popular Music of the Olden Time,* 1855–1859.

Wel-come, welcome, roy - al May! Wel-come long de-sir-ed day!

Man-y Springs and Mays we've seen Have brought forth what's gay and green,

But none like this glorious Spring Which brings forth our gra-cious King: Then

ban - ish care, And let us sing, We have our laws, And we have our King.

361

"The Twenty-ninth of May" was printed in Playford's *English Dancing Master,* 1686, and in every subsequent edition, sometimes twice in the same edition with different names, such as "May Hill," "The Jovial Beggars," "The Jovial Crew," "The Restoration of King Charles." In *Old English Country Dances,* 1890, Frank Kidson calls this an "exceedingly fine and marked air of Charles the Second's time." Cecil J. Sharp who arranged it for piano in *Country Dance Tunes,* Vol. IV, gave the characteristics of a country dance as "simplicity and gaiety," qualities well-exemplified in ROYAL OAK. This tune was set to a song entitled "Royal Oak Day" in *Songs of the British Islands,* 1903, edited by William H. Hadow for use in English schools. The title refers to the famous oak in which Charles II hid during his flight after the battle at Worcester in 1651. After the Restoration in 1660, May 29 was celebrated as "Royal Oak Day" or "Oak Apple Day" on which, formerly, country boys wore oak apples or sprigs of oak to commemorate the King's hiding place. See No. 106 for comments on Martin Shaw.

479 Father, We Thank Thee for the Night

Although Rebecca J. Weston (dates unknown) is usually credited with this hymn, there is no evidence to support the claim, nor is anything known of her life. The hymn first appeared in Daniel Batchellor's and Thomas Charmbury's *Manual for Teachers, and Rote songs to accompany the Tonic sol-fa music courses for schools,* 1884, Boston, and it was also included in *Kindergarten Chimes,* 1887, edited by Kate Douglas Wiggin.

ONSLOW   The only available information about this tune is that it was the setting for the present text in Part I of a *Manual for Teachers, and Rote songs,* 1855. Rev. Daniel Batchellor was the composer. Tune and words were also included in *Songs and Games for Little Ones,* 1909.

480 I Love to Think That Jesus Saw

The wife of the Rev. J. G. Skemp, a Baptist minister in England, Ada Skemp (1857–1927) was active both in the churches her husband served and in the teaching profession. She was co-principal of Hale High School in Cheshire for several years and later was co-principal of Ansdell College, Lytham St. Anne's, Lancashire. Her hymn was first published in Carey Bonner's *Child Songs,* 1908, and later appeared in *School Worship,* 1926. The hymn imaginatively represents the simple thoughts of a child looking at the past, and thereby gives biblical events a fresh contemporaneity.

CHILDHOOD   In *A Students' Hymnal,* 1923, this tune is attributed to the "University of Wales," and is one of several in that collection that were composed not by one individual but by several working together. The hymnal was compiled by and for the students under the supervision of Sir Walford Davies, their professor of music, who said in the preface that in two cases at least, five students had contributed to one four-line melody. CHILDHOOD shows that such cooperation can be fruitful. It was written for "It fell upon a summer day," Stopford Brooke's hymn about Jesus blessing the children. (Mark 10:13–15) It is also associated with the present text in some English hymnals and in at least one American collection for use in Sunday Schools, *Hymns for Primary Worship*, 1946.

481 I Sing a Song of the Saints of God

This hymn by Lesbia Scott (1898–   ) "was meant for use on Saints' days, to impress the fact that sainthood is a living possibility today." As were most of her hymns, it was written for her own children "not for publication, but for use in our own nursery, as an expression of the faith we were trying to give the children." "Most of them," she related, "came in response to the children's own demands. 'Make a hymn for a picnic,' 'Make a hymn for a foggy day.'" The hymns were later published by the Morehouse-Gorham Company, *Everyday Hymns for Children*, 1929. She was born in London and educated at Raven's Croft School in Sussex, and married John Mortimer Scott, a British naval officer. Interested in amateur theatricals, she has done a considerable amount of writing, especially of religious dramas. Among her works are *Malta Cathedral Nativity Play*, 1931; *That Fell Arrest*, 1937; and *Then Will She Return*, 1946.

GRAND ISLE was composed in 1940 by a nephew of the man who wrote both words and music of "We three kings of Orient are." (143) It appeared with the present text in *The Hymnal 1940*. John Henry Hopkins (1861–1945), son of a clergyman, and a grandson of the second bishop of Vermont, was educated at the University of Vermont and at General Theological Seminary where he served as organist in his student days. In 1910 he was honored with an S.T.D. (Doctor of Sacred Theology) degree by Western Theological Seminary. After ordination in 1891, he served in several churches in the Middle West, becoming rector of the Church of the Redeemer, Chicago, in 1910. Dr. Hopkins wrote a number of articles and books for his denomination including *The Great Forty Years of the Diocese of Chicago*, 1936. Throughout his life he found time for his musical interests, serving as organist in several churches from 1878 until his ordination, and composing various works for use in church. He was a member of the National Association of Organists. In 1937 he was appointed a member of the Joint Commission on the Revision of the Hymnal, took an active part as one of the Committee on Tunes for *The Hymnal 1940*, and said that his work with the latter group was the crowning joy of his career. GRAND ISLE was named for Grand Isle, Vermont, on Lake Champlain, where Dr. Hopkins lived after his retirement in 1929, serving in the Log Chapel there until his death in 1945.

482 Little Jesus, Sweetly Sleep

Of unknown authorship, this traditional Czechoslovakian carol, popularly called "the rocking carol," was translated by Percy Dearmer and first published in *The Oxford Book of Carols*, 1928, which he jointly edited with

363

Ralph Vaughan Williams and Martin Shaw. See No. 112 for comments on Dearmer.

ROCKING   Martin Shaw's arrangement of this melody for the Czech carol "Hajej, nynjej" (literally: "You can sleep and dream") is from *The Oxford Book of Carols*, 1928. Anyone who has ever sung this charming carol can never forget it. Pianists should play it lightly and smoothly remembering that it is a lullaby. The melody, not the chordal accompaniment, should be the main concern. Those who teach the words should make sure that the repeated "rock you's" are sung gently and do not degenerate into jerky "rah-cues" with the accent on "cue"! In the *Companion to Congregational Praise*, 1953, Erik Routley comments on the family resemblance of this tune to the familiar melody for "Twinkle, twinkle, little star." See No. 106 for comments on Martin Shaw.

483   I Think When I Read That Sweet Story

The words of this children's hymn were written by Jemima Thompson Luke (1813–1906) while she rode in a stagecoach from Taunton to Wellington to attend a missionary meeting. Sometime earlier she had heard a Greek marching tune, SALAMIS, that had appealed to her, and she had tried unsuccessfully to find a hymn to which it could be sung. It was with the tune in mind that she penciled these lines. Writing of the experience to a friend, she said: "It was a beautiful spring morning, it was an hour's ride, and there was no other inside passenger. On the back of an old envelope I wrote in pencil the first two of the verses now so well known, in order to teach the tune to the village school supported by my stepmother, and which it was my province to visit." She later added a third stanza to make it a missionary hymn, but this has not been included here. It first appeared in the *Sunday-School Teachers' Magazine,* March 1841. Mrs. Luke was the wife of the Reverend Samuel Luke, a Congregational minister. She published several books and frequently contributed articles to religious periodicals, especially on the subject of foreign missions. Her father, Thomas Thompson, was a leading figure in founding the British and Foreign Sailors' Society, the Sunday School Union, and the Bible Society. She died on the Isle of Wight, February 2, 1906, at the age of ninety-three.

SWEET STORY (LUKE), from *Oriola,* 1859, a book of Sunday School songs edited by William B. Bradbury (see No. 178), was his arrangement of the Greek air which prompted Mrs. Luke to write this hymn. The melody had the following form when it was published in the *Sunday-School Teachers' Magazine,* March, 1841.

When one compares SWEET STORY with the Greek melody, named SAL–
AMIS or ATHENS in English usage, he realizes that it is much more Bradbury than Greek. In *Oriola* the tune was arranged in three parts with suc-
cessions of double thirds between the soprano and alto parts. The present
arrangement, made by the writer, is basically Bradbury's, cast into 2/2 time,
with his harmonies outlined, with many repeated notes in the under parts
eliminated and with three dotted notes made even, all in order to simplify
and to make the music less "busy." Two current English hymnals include
Mrs. Luke's text with a slightly altered form of the Greek air, named
ATHENS. In *The English Hymnal,* 1906, the words were set to EAST
HORNDON, Ralph Vaughan Williams' arrangement of an English traditional melody.

484 Remember All the People

This children's missionary hymn was written by Percy Dearmer in 1929 at
the request of the Church Missionary Society for its children's magazine, *The
Round World,* and was reprinted in *Songs of Praise for Boys and Girls,* 1930.
Its vivid imagery and fresh style make it one of the finest modern missionary
hymns written for children. See No. 112 for comments on Dearmer.

FAR–OFF LANDS This bright tune, arranged for Percy Dearmer's text
by C. Winfred Douglas in *The Hymnal 1940,* is a melody of the Bohemian
Brethren which was set to "Hur Ljuvt det är att komma" in the Swedish
Hemmets Koralbok, 1921. FAR–OFF LANDS is easily learned because
three of its phrases are identical. A tune like this in A A B A form is a good
one to use in explaining the principles of repetition and contrast which play
such an important part in music. By singing the whole hymn through to the
melody of the first phrase, children and adults quickly recognize how monotonous this becomes and how much variety is brought in by the four measures of the third phrase.

485 This is My Father's World

During his first pastorate in a Presbyterian church in Lockport, New York,
Maltbie Davenport Babcock (1858–1901) often went for a walk early in the
morning to a nearby hill to enjoy the sweeping view of Lake Ontario and the
surrounding countryside, saying as he left the house, "I am going out to see
my Father's world." This hymn may have been inspired by that experience.
After graduating from Syracuse University, where he won honors as a stu-

dent, athlete, and campus leader, and was a member of the drama and glee clubs, he attended Auburn Theological Seminary (now associated with Union Theological Seminary). He had two notable pastorates, at the Brown Memorial Presbyterian Church in Baltimore and The Brick Presbyterian Church in New York City, in addition to his ministry in Lockport. So popular was he with the students of Johns Hopkins University that a room was reserved for his use in order that they might have a place to talk with him in private. All sorts and conditions of men and women sought his counsel and benefited from his keen insights and dynamic personality. He died in Naples, Italy, May 18, 1901, while on a Mediterranean tour. His hymns were published posthumously in a small book of religious poems, *Thoughts for Everyday Living,* 1901. The present hymn, consisting originally of sixteen four-line stanzas, is from this collection and is a cento of stanzas two and three, four and five, and fourteen and sixteen.

TERRA BEATA (TERRA PATRIS) (translated, "blessed earth," "Father's earth")   A number of years ago the writer was looking through the *English Hymnal* and came upon a tune named RUSPER which seemed strangely familiar. Its heading was, "From an English Traditional Melody." Soon she realized that it must be the melody that Franklin L. Sheppard said he had learned from his mother as a boy and later adapted for the present text written by his friend Maltbie Babcock. Sheppard was editor of *Alleluia,* 1915, a hymnal "for use in schools, in the home, in young people's societies and devotional meetings" in which TERRA BEATA appeared, captioned "Traditional English Melody arranged by S.F.L." In spite of Sheppard's insistence that the melody was not original with him, there were those who stated categorically that he was its creator. A glance at RUSPER will show that S.F.L. knew what he was talking about.

Franklin L. Sheppard (1852–1936), born in Philadelphia, was graduated from the University of Pennsylvania at the head of his class (1872) and was a charter member of the university's chapter of Phi Beta Kappa. He spent much of his life in Baltimore as manager of the foundry of his father's firm

366

but seemed always to be active in church work, first as a member and vestry-man of the Zion Protestant Episcopal Church, later as a Presbyterian. In the Second Presbyterian Church of Baltimore he was an elder, director of the music, and active in the Sunday school. He was a lay delegate several times to the General Assembly, and was also a member of the Board of Publication and Sabbath-School work, later becoming its president. His vision and leadership had much to do with the erection of the Witherspoon Building in Philadelphia, which serves as denominational headquarters. Although not a professional musician, Mr. Sheppard served as organist in the church in which he was confirmed and throughout his life was deeply interested in music. He was a member of the committee that edited and published the Presbyterian *Hymnal* of 1911.

486 Golden Breaks the Dawn

This delightful Chinese hymn with its elemental, unaffected simplicity is from *Hymns of Universal Praise*, 1936, a notable collection published as a cooperative project by six major church bodies in China. The volume contained more than four hundred hymns of Western Christendom translated into Chinese. It also included sixty-two hymns written by Chinese Christians and seventy-two tunes of Chinese origin or composition. From the latter group of this collection Frank W. Price (1895–   ) selected and translated twenty-three hymns which he published in booklet form as *Chinese Christian Hymns*, 1953. (Educational Department, Board of World Missions, Presbyterian Church in the United States, Box 330, Nashville, Tennessee.) The present hymn is from this booklet. Dr. Price was a missionary in China for thirty years. After three years of detention by the Communists, he returned to the United States in 1952. He was director of the Missionary Research Library at Union Theological Seminary in New York City until 1961, and since then has been living in Lexington, Virginia.

The author, T. C. Chao (1888–   ), is one of the most brilliant Chinese theologians of the twentieth century. He attended the interdenominational Missionary Council in Jerusalem in 1928 and in Madras in 1939, giving one of the major addresses at the latter conference; and he was elected one of the six vice-presidents of the World Council of Churches at its inaugural meeting in Amsterdam in 1948. From 1928 until 1953 he was dean of the School of Religion of Yenching University, and when the school was reorganized as the Yenching Union Theological Seminary under prodding of the Communists, he continued on the faculty until his retirement in approximately 1956. There are conflicting reports as to whether he embraced or disavowed the Communist revolution, although it is known that he resisted the takeover of Yenching University and that he was subjected to severe and constant attack because of his ecumenical connections. The truth may never be disclosed and little is known of his present status. His hymns, however, of which there are ten in Dr. Price's booklet, are a living legacy of his Christian faith.

LE P'ING is a hexatonic melody, technically, because it uses a six-tone scale. However, the fourth degree of the scale, *c* in this case, comes into the melody only once (measure ten), which accounts for its predominantly pentatonic flavor. Translated, LE P'ING, the name of this old folk melody, means "Happy Peace." Both LE P'ING and HSUAN P'ING are from the booklet *Chinese Christian Hymns,* 1953.

487 Praise Our God Above

Entitled "Harvest Song" in Frank Price's *Chinese Christian Hymns,* 1953, this is another of T. C. Chao's hymns taken from *Hymns of Universal Praise,* 1936. See No. 486 for comments on T. C. Chao and Frank Price.

HSUAN P'ING is a pentatonic melody. The writer has found that children and young people who have not even had music lessons enjoy picking out pentatonic melodies on the black keys of the piano if they are shown how easily this can be done. To play No. 487 on the black keys, start on *e* flat. HSUAN P'ING carries the meaning of a kind of proclamation of peace. As the heading states, it is a Confucian temple chant.

These two Chinese melodies, LE P'ING and HSUAN P'ING, have been printed without harmonies because the music editors felt that their distinctive character is more apparent when they are sung in unison.

488 Go, Tell It on the Mountain

Several versions of this joyous Negro spiritual have appeared in different collections. This has been taken from *American Negro Songs and Spirituals,* 1940, edited by John W. Work. The first line of this spiritual was used by a young Negro war veteran, James Baldwin, in 1953 for an autobiographical novel which won wide recognition as one of the finest books dealing with the problems faced by Negroes in contemporary American life. It portrays a Negro family turning to religion out of its disillusionment in finding no more acceptance in the North than in the South. Mr. Baldwin became one of America's leading novelists and a brilliant interpreter of racial conflicts and tensions. See No. 179 for comments on the Negro spiritual.

GO TELL IT ON THE MOUNTAIN, a Negro spiritual for Christmas, was included in this section of the hymnal because of young people's delight in singing it. In *White and Negro Spirituals,* George Pullen Jackson has shown that the tune to which the stanzas of this spiritual are sung is very much like part of a white spiritual "We'll march about Jerusalem"; and William Arms Fisher comments on the similarity of the refrain to that of George F. Root's "Tramp, tramp, tramp, the boys are marching." In spite of these echoes of other tunes, GO TELL IT ON THE MOUNTAIN has an individuality of its own and a spirit which suggests the wonder and the excitement occasioned by the news of Jesus' birth. Like the Chinese melody at No. 486, this melody is hexatonic, and similarly the fourth degree of the scale appears only once (in the last measure of the refrain) and the pentatonic flavor predominates.

489 I Would Be True

One of the most popular hymns among young people during the past several decades is this hymn by Howard Arnold Walter (1883–1918), written when he was twenty-three years old. At the time, he was teaching English at Waseda University in Tokyo, a position he had accepted after completing his first year of studies at Hartford Seminary Foundation in Hartford, Connecticut. He entitled the poem "My Creed" and sent it to his mother, who in turn submitted it to *Harper's Magazine*. It appeared in the May, 1907, issue and has since been reprinted in various hymnals and song booklets. In elevating laughter into a high virtue the hymn is rather distinctive. After graduating from Hartford in 1909 and winning a two-year fellowship, Walter studied in Scotland and in Germany. Upon his return to America he became the assistant minister in the Asylum Hill Congregational Church in Hartford. Because of his interest in the foreign mission field, he applied for an appointment as a missionary but was turned down because of a weak heart. He volunteered to go to India for the Young Men's Christian Association, and was assigned to work among the Muhammadan students in Foreman Christian College in Lahore. His weak constitution and an influenza epidemic caused his untimely death on November 1, 1918. A memorial tablet with the words of this hymn inscribed on it was placed in his honor in his home church, First Church of Christ (Congregational), New Britain, Connecticut, February 14, 1926.

PEEK was written by Joseph Y. Peek (1843–1911) for the present text which had been given to him by its author whom he met in 1909 at the Nostrand-DeKalb Methodist Church in Brooklyn, after a midweek evangelistic service. The words were printed on a card with the caption "My Creed." Peek, impressed with the ideas expressed in the words, felt that they would have wider use if set to music, and soon found that a melody for them kept running through his head. Not being a musician, he whistled the tune to an organist friend who jotted down the notes for him. A veteran of the Civil War, Peek worked at a number of occupations before becoming a florist by trade and a horticulturist of note. In 1904 he decided to become a Methodist minister, gave up his successful business which had flourished since 1881, spoke as a lay preacher in churches in Maine, Florida, and California, and was ordained at St. Petersburg, Florida, two months before his death. Although he had no formal musical training he played the piano, violin, and banjo and was an enthusiastic amateur.

490 Now in the Days of Youth

After being shipwrecked as a young man and impressed into service in the Brazilian Army, Walter John Mathams (1853–1932) made his way back to England and prepared himself for the ministry. He was the pastor of three Baptist churches and for three years served as a chaplain with the British Army in Egypt. Following this he became a minister of the Church of Scotland and devoted ten years of his life to the Mallaig mission church. He was the author of several books and a considerable number of hymns. The present hymn was written for use at Sunday school and Christian Endeavor meetings. For a time he forgot that he had written it until a friend called it to his attention. *Worship and Song*, 1913, was the first hymnal in which it appeared.

DIADEMATA Although the music editors tried to avoid the overuse of any tune, they felt that this setting for Mathams' hymn from the *Pilgrim Hymnal*, 1931, was justifiable because of its connection with Charles Wesley's hymn "Soldiers of Christ, arise." Both hymns express in a different way the necessity of girding oneself with "the whole armor of God" in order to be "prepared for larger years to come." See No. 199 for comments on DIADE–MATA.

491 O God of Youth, Whose Spirit

Adopted as the official hymn of the National Federation of Young People, this hymn by Bates Gilbert Burt (1878–1948) was written to be sung at a high school commencement in Pontiac, Michigan, in 1935. Burt was then the rector of All Saints' Church in Pontiac, a position he held from 1922 until 1947. Previously he had served as a chaplain in France, 1918–19. In 1946 he was made a member of the Joint Commission on the Revision of the Hymnal of The Protestant Episcopal Church. He died in St. Mary's rectory, Edgewood, Maryland, April 5, 1948.

LYNNE was composed for this hymn by its author in 1940 and named in honor of a baby granddaughter. Although this fine unison tune has no regularly recurring accent in the way of strictly measured music, it is easy to learn and to sing because of its syllabic style (one note to a syllable) and also because of its stepwise movement. There are only four skips within the phrases themselves. Those that come between two of the four phrases are major thirds which present no difficulty.

492 O Gracious God, Whose Constant Care

Few churchmen during the first half of the twentieth century devoted themselves with greater dedication and effectiveness to the religious training of American young people than Harry Thomas Stock (1891–1958). Following graduation from Chicago Theological Seminary in 1916 and a year of post graduate study at the University of Chicago, he served for five years as associate professor of church history at the Seminary. From 1922 to 1938 he was Secretary of the Department of Student Life and Young People's Work, Congregational Education Society; and for two decades, until his death in 1958, he served with distinction as General Secretary of the Division of Christian Education of the Board of Home Missions of the Congregational Christian Churches. His books include *Church Work with Young People*, 1927; *Problems of Christian Youth*, 1928; *So This Is Missions*, 1938; and *Preparing for a Life Work*, 1936. He wrote the present hymn for a vesper service at a summer youth conference, and it was first published in *The Con-*

gregationalist, February 12, 1931. *The Hymnal*, 1941 (Evangelical and Reformed Church), was the first denominational book to include it. One stanza has been deleted and "vesper hour" was changed to "sacred hour" in the third stanza to make it more suitable for general use.

LOBT GOTT IHR CHRISTEN (NICOLAUS; HERMANN; ST. GEORGE'S; BRAY) "Let all together praise the Lord" is one translation of the first line of Nicolaus Hermann's joyful Christmas hymn "Lobt Gott, ihr Christen alle gleich" from which the tune name is taken. The melody, composed by him, was first published in a 1554 tract, set to one of his hymns for children. In his collection *Die Sontags Evangelia uber das gantze Jar*, 1560, it was set to "Lobt Gott," the first of "Three Spiritual Christmas Songs of the newborn child Jesus, for the children in Joachimsthal." It has continued in use through the centuries and is a favorite German Christmas hymn. Nicolaus Hermann (c. 1485–1561), born near Nürnberg, spent much of his life in Joachimsthal in Bohemia (a German-speaking area which had been a stronghold of John Huss' followers) where he became known and loved as teacher, organist, cantor, composer, hymn writer. There was close cooperation between him and Johannes Mathesius, rector of the Latin school where Hermann taught and pastor of the Lutheran church where he was organist. Mathesius, a pupil and intimate friend of Martin Luther and ordained by him, had at one time lived as a member of Luther's household. Hermann was deeply interested in the religious education of children and young people and wrote most of his hymns for their use. Ideas from particularly inspiring sermons of Pastor Mathesius were often incorporated into hymns by his organist. This church musician was so passionately fond of music that in his old age he used to dream of heaven as a place where every organist and lutenist would "take some holy text, and strike upon his organ or his lute; and everyone will be able to sing at sight and by himself four or five different parts. There will be no more confusion and mistakes, which now often put many a good musician quite out of heart, especially when he has to begin several times over." He is not the only church musician to have had such dreams!

Bach used Herman's melody in Cantatas 151 and 195 (No. 1 of the Wedding Cantatas) and in two chorale preludes for organ: one in the *Orgelbüchlein* and one in the miscellaneous Preludes. There are two harmonizations in the *Choralgesänge*. Hermann's original melody is given below. (Zahn 198)

Kommt her, ihr lie-ben Schwe-ster - lein, an die - sen A bend - tanz; lasst
Lobt Gott, ihr Chri-sten al - le gleich, in sei-nem höch-sten Thron, der

uns ein geist-lichs Lie-de - lein sin - gen um ei-nen Kranz, sin-gen um ei-nen Kranz.
heut auf-schleusst sein Kö-nig-reich und schenkt uns sei-nen Sohn, und schenkt uns sei-nen Sohn

LOBT GOTT IHR CHRISTEN does not appear in the majority of contemporary denominational hymnals of the United States. Yet in the late eighteenth and early nineteenth centuries it was included in many American collections with various modifications, a variety of texts, and the names ST. GEORGE'S, BRAY, LÜTZEN. In *The Mozart Collection*, 1846, edited by Elam Ives, Jr., BRAY had the present Bach harmonization from Cantata 151.

493 When Stephen, Full of Power and Grace

In honor of Stephen, the first Christian martyr, Jan Struther wrote this hymn for *Songs of Praise*, 1931. The words recapture in a remarkably effective way the undying spirit of the martyred saint (Acts 7:54–60). See No. 42 for comments on Jan Struther.

WELLINGTON SQUARE is a resolute, unison tune that captures and reinforces the spirit of Jan Struther's hymn for which it was written and with which it appeared in *Songs of Praise*, 1931. It has some of the flavor and simplicity of structure characteristic of many English folk tunes; three of its phrases are practically identical melodically. The composer, Guy Warrack (1900–   ) was born in Edinburgh, educated at Winchester College, and Magdalen College, Oxford, and at the Royal College of Music where he studied composition with Vaughan Williams, and from 1925 to 1935 was a member of the teaching staff. He has served as a conductor of the Oxford Orchestral Society, the Handel Society, the B.B.C. Scottish Orchestra (1936–1945), and as musical director of Sadler's Wells Ballet Theatre (1948–1951). In addition to his activities in London and the provinces, he has conducted concerts and broadcasts in Ceylon, New Zealand, and South Africa. His compositions include orchestral and choral works, songs, and music for many films including *A Queen Is Crowned*, the Technicolor film of the coronation of Queen Elizabeth II, 1953. He is the author of *Sherlock Holmes and Music*, 1947, and of numerous articles for papers and periodicals and has served as president of the International Council of Composers, chairman of the Composers' Guild of Great Britain, and Chairman of the Sherlock Holmes Society of London. In answer to an inquiry about the name of this tune he wrote: "Jan Struther was the wife of an old friend and neighbour of mine and at the time the hymn was written and composed we all lived in Wellington Square, Chelsea."

494 We Would Be Building

During a year of graduate study in Edinburgh, 1931–1932, Purd Eugene Deitz (1897–   ) first heard the tune FINLANDIA and, as he later said, was quite carried away by its possibilities. Upon his return to this country, he was made chairman of a committee to plan for a youth conference to be held in Philadelphia, where he served as pastor of Trinity Reformed Church. Because the worship committee had been unable to find a hymn suitable for the conference theme, "Christian Youth Building a New World," Dr. Deitz wrote this hymn one Saturday evening with the tune FINLANDIA in mind. The new hymn was an immediate success and spread quickly over the country through youth groups and then to mission fields abroad. In 1937 it was sung in English, French, and German at the World Conference of Christian Youth in Amsterdam. The first official denominational hymnal to include it was *The Hymnal*, 1941, of the Evangelical and Reformed Church, although it had been printed earlier in *Follow Me,* 1936, a Presbyterian daily devotional book for youth, widely used by many denominational groups. Dr. Deitz's first pastorate was at Fourth Reformed Church in Dayton, Ohio, following which he spent thirteen years at Trinity Reformed Church. From 1938 to 1949 he was professor of practical theology at Eden Theological Seminary, Webster Groves, Missouri, and in 1949 was elected the Executive Secretary of the Board of National Missions of the Evangelical and Reformed Church, later serving as the General Secretary of the Division of Church Extension of the Board for Homeland Ministries of the United Church of Christ in New York City.

FINLANDIA   See No. 77 for comments on the tune.

495 We Are Climbing Jacob's Ladder

This hymn has been taken from *American Negro Songs and Spirituals,* 1940, edited by John W. Work. The text was undoubtedly inspired by the Scriptural account of Jacob's dream at Bethel (Genesis 28:10–17). See No. 179 for additional comments on the Negro spiritual.

JACOB'S LADDER   In singing this slow sustained spiritual, which is simple, descriptive music, a strict rhythm should be maintained throughout. One hears it sung by groups who fail to give full value to the dotted half notes. This may be due to carelessness or it may show the influence of a 3/4 version of the melody which appears in some books. In the Preface to *Jubilee Songs,* 1872, Theodore F. Seward wrote that one of the noticeable features of the melodies in that collection was the complete absence of triple time. And Professor John W. Work said in his paper "The Negro Spiritual," which he read before the International Hymnological Conference, held in 1961, in New York City: "A few spirituals appearing in collections are written in 3/4 and 6/8 meter. These are rare and atypical — and probably non-Negro." The rhythmic pattern ♩ ♩. which appears in every measure except the last of JACOB'S LADDER suggests climbing a rung, pausing for breath, and getting ready for the next rung.

496 The National Anthem

An incident in the War of 1812 led Francis Scott Key (1779–1843) to write what officially became the national anthem of the United States by Act of Congress, March 3, 1931. Key had been authorized by President Madison to negotiate the release from a British ship of Key's physician friend, a Dr. Beanes, arrested by the British after their Washington raid and the burning of the Capitol and the White House. Key was able to reach the British fleet near the mouth of the Potomac and to secure the release of his friend, but Key and his party were ordered to wait under guard aboard a ship, so as not to give warning of preparations they had observed for an imminent attack on Baltimore. On September 13, 1814, the British fired about eighteen hundred bombs at Fort McHenry which guarded the Baltimore harbor. Watching this cannonading, Key and his friends anxiously awaited the outcome, especially when the shore fortifications ceased to return the fire during the early morning hours. However, as dawn finally came through a misty drizzle on September 14, to their joy they caught a glimpse of the oversized flag of their country still flying. Realizing that Baltimore was strongly defended, the British withdrew. When Key saw that the attack was over, he immediately began to jot down the words of "The Star-Spangled Banner" on the back of an old letter and completed the song in Baltimore during that city's victory celebration. A fresh copy made in his hotel on the evening of the fourteenth is probably the one now preserved in Baltimore's Walters Art Gallery. The next morning the Baltimore *American* printed the words as a handbill, and the poem immediately made its appearance in other newspapers across the country and within the year was included in three songbooks. Key, a lay reader in the Episcopal Church, served on the committee to prepare a new hymnal for his denomination in 1823. Born in Frederick, Maryland, the son of a distinguished officer in the Revolutionary War, Key became a lawyer and was United States district attorney three times. Although living in a slave state, he finally freed his own slaves and worked to improve conditions under which other Negroes had to live.

STAR–SPANGLED BANNER (THE NATIONAL ANTHEM) The tune for our national anthem may have been "made in England" but when and by whom no one knows. It has been the subject of much research and controversy in England and America for it was well-known in both countries when "The Star-Spangled Banner" was written. "To Anacreon in Heaven," the text with which the tune was sung in England from about 1775, was written by Ralph Tomlinson for the Anacreontic Society of London (in existence c. 1766–c. 1794) which he served for a time as president. The first known dated appearance of his text was in *The Vocal Magazine,* August, 1778. It became the official song of this fashionable, exclusive club of wealthy and aristocratic gentlemen and was sung at each of their fortnightly meetings held from mid-November to mid-May. Meetings consisted of a grand concert (in which professional musicians, who were honorary members, took part), an elegant dinner, and a concluding session of singing and varied entertainment. Oscar G. T. Sonneck says that the wide range of the melody (an octave and a fifth) was "considered the sine qua non of effective drinking songs of the period."

Like many other British products, the tune (and the idea of Anacreontic Societies) crossed the Atlantic, came into use in America some time after 1790, and by 1796–1797 was appearing in American collections of popular secular songs, often with patriotic parodies, rarely with Tomlinson's poem. It became a favorite after its publication in the *American Musical Miscellany,* 1798, with "Adams and Liberty," a patriotic ode written for the fourth anniversary of the Massachusetts Charitable Fire Association in Boston by Thomas (Robert Treat) Paine whose father was one of the signers of the Declaration of Independence. The success of Paine's song caused other poetically inclined patriots to use it as a model even though the meter and tune were rather involved. It has been estimated that at least a hundred of these patriotic parodies have survived. Francis Scott Key, himself, wrote one, "When the Warrior returns from the battle afar," which was sung at a dinner in Georgetown, D. C., in 1805, honoring the naval commander Stephen Decatur. This parody contained phrases and rhymes used later in the song that became the national anthem. The tune was steeped in patriotic associations.

Although no composer's name appears with the tune in any of the extant eighteenth-century copies of "To Anacreon in Heaven," it is attributed often to John Stafford Smith (1750–1836) because it was in his *Fifth Book of Canzonets, Catches, Canons & Glees*, London, 1799. All of the other music in this collection is known to have been composed by Smith, and this fact coupled with the statement "harmonized by the Author" on page 33, where "The Anacreontick Song" appears in a three-part arrangement, has convinced some that the tune was his. Since Smith used the word *author* in the title, the copyright entry, and the dedication, it has been assumed that for him, as for other eighteenth-century composers, that term was sometimes used as the equivalent of composer. In *The Star-Spangled Banner*, Washington, 1914, Oscar G. T. Sonneck, the first Chief of the Music Division of the Library of Congress wrote: "Available evidence, and a more thorough study of it, than in 1909 . . . compel me to believe that the music of Ralph Tomlinson's poem 'To Anacreon in Heaven' was indeed composed by John Stafford Smith. Words and music of this song, later on popularly known as 'The Anacreontick Song,' probably originated about the year 1775." There is by no means full agreement among scholars with Sonneck's deductions and conclusions. Some call his attribution of the tune to Smith mistaken and say that the actual origin of the tune is unknown.

497 Praise to the Holiest in the Height

These lines are from John Henry Newman's poem, *The Dream of Gerontius*, written in 1865 and printed in his *Verses on Various Occasions*, 1868. The hymn attained wide popularity among the free churches after its appearance in the Appendix to *Hymns Ancient and Modern*, 1868. William Gladstone prized it highly, second only to "Rock of Ages," and it was sung at his funeral. See No. 215 for comments on Newman.

ST. MARY (HACKNEY; GERMAN AIR; PLAYFORD'S) In Lowell Mason's *The Modern Psalmist*, 1839, the following comment appeared above ST. MARY: " 'This tune,' says Mr. Horsley, 'is, perhaps, the finest in our service.' " Just who Mr. Horsley was is not indicated, but from his appraisal of ST. MARY one would have to say that his taste in hymn tunes was commendable. The tune has had long and continued use in English hymnody. It was one of the most frequently sung psalm tunes in seventeenth- and eighteenth-century New England, and one of the thirteen tunes in the ninth edition of the Bay Psalm Book, 1698. Its inclusion in collections edited by Hastings, Mason, Abner Jones, Joshua Leavitt, in the nineteenth century indicates that it continued in use in the United States for a long time. It is a striking tune with marked individuality. In English hymnody it was often associated with John Marckant's hymn "O Lord, turn not thy face" (580) and in the eighteenth century with "Our God, our help in ages past."

ST. MARY was the tune for Psalm 2 in Archdeacon Edmund Prys' Psalter, *Llyfr y Psalmau,* 1621, which contained a Welsh metrical version of all the psalms and a few canticles, nearly all of them in Common Meter which Prys used in order to promote congregational singing. Many of his versions are still sung in Welsh churches and his Psalter is said to be one of the chief treasures of Welsh hymnody. Prys (1541–1624), educated at St. John's College, Cambridge, served in several chapels and churches before becoming archdeacon of Merioneth (see 426) and chaplain to Sir Henry Sidney, Lord President of Wales. In 1602 he was made a canon of St. Asaph's Cathedral in North Wales.

Originally there was no *b* flat in the signature of ST. MARY. Whether this omission was intentional or due to faulty printing is not known; without the *b* flat the melody is in the Dorian mode. The third note in measure three was originally *g*. The tune became popular in England after its appearance in its present form in John Playford's *Whole Book of Psalms,* 1677, where it was called ST. MARY'S. However, through its inclusion in that book, which became the standard for the rest of the seventeenth century and for most of the eighteenth in England, it acquired the name PLAYFORD'S. In Miller's *Psalms of David,* 1790, the tune was called an old German melody by Rathiel, a German musician who was organist of St. John's, Hackney, in London, around 1750 — which accounts for another of its names.

498 Each Morning Brings

After studying at the universities of Basel, Freiburg, Paris, and Padua, Johannes Zwick (c. 1496–1542) was for some time a tutor in law at Basel and Freiburg before entering the priesthood in 1518. Because of his Lutheran sympathies, he was later forbidden to officiate and his charge was taken from him. Returning to his birthplace, Constance, he was named one of the town preachers and devoted himself selflessly to the care of the poor and dispossessed. When the pastor in the town of Bischofszell lost his life as a result of the plague, Zwick offered to take his place and labored there for several months until he fell ill and died in the same year. In Herzog's *Real-Encyklo-pädie,* it is said that he "was one of the leaders of the Swiss Reformation" and "ranks next to Blaurer as the most important of the early hymn writers of the Reformed Church." This hymn first appeared in the third edition of the *Nüw Gesangbüchle,* 1545, the hymnal of the Reformed Church in Constance. The present translation is taken from *Cantate Domino,* 1951. The translator, Margaret Barclay (1932–   ) also translated several other German hymns and a Chinese hymn into English for *Cantate Domino.* She was on the staff of the World Council of Churches as an English translator from 1947 to 1953 and since 1954 has served in the same capacity with the

High Authority of the European Coal and Steel Community, a branch of the Common Market, in Luxembourg. She is a Fellow of the Institute of Linguists in London, the British professional translators' and interpreters' association. She wrote in a letter, "The hymns in *Cantate Domine* represent the only occasion when I burst into print, though I did write a dozen or so publicity articles long ago for the World Council."

ALL MORGEN IST   When the music editors heard this engaging melody for the first time in the home of Pastor Ernest Muller in Bouxwiller, near Strasbourg, they were struck with its fitness for an introit in a morning service. Not long afterward they heard it sung as the introit at a Sunday morning service in the Dreikönigskirche in Frankfurt am Main. In current German hymnals and in *Cantate Domino,* the hymnal of the World Student Christian Federation, it appears with the German original of the present text which has been associated with it since 1934. This anonymous melody was set to Luther's hymn "Vom Himmel hoch" in the *Wittenbergisch Gesangbüchli,* 1537 (Zahn 345), one of several hymnals edited by Johann Walther (1496–1570), Luther's friend and principal collaborator in organizing and laying the foundations for Lutheran church music. From 1517 to 1525 he was bass singer in the chapel of Elector Frederick the Wise at Torgau, and from 1548 to 1554 directed the music in the court chapel at Dresden for Moritz, Elector of Saxony. As director of the Torgau singing school, the first Lutheran cantorate established in Germany, he became the first Lutheran cantor. The Torgau school, founded with Luther's encouragement, became famous throughout Germany for the high quality of its music training and traditions. A complete edition of Walther's works is in process of publication.

499   Lo, God Is Here!

Two translations of this hymn by Gerhardt (or Gerhard) Tersteegen appear in this hymnal, the other being found at No. 3. John Wesley's translation was first published in *Hymns and Sacred Poems,* 1739. The present version includes the first two stanzas. See No. 3 for comments on Tersteegen and No. 9 for comments on Wesley.

AUS GNADEN SOLL ICH, composed in 1796 by Justin H. Knecht (1752–1817), was in *Vollständige Sammlung . . . Choralmelodien,* Stuttgart, 1799, set to "Dein Heil, O Christ, nicht zu verscherzen" by Christian F. Gellert. (Zahn 2897) Zahn lists four other texts with which the tune was sung in Germany including "Aus Gnaden soll ich selig werden." See No. 243 for comments on Knecht.

500   Lord God of Morning and of Night

Famous as the editor of *The Golden Treasury of the Best Songs and Lyrical Poems in the English Language,* 1861, which went through many editions and still continues in use, Francis Turner Palgrave (1824–1897) served for a time as private secretary to William Gladstone. For many years he held various positions in the government education department, eventually becoming assistant secretary, and from 1885 to 1895 he was professor of poetry at Oxford. He published several volumes of essays and poems, including *Hymns,* 1867, *Lyrical Poems,* 1871, and *The Children's Treasury of English Song,* 1875. He also held the position of art critic on the *Saturday Review.* He wrote the present hymn in 1862, and it appeared in Lord Selborne's *Book of Praise,* 1863, and in Palgrave's *Hymns.* Though it consisted originally of five stanzas, only the first and last stanzas are included here.

MACH'S MIT MIR, GOTT is discussed at No. 99. (Zahn 2383) It was set to Palgrave's text in *Hymnal for Colleges and Schools,* 1956.

501 Lord, for the Mercies of the Night

John Mason (c. 1646–1694) belongs to the select group of men in England who preceded Isaac Watts in introducing hymns into the worship of the church. When his *Spiritual Songs, or Songs of Praise to Almighty God upon Several Occasions,* 1683, appeared, congregational singing was limited to the metrical psalms. His volume of hymns went through twenty editions and had a marked influence on Watts and Wesley. Richard Baxter described him as "the chief glory of the Church of England" and wrote of him: "The frame of his spirit was so heavenly, his deportment so humble and obliging, his discourse of spiritual things so weighty, with such apt words and delightful air, that it charmed all that had any spiritual relish." During his tenure as rector of the parish church in Water-Stratford where he spent the last twenty years of his life, his sermons increasingly took on an imminent premillenarian cast. Huge crowds gathered to hear him preach, and his services became in many respects prototypes of the nineteenth-century camp meetings. Even after his death, people continued to meet for several years near his church on a spot called Holy Ground, awaiting Christ's return to earth. The present morning hymn is from his *Spiritual Songs.*

FARRANT   For a long time this tune has been named for and attributed to Richard Farrant (d. 1581) who, it was thought, composed the anthem "Lord, for thy tender mercies' sake" from which the hymn tune was adapted. In *Songs of Praise* the heading is: "Adapted from an Anthem of the school of R. Farrant." However, Edmund H. Fellowes states in *Grove's Dictionary* (1954 edition) that there can be no doubt that John Hilton, the Elder (d. 1608), was the composer of the anthem. In *English Cathedral Music,* 1941, Fellowes writes:

John Hilton's work dates from the best period of the Elizabethan School. The date of his birth is unknown. He is first heard of as a lay-clerk at Lincoln Cathedral in 1584. In 1594 he became Organist of Trinity College, at Cambridge. He died at Cambridge in 1608. His anthem *Lord, for thy tender mercy's sake* is among the most beautiful things in English Church music. It is a perfect setting of a penitent's prayer; lovely in melody and tender in expression. The name of Farrant is not known to have been associated with this anthem till 1778. It is ascribed in all earlier manuscripts to Hilton, and there is no reason whatever to doubt that he was the composer.[31]

In William H. Havergal's *Old Church Psalmody*, 1847, the source of the present harmonization of FARRANT, each phrase starts with and ends with a long note. In "Notes on Certain Tunes" in *Old Church Psalmody* Havergal wrote of FARRANT:

> This is a compilation from the beautifully "serene" anthem, "Lord, for thy tender mercies' sake." With slight exceptions in the parts, the tune was compiled by the editor's worthy friend, Dr. Edward Hodges, whom England has lost, and New York has gained.

Hodges was organist and choirmaster of Trinity Church in New York from 1846 to 1863.

502 We Praise Thee, Lord

Consisting originally of eight stanzas, this hymn by Johann Franck, originally beginning "Dreieinigkeit der Gottheit wahrer Spiegel," was first published in C. Peters' *Andachts-Zymbeln*, Freiberg, 1655 in the section entitled, "On the Holy Trinity." Catherine Winkworth translated stanzas one to three, seven, and eight in her *Lyra Germanica*, Second Series, 1858. Stanzas two, seven, and eight of her translation, slightly altered, were included in *Hymns of the Spirit*, Boston, 1864, edited jointly by Samuel Longfellow and Samuel Johnson. The present version uses stanzas two and seven of Miss Winkworth's translation taken from *Hymns of the Spirit*. See No. 222 for comments on Franck and No. 2 for comments on Miss Winkworth.

AINSWORTH 97 was the tune assigned to Psalms 95, 97, 146, and 150 in Ainsworth's *Book of Psalmes: Englished both in Prose and Metre*, printed at Amsterdam in 1612. It was prepared by Henry Ainsworth (c. 1571–1622 or 1623) for the English Separatists who had gone from London to Amsterdam, thence to Leyden, and from whose number the Pilgrims came. It was the psalter they used at Plymouth until 1692. Ainsworth, minister, Hebrew scholar, Biblical commentator, has been described as "the most steadfast and cultured champion of the principles represented by the early Congregationalists." AINSWORTH 97 had its origin in the tune for Psalms 74 and 116 in the 1562 Genevan Psalter. It was set to the same Psalms in Lobwasser's German psalter (1573) and came to be used with a number of texts in later German collections. (Zahn 859) The meter of the Genevan tune was 10.11.11.10. In order to adapt it to the four Psalms mentioned above, which were in 10.10.10.10., Ainsworth omitted three notes of the original melody. The following stanza from Ainsworth's metrical version of Psalm 150, sung in unison, unaccompanied, to the tune as it appears here, makes an appropriate introit for a Thanksgiving Day service.

> O praise Him with sound of the trumpet shrill;
>> Praise Him with harp and the psalterion;
> O praise Him with the flute and tymberil;
>> Praise Him with virginals and organon!

379

The harmonies given here are from one of Claude LeJeune's numerous settings of Genevan psalm tunes. Those contained in his best-known collection, published in 1613, were much used in the Reformed churches of France, Holland, and Germany. LeJeune (c. 1528–1600), renowned in his day, composed a great variety of secular vocal music. During the siege of Paris in 1588 he fled, being a Protestant, carrying with him many of his manuscripts. He was arrested and his music would have been burned but for the intervention of a Catholic fellow musician, Jacques Mauduit.

The Music of the Pilgrims, 1921, by Waldo Selden Pratt describes the psalmbook brought to Plymouth in 1620. In it are the thirty-nine melodies from the psalter in modern notation with brief notes on their sources and previous usage, a short sketch of Ainsworth's life, and comments on the psalm singing of the Pilgrims, on the format of the psalter, and on the literary quality of its texts.

503 Open Now Thy Gates of Beauty

Bearing the title, "Appearing before God," this hymn by Benjamin Schmolck was first published in his *Kirchen-Gefährte,* 1732, with seven stanzas. The translation is by Catherine Winkworth from her *Chorale Book for England,* 1863. See No. 279 for comments on Schmolck and No. 2 for comments on Miss Winkworth.

UNSER HERRSCHER was one of the tunes in Joachim Neander's *Glaub- und Liebesübung,* 1680, where it was set to his hymn "Unser Herrscher, unser König" (Our Ruler, our King). (Zahn 3735) The present harmonization is largely that found in *The Chorale Book for England,* 1863. (No. 15) See No. 3 for comments on Neander.

504 This Is the Day the Lord Hath Made

Based on Psalm 118:24–26, this free paraphrase by Isaac Watts is from his *Psalms of David,* 1719. It was entitled "Hosanna; the Lord's Day; or, Christ's resurrection and our salvation," and consisted of five stanzas, of which the present version uses the first and last. See No. 1 for comments on Watts.

NUN DANKET ALL' See No. 241 for comments on the tune.

505 You That Have Spent the Silent Night

Described by John Julian as one of the earliest English dramatists, the first English satirist, and the first English critic in poetry, George Gascoigne (c. 1525–1577) led a tempestuous life. Educated at Trinity College, Cambridge, he decided to study law; but because of his extravagant ways he was disinherited by his father. He represented Bedford in Parliament in 1557–1558 and was returned again in 1572 from Midhurst but did not take his seat because of objections that were raised about his character. Serving under William of Orange in Holland, he distinguished himself by his gallant conduct in the field and was appointed a captain. He was later captured by the Spanish forces and returned to England. Thereafter he led a literary life and seems to have been attached to Elizabeth's court. The present hymn, considerably revised, is from his poem, "Good Morrowe," originally entitled "Gascoignes good morrow" as given in his book *A Hundredth sundrie Floures bound up in one small Poesie,* 1573. The hymn in its present form has been taken from *The Oxford Hymn Book,* 1908.

OLD 22ND   See No. 259 for comments on the tune.

506   Come, My Soul, Thou Must Be Waking

Friedrich R. L. von Canitz (1654–1699), referred to as an ornament of the aristocracy, was a skilled diplomat, generous philanthropist, and devout Christian. He held several important positions under Elector Friedrich Wilhelm of Brandenburg and his successor, Friedrich III, was given the title of baron in 1698 by Emperor Leopold I, and traveled all over Europe on state missions. On the morning he died, August 11, 1699, he asked to be carried to an open window so that he might see the sun rise again and exclaimed, "Oh! if the appearance of this earthly and created thing is so beautiful and quickening, how much more shall I be enraptured at the sight of the unspeakable glory of the Creator Himself." This lovely morning hymn, originally containing fourteen six-line stanzas and beginning, "Seele, du musst munter werden," was first published anonymously in *Nebenstunden unterschiedener Gedichte,* 1700, a posthumous collection of his hymns, edited by Joachim Lange. It was first translated anonymously into English in the July, 1838, issue of the *British Magazine* and appeared in shortened form as a note in Thomas Arnold's book of sermons, *Christian Life: its Cause, its Hindrances, and its Helps,* 1841. Most authorities now credit the translation to Henry J. Buckoll (1803–1871), assistant headmaster of Rugby who remained there for forty-five years and who probably edited the first edition of *Psalms and Hymns for the use of Rugby School Chapel.* He later included the hymn in his *Hymns Translated from the German,* 1842.

VENI, ANIMA MEA was selected from several tunes submitted anonymously to the *Pilgrim Hymnal* committee for use with this text. It was composed by Mark Dickey (1885–1961) whose musical career was closely connected with the church. He was born in Ludlow Center, Massachusetts, and had his schooling there and in Milton, New Hampshire, where his father was minister of the Congregational Church. He began regular music study at eight, and after graduating from high school studied at the New England Conservatory of Music in Boston. He served as organist and choir director of Congregational churches in Massachusetts, New Hampshire, and Maine. Dickey's compositions include works for piano, organ, recorder, and for various instrumental combinations; hymns, anthems, sacred and secular songs, and carols for Christmas and Easter. In 1932 his anthem "Let not your heart be troubled" won the H. W. Gray prize in a national competition sponsored

381

by the American Guild of Organists. On his seventy-fifth birthday he was honored by the Boston Chapter of the Guild and presented with a citation which read in part:

> The contribution you have made in promoting fine music through your playing and composing can hardly be measured. . . . We honor you for your devotion to the highest ideals of our profession.

507 To Thee Before the Close of Day

This office hymn, long used by the Western Church in the last service of the day, compline, is of unknown authorship, dating from the seventh century. Many translations have appeared. The present translation is by John David Chambers (1805–1893) from his *Psalter, or Seven Ordinary Hours of Sarum, with the Hymns for the Year, and the Variations of the York and Hereford Breviaries*, 1852. Chambers was appointed recorder of New Sarum (Salisbury) in 1842. He wrote several scholarly volumes in the field of liturgical and ecclesiastical lore. John Julian comments in the *Dictionary of Hymnology:* "Chamber's publications and translations have had no small part in stimulating the great change which has taken place in the mode of worship in the Church of England. His translations of Latin hymns are close, clear and poetical; they have much strength and earnestness, and the rhythm is easy and musical."

JAM LUCIS is a simple, syllabic plainsong with a compass of four notes. As its name indicates, the melody had long association with "Jam lucis orto sidere" ("Now that the daylight fills the sky"), a traditional office hymn for prime. Like many plainsong tunes it was used with a number of diverse texts. The present arrangement of the melody by Winfred Douglas is from *The Hymnal 1940*. In some English hymnals JAM LUCIS is arranged as an Anglican chant.

508 Before the Day Draws Near Its Ending

Written for a Festival of Choirs at Nantwich, England, April 22, 1880, by John Ellerton, with the heading "Afternoon," this hymn was first published in the *Nantwich Festival Book*, 1880. See No. 47 for comments on Ellerton.

RENDEZ À DIEU See No. 282 for comments on the tune.

509 Again, as Evening's Shadow Falls

In a letter dated February 11, 1890, Samuel Longfellow wrote, "My two favorites among my hymns are the vesper hymn, 'Again, as evening's shadow falls,' and the one beginning, 'I look to Thee in every need.'" (No. 92) The former was entitled "Vesper Hymn" and first appeared in his book, *Vespers*, 1859, a small collection of hymns which he published for use in his church in Brooklyn. See No. 46 for comments on Longfellow.

SONG 5 is another of Orlando Gibbons' melodies from *Hymnes and Songs of the Church* (see No. 162) where it was the setting for Wither's paraphrase, "The Lamentation of David over Saul and Jonathan." (II Samuel 1:19 f.)

> Thy beauty, Israel, is gone;
> Slaine in the Places high is he:
> The Mighty now are overthrowne.
> Oh, thus how cometh it to be!

SONG 5 was used for "O Prince of peace, who man was born" in *The Yattendon Hymnal,* edited by Robert Bridges, and for Tennyson's "Strong Son of God, immortal love" in *The English Hymnal,* 1906, edited by Percy Dearmer and Ralph Vaughan Williams.

510 Now the Day Is Over

This hymn by Sabine Baring-Gould was written for the children of Horbury Bridge, Yorkshire, a mission church under his care, while he was the curate of Horbury. First published in *The Church Times,* February 16, 1867, it was included the following year in the Appendix to *Hymns Ancient and Modern,* 1868. It is based on Proverbs 3:24 ("When thou liest down, thou shalt not be afraid: yea, thou shalt lie down, and thy sleep shall be sweet"). See No. 51 for comments on Baring-Gould.

EUDOXIA   In five standard English hymnals EUDOXIA is the only tune given with Sabine Baring-Gould's evening hymn. Although listed as the composer of the melody, he said himself that after it was published he realized how much it resembled a German tune he had known as a child, but was unable to identify. In the 1935 Supplement to the *Handbook to the Church Hymnary,* Millar Patrick printed the words and melody of "The Cricket," a song which was widely taught in English schools around the middle of the nineteenth century. Both he and Anne G. Gilchrist, who discovered the tune (by A. Weber), felt that it was in all probability the German air, echoes of which Baring-Gould detected in EUDOXIA. After pointing out that the meter of "Now the day is over" is the same as that of "The Cricket," and that its mood might have been suggested subconsciously by the line "While the world is sleeping," Miss Gilchrist concludes: "But a 'reminiscence' is a long way from an adaptation, and I think Baring-Gould had a right to call the tune he made for his hymn his own."

511 Gloria Patri

Known as the Lesser Doxology to distinguish it from the *Gloria in excelsis,* or Greater Doxology, this ancient canticle is an ascription of praise to the Trinity. The first part, "Glory be to the Father, and to the Son, and to the Holy Ghost," is based on the commission to baptize all nations (Matthew 28:19) and may have come into use in both East and West as early as the second century. The second part, "As it was in the beginning, is now, and ever shall be," is of later origin and was added during the Arian controversy in the fourth century to affirm that the triune God of the New Testament is the same divine being as the God of the Old Testament. The Arians denied this. From earliest times it has commonly been sung after the psalms to give them a Trinitarian character and ending. In support of this usage, Henry Sloane Coffin declared in *The Public Worship of God*, 1946, "In view of the origin of the Gloria Patri and its long historical association with the Psalms, it is vandalism to tear it from its proper context, and attach it to something else in the service." [32] At the close of Isaac Watts' *Hymns and Spiritual Songs*, 1707–1709, there are twenty versions of the canticle prefaced with the comment: "Though the Latin name of it, *Gloria Patri*, be retained in our nation from the Roman Church; and though there may be some excess of superstitious honour paid to the words of it, which may have wrought some unhappy prejudices in weaker Christians, yet I believe it still to be one of the parts of Christian worship." The *Gloria Patri* is today, as it has been for centuries, the most widely known and frequently sung canticle of the early church.

The *Gloria Patri* is set here to the first section of "Old Scottish Chant" ("Old Chant"), the source of which has never been identified. Its full form is given at No. 554 with *Gloria in excelsis*, with which it has been widely and continuously associated in English-speaking countries.

512 Gloria Patri

See No. 511 for comments on the text.

This setting for the *Gloria Patri* is from the *Pilgrim Hymnal*, 1931, where no source was given for it. It seems to have been derived from the first Gregorian Psalm Tone, one of eight melodic formulas used for chanting the psalms. (See No. 177.)

513 Gloria Patri

See No. 511 for comments on the text.

GLORIA PATRI, retained from the *Pilgrim Hymnal*, 1931, is from Henry W. Greatorex's *Collection of Psalm and Hymn Tunes*, 1851, published when he was organist and director of the music at Calvary Episcopal Church in New York City. This book, one of the best collections of its time, went through a number of editions and in general had a beneficial effect on church music.

Greatorex (1815–1858), born in England, was the son and pupil of Thomas Greatorex, well-known teacher, composer, conductor, and organist of Carlisle Cathedral and later of Westminster Abbey. The son came to the United States in 1839, served for two years as organist in the Center Congregational Church in Hartford, Connecticut, and later at St. John's Church in the same city. From 1846 to 1848 he was organist at St. Paul's Chapel in New York City and presumably went from there to Calvary Church. In 1853 he left New York for Charleston, South Carolina, serving there in an Episcopal church until his death from yellow fever in 1858. Although Greatorex's GLORIA PATRI is widely used in free churches in the United States, it is giving place in many quarters to the chant at No. 511.

514 Praise God From Whom All Blessings Flow

This is the last stanza of each of three hymns that Thomas Ken wrote for the schoolboys of Winchester College. The hymns appeared as an Appendix in his *Manual of Prayers for the Use of the Scholars of Winchester College*, 1695 edition. They were, "Awake, my soul, and with the sun" (Morning, No. 32); "All praise to thee, my God" (Evening, Nos. 56 and 57); and "My God, now I from sleep awake" (Midnight). This doxology is unquestionably the best known and most widely sung of all English metrical doxologies and is used in many Protestant churches at the beginning of worship or when the offering is received.

See No. 32 for further comments on Ken.

OLD HUNDREDTH is given here as it appeared with Bèze's version of Psalm 134 in the 1551 edition of the Genevan Psalter. (See No. 4.) It differs from the English form of the melody in the rhythm of the first two notes in measure ten — a rhythm which gives it variety and distinctiveness.

The original form of the melody has been retained in psalters used in Europe. In France OLD HUNDREDTH is now sung with Valentin Conrart's version of Psalm 134, the first stanza of which follows.

> Vous, saints ministres du Seigneur,
> Qui, dé-vou-és a son hon-neur,
> Nuit et jour gardez sa maison,
> Présentez-lui votre o-rai-son.

Les Psaumes en vers françois, retouchéz sur l'ancienne version, 1679, was largely the work of Conrart (1603–1675), one of the founders of the French Academy. The meters of Clément Marot's and Bèze's versions as well as some of their phrases were preserved but Conrart's revision is in fact the French "New Version" of the Psalms.

515 Praise God From Whom All Blessings Flow

See No. 514 for comments on the text.

OLD HUNDREDTH   The present form of this famous hymn tune, with all the notes of equal length, is the one most commonly sung in American churches. The form of the melody at No. 4, however, is coming into use in more and more churches and schools.

516 Thy Word Is a Lamp Unto My Feet

The text, Psalm 119:105, is from the King James Version.

This response, for use before the responsive reading, was written by Hugh Porter (1897–1960) for the choir of the Collegiate Church of St. Nicholas, formerly on Fifth Avenue and Forty-eighth Street, New York City, where he was organist and choirmaster from 1936 to 1947. Hugh Porter, son of a Methodist minister, was born in Heron Lake, Minnesota, but grew up in towns in Colorado, Illinois, and Indiana. He had good, early musical instruction from two teachers who had been assistants to Theodor Leschetizky, and even as a young boy played for church services as a substitute organist. When he applied for his first regular organ position at age fourteen, the church authorities were dubious; but when he not only played the service well but also repaired a faulty pipe during the sermon, they hired him on the spot. From that time until his death he served as organist in a number of Protestant churches. At sixteen he toured as accompanist with The Flying Squadron, a Prohibition group which held meetings in every state of the Union. Dr. Porter received the B.Music degree with honors at the American Conservatory in Chicago in 1920; the A.B. at Northwestern University in 1924, where he was chapel organist; and on Sundays served churches in the Chicago area. In 1924 he went to New York, was granted a fellowship by the Juilliard Musical Foundation (before the Graduate School had been established), studied privately with Lynnwood Farnam, Frank LaForge, and Rosario Scalero at the David Mannes School, and taught there for one year. He was a student of Albert Stoessel in choral conducting. During the period from 1920 to 1952 he taught at the American Conservatory; at New York University; was organist for the Oratorio Society of New York and of the Chautauqua Institution; was head of the organ department of the Juilliard Summer School (1932–1945), and conductor of the Lutheran and Washington Heights Oratorio Societies. He served as organist of the New First Congregational Church, Chicago; Calvary Episcopal Church and Church of the Heavenly Rest in New York City; and as organist-choirmaster at the Second Presbyterian Church, New York, and for the Sunday services at Union Theological Seminary (1947–1960). He was a Fellow of the American Guild of Organists, and as a recitalist was well-known throughout the country.

For a number of years Dr. Porter was torn between music and the ministry. In 1927, he resigned as organist of Calvary Church, gave up teaching, and entered Union Theological Seminary as a ministerial candidate. The following year, when the School of Sacred Music was founded, he was persuaded by Dr. Henry Sloane Coffin, president of the seminary, to enroll in its first class. He received the M.S.M. degree in 1930, the S.M.D. in 1944, was on the faculty from 1931 until his death, and became director in 1945. In 1947 he was appointed Clarence and Helen Dickinson Professor of Sacred Music, the first full professor of music on the seminary faculty. During his fifteen years as director, the program of the school was broadened, its requirements raised, the faculty was enlarged, equipment and facilities for teaching and practice were greatly improved, summer sessions were established with notable success, musical performances reached new heights, and the school attained new musical dimension and status. Dr. Porter considered his work on the *Pilgrim Hymnal*, 1958, one of the most rewarding assignments of his career. He died suddenly, September 22, 1960, in the organ loft of James Chapel at Union Seminary where he had gone in response to a call for help to find and repair a cipher so that a student organist could play for the morning service. In a memorial minute adopted by the faculty of Union Theological Seminary, Dr. Morgan Noyes wrote:

> The School of Sacred Music gave Dr. Porter the ideal setting for the employment of his great gifts in the service of the two dominant loyalties of his life — music and the church. He served them with a complete devotion which asked for nothing save the opportunity to give himself without reservation. Modest and unassuming, apparently impervious to personal ambition and unconcerned with professional honors and public recognition, he was able to draw out the best in others because he gave so lavishly of his own best to them.

The following tribute from Nadia Boulanger was one of several included in a memorial booklet issued by the Seminary:

> Hugh Porter was many years ago my student. At once his talent, his integrity, his moral value struck me. We became soon friends, quite naturally, and always remained. And during all this time, I did not cease to see him grow, as an artist, as a man. Exacting to himself, generous and indulgent for others, always faithful to his creed.

5 I 7   Teach Me, O Lord, the Way of Thy Statutes

The text, Psalm 119:33, is from the King James Version.

"Teach me, O Lord, the way of thy statutes" is from Thomas Attwood's well-known anthem of that name. Attwood (1765–1838), the son of a coal merchant who played viola and trumpet in the Royal Band and was an underpage to George III, became a chorister in the Chapel Royal when he was nine. His gifts and abilities were noted by the Prince of Wales (later George IV) who decided to send him abroad at his own expense in order to further his musical education. Accordingly, in 1783, Attwood went to Italy, studied in Naples for two years, then went on to Vienna where he became one of Mozart's favorite pupils.

After returning to London in 1787, Attwood became an important figure in the musical life of England and filled a variety of posts as music teacher to the Duchess of York and the Princess of Wales, organist of St. Paul's Cathedral, composer to and organist of the Chapel Royal, organist for George IV's private chapel at Brighton, and a professor in the newly founded Royal Academy of Music. He was one of the founders of the London Philharmonic Society. His compositions included operas, piano sonatas, anthems, chants, service music, songs, and glees. He became a close friend of Mendelssohn and was his host on numerous occasions. When in London, Mendelssohn would sometimes accompany Attwood to St. Paul's on Sunday and play the organ at the conclusion of the service. It was his playing of Bach's organ works that kindled Attwood's enthusiasm for these compositions and broke down his considerable prejudice against them. Mendelssohn's *Three Preludes and Fugues* for organ were dedicated to Attwood *mit Verehrung und Dankbarkeit* (with admiration and gratitude).

518 Let Thy Word Abide in Us, O Lord

Nothing is known of the author of this brief response, D. Tait Patterson (1877–1956), other than his name and the dates of his birth and death.

This chant was composed by George Dyson (1883–1964), English composer, teacher, organist, and author. He was a scholarship student at the Royal College of Music from 1900 to 1904. After winning the Mendelssohn Scholarship he continued his studies on the Continent for four years. In 1918 he received the Doctor of Music degree at Oxford. A gifted teacher, Dyson was music master at Osborne, Marlborough, and Rugby, and was director of music at Wellington College (1921–1924) and Winchester College (1924–1937). In Winchester he took an active part in the musical life of the town, conducting its choral society, amateur orchestra, and the annual competition festivals. His appointment as director of the Royal College of Music in 1937 marked the first time in the history of the school that a former student was so honored. During his years there (1937–1952) he reorganized and strengthened the curriculum and did much to improve the equipment and buildings. In 1941 he was knighted. His compositions include vocal and instrumental works, church music, chamber music, and large-scale choral and orchestral works. He was a brilliant and witty lecturer and the author of *The New Music,* 1924; *The Progress of Music,* 1932; *Fiddling While Rome Burns,* 1954; and *Grenade Fighting,* a manual adopted by the British War Office in World War I.

519 To My Humble Supplication

Beyond the fact that he lived in the seventeenth century and wrote some metrical paraphrases, little is known of Joseph Bryan. This prayer is the first stanza of a cento of one of his poems, based on Psalm 86, and was made by Percy Dearmer for *The English Hymnal,* 1906. A collection of Bryan's poems exists in a manuscript, c. 1620, in the British Museum, from which Dearmer prepared his cento.

MON DIEU, PRÊTE–MOI L'OREILLE (PSALM 86; GENEVA 86). The music for this response is the first half of the setting for Clément Marot's version of Psalm 86 in various French psalters issued after 1543, the year in which the text was first published in *Cinquante Pseaumes en françois.* An edition of these fifty psalms with music, published later that year, accounts for the date 1543 given with the tune by Douen and other editors, even though there is no extant copy of the book. The earliest date given for the melody in Pidoux's *Le Psautier Huguenot,* 1962, is 1545, that of a psalter published at Strasbourg. The melody was given its present form in the Genevan Psalter of 1551. It was used also for Psalm 77 in the complete psalter of 1562. Douen attributed the adaptation or the composition of the melody to Bourgeois and traced parts of it to a secular chanson. The tune was taken into the psalter of the Reformed church of Germany, into the Anglo-Genevan Psalter of 1561, and into the 1564 Scottish Psalter. After 1587 it passed into Lutheran use and was the setting for several texts. There is a harmonization of the melody by Bach in his *Choralgesänge* for the hymn "Lass, O Herr, dein Ohr sich neigen." Gustav Holst used the tune in the first of his *Two Psalms* for mixed voices with strings and organ. The present harmonization is from *The English Hymnal,* 1906, in which the complete melody was set to Heber's hymn "Virgin-born, we bow before thee." In *Songs of Praise,* 1925, the same harmonization appeared with the present text and other stanzas of Bryan's paraphrase of Psalm 86.

520 Almighty Father, Hear Our Prayer

The source of the text is unknown.

The setting for these words, retained from the *Pilgrim Hymnal,* 1931, is adapted from Elijah's and the people's petitions for help in Mendelssohn's *Elijah.* (Part I, No. 19.) See No. 120 for comments on Mendelssohn.

521 Lord Jesus Christ, Be Present Now

Of unknown authorship, although it is sometimes credited to Wilhelm II, Duke of Saxe-Weimar (1598–1662), this hymn, originally beginning "Herr Jesu Christ, dich zu uns wend," first appeared in Johann Neidling's *Lutherisch Handbüchlein,* 1648, second edition. John Julian wrote, "Whoever the author was the hymn soon became justly popular, and in 1678 was formally directed to be sung in all the churches in Saxony on all Sundays and festivals. It is a simple and forcible hymn, which survived the Rationalistic period, and is found in all recent German hymn-books." The translation is by Catherine Winkworth from her *Chorale Book for England,* 1863. See No. 2 for comments on Miss Winkworth.

HERR JESU CHRIST was one of eighty melodies included without text in the Appendix of *Pensum sacrum,* 1648, a collection of Latin odes written by professors of the University of Prague. In *Cantionale sacrum,* Gotha, 1651, the tune was set to "Herr Jesu Christ, dich zu uns wend," the hymn with which it has been associated ever since. According to Zahn the tune undoubtedly had older roots. Koch gives *Cantional Germanicum,* Dresden, 1628, as its source. In *The Story of Our Hymns,* 1952, Armin Haeussler mentions a tradition that traced the tune back to John Huss. In several of Lowell Mason's collections, the tune, in varied forms, named HAGUE or IOSCO, carries the heading: "Melody by John Huss Burnt as a Martyr, 1415." There is one harmonization of the melody in Bach's *Choralgesänge* and there are four chorale preludes on it for organ: one in the *Orgelbüchlein,* one in the *Eighteen Chorales,* and two in the miscellaneous Preludes. Writing of these preludes Charles Sanford Terry says in *Bach's Chorals,* Part III:

> Probably it is not an unrelated coincidence that the number of Bach's Organ movements upon the melody equals the number of stanzas of the hymn. Their differing moods and appropriateness to a particular stanza support the assumption that Bach had the text of the hymn before him and followed it closely.

HERR JESU CHRIST, as it appeared in *Pensum sacrum,* is given below with the text from *Cantionale sacrum.* (Zahn 624) The *c*-sharp did not appear in all versions. There is a later form of melody at No. 537.

Herr Je - su Christ, dich zu uns wend, dein heil-gen Geist du zu uns send,

mit Hilf und Gnad, Herr, uns re-gier und uns den Weg zur Wahr-heit führ.

522 Let the Words of My Mouth

The text, Psalm 19:14, is from the King James Version.

This double chant, often referred to as "Langdon in F" was one of twenty chants given at the end of Richard Langdon's *Divine Harmony, a Collection, in Score, of Psalms and Anthems,* 1774. Although no names appeared with the chants, it is thought that Langdon composed this particular one. A graduate of Oxford (Bachelor of Music, 1761), he served as organist of Exeter Cathedral (1753–1777), of Ely Cathedral for a few months, of Bristol Cathedral (1778–1782), and of Armagh Cathedral (1782–1794).

A single Anglican chant consists of seven measures of melody harmonized in four parts, comprising two phrases of three and four measures respectively. The first measure of each phrase contains the reciting note followed by the inflection and cadence in the remaining measures. It serves for one verse of the text. A double chant, as its name implies, is fourteen measures long and is sung to two verses.

523 May the Words of Our Mouths

The text is a slightly altered version of Psalm 19:14, using the words *our* for my, *mouths* for mouth, and *hearts* for heart, from the King James Version.

The setting for this response was one of those submitted anonymously to the Pilgrim Hymnal Committee. Only when copy was being prepared for the printer did the music editors learn that its composer had been a student at the School of Sacred Music of Union Theological Seminary and an organ pupil of the director of that school, Dr. Hugh Porter. Alan Walker (1927–   ) received a Bachelor of Music degree at Boston University in 1951 and a Master of Sacred Music at Union Theological Seminary in 1953. He has been organist and choir director in Lutheran, Episcopal, Congregational, and Presbyterian churches in Massachusetts, New Jersey, and North Carolina. Since 1956 he has been director of music at Central Church, Worcester, Massachusetts; he also directs the glee club at Becker Junior College, Worcester. From 1960 to 1962, he served as dean of the Worcester chapter of the American Guild of Organists. This unison response was written for the adult choir at Howard Memorial Presbyterian Church, Tarboro, N.C., where Allen was organist and choirmaster from 1953 to 1956.

524 Lead Me, Lord

The text, based on Psalm 5:8 and 4:8, is from the King James Version.

This setting for "Lead me, Lord" is an abridged form of Samuel S. Wesley's anthem of the same name. The introduction and two solo passages have been omitted. Brief comments on some of the features of Wesley's anthems are given by Edmund H. Fellowes in his *English Cathedral Music*, 1941. He says that it was during Wesley's six years at Exeter Cathedral that "he earned the position of the foremost composer of English Cathedral music as well as the best executant on the organ." See No. 260 for comments on S. S. Wesley.

525 Come, and Let Us Sweetly Join

When John and Charles Wesley's *Hymns and Sacred Poems* appeared in 1740, it contained a hymn of twenty-two double stanzas written by Charles Wesley and called "The Love Feast." It was divided into five parts. The present hymn is taken from part one, which was printed separately in the *Wesley Hymn Book*, 1780. The first stanza is given here. See No. 43 for comments on Charles Wesley.

SAVANNAH   See No. 458 for comments on the tune.

526 O Thou Who Hearest Prayer

This combination of text and tune with the present harmonization, and captioned *Welsh Melody*, was sent to the Pilgrim Hymnal Committee early in its deliberations with no indication as to the source of the words or the music. The editors were unable to learn who was responsible for this fine hymn and would be grateful for information concerning it.

527 Enrich, Lord, Heart, Mouth, Hands in Me

This has been taken from George Herbert's poem "Trinitie Sunday" which appeared in a collection of his poems, *The Temple,* published in 1633, a year after his death, by his friend, Nicholas Farrar. In giving permission to have his poems published, he did so "if he [Farrar] can think it may turn to the advantage of any dejected soul." See No. 401 for comments on Herbert.

WULFRUN, one of a number of hymn tunes composed by George Wallace Briggs, author of Hymns 198, 286, 308, was written for these words and first published in *Hymns for Little Children.* In *Songs of Praise for Boys and Girls,* 1929, there are several hymns and tunes by Briggs, who played an important part in educational work in England through the collections of hymns, prayers, and liturgical services which he edited for use in schools. He was one of the founders of the Hymn Society of England. In *The Hymn,* October, 1950, Canon Briggs wrote: "The study of hymns is a valuable part of religious education. Moreover, there is nothing which helps more towards Christian unity, for there are no denominational frontiers in hymnology."
See No. 198 for further comments on Briggs.

528 Create in Me a Clean Heart, O God

The text, Psalm 51:10–12, is from the King James Version and is the basis of the Miserere (a penitential psalm and prayer of supplication).

Tonus Regius (Royal tone) designated also as Tonus Parisianus, French Chant, Parisian Tone, and simply Gregorian, is said to be the modern form of Tone VI, one of the eight Gregorian psalm tones. The names would seem to imply that it is a French adaptation used in the diocese of Paris, probably in the Royal Chapel. The present harmonization of the chant is from *The Common Service Book with Hymnal,* 1917 (United Lutheran Church in America), where it is set to the verses for use at the offertory in the Communion Service.

529 The Sacrifices of God

The text, Psalm 51:17, is from the King James Version.

Tonus Regius   See No. 528 for comments on the tune.

530 O Thou By Whom We Come to God

See No. 336 for comments on the text.

WIGTOWN was the setting for "Prayer is the soul's sincere desire" in the *English Hymnal,* 1906. The stanza given here is the seventh of Montgomery's well-known hymn on prayer. See No. 330 for comments on the tune.

531 The Lord Be With You

These versicles have been taken and adapted from *The Book of Common Prayer,* 1549 (also called The First Prayer-Book of Edward VI). They are found in "An Order for Matins" between the Lord's Prayer and the closing collects and are based on Psalm 85:7 and Psalm 51:10–11. The practice of having the priest or minister sing or read a short sentence followed by the response of the congregation is of ancient derivation, going back to the Middle Ages when it became customary to add to the daily offices a few brief verses, responses, and prayers. The salutation and response by priest and people was also used in the mass to introduce the different parts of the liturgy. Cyprian refers to his fellow Christians greeting one another with the words, "The Lord be with you." An even earlier account of the same practice is found in the Old Testament (Ruth 2:4): And, behold, Boaz came from Bethlehem, and said unto the reapers, The LORD be with you. And they answered, The LORD bless thee.

The settings for these versicles and responses which follow the creed in the services of Morning and Evening Prayer in the Anglican church, are from Thomas Tallis' *Festal Responses* (c. 1564), harmonizations of the plainsong melodies in Merbecke's *Booke of Common Praier Noted,* 1550. (See No. 545.) The melodies from Merbecke's *Booke* are in the tenor of Tallis' harmonized responses. The present arrangement of the responses is by Joseph Barnby. (No. 35) In the "Historical Notes" of the *Temple Choral Service Book,* second edition, 1869, the editor, E. J. Hopkins (see No. 60) wrote:

> Portions of the Liturgy were harmonized, separately, by numerous writers, whose names occupy a conspicuous place in the list of cathedral composers. Tallis's complete settings . . . however, proved so superior in treatment to the combined productions of all other pens — on account of their greater devotional character, religious beauty, and expressive appropriateness — that they gradually met with general favour, and . . . ultimately were universally accepted and adopted for use on the Church Festivals. . . . It formed no part of Tallis's design to supersede or silence the Congregational song during the celebration of Divine Service on the Church Festivals, but, on the contrary, to clothe it, as the audible medium through which prayer and praise were offered up, in the most devotional and edifying harmony his great knowledge of the musical art was capable of producing.

Although the versicles bear the directive "To be said or sung," proper liturgical practice specifies that when versicles are read, responses should be spoken, not sung. In *The Choral Service,* 1927 (revised 1930), issued by the Joint Commission on Church Music of the Protestant Episcopal Church in the United States, under "Notes to Choirmasters" is the following:

> The singing of Responses when the Versicles are read, or of Amens to Collects and Prayers which are recited, although a common practice, is inconsistent with the theory and rationale of choral service.

See No. 18 for comments on Tallis. See No. 533 for another setting of the versicles and responses.

393

532 Have Mercy Upon Us

The source of the text is unknown. This is a response to be sung by the congregation as part of the litany.

In *The Hymnal,* 1941 (Evangelical and Reformed) the music for this response is attributed to "H.S.," presumably Henry Schwing (1825–1907), organist, teacher, author, editor. He spent much of his life in Baltimore where he settled in 1848. He taught theory at the Woman's College of Baltimore (Goucher College) for one year and directed its music department from 1892 to 1894. For twenty-five years he was organist of the Mount Vernon Place Methodist Episcopal Church. He wrote books on music theory, piano instruction, improvisation, and modulation, and was mainly responsible for harmonizing the melodies in *Tunes for Worship,* 1884, a companion volume to *Hymns of the Reformed Church in the United States,* 1874; twenty-five of the 218 tunes in the book were composed by Schwing. He was music editor of *The Hymnal,* 1890, of the Reformed Church.

533 The Lord Be With You

See No. 531 for comments on the text.

This is a setting of the ferial responses, for use on week days and ordinary holidays marked by no special observance. The plainsong congregational melodies from Merbecke's *Booke of Common Praier Noted,* 1550, are in the soprano. "And" in the first response was sung to *e* in Merbecke's setting. (See the tenor of No. 531.) Other slight alterations are mentioned at No. 531. This arrangement of the responses is from *The Cathedral Prayer Book,* 1891. A note in the preface states that "the Versicles and Responses . . . are from the arrangement used in St. Paul's Cathedral (Stainer and Martin, founded on Goss)." In *The Hymnal 1940,* the ferial and festal responses are printed side by side at Nos. 601 and 602, an arrangement which enables one to compare the two forms at a glance. In the Historical Introduction to the *Temple Choral Service Book,* 1869, Dr. E. J. Hopkins made the following comments:

> The Ferial Responses are founded on a series of simple and impressive melodies to which the Liturgy of the Church of England has been recited from the earliest days of the Liturgy itself. The origin of these melodies, however, does not date back simply to the period of the Reformation; they are, in fact, an adaptation, to the English Service, of intonations that had been in use in the Church in England from time immemorial.

534 O Lord, Open Thou Our Lips

The Morning Office ("Matins") from earliest times has opened with these words, taken from Psalm 51:15. In the current American *Book of Com-*

mon Prayer, these versicles come after the Lord's Prayer and are followed by the *Gloria Patri* and the *Venite.*

In Merbecke's *Booke of Common Praier Noted,* 1550, the first versicle and response given here were set to one tone. "My," not "our," was used in the text. The present setting is from Tallis' harmonization of the words "World without end, Amen" at the end of the *Gloria Patri* in the *Festal Responses.* (See No. 531.) The second versicle and response (which were not in Merbecke's *Booke*) are from the same source.

535 We Give Thee But Thine Own

Written by William Walsham How in 1858, this hymn originally had six stanzas and was first published in *Psalms and Hymns,* 1864, which How edited jointly with Thomas Baker Morrell. This is the first stanza. See No. 252 for comments on How.

YATTENDON 46   This tune by Harry E. Wooldridge (1845–1917) was No. 46 in the *Yattendon Hymnal,* 1899, set to Lyte's hymn "Far from my heav'nly home," for which it had been composed originally. It was set to the present text in *The Hymnal 1940.* Six of the one hundred tunes in the *Yattendon Hymnal* were by Wooldridge, and a large number of the others were arranged by him. This hymnal was edited by Robert Bridges in close collaboration with Wooldridge, a lifelong friend. As a student at Trinity College, Oxford, Wooldridge became deeply interested in art and music, and while studying painting at the Royal Academy of Art also carried on musical research. He became an expert in polyphonic music of the medieval period and the author of the first two volumes of the *Oxford History of Music,* published in 1901 and 1905. In 1893 he revised and re-edited Chappell's *Popular Music of the Olden Time,* giving it the title *Old English Popular Music.* From 1895 to 1904 he was Slade Professor of Fine Art at Oxford. With E. E. P. Arkwright he edited three volumes of Purcell's church music.

536 All Things Come of Thee, O Lord

The text, 1 Chronicles 29:14, is from the King James Version, omitting the first part of the verse and adding the words "O Lord" between the two phrases.

The music for this offertory response has been attributed to Beethoven but its source has not been identified. Presumably the arrangement was made by E. J. Hopkins (See No. 60), editor of *The Temple Choral Service Book,* 1867, in which it was used for the responses to the Decalogue in the Communion service. Its heading was "From Beethoven."

537 All Things Are Thine

John Greenleaf Whittier wrote this hymn in 1873 for the dedication of Plymouth Congregational Church in St. Paul, Minnesota. First published in

Hazel Blossoms, 1875, it was also included in W. Garrett Horder's *Congregational Hymns,* 1884. Consisting originally of five stanzas, the hymn concluded with the lines:

> O Father, deign these walls to bless;
> Fill with thy love their emptiness;
> And let their door a gateway be
> To lead us from ourselves to thee.

See No. 224 for comments on Whittier.

HERR JESU CHRIST is a later form of the melody discussed at No. 521. The harmonization is from *The Hymnal,* 1941. (Evangelical and Reformed.)

538 Bless Thou the Gifts

This is the last stanza of a four-stanza hymn that Samuel Longfellow wrote in approximately 1886 for the dedication of the Cambridge Hospital in Cambridge, Massachusetts. It first appeared in his *Hymns and Verses,* 1894, edited by his niece, Alice M. Longfellow. See No. 46 for comments on Longfellow.

BRESLAU is a later form of the melody traditionally associated with "O (Herr) Jesu Christ, mein's Lebens Licht" discussed at No. 67. The 4/4 version of the tune which Bach used in Cantatas 3 and 44 is practically identical with the version at No. 67. The 4/4 version used by Mendelssohn for the chorale "O Thou, the true and only light" in the oratorio *St. Paul* is the same as BRESLAU.

539 May the Grace of Christ Our Savior

Listed as one of the "Short Hymns" in the *Olney Hymns,* 1779, this paraphrase of 2 Corinthians 13:14 (The grace of the Lord Jesus Christ, and the love of God, and the communion of the Holy Ghost, be with you all) was written by John Newton as a closing hymn. It has been translated into many languages and was sung for many years at the conclusion of the weekly meeting of Presbyterian ministers in New York City. It is also used on occasion as a wedding hymn. See No. 221 for comments on Newton.

OMNI DIE was the melody for "Omni die dic Mariae" in the 1631 edition of *Grosscatholisch Gesangbuch* published at Nürnberg in 1625. Known also in a vernacular version, this hymn was one of numerous *Marienlieder* (songs to or about the Virgin Mary) which were popular among German Catholics. They were often set to folk melodies. The *Grosscatholisch Gesangbuch* and *Geistliche Nachtigal,* 1649, both compiled by David Gregor Corner (1585–1648) from various sources, were important collections of Catholic hymns and tunes which went through several editions in the seventeenth century.

The present harmonization of OMNI DIE was made by Hubert Lamb (1909–   ) for use with the present text in *The Middlesex Hymn Book,* 1952. Professor Lamb, a graduate of Harvard University and the recipient of the John Knowles Paine traveling fellowship for two years, taught at the Longy School of Music in Cambridge, Massachusetts, from 1934 to 1945. In 1935 he became a member of the faculty of Wellesley College where he was appointed Hamilton C. Macdougall Professor of Music in 1957 and subsequently became head of the music department. In 1948 he was granted a Guggenheim fellowship. His compositions include works in a variety of forms for unusual and varied vocal and instrumental combinations.

540   Father, Give Thy Benediction

This response consists of the first four lines of an eight-line hymn by Samuel Longfellow which was first published anonymously in *Hymns of the Spirit,* 1864, a collection edited jointly by Longfellow and Samuel Johnson. See No. 46 for comments on Longfellow.

ALTA TRINITA BEATA   See No. 403 for comments on this tune which has been abridged to fit the present text.

541   Thou Wilt Keep Him in Perfect Peace

The text, Isaiah 26:3, omitting the last phrase, "because he trusteth in thee," is from the King James Version.

DUKE'S TUNE   The setting for these words is made up of the first and last phrases of DUKE'S TUNE, one of the twelve Common Tunes (for use with Common Meter versions) in Andro Hart's *The CL Psalmes of David,* 1615. In Ravenscroft's Psalter, 1621, it was listed among Scottish Tunes and was harmonized by the editor for Psalms 33 and 87.

542   Sweet Savior, Bless Us Ere We Go

First published in his *Jesus and Mary,* 1849, this hymn by Frederick W. Faber was entitled "An Evening Hymn at the Oratory" and consisted originally of seven four-line stanzas with a refrain. Only the first stanza and refrain are included here. The omitted fourth stanza reads:

> Do more than pardon; give us joy,
> Sweet fear and sober liberty,
> And simple hearts without alloy,
> That only long to be like Thee.

See No. 101 for comments on Faber.

GOTTLOB, ES GEHT   See No. 468 for comments on the tune.

543 God Be in My Head

See No. 393 for comments on the text.

GOD BE IN MY HEAD was composed by Henry Walford Davies (1869–1941) whose name and voice and teaching were known to thousands who listened to his broadcasts over BBC (British Broadcasting Corporation) for seventeen years (1924–1941). He was born in Oswestry, Shropshire, near the Welsh border. At twelve he was accepted as a chorister at St. George's Chapel, Windsor, and later became student assistant to Walter Parratt with whom he studied organ for seven years. In 1890 he won a scholarship in composition at the Royal College of Music and remained for four years, studying with Stanford and Parry. He received the Mus.B. and Mus.D. degrees from Cambridge University in 1891 and 1898. In the latter year he succeeded E. J. Hopkins as organist and director of the choir at the Temple Church in London, a post which he filled with distinction for twenty-five years. One of his choristers and student assistants was Leopold Stokowski who said in a letter to Davies in 1902, telling of his appointment as organist of St. James' Church, Piccadilly: "I can never, of course, repay in any way your kindnesses to me. I can only hope to have an opportunity of passing them on to another." For eight years Davies taught counterpoint at the Royal College of Music and from 1902 to 1907 was conductor of the Bach choir.

During World War I Davies organized music for British troops, and in 1918 was appointed musical director to the Royal Air Force. In 1919 he became professor of music at University College, Aberystwyth, and director of music and chairman of the National Council of Music for the University of Wales. The latter post, which he held until his death, involved organizing music education in schools throughout Wales, teacher training, and conducting and judging at Eisteddfodau. He was knighted in 1922, in 1927 became organist of St. George's, Windsor, and in 1934 succeeded Sir Edward Elgar as Master of the King's Music. He was given honorary degrees by the universities of Leeds, Glasgow, Dublin, and Oxford. At the outbreak of World War II in 1939, Davies went with the BBC to Bristol to continue his broadcasting. Two of the best-known of his numerous compositions are the cantata *Everyman* (his first notable success) and *A Solemn Melody* for organ and strings. The little introit "God be in my head" was sung at his wedding in 1924. Davies was among those who gave enthusiastic support to the founding of the Royal School of Church Music.

544 Lord, Have Mercy Upon Us

The custom of singing the *Kyrie eleison* ("Lord, have mercy") after each commandment was introduced by Calvin in 1540 in his Strasbourg liturgy. He was also responsible for putting the Decalogue into metrical form and including it in the service. In The Second Prayer Book of Edward VI, 1552, Cranmer followed Calvin's precedent, partly to appease the more radical wing of the Puritan party who wanted to model English worship on the pattern established in Geneva. It was Cranmer who added the words, "upon us" and "incline our hearts to keep this law." The Decalogue interspersed with the *Kyries* is part of the Order of Holy Communion in *The Book of Common Prayer*, 1928, of the Protestant Episcopal Church in the United States. See also No. 545.

The chant given here appeared in its present form with the *Venite* in the section devoted to Tallis' service music in Volume I of *Cathedral Music*, 1760, edited by William Boyce. (See No. 562.) In some hymnals it is called "Tallis' Chant." In others the headings "Ancient Melody" and "Old Melody" indicate that its roots, at least, are older than Tallis or Boyce. Many early Anglican chants were harmonizations of traditional Gregorian tones. This chant is an adaptation of Tone I. In Tallis' harmonization, made in 1550, the melody was in the tenor. Boyce transferred it to the treble part. The chant and psalm tone are shown together in the article "Anglican Chant and Chanting" in *The Oxford Companion to Music*, and on pages 128–129 in *Church Music in History and Practice*, 1937. In the last-named book (p. 109) the author, Winfred Douglas, shows the close resemblance of Tone I to "a melody of the oldest Hebrew musical tradition, that of the Persian Jews" for chanting the Shema.

545 Lord, Have Mercy Upon Us

The *Kyrie eleison* ("Lord, have mercy") is one of the oldest forms of prayer and liturgical responses in Christian worship. Originating in the Eastern Church as a response by the people to the litanies, it was taken over later by the West. Gregory the Great (c. 540–604) changed the second *Kyrie* to *Christe* and indicated that the phrases were to be sung antiphonally by clergy and congregation. It is the only Greek used in the canon of the mass. In his book, *An Outline of Christian Worship*, 1936 (1955 edition), William Maxwell describes the Clementine Liturgy of the fourth century and makes the comment: "To each clause of the litanies all made the reply, *Kyrie eleison,* and a charmingly intimate touch is found in the rubric, 'more especially let the little children answer.' It is a homely picture, the children 'standing by under the charge of their fathers and mothers' and taking their part in the worship of the Church." [33] See also No. 544.

This *Kyrie,* adapted from a tenth century Sarum mass for the dead, is from John Merbecke's *Booke of Common Praier Noted,* 1550, the first complete musical setting of the English liturgy as authorized by the Act of Uniformity in 1549. Archbishop Cranmer, compiler of the first English prayer book, selected Merbecke, organist of St. George's Chapel at Windsor, to provide suitable music for the portions of the service which were to be sung, specifying that the melodies should not be "full of notes, but as near as may be, for every syllable a note; so that it may be sung distinctly and devoutly." The simple, syllabic, unison, and unaccompanied melodies which Merbecke set to the English words were adaptations largely of traditional plainsong melodies, some bearing only a faint likeness to the originals and some being his own composition. Because of opposition to the sung service on the part of extremists in the reforming party and the subsequent deletion in the second prayer book, 1552, of the rubrics enjoining the singing of certain parts of the service, Merbecke's *Booke* had little use and was soon forgotten except by antiquarians and historians. After a lapse of three centuries it came into use again when the leaders of the Oxford Movement sought to revive the ancient principles of choral worship and to restore the sung Eucharist. Since then Merbecke's liturgical music has had wider and wider use.

Although Merbecke (c. 1510–c. 1585) is relatively unimportant as a composer, the use of his music for the liturgy in English and American churches has made him one of the best-known Tudor musicians. A mass, two motets, and a carol are all that remain of his works. The dates of his birth, death, and various appointments are not known, but what records there are suggest that he spent his life at Windsor where he was a chorister, lay clerk, and organist at St. George's Chapel. A man of piety and learning, an enthusiastic Biblical scholar with a great interest in the principles promulgated by the Reformers, he studied Calvin's treatises and started to make a concordance to the English Bible. When he was half way through this enterprise, ecclesiastical commissioners came to Windsor to hunt for heretics and heretical writings. Their discovery in Merbecke's home of the concordance, and of his hand-written copy of one of Calvin's epistles against the mass, resulted in his arrest and imprisonment along with a "singing man," a priest, and a tailor. After months in Marshalsea prison, the men were tried, convicted of heresy, and condemned to death at the stake. On the day following the trial, three of the men were put to death; but through the intervention of Bishop Gardiner of Winchester, Merbecke was pardoned by Henry VIII. Although he openly espoused the Reformed doctrines when Edward VI came to the throne, Merbecke managed to escape persecution and possible death in the reign of Queen Mary. During the last thirty-five or forty years of his life he abandoned music entirely, even writing regretfully of his "study of Musike and plaiyng Organs wherin I consumed vainly the greatest part of my life." In 1550, the year of the publication of the *Booke of Common Praier Noted,* his concordance, which he started again from scratch, was also completed. His was the first concordance to the entire English Bible. He also wrote many controversial books on theology, but it is as a composer and not as a theologian that this Tudor musician is best known today. There are various spellings of the name: Merbecke, Marbeck, Marbecke. In Volume Ten of *Tudor Church Music* the editors have used the form Marbeck because it "has the advantage of indicating the pronunciation of the name however spelt." At the end of the *Book of Common Praier* the name is given as John Merbecke.

546 Glory Be to Thee

Of ancient origin, the *Gloria tibi* ("Glory be to thee, O Lord") is from the Sarum Missal and was originally sung by the people in response to the announcement of the Gospel reading in the Roman liturgy. Such responses were common in both the Greek and Latin rites. Cranmer included it in the prayer book of 1549, and it is in *The Book of Common Prayer,* 1928, of the Protestant Episcopal Church.

The music for this *Gloria tibi* has been arranged from Tallis' setting of the words "And our mouth shall show forth Thy praise" in his *Festal Responses*. The plainsong melody from Merbecke is in the tenor. (See Nos. 531 and 545.) The arranger is unknown.

547 Glory Be to Thee

See No. 546 for comments on the text.

The composer of this setting of the *Gloria tibi* is unknown.

548 Thanks Be to Thee

The *Gratia tibi* ("Thanks be to thee, O Christ") is a response to be said or sung after the reading of the Gospel.

Like the music for the first response at No. 534, this has been adapted from the *Gloria Patri* in Tallis' *Festal Responses*. It was set to the present words in *The Methodist Hymnal*, 1935.

549 Praise Be to Thee

The *Laus tibi* ("Praise be to thee, O Christ") is a response to be said or sung after the reading of the Gospel. It was so used in The First Prayer Book of Edward VI, 1549, and is found in *The Book of Common Prayer*, 1928, of the Protestant Episcopal Church.

This combination of text and tune was taken from *The Hymnal*, 1941, (Evangelical and Reformed). No indication of the source of the tune, other than the composer's name and dates, is given in *The Story of Our Hymns*, the handbook for that hymnal.

550 Holy, Holy, Holy

Known as the seraphic hymn, from Isaiah's vision in the temple, Isaiah 6:1–3, this exalted hymn was sung as a doxology in Hebrew worship long before the Christian era. It was taken over by the church before the end of the third century, possibly as early as the first century, and adapted for use in Eucharistic worship. Clement of Rome alludes to it in his letter to the Corinthians in 96 A.D. The vision of John in Revelation 4:8 and 11 bears a striking similarity to Isaiah's vision. *Sanctus* is the Latin word for "holy." In some liturgies the acclaim of the multitudes at Jesus' triumphal entry into Jerusalem (Matthew 21:9) is attached to the traditional words, as found in The First Prayer Book of Edward VI, 1549, where it follows the Preface and precedes the Prayer for the Whole State of Christ's Church. The Sanctus, because of its rich historical associations and great beauty, is the communion hymn par excellence.

Through this Sanctus we meet "one of the most original and remarkable men of his time," Samuel Wesley (1760–1837), son of Charles Wesley the hymn writer, nephew of John Wesley the founder of Methodism, and father of Samuel Sebastian Wesley, organist and composer. "Old Sam," as he was called after his son had become famous, was the most brilliant organist and finest improviser of his day, unrivalled in his performance of fugues by Bach and Handel. He was also an excellent violinist and harpsichordist as well as a classical scholar and a good linguist, a man of wide culture with fine taste in literature as in music. He and his older brother Charles were two of the most extraordinary child prodigies of the eighteenth century. Anecdotes of their musical gifts and attainments abound and astonish. For instance, before Samuel was five years old he taught himself to read, and later to write, by poring over the score of Handel's *Samson* which he came to know by heart.

During late adolescence, Samuel began to attend services at the chapel of the Portuguese Embassy, attracted particularly by the music, and in 1784 became a Roman Catholic. In thanksgiving for his conversion he composed a mass and sent it to Pope Pius VI, who duly acknowledged it. In the ensuing years Wesley wrote a considerable amount of music for the Catholic service. He always insisted, however, that it was the music in the Catholic Church that had drawn him to it. Throughout most of his life he considered himself a member of the Church of England.

One night in 1787, Wesley fell into a deep excavation and lay there unconscious until daylight. When it was discovered that he had suffered serious skull injuries, surgery was recommended but he refused to have the necessary operation. Although the wound healed, throughout the rest of his life he suffered recurrently from long periods of nervous and mental instability which had a deleterious effect on his career. In spite of continuing physical, domestic, matrimonial, and professional setbacks, in spite of poverty and neglect, Wesley kept going — performing, lecturing, conducting, composing, teaching for twenty-five years at a girls' school (sheer drudgery for him), and waging a winning battle for his hero, Johann Sebastian Bach, to whose music he had been introduced around 1800. His boundless enthusiasm for Bach stemmed from his own systematic study and analysis of works then available. He said that Bach's compositions opened to him an entirely new musical world. Wesley's campaign in Bach's behalf was carried on through performances of his works, lecturing, writing, and editing. As early as 1802 he proposed that an English translation of Forkel's *Life of Bach* be made available. It was finally published in 1820. With C. F. Horn, Wesley brought out an edition of the *Well-Tempered Clavichord*, issued in four parts between 1810 and 1813. In 1809 he edited Bach's "Organ Trios, adapted for three hands upon the Pianoforte," and in 1809 directed the first performance in England of Bach's motet, "Jesu, meine Freude." So much has been written about Mendelssohn's part in the revival of interest in Bach's music that Samuel Wesley's share in that revival has been overshadowed. Yet he was trying to convince others of Bach's greatness before Mendelssohn was born.

Wesley was a prolific composer. His compositions — over seventy per cent are still in manuscript — include orchestral and chamber music, choral works, service music, songs, glees, works for organ and piano. In a lecture on Wesley in 1927 Gustav Holst said, "Every artist should be judged by his best work. And Wesley's best work is superb." James T. Lightwood's biography, *Samuel Wesley: Musician,* 1937, gives an illuminating picture of this remarkably gifted man.

551 Holy, Holy, Holy

See No. 550 for comments on the text.

Many people in the Chicago area knew the composer of this Sanctus as Dean Lutkin because of his identification with the School of Music of Northwestern University in Evanston. Many have vivid memories of this rather short but commanding musician with his delightful sense of humor and his great gift for conducting large or small choral groups. Peter Christian Lutkin (1858–1931), the youngest of six children, was born in Thompsonville, Wisconsin, of Danish parents. In 1871, two years after the family moved to Chicago, both parents died suddenly and young Peter had to make his own way. He attended public school and the choir school at St. James' Church where at fourteen he became organist even though he had had little technical training. He held this position for nine years, and for two years taught piano at Northwestern, although at that time there was no music department at the university. His musical talents brought him recognition and unusual opportunities for instruction by prominent Chicago musicians through whose interest and support he was enabled to study in Europe for three years. On his return to Chicago in 1884, he served as organist and choirmaster at St. Clement's and St. James', and was also director of the theory department of the American Conservatory from 1885 to 1895.

When the School of Music was founded at Northwestern University in 1896, Lutkin was named its first dean. Under his direction it became one of the leading musical institutions in the Middle West and had great influence on the development of music education in colleges throughout the country. The A Cappella Choir which he founded and directed was noted for the quality of its programs and performances. In 1908, with the financial aid of influential friends, Dean Lutkin established the Chicago North Shore Music Festivals, directing them until 1930. He helped found the American Guild of Organists, and was active in the Music Teacher's National Association serving as its president in 1911 and 1920. His deep concern for music in the church accounts for the strength of the department of church and choral music at Northwestern University which he directed until a year before his death. In 1900 he was granted the D.Mus. degree by Syracuse University. He helped edit the *Methodist Hymnal,* 1905, and the *New Hymnal* (Episcopal), 1918.

552 Lift Up Your Hearts

Dating from the third century, the *Sursum corda* ("Lift up your hearts") has provided from earliest times to the present day the fitting opening and invitation to the Lord's Table. In all the great liturgies, both of East and West, these are the words that have been used to introduce the prayer of consecration. The note of thanksgiving at this point in the Communion service is in keeping with Jesus' act of giving thanks before breaking the bread. It is from this prayer of thanksgiving, *eucharisteō* ("I give thanks"), that the Communion service takes its name, the Eucharist.

The music, as well as the text of *Sursum Corda,* is very ancient. Winfred Douglas has commented, "There is every reason to believe that the traditional chant . . . in its simpler forms long antedates St. Gregory, and that by his time this richer festal form had been developed." The present version is less florid than some; the harmonization of the responses is from the *Common Service Book of the Lutheran Church,* 1917. (United Lutheran Church in America.)

553 Holy, Holy, Holy

See No. 550 for comments on the text.

In Pope Gregory's time (590–604) the Sanctus was one of three portions of the service of Holy Communion that were sung by the congregation. The other two were *Kyrie eleison* and *Gloria in excelsis.* The present setting of the Sanctus is Merbecke's adaptation of an ancient melody from a tenth century English requiem. Except for the first four chords, the arrangement given here is by Winfred Douglas from the First Communion Service in *The Hymnal 1940.* In Merbecke's *Booke of Common Praier Noted,* 1550 (see No. 545), there was a fermata over the second syllable of each "holy," over "hosts," and over the second syllable of "highest." The words of the last phrase, "Osanna in the highest," were set as follows, with no Amen.

O - san - na   in   the highest.

Merbecke's setting of the last phrase, adapted to the present words, is given in *The Hymnal,* 1933, *The Hymnbook,* 1955, and in *The Office of the Holy Communion as set by John Merbecke,* edited by Edmund H. Fellowes in 1949.

554 Glory Be to God on High

Known as the Greater Doxology (see comments at No. 511), this ancient canticle dating back to the second century in its earliest Greek form is an elaboration of the angel's song as recorded in Luke 2:14. Athanasius (c. 295–373) is often credited with preparing the first Latin translation. In the Roman and Lutheran liturgies and in The First Prayer Book of Edward VI, 1549, the *Gloria in excelsis* follows the *Kyrie* at the start of Holy Communion but beginning with The Second Prayer Book of Edward VI, 1552, and continuing to the present American Prayer Book of 1928, it is a part of the post-Communion thanksgiving at the close of the service. It has been used in the Eastern Church since the fourth century in the Daily Offices. Luther declared, "It did not grow nor was it made on earth: it came down from heaven."

See No. 511 for comments on "Old Scottish Chant."

555   O Lamb of God

Derived largely from the salutation of John the Baptist, "Behold the Lamb of God, which taketh away the sin of the world" (John 1:29), the *Agnus Dei* was introduced into the Roman liturgy in 687 A.D. by Pope Sergius I. He directed that it be sung antiphonally by clergy and congregation at the time of the breaking of the consecrated Host, and it is now part of the ordinary of the mass, that is, those parts of the mass with an invariable text, namely, the *Kyrie, Gloria, Credo, Sanctus,* and *Agnus Dei.* In *The Book of Common Prayer* since 1552, it is found in inverted order before the *Kyrie* at the climax of the litany and is included in altered form after the *Gloria* in the Holy Communion. One of the most moving accounts of the interpretation of the idea of Jesus as the Lamb of God is given in the story of Philip and the Ethiopian eunuch, Acts 8:26–39. There are numerous other scriptural references to the same idea. The *Agnus Dei* was restored in the worship of the Church of Scotland in 1929, and it is finding wider and increasing use in other major communions.

In his essay on John Merbecke which is included in *A Forgotten Psalter and Other Essays,* 1929, Sir Richard R. Terry says that the melody for this *Agnus Dei,* given in *The Booke of Common Praier Noted,* 1550, for use at the Communion, is based on a Sarum melody. Others have considered it an original melody, Gregorian in character. Merbecke placed a fermata over each "us" and over "peace." With the exception of the first two chords and those for "grant us," the present arrangement by Winfred Douglas is from *The Hymnal 1940.* See No. 545 for comments on Merbecke.

556   O Christ, Thou Lamb of God

This is an altered form of the *Agnus Dei.* See comments at No. 555.

"Christ, Thou Lamb of God" is an arrangement by Healey Willan of "Christe, du Lamm Gottes" from a communion service in *Kirchenordnung,* 1528, a service book prepared by Johann Bugenhagen and Martin Luther for the city of Brunswick. In some German hymnals Luther is named as the arranger of the chant.

Healey Willan (1880–   ), distinguished Canadian organist, teacher, composer, church musician, was born in London, England. At eight he became a chorister at St. Saviour's, Eastbourne, remained there for seven years, and later served as organist and choirmaster in three English churches before

405

coming to Toronto in 1913 to be head of the theory department at the Toronto Conservatory. He was its vice-principal from 1920 to 1936. His long connection with the University of Toronto dates from his appointment in 1914 as a lecturer and examiner; he was organist from 1932, and professor of theory from 1937 until his retirement in 1950. The university granted him an honorary doctorate in music in 1921. From 1919 to 1925 he was music director of the Hart House Players and wrote incidental music for fourteen of the classical plays in their repertoire. As organist and choirmaster at St. Paul's Church from 1913 to 1921, and subsequently at the Church of St. Mary Magdalene, both in Toronto, he became noted for his use of plainsong and polyphonic music of the Tudor and Renaissance periods and for his deep interest in the revival and use of the liturgical modes. His compositions include two symphonies, a concerto, chamber music, songs, music for piano and organ, three radio operas commissioned by the Canadian Broadcasting Corporation, and much church music. Dr. Willan was the only musician from outside the British Isles commissioned to write an anthem for the coronation of Queen Elizabeth II.

"Christe, du Lamm Gottes," the melody of a pre-Reformation *Agnus Dei,* was used by Bach in Cantatas 23 and 127, in the *Kyrie* of the Mass in F, and for a chorale prelude in the Orgelbüchlein.

557 Here, O My Lord, I See Thee

See No. 287 for comments on the text.

ADORO TE is the plainsong melody traditionally sung with St. Thomas Aquinas' hymn "Adoro te devote, latens veritas" ("Humbly I adore thee, Verity unseen"). It appeared with the present text in the *Hymnal for Colleges and Schools,* 1956, from which the greater part of the harmonization was taken. Although often listed as a thirteenth-century plainsong, it has been called modern by Dom J. Gajard, who wrote the notes for a recording of Gregorian chants made by the monks of Solesmes. Cyril Pocknee says in *French Diocesan Hymns and their Melodies* that it cannot be found before the *Paris Processional,* 1697, where it was set to a neo-Gallican version of Aquinas' hymn. The melody gives a strong feeling of the major mode and suggests the I–IV–V harmonies that became established in the seventeenth century. The form of the melody given here for ADORO TE is the Solesmes version. Since 1833 the Benedictine monks of St. Pierre de Solesmes Abbey have devoted their energies to liturgical studies and research in Gregorian chant in an effort to determine the true form of the ancient melodies, the meaning of the neumes and the rhythmic signs, and to discover and further the proper way of singing this music.

558 'Twas on That Dark and Doleful Night

This communion hymn by Isaac Watts bore the caption in his *Hymns and Spiritual Songs,* 1709, Book III, "The Lord's Supper Instituted. I Cor. xi. 23, etc." It has been taken in its present form from *The Hymn*, Vol. 4, No. 1 (January, 1953), published by The Hymn Society of America. See No. 1 for comments on Watts.

BOURBON, a pentatonic melody found with sacred texts in a number of shape-note books (see No. 165), was harmonized by Louise McAllister (1913–1960), pianist, composer, teacher, writer. She was born in Louisville, Kentucky, where her father was professor of English Bible at the Louisville Presbyterian Theological Seminary. In 1925 the family moved to Richmond, Virginia, where Dr. McAllister became a member of the faculty at Union Theological Seminary and where Miss McAllister spent the rest of her life, taking an active part in musical and church activities. She was graduated with highest honors from the Collegiate School in Richmond and attended Mary Baldwin College in Staunton, Virginia, for part of a year, being unable to continue because of an injury to her hands. She studied privately with Mrs. Crosby Adams for many years and with John Powell for nearly a decade after 1949. A number of her compositions for piano have been published and have had wide circulation. Her harmonizations of folk-hymn melodies have been included in various hymnals; three appeared in *The Hymn*, January 1953. In an article on harmonizing modal tunes (*The Hymn*, January 1953) Miss McAllister wrote: "The ultimate value in the introduction of these tunes to an increasing number of modern hymn-singers lies in acquainting them with their own rich Anglo-American heritage which has stood the test of time." Like many other folk-hymn melodies, BOURBON has been found also with secular words.

559 We Praise Thee, O God

Coming from the earliest period of Latin hymnody and universally recognized as one of the greatest of all hymns, the "Te Deum laudamus" has been called "the masterpiece in the hymnody of the Christian church." Luther ranked it next in importance to the Apostles' Creed and the Nicene Creed as a confession of faith and a hymn of praise. The story that it was improvised by Ambrose and Augustine at the time of the latter's baptism, each of them singing spontaneously alternate phrases, is unfortunately nothing more than a delightful legend. For many centuries it was called the Canticle of Ambrose and Austin (or Augustine) in the old breviaries. Many scholars assign its authorship to Niceta, Bishop of Remesiana in Dacia (now Yugoslavia) from 392 to 414, a friend of Aurelius Clemens Prudentius and a contemporary of Jerome (c. 340–420), although other scholars believe it to be composite in origin. It is drawn in large part from the Apostles' Creed, the *Gloria in excelsis* and Sanctus, and the Psalms. In structure, it consists of two distinct hymns and a litany. The first part is a hymn of praise to God (lines 1 through 6); the second extols Christ as the King of glory (lines 7 through 12); the last contains a series of versicles and responses (lines 13 through 16). Millar Patrick has said of the "Te Deum laudamus": "Its comprehensiveness, the grandeur of its conceptions, the incomparable dignity of its language, the moving transition from adoration to confession and supplication, and the final mounting of its confidence to the quiet but firm assertion of the faith that a soul settled on the rock of these triumphant certainties will never be confounded — *In te, Domine, speravi: non confundar in aeternum* — combine to give it an unchallenged place as the greatest of all the hymns of 'the holy church throughout all the world.' " [34]

Organist, teacher, and church musician, Edwin G. Monk (1819–1900) had his first musical instruction from his father, an amateur. Subsequently he studied piano, voice, and organ in London, and served as organist in two churches before becoming in 1844 the first organist, precentor, and music master at the newly founded St. Columba's College, Stackhallan (later removed to Rathfarnam near Dublin), the first Anglican public school in Ireland. In 1847 Monk went to Oxford where he conducted the Motet and Madrigal Society, taught singing, and earned his B.Mus. and D.Mus. degrees. From 1847 to 1858 he was organist and music master at St. Peter's College, Radley; from 1858 to 1881, organist of York Minster; and from 1871 to 1883 was one of the examiners for musical degrees at Oxford. He composed songs and anthems, edited a number of service books and chant collections, and wrote the librettos for three oratorios of Sir George MacFarren with whom he had studied harmony and composition. That music did not take all his time is shown by his election in 1871 as a Fellow of the Royal Astronomical Society. See No. 1 for comments on William Croft.

560 We Praise Thee, O God

See No. 559 for comments on the text.

Sir Frederick Arthur Gore Ouseley (1825–1889), teacher, scholar, author, organist, composer, was educated privately and at Christ Church, Oxford, was ordained in 1855, and in that year became precentor of Hereford Cathedral and professor of music at Oxford. In 1854 he founded St. Michael's College, Tenbury, "to prepare a course of training and to form a model for the choral service of the church . . . and to train boys in such religious, musical, and secular knowledge as shall be conducive thereto." The college was built on an estate of Ouseley's and generously endowed by him. The large collection of manuscripts and printed music which he amassed and gave to St. Michael's is described in *Grove's Dictionary* (1954) as being "by far the most important private music library in the United Kingdom." One of its treasures is the copy of the *Messiah* which Handel used when he conducted the first performance of the work in Dublin. At Oxford, Ouseley raised the requirements for examinations and degrees and gave music a new status at the university. He wrote quantities of church music, was the author of textbooks on harmony, counterpoint, and fugue, edited Gibbon's sacred works, an edition of Naumann's *History of Music,* and was closely associated with the original edition of *Hymns Ancient and Modern,* 1861. In the article "Absolute Pitch" in *The Oxford Companion to Music,* a paragraph is devoted to Ouseley's phenomenal sense of pitch. See No. 237 for comments on Crotch.

561 We Praise Thee, O God

See No. 559 for comments on the text.

Stephen Elvey (1805–1860), the elder brother of Sir George Elvey (No. 199), received his first musical training as a chorister at Canterbury Cathedral. Later he went to Oxford, became organist of New College in 1830, and in subsequent years of St. Mary's University Church and St. John's College. In 1831 and 1838, respectively, he received the Bachelor's and Doctor's degrees in music, and in 1848 became choragus of the University. His *Psalter and Canticles Pointed,* edited in collaboration with Ouseley, was well-known, as was his Evening Service, composed as a continuation of Dr. Croft's Morning Service in A.

Comparatively little is known about Richard Farrant (c. 1530–1580), a gentleman of the Chapel Royal in the reigns of Edward VI, Mary, and Elizabeth I. In 1564, when appointed organist and master of the choristers at St. George's Chapel, Windsor, he resigned his post in the Chapel Royal, but was reappointed in 1569. Farrant's duties at St. George's and at the Chapel Royal included the preparing of plays or interludes which were customarily performed by the choristers before royalty. On two occasions in 1568, he presented his musicians in a play before Queen Elizabeth at Windsor. Edmund H. Fellowes suggests that these dramatic activities may have curtailed his composing. "His output seems surprisingly small when it is remembered that he was engaged upon choir work for the greater part of his life in association with Marbeck at St. George's Chapel, Windsor." [31] Farrant's Service in A minor and his two short anthems, *Hide not thou thy face,* and *Call to remembrance,* which, in Fellowes' opinion are "among the most beautiful things of the kind in the entire repertory of English Church music" have continued in use in Cathedrals and churches ever since they were written.

562 O Come, Let Us Sing

The *Venite, exultemus Domino* (Psalm 95) was the battle song of the Knights Templars during the crusades. It was and still is sung in the liturgies of the Roman Catholic and Anglican churches in its entirety at the beginning of matins. When *The Book of Common Prayer* of the Protestant Episcopal Church in the United States was revised in 1789, the last four verses of the psalm were dropped, and verses nine and thirteen of Psalm 96 were put in their place. The change was made to give the *Venite* a more exalted and appropriate ending than was provided by the original verses. It is this form that appears here. The version used is from *The Great Bible,* 1539, the translation of which was largely the work of Miles Coverdale (c. 1488–1569). All the psalter selections and canticles in *The Book of Common Prayer* are from this version.

William Boyce (c. 1710–1779), the composer of this double chant, has been described by Edmund H. Fellowes as "the leading personality in English music in the eighteenth century after the decline of the Restoration School." Boyce, the son of a cabinetmaker, had his early musical training as a chorister at St. Paul's Cathedral. When his voice changed he was apprenticed to Maurice Greene, organist of the Cathedral. Even during his apprenticeship Boyce's hearing was impaired but this did not discourage or deter him from continuing his musical studies and activities. After leaving Greene he studied with the celebrated John Pepusch. He served as organist in several churches, gave harpsichord lessons in private schools and seminaries, was appointed composer to the Chapel Royal and conductor of the Three Choirs Festivals, and succeeded Greene as one of the organists of the Chapel Royal and as master of the King's band. In 1749 he was given a doctor's degree by Cambridge University. In his late fifties increasing deafness made it necessary for him to give up teaching and most of his posts. He moved to Kensington and devoted his energies to compiling the work by which he is best known, *Cathedral Music, being a Collection in Score of the most Valuable and Useful Compositions for that Service by the Several English Masters of the Last Two Hundred Years*. The three volumes, published in 1760, 1768, and 1778, constitute a monumental work. It has been said that if Boyce had composed no music, his name would have been perpetuated through this great collection which had enormous influence in determining the repertory of cathedral choirs for 150 years after its publication. Boyce was a good friend of Charles Wesley who consulted him about the course to follow in educating his two gifted sons, Charles and Samuel. (See No. 550.) After Boyce's death Wesley wrote: "A more modest man than Dr. Boyce I have never known. I never heard him speak a vain or ill-natured word, either to exalt himself or depreciate another."

563 O Come, Let Us Sing

See No. 562 for comments on the text.

There seems to be no available information about the composer of this chant.

564 O Come, Let Us Sing

See No. 562 for comments on the text.

This single chant is attributed to Richard Goodson, the elder (1655–1718) who was appointed organist of New College, Oxford, in 1682, the year in which he succeeded Edward Lowe as organist of Christ Church Cathedral and professor of music in the university. At his death a son of the same name followed him in both of these posts.

565 O Be Joyful in the Lord

Introduced into *The Book of Common Prayer* in 1552 as an alternative to the *Benedictus* in Morning Prayer, the *Jubilate Deo* is the well-known Psalm 100. This is the Coverdale translation from The Great Bible, 1539.

The composer of this double chant was a remarkably versatile man with many interests and gifts. He was theologian, scholar, architect, an authority on heraldry, author of a little handbook on logic that was still in use in the second part of the nineteenth century, and a composer of anthems, service music, and rounds and catches. Henry Aldrich (1647–1710) spent the greater part of his life at Christ Church, Oxford, going there as a student in 1662 and becoming successively tutor, canon, dean (1689 until his death), and vice-chancellor of the university (1692–1695). The Church of All Saints, Oxford, and three sides of the Peckwater Quadrangle of Christ Church were built according to his designs. He took time to study and cultivate music, feeling that as dean of a college and cathedral he should do all he could to advance church music. His own compositions were not strikingly original but were quite an achievement for one not trained as a musician. He adapted English words to a large number of works by Byrd, Tallis, Palestrina, Carissimi, and others, which had been set originally to Latin words for use in Roman Catholic services. With less skill, he altered the music as well as the text in many instances. His large and valuable collection of music was bequeathed to the library of Christ College, Oxford. In his *General History of Music*, Burney says of Aldrich: "He not only had concerts and rehearsals at his apartments weekly, but established a music-school in his college. . . . Music perhaps never flourished so much at Oxford as under his example, guidance and patronage."

566 O Be Joyful in the Lord

See No. 565 for comments on the text.

Oxford Chant is an anonymous composition.

567 O Be Joyful in the Lord

See No. 565 for comments on the text.

See No. 199 for comments on Sir George J. Elvey.

568 Blessed Be the Lord God

The *Benedictus* or "Song of Zacharias" (Luke 1:68–79) heralding the ministry of John the Baptist is one of three canticles found in the Lucan account of the nativity, the other two being the *Magnificat* (Luke 1:47–55) and the *Nunc dimittis* (Luke 2:29–32). These are among the oldest Christian hymns, both in terms of origin and continuous use. The *Benedictus* was sung in Christian worship as early as 800 A.D. and came after the short scripture lesson in lauds in the medieval offices. It is especially appropriate for use following a reading from the Psalter and during Advent.

See No. 35 for comments on Joseph Barnby.

569 Blessed Art Thou, O Lord

In the Greek version of the Old Testament, the Septuagint, a poetic interpolation occurs following Daniel 3:23, known as the Song of the Three Holy Children. It is a hymn of praise sung by Azariah, Hananiah, and Mishael in gratitude for their deliverance from the "burning fiery furnace" to which they had been consigned for defying Nebuchadnezzar. The present canticle, *Benedictus es Domine,* is taken from this song and consists of verses 29–34. The *Benedicite, omnia opera Domini* ("O all ye works of the Lord, bless ye the Lord") also comes from the same source. The *Benedictus es Domine* is sung daily, with the *Benedicite,* in the Ancient Mozarabic liturgy of the church in Spain for lauds and is used as a shorter alternative for the "Te Deum" or the *Benedicite* in the American Prayer Book, following the First Lesson in Morning Prayer.

John Randall (1715–1799) is best known for two double chants, one of which is given here. He started out as a chorister in the Chapel Royal, later received Mus.B. and Mus.D. degrees at Cambridge and served as organist of King's, Trinity, and St. John's colleges and of the university. In 1755 he succeeded Dr. Maurice Greene as professor of music at Cambridge. On Handel's forty-seventh birthday, February 23, 1732, his oratorio *Esther* was presented with scenery, costumes, and acting, in the home of Bernard Gates, master of the choristers of the Chapel Royal. Randall was the chorister who sang the part of Esther.

570 My Soul Doth Magnify the Lord

First sung by Mary on the occasion of her visit to Elizabeth, the mother of John the Baptist, the *Magnificat* (Luke 1:46–55) has been in use at vespers in the Western Church since the time of Benedict in the sixth century. In the American Prayer Book it precedes the reading of the New Testament Lesson in Evening Prayer. During the later Middle Ages it was the most popular of all the canticles due, in part, to the veneration of Mary that prevailed in those centuries. It is unusual and distinctive in its combined moods of exaltation, thanksgiving, quiet submissiveness, and daring concern for social justice.

Robinson's Chant in E-flat, said to have been the favorite of King George III, was one of several pieces which young Samuel Wesley copied out by hand in his "First Music Book," now in the British Museum. John Robinson (1682–1762), a chorister in the Chapel Royal under Dr. Blow and also one of his organ students, became organist of St. Lawrence, Jewry, in 1710 and of St. Magnus the Martyr, London, in 1713. He was assistant to Dr. William Croft for a number of years and became his successor at Westminster Abbey in 1727, remaining there until his death and retaining the posts in the two parish churches as well. In his *History,* Sir John Hawkins described Robinson as a "very florid and elegant performer on the organ," and as "highly celebrated as a master of the harpsichord." But he disapproved of Robinson's practice of introducing into the church services music of a lighter type better suited to the harpsichord than to the organ.

571 My Soul Doth Magnify the Lord

See No. 570 for comments on the text.

Henry Lawes (1596–1662), composer of this double chant, served as one of the gentlemen in Charles I's Chapel Royal, as an epistler (one who reads the Epistle at the Communion service), as clerk of the cheque, and in the King's Band. He became music master to the family of the earl of Bridgewater who commissioned him to write and direct the music for a masque to be performed as part of the festivities connected with the earl's assumption of the office of lord president of Wales. Lawes asked his friend, John Milton, with whom he had collaborated before, to write the words, and at Ludlow Castle on Michaelmas night, September 29, 1634, *Comus* was given its first performance with Lawes in the role of the attendant spirit. It was Lawes who first published the work, in 1637, in response to many demands for the music. He was highly esteemed by his contemporaries, especially by the poets (including Herrick, Carew, Milton, and Cartwright) who were eager to have him supply music for their poems and plays because of the care he gave to the proper setting of the words. He is best known as a song writer. Because a number of his tunes were for unusual meters, they never had wide use in church.

Lawes lost all his court appointments during the Protectorate, but regained them at the Restoration and wrote an anthem for the coronation of Charles II. Vaughan Williams' use of five of Lawes' hymn tunes in *The English Hymnal,* 1906, has brought them into wider circulation in England and America.

572 Lord, Now Lettest Thou Thy Servant Depart in Peace

The *Nunc dimittis* or Song of Simeon (Luke 2:29–32) has been called the greeting of the Old Dispensation to the New. The devout and aged Simeon spoke these words on the occasion of the presentation of the infant Jesus in the temple in Jerusalem. The canticle is one of the earliest New Testament songs to be used in Christian worship. It has been sung at the evening service of compline since the fourth century. Calvin included it in his *Aulcuns Pseaulmes et Cantiques/ mys en Chant,* 1539, and in his *La Forme des Prières Ecclésiastiques,* 1540. A metrical version of the *Nunc dimittis* was included in the Genevan Psalter.

The canticle follows the reading of the New Testament lesson in Evening Prayer in the American Prayer Book.

See No. 35 for comments on Joseph Barnby.

573 Lord, Now Lettest Thou Thy Servant Depart in Peace

See No. 572 for comments on the text.

See No. 561 for comments on Richard Farrant.

574 Lord, Now Lettest Thou Thy Servant Depart in Peace

See No. 572 for comments on the text.

See No. 528 for comments on this chant.

575 Come, Holy Ghost, Our Souls Inspire

See No. 231 for comments on the text.

Plainsong tunes have been called noble melodies which have stood the wear and tear of ages. Surely VENI CREATOR fits this description. It has served Catholics and Protestants alike. It has been associated with the Latin text from its earliest use (probably in the tenth century), and before that was sung with the Ambrosian Easter hymn, "Hic est dies verus Dei." The earliest liturgical use of "Veni Creator Spiritus" was at Vespers on Whitsunday. Later it became the office hymn for terce on that day, to commemorate the outpouring of the Holy Spirit at "the third hour" (Acts 2:15). Since the eleventh century it has been used for ordinations and for centuries has been the chosen hymn for use at church councils, dedications, the laying of cornerstones, coronations, and at those "solemn functions of the Church when the grace of the Holy Spirit is sought." German translations of "Veni Creator Spiritus" were made from the thirteenth century on. Luther's version, "Komm, Gott Schöpfer, heiliger Geist" ("Come, God Creator, Holy Ghost"), appeared in the Erfurt *Enchiridion,* 1524, with an adaptation of the traditional melody. (Zahn 294) A different version of this plainsong, with Luther's text, appeared in Klug's *Geistliche Lieder,* 1535, and this has become the best-known and most widely used. It is given below. (Zahn 295)

Komm Gott Schöp-fer, hei - li - ger Geist, be-such das Herz der Men-schen dein,

mit Gna-den sie füll, wie du weisst, dass dein Ge-schöpf vor-hin sein.

Bach composed two choral preludes on "Komm, Gott Schöpfer," one in the *Orgelbüchlein,* one in the *Eighteen Chorales.* There are two harmonizations of the tune in the *Choralgesänge.*

The present form of the melody is basically that found in the *Vesperale Romanum,* published at Mechlin (Malines), Belgium, in 1848, one of several editions of plainchant which appeared in Europe in the nineteenth century. The Mechlin version came into use in England through the *Hymnal Noted* and *Hymns Ancient and Modern.* The present version is less strictly measured. The Solesmes version is given on page 885 of *Liber Usualis.*

576 Lord, Thou Hast Searched Me

This modern paraphrase of Psalm 139:1–12 has been taken from *The Psalter Hymnal*, 1927, a hymnal of the United Presbyterian Church. The author is unknown.

In George Pullen Jackson's *White Spirituals in the Southern Uplands*, 1933, TENDER THOUGHT is included in a list of eighty of the most popular tunes found in fifteen shape-note books used in the rural South in pre-Civil War days. This tune appeared in *Kentucky Harmony, A Choice Collection of Psalm Tunes, Hymns and Anthems*, c. 1815, compiled by Ananias Davisson (1780–1857) who claimed it and fourteen others as his own. In Dr. Jackson's opinion they are among the best tunes in the book. Davisson obviously knew the kind of melodies that appealed to his particular constituency for many of them became stock-in-trade for later editors whose choice of materials was based on what was most popular with singers. Some of Davisson's own tunes attained unique popularity. Little is known of his life. In the preface to his *Supplement to the Kentucky Harmony*, 1820, he wrote that he "spent the Morning of Life in the modest circles of the Musical World," referring in all likelihood to his teaching in singing schools. William B. Blake, in the *Musical Million*, Dayton, Virginia, 1884, described Davisson as "a man of unaffected piety, a ruling elder in the Presbyterian Church of Dayton . . . well and favorably known forty years ago up and down our valley," — the Shenandoah, in northwestern Virginia.

In Blake's comments on Davisson, mentioned above, *Kentucky Harmony* was said to be "characteristic of that period, abounding in minor tunes." TENDER THOUGHT is one of these, a haunting melody, with "Dorian implications" (Jackson) even though the characteristic sixth degree of the first mode does not occur in it. It is in A A B A form. The tune's name comes from its frequent association in the shape-note books with Philip Doddridge's hymn, "Arise, my tend'rest thoughts, arise." TENDER THOUGHT was set to the paraphrase of Psalm 139 in *Hymnal for Colleges and Schools*, 1956.

577 Great God Who Hast Delivered Us

When Clément Marot died in 1544, he had translated fifty of the psalms into French and put them into metrical form for the Genevan Psalter. John Calvin subsequently appointed Théodore de Bèze (1519–1605) to complete the task of translating the remaining one hundred psalms. Bèze was a noted theologian, biblical scholar, and gifted poet who succeeded Calvin in leadership after the latter's death in Geneva. He finished his work in several installments, and the completed Genevan Psalter appeared in 1562. Psalm 68 was among the psalms presumably translated by Bèze, beginning with the words "Que Dieu se montre seulement." The third stanza of his translation is the basis of the present hymn. The full text of Bèze's translation is given in *Cantate Domino*, 1951, Number 69. The author of the English translation is unknown.

PSALM 36 (68) (OLD 113TH; ES SIND DOCH SELIG ALLE; GENEVA 68) This famous tune, attributed to Matthäus Greiter (c. 1490–

1550), has been sung by Protestants for over four hundred years. It appeared in a Strasbourg service-book, *Teutsch Kirchenam(p)t,* 1525, with Greiter's version of Psalm 119, "Es sind doch selig alle, die," words still found with it in German hymnals. In Calvin's first psalter, *Aulcuns Pseaulmes et Cantiques mys en chant,* Strasbourg, 1539, it was set to Psalm 36, an association maintained through all subsequent French psalters down to the present. Bèze's version of Psalm 68, "Que Dieu se montre seulement," written to fit this tune, and sung by French Protestants during persecutions, battles, trials and victories, has been called "The Marseillaise of the Huguenots." In the Anglo-Genevan psalter of 1561 and in later English and Scottish psalters, its use with Psalm 113 gave the tune its English name, OLD 113TH. It was one of John Wesley's favorite hymn tunes, included in all the Methodist tune books issued during his lifetime, and sung by him the day before he died to Isaac Watts' "I'll praise my Maker while I've breath." In English usage it was often shortened to half its length. In *The Yattendon Hymnal,* 1899, Robert Bridges restored the melody to the form it had in the Genevan tradition after what he called "330 years of abuse" in English hymnody.

In Germany the tune was set to Psalms 36 and 68 in Lobwasser's Psalter, 1573, and from c. 1584 was associated with "O Mensch, bewein dein' Sünde gross" ("O man, thy grievous sin bemoan"), stanzas of which were sung between portions of the story of the Passion during Holy Week in Lutheran churches. Bach used the melody in the concluding chorus of Part I of the *St. Matthew Passion,* and for one chorale prelude in the *Orgelbüchlein.* PSALM 36 came to America in the psalter used by the Pilgrims at Plymouth, set to Ainsworth's versions of Psalms 84 and 136. (See No. 502.) In *Harmonia Sacra,* Andover, Massachusetts, 1816, the tune had substantially its present form, but in later American collections was considerably altered.

Bavarian-born Matthäus Greiter (his name appears in a variety of forms) was a monk and precentor in Strasbourg Cathedral before becoming a Protestant in 1524. Thereafter he served in four Lutheran churches in various capacities: singer, deacon, curate, minor canon, and chaplain. Four tunes attributed to him were included in Calvin's 1539 psalter and taken into the Genevan psalter of 1542. Greiter, a gifted musician, was regarded by his contemporaries as one of the best composers of his time. Between 1538 and 1550 he taught music at the Gymnasium Argentinense, a classical school where Latin and German psalms were sung daily, and Saturday afternoons were devoted entirely to instruction in music. In 1548, when Catholic services were resumed in the Cathedral during the Interim (one of three periods when Charles V attempted by compromises to settle temporarily the controversies between Catholics and Protestants), Greiter and Wolfgang Dachstein, a Protestant colleague, collaborated with the Catholics and founded a choir school to provide music for their services. This aroused the hostility of fellow Protestants and the town council; nevertheless, during this time Greiter kept his position at the Lutheran Church of St. Stephen. After his teaching at the gymnasium was terminated in 1550, he returned to the Roman Catholic faith. In December of the same year he died of the plague. In addition to composing music for use in church, Greiter made polyphonic settings of a number of secular songs, one of which, *Fortuna,* has been called astonishing, extraordinary, and "the only chromatic experiment by a German composer of that time known so far." (See *The Musical Quarterly,* October, 1956; January, 1957.)

578 I Sought the Lord, and Afterward I Knew

See No. 408 for comments on the text.

PEACE was adapted by George Brandon (1924–   ) from the following unharmonized pentatonic melody in *The Revivalist,* 1869, "a collection of Choice Revival Hymns and Tunes original and selected, edited by Joseph Hillman." The Rev. L. Hartsough was musical editor of the collection.

O that my load   of   sin were gone! O that I   could   at last sub-mit

At   Je-sus' feet to   lay it down! To lay my soul   at   Je-sus'   feet.

No source was given for the words or the tune, which was named PEACE. In George Pullen Jackson's *Down-East Spirituals and Others,* the tune is in 6/4 and the hymn is identified as one of Charles Wesley's. Brandon came upon the tune in 1950, wrote a set of variations on it for clarinet and piano (or organ), and used his harmonized version of the melody for the hymn tune which was submitted anonymously to the Pilgrim Hymnal Committee. A native of Stockton, California, Mr. Brandon was educated at the College of the Pacific (A.B. 1945) and at Union Theological Seminary (M.S.M. 1952, M.R.E. 1957). He has played the organ and directed choirs in churches of various Protestant denominations, has been instructor in music and religion and director of chapel music at Eureka College, Eureka, Illinois (1957–1959), associate professor of music and chairman of the fine arts department at William Penn College, Oskaloosa, Iowa (1959–1962), and has done advanced study at the University of California. A number of his anthems, some responses, and two hymn tunes have been published. He is a member of the American Guild of Organists, was former dean of the Central California chapter, and is a member of the executive committee of the Hymn Society of America.

579 Summer Ended, Harvest O'er

As joint editor with Hyde W. Beadon and James R. Woodford of *The Parish Hymn Book,* 1863, Greville Phillimore (1821–1884) contributed several original hymns and a number of translations of Latin hymns. This was one of the first hymnals to include some of John Mason Neale's translations of early Greek hymns. Phillimore was ordained in 1843 and served three Anglican parishes, Down Ampney, Henley on Thames, and Ewelme. He published two books, *Parochial Sermons*, 1856, and *Sermons and Hymns*, 1884. The present hymn is from *The Parish Hymn Book* where it appears with eight four-line stanzas under the caption "Harvest" and the text "He reserveth unto us the appointed weeks of the harvest" (Jeremiah 5:24). Stanzas one and two are included here. Woodford, later Bishop of Ely, is credited with lines three and four of the first stanza.

FREUEN WIR UNS ALL IN EIN'   This attractive Aeolian melody, attributed to Michael Weisse (see No. 113), was set to his hymn "Freuen wir uns all in ein'" ("Let us rejoice with one accord") in *Ein New Gesengbuchlen,* 1531, which he edited. "Summer ended, harvest o'er" was one of two texts set to this tune in *Songs of Syon,* 1910, edited by George R. Woodward. See No. 144 for comments on Woodward.

580   O Lord, Turn Not Thy Face From Them

Described by Charles L. Atkins as "probably the oldest English hymn in continuous use," this hymn by John Marckant (sixteenth century) was first published as one of the "Songs" appended to John Day's edition of the Old Version, 1561, with the letter *M* in place of a signature, and entitled "The Lamentation of a Sinner." The full name appears in the 1565 edition of the Old Version and in subsequent editions. The version used here is a composite one taken largely from John Playford's *The Whole Book of Psalms,* 1677, and the Supplement to the *New Version,* 1708. The hymn is often found in old copies of *The Book of Common Prayer* bound in with the psalms, both the Old Version and the *New Version.* Marckant, sometimes spelled Market and Marquaunt, served Anglican churches in Clacton Magna and Shopland and produced two or three minor literary works.

CONTRITION   Vincent Persichetti (1915–   ), one of America's outstanding contemporary composers, describes CONTRITION as a quiet Lenten hymn moving in solemn quarter notes, and says further, "It is strictly diatonic until a chromatically altered chord is generated by the word 'sinful'. The Amen is built upon the first three chords of the Hymn." CONTRITION is from Persichetti's *Hymns and Responses for the Church Year,* 1956, in which the composer comments: "Each piece is a musical entity, complete but compressed. . . . Amens at the ends of the hymns are integral parts of the music and are not to be sung as afterthought; the Hymn is usually incomplete harmonically until the Amen has been sounded." Persichetti, born in Philadelphia, had an early start in music and was playing the piano in local orchestras by the time he was eleven. When he was fifteen he was appointed organist of St. Mark's Reformed Church, Philadelphia, and for the next eighteen years served as organist and choirmaster in various churches to help pay for his education. He became familiar with the services and liturgy of many churches and, as he comments, "played what were probably several thousand services and innumerable organ recitals." After undergraduate work at Combs College (B.Mus., 1936) he studied at the Curtis Institute of Music for two years, working with Fritz Reiner and graduating in 1938 with a diploma in conducting. In 1939 he was given a scholarship at the Philadelphia Conservatory of Music for piano study with Olga Samaroff-Stokowski and composition with Paul Nordoff. In 1942 he was appointed head of the composition department of the Philadelphia Conservatory, and in 1947 joined the faculty of the Juilliard School of Music as a teacher of composition. His compositions have been performed in this country and abroad and have brought him much recognition and many awards. He is the author of *Twentieth Century Harmony; Creative Aspects and Practice,* 1961.

581 All Hail the Power of Jesus' Name

See No. 195 for comments on the text.

CORONATION   See No. 195 for comments on the tune. See No. 340 for comments on David McK. Williams.

582 Christ the Lord Is Risen Today

See No. 182 for comments on the text.

This descant was written by Hugh Porter and his wife for an Easter service at the Collegiate Church of St. Nicholas, New York City.

Ethel K. (Flentye) Porter, born in Wilmette, Illinois (1901), did her undergraduate work at Northwestern University (A.B. 1923) where she and her husband were classmates. In 1927 she received a B.M. degree from the American Conservatory of Music in Chicago, graduating with honors. In that same year she received second place (piano division) in the finals of the Young Artists' Auditions sponsored by the National Federation of Music Clubs. From 1927 to 1931 she had a fellowship in the Graduate School of the Juilliard Musical Foundation in New York City, studying piano with Olga Samaroff-Stokowski and serving two years as accompanist for Francis Rogers' voice pupils. During the summer of 1930 she was given a scholarship for study with Isidor Philipp and Nadia Boulanger at the American Conservatory in Fontainebleau, France. Persuaded by Mme. Samaroff-Stokowski to teach music at the Dalton School in New York City along lines then being followed in the Layman's Music Courses, she continued there from 1931 to 1945. She gave up teaching at Dalton when her husband became director of the School of Sacred Music at Union Theological Seminary in 1945, and from then until his death in 1960 collaborated with him in a number of ways, notably in their joint service as music editors of the new *Pilgrim Hymnal* which appeared in 1958. She has given a course on music for children at the School of Sacred Music, has lectured for church groups and at workshops, and for several years has taken an active part in the music program for children in the Sunday school of the Riverside Church in New York City.

See No. 516 for comments on Dr. Porter.

583 Our God, Our Help in Ages Past

See No. 1 for comments on the text.

The descants for ST. ANNE (583) and HANOVER (584) are from Donald Kettring's *Descants on Familiar Hymns*, 1956, which he says " 'grew up' in the various churches I have served as a device to help vitalize congregational singing. We have used them consistently but sparingly and if the descant is sung in a full natural voice and does not overpower the hymn tune I believe it introduces variety and accentuates the climax stanzas." Donald D. Kettring (1907–   ), an ordained minister and a church musician, did his undergraduate work at Ohio Wesleyan University with majors in Bible and music, and his graduate work at McCormick Theological Seminary and Union Theological Seminary (M.S.M. and B.D.). He was ordained to the Christian ministry (Congregational-Christian) in 1945, and in 1956 was granted an honorary Mus.Doc. degree by Grove City College. He has served as organist and choir director at the Market Square Presbyterian Church, Harrisburg, Pennsylvania; Westminster Presbyterian Church, Lincoln, Nebraska; First Congregational Church, Columbus, Ohio; and since 1948 at the East Liberty Presbyterian Church, Pittsburgh, Pennsylvania, where in 1958 he was installed as associate minister. He has had much experience and success in organizing and administering choir programs in churches and has taken part in workshops and church music institutes throughout the country, appearing also as guest speaker, organist, and choral director for various chapters of the American Guild of Organists. His book *Steps Toward a Singing Church*, 1948, has become a standard text for those interested in organizing and establishing multiple choir programs in churches. A number of his anthems have been published.

584 Ye Servants of God, Your Master Proclaim

See No. 206 for comments on the text.

See No. 583 for comments on Kettring.

585–594 Amen

In ancient Jewish worship it was customary for the people to sing or say the Amen meaning "So be it!" after prayers were offered, to affirm their own endorsement of and commitment to what had been sung or spoken. It was intended primarily as a response of faith on the part of the congregation, uniting the worshipers with what they had heard or uttered, and not as a conventional way of marking the end of a prayer or song of praise or something performed by the minister alone. This practice was taken over by the early church and, later on, by Islam. St. Paul in dealing with the problem of speaking in tongues wrote to the Christians in Corinth, "I will sing with the spirit and I will sing with the mind also. Otherwise, if you bless with the spirit, how can any one in the position of an outsider say the 'Amen' to your thanksgiving when he does not know what you are saying? For you may give thanks well enough, but the other man is not edified." The Amen inherently involved giving assent and support by the people to what had been said or sung. In more recent times, James Moffatt urged the continuance of this ancient custom, saying, "It is like signing one's name to a document, not a thing to be done casually." He observes, "Yet in many congregations the 'Amen' is left at the end of the prayers and the benediction, to the minister, or, if it is used, it is uttered with an offhand air, so that it sounds like an anticlimax, whereas it should gather up the full heart of the people." [1]

The first recorded use of the Amen in print at the end of a hymn occurs in an unusual sixteenth-century English hymnal bearing the doleful title, *Seven Sobs of a Sorrowfull Soule for Sinne!*, 1583. Most present-day editors and hymnologists recommend that the Amen be sung only at the end of hymns of prayer or praise or of those addressed to God. In general, with some exceptions, this has been followed in the present *Pilgrim Hymnal*.

The source of this Amen (585) is unknown.

The twofold Amen at No. 586 was composed by Robert Ramsey (c. 1600– c. 1650) who received his Bachelor of Music degree from Cambridge in 1616, was organist of Trinity College, Cambridge, from 1628 to 1644, and master of the choristers from 1637 to 1644. He composed service music, anthems, madrigals, and songs. Originally this setting was for a single Amen.

The Greek liturgy is given as the source for this twofold Amen, No. 587.

Johann Gottlieb Naumann (1741–1801), who wrote much church music and a number of successful operas, is believed to have composed this Amen at No. 588. It acquired the familiar title "Dresden Amen" from being sung in the Royal Chapel at Dresden. Mendelssohn used it in his *Reformation Symphony*, and Wagner incorporated it in the Grail motive of *Parsifal*.

There seems to be no available information about this traditional threefold Amen, No. 589.

According to R. G. McCutchan in *Our Hymnody*, this threefold Amen, No. 590, Danish in origin, is much used in Lutheran churches in Denmark.

This fourfold Amen (No. 591) was written by Prof. Robert G. Barrow (1911–   ) for the choir in the First Congregational Church, Williamstown, Massachusetts, where his wife, Esther Barrow has been organist and choirmaster since 1940. Prof. Barrow, chairman of the department of music at Williams College from 1949, also lectures on the theory and history of music and directs the Williams Glee Club. He did his undergraduate and graduate work at Yale, was awarded the Ditson Fellowship for foreign study, and studied abroad with Louis Vierne, Ralph Vaughan Williams, Paul Hindemith, and Sir Henry Wood. For four years he was organist and choirmaster at the National Episcopal Cathedral in Washington, D.C. He has been conductor of the Berkshire Choral Society, national secretary for the College Music Association, and lecturer in music on the John Hay Fellows Program for high school teachers sponsored by the Ford Foundation. His compositions include works for organ, chorus, strings, and small orchestra. His published works include a Christmas and an Easter Cantata, a suite for organ, and an organ sonata. He is the editor of the "Williams Series" of music for men's voices.

See No. 580 for comments on Vincent Persichetti, composer of the "Two-fold Amen" (No. 592) and the "Threefold Amen" (No. 593).

John Stainer (1840–1901), one of the best-known English church musicians of the Victorian era, composed this sevenfold Amen for use after the prayer of consecration at Holy Communion. Stainer had good early musical training from his father, a parish schoolmaster, and was an accomplished player and sight reader by the time he was accepted as a chorister at St. Paul's Cathedral when he was seven. At fourteen he had his first position as a church organist, and at sixteen was chosen by Ouseley to be the first organist of St. Michael's, Tenbury. (See No. 560.) In 1859, shortly after receiving his B.Mus. degree at Christ College, Oxford, Stainer was appointed organist of Magdalen College where for thirteen years he did outstanding work with the choir. He received the B.A., M.A., and D.Mus. degrees at Magdalen and was the acknowledged leader of musical life at Oxford. In 1872 he succeeded his former master, Sir John Goss, as organist of St. Paul's. Under Stainer's direction the choir became the best in England, the quality of the repertoire was greatly improved, and the revitalized services became the model for churches and cathedrals throughout the country. In 1881 he became principal of the National Training School (later the Royal College of Music) where he had taught since its founding. He resigned his post at St. Paul's in 1888, the year in which he was knighted by Queen Victoria. The following year he succeeded Ouseley as professor of music at Oxford and continued teaching there until his death. Stainer composed cantatas, anthems, service music, hymn tunes; edited hymnals; wrote textbooks on organ, harmony, counterpoint and musical terms; engaged in valuable musical research; and with the Rev. H. R. Bramley edited *Christmas Carols, New and Old,* 1871, which revived a large number of traditional carols. (See No. 122.)

ACKNOWLEDGMENTS

The publishers wish to express sincere gratitude and appreciation to those publishers who kindly granted permission for use of their copyrighted materials. Every effort has been made to trace the ownership of all copyrighted material, although in some instances exact ownership is obscure. If any omissions have been made, it is hoped that these will be brought to our attention so that proper acknowledgment may be made in future editions of the book.

1. From *Handbook to the Church Hymnary*, 1927. Edited by James Moffatt and Millar Patrick. Reprinted by permission of Oxford University Press, London.

2. From *Hymns in Christian Worship* by H. A. L. Jefferson. Barrie & Rockliff, London, 1950. Used by permission.

3. From *The Harvard University Hymn Book,* Harvard University Press, Cambridge, 1926. Used by permission.

4. From *Jewish Music* by A. Z. Idelsohn. Holt, Rinehart and Winston, Inc., New York, 1929. Used by permission.

5. From *Sibelius* by Harold E. Johnson. Alfred A. Knopf, Inc., New York, 1959–1960, and Faber and Faber, Ltd., London. Used by permission of the publishers.

6. From *The Yattendon Hymnal*, 1899. Edited by Robert Bridges and J. Ellis Wooldridge. Reprinted by permission of Oxford University Press, London.

7. From *Fugitive Notes on Certain Cantatas and the Motets of J. S. Bach* by W. G. Whittaker. Reprinted by permission of Oxford University Press, London.

8. From *Songs of Praise Discussed,* 1933. Compiled by Percy Dearmer. Reprinted by permission of Oxford University Press, London.

9. From *Music, History and Ideas* by Hugo Leichtentritt. Harvard University Press, Cambridge, 1938, 1944. Used by permission.

10. From *The Story of Christian Hymnody* by Ernest E. Ryden. Fortress Press, Philadelphia, 1959. Used by permission.

11. From *Studies of Familiar Hymns,* Second Series, 1923, by Louis F. Benson. Published by the Board of Christian Education of the Presbyterian Church, Philadelphia.

12. From *The English Hymnal,* 1906. Reprinted by permission of Oxford University Press, London.

13. From *The Story of Our Hymns* by Armin Haeussler. Eden Publishing House, St. Louis, 1952. Used by permission.

14. From *The Hymnal 1940 Companion* edited by Leonard Ellinwood. The Church Pension Fund, New York, 1949, 1951. Used by permission.

15. From *The Negro in American Culture* by Margaret Just Butcher. Alfred A. Knopf, Inc., New York, 1956. Used by permission.

16. From *The Book of American Negro Spirituals* by James Weldon and J. Rosamond Johnson. The Viking Press, Inc., 1944. Used by permission.

17. From *Hymns We Love,* by Cecil Northcott. Published U.S.A. 1955, The Westminster Press, Philadelphia. Used by permission.

18. From *Response,* Vol. IV, No. 11, Advent 1962. Lutheran Society for Worship, Music and the Arts, St. Louis. Used by permission.

19. From *Lowell Mason: An Appreciation of His Life and Work* by Henry Lowell Mason. The Hymn Society of America, New York, 1941. Used by permission.

20. From *The Handbook to the Hymnal,* William Chalmers Cobert, Ed. Copyright 1935, by the Presbyterian Board of Christian Education. Copyright renewed 1963. Used by permission.

21. As quoted in *Handbook to the Church Hymnary,* 1927. Edited by James Moffatt and Millar Patrick. Reprinted by permission of Oxford University Press, London.

22. From *The Music of the French Psalter of 1562* by Waldo Selden Pratt. Columbia University Press, New York, 1939. Used by permission.

23. From *Four Centuries of Scottish Psalmody,* 1941, by Millar Patrick. Reprinted by permission of Oxford University Press, London.

24. From *Music in Western Civilization* by Paul Henry Lang. W. W. Norton & Company, Inc., New York, 1941. Used by permission.

25. From *Johann Sebastian Bach* by Philipp Spitta, Dover Publications, Inc., New York.

26. From *Church Music in History and Practice* by Winfred Douglas. Charles Scribner's Sons, New York, 1937. Used by permission.

27. From *J. S. Bach* by Albert Schweitzer. A. & C. Black Ltd., London, 1905, and The Macmillan Company, New York. Used by permission of the publishers.

28. William Boyd in *The Musical Times,* XLIX, 1908. Novello & Company Ltd., London. Used by permission.

29. From *The History of the Choir and Music of Trinity Church* by Arthur H. Messiter. Edwin S. Gorham, New York, 1906. Used by permission.

30. From *Collected Hymns* by John Haynes Holmes. Beacon Press, Boston, 1960. Used by permission.

31. From *English Cathedral Music* by Edmund H. Fellowes. Methuen & Company, Ltd., London, 1941. Used by permission.

32. From *The Public Worship of God,* by Henry Sloane Coffin. Copyright 1946, by W. L. Jenkins. The Westminster Press, Philadelphia. Used by permission.

33. From *An Outline of Christian Worship,* 1936, by William Maxwell. Reprinted by permission of Oxford University Press, London.

34. From *The Story of the Church's Song* by Millar Patrick. Revised edition. John Knox Press, Richmond, 1962. Used by permission.

BIBLIOGRAPHY

Handbooks

COVERT, WILLIAM C., AND LAUFER, CALVIN W., *Handbook to the Hymnal* (Presbyterian). Presbyterian Board of Christian Education, Philadelphia, 1935.

DEARMER, PERCY, AND JACOB, ARCHIBALD, *Songs of Praise Discussed.* Oxford University Press, London, 1933.

DOUGLAS, WINFRED; ELLINWOOD, LEONARD; FARLANDER, ARTHUR; AND OTHERS, *The Hymnal 1940 Companion.* The Church Pension Fund, New York, 1949.

FRERE, WALTER H., AND OTHERS, *Hymns Ancient and Modern* (Historical Edition). William Clowes & Sons, Ltd., London, 1909.

FROST, MAURICE, *Historical Companion to Hymns Ancient and Modern.* William Clowes & Sons, Ltd., London, 1962.

HAEUSSLER, ARMIN, *The Story of Our Hymns* (Handbook for *The Hymnal,* 1941, Evangelical and Reformed Church in the United States). Eden Publishing House, St. Louis, 1952.

McCUTCHAN, ROBERT G., *Our Hymnody; A Manual of the Methodist Hymnal* (Second Edition). Abingdon-Cokesbury Press, New York and Nashville, 1942.

MOFFATT, JAMES, AND PATRICK, MILLAR, *Handbook to the Church Hymnary.* Oxford University Press, London, 1935.

PARRY, K. L., AND ROUTLEY, ERIK, *Companion to Congregational Praise.* Independent Press, Ltd., London, 1962.

POLACK, WILLIAM G., *The Handbook to the Lutheran Hymnal.* Concordia Publishing House, St. Louis, 1942.

Reference Books

BAKER, THEODORE, *Baker's Biographical Dictionary of Musicians* (Fifth Edition). G. Schirmer, Inc., New York, 1958.

BÄUMKER, WILHELM, *Das katholische deutsche Kirchenlied* (four volumes), Freidberg, 1896–1911. Reproduced by G. Olm, Hildesheim, 1962.

BLOM, ERIC, ED., *Grove's Dictionary of Music and Musicians* (Fifth Edition, nine volumes). Macmillan and Co., Ltd., London, 1954. Earlier editions useful.

JULIAN, JOHN, ED., *A Dictionary of Hymnology.* J. Murray, London, 1892–1925. (Reprint, Dover Publications, New York, 1957.)

SCHOLES, PERCY A., *Oxford Companion to Music.* Oxford University Press, New York, 1938. (Eighth Edition, 1950.)

ZAHN, JOHANNES, *Die Melodien der deutschen evangelischen Kirchenlieder* (six volumes). Gutersloh, 1889–1895.

General

BENSON, LOUIS F., *The English Hymn.* George H. Doran Co., New York, 1915. (Reprint, John Knox Press, Richmond, Virginia, 1962.)

DOUGLAS, CHARLES WINFRED, *Church Music in History and Practice.* Charles Scribner's Sons, New York, 1937. (Revised by Leonard Ellinwood, 1962.)

FROST, MAURICE, *English and Scottish Psalm and Hymn Tunes.* Oxford University Press, London, 1953.

GROUT, DONALD JAY, *A History of Western Music.* W. W. Norton & Company, Inc., New York, 1960.

JACKSON, GEORGE P., *White Spirituals in the Southern Uplands.* The University of North Carolina Press, Chapel Hill, North Carolina, 1933.

———, *White and Negro Spirituals.* J. J. Augustin, Inc., New York, 1944.

LANG, PAUL HENRY, *Music in Western Civilization*. W. W. Norton and Co., Inc., New York, 1941.

LEICHTENTRITT, HUGO, *Music, History and Ideas*. Harvard University Press, Cambridge, 1944.

LIGHTWOOD, JAMES T., *Hymn Tunes and Their Story*. The Epworth Press, London, 1935.

PATRICK, MILLAR, *Four Centuries of Scottish Psalmody*. Oxford University Press, London, 1949.

————, *The Story of the Church's Song*. Scottish Churches Joint Committee on Youth, Edinburgh, 1927. Revised for American use by James Rawlings Sydnor. John Knox Press, Richmond, 1962.

PHILLIPS, CHARLES S., *Hymnody Past and Present*. The Macmillan Company, New York, 1937.

PIDOUX, PIERRE, *Le Psautier Huguenot du XVIe Siecle*. Edition Bärenreiter, Basel, 1962.

POCKNEE, CYRIL E., *The French Diocesan Hymns and Their Melodies*. Morehouse-Gorham Co., Inc., New York, 1954.

PRATT, WALDO SELDEN, *The Music of the Pilgrims: A Description of the Psalm-book Brought to Plymouth in 1620*. (Ainsworth Psalter) Oliver Ditson Co., Boston, 1921.

————, *The Music of the French Psalter of 1562*. Columbia University Press, New York, 1939.

ROUTLEY, ERIK, *Hymns and Human Life*. The Philosophical Library, Inc., New York, 1953.

SYDNOR, JAMES R., ED., *A Short Bibliography for the Study of Hymns*. The Hymn Society of America, Paper XXV, New York, 1964.

TERRY, CHARLES SANFORD, *Bach's Chorals*, Parts I, II, III. Cambridge University Press, Cambridge, 1921.

INDEX

All references are to page numbers. Roman numerals refer to introductory articles.

Names of tunes are in capitals and small capitals. Titles of books and their common designations are in italics.

Abbreviations: abridged, abr.; adapted, adap.; altered, alt.; arranged, arr.; attributed, attrib.; author, auth.; biography, biog.; composer, comp.; editor, ed.; harmonized, harm.; paraphrase, para.; pseudonym, pseud.; quoted, quot.; translator, trans.

An asterisk [*] denotes material under another number, usually signified by "see" comments on the text or tune.

A Mighty Fortress Is Our God, xv, 282–284
ABBEY, 247
Abelard, Peter, biog., 128; 244
ABERYSTWYTH, 87, 169
Abide With Me, 35, 167, 230
According to Thy Gracious Word, 228
ACH BLEIB BEI UNS, 48
ACH GOTT UND HERR, 360
Adams, Sarah Flower, 273
Addison, Joseph, 58, 76, 183
ADESTE FIDELIS (PORTUGUESE HYMN), 109, 110, 293
Adler, Felix, 327
ADORO TE, 406
Again, as Evening's Shadow Falls, 41, 382
AGINCOURT HYMN; see DEO GRACIAS
Agnus Dei, discussion of, 405
Ah, Holy Jesus, How Hast Thou Offended, 131
Ah! Think Not the Lord Delayeth, 91
Ahle, Johann Rudolf, 169, *204
Ainger, Arthur Campbell, 237
AINSWORTH 97, 379
Ainsworth Psalter (1612), 39, 43, 181, 263, 358, 359, 416
ALBANY; see ANCIENT OF DAYS

Albert, Heinrich, 254
Alchemy (philosophers' stone), 311
Aldrich, Henry, 411
Alexander, Mrs. Cecil F., biog., 138; 253, *254, 361
Alexander, James W., trans., 135
"Alexander's Ragtime Band," 168
ALFORD, 245
Alford, Henry, biog., 245; 352, 353
Alington, Cyril, 149
All Beautiful the March of Days, 349
All Creatures of Our God and King, 14, 55
All Glory Be to God on High, 3
All Glory, Laud, and Honor, 125
All Hail the Power of Jesus' Name, 157, 158, 419
ALL MORGEN IST, 377
All My Heart This Night Rejoices, 100
All My Hope on God is Founded, 266
All People That on Earth Do Dwell, xii, 5, 7
All Praise to Thee, for Thou, O King Divine, 120
All Praise to Thee, My God, 49, 50, 385
ALL SAINTS NEW, 302
All Things Are Thine, 395

All Things Bright and Beautiful, 361
All Things Come of Thee, O Lord, 395
ALLEIN GOTT IN DER HÖH', 3
Alleluia! Alleluia! Hearts to Heaven, 145
Alleluia! The Strife is O'er, 146
ALLES IST AN GOTTES SEGEN, 91
Almighty Father, Hear Our Prayer, 389
Alone Thou Goest Forth, O Lord, 128
ALTA TRINITA BEATA, 312, 397
Ambrose (Saint), 35, 37, 407
Amen, discussion of, 420
AMERICA (National Anthem), 336
ANCIENT OF DAYS, 201
Ancient of Days, Who Sittest Throned in Glory, 201, 236
And Now, O Father, Mindful of the Love, 234
Anderson, James, adap., 134
ANGELIC SONGS; see TIDINGS
Angels, From the Realms of Glory, 94
Angels Holy, High and Lowly, 60
ANGEL'S STORY, 174
Angels We Have Heard on High, 93
ANGELUS (WHITSUN HYMN), 49
Anglo-Genevan Psalter (1551), 83; (1556), 209, *324, *381, (1561), 5, 83, 190
Anne (Queen of England), 1, 19
Antes, John, biog., 353
ANTIOCH (COMFORT; HOLY TRIUMPH), 107
AR HYD Y NOS, 51
ARFON, 139
Arnold, Matthew, quot., 322
ARNSBERG (GRÖNINGEN), 4
Arnulf of Louvain, 135
ARTHUR'S SEAT, 298
As Hymnodus Sacer (1625), 56, 360
As Pants the Hart, 303
As the Sun Doth Daily Rise, 31
As With Gladness Men of Old, 96
At Even, Ere the Sun Was Set, 48
At the Name of Jesus, 159

Atkinson, Frederick C., biog., 187
Attwood, Thomas, biog., 387
Augustine (Saint), xv, 37, 407
AURELIA, 209
AUS DER TIEFE; see HEINLEIN
AUS GNADEN SOLL ICH, 377
AUSTRIA (AUSTRIAN HYMN), 215, 216, 337, 338
Ave Hierarchia (1531), 207
AVE VIRGO VIRGINUM (GAUDEAMUS PARITER), 151
Awake, Awake to love and Work!, 32
Awake, My Soul, and With the Sun, 29, 74, 385
Awake, My Soul, Stretch Every Nerve, 282
AWAY IN A MANGER, 113
AZMON, 179, 271

Babcock, Maltbie Davenport, 365
Bach, Johann Sebastian, biog., 225 f.; 3, 23, 265; harm., 72, 112, *243, *398; Cantatas: No. 1: 119; No. 3: 56, 396; No. 6: 48; No. 12: 78, 179; No. 13: 47, 83; No. 19: 83; No. 21: 69; No. 23: 406; No. 24: 203; No. 25: 83, 136; No. 27: 69; No. 30: 83; No. 36 (Advent): 119; No. 37: 119; No. 39: 83; No. 40: 266; No. 44: 47, 56, 396; No. 45: 160; No. 48: 360; No. 49: 119; No. 57: 17; No. 58: 56; No. 61: 119; No. 64: 160, 179; No. 65: 276; No. 66: 149; No. 69: 78; No. 70 (Advent): 83, 221; No. 71: 203; No. 72: 276; No. 75: 78; No. 79 (Reformation): 27; No. 80: 284; No. 81: 179; No. 84: 3, 69; No. 87: 179; No. 90: 40; No. 92: 276; No. 93: 69; No. 94: 160; No. 95: 126, 293; No. 97: 47; No. 98: 78; No. 100: 78; No. 101: 40; No. 102: 40; No. 103: 276; No. 104: 3; No. 111: 276; No. 112: 3; No. 118: 56; No. 122: 189; No. 127: 406; No. 128: 3, 160; No. 129: 160; No. 135: 136; No. 137: 17; No. 139: 80; No. 140: 23, 86;

Bach, Johann Sebastian *Cont.*
No. 144: 78, 276; No. 151: 371;
No. 153: 56, 136; No. 156: 80;
No. 161: 136; No. 162: 58; No.
166: 69; No. 172: 119; No. 179:
69; No. 192 (Nun danket alle
Gott): 27; No. 194: 83; No. 195:
371; No. 197: 69.
Cantata (unfinished) "Herr Gott,
Beherrscher aller Dinge," 17
Cantata (unfinished) "Ehre sei
Gott in der Höhe," 160
Choralgesänge, 3, 27, 40, 43, 47,
48, 57, 69, 91, 100, 119, 126, 135,
136, 149, 170, 178, 186, 203, 221,
276, 284, 289, 293, 357, 360, 371,
389, 414, 416
Chorale Partita ("O Gott du from-
mer Gott"), 71
Chorale Preludes (*Orgelbüchlein*),
40, 43, 58, 69, 81, 92, 99, 102,
149, 170, 179, 208, 371, 390, 406,
414, 416
Christmas Oratorio, 95, 99, 100,
136, 221, 254
Clavierübung, 3, 40, 90, 135
Eighteen Chorales for Organ, 3,
27, 40, 43, 126, 135, 414
Miscellaneous Chorale Preludes, 3,
40, 69, 102, 170, 179, 221, 360,
371, 390
Motet No. 4, 100
Motet ("Jesu meine Freude"), 179
Musikalisches Opfer, 188
Passion According to St. John, 33,
40, 47, 80, 126, 132
Passion According to St. Matthew,
33, 47, 98, 132, 136, 276, 416
Prelude and Fugue (St. Anne), 2
Schübler Chorales, 17, 23, 48, 69
Three Wedding Chorales, 27, 78
Well-Tempered Clavichord (Bk.
II), 188
Bacon, Leonard, 236; biog., 337
Baker, Henry, comp., 345
Baker, Henry Williams, 48, 66, 344,
353; quot., 245; trans., 89
Baker, Theodore, trans., 21, 108
Bambridge, William S., 301

BANGOR, 2, 122, 129, 228
Barbauld, Anna Laetitia Aiken, 353,
354
Barclay, Margaret, trans., 376
Baring-Gould, Sabine, biog., 45, 298,
383; trans., 301
Barnby, Joseph, biog., 33; 45, 151,
237, 242, 297, 355, 393, *411,
*413
Barrow, Robert G., 421
Barthelemon, Francois H., biog., 30;
*314
Barton, Bernard, 205
Batchellor, Daniel, 362
Bates, Katherine Lee, 338
BATTLE HYMN OF THE REPUBLIC,
341
BATTY; *see* RINGE RECHT
Bax, Clifford, 347
Baxter, Richard, 22
"Bay Psalm Book" (1640), 39, 43,
73, 77, 181, 358, *359; (1698),
376
Bayeux Antiphoner (1739), 52
Bayley, Daniel, 332
Bayly, Albert F., 240, 348
Beach, Curtis, 25, *61
Be Known to Us in Breaking Bread,
225
Be Still, My Soul, 63
Be Thou My Vision, 303
BEATITUDO, 273
BEECHER, 183
Beecher, Henry Ward, 34, 167,
183 f., 207, 274
Beecher, Lyman, 207
Beethoven, Ludwig van, biog., 11;
337; attrib., 395; *Ninth Symph.,*
68
Before Jehovah's Aweful Throne, 12,
13
Before the Cross of Jesus, 130
Before the Day Draws Near Its End-
ing, 382
Behold Us, Lord, A Little Space, 307
Bell, Maurice F., harm., 21, *256
Beneath the Cross of Jesus, 129
BENEDIC ANIMA MEA; *see* PRAISE MY
SOUL

Bennett, William Sterndale, 264
Bernard of Clairvaux, 135, 180, *181
Bernard of Cluny, 243
Berwick Hymnal (1886), 262
BETHANY, 274
Bèze, Théodore de; *see Genevan Psalter*
Bianco da Siena, 192
Bible references; *see* Scriptural texts
BISHOPGARTH, 276
BISHOPTHORPE, 222
Blackie, John Stuart, 60
BLAENHAFREN, 330
Blanchard, Ferdinand Q., 130
Bless Thou the Gifts, 396
Blessed Art Thou, O Lord (Benedictus es, Domine), 412
Blessed Be the Lord God (Benedictus), 411
Blessed Jesus, at Thy Word, 169
Blessed Jesus, Here Are We, 224
Blest Are the Pure in Heart, 171
Blest Be the Tie That Binds, 221
Blow, John, 2, 65
Bode, John Ernest, 174
Bohemian Brethren (Unitas Fratrum), x, 20, 51, 92, 151, 207, *256, 365
Boleyn, Anne, 19
Bonar Horatius, biog., 79; 94, 230, 308, 318, 345, *406
BONN; *see* WARUM SOLLT ICH
Book of Books, Our People's Strength, 204
Borthwick, Jane L., and Sarah, trans., 63, 234
Bortniansky, Dmitri S., 45
Bos, Coenraad V., 21
Boston Handel and Haydn Society, *see* Handel and Haydn Society
BOURBON, 407
Bourgeois, Louis, biog., 6; 166, *333; attrib., 315; adap., 42, 44, 132, 190, 227, *231, 262, *309, *342, *347, *357, *382; *see also French Psalter*
Bourne, George, 233
Bowie, Walter Russell, biog., 256; 324, 333

Bowring, John, 86, 127
Boyce, William, biog., 409; 266
Boyd, William, 287; quot., 288
BOYLSTON, 222
BRADBURY, 257
Bradbury, William B., biog., 143; 252, 290, 300, 364
Brahms, Johannes (Op. 122), 47, 136
Brandon, George, adap., 417
Bread of Heaven, on Thee We Feed, 225
BREAD OF LIFE, 204
Bread of the World, in Mercy Broken, 227, 228
Break Forth, O Beauteous Heavenly Light, 95
Break Thou the Bread of Life, 204
Breathe on Me, Breath of God, 187, 188
BRESLAU, 396
Bridges, Matthew, 160, 253
Bridges, Robert, biog., 331; para., 46; quot., 65, 142; trans., 36, 44, 131. *See also Yattenden Hymnal*
Briggs, George W., 160, 229, 243, 392
Bright, William, 234
Brightest and Best of the Sons of the Morning, 103
Bring a Torch, Jeannette, Isabella, 101
Britten, Benjamin, 248
Brooke, Stopford A., 57
Brooks, Phillips, biog., 110
Browne, Simon, 191
Brownlie, John, trans., 161, 315
Bryan, Joseph, 388
BRYN CALFARIA, 233
Buchanan, Annabel Morris, arr., 246
Buck, Zechariah, 174, 187
Buckham, John Wright, 236
BUCKLAND, 190
Buckoll, Henry J., trans., 381
Budry, Edmond L., 155
Built on the Rock, 218
BUNESSAN, 35
Bunyan, John, biog., 290
Burleigh, Harry T., biog., 320 f.

Burleigh, William H., 295
Burnap, Uzziah C., 185, 298
Burney, Charles, quot., 198, 282, 312, *397
Burt, Bates Gilbert, 370
Butler, Henry Montagu, 274
Buxtehude, Dietrich (*Chorale Fant.*), 119
Byrne, Mary E., 303
Byrom, John, biog., 104

CAITHNESS, 273
Calkin, John Baptiste, 230, 236
Calvin, John, 165, 258
Calvisius (Seth Kallwitz), biog., 48; attrib., 48; 275
Campbell, Jane M., trans., 351
Canitz, Friedrich R. L. von, 381
Cannon, Mrs. Ross, quot., 306
CANONBURY, 41, 308
CANTERBURY; *see* SONG 13
Cantica Spiritualis (1847), 49
CARLISLE (INVOCATION), 24
CAROL, 106
Caswall, Edward, trans., 32, 180, 247
Catholicum Hymnologium Germanicum (1584) (Leisentritt), 152
Chadwick, John W., 222
Chambers, John David, trans., 382
Chao, T. C., 367, 368
Charpentier, Marc-Antoine, 101
Chatfield, Allen W., trans., 248
CHAUTAUQUA, 41
Chautauqua Assembly, 29, 41
Chesterton, Gilbert Keith, 335
CHILDHOOD (Tune), 362
Chinese Christian Hymns, 1953, 367, 368
Chinese melodies, 368
CHINESE MELODY (P'U T'O), 58
Choir School, first in U. S., 228
Chorale Book for England (1863); *see* Winkworth, Catherine
Chorley, Henry F., 343
Christ for the World We Sing!, 235
Christ Is Made the Sure Foundation, 212
Christ Is the World's True Light, 160
CHRIST IST ERSTANDEN, 148

Christ lag in Todesbanden, 148
Christ the Lord Is Risen Again, 148
Christ the Lord Is Risen Today, 147, 156, 419
Christ, Whose Glory Fills the Skies, 38
CHRISTE SANCTORUM, 37
Christian, Dost Thou See Them, 285
Christian Lyre, The (1830), 136; 15, 51, 125, 221, 316, 337
Christian, Rise and Act Thy Creed, 322
Christians, Awake, Salute the Happy Morn, 104
CHRISTMAS (SANFORD; LUNENBERG), 282
Churchill, Winston, 2, 160, 291, 341
Chute, Marion Jean, 307
City of God, How Broad and Far, 211
Civil War, hymns influenced by, 222, 340
Clark, Alden H., trans., 305
Clark, Mrs. Alden, adap., 306
Clarke, Jeremiah, biog., 65; 2, 74, *161, 176, 222, *348
Claudius, Matthias, 351
Clausnitzer, Tobias, 169, 201, *225
Clement of Alexandria, 132
Clephane, Elizabeth C., 129
CLOISTERS (Tune), 297
Coffin, Charles, 93, 117, *152
Coffin, Henry Sloane, xiv, 324; trans., 88; quot., 384
Collection of Psalms and Hymns; see Wesley, John
Collyer, Robert, 223
Columba (Saint), 67, 200
Come, and Let Us Sweetly Join, 391
Come Down, O Love Divine, 192
Come, Gracious Spirit, Heavenly Dove, xii, 191
Come, Holy Ghost, Our Souls Inspire, 186, 287, 414; *see also* Veni Creator Spiritus
Come, Holy Spirit, God and Lord!, 189
Come, Holy Spirit, Heavenly Dove, 194

Come, Labor On, 234
Come, Let Us Join with Faithful Souls, 271
Come, My Soul, Thou Must Be Waking, 381
Come, Risen Lord, 229
Come, Thou Almighty King, 198
Come, Thou Long-Expected Jesus, 82
"Come Unto Me, Ye Weary," 248
Come, Ye Faithful Raise the Strain, x, 150, 151
Come, Ye Thankful People, Come, 352; Thanksgiving version, 353
Comfort, Comfort Ye My People, 83
CONDITOR ALME, 91
Conder, Josiah, 225
Conkey, Ithamar, 127
CONSOLATION (BERLIN, EPIPHANY), 34
CONTRITION, 418
Converse, Charles C., biog., 263
CORDE NATUS; see DIVINUM MYSTERIUM
CORINTH; see DULCE CARMEN
Corner, David Gregor; see Grosscatholisch Gesangbuch
CORONAE, 163
CORONATION, 158, 419
Cory, Julia Bulkley Cady, 21
Cosin, Bishop John, trans., 186, *414
Coster, George Thomas, 297
Cotterill, Thomas, biog., 164
Courteville, Raphael, 215
Cowper, William, biog., 72; 215, *273, 312
Cox, Frances Elizabeth, trans., 20
Coxe, Arthur Cleveland, 213, 330
CRANHAM, 105
CRASSELIUS; see WINCHESTER NEW
Create in Me a Clean Heart, O God, 392
CREATION, 59, 337; see also Haydn, Franz
Creation's Lord, We Give Thee Thanks, 239
Creator of the Stars of Night, 91
CRIMOND, 70

Croft, William, biog., 2; attrib., 165, *213, *420; comp., 184
CROFT'S 136TH, 184
Croly, George, attrib., 187
Crossman, Samuel, 135
Crotch, William, biog., 190; *408
Crown Him with Many Crowns, 160, 300
Crüger, Johann, biog., 27; 132, 136, 178, 194, *205, 288, *380
"Crusader's Hymn," 182; see also SCHÖNSTER HERR JESU
Cummings, William H., biog., 97
CUSHMAN, 124
Cutler, Henry, biog., 302
CWM RHONDDA, 76, 287
Czechoslovakian carol, 363

Damon's Psalter (1579), *282
DANBY, 348
Darwall, John, 22
DARWALL'S 148TH, 22, 164
DAS NEUGEBORNE KINDELEIN (JENA), 189
DAS WALT' GOTT VATER, 186, 334
Davies, Henry Walford, xv; biog, 398; 111, 362
Davies, Hugh, harm., 139
Davis, Ozora Stearns, 175
Davison, Archibald T., 163; quot., 21
Davisson, Ananias, 32, *325, 415
DAWN (WATCHMAN), 38
Day Is Dying in the West, 40
Day's Psalter (1561), 418
Dear Lord and Father of Mankind, 267
Dear Master, in Whose Life I See, 166
Dearmer, Geoffrey, para., 312
Dearmer, Percy, biog., 91; 85, 204, 340, 365, 388; quot., 9, 38, 116, 233, 274, 280, 299, 307, 332; trans., 37, 157, 363
Decius, Nicolaus, 3
DENNIS, 63, 221
DEO GRACIAS (THE AGINCOURT SONG), 123
DEUS TUORUM MILITUM, 123, 348
DIADEMATA, 161, 299, 370, 411

Dickey, Mark, 381
Dietz, Purd Eugene, 372
DIVA SERVATRIX, 52
DIVINUM MYSTERIUM (CORDE NATUS), 89
DIX, 56, 96, 355
Dix, William Chatterton, 56, 96, 115, quot., 248
Doane, George Washington, biog., 236
Doane, Bishop Wm. Croswell, biog., 201; 236
Doane, William Howard, biog., 310
Doddridge, Philip, xxi; biog., 63; 282, 303, 348
DOMINUS REGIT ME, 66
DONNE SECOURS (GENEVA 12), 262, 309
Douglas, C. Winfred, biog., 291; harm., 32, 37, 90, 235, *325; arr., 365, 382, 404; quot., 274, 352; trans., 225
Döving, Carl, trans., 219
Dowland, John, biog., 7; harm., 8
DOWN AMPNEY, 192
Doxology; see OLD HUNDREDTH
Draper, William Henry, biog., 134; 55
Draw Nigh to Thy Jerusalem, 127
Draw Thou My Soul, O Christ, 251
DRESDEN; see WIR PFLÜGEN
DU MEINE SEELE, SINGE, 153
Duché, Jacob, biog., 31
Duffield, George, 300
DUKE STREET, 162, 236, 338
DUKE'S TUNE, 397
DULCE CARMEN (CORINTH), 269
DUNDEE (FRENCH), 2, 71, 73, 303
DUNFERMLINE, 307
Dunkerley, William A. (Pseud. John Oxenham), xxi, 213, 319, 320
DURHAM; see INNOCENTS
DURROW, 200
Dutch melodies, 21, 61, 82
Dwight, Timothy, xx, xxi; biog., 217
Dyer, Samuel, 191, *361
Dykes, John Bacchus, biog., 66; 132, 141, 173, 180, *194, 202, 245, 273, 285, 331
Dyson, George, biog., 388

Each Morning Brings, 376
EASTER HYMN (WORGAN), 147, *155
Ebeling, Johann G., 100, 153
EBENEZER (TON-Y-BOTEL), 340
Ecclesiasticus, 44:1–7, 360; 44:1–16, 243; 50:22–24, 27
ECUMENICAL; see SURSAM CORDA
Edmeston, James, 269
Edward VII (Prince of Wales), 301, 302
Edwards, Frank L., 249
Edwards, John D., *355
EIN' FESTE BURG (A Mighty Fortress), 283
Ein New Gesengbuchlen (Weisse) (1531), 92, 148, 207, 418; see also Bohemian Brethren
EISENACH (MACH'S MIT MIR; LEIPSIC), 80, 223
Ein schön geistlich Gesangbuch (1609) (Vulpius), 189, 293
Elizabeth I (Queen of England), 7, 19, 77, 381
Elizabeth II (Queen of England), 18, 71, 372, 406
ELLACOMBE, 57, 351
ELLERS, 52
Ellerton, John, 42, *43, 52, 139, 307, 343, 356, 382
ELTON, 346
Elliott, Charlotte, 251, *253
Elliott, Emily E. S., 256
Elvey, Sir George, biog., 161; 253, *300, *352, *370, 411
Elvey, Stephen, 409
England, Paul, trans., 22
ENGELBERG, 120
English Hymnal (1906), 10, 14, 15, 21, 28, 37, 53, 61, 67, 74, 75, 85, 91, 105, 108, 111, 117, 123, 125, 135, 139, 151, 166, 180, 193, 211, 221, 222, 233, 234, 273, 301, 316, 318, 328, 335, 340, 349, 350, 365, 389; see also Vaughan Williams, Ralph
English melodies, 115, 348, *349, 361, 366
English Psalters; see Sternhold and

434

Hopkins; Ravenscroft; Playford; Tate and Brady

Enrich, Lord, Heart, Mouth, Hands in Me, 392

Erbaulicher Musicalischer Christen-Schatz (1745), 261 f

ERFURT, *see* VOM HIMMEL HOCH

ERIE (WHAT A FRIEND), 263

ERMUNTRE DICH (SCHOP), 95

ES IST EIN' ROS', 108

EST IST GEWISSLICH, *see* NUN FREUT EUCH

Essay on the Church Plain Chant (1782), 269

Este's Psalter (*The Whole Booke of Psalmes,* 1592), 7, 43, 119, 181, 209

Eternal Father, Strong to Save, 331

Eternal God, Whose Power Upholds, 234

Eternal Ruler of the Ceaseless Round, 222

EUCHARISTIC HYMN, 383

EUDOXIA, 282

European Psalmist (1872), 210, 214

Evans, David, biog., 35; arr., 174, 269, *304; comp., 134; harm., 139, 200, 249, *327

EVENSONG, *see* LANGRAN

EVENTIDE, 167

EWING, 243

Ewing, Alexander, 244

Faber, Frederick Wm., 81, 132, 239, 286, 289, 397

Fairest Lord Jesus, 182

Faith of Our Fathers, 286

FAR-OFF LANDS, 365

FARRANT, 378

Farrant, Richard, biog., 409; attrib., 378; 413

Farjeon, Eleanor, 35

Farrington, Harry Webb, 121

Father Almighty, Bless Us with Thy Blessing, 262

Father Eternal, Ruler of Creation, 342

Father, Give Thy Benediction, 397

Father, Hear the Prayer We Offer, 288

Father in Heaven, Who Lovest All, 304

Father, in Thy Mysterious Presence, 262

Father, to Thee We Look in All Our Sorrow, 355

Father, We Praise Thee, Now the Night Is Over, 37

Father, We Thank Thee for the Night, 362

Father, We Thank Thee Who Hast Planted, 231

Fawcett, John, biog., 54; 221

FEDERAL STREET, 232, 312

FESTAL SONG, 238

FESTGESANG; *see* MENDELSSOHN

FFIGYSBREN, 175

FIELD, 325

Field, Herbert H., 325

Fight the Good Fight, 287

Fill Thou My Life, O Lord, 308

"FINLANDIA," 64, 372; *see also* Sibelius, Jan

FINLAY, 25

Finlay, Terence J., 25

Finnish melodies, 269

Fischer, William Gustavus, 250

Flemming, Friedrich F., 262

FLORENCE; *see* ALTA TRINITA BEATA

Fling Out the Banner!, 236

FOLKINGHAM, 333

For All the Saints, 120, 242

For the Beauty of the Earth, 55

For the Brave of Every Race, 243

FOREST GREEN, 349

Forgive, O Lord, Our Severing Ways (O mensch sieh), 212

Forth in Thy Name, O Lord, I Go, 314

Forty Days and Forty Nights, 121

Forward Through the Ages, 299

Fosdick, Harry Emerson, 286, 335

Foster, Bishop Fredk. W., trans., 4

Founded on Thee, Our Only Lord, 360

Foundery Collection (1742); *see* Wesley, John

Foundling Hospital Collection (1796), 14
FRANCONIA, 171
Franck, Johann, 177, 379
FRANKFORT; *see* WIE SCHÖN LEUCHTET
FRENCH; *see* DUNDEE
French carols, 86, 93, 101, 139
French church melodies, 37, 52, 123, 154, 244, 297; *see also* Genevan Psalter; Bourgeois, Louis
French Psalter, 6, 43; (1545), 165, 347; (1562), 415; *see also* Bourgeois, Louis
French Revolution, 12
FREU DICH SEHR; *see* PSALM 42
FREUEN WIR UNS ALL IN EIN, 418
Freylinghausen, Johann A. (*Gesangbuch*, (1704), biog., 62; *see also* *Geistriches Gesangbuch* (1704)
Friedell, Harold, 25
Fritsch, Ahasuerus, 160
From All That Dwell Below the Skies, 13
From Heaven Above to Earth I Come, 98

Gaelic melodies, 35
Gajard, Dom J., 406
GALILEE, 253
Gannett, William Channing, 299, 349; alt., 350
GARDINER; *see* GERMANY
Gardiner, William, biog., 8; rel. with Beethoven, 216; *Sacred Melodies*, 8, 13, 59, 255, 326
Gascoigne, George, alt., 380
Gastorius, Severus, 77, 78
GAUDEAMUS PARITER; *see* AVE VIRGO VIRGINUM
Gauntlett, Henry J., harm., 81, *82
Gay, Annabeth McClelland, 258
Geer, E. Harold, trans., 111
Geistliche Kirchengesäng (1623), 13, *55
Geistliche Lieder (1535) (Klug), 99, 102, 149, 220, 283, *340, 414
Geistliche Lieder (1539) (Schu-

mann), 3, 39, 99, *224; (1589), 48
Geistreiches Gesangbuch (1704) (Freylinghausen), 18, 39, 265
GELOBT SEI GOTT, 149, 357
GENEVAN PSALM 22, 315
Genevan Psalter (1551), xix, 5, 42, 83, 190, 227, 262, *309, 333, *342, 347, 356, *357, 385, 389; (1562 complete), 14, 21, 92, 379, 415; *see also* Bourgeois, Louis; Marot, Clement
George, Graham, 141
GEORGETOWN, 267
Gerhardt, Paul, 46, 100, 126, 135, 178, 265
German melodies, 46, 108, 178, 182, 350, *361
GERMANY (GARDINER, WALTON), 326
GETHSEMANE; *see* REDHEAD NO. 76
Giardini, Felice de, 198, *235, *358
Gibbons, Orlando, biog., 131; 68, 130, 166, 223, 234, 264, *281, *301, 383
Gill, Thomas H., 220
Gillman, Frederick John, 334
Gilmore, Joseph H., 289
Give to the Winds Thy Fears, 265
Gladden, Washington, xxi, 323
Gläser, Carl G., 179, *271
GLORIA, 93
Gloria patri, discussion of, 383 f.
Gloria tibi, discussion of, 400
Glorious Things of Thee Are Spoken, xii, 215
Glory Be to God on High, 55
Glory Be to God on High (Gloria in Excelsis), 404
Glory Be to the Father; *see* Gloria Patri
Glory Be to Thee (Gloria tibi), 400, 401
GO DOWN MOSES, 330; *see also* When Israel Was in Egypt's Land
Go, Tell It on the Mountain, 368
GO, TELL IT ON THE MOUNTAIN, 368
Go to Dark Gethsemane, 128
God Be in My Head, 304, 398

GOD BE IN MY HEAD, 398
God Be With You Till We Meet Again, 53
God Himself Is With Us, 4
God Is My Strong Salvation, 293
God Is Working His Purpose Out, 237
God Moves in a Mysterious Way, 72, 73
God of Earth and Sea and Heaven, 249
God of Grace and God of Glory, xii, 286, 335
God of Our Fathers, Known of Old, 333
God of Our Fathers, Whose Almighty Hand, 334
God of Our Life, Through All the Circling Years, 78
God of the Earth, the Sky, the Sea, 56
God of the Living, in Whose Eyes, 356
God of the Nations, Who from Dawn of Days, 333
God of the Prophets, 357
GOD REST YOU MERRY, 100
God Rest You Merry, Gentlemen, 100
God Send Us Men Whose Aim 'Twill Be, 334
God, That Madest Earth and Heaven, 50
God the Omnipotent, 343
God's Glory Is a Wondrous Thing, 289
Golden Breaks the Dawn, 367
Good Christian Men, Rejoice, 102
Good Christian Men Rejoice and Sing!, 149
Goodson, Richard, 410
Goss, John, biog., 17; 151, 298; harm., 35
GOTT DES HIMMELS (SILESIA; WALTHAM), 254
GOTT SEI DANK (PITTSBURGH), 61
GOTTLOB, ES GEHT (WEISSE), 356, 397
GOTTSCHALK; see MERCY

Gottschalk, Louis Moreau, biog., 195 f.
Goudimel, Claude, adap., 44, 83
Gould, John Edgar, biog., 171; 251
Gower, John Henry, 138
GRACE CHURCH (NAPLES), 255
Gracious Spirit, Dwell with Me, 197
GRAEFENBERG; see NUN DANKET ALL'
GRAND ISLE, 363
Grant, David, 70
Grant, Robert, 8, 165
Great God, We Sing That Mighty Hand, 348
Great God Who Hast Delivered Us, 415
Greatheed, S. S., arr., 94; harm., 245
Greatorex, Walter, biog., 384; 127, *275
Greek hymns, 28, 155, 161, 285, 365
Greenaway, Ada Rundall, 139
GREENLAND, 153
GREENSLEEVES, 115
Gregorian chant, discussion of, 90
Gregory, A. S., xvi
Gregory, Philip E., 223
Gregory the Great, 37
Greiter, Matthäus, biog., 416
Grenoble church melody, *348
GRÖNINGEN; see ARNSBERG
Grosscatholisch Gesangbuch (1649) (Corner), 14, 396
GROSSER GOTT, WIR LOBEN DICH, 199, *200
Grubb, Edward, 71
Gruber, Franz, 114, *115
Grundtvig, Nicholai Frederik Severin, 218
Gurney, Dorothy Frances, 355
Gurney, John Hampden, biog., 271; 22
Guide Me, O Thou Great Jehovah, 75, 197
GWALCHMAI, 55, 164

Hail the Day That Sees Him Rise, 164
Hail the Glorious Golden City, 327
Hail to the Lord's Anointed, 83

Hale, Edward Everett, 40
HALIFAX, 235
Hall, William J., 171
HAMBURG, 142
Handel, Georg F., biog., 156; 32, 282; *Chandos*, 2; *Dettingen Te Deum*, 68; *Judas Maccabaeus*, 155; *Messiah*, 15, 107; *Siroe*, 282; *Susanna*, 235
Handel and Haydn Society Collection of Church Music (1822), 9, 12, 206, *222, 255, 270; (1828), 69, 142; (1830), 44; *see also* Mason, Lowell
HANKEY, 250
Hankey, Arabella Katherine, 250
HANOVER (ST. GEORGE'S), 165
Harding, James (John) P. and W. Edmond, 103
HAREWOOD, 315
Hark! the Herald Angels Sing, 96, 156
Harkness, Georgia, 308
Harmonia Sacra (Butts), 147, 235
Harmonischer Lieder-Schatz (1738), 91, 171
Hart, Andro (*The CL Psalmes of David . . . 1615*), 73
Hartsough, L., 417
Hassler, Hans Leo, biog., 137; harm., 149
Hast Thou Not Known, 65
Hastings, Thomas, biog., 280; 250; *Musical Miscellany I* (1836), 168; *Manhattan Coll.* (1838), 200
Hatch, Edwin, 187, *188
Hatton, John (not John Liptrott), 163, *236, *338
Have Faith in God, 281
Have Mercy Upon Us, 394
Havergal, Frances R., biog., 308; 313
Havergal, Wm. H., biog., 171; 13, 39, 81, 308; harm., 62; quot., 195, 379
Haweis, Thomas, 211
Hawks, Annie Sherwood, 268
Haydn, Franz Josef, biog., 60, 216; *217, 255, 299, 337, *338; CREATION, 59

Haydn, Johann Michael, biog., 153; 8
Hayne, Leighton G., 190, 345
HE LEADETH ME, 143
He Leadeth Me, O Blessed Thought!, 289
He Who Would Valiant Be, 290
Heart and Mind, Possessions, Lord, 305
Heaven and Earth, and Sea, and Air, 61
Heber, Bishop Reginald, biog., 50; 103, 155, 202, 227, *228, 302
Hebrew melodies (LEONI), 15; (ROCK OF AGES), 25
Hedge, Frederick H., 283
Heermann, Johann, biog., 131; 71, 160, 166, 203
HEINLEIN (AUS DER TIEFE), 121
Helmore, Thomas, biog., 89; 90, 102, 151, 244
Hemy, Henri F., 286
Herbert, George, biog., 311; alt., 392
Herbert, Petrus, 51
Herbst, Martin, 121
Here, O My Lord, I See Thee Face to Face, 230, 406
Hermann; *see* LOBT GOTT IHR CHRISTEN
Hermann, Nicolaus, biog., 371
HERMON, 176
Hernamann, Claudia Frances, 125
HERR JESU CHRIST, 389 f., 396
HERR JESU CHRIST, MEIN'S LEBENS LICHT, 56
Herrnschmidt, Johann Daniel, 18
HERZLICH TUT MICH VERLANGEN; *see* PASSION CHORALE
HERZLIEBSTER JESU, 132
HESPERUS (WHITBURN; QUEBEC), 345
High in the Heavens, Eternal God, 68
High O'er the Lonely Hills, 38
HILARITER, 157
Hills of the North, Rejoice, 84
Hintze, Jacob, 57, *243
Hodges, Edward, 238, 379; arr., 11
Hodges, John Sebastian Bach, 228

Holden, Oliver, biog., 158; *419
Holland, Henry Scott, 335
Holmes, John Haynes, 324, 329
Holmes, Oliver Wendell, biog., *74; 279, 337
Holst, Gustav, biog., 105; 10, 85, 347, 389
Holy God, We Praise Thy Name, 199
Holy, Holy, Holy! Lord God Almighty, 202
Holy, Holy, Holy (Sanctus), 401, 404
HOLY NIGHT; see STILLE NACHT
Holy Spirit, Truth Divine, 195
Hope of the World, 308
Hopkins, Edward J., biog., 52; 190, 395
Hopkins, John Henry, biog., 363
Hopkins, Jr., John Henry, biog., 116
Hopper, Edward, 170
Horder, W. Garrett, 9, 222, 268, 322; arr., 77, 340; 345; quot., 220
HORSLEY, 138
Horsley, William, 138
Hosmer, Frederick Lucian, biog., 299; 50, 345, 350, 355, 357
Housman, Laurence, 342
How, Bishop Wm. W., xvi; biog., 203; 120, *242, 257, 258, 275, 276, 395
How Brightly Shines the Morning Star; see O Morning Star
How Firm a Foundation, 292
How Gentle God's Commands, 63
How Lovely are Thy Dwellings Fair, 222
How Sweet the Name of Jesus Sounds, 176
Howard, Samuel, 266
Howe, Julia Ward, 340
Hoyle, Richard Birch, trans., 155
HSUAN P'ING, 368
Hughes, John, 76, *287
HUMMEL, 289
Hungarian melody, 296
Hunter, John, biog., 166
Huntingdon, Countess of, 159, 211
HURSLEY, 44
Husband, Edward, 259

Huss, John, 389
Hutcheson, Charles, 204
Hutchins, Charles L., 294
Hutton, Frances A., 294
Hutton, Henry Wollaston, 294
Hyde, William DeWitt, biog., 239
HYFRYDOL, 15
HYMN TO JOY, 10
Hymns Ancient and Modern (1859) 126; (1861), 2, 32, 34, 44, 56, 57, 81, 105, 119, 121, 126, 130, 132, 146, 148, 167, 177, 195, 202, 207, 244, 245, 262, 270, 331, 344, 352, 353; Appendix (1868), 45, 48, 52, 57, 66, 138, 161, 209, 259, 270, 285, 297, 298, 375, 383; (1875), 68, 125, 234, 238, 245, 273; (1889), 42; (1904), 120, 317; (1909), 132, 209, 244
Hymn Tunes of the United Brethren (1824), 353

I Greet Thee, Who My Sure Redeemer Art, 165
I Know Not How That Bethlehem's Babe, 121
I Look to Thee in Every Need, 75, 382
I Love Thy Kingdom, Lord, 217
I LOVE TO TELL THE STORY; see HANKEY
I Love to Think That Jesus Saw, 362
I Need Thee Every Hour, 268
I Sing a Song of the Saints of God, 363
I Sing the Mighty Power of God, 57
I Sought the Lord, and Afterward I Knew, 315, 417
I Think When I Read That Sweet Story, 364
I to the Hills Will Lift Mine Eyes, 71
I WANT TO BE A CHRISTIAN, 275
I Would Be True, 369
ICH HALTE TREULICH STILL, 265
If Thou But Suffer God to Guide Thee, 69
Immortal, Invisible, God Only Wise, 9

Immortal Love, Forever Full, 180, 185

IN BABILONE, *25, 61, *82

In Christ There Is No East Or West, 319, 320

IN DULCI JUBILO, 102

In Heavenly Love Abiding, 268

In the Bleak Midwinter, 105

In the Cross of Christ I Glory, 127

In the Hour of Trial, 294

Indian (Asiatic) melodies, 306

Ingelow, Jean, attrib., 315, *417

Ingemann, Bernard Severin, 301

Ingham, T. H., 38

INNOCENTS (DURHAM; ALL SAINTS), 31, 322

INNSBRUCK (NUN RUHEN ALLE WÄLDER), 46

INTEGER VITAE (FLEMMING), 262

INTERCESSOR, 317

IRIS; see GLORIA

Irish melodies, 67, 174, 200, *304, 322; see also Gaelic

Irvine, Jessie Seymour, 70

Isaak, Heinrich, biog., 47; attrib., 46

ISTE CONFESSOR (ROUEN), 297

It Came Upon the Midnight Clear, 106

ITALIAN HYMN, 198, 214, 235, 358

IVES (GREENWOOD, BEULAH), 328

Ives, Jr., Elam, biog., 328 f.; 11

Jackson, George Pullen, 144, 417

Jackson, Robert, 188

JACOB'S LADDER, 373

JAM LUCIS, 382

James I (King of England), 131, 311

Jeffery, J. Albert, 201

JENA; see DAS NEUGEBORNE KINDE-LEIN

Jenkins, David, 277

JERUSALEM; see LEONI

Jerusalem, My Happy Home, 245

Jerusalem the Golden, 243

JESU, MEINE FREUDE, 178

Jesus Calls Us, O'er the Tumult, 253, 254

Jesus Christ Is Risen Today, 152

Jesus, Friend, So Kind and Gentle, 223

Jesus, in Thy Dying Woes, 133, 134

Jesus, Lover of My Soul, 168, 169

Jesus, Priceless Treasure, 177

Jesus, Savior, Pilot Me, 170

Jesus Shall Reign Where'er the Sun, xii, 162

Jesus, the Very Thought of Thee, 180, 181

Jesus, Thou Divine Companion, 315

Jesus, Thou Joy of Loving Hearts, 231

Jesus, Where'er Thy People Meet, 312

Jesus, With Thy Church Abide, 238

Jeszensky, Karoly, 296

Jewish melodies; see Hebrew melodies

JOANNA; see ST. DENIO

John of Damascus (Mansur), 150, 155

Johnson, Samuel (of Salem), 41, 189, 211, 262, 288, 379

Join All the Glorious Names, 184

Jones, Darius E., 168, 293

Jones, John, 277

Jones, Joseph D., 55, *164

Jones, William (Jones of Nayland), 162, 253

Joseph, Georg, 49

Joseph, Jane Marion, trans., 112

Joy Dawned Again on Easter Day. 152

Joy to the World! the Lord Is Come, 107

Joyful, Joyful, We Adore Thee, 10

Judah, Daniel ben, 15

JUDAS MACCABEUS, 155; see also, Handel

Jude, William H., 254

Judge Eternal, Throned in Splendor, 335

Just As I Am, Without One Plea, 251, 253

Katholisches Gesangbuch (c. 1774), 199

Keble, John (*Christian Year*), 33, 44, 171, 236, 304
KEDRON, 133
Keen, Robert ("K."?), 293
Kelly, Thomas, 161, 163
Ken, Bishop Thomas, biog., 29; 385
Kennedy, Benjamin H., trans., 275
Kennedy, President John F., 47, 183, 200, 331
Kentucky Harmony (1816), 32, *325
Kerr, Hugh Thompson, 78
Kethe, William, xii, 5; para., 8
Kettring, Donald D., 420
Key, Francis Scott, 373
Kierkegaard, Sören, 218
KINGS OF ORIENT, 117
KING'S WESTON, 159
KINGSFOLD, 318
Kingsley, Charles, biog., 322; 248, 324
Kipling, Rudyard, biog., 304; 333
Kirchengesangbuch, 153; (1699), 201
KIRKEN DEN ER ET, 219
Knapp, Shepherd, 317
Knapp, William, 332, *360
Knecht, Justin Heinrich, 196, *238, 259, 314, 377
Kocher, Conrad, biog., 56; *96, *355
König, Johann B., 91, 171
Komm, Gott Schöpfer, heilige Geist, 414
KREMSER, 21; *see also* Dutch melodies
Kyrie eleison, discussion of, 398, 399

La Feillée (*Méthode du Plain-Chant,* 1782), 37, 154, 245
Lamb, Hubert, biog., 397
Lamp of Our Feet, Whereby We Trace, 205
LANCASHIRE, 295
LAND OF REST, 246
Landsberg, Max, trans., 15
Lane, Spencer, 294
Langdon, Richard, 390
LANGHAM, 343
LANGRAN, 230, 295

Langran, James, 230
Larcom, Lucy, 251
LASST UNS ERFREUEN (VIGILES ET SANCTI), 13, 55
Lathbury, Mary A., 204
Latin carols and melodies, 31, 33, 37, 102, 116, 123, 135, 146, 152, 178, 180, 186, 212, 231, 414
LATROBE, 350
LAUDA ANIMA; *see* PRAISE MY SOUL
LAUDES DOMINI, 33
Laudi Spirituali, discussion of, 192, 313
Laudi Spirituali (Ms. collection), 312, *397
Laudi Spirituali (1851), 192
Laufenburg, Heinrich von, 224
Laufer, Calvin Weis, biog., 325; quot., 1
Laus tibi, discussion of, 401
Lawes, Henry, 2; biog., 413
LE P'ING, 367
Lead, Kindly Light, 78, 172, 173
Lead Me, Lord, 391
Lead On, O King Eternal, 295
Lead Us, Heavenly Father, Lead Us, 269
Lead Us, O Father, 295
Leavitt, Joshua, biog., 316
Leisentritt's Gesangbuch (1584), *see* Catholicum Hymnologium Germanicum
LeJeune, Claude, harm., 380
LEONI (YIGDAL), 15
LES COMMANDEMENS DE DIEU, 42
Let All Mortal Flesh Keep Silence, 85
Let the Whole Creation Cry, 57
Let the Words of My Mouth, 390
Let There Be Light, Lord God of Hosts, 345
Let Thy Word Abide in Us, O Lord, 388
LET US BREAK BREAD TOGETHER, 231
Let Us With a Gladsome Mind, 58
Ley, Henry G., harm., 357
LIEBSTER JESU, 169, 204, 225
Life of Ages, Richly Poured, 189

Lift Thy Head, O Zion, Weeping, 296

Lift Up Your Heads, Ye Mighty Gates, 93

Lifts Up Your Hearts!, 274

Lift Up Your Hearts (SURSUM CORDA), 403

Lift Up Your Hearts, Ye People, 152, 153

Lighten the Darkness, 300

Lindemann, Ludvig Mathias, biog., 219

Liszt, Franz, 182

LITTLE CORNARD, 85, *157

Little Jesus, Sweetly Sleep, 363

Littledale, Richard F., 192

LLANFAIR (BETHEL), 19, 152

LLANGLOFFAN, 336

LLANHERNE, 60

LLANLLYFNI, 277

LLANSANNAN, 249, 327

Lloyd, John Ambrose, 249, *327

Lloyd, William, 329

Lo, God Is Here!, 377

Lo, How a Rose E'er Blooming, 108

LOBE DEN HERREN, 16

LOBE DEN HERREN, O MEINE SEELE, 18

LOBT GOTT IHR CHRISTEN (HERMANN), 371

Lobwasser, trans., 7, 83, 191, 195; *Psalter* (1573), 43, 227, 356, 379, 416

Lock Hospital Collection (1769), see Madan, Martin

Lockhart, Charles, 24

LOMBARD STREET, 326

L'OMNIPOTENT, 356

Longfellow, Henry Wadsworth, quot., 26, 351, 358

Longfellow, Samuel, 41, 45, 56, 75, 130, 195, *196, 214, 288, 348, 349, 379, 382, 396, 397

Look, Ye Saints, the Sight Is Glorious, 163

Lord, As to Thy Dear Cross, 271

Lord Christ, When First Thou Cam'st, 256

Lord, Dismiss Us With Thy Blessing, 54

Lord, Enthroned in Heavenly Splendor, 233

Lord, for the Mercies of the Night, 378

Lord God of Hosts, How Lovely; see How Lovely Are Thy Dwellings

Lord God of Hosts, Whose Purpose, 317

Lord God of Morning and of Night, 377

Lord, Have Mercy Upon Us, Kyrie, 398, 399

Lord, I Want to Be a Christian, 275

Lord Jesus Christ, Be Present Now, 389

Lord Jesus Christ, Our Lord Most Dear, 224

Lord Jesus, in the Days of Old, 39

Lord Jesus, Think on Me, 248

Lord, Now Lettest Thou Thy Servant Depart in Peace (Nunc dimittis), 413, 414

Lord of All Being, Throned Afar, 74

Lord of All Hopefulness, 173

Lord of Our Life, and God of Our Salvation, 296, 297

Lord of True Light, We Gratefully Adore Thee, 357

Lord, Save Thy World, 348

Lord, Speak to Me, That I May Speak, 308

Lord, Teach Us How to Pray Aright; see O Thou By Whom We Come to God

Lord, Thou Hast Known Our Joy, 358

Lord, Thou Hast Searched Me, 415

Lord, Through This Holy Week, 134

Lord, Thy Mercy Now Entreating, 261

Lord, Thy Word Abideth, 207

Lord, We Thank Thee for Our Brothers, 217

Lord, Who Throughout These Forty Days, 125
LOUVAN, 74
Love Divine, All Loves Excelling, 15, 183
LOVELY; see RHOSYMEDRE
LOVE'S OFFERING, 314
Lowell, James Russell, 327, 330, 340
Löwenstern, Matthäus Apelles von, 296
Lowry, Robert, biog., 261; 258, 268, 310
Lowry, Somerset, 319
Luke, Jemima Thompson, 364
Luther, Martin, biog., 98; x, 39, 135, 189, 221, *340, 377; "Cradle hymn," 113; EIN' FESTE BURG, 282–284; quot., 149; attitude toward music, xvi, 285
Lutherisch Handbuchlein (1638), 389
LUTHER'S HYMN; see NUN FREUT EUCH
Lutkin, Peter Christian, biog., 403; xvi
LUX BENIGNA, 173
Lvov, Alexis F., biog., 344
Lynch, Thomas Toke, 197, 298
LYNNE, 370
Lyon, Meyer (Meier Leon), 15, 16
LYONS, 8, 165
Lyra Davidica (1708), 147, 152, *419
Lyra Germanica; see Winkworth, Catherine
Lyte, Henry Francis, 17, 19, 167, 257, xii
LYTLINGTON, 304

McAllister, Louise, 407
Macgregor, Duncan, trans., 200
MACH'S MIT MIR, GOTT, 378
McKEE, 320, 321
McKee, Elmer, 320
Macnicol, Nicol, trans., 260
Madan, Martin, biog., 24; 147, 198, 211
Magdeburg, Joachim, 275
MAGYAR, 296

Make Me a Captive, Lord, 276
Maker, Frederick C., biog., 79; 129, *130, 268, 334
Mann, Arthur H., 174
Mann, Newton, trans., 15
Maraucher, Karl, 114
March on, O Soul, With Strength, 297
Marckant, John, 418
MARGARET (ELLIOTT), 257
MARION, 270
Marot, Clement, 166, 227, 388, 415; see also French Psalter
Marsh, Simeon B., 168
MARTYN, 168
MARTYRDOM (FENWICK; AVON), 228, 303
MARYTON, 323
Mason, Henry Lowell, 205, 222
Mason, John, 378
Mason, Lowell, biog., 205; 13, 34, 62, 63, 107, 172, 179, 202, 214, *221 222, 250, 272, 274, 307, 328 336, 389; quot., 172, 206, 214; 307, 308, 375; Boston Academy Collection (1835), 346; Carmina sacra (1841), 179; The Choir (1832), 51, 62, 214, 222; (1883) 59, 136, 191, 346; Church Psalmody (1831), 214; The Hallelujah (1854), 346; Modern Psalmist (1839), 45, 69, 83, 179, 191, 205, 214, *271, 375; (1841), 346; Musical Letters from Abroad (1852, 172; National Psalmist (1848), 43, 60, 81, 131, 181, 203, 214, 248, 307, 333; The People's Tune Book (1860), 307; The Psaltery (1845), 307; Sabbath Hymn and Tune Book (1859), 191; Spiritual Songs for Social Worship (1832), 62; see also Handel and Haydn Society Collection.
Master, No Offering Costly and Sweet, 314
MATERNA, 339
Mathams, Walter John, 369
Matheson, George, 276, 309

Matthews, Timothy R., biog., 257; 304

Matutinus altiora (Latin hymn), 31

Maurus, Rhabanus, 186, *414

May the Grace of Christ Our Savior, 270, 396

May the Words of Our Mouths, 390

MEDITATION, 138

MEIN LEBEN (VULPIUS), 293

MEINE HOFFNUNG, 266

MEIRIONYDD, 329

Melanchton, Philipp, 47

MELCOMBE (NAZARETH), 33, 109, 237

MELITA, 331

MELROSE, 334

Men, Whose Boast It Is, 327

MENDELSSOHN, 96

Mendelssohn-Bartholdy, Felix, biog., 97; 3; arr., 35; "Allein Gott in der Höh," 3; Elijah, 98, 203, 389; Festgesang, 97; Lobegesang (Hymn of Praise), 27; Reformation Symphony, 421; St. Paul, 3, 69, 396; Sixth Organ Sonata, 40; use of "Ein' feste Burg" 284

MENDON, 191, 361

Merbecke, John, biog., 399 f.; 393, 404, 405

MERCY (GOTTSCHALK), 195

MERRIAL, 45

Merrill, William Pierson, 237, 338

Messiter, Arthur H., biog., 270; quot., 302

Meter, discussion of, xviii

Methode du Plain-Chant (1782); see La Feillée

Methodists, 12, 76, 158 f., 165, 235, 265, 326, 350, 401, 416; see also Wesley, John

MILES LANE, 158

Miller, Edward, biog., 279

Mills, Charles Smith, 358

Milman, Henry Hart, 140, *141

Milton, John (poet) biog., *58; 77, 222; para., 353

Milton, John (father of poet), harm., 77, *359

Mine Eyes Have Seen the Glory, 340

MIT FREUDEN ZART (BOHEMIAN BRETHREN), 20, 256

Mohr, Joseph, 114

MON DIEU, PRÊTE-MOI L'OREILLE (PSALM 86; GENEVA 86), 388

Monk, Edwin G., biog., 408

Monk, Wm. Henry, biog., 163; 32, 234; arr., 56, *96, 146; comp., *58, 167; harm., 57, 270, *351; see also Hymns Ancient and Modern; The Parish Choir

MONKLAND, 353

MONSELL, 29

Monsell, John S. B., biog., 29; 287

Montgomery, James, biog., 24; 83, 94, 128, 225, 228, 237, 264, 294, *392; arr., 104, 293

Moravians, 4, 12, 19, 24, 51, 92, 103, 255, 261, 350, 353, *391

MORE LOVE TO THEE, 310

More Love to Thee, O Christ, 310

MORECAMBE, 187

Morning Has Broken, 35

MORNING HYMN (MAGDALENE), 30, 314

MORNING LIGHT, 241, 300

MORNING SONG (CONSOLATION), 32, 325

MORNING STAR, 103

MORNINGTON, 311

Mornington, Earl of; see Wellesley, Garrett

MOSCOW; see ITALIAN HYMN

Most Perfect Is the Law of God, 204

Moultrie, Gerard, trans., 85

Moxley, Henry Roberts, 357

MUNICH (KÖNISBERG), 203

Musicalischer Christen-Schatz (1745); see Erbaulicher

Musicalisch Hand-Buch (1690), *93

My Country, 'Tis of Thee, 240, 336

My Faith, It Is an Oaken Staff, 298

My Faith Looks Up to Thee, 272

My God, Accept My Heart This Day, 253

My God, I Love Thee, 247

444

My God, I Thank Thee, Who Hast Made, 79
My Song Is Love Unknown, 135
My Soul Doth Magnify the Lord (Magnificat), 412, 413

Nägeli, H. G., biog., 63; *198, *221
National Anthem, United States, 373 f.
NATIONAL HYMN, 334
Naumann, Johann Gottlieb, 421
Nazianzen, Gregory, 314
Neale, John Mason, biog., 88; auth., 125, 359; quot., 244; trans., 87, 89, 91, 102, 126, 150, 152, 154, 155, 213, 244, 269, 417
Neander, Joachim, biog., 16; comp., 5, 39, 61, 380
Nearer, My God, to Thee, 273
NEED, 268
Nelson, Horatio, 31
Netherlands Folk Song; see Dutch melodies
New Ordentlich Gesangbuch (1646), 71
Neues Geistreiches Gesangbuch (Freylinghausen); see Geistreiches Gesangbuch
NEUMARK (BREMEN), 69
Neumark, Georg, biog., 69
New Every Morning Is the Love, 33
New Version (1696); see Tate and Brady
Newman, John Henry, 160, 172, *173, 375; Apologia pro Vita Sua, 322
Newton, John, 176, 215, 312, 396
NICAEA, 202
NICHT SO TRAURIG, 225
Nicolai, Philipp, 22, 86, 118, *197
Nicolson, Sydney H. biog., 304
Noble, James Ashcroft, 39
Noble, T. Tertius, biog., 84; 234
Noel, Caroline, 159
North, Frank Mason, biog., 326
Not Alone for Mighty Empire, 338
Now Cheer Our Hearts This Eventide, 47
Now God Be with Us, 51

Now in the Days of Youth, 369
Now Let Every Tongue Adore Thee!, 22
Now, on Land and Sea Descending, 45
Now Praise We Great and Famous Men, 360
Now Thank We All Our God, 27
Now the Day Is Over, 45, 383
NUN DANKET, 27
NUN DANKET ALL' (GRÄFENBERG), 194, 205, 380
NUN FREUT EUCH (ES IST GEWISSLICH) (LUTHER'S HYMN), 220, 340
NUN RUHEN ALLE WÄLDER; see INNSBRUCK, 46
NUNC DIMMITTIS, ix, 44
Nunn, E. Cuthbert, trans., 101
NYLAND, 269

O Be Joyful in the Lord!, 25
O Be Joyful in the Lord (Jubilate Deo), 410, 411
O Beautiful for Spacious Skies, 338
O Brother Man, Fold to Thy Heart Thy Brother, 316
O Christ, Thou Lamb of God, 405
O Come, All Ye Faithful, 108
O Come and Mourn With Me Awhile!, 132
O Come, Let Us Sing (Venite), 409
O Come, O Come, Emmanuel, 87
O Day of God, Draw Nigh, 342
O FILII ET FILIAE, 154
O for a Closer Walk With God, 273
O for a Thousand Tongues to Sing, 179
O Gladsome Light, 43
O God, Above the Drifting Years, 236
O God, Beneath Thy Guiding Hand, 236, 337
O God of Bethel, By Whose Hand, 303
O God of Earth and Altar, 335
O God of Love, O King of Peace, 344
O God of Youth, Whose Spirit, 370

O God, Thou Art the Father, 200
O God, We Praise Thee, and Confess, 19
O God, Within Whose Sight, 213
O GOTT, DU FROMMER GOTT (ROCHESTER; DARMSTADT), 71, 160, 203
O Gracious God, Whose Constant Care, 370
O HAUPT VOLL BLUT UND WUNDEN; see PASSION CHORALE
O Holy City, Seen of John, 324
O Holy Spirit, Enter In, 197
O How Glorious, Full of Wonder, 25, 61
O JESU, 75
O JESU CHRISTIE, WAHRES LICHT, 166
O Jesu Sweet, O Jesu Mild, 111
O JESULEIN SÜSS, 111
O JESUS, I Have Promised, 174
O Jesus, Thou Art Standing, 258
O Lamb of God (Agnus Dei), 405
O Light That Knew No Dawn, 314
O Little Town of Bethlehem, 110
O Lord, Almighty God, Thy Works, 358, 359
O Lord and Master of Us All, 180
O Lord of Hosts, Whose Glory Fills, 359
O Lord of Life, Where'er They Be, 357
O Lord, Open Thou Our Lips, 394
O Lord, Turn Not Thy Face from Them, 418
O Love, How Deep, How Broad, How High, 123
O Love of God, How Strong and True, 79
O Love That Wilt Not Let Me Go, 309
O Master, Let Me Walk With Thee, 323
O Master Workman of the Race, 318
O MENSCH SIEH (BOHEMIA), 212
O Morning Star, How Fair and Bright, 118
O My Soul, Bless God, the Father, 81

O PERFECT LOVE (SANDRINGHAM), 355
O QUANTA QUALIA (REGNATOR ORBIS), 244
O Sacred Head, Now Wounded, 135
O Say Can You See; see Star-Spangled Banner
O Sons and Daughters, Let Us Sing! (O filii et filiae), 154
O Spirit of the Living God, 237
O Splendor of God's Glory Bright, 35, 37
O Thou By Whom We Come to God, 264, *392
O Thou Great Friend, 175
O Thou to Whose All-Searching Sight, 254
O Thou Who Hearest Prayer, 391
O Thou Who Through This Holy Week, 125
O What Their Joy and Their Glory Must Be, x, 244
O Where Are Kings and Empires Now, 213
O Word of God Incarnate, xii, 203
O Word of Pity, for Our Pardon Pleading, 134, 139
O Worship the King, All Glorious Above, 8, 165
O Zion, Haste, Thy Mission High Fulfilling, 238
Oakley, Charles Edward 84
Oakeley, Frederick, trans., 108, *110, 128
Of the Father's Love Begotten, 89
OLD HUNDREDTH, 5, 7, 13, *359, 385
OLD 22ND, 209, 324, 381
OLD 124TH, 347
OLD 134TH; see ST. MICHAEL
Olearius, Johann, 83
Oliver, Henry Kemble, biog., 232; *312
OLIVE'S BROW, 143
Olivers, Thomas, 15
OLIVET, 272
OMNI DIE, 396
On Jordan's Bank the Baptist's Cry, 93
446

On This Day Earth Shall Ring, 112
Once to Every Man and Nation, 339
One Holy Church of God Appears, 214
One Who Is All Unfit to Count, 259
ONSLOW, 362
Onward, Christian Soldiers, 298
Open Now Thy Gates of Beauty, 380
ORA LABORA, 234
Organists, longevity of, 215, 231
Our Father, By Whose Name, 355
Our God, Our Help in Ages Past, xiii, 1, 420
Our God, to Whom We Turn, 71
Ouseley, Frederick Arthur Gore, biog., 408
Owen, Frances Mary, 300
Owen, William, 233
Oxenham, John (pseud.); see Dunkerley, Wm., A.
Oxford Book of Carols, 85, 91, 94, 100, 102, 108, 112, 114, 115, 117, 157, 193, 319, 349, 363
Oxford Chant, 411
Oxford Movement, 32, 33, 89, 160, 172, 236, 302

Pachelbel, Johann, 78, 99
Palestrina, da, Giovanni Pierluigi, biog., 146; see also VICTORY
Palgrave, Francis Turner, 377
Palmer, George H., 122; arr., 170
Palmer, Ray, xxi, 231, 272
Parish Choir, The (1850), *58, *322; see also Monk, Wm. Henry
Park, John Edgar, 124
PARK STREET, 13
Park Street Church, 13, 232
Parker, Edwin Pond, 314
Parker, Theodore, 175
Parr, Leonard A., 152, *153
Parry, C. Hubert H., biog., 317
Parry, Joseph, biog., 87; comp., 169
PASSION CHORALE (HERZLICHT TUT MICH VERLANGEN), 136
Patterson, D. Tait, 388

PEACE, 417
Peace, Albert Lister, 309
PEEK, 369
Peek, Joseph Y., 369
PENITENCE (LANE), 294
Pensum Sacrum (1648), 389, *396
PENTECOST, 287
Percy, William Alexander, 266
Perischetti, Vincent, biog., 418; 422
Perronet, Edward, 157, *419
PERSONENT HODIE (THEODORIC), 112
PETRA; see REDHEAD No. 76
Petri, Theodoric, 112
Petrie, George, 67
Pfatteicher, Carl F., trans., 18
Phelps, Sylvanus Dryden, alt., 261
Phillimore, Greville, 417
Piae Cantiones (1582), 102, 112, 116, 134
PICARDY, 85
Pierpont, Folliott Sandford, 55
Pilgrim Hymnal (1904), 298, 315, 322; (1912), 238; (1931), 75, 135, 186, 304, 311, 318, 329, 334, 358, 370, 384, 389; (1958), xvii, xviii, 53, 387, 419
PILOT, 171
Plainsong, discussion of, 90
Playford's Psalter (1671), 43, *401; see also Sternhold and Hopkins; Ravenscroft; Tate and Brady
PLEADING SAVIOR (SALTASH), 316
Pleyel, Ignaz, biog., 255
Plumptre, Edward H., 270
Plymouth Collection (1855), 34
Pollock, Thomas Benson, 133, 238
Pope Paul VI, 16
Porter, Ethel K. (Flentye), biog., 419; xviii
Porter, Hugh, biog., 386; 78, *419
PORTUGUESE HYMN; see ADESTE FIDELES
POTSDAM, 188
Pott, Francis, trans., 146; 121
Powell, Roger K. 217
Praetorious, Michael, biog., 36; adap., 36, 117; arr., 108
Praise Be to Thee (Laus tibi), 401

Praise God From Whom All Bless-
  ings Flow, 29, 385; *see also* OLD
  HUNDREDTH
PRAISE, MY SOUL (BENEDIC ANIMA
  MEA), 17
Praise, My Soul, the King of Heaven,
  17
Praise, O Praise Our God and King,
  353
Praise Our God Above, 368
Praise the Lord, His Glories Show,
  19
Praise the Lord! Ye Heavens, Adore
  Him, 14
Praise Thou the Lord, O My Soul,
  Sing Praises, 18
Praise to God, Immortal Praise, 354
Praise to God, Your Praises Bring,
  350
Praise to the Holiest in the Height,
  375
Praise to the Lord, the Almighty,
  16
Prayer of Thanksgiving, 21
Prentiss, Elizabeth P., 310
Presbyterian Hymnal (1876), 95;
  (1911), 367; (1933), 330
Price, Frank W., trans., 58, 367, 368
Prichard, Rowland H., 15
Procter, Adelaide Ann, 79
Prudentius, Aurelius Clemens, 89
Pry's Psalter (1621), 376
PSALM 36 (OLD 113TH), 415
PSALM 42 (FREU DICH SEHR, O
  MEINE SEELE), 83
PSALM 80, 134
Psalm in worship, place of, xiii
Psalm Tunes (William Anchor, c.
  1721), 125, *180
Psalms (for other texts, *see* Scrip-
  tural Texts)

Psalms	Page
4:8 and 5:8	391
8	61
19:1-6	59
19:7-9, 14	204, 205, 390
23	66, 70, 162, 289, 307
24	93
27	293

Psalms	Page
34	68
36	68, 73
37:5	265
42	83, 303
46	282
51:10-12	392, *393, 394
51:15	394
51:17	392
72	83
82	77
84	222
85	77, *393, 394
86	77
87	215
90	1, 220
91	75
92	162
95	409
98	107
100	5, 12, *13, *25, *411
103	17, 81
104	8, 165
117	13, 14, 65
118:24-26	380
119:105	207, 386
121	71
136	58, 353
139:1-11	415
139:18	34
146	18
147	350
148	14, 22, 57
150	19

Psalter (1912), 204
Psalter Hymnal (1927), 415
PUER NOBIS, 116
PUER NOBIS NASCITUR, 36, 152
Purcell, Henry, 85; attrib., 65, 125
Purday, Charles Henry, 78, *173
PURPOSE, 237
Pusey, Edward B., 296
Pusey, Philip, para., 296
QUEBEC; *see* HESPERUS

Ramsey, Robert, 421
RAMWOLD, 239
Randall, John, biog., 412
RANDOLPH, 53

Rankin, Rankin, Jeremiah E., biog., 53

RATHBUN, 127

RATISBON, 39

Ravenscroft (Whole Booke of Psalmes) (1621), 5, 8, 43, 49, 73, 119, 125, 172, 181, 209, *225, 247, 248, 307, 359

Ravenscroft, Thomas, biog., 73

RAVENSHAW, 207

Rawson, George, 208

"Recessional" (Kipling), 333

REDHEAD NO. 76 (PETRA, GETHSEMANE), 128, *198

Redhead, Richard, biog., 128; *198

Redner, Lewis N., 110

Reed, Andrew, 194

Rees, Bryn Austin, 281

Rees, E., 134

REGENSBURG, 288

REGENT SQUARE, 94, 213

REGNATOR ORBIS; see O QUANTA QUALIA

Reimann, Balthasar, biog., 75

Reinagle, Alexander R., biog., 177; *319

Rejoice O Land, in God Thy Might, 331

Rejoice, O People, in the Mounting Years, 240

Rejoice, the Lord Is King!, 164, 315

Rejoice, Ye Pure in Heart, 270

Remember All the People, 365

REMEMBER THE POOR, 322

RENDEZ À DIEU (GENEVA 118), 227, 231, 382

REST (ELTON), 268

Revivalist, The, 417

RHOSYMEDRE (LOVELY), 135, 355

RHUDDLAN, 335

Richardson, John, 272

RICHMOND, 211

Ride On, Ride On in Majesty, 13, 140, 141

Riley, J. Athelstan, 28

Rinckart, Martin, 27

Ring Out, Wild Bells, 348

RINGE RECHT (BATTY), 261

Rise Up, O Men of God!, 337

Rist, Johann, 95

Robbins, Howard Chandler, trans., 132; quot., 338

Roberts, Daniel Crane, 334

Robinson, John, 412

ROCK OF AGES, 25, 128, 279–281

ROCKING, 364

ROCKINGHAM (MAYHEW), 278

ROCKPORT, 84

Rodigast, Samuel, 77

Röntgen, Julius, 61, *82

Roman Catholic melodies and sources, xi, 14, 32, 47, 57, 109, 111, 132, 134, 154, 183, 199, 216, 262, 271, 286, 414

Ronander, Albert C., vi. xii, xxv

Roosevelt, President Franklin Delano, 160, 331

Root, George F., 258

Rosetti, Christina Georgina, 105, 348

ROUEN; see ISTE CONFESSOR

ROYAL OAK, 361

Russell, Francis Albert Rollo, 322

Russell, Frederick George, 326

Russian Hymn, 344

Saboly, Nicholas, 101

Sacred Melodies; see Gardiner, William

ST. AGNES, 180, *191, 194

St. Ambrose; see Ambrose

ST. ANDREW OF CRETE, 285

ST. ANNE, 1, 213, 420

ST. ASAPH, 301

St. Augustine; see Augustine

ST. BERNARD, 271

ST. BRIDE (ALL SAINTS), 265

ST. CATHERINE (TYNEMOUTH), 286

ST. CECILIA, 345

ST. CHRISTOPHER, 129, 130

ST. CLEMENT, 43

ST. COLUMBA (ERIN), 67

ST. CRISPIN, 253

ST. CROSS, 132

ST. DENIO (JOANNA), 9

ST. DROSTANE, 141

ST. DUNSTAN'S, 291

ST. EDITH; see ST. HILDA

St. Edmund (Fatherland, Pilgrimage), 251
St. Flavian, 125, 225
St. Francis (Assisi), 55
St. Francis Xavier, 247
St. George's Windsor, 352
St. Gertrude, 299
St. Hilda (St. Edith), 259
St. James, 215
St. Kevin, 150
St. Louis, 110
St. Magnus (Nottingham), 65, 161
St. Margaret, 309
St. Mary (Hackney; German Air), 2, 375
St. Matthias; see Song, 67
St. Michael (Old 134th), 190, 342
St. Peter, 177
St. Stephen (Nayland; Newington), 162, 253
St. Theodulph (Valet will ich dir geben), 126
St. Thomas (Williams), 218
Salzburg, 57, 243
Sandon, 78, 173
Sangle, Krishnarao Rathnaji, 305
Sante, Pierluigi Giovanni; see Palestrina
Sarum Hymnal, 242
Sarum Antiphoner, 37
Sarum Primer (1558), 304, *398
Savannah (Herrnhut), 350, 391
Savior, Again to Thy Dear Name, 52
Savior, Like a Shepherd Lead Us, 257
Savior, Thy Dying Love, 261
Saxby, 304
Scheffler, Johann (Silesius), 49
Scheidt, Samuel, 111
Schein, Johann Hermann, biog., 80; *223, *378
Schicht, Johann G., biog., 139; 199
Schirmer, Michael, 197
Schlegel, Katharina von, 63
Schmolck, Benjamin, biog., 224; 380
Schönster Herr Jesu (Crusader's Hymn), 182, 183
Scholefield, Clement C., 43

Schop: see Ermuntre dich
Schop, Johann, biog., 95
Schütz, Johann Jacob, 20
Schulz, Johann Abraham Peter, 351
Schumann, Robert, biog., 41; arr., 41, *308
Schumann-Heink, Mme. Ernestine, 115
Schweitzer, Albert, quot., 179, 188, 265, 283
Schwing, Henry, 394
Scott, Lesbia, 363
Scott, Robert B. Y., 342
Scott-Gatty, Alfred, 318, *358
Scottish Psalter (1564), 5, 43, 83, 134, 227, 347, 356; (1615), *303, *307, *359; (1635), 260, *308, *392, 397; (1650), 5, 70, *71, 75, 204
Scottish Translations and Paraphrases (1745, 1781), 65
Scriptural Texts:
Genesis 1:31, p. 361; 5:24, p. 273; 11:20 (Serug), p. 214; 28:10-17, p. 373; 28:10-22, p. 274; 28:20-22, p. 303
Exodus 15:1, 2 (Song of Moses), p. 222
Numbers 34:4, 5, p. 179
Judges 5:21 (Am. Rev.), p. 297
Ruth 2:4, p. 393
I Chron. 29:14, p. 395
Job 38:7, p. 103
Psalms; see Psalms
Proverbs 3:24, p. 383
Song of Solomon 1:3, p. 176
Isaiah 6:1-3, pp. *401, 403; 6:8, p. 329; 9:2-7, p. 95; 14:12, p. 103; 21:11-12, p. 87; 26:3, p. 397; 33:20-21, p. 215; 40:1-8, p. 83; 40:28-31, p. 65; 43:12, p. 293; 52:8, p. 86
Jeremiah 5:24, p. 418
Lamentations 3:22-23, p. 33
Daniel 3:23, p. 412; 7:9, p. 201
Habakkuk 2:14, p. 237
Malachi 4:2, p. 39
Matthew 1:23, p. 88; 4:18-20, pp. 253, 254; 13:36-43, p. 352;

14:22-32, p. 315; 21:9, p. 401; 22:9, p. 326; 25:1-13, p. 86; 28:19, p. 383
Mark 1:16-20, p. 266; 1:32, p. 48; 10: 13-15, p. 363
Luke, Chapters 1, 2, p. 108; 1:46-55, pp. 412, *413; 1:68-79, p. 411; 2:7, p. 257; 2:8-14, pp. 119, 404; 2:29-32, pp. 44, *413, *414; 3:35 (Serug), p. 214; 18:13, p. 231; 22:19, p. 228; 22:32, p. 294; 23:46, p. 133; 24:28 ff., p. 229; 24:29, pp. 44, 47; 24:30-31, p. 225
John 1:29, p. 405; 18:1, p. 133; 6:51-54, p. 225; 15:1, p. 225
Acts 2:15 (2:4 King James), p. 414; 7:54-60, p. 372; 17:27, p. 262; 28:1, p. 331
Romans 14:7, p. 308
I Cor. 9:24, 26, pp. 282, 287
II Cor. 13:14, p. 396
Galatians 3:28, p. 319; 5:25, p. 187; 6:14, pp. 127, 142
Ephesians 2:20-22, p. 212; 3:1, p. 277; 3:13, p. 287; 5:14, p. ix; 6:10-18, p. 299; 6:14, p. 300
Phil. 2:5-11, p. 120; 3:12-14, p. 282; 3:13-14, p. 282; 4:4, p. 164
Col. 3:16, p. ix
I Tim. 1:17, p. 9; 3:2-7, p. 248; 3:16, p. ix; 6:12, p. 287; 6:17, p. 266
II Tim. 2:19, p. 293; 4:7-8, p. 287
Hebrews 12:1, p. 282; 13:5, p. 293
James 1:27, p. 317
I Peter 2:4-6, p. 212
Revelation 3:20, p. 258; 4:10, p. 282; 4:8-11, p. 202; 7:9-15, p. 163; 15:3-4, p. 359; 19:6-9, p. 86; 21:21-22, pp. 212, 324
Scriven, Joseph, 263
Sears, Edward Hamilton, alt., 106
Selnecker, Nicolaus, 47
Send Down Thy Truth, O God, 190
Sequence, description of, 148
Seraphic hymn, meaning of, 401

SERENITY, 185
Sermisy, Claude de, 276
SERUG, 214
Shape-note hymbooks, 32, 133; *see also* Spirituals, White
Shaw, Geoffrey T., biog., 343; arr., 116; harm., 205
Shaw, Martin, biog., 85; arr., 157, 361, 364; comp., 237, 347
SHEPHERDS' PIPES, 258
Sheppard, Franklin L., biog., 366
Sherwin, Wm. Fiske, biog., 29; 41, 204
Shrubsole, William, biog., 158; xv
Shurtleff, Ernest Warburton, 295
Sibelius, Jean, biog., 64; *373; *see also* "Finlandia"
SICILIAN MARINERS, 54, 224
Sicilian melody, 54
Sidebotham, May Ann, 261
Siena, Bianco da; *see* Bianco da Siena
Silent Night, Holy Night, 114
Silesian melody, 182
Sill, Edward Rowland, 190
SINE NOMINE, 242
Sing Praise to God Who Reigns Above, 20
Skemp, Ada, 362
SLANE, 174, 304
SLEEPERS, WAKE; *see* WACHET AUF
Smart, Sir George, biog., 68
Smart, Henry, biog., 94; 155, *213, *295
Smith, Alfred Morton, biog., 229
Smith, Elizabeth Lee, trans., 166
Smith, Henry Percy, 323
Smith, John Stafford, attrib., 375
Smith, Samuel Francis, biog., 240; 336, 360
Smith, Walter Chalmers, 9
Smyttan, George Hunt, adap., 121
Soldiers of Christ, Arise, xii, 299, 370
Solesmes, Gregorian chant at, 406
SOMETHING FOR JESUS, 261
Son of God, Eternal Savior, 319
SONG 1, 222, 234
SONG 5, 383
SONG 13 (CANTERBURY), 130
SONG 24, 166, 301

451

Song 67 (St. Matthias), 264, 281

Sonneck, Oscar G. T., 374, 375

Southwell, 248, 282

Spirit Divine, Attend Our Prayers, 194

Spirit of God, Descend Upon My Heart, 187

Spirituals, Negro, 144, 231, 275, 320, 330, 368, 373

Spirituals, White, 133, 407, 415

Splendor Paternae, 37

Stainer, John, biog., 422; harm., 100, 102; quot., 404; 317

Stand Up and Bless the Lord, 24

Stand Up, Stand Up for Jesus, 300

Stanford, Charles V., 67, 84, 120

Star-Spangled Banner, story of, 374

Steadfast, 71

Sternhold and Hopkins' Psalter (1562), 5, 67, 125, *225, 359

Stevenson, John, arr., 45

Still, Still with Thee, 34

Stille Nacht (Holy Night), 114, 115

Stock, Harry Thomas, 370

Stocking, Jay Thomas, 318

Stockport; see Yorkshire

Stone, Samuel J., 209

Stork, Charles Wharton, trans., 26

Stowe, Harriet Beecher, 34, 207

Stracathro, 204

Stralsund Gesangbuch (1665), 17

Strong Son of God, Immortal Love, 278, 383

Struther, Jan, 38, 173, 372

Stubbs, Simon, harm., 359

Studdert-Kennedy, Geoffrey A., 32, 326

Student's Hymnal (1923), 362

Stuttgart, 81, 82

Sullivan, Arthur, biog., 150; 43, 251, 276, 288, 299; quot., 18; adap., 107

Summer Ended, Harvest O'er, 417

Sun of My Soul, Thou Savior Dear, 44, 323, 345

Sunset to Sunrise Changes Now, 132

Supplement to the New Version (1708), 418

Sursum corda, 229

Sursum Corda, 274; definition of, 403

Swedish Litany, 133

Swedish melodies, 26, 133

Sweet Savior, Bless Us Ere We Go, 397

Sweet Story, 364

Swiss Folk tune, 298

Symonds, John, biog., 346

Synesius of Cyrene, 248

Take My Life, and Let It Be, 313

Tallis' Canon, 49, 50, 75

Tallis' Ordinal, 19, 76

Tallis, Thomas, biog., 49; 19, 393, *394, 395, 399, *400, 401

Tana mana dhana (Marathi), 306

Tans'ur, William, biog., 122, *129, *228, 332

Tantum ergo; see Dulce carmen

Tappan, William Bingham, 143

Tarrant, William George, 271, 360

Tate and Brady (1696), 5, 22, 67, 303; Supplement (1703), 19, 119, 333

Taylor, Bishop Jeremy, 127

Taylor, Thomas R., 251

Taylor, Virgil C., 74

Teach Me, My God and King, 311

Teach Me, O Lord, the Way of Thy Statutes, 387

Te Deum laudamus, origin of, 407; 19, 26

Ten Thousand Times Ten Thousand, 245

Tender Thought, 415

Tennyson, Alfred, Lord, biog., 278; 202, 348

Terra beata, 366

Tersteegen, Gerhard (or Gerhardt), 4, 377

Teschner, Melchior, 126

Tisserand, Jean, 154

Thalben-Ball, George T., biog., 60

Thanks Be to Thee (Gratia tibi), 401

452

THE AGINCOURT SONG; *see* DEO GRACIAS
The Church's One Foundation, 209
The Day of Resurrection!, x, 155
The Day of the Lord Is at Hand, 322
The Day Thou Gavest, Lord, Is Ended, 42
The Duteous Day Now Closeth, 46
THE FIRST NOWELL, 115
The God of Abraham Praise, 15
The Head That Once Was Crowned with Thorns, 161
The Heavens Declare Thy Glory, Lord, 205
The King of Love My Shepherd Is, 66, 67
The King Shall Come When Morning Dawns, 161
THE KING'S MAJESTY, 141
The Lord Be with You, 393, 394
The Lord Is Rich and Merciful, 258
The Lord Will Come and Not Be Slow, 77
The Lord's My Shepherd, 70, 303
The Man Who Once Has Found Abode, 75
The Morning Light is Breaking, 240, 300
The Sacrifices of God, 392
The Son of God Goes Forth to War, 302
The Spacious Firmament on High, 58, 163
THE STAFF OF FAITH, 298
The Strife Is O'er; *see* Alleluia! The Strife Is O'er
The Summer Days Are Come Again, 349
The Voice of God Is Calling, 329
The Whole Bright World Rejoices Now, 157
THEODORIC; *see* PERSONENT HODIE
Theodulph, Bishop of Orleans, 125
There Is a Green Hill Far Away, 138
There's a Wideness in God's Mercy, 81, 82
These Things Shall Be, 346

They Cast Their Nets in Galilee, 266
Thilo, Valentin, 111
Thine Is the Glory, 155
Thirty-Years' War, 27, 69, 160, 197, 220, 296
This Is My Father's World, 365
This Is the Day the Lord Hath Made, 380
Thomson, Mary Ann (Mrs. John), 238
Those Who Love and Those Who Labor, 312
Thou Didst Leave Thy Throne, 256
Thou God of All, Whose Spirit Moves, 324
Thou Judge By Whom Each Empire Fell, 340
Thou Wilt Keep Him in Perfect Peace, 397
Thring, Godfrey, 160, 294
Throned Upon the Awful Tree, 139
Through All the Changing Scenes, 67
Through the Night of Doubt and Sorrow, 301
Thrupp, Dorothy Ann, attrib., 257
Thy Kingdom Come, O Lord, 345
Thy Word Is a Lamp Unto My Feet, 207, 386
TIDINGS (ANGELIC SONGS), 239
'Tis Midnight, and On Olive's Brow, 143
'Tis Winter Now; the Fallen Snow, 348
Tilak, Narayan Vaman, 259
"To Anacreon in Heaven," 374
To My Humble Supplication, 388
To Thee Before the Close of Day, 382
TOCHTER SION (1741), *319
Tomer, William G., biog., 54
Tomlinson, Ralph, 374
TON-MÂN, 134
Tonus Regius, 392
TON-Y-BOTEL; *see* EBENEZER
Toplady, Augustus M., 279, *281
TOPLADY (ROCK OF AGES), 280
Toth, William, trans., 296
TOULON, 333, 357

Tourjée, Eben, biog., 82
Tourjée, Lizzie S., 82
TRENTHAM, 188
TRINITY; see ITALIAN HYMN
Trinity Church (New York), choir of, 270, 302
Trope, defined, 89
Troutbeck, John, trans., 95
TRURO, 68, 93, 346, 348
Tucker, F. Bland, 120, 355; trans., 129, 231
Turn Back, O Man, Forswear Thy Foolish Ways, 347
Turner, Herbert B., 124
'Twas On That Dark and Doleful Night, 406
Tweedy, Henry Hallam, xxii, 234
Twells, Henry, 48
Tye, Christopher, 120
Tyng, Dudley Akins, 300

UFFINGHAM, 74, 348
Unitas Fratrum; see Bohemian Brethren
United Presbyterian Book of Psalms U. S. A. (1871), 75
UNSER HERRSCHER, 380
Unto Thy Temple, Lord, We Come, 223
Unto Us a Boy Is Born!, 116
"Unto us a boy is born"; see PUER NOBIS NASCITUR
UXBRIDGE, 205

VALET WILL ICH DIR GEBEN; see ST. THEODULPH
Van Dyke, Henry, biog., 10; 315
VATER UNSER, xvii, 39
Vaughan Williams, Ralph, xv; biog., 192 f.; arr., 7, 318, 348, *349; comp., 53, 159, 192, 242; quot., 192; Three Preludes, 135; see also English Hymnal (1906)
VENI, ANIMA MEA, 381
VENI CREATOR, 414
Veni, Creator Spiritus, x, 19, 186, 287, 414
VENI EMMANUEL, 88
Venua, Frédéric Marc-Antoine, 13

VESPER HYMN, 45; see also Again, As Evening's Shadow Falls
Vesperale Romanum (1848), 414
VI LOFVE DIG, O STORE GUD, 26
Victoria, Queen of England, 18, 27, 42, 161, 276, 333, 342, 422
VICTORY (Palestrina), 146
VIENNA (RAVENNA, KNECHT), 196, *238, 313
VIGILES ET SANCTI; see LASST UNS ERFREUEN
VOM HIMMEL HOCH (ERFURT), 99, *224
Vories, William Merrill, 345
Vulpius, Melchoir, 149, 189, 293, *357; see also MEIN LEBEN

WACHET AUF (SLEEPERS, WAKE), 22, 86
Wade, John F., 108, *293
Wagner, Richard (Dresden "Amen"), 421
Wainwright, John, 104, *240
Wake, Awake, for Night Is Flying, 22, 86
Walch, James, 239
Walker, Alan, 391
Wallace, William Vincent, biog., 185
Wallin, Johan Olaf, 26
WALSALL, 125, 180
Walter, Howard Arnold, 369
Walter, Wm. Henry, biog., 238
Walther, Johann, 39, 135, 377
WALTHAM (DOANE; CAMDEN), 236
WALTON; see GERMANY
Walton, James G., 286
Walworth, Clarence, trans., 199
Ward, Samuel A., 339
WAREHAM, 332, 360
Waring, Anna Laetitia, 268
Warner, Richard, 240
Warrack, Guy, 372
Warren, George W., 334
WARUM SOLLT ICH (BONN, EBELING), 11, 100
WAS GOTT TUT (BADEN; PACHELBEL), 78
Was Gott tut, das ist wohlgethan, 78

WAS MEIN GOTT WILL (ST. LUKE'S), 276

WATCHMAN; see DAWN

Watchman, Tell Us of the Night, 86

Watts, Isaac, biog., 1; xix ff., 57, 184, 194, 406, *420; para., 12, *13, 65, 107, 127, 142; *Psalms of David* (1719), 1, 68, 107, 162, 205, 350, 380; quot., xix f., xxi, 58

We All Believe in One True God, 201

We Are Climbing Jacob's Ladder, 373

We Are Living, We Are Dwelling, 330

We Bear the Strain of Earthly Care, 175

We Come Unto Our Fathers' God, 220

We Gather Together, 21

We Give Thee But Thine Own, 395

We Limit Not the Truth of God, 208

We May Not Climb the Heavenly Steeps; see Immortal Love, Forever Full

We Plow the Fields and Scatter, 351

We Praise Thee, Lord, 379

We Praise Thee, O God, Our Redeemer, 21

We Praise Thee, O God (Te Deum laudamus), 407, 408, 409

We Thank Thee, Lord, Thy Paths of Service, 325

We Three Kings of Orient Are, 116

We Worship Thee, Almighty Lord, 26

We Would Be Building, 372

We Would See Jesus; Lo! His Star Is Shining, 124

WEBB (MORNING LIGHT), 241, 300

Webb, Benjamin, biog., 123; ed., 33; trans., 123

Webb, George J., biog., 241

Webbe, Samuel, 32, 33, *237, 269

Weise, Christian, 357

Weisse, Michael, 212; see also *Ein New Gesengbuchlen;* Bohemian Brethren

WEISSE FLAGGEN, 145, 319

Weissel, Georg, 93

WELLESLEY, 82

Wellesley, Garrett (Earl of Mornington), 311

WELLINGTON SQUARE, 372

Welsh melodies, 9, 15, 19, 51, 55, 60, 76, 87, 135, 140, 175, 233, 249, *327, 329, 335, 336, 340, *355, 391

WELSH MELODY, 391

WELWYN, 244, 318, 358

WENTWORTH, 79

Wer nur den lieben Gott lasst walten (Neumark), 12, 69

Were You There, 144

Werner's *Choralbuch* (1815), 39

Wesley, Charles, 38, 82, 96, 147, 152, 164, 168, 179, 183, 299, 314, 391, 410, 417, *419, *420

Wesley, John, 1, 19; *Collection of Psalms and Hymns* (1737), 13; alt., 265, 377; *Foundery Tune Book,* 12, 40, 350, *391

Wesley, Samuel Sebastian, biog., 402; 210, 315, 317, 391, 410

Weston, Rebecca J., 362

WHAT A FRIEND; see ERIE

What Child Is This, Who, Laid to Rest, 115

What Star Is This, With Beams So Bright, 117

Whate'er My God Ordains Is Right, 77

When All Thy Mercies, O My God, 76

When I Survey the Wondrous Cross, xxi, 127, 142, 279

When Israel Was in Egypt's Land, 330

When Morning Gilds the Skies, 32

When My Love to God Grows Weak, 130

When Stephen, Full of Power and Grace, 372

When Through the Whirl of Wheels, 326

Where Cross the Crowded Ways of Life, 326

While Shepherds Watched Their Flocks, 119, 215, 282
White Spirituals; *see* Spirituals
WHITFORD, 249
Whiting, William, 331
Whittier, John Greenleaf, biog., 180; 185, 212, 222, 267, 281, 316, 395
Who Trusts In God, a Strong Abode, 275, 276
WIE SCHÖN LEUCHTET (FRANKFORT), 118, 197
WIGTOWN, 260, 308, 392
Wile, Frances Whitmarsh, 349
Wilhelm II., Duke of Saxe-Weimar, 389
Wilkes, John, arr., 353
Willan, Healey, arr., 405
Williams, Aaron (*New Universal Psalmist*) (1770), 22, 218
Williams, David McK., biog., 267; 26, 419
Williams, Peter, trans., 76
Williams, Robert, 19, *152
Williams, Theodore C., 55
Williams, Thomas J., 340, 346; *Psalmodia Evangelica* (1789), 68, *346, *348
Williams, William, 75
Willis, Love, 288
Willis, Richard Storrs, 106, 182
Wilson, Hugh, 229, *303
WILTSHIRE, 68
WINCHESTER NEW (CRASSELIUS), 12, 93
WINCHESTER OLD, 119
WINDSOR (DUNDEE; ETON), 181
Winkworth, Catherine, biog., 3; 224; *Chorale Book for England* (1863), 16, 17, 52, 57, 69, 83, 93, 118, 132, 178, 197, 201, 203, 266, 289, 380, 389; *Lyra Germanica* (1855), 93, 99, 189; (1858), 27, 86, 100, 148, 169, 379
WIR GLAUBEN ALL' AN EINEN GOTT, 201
WIR PFLÜGEN (DRESDEN; CLAUDIUS), 351

With Songs and Honors Sounding Loud, 350
Within the Maddening Maze of Things, 281
Witt, Christian F., biog., 81
Wolcott, Samuel, 235
WOODLANDS, 127, 275
Woodward, George R., biog., 117; 135, *152, 418
WOODWORTH, 143
Wooldridge, Harry E., 395
Wordsworth, Christopher, adap., 145
WORGAN; *see* EASTER HYMN
Work, John W., ed., 368; quot., 373
Worship the Lord in the Beauty of Holiness, 29
Wortman, Denis, biog., 357
Wreford, John R., 130
WULFRUN, 392
WUNDERBARER KÖNIG; *see* ARNSBERG

YATTENDON 46 (Tune), 395
Yattendon Hymnal, 36, 44, 46, 48, 131, 222, 266, 332, 383, 395, 416; *see also* Bridges, Robert
Ye Holy Angels Bright, 22
Ye Servants of God, Your Master Proclaim, 164, 420
Ye Watchers and Ye Holy Ones, 14, 28
YIGDAL; *see* LEONI
YORK (THE STILT), 77, 359
YORKSHIRE (STOCKPORT), 104, 240
You That Have Spent the Silent Night, 380
Young, Bishop John Freeman, trans., 114

Zeuner, Heinrich C., 289
Zinsendorf, Nicolaus Ludwig von, 254
ZU MEINEM HERRN, 139
Zundel, John, 183
Zwick, Johannes, biog., 376